The Politics of Democratic Consolidation

The New Southern Europe

P. Nikiforos Diamandouros and Richard Gunther

General Series Editors

The Politics of Democratic Consolidation

Southern Europe in Comparative Perspective

Edited by Richard Gunther,
P. Nikiforos Diamandouros,
and Hans-Jürgen Puhle

The Johns Hopkins University Press
Baltimore and London

Sponsored by the Subcommittee on the Nature and Consequences of Democracy in the New Southern Europe of the Joint Committee on Western Europe of the American Council of Learned Societies and the Social Science Research Council

 Published 1995
Printed in the United States of America on acid-free paper
04 03 02 01 00 99 98 97 96 95 5 4 3 2 1

The Johns Hopkins University Press
2715 North Charles Street
Baltimore, Maryland 21218-4319
The Johns Hopkins Press Ltd., London

ISBN 0-8018-4981-0
ISBN 0-8018-4982-9 (pbk.)

Library of Congress Cataloging-in-Publication Data will be found at the end of this book.

A catalog record for this book is available from the British Library.

Contents

Figures and Tables

Figures

Tables

Preface

The "New Southern Europe" project, of which this volume is the first in a series, moves beyond the study of transitions to democracy and focuses instead on the circumstances under which the consolidation of democracy is achieved and the preconditions for democratic persistence are met. It links the insights and knowledge derived from the exploration of this topic to broader concerns regarding the nature of democratic politics and, indeed, of contemporary democratic theory. It highlights the lessons drawn from such an undertaking, in the hope that they will prove useful to policy makers attempting to navigate the uncharted and unpredictable waters of democratization in their own countries, and that they can contribute, however modestly, to the promotion of the democratic enterprise, wherever it is being pursued.

We have chosen Greece, Italy, Portugal, and Spain—defined here as Southern Europe, for reasons extensively discussed in this volume—as the empirical universe from which to derive insights and upon which to test the project's major working hypotheses. The choice was the result of three important developments that have affected the region in recent decades. First, the dramatic socioeconomic transformation of these countries over the past four decades has brought about their incorporation into the privileged domain of the so-called First World, making them, along with Japan, the only ones to have achieved this since the end of the Second World War. Second, the transition to democratic politics in Greece, Portugal, and Spain during the 1970s placed the region in the forefront of what has been called the "third wave of democratization."[1] Finally, of all the countries that have recently embarked upon the long and uncertain journey towards democracy, these four have traveled the farthest, and they have successfully consolidated their democratic political systems. Accordingly, it is possible to examine their full democratization trajectories, up to and including the crucial consolidation process, successful completion of which helps make possible the persistence and long-term stability of new democratic regimes. The Southern European experience can provide unique in-depth insights into processes that have only just begun in other recently democratized or redemocratized polities. Rapid and far-reaching socioeconomic change, a decisive break with traditions of underdevelopment and authoritarianism, and the success of their democratic transition and consolidation processes lend the notion of the "New Southern Europe" credibility and timeliness as both an object of study and the title of this series.

The Problem

The resurgence of democracy and its "rediscovery" by the scholarly community as a field worthy of attention pose intriguing questions for the student of the sociology of knowledge. To be sure, the neglect which had marked the study of democratic institutions and politics in the aftermath of the Second World War reflected the political realities of that period and the priorities which the Cold War had imposed upon its intellectual interpreters. Put otherwise, the perceived threat to democracy posed by the emergence and proliferation of totalitarian and authoritarian regimes acted, at the time, as a powerful impetus for shifting the focus of political inquiry towards non-Western and nondemocratic systems. In addition, the failure, during the 1960s and early 1970s, of democratic experiments in Latin America, Africa, and Asia tended to give rise to a certain degree of pessimism concerning the prospects for democracy "outside the West" (as a culturally introverted formulation would have it). Struggling with the question of whether democracy was more attuned to particular types of social and cultural settings gave rise to the significant literature on the prerequisites or, in Seymour Martin Lipset's more careful and more sophisticated construction, "social requisites" of democracy. In part, the emphasis on the socioeconomic preconditions for the emergence of democracy reflected the Marxist or neo-Marxist influence on theorizing concerning the salience of socioeconomic factors for political development, underdevelopment and, more generally, change.

The empirical world on which these analytical perspectives had been based changed abruptly during the 1970s, giving rise to a significant reorientation in the nature and scope of political science inquiry. Democratic politics (re)emerged initially in Southern Europe and subsequently in Latin America, Central America, and East Asia, rekindling interest in democracy as a political system, in its attributes and properties, and in its theoretical implications. A pioneering effort in this regard was Juan Linz's *Crisis, Breakdown, and Reequilibration,* which, as part of the larger project (with Alfred Stepan) "The Breakdown of Democratic Regimes," helped refocus attention on the underpinnings of the stability and survival of democratic regimes.[2] During the following decade, a wave of studies analyzed in considerable detail the breakdown of nondemocratic regimes and transitions to democracy. These studies (particularly the influential *Transitions from Authoritarian Rule,* edited by Guillermo O'Donnell, Philippe C. Schmitter, and Laurence Whitehead)[3] focused on a set of central attributes (uncertainty, fluidity, and contingency) which shifted the emphasis in comparative political analysis from socioeconomic structures to politics, leadership and, more generally, human resourcefulness and ingenuity—*virtù,* in Machiavelli's terminology. Acknowledging the critical role of politics in the negotiation of successful transitions, the main emphasis of comparative studies in the 1980s focused on the role of elite actors in steering through the turbulent and uncharted waters of regime change, and on the central significance of pacts and/or elite settlements involving the major players in a democratic transition for the eventual consolidation of democratic politics in a given country.

Such a reorientation in analytical focus was certainly based on, and justified by, the very nature of the transition as a historical period in which the salience of long-term, structural constraints becomes most attenuated, their capacity to act as "confining conditions" to change is greatly reduced, and conjunctural factors privileging political initiative and human engineering gain maximum room for maneuver. In the East European context, this was manifested in the ascendance of the so-called Sinatra doctrine as an analytical perspective.

Faced with the considerable flux characteristic of regime transitions, analysts searched for patterns of behavior and distinct paths to democracy that might be conducive to abstraction and theory building. This search constituted an implicit acknowledgment of the belief in a subtle but complex interplay between diachrony and synchrony, macrostructures and conjuncture, the interaction of which produced different and distinct transition trajectories even among cases not sharing specific empirical properties. Seen in this light, the dynamics of regime transition should be regarded as a critical part, but nevertheless only a part, of a broader and longer-term process of regime change, involving the end of the predecessor regime, the establishment of a new regime, the consolidation of democracy, and democracy's persistence. Over time, deconsolidation may occur and may result in either reequilibration or expiration, leading to a new cycle of regime rise and decline. The shifting relationships of domination within each phase of the long cycle become the key to understanding the specific paths or trajectories traveled by individual societies as they negotiate their way through the uncertainties of regime change that lead to democratic politics.

Several important questions are inherent in the use of paths or trajectories as convenient heuristic devices to facilitate our understanding of the evolution of democratic regimes: Does the particular way in which a nondemocratic regime unravels have an impact (direct or indirect) on the subsequent trajectory followed by a country in its transition to democracy? Do the generic attributes of a particular type of transition influence the type of democracy ultimately issuing from it? Do the specific characteristics of the emerging democratic regime have a marked effect on the nature of its consolidation process? Finally, does the quality of democracy and of democratic institutions established through this overall process reflect or bear the lasting imprint of the particular trajectories leading to it? These questions acquired increasing salience as ever larger numbers of formerly nondemocratic political systems passed through the early (i.e., transition) phase of the democratization process and as democratic consolidation (and, hence, the long-term prospects for regime survival) became the first concern of fledgling democracies moving beyond the preoccupations of the transition. These questions highlighted the need to conceptualize more distinctly those properties defining the various aspects of the overall democratization process—the breakdown of the previous regime, democratic transition, regime consolidation, and democratic persistence.

It is particularly important to distinguish between transition and consolidation processes. Regime transition entails the creation of the basic political institutions of a new democratic system and the drafting of new rules for regulating the political behavior of citizens, organizations, and governing elites. Democratic consolidation, which we define in considerable detail in the introductory chapter of Volume 1 of this series, involves the legitimation of those institutions and the widespread internalization of the new democratic regime's basic behavioral norms. It is important to note that transition and consolidation are conceptually distinct but that, in reality, they may temporally overlap or even coincide. To be sure, the transition process must obviously begin prior to consolidation, and the consolidation process usually requires a longer period of time to reach completion, particularly with regard to the attitudes and behavioral norms of mass publics as compared with those of political elites and organizations. But, in all four Southern

European countries, consolidation processes were set in motion or were well advanced prior to the end of their respective transitions; and in some cases, such as the negotiated transition to democracy in Spain, the same procedures through which new democratic institutions were created also helped to forge a broad elite-level consensus acknowledging the legitimacy of those institutions and respecting their associated rules of the game. In other words, specific features of a democratization process may contribute positively to both the successful completion of the transition and to consolidation of the new regime. Accordingly, transition and consolidation processes usually overlap temporally; in some cases they may coincide, while in others they may occur sequentially. Thus, while it is necessary to establish the conceptual boundaries between the two processes, it would not be correct to conceive of consolidation as a stage that neatly follows the completion of the transition phase.

Similarly, the distinction between consolidation and what we call democratic persistence is worthy of mention at this point. The concept of democratic persistence represents the end product of a long democratization process, whose attainment is contingent upon the successful negotiation of transition and consolidation by a multitude of actors in a given society. Consolidation, whatever its actual temporal length—and, as volume one in our series demonstrates, there are minimalist and maximalist views on this subject—should be conceived of as reaching closure at one point in time or another. To do otherwise would be to adopt a logically problematic position assigning to consolidation an open-ended quality which would severely impair our ability to analyze processes of regime deconsolidation, reequilibration, and breakdown. As would be clear from even a cursory comparison of our analysis of consolidation processes with the classic study of regime breakdowns by Linz and Stepan, we believe that the dynamics of regime consolidation and regime breakdown are entirely distinct: the one is not simply a mirror image of the other. Consolidation should be viewed as anterior to and distinct from democratic persistence. Consolidation can contribute substantially to a democratic regime's capacity to persist in the face of even severe challenges, to adjust and to survive. But by no means does consolidation at one point in time guarantee that a particular regime will survive indefinitely. Moreover, studies of democratic persistence open up an entirely new set of questions, pertaining to such matters as the quality of democracy in a given regime and the performance of its political institutions. In this sense, the qualitative aspects of Southern European democracies and, more generally, the attributes of democratic persistence, deconsolidation, reequilibration or recrafting of a democratic regime in the region should become the next natural area of inquiry.

Three perspectives—two methodological and one theoretical—were, from the outset, central to the definition of our project's intellectual agenda. First, a rigorously comparative mode of inquiry was adopted as a means of transcending the methodological constraints implicit in single-country studies. Accordingly, we have undertaken intraregional comparative analysis in an effort to identify and explain both convergences and divergences in the developmental experiences of these countries. Second, an interregional perspective has been maintained as a means of ensuring that the insights derived from the study of this particular cluster of cases could be validated, modified, or negated by lessons drawn from the study of similar developments in other regions of the world. Explicit and detailed comparisons with relevant cases in Latin America, Eastern Europe, and other industrialized countries served as a corrective backdrop to this regionally focused project. The theoretical perspective that distinguishes our multivolume exploration of social, economic, cultural, and political change is the attempt to draw from the Southern European experience substantive implications for the construction and nature of democracy throughout the contemporary world, that is, for democratic theory in general.

Viewed from the perspective of these central concerns, the four countries on which our inquiry became focused proved to be ideally suited to the task. To begin with, as Edward Malefakis argues in his contribution to the first volume, their historical and developmental trajectories since the beginning of the nineteenth century, provide, in both their converging and their diverging moments, sufficient evidence of similarities at the socioeconomic and political levels alike to invite and facilitate intraregional comparison. The transition to socioeconomic and political modernity that occurred in all four countries during the postwar period greatly enhanced the value of such a comparison and the lessons to be derived from it. In a very real sense, rapid, accelerated, indeed compressed change at the cultural, economic, social, and political levels became the hallmark of Southern Europe during this period. In many ways, it appeared that the passage from a state of protracted and painful underdevelopment, replete with the structural rigidities which this implies, to the fluidity and resilience characteristic of modernity was the result of an atypical trajectory of change that had involved skipping over developmental stages that had characterized processes of socioeconomic and political change in most other Western countries earlier in the twentieth century. With some justification, therefore, we have referred to this as "leap-frogging." It was, most of all, this peculiarity which convincingly shattered longstanding stereotypes concerning the backwardness of the region and gave the New Southern Europe a broader theoretical significance than its geographical boundaries might otherwise imply.

An additional by-product of this remarkable transition to socioeconomic modernity was that, by the 1970s, the Southern European societies and economies had, to a qualitatively significant degree, overcome the profound and rigid social and economic inequalities which, for more than a century, had constituted the major structural flaw upon which earlier efforts at democratization had ingloriously foundered. Despite the persistence to this day of pockets or enclaves of poverty and premodern, even preindustrial structures within each country, the benefits of economic development have been widely distributed.

The success with which the New Southern Europe has managed its democratization process and, conversely, the continuing uncertainty still surrounding consolidation processes in Latin America, Eastern Europe, and East Asia have heightened interest in the lessons to be learned from the study of particular transition and consolidation trajectories. Our search for such lessons took two distinct but clearly complementary routes: The first adopted a prospective viewpoint and sought, through a systematic and comparative study of transition and consolidation paths in Greece, Italy, Portugal, and Spain, to identify the distinguishing properties of each and to formulate more general propositions concerning the particular ways in which the nature, content, and evolution of a transition affected both the ensuing consolidation and the democracy issuing from it. The second route moved in a retrospective mode, with an eye to determining the relative impact of structures and forces operating prior to the onset of regime change on transition, consolidation, and democratic persistence. The circumstances of the demise of the preceding nondemocratic regime, the way in which the expiration of that regime is linked to its foundation, and the impact of the longer-term heritage of state-society relations upon transition and consolidation are some of the central concerns of this inquiry.

These two perspectives, though distinguishable in terms of the relative emphasis each places on particular aspects of the overall democratization process, are clearly complementary: taken together, they serve to expand the conceptual time horizons upon which to base the search for analytical categories capable of rendering the notion of trajectories more intelligible. Thus, the prospective viewpoint's greater emphasis on conjunctural aspects of change—such as politics, leadership, fluidity, uncertainty, and contingency—is balanced by the greater concern of the retrospective mode of analysis in identifying long-term structural factors, such as socioeconomic parameters, legacies of the predecessor regime, or simply historical heritage.

A word of caution is in order at this point. Our concern with, and emphasis on, trajectories of democratic transitions and consolidations and, especially, our focus on the ways in which the dynamics shaping particular phases in the overall democratization process tend to affect subsequent ones should in no way be understood as implying a deterministic conceptual bias. On the contrary, the whole purpose of the notion of trajectory is to facilitate the categorization and abstraction conducive to taxonomy, while recognizing that individual moments in the overall process are structured so as to maximize (as during transitions) or to place greater constraints on (as during consolidations) the freedom of movement enjoyed by the actors involved in them. Put otherwise, the concept of trajectory is meant to capture and highlight the particular combination and interplay of freedom and constraint at each successive stage of the democratization process. This approach is a variety of "path dependent" analysis. The heir of a distinguished tradition in historical sociology and political science, this approach figures prominently in the recent and influential literature on "new institutionalism."

Projected Volumes in This Series

One of the central features of the arrival of socioeconomic modernity in the New Southern Europe was the emergence of a notable degree of pluralism, which, with inevitable but not excessive variations, became a distinguishing trait of the societies and economies of the four countries we examine here. Put somewhat differently, the advent of socioeconomic modernity implied the gradual assertion of civil society in these countries. In turn, this socioeconomic pluralism served as a major asset when these countries embarked upon the delicate and fragile processes of regime transition and consolidation. At the same time, concern over the potentially adverse effects of accelerated and "leapfrogging" change on the prospects for democratic consolidation rendered the Southern European democratization experience doubly interesting to observers and scholars interested in the more theoretical aspects of this subject. How would the recent (re)establishment of modern democratic parties affect the prospects for democracy in the region? What would be the impact on democratic consolidation of the general weakness of secondary organizations in Greece, Portugal, and Spain? Would the combination of weak secondary organizations and powerful mass communications media in these relatively modern and affluent societies leave its imprint on the nature of democratic politics or on the processes shaping attitudes, values, and solidarities among citizens? If so, how would the Southern European democratization experiences differ from those of other Western countries, whose democratic systems had been established in the first decades of the twentieth century, prior to the advent of electronic mass media, or in the wake of the devastation brought about by the Second World War? More broadly, what kinds of cultural, economic, social, and political arrangements would the consolidation of democracy in the region produce? How would these arrangements differ from those which had prevailed in the region's predemocratic political systems, or from those which became dominant in the societies of Northern and Western Europe after the end of the Second World War? Would the new democracies of Southern Europe experience the same processes of drift, dealignment, disaffection, disorganization, and dissolution of traditional solidarities—a syndrome sometimes associated with "the new democratic politics"—that have taken place in other industrialized societies since the end of the Second World War? Indeed, the fragile political attachments and low levels of adherence to secondary organizations so distinctive of politics in the New Southern Europe suggested that the region might have leap-frogged into the era of new democratic politics without prior exposure to, or immersion in, the type of stable political structures that had accompanied the construction of politics in Northern and Western Europe.

The first two volumes in this series will analyze, from a variety of perspectives, the processes of political change and the nature of political institutions and behavior in Greece, Italy, Portugal, and Spain. Volume 1, *The Politics of Democratic Consolidation: Southern Europe in Comparative Perspective,* begins by examining Southern Europe as a distinct conceptual entity and by tracing its patterns of social and political change over more than a century. This historical background serves as the starting point for describing the long-term trajectory of political change in the region. The bulk of this volume focuses on the problems and nature of democratic consolidation in Southern Europe. Given the widely acknowledged success of this process within the newly redemocratized polities in the region, one of the first volume's goals is to derive analytical insights into consolidation processes in general and, specifically, to generate hypotheses about factors which are conducive to or which impede successful achievement of democratic consolidation. Towards this end, each chapter's author undertakes a rigorous intraregional comparative analysis, taking advantage of substantial variations in transition trajectories and other relevant factors. Some chapters broaden the geographical scope of this analysis by systematically comparing Southern European consolidation experiences with those of countries in Latin America's Southern Cone and in Eastern Europe which have recently undergone regime change. In this context, it is worth emphasizing that the literature on democratization is only now beginning to focus on issues of democratic consolidation and that published comparative studies of this process are rare. To be sure, the collective volumes edited by John Higley and Richard Gunther, Ulrike Liebert and Maurizio Cotta, and Geoffrey Pridham have gone a long way in exploring the impact of specific sets of actors and institutions (political elites, parliaments, and political parties) on consolidation.[4] To our knowledge, however, *The Politics of Democratic Consolidation* is the first in-depth and multidimensional comparative analysis of the phenomenon. Individual chapters focus on the impact on consolidation of civil-military relations, the nature of the outgoing nondemocratic regime, political parties, international factors, key central government institutions, social movements, and other collective actors. One chapter presents an analysis of survey data documenting the extent of legitimacy achieved by these regimes by the 1980s, as well as the differing conceptualizations of democracy held by Southern Europeans. Finally, the volume takes the first step beyond the achievement of consolidation by examining three important features of the types of democracy that have emerged in these Southern European countries: it describes the basic patterns of legislative-executive relations in these democracies, the configuration of interest groups, and the structure of political parties and party systems.

The second volume, *Democratic Politics in the New Southern Europe,* will carry one step further this effort to examine key features of these consolidated democracies, by exploring in considerable detail the nature of politics and political behavior in Southern Europe. A central theme of the volume will be the impact of socioeconomic change and specific trajectories of political change on political institutions, agendas, beliefs and ideologies, and political participation. Apart from undertaking a rigorous intraregional comparative analysis, the chapters in the second volume will draw upon data from and studies of other democracies in advanced industrialized countries (in Northern and Western Europe, North America, and elsewhere).

Volume 3, *Economic Change in the New Southern Europe,* will examine commonalities and divergences in the economic structures and policies of the four Southern European countries. As with all of the volumes in this series, two unifying themes pertain to the impact of socioeconomic modernization and the implications of democratization for the various sectors of society and dimensions of social life—in this instance, for the economic sphere. Certain aspects of the Southern European experience, such as the rapid and leap-frogging character of socioeconomic change and recent accession to membership in the European Community by three of the four Southern European countries, make this region a particularly suitable subject. In addition, the economies of the region have certain structural features that are more pronounced than elsewhere: a predominance of small and medium-size firms and powerful underground or shadow economies; a multifaceted impact of tourism and very large tertiary sectors on these societies; and long-term implications of deruralization and of its concomitant, an explosive urbanization, which, while producing some of the well-known problems of major conurbations around the world (ecological damage, traffic problems, atmospheric pollution), has eschewed the associated pathologies that have materialized in rapidly urbanizing Latin American countries (e.g., extreme poverty, extensive shanty towns and crime).

The Changing Functions of the State in the New Southern Europe, Volume 4 in the series, will examine the impact of democracy on the nature and dynamics of state responsibilities. Here the major areas of concern are two: First, how, if at all, did democratization affect what traditionally had been perceived as distant and unresponsive states in the region? Would the strengthening of civil society bring about a restructuring in traditional state-society relations, or substantially alter the longstanding characterization of the region as involving state-heavy and yet weak-state societies? What were the implications of such changes for the quality, content, and thrust of public policy in these countries, for the overinflated parastate sector, and for the nature of welfare services in the region? Second, what comparative insights and lessons can be derived from the Southern European experience for the study of the challenges confronting the policy instruments of organized capitalism in advanced industrial societies since the mid-1970s? More generally, has the Southern European state and its policies (especially social policies) come to resemble more closely its northern counterparts, or has it retained some of the features of late development that so distinguished it in the 1950s from the welfare states of Western and Northern Europe and other parts of the industrialized and democratic world?

Leap-frogging has perhaps been most visible in the dramatic transformation of the relationship between politics and culture in Southern Europe. Having greatly benefited from pluralism, tolerance of others, moderation, a distinct preference for positive (rather than zero-sum) approaches to conflict management, and the system of shared assumptions which these imply, democratic consolidation, in turn, decisively strengthened these and other salient attributes of democracy in the four countries under study, in the process providing for both the expansion of their scope as well as for their rooting and deepening. Illustrative examples of this process include the continuous and profound (but inadequately understood) redefinition and renegotiation of collective identities in each country, which helped supersede deep cleavages that had long impeded modernization in the region, facilitated further integration into the modern world, and promoted convergence with trends observable in Northern and West European societies. At the same time, incorporation into the European Community has tended to strengthen and accelerate the processes of cultural diffusion contributing to these changes and to support their extension to new areas, including those affecting the role of women, giving rise to a new sensitivity concerning environmental issues and recognizing the need to respect and safeguard cultural diversity within Southern European societies. A specific theme that serves as a major anchoring device for Volume 5, *Culture Change in the New Southern Europe,* is the extent to which socioeconomic development, cultural change, and democratic consolidation have helped overcome the profound cultural dualism which the encounter of modernity with tradition brought about in the region, from the beginning of the nineteenth century to the very recent past. Poignantly evoked in, among others, Giuseppe di Lampedusa's *The Leopard,* the theme of cultural dualism centers on the conflict between liberalism and the Enlightenment against absolutism and traditional authority and has helped spawn an influential literature on "the two Spains," "the two Greeces," "the two Portugals," and, most certainly, "the two Italies." As such, it is a theme which goes to the heart of the political and cultural dilemmas the region confronted as, with inevitable intraregional variations, it negotiated its transition to the modern world of advanced industrial capitalist societies and values, in the decades following the Second World War. An additional, distinctive characteristic of this final volume in the series will be its combination of micro and macro perspectives, derived from studies focusing on change at the local, regional, and national levels. The particular ways in which the shifting relationship between politics, social relations, and culture affects, and is affected by, democratic consolidation as well as the implications of this relationship for democratic theory constitute additional questions explored in Volume 5.

The Contents of This Volume

As already indicated, Volume 1 in this series undertakes a systematic examination of the processes by which the Southern European democracies became consolidated. The central purpose of the introductory chapter is to provide a theoretical discussion of the concept of consolidation. To that end, it defines that concept, examines the role of elite and mass actors in consolidation processes, identifies salient indicators of consolidation, and looks at the different trajectories traveled by the four Southern European democracies on their way to consolidation.

In the second chapter, Edward Malefakis explores the long-term socioeconomic and historical settings out of which recent developments have evolved. The chapter is not primarily concerned with democratic consolidation as such, but with trying to establish structural similarities and historical parallels among the Southern European nations, and with showing how, especially during the past two centuries, they acquired an identity which distinguished them from both Eastern and Western Europe. One of the major points Malefakis makes is that political consolidation of any kind—absolutistic, liberal, democratic, or dictatorial—was less customary in Southern Europe than elsewhere. Because of the great complexity and variety of the socioeconomic structures of the region, the precocity with which its inhabitants were exposed to all of the major political movements of modern times, and its unique historical past, no stable political equilibrium of more than a few decades duration could be established during the nearly two centuries between the 1790s and the 1970s. The legitimacy of every regime was constantly challenged by important sectors of society, and they all faced repeated attempts to overthrow them. Several of these attempts succeeded, giving an unparalleled instability to Southern European politics during much of the nineteenth and twentieth centuries. This history accentuates the uniqueness of the democratic consolidation achieved during the past few decades and makes the process by which consolidation was secured all the more interesting.

Malefakis's historical background is followed by five chapters that set forth new perspectives on recent democratic consolidation processes in Southern Europe. Some of these chapters explore areas largely neglected in party-elite centered explanations of those processes. Juan Linz, Alfred Stepan, and Richard Gunther contrast the success of Southern European consolidation processes with the failure of most such efforts in Latin America and the extreme obstacles impeding democratic consolidation efforts in Eastern Europe. The nature of the outgoing authoritarian regime, a factor largely unexplored in previous analyses, emerges as a powerful determinant of the prospects for success in democratic consolidation. The authors build upon Linz's earlier typology of political regimes by breaking down the heavily populated category of authoritarian systems into three separate regime types—sultanistic, posttotalitarian, and authoritarian. They point out that democratic consolidation was greatly facilitated in the three most recent Southern European transitions by the relatively high level of pluralism that had emerged in the final years of the former authoritarian regime. This contrasts sharply with most of the East European transitions, where democratization itself (let alone consolidation) has been enormously impeded by an absence of institutionalized pluralism characteristic of posttotalitarian and sultanistic regimes. Another aspect of the former regime that can greatly affect these processes, as it has in Latin America, is the extent to which the regime had been dominated by hierarchical (versus nonhierarchical) military officers. Other potentially serious impediments to successful democratization include the extent to which regime transformation is accompanied by a crisis of what Linz, Stepan, and Gunther call stateness (in which nationalist minorities challenge the continuing existence of a multinational state) or by crises arising out of simultaneous efforts to radically restructure the economy. Their argument implies that attempts to export a Southern European model of transition to these greatly differing contexts should be undertaken with great caution.

Felipe Agüero undertakes a systematic comparative analysis of the role of the military in regime change. While a few monographic studies have analyzed the involvement of the military in transition processes or the extrication of the military from civilian politics in Southern Europe,[5] there have been no systematic comparative analyses of the military's role in all of the three recent Southern European transitions. The scope of Agüero's analysis is further broadened through an explicit comparison of Southern Europe with several Latin American cases, where success in consolidating new democracies has been more limited. Agüero makes the case for the need to integrate the military dimension into studies of democratization and democratic consolidation. He maintains that without such an integration it is simply not possible to make accurate assessments of the outcomes of democratization in Southern Europe and South America. He argues that these outcomes are heavily influenced by the nature of military participation in the preceding authoritarian regime, as well as by the nature of the elites who control the transition and set the agenda for the ensuing changes. Starting from different points than did Southern European regimes, South American regions faced greater barriers to democratization, although these barriers do not foreclose chances of success over the long term.

Geoffrey Pridham explores the impact of international factors on consolidation. He analyzes the long-term processes of deepening or rooting of democratic attitudes, norms, and practices. Virtually all other analyses of consolidation processes terminate at the point when the regime has become "sufficiently consolidated." Pridham argues that this more restricted focus overlooks longer-term processes that can reinforce the consolidation of new democracies and remold their political cultures. Other analyses also ignore the possibility that various developments could trigger the deconsolidation of regimes in the future.[6] To the extent that integration within the European Community can forge linkages with other, more established, West European democracies, a resocialization of Southern European citizens may reduce sources of alienation and more firmly anchor these democratic systems over the long term. Pridham concludes that, in the interdependent world of the 1980s and 1990s, the international context is crucial in analyzing the processes of democratic consolidation. This is especially the case for member states of the European Community, where internal and external factors are progressively more interconnected.

Sidney Tarrow examines the roles of mass movements and popular mobilizations in transitions to democracy. While many of the elite-oriented analyses that dominate the literature on democratic consolidation in Southern Europe acknowledge the potential or actual significance of the role of the masses in transition processes, none have dealt with this factor to this point. Tarrow analyzes the roles played by popular mobilizations in two transitions that had greatly different outcomes: the highly successful transition to democracy in Spain and the collapse of Italian democracy following the First World War. He argues that such mobilizations were more significant for success or failure in democratization than has been acknowledged in most previous work on regime transitions, and that elite interactions may be sharply constrained by their respective social, cultural, and political contexts. While most of his analysis focuses on the role of mass mobilization in transitions to democracy, particularly as it concerns the breakdown of former authoritarian regimes and the early stages of the emergence of democracy, his findings have clear implications for processes of consolidation. He points out that widespread mobilizations may be necessary to initiate the breakdown of nondemocratic regimes and to sustain progress towards democratization but that tactical demobilization may facilitate consolidation processes at certain key stages. This pathway to democratic consolidation, however, may have lasting implications for the structure and quality of political behavior in the new democracy: specifically, a regime founded through elite-level pact making and the demobilization of popular forces may contribute to the emergence of a poorly organized working class, such that collective action is often crude, interest-based, and intolerant of the rights of others.

Leonardo Morlino and José Ramón Montero undertake an empirical analysis of mass-level attitudes towards the legitimacy of democracy and the democratic regimes of Greece, Italy, Portugal, and Spain. They reaffirm our assessment that support for democracy is strong in all four countries, but they come to mixed conclusions concerning the extent to which fully democratic political cultures have emerged in these countries. They point out that citizens in these Southern European countries conceive of democracy in different ways, and they develop a typology describing these different conceptualizations. They also find that perceptions of the efficacy of democracy in some cases, particularly Italy, are strikingly low. This raises important questions concerning the relationship between perceived efficacy and regime legitimacy, which are then discussed. These findings (based on 1985 opinion surveys) appear to have captured a dimension of public ambivalence towards party politics in Italy that acquired great salience in the late 1980s and early 1990s, contributing to a deconsolidation of several important political subsystems (or what Schmitter, in this volume, calls partial regimes). More broadly, cynicism towards political parties emerges from their study as a general characteristic of political culture in Southern Europe.

The concluding three chapters of this book look beyond the processes by which these Southern European democracies were consolidated to the kinds of democracies which emerged from these processes. To date, very few comparative studies of Southern European democratic institutions have been undertaken,[7] and even monographic studies of political institutions in the new Southern European democracies are few and far between. In sketching out descriptions of key institutions of these democracies (executive and legislative relations in varying institutional contexts, interest groups, and parties and party systems), the closing chapters also address a specific theoretical issue: to what extent have differing regime transition and consolidation trajectories affected the basic character of these new democracies?

Gianfranco Pasquino explores the nature of executive-legislative relations in Southern Europe. This is a subject that has generally been ignored in the comparative politics literature and has not previously been the focus of studies of democratization processes. Building upon Karl Loewenstein's earlier work, Pasquino focuses on the distinction between concentration of power in the executive, which contributes to governmental stability and efficacy, and the dispersion of power, which enhances representativeness and opens channels of communication between the legislature and the executive. He argues that a particular pattern of executive-legislative relations may be functional at one stage in the democratization process but dysfunctional at another. Specifically, he argues that openness and representativeness may be crucial during that phase of the transition when new democratic institutions are being fashioned but that government stability and decisional efficacy enhance the prospects for democratic consolidation. In this respect, Italy's consolidation was complicated and made more protracted by its greater dispersion of decision-making authority and its high levels of government instability. These same problems also contributed to the rise of cynicism towards parties and politicians that culminated in the early 1990s in deconsolidation and restructuring of the electoral and party systems and that fed northern resentment towards the inefficiency and corruption of the government in Rome.

Philippe Schmitter draws an important distinction between the consolidation of democracy, on the one hand, and the consolidation of "partial regimes," such as those encompassing parties and party systems, patterns of interest intermediation, and territorial or regional administration, on the other. He contends that the consolidation of partial regimes (i.e., the emergence of stable institutions and patterns of interaction within these respective spheres) has an important impact on the type of democracy that emerges from the consolidation process. Focusing on business and labor organizations, he concludes that the four democracies of Southern Europe vary substantially with regard to the extent of institutionalization of interest associations. He further contends that the consolidation of these partial regimes will primarily affect the nature of social, political, and economic interactions within these systems. Specifically, he argues that the consolidation of partial regimes, encompassing trade unions, business associations, and agricultural interest groups, has an important impact on the distribution of benefits, formulas of legitimation, and the level of citizen satisfaction in each country. In other words, partial regimes have a long-term impact on the type of democracy which has taken shape. The short-term impact of these interest groups on the transition to or consolidation of democracy, however, was limited.

Leonardo Morlino's exploration of the partial regime involving political parties and party systems, in contrast, concludes that parties played central roles in all four of these democratic consolidation processes. Thus, the consolidation of these partial regimes affected the type of democracy that emerged in each case, and parties had a direct impact on the consolidation of democracy itself. Morlino distinguishes among differing aspects of the consolidation process. One of these pertains to the legitimation of democratic institutions and practices. Here, parties and party elites play the leading role in channeling and remolding the opinions and attitudes of their followers towards the emerging regime. In Greece, Portugal, and Spain, semiloyal or antisystem parties were negligible and largely disappeared after the first one or two elections; so the basic stands of political parties decisively contributed to popular acceptance and legitimation of these new democratic regimes. In Italy, however, antisystem or semiloyal stands by parties on both the left and the right continued to pose challenges to regime legitimation for decades, greatly protracting the consolidation process. Italian democracy was eventually consolidated, but by a different process, in which the extensive structuring of political parties and their domination of their respective segments of civil society played key roles.

In the last chapter three tasks are undertaken: drawing together the more important insights contained in the preceding chapters, interpreting them in a broader comparative context conducive to theoretical generalization, and suggesting questions which subsequent volumes in this series and future research building upon these findings need to address.

Taken together, the contributions in Volume 1 confront two sets of issues. First, they explore those factors that facilitate or impede democratic consolidation. Taking advantage of the nearly unique status of these Southern European countries as fully consolidated but relatively recently established democracies, they systematically examine those aspects of Southern European societies and polities that have helped advance those countries' consolidation processes and contrast them with characteristics of some South American and East European countries that have recently undergone transitions from nondemocratic regimes. They also compare the four Southern European cases with each other in an effort to explain variations in their respective consolidation experiences—hypothesizing, for example, about why Italy's consolidation process was so difficult and protracted, as compared with those of Greece and Spain. In this respect, the consolidation of democracy serves as a *dependent* variable in a wide variety of analyses. And, as we argue in the introductory chapter, we believe that, in turn, the consolidation of a new democracy (which involves the widespread legitimation of its key political institutions and behavioral norms) will contribute to the persistence of these regimes, enabling them to remain stable even in the face of serious challenges.

The second set of questions addressed in some of these chapters treats transition and consolidation processes as *independent* variables: it relates to the "trajectories" notion set forth above insofar as it explores the extent to which lasting features of political or social relations within a particular democratic regime are affected by important characteristics of its processes of regime change and consolidation. In this volume, we limit this exercise to the impact of transition and consolidation experiences on the basic executive and legislative institutions of each country's central government, on the development of interest groups and patterns of interest intermediation, and on the party system. Subsequent volumes in this series will broaden the scope of this enquiry to include the possible impact of these transition trajectories on other aspects of political behavior, on economic policies, on the evolution of public policy and the public sector in general, and on the political culture of each Southern European country.

The History of This Project

The intellectual history of the various initiatives which, eventually, gave rise to this project is, perhaps, worth recounting briefly. The initial stimulus for the creation of a committee of social scientists interested in studying the evolution of the Southern European transitions to democracy was provided by the events in Greece and Portugal in 1974 that toppled the authoritarian regimes of those countries. Following a series of formal and informal meetings over the ensuing two years, a research group was formed, called the Committee on Southern Europe (COSE), whose purpose was to promote the systematic study of the region over the period from the end of the Napoleonic Wars to the present. Initial participants in this effort were Douglas A. Chalmers, P. Nikiforos Diamandouros, Giuseppe Di Palma, James R. Kurth, Juan J. Linz, Edward E. Malefakis, Joyce F. Riegelhaupt, and Philippe C. Schmitter. The eventual product of this initiative was the creation and persistence of an informal, interdisciplinary network of scholars interested in both Southern Europe as a region and in the particular historical or political processes it exemplifies best, such as rapid and profound socioeconomic transformation in late-developing societies and successfully negotiated transitions to democracy. While COSE's institutional life proved to be short, most of its members, acting as individuals, remained in relatively close contact and, through their scholarly work and professional activities, substantively contributed, during the late 1970s and the early 1980s, to the expansion and, especially, the internationalization of the network to include European and Latin American social scientists working on either Southern Europe or on democratic transitions.

It was, at least in part, thanks to these efforts that, during the same period, Southern Europe as a region and the individual countries separately acquired greater visibility in meetings of professional associations at the national level (in particular, the political science and sociological associations in Europe and the United States, including the Council of European Studies in the latter), the regional level (e.g., the European Consortium for Political Research, where a separate Southern European Study Group was set up in the early 1980s), and international level (e.g., International Political Science Association and the International Sociological Association). The result was a significant accumulation of knowledge on various dimensions of the polities, economies, and cultures of Southern European societies, with significant spill-over effects for both area studies and comparative analysis.

This burgeoning activity came to happy fruition in 1987–88. Two informal meetings served as the immediate stimulus for a new round of activity: the first took place in the context of a conference on transition and consolidation in Latin America and Southern Europe, organized by Guillermo O'Donnell and Philippe Schmitter at the Kellogg Institute of the University of Notre Dame in April 1987. There a small group consisting of Maria Carrilho, P. Nikiforos Diamandouros, Richard Gunther, Juan Linz, and Philippe Schmitter intensively explored available options for a new initiative and extensively deliberated the requisites and content of its intellectual agenda. Issuing directly from this first meeting, a second one, made possible through Schmitter's energies and capacity to secure the required financial support, brought together a larger number of European and American specialists on Southern Europe to the magnificent setting of the European University Institute, in San Domenico di Fiesole, near Florence, in September 1987. It was in the sedate and austere premises of the institute that the central themes informing this project were initially articulated and widespread consensus was reached on the desirability of focusing not on transition but, rather, on consolidation, whose qualitatively different attributes and properties had yet to be seriously studied and analyzed.

It was at this time, finally, that the decision was taken to approach the Joint Committee on Western Europe of the American Council of Learned Societies (ACLS) and the Social Science Research Council (SSRC) with the idea of their sponsoring this activity. The Joint Committee's prior interest in democratization and regime transition in Southern Europe (in November 1981, it had sponsored a conference by that name in Madrid) made it an appropriate vehicle for a larger undertaking centered on democratic consolidation.

Endorsing the idea for such an initiative, the Joint Committee, in December 1987, proposed to the boards of the ACLS and SSRC establishment of the Subcommittee on the Nature and Consequences of Democracy in Southern Europe, which, following approval, formally came into being in April 1988. Co-chaired by P. Nikiforos Diamandouros (University of Athens) and Richard Gunther (Ohio State University), the subcommittee consisted of the following members, drawn from Greece, Italy, the Federal Republic of Germany, France, Portugal, Spain, the United Kingdom, and the United States: Manuel Villaverde Cabral (University of Lisbon), Maria Carrilho (Advanced Institute of Labor and Enterprise Sciences, Lisbon), Juan J. Linz (Yale University), Carmelo Lisón Tolosana (University of Madrid-Complutense), Edward E. Malefakis (Columbia University), George Th. Mavrogordatos (University of Athens), Yves Mény (Institut d'Etudes Politiques, Paris), José Ramón Montero (Autonomous University of Madrid), Leonardo Morlino (University of Florence), Gianfranco Pasquino (University of Bologna), Víctor Pérez-Díaz (Juan March Center for Advanced Study in the Social Sciences, Madrid), Hans-Jürgen Puhle (University of Bielefeld), Sidney Tarrow (Cornell University), and Loukas Tsoukalis (St. Antony's College, Oxford).[8]

The subcommittee's charge was dual: "(1) to engage in a systematic study of the nature of democratic consolidation in Greece, Portugal, Spain, and postfascist Italy, by exploring its cultural, economic, political, and social dimensions; and (2) to use the insights derived from this regional case study to contribute to the emergent, more general, theoretical debate concerning the properties of, and processes involved in, the consolidation of democracy." The interrelated dimensions of change in the New Southern Europe which the subcommittee was to explore were five: processes of democratic consolidation, the new democratic politics, economic and social relations in the region, the changing functions of the state in the post-Keynesian era, and the dynamics of cultural change.[9]

The final step towards the realization of what had, for more than a decade, been an elusive goal came in May 1988. At that time, the Stiftung Volkswagenwerk, underscoring its role as a preeminent European institution committed to the fostering of social science knowledge across national borders, agreed to provide generous support for a five-year program of research, conferences, and publication activities designed to produce five and possibly six collective volumes dealing with the five interconnected dimensions of change mentioned above and drawing together the major theoretical findings issuing from the project. It was through additional German support, provided by the Werner-Reimers Stiftung and the German Social Science Study Group on Spain and Portugal, that the project received its informal launching, in July 1989. Coordinated by Hans-Jürgen Puhle, who was greatly instrumental in steering the subcommittee's project through the German foundation world, this meeting brought the two co-chairs and a number of subcommittee members to Bad Homburg to prepare for the first conference in the series, which was held a year later in Madrid.

Volume 1 of the series is the product of an initial general conference, held in Madrid at the Juan March Center for Advanced Study in the Social Sciences in July 1990, and of a follow-up authors' meeting hosted by the Department of Sociology, University of Rome, in December of the same year. The second volume was made possible by an initial meeting held at the European Cultural Center, in Delphi, Greece, in July 1991, and a follow-up authors' conference sponsored by the Institute Clingendael, in The Hague in March 1992. Volume 3 also issued from a twin set of conferences: the first was held in Sintra, Portugal, in July 1992, while the authors' follow-up session was hosted by the Levi Foundation, in Venice in April 1993. The initial conference leading to Volume 4 was sponsored by the Zentrum für interdisziplinäre Forschung of the University of Bielefeld, Germany, in July 1993, and the authors' meeting was held at Boğaziçi University in Istanbul in July 1994. It is hoped that these conferences and the resulting published volumes will serve to more fully integrate Southern Europe into the mainstream of comparative social science research.

P. Nikiforos Diamandouros and Richard Gunther
General Series Editors

Acknowledgments

The debts to be acknowledged in an enterprise as large as this one are inevitably so many that it becomes virtually impossible to do justice to all those who, in a variety of ways, contributed to the initial conception, subsequent articulation, and eventual realization of the project. This notwithstanding, it behooves us to single out those few individuals whose critical support ensured the success of our common enterprise. From the very beginning, Juan J. Linz and Philippe C. Schmitter played a pivotal role in promoting the idea of such a project. Each in his own way provided both intellectual and organizational support and encouragement which proved critical to the successful launching of the subcommittee and invaluable for the articulation and elaboration of its intellectual agenda. Hans-Jürgen Puhle's multiple contributions to our efforts have been equally crucial. Besides acting as author and coeditor, as well as organizer and gracious host of the subcommittee's meetings in Bad Homburg and Bielefeld, he played a central role in securing financial support for this multiyear project. Above all, however, he has served, from the beginning, as an invaluable source of advice, stimulation, moral support, and guidance on both intellectual and organizational matters confronting the co-chairs.

Grateful thanks are also due those members of the subcommittee who faithfully attended conferences, contributed to deliberations, read papers, acted as a board of advisors, served as resource persons in a multiplicity of ways, and, above all, stood by us as friends.

Both at the time of the proposal's submission and, especially, since its approval, the subcommittee profited greatly from the friendly encouragement, discrete presence, and professional support extended to it by Dr. Alfred Schmidt and subsequently by Dr. Helga Junkers of the Volkswagen Foundation, who monitored the subcommittee's activities.

To them and the foundation itself we wish to express our most sincere appreciation.

The Social Science Research Council (SSRC) and its professional and support staff have, from the outset, provided invaluable organizational support for this project. Peter A. Gourevitch, Peter A. Hall, and Peter Lange served successively as chairs of the subcommittee's parent body, the Joint Committee on Western Europe of the ACLS/SSRC, during the life of this project. Their genuine interest in the affairs of the subcommittee and their willingness to offer advice and support when needed served as a source of comfort and reassurance for the co-chairs. Yasmine Ergas and Kent Worcester, the SSRC professional staff responsible for the subcommittee, and their assistants, Elizabeth O'Brien, David Terrien, and Justin Powell deserve mention for providing the requisite organizational support for the many conferences, authors' meetings, and editors' requests which this project entailed.

An expression of thanks should also go to those institutions and organizations in Germany, Greece, Italy, the Netherlands, Spain, and Turkey which graciously acted as hosts to, and partial sponsors for, preliminary meetings leading up to the establishment of the subcommittee as well as subsequent conferences and authors' meetings. These are Boğaziçi University, the Center for Interdisciplinary Research at the University of Bielefeld, the Clingendael Institute in The Hague, the European Cultural Centre of Delphi, the European University Institute, the German Social Science Study Group on Spain and Portugal, the Center for Advanced Study in the Social Sciences of the Juan March Institute in Madrid, the Helen Kellogg Institute for International Studies at the University of Notre Dame, the Ugo and Olga Levi Foundation in Venice, the University of Rome, and the Werner-Reimers Foundation in Bad Homburg.

The Mershon Center of the Ohio State University provided very generous support, making possible the extensive work of editorial revision and production of the manuscript for the first volume of this series. In particular, the assistance provided by Neovi Karakatsanis was invaluable, both for the extraordinary care and diligence she brought to bear in editorial tasks and for the insightful criticisms that helped to improve the manuscript. Jonathan Swarts also made a substantial contribution to this book, particularly regarding preparation of the index.

One of the most impressive aspects of this enterprise was the degree of genuine interest, support, and oftentimes enthusiasm which it generated among social scientists from different disciplinary backgrounds, who were called upon to act as contributors to individual volumes, discussants in conferences and authors' meetings, resource persons, or simply friendly advisors. Taken together, this wider circle of scholars deserves credit for having helped create an international and interdisciplinary network of social scientists actively committed to the generation of scholarly knowledge on Southern Europe, democratic consolidation, and more generally, democratization. Whether through institutional structures or informal contacts, the persistence of this network will constitute a reminder and compelling evidence that this ACLS/SSRC initiative was very much worth undertaking. For this, they have our heartfelt appreciation and thanks.

The Politics of Democratic Consolidation

1 Introduction

Richard Gunther, Hans-Jürgen Puhle, and P. Nikiforos Diamandouros

The reemergence of democratic regimes in Greece, Portugal, and Spain in the mid-1970s appeared at first as an aberrant departure from a worldwide trend in the direction of authoritarianism. The large number of democratic breakdowns in postcolonial African states and the emergence in Latin America of unprecedentedly harsh forms of authoritarian rule suggested that democracy might survive only in certain kinds of societies at certain times and that stable democratic regimes would remain, for the foreseeable future, a luxury that might be enjoyed by only a handful of societies.

In retrospect, however, the redemocratization of Southern Europe can more properly be regarded as a harbinger of things to come: it was the first trickle in what would later become a "third wave" of democratization.[1] This trend reached its apex in 1989, with the collapse of nondemocratic communist regimes throughout Eastern Europe and the Soviet Union. In this greatly altered circumstance, the democracies which emerged in "The New Southern Europe" took on added salience and presented themselves as invaluable objects for social science analysis. Unlike virtually all of the other recent cases of redemocratization, Greece, Portugal, and Spain had not only completed their transitions to democracy, but by the middle to late 1980s all of their new democratic regimes had become fully consolidated. The politics of democratic consolidation in Southern Europe can therefore provide analysts and political actors alike with a unique laboratory for the testing of propositions relevant to theories of redemocratization and democratic stability.

This volume will analyze the processes of consolidation of democratic regimes in Southern European countries in a comparative perspective, identifying similarities and differences and using them for the elaboration of theoretical propositions that can be applied and tested elsewhere. We will add an analysis of the earlier redemocratization of Italy to those of Greece, Portugal, and Spain. Since, as Edward Malefakis argues in the following chapter, these four Southern European countries have displayed such significant parallels in their previous social, economic, and political development, the systematic incorporation of Italy within this framework will enable us to undertake an analysis of "most similar systems." At the same time, the fact that Italy had undergone redemocratization three decades earlier, under very different circumstances (the extreme poverty of the postwar era, the outbreak of the Cold War, etc.) allows us to introduce variations in theoretically significant dimensions to test their impact on consolidation processes and other aspects of democratic politics. Several of the chapters in this volume also make explicit comparisons with recent democratization and redemocratization processes in Latin America and Eastern Europe, making it clear that some of the theoretical insights derived from the study of these Southern European cases are, indeed, exportable to other regions. At the same time, these writers underline the methodological risks inherent in exporting Southern European models of transition or consolidation to regions with greatly different socioeconomic structures, cultures, and political traditions.

For three reasons, in particular, we believe that this book on democratic consolidation in Southern Europe is timely and will be extremely useful. First, while there has been a tremendous proliferation of fine academic studies of democratization in the late twentieth century, nearly all of this literature has focused on the demise of authoritarian or communist regimes and on the *transition* to democracy, and does not entail a systematic analysis of democratic *consolidation* processes. Second, the Southern European countries present a unique opportunity for the study of consolidation processes, which are only just beginning or only partly under way in most other recently redemocratized countries. Third, unlike all previous cases of successful democratization (including the postwar democratization of Germany, Italy, and Japan), redemocratization processes in Southern Europe have been subjected to rigorous analysis, from a variety of perspectives, using the full panoply of modern social science research techniques: the testing of hypotheses has proceeded on the basis of both quantitative data (including public opinion surveys replicating the administration of similar questionnaire items throughout all four countries in the region, and even parallel questionnaires, on occasion) and qualitative approaches (such as in-depth case studies and systematic elite interviews). Since many of these studies were conducted by several of the contributors to this volume, these researchers are well positioned to carry out comparative analyses that are firmly grounded in a rich empirical literature.

Transitions to Democracy

Transition and consolidation are conceptually distinct aspects of democratization, although in practice they may temporally overlap or sometimes even coincide. Transition begins with the breakdown of the former authoritarian regime and ends with the establishment of a relatively stable configuration of political institutions within a democratic regime. Consolidation (which will be more extensively defined below) refers to the achievement of substantial attitudinal support for and behavioral compliance with the new democratic institutions and the rules of the game which they establish. In most cases, the consolidation of democracy requires more time than the transition process (although the amount of time required for consolidation varies, depending upon whether maximalist or minimalist definitions of it are adopted, as will be discussed at greater length below); consolidation is much more complex, and it involves a much larger number of actors in a wider array of political arenas. The outcomes of these processes are also distinct: transition results in the creation of a new regime; consolidation results in the stability and persistence of that regime, even in the face of severe challenges. The endpoints of the two processes may differ in another way as well. Transition may culminate in a new regime, but that regime may not even be fully democratic; democratic consolidation, as we define it, requires full conformity with all the criteria inherent in a demanding, multifaceted procedural definition of democracy. Key explanatory variables may differ significantly between the two processes: confining conditions of a transition may be renegotiated and made irrelevant through the subsequent consolidation process; conversely, factors such as the social requisites for democracy, which could be partly neglected during the transition, may become highly relevant subsequently, as mass support for the new regime becomes a significant consideration.[2] In short, what matters for the transition may be less relevant or irrelevant for democratic consolidation, and vice versa. Finally, it is important to distinguish conceptually between transition and consolidation insofar as these two distinct aspects of the broader democratization process may interrelate with one another in subtle but important ways: indeed, one of the unifying themes of this series of volumes is that the transition trajectory followed by a political system may have a multifaceted impact on the consolidation process or on the character of the democracy which is ultimately established.

To this point, the comparative literature on democratization has focused almost exclusively on transition processes. The early and classic analyses of transitions from authoritarian rule, focused exclusively on processes relating to the demise of authoritarian regimes and those regimes' characteristics, coalitions and factions, their various ways of extricating the military from government and politics, elite pacts or settlements (if there were any), founding coalitions and elections, the framing of the constitution and of the new democratic institutions, and/or the national and international context within which these processes unfolded.[3]

Most of the monographic literature on democratization in Southern Europe has also centered much more around the transition than around the consolidation of the new democracies.[4] In some respects, an exception to this generalization is the case of Spain, which, for various reasons, has been studied most extensively and has been regarded as the ideal type of a negotiated transition, as well as a successful and relatively unproblematic consolidation of democracy. Research on Spain has, from early on, gone beyond the narrow scope of the transition.[5] It has dealt extensively with the broader and more complex problems of democratic consolidation, the stability of institutions, electoral coalitions, and the political class.[6] At a different level, it has focused on economic and social policies, "corporatism," and the long-term impact of social and cultural change.[7] Studies of Greece and Portugal are fewer in number and more limited in scope, largely focusing on transition processes.[8]

Nevertheless, while some monographic studies have gone beyond the traditional focus on transition to explore processes of democratic consolidation, there have been very few explicitly comparative studies that do so. Most of the comparisons between Southern Europe and Latin America, and increasingly since 1989 Eastern Europe, have so far not gone much beyond typological comparisons,and have principally focused on the problems of the transition and (in Eastern Europe) the beginnings of the economic transformation.[9] A number of important parameters of the consolidation process have been addressed in more recent work on different types of democracies.[10] The historical, institutional, social, and cultural traditions of the societies involved and their broader environment have also been touched upon in this emerging literature.[11] The more general problem of mediation between democracy, formal and substantive, has been the object of yet another small body of published studies.[12] Those few studies published to date which have conceptualized the consolidation of (a particular type of) democracy as a distinct process categorically different from (but nevertheless to a still unclear extent influenced by) the transition have not gone beyond noting the structure of the problem and asking important questions.[13]

Thus, it is desirable at this stage to go beyond typological assumptions to develop a more consistent theoretical argument concerning consolidation processes supported by empirical data and comparative analysis. For the reasons listed above, Southern Europe is the ideal laboratory for this more ambitious social science enterprise. The first steps in this direction have been taken recently in a handful of studies, but their scope has largely been restricted to only a few aspects of these complex processes, such as the specific roles played by elites, parliaments, political parties, interest groups, and modes of interest intermediation in democratic consolidation. To date, none has attempted a multidimensional assessment of the processes of democratic consolidation.[14]

On Democratic Consolidation

The extent to which new democracies have become consolidated is of both practical and theoretical significance and has given rise to considerable scholarly debate. Although, in some respects, this debate is a reflection of differing substantive conclusions about the extent of consolidation of various democratic regimes, it is also clear that one reason why no clear consensus has emerged is that scholars have used different definitions of democratic consolidation. In order to limit the confusion that would result from analysts talking past each other in this manner, we believe that it is desirable to begin by explicitly setting forth a definition of this key concept.

Our starting point is recognition of the fact that the concept of democratic consolidation is double-barrelled—it joins two distinct concepts that must be assessed separately in analyzing the status of political regimes. In order to conclude that democratic consolidation has succeeded in a particular case, it is necessary first to ascertain whether the regime is fully democratic and then to determine if that regime is consolidated. In our conceptualization, both democracy and consolidation are ideal types, and both must be closely approximated before one can conclude that democratic consolidation has occurred.

The definition of democracy that we will use in this book is the procedural conceptualization of Juan Linz. In setting forth his classic regime typology, Linz stated that a system can be regarded as democratic "when it allows the free formulation of political preferences, through the use of basic freedoms of association, information, and communication, for the purpose of free competition between leaders to validate at regular intervals by nonviolent means their claim to rule, . . . without excluding any effective political office from that competition or prohibiting any members of the political community from expressing their preference."[15] In collaboration with Alfred Stepan, Linz has slightly modified this definition by adding that, if certain policy domains are "off limits" and not under the effective authority of elected officials, or if electorally unaccountable elites retain "reserve powers" that can block policy initiatives by elected officials, then the system should be regarded as falling significantly short of the democratic ideal type.[16]

With one partial exception, all four of the Southern European regimes analyzed in this volume had become fully democratic by the late 1970s, according to each of the demanding criteria set forth by Linz: elections were held at regular intervals and under universal suffrage; full civil and political liberties were enjoyed by Portuguese, Spanish, Italian, and Greek citizens; no political parties or ideological orientations were banned or otherwise excluded from electoral competition; and electoral fraud which might have inhibited or invalidated expressions of citizen preferences was minimal. The one partial exception was Portugal. The existence of the Portuguese Council of the Revolution (consisting of *nonelected* military officers with extensive powers, including those of judicial review of parliamentary legislation) initially violated the clause pertaining to the exclusion of "any effective political office from that competition." With the constitutional reforms of 1982 eliminating the Council of the Revolution, however, this limitation on Portuguese democracy was removed. The 1976 Portuguese constitution also included clauses that violated the ideal-type definition insofar as they removed a wide range of economic policy issues from effective control of elected officials. In an effort to make permanent some of the revolutionary conquests of 1974–75, the constitution explicitly endorsed socialism and prevented privatization of nationalized or collectivized agricultural, industrial, and financial properties.[17] The reforms of 1989, however, removed most of the relevant clauses of the constitution, thus opening up the full range of policy options to democratically elected officials. With these reforms, Portugal could be regarded as completely democratic.

To what extent have these four democratic regimes become consolidated? Before addressing this question, we must clearly define consolidation and contrast our definition with several treatments of this concept in the newly emerging literature on democratic consolidation. Some of these definitions are minimalist in scope, nature, and duration.[18] Others are extensive in terms of the range of social and political institutions involved,[19] in terms of the amount of time required before consolidation is achieved,[20] or both. Our definition is middle range and focuses primarily on political institutions and norms of behavior. It derives from the simple notion that the most fundamental problem confronting recently democratized political systems pertains to the resilience of the political regime itself and its ability to remain stable and to develop even in the face of severe challenges.

Most definitions of consolidation involve the stabilization, routinization, institutionalization and/or legitimation of patterns of politically relevant behavior. As Philippe Schmitter notes, "the basic idea common to all of these is that social relations can become social structures, i.e., patterns of interaction can become so regular in their occurrence, so endowed with meaning, so capable of motivating behavior that they become autonomous in their internal function and resistant to externally induced change."[21] Laurence Whitehead asserts that the essence of the consolidation process is that "the new regime becomes institutionalized, its framework of open and competitive political expression becomes internalized."[22] Adam Przeworski states that "democracy is consolidated when under given political and economic conditions a particular system of institutions becomes the only game in town, when no one can imagine acting outside the democratic institutions, when all the losers want to do is to try again within the same institutions under which they have just lost."[23] Other definitions of democratic consolidation that are similar to or entirely compatible with ours are set forth by Scott Mainwaring, Guillermo O'Donnell, and Samuel Valenzuela.[24]

We consider a democratic regime to be consolidated when all politically significant groups regard its key political institutions as the only legitimate framework for political contestation, and adhere to democratic rules of the game. This definition thus includes an attitudinal dimension, wherein existing political institutions are regarded as acceptable and without legitimate alternatives, as well as a behavioral criterion, according to which a specific set of norms is respected and adhered to by all politically significant groups.[25] It should be noted that use of the term *politically significant* builds into the definition a degree of flexibility, a necessary feature of all ideal-type conceptualizations. As with all ideal types, there is no real-world case in which *all* citizens or political groups strictly obey democratic rules of the game and fully acknowledge the legitimacy of the political institutions and principles under which they live—every fully democratic society will include some political dissidents or social deviants who reject or violate these criteria. While these inevitable departures from strict conformity with the ideal type do not undermine the utility of such concepts in comparative analysis, they do sometimes make it difficult to locate with precision the dividing line between (in this instance) consolidated and unconsolidated democratic regimes. Since regime sustainability is our principal concern, we would place that dividing line at the point where democratic regimes are *sufficiently consolidated* so as to survive and remain stable in the face of such serious challenges as major economic or international crises, or even serious outbreaks of terrorist violence. Accordingly, a regime may be regarded as sufficiently consolidated even if some of its citizens do not share in the democratic consensus or regard its key institutions as legitimate, as long as those individuals or groups are numerically insignificant, basically isolated from regime-supporting forces, and therefore incapable of disrupting the stability of the regime. The broader the scope of that democratic consensus, however, the closer the regime will be to full conformity with our ideal-type definition of democratic consolidation.

This criterion of political significance thus includes a numerical component.[26] The strategic location of antidemocratic forces is also relevant: a handful of dissidents on the fringes of a polity would not normally be regarded as politically significant. If those individuals were the commanders of key military units near a nation's capital, however, their disruptive potential would be much greater. Accordingly, a democratic system may be regarded as consolidated if the legitimacy of its key institutions is not challenged or if its basic rules of political behavior are not regularly violated by politically significant groups. Geoffrey Pridham, in this volume, refers to this degree of consolidation as "negative consolidation;" it is negative insofar as it involves the discrediting and neutralization of any real threat of collapse and replacement by another regime. Using this definition, we regard all four of the Southern European regimes analyzed here as consolidated by the early to middle 1980s.

This is not to say that significant qualitative and quantitative changes may not still take place. The quality of democracy in each country may still be improved (moving it closer to the ideal type) or undermined. And support for existing democratic institutions and practices may increase, either through continuing efforts to inculcate democratic values into populations initially socialized under authoritarian regimes or through the progressive integration of once isolated societies into the core of Western Europe through the proliferation of linkages with the European Community. Pridham refers to this as "positive consolidation." He analyzes international influences of this kind that have set in motion ongoing processes that will progressively reinforce the consolidation of the new Southern European democracies over the course of several decades. We regard continued movement towards the ideal type of democratic consolidation in these systems as very significant. However, we believe that these longer-term processes should be regarded as broadening and deepening system support and as enhancing democratic legitimacy within regimes that by the mid-1980s were already sufficiently consolidated to have survived strong challenges.[27]

The key point is that, in several ways, the basic character of politics within consolidated democracies is different from political interactions within unconsolidated systems, and this enhances the prospects for stability and long-term survival of consolidated systems. First, acknowledging the legitimacy of democratic institutions and respecting rules of democratic procedure discourages governing elites in new democracies from trampling on the rights of opposition groups. A lack of such commitment, in contrast, could be compatible with an abridgment of democracy that might ultimately culminate in its transformation into a limited democracy or an authoritarian regime.[28] The coup-from-above executed by Peruvian president Alberto Fujimori in 1992 is an excellent example of such behavior in an unconsolidated democratic system.[29] Governing elites in consolidated democratic regimes share in the consensus supporting a democratic regime and respect its norms and institutions. This serves as a check on abuses of executive power.

Democratic consolidation also contributes to stability by reducing the intensity of the expression of political conflict and by restricting it to peaceful institutionalized channels. Acknowledgment of a common set of democratic norms of behavior reduces uncertainty about what constitutes proper or improper behavior and contributes to the routinization of nonviolent and mutually respectful expressions of political conflict. Insofar as these norms eschew violence, intimidation, and the like, their widespread acceptance reduces mutual fears and suspicions. And insofar as losing in a political conflict is not usually perceived as posing a direct threat to the physical or material well-being of either side, the intensity of the conflict is mitigated and incumbents who lose an election are more willing to step down, confident that they will survive and perhaps return to power at some point in the future. Acknowledgment of the legitimacy of governmental institutions in a new democracy also increases the probability that conflict will be channeled as a matter of choice through democratic, representative institutions, rather than into unregulated extraparliamentary arenas. This stands in sharp contrast with several European democracies in the interwar period and with several new democracies in postcolonial Africa, in which democratic norms were not widely internalized, violent extraparliamentary behavior was common, and elites who lost power were, indeed, denied civil and political rights, having no real prospect of returning to power through the regime's "representative" institutions. More recently, the absence of consensual adherence to democratic norms has contributed to high levels of violence in several East European countries (especially in several parts of what had been Yugoslavia and the Soviet Union).

The dynamics of political conflict in unconsolidated democratic regimes are distinct in several ways. Important and powerful elites and their supporters deny the legitimacy of the existing regime and may seek to overthrow it. Challenges to regime legitimacy and the absence of consensual acceptance of democratic norms of behavior also impart a tenuous, conditional, and mutually suspicious quality to expressions of political conflict. Few political actors are prepared to stake their futures on the workings of democratic institutions; they look for other, frequently illegal and antidemocratic, ways to shore up their positions, engaging in democratic processes only as long as such activities are useful in advancing their interests. And, because they also perceive rival political parties as conditional in their support for democracy and equivocal in their commitment to democratic rules of the game, political competition and conflict are fraught with suspicion and distrust. Insofar as mass mobilizations in the streets take the place of bargaining among representative elites and become the principal form of "dialogue" between government and opposition (or even between rival opposition groups), a self-reinforcing cycle of protest-repression-protest may be set in motion that progressively polarizes relations among groups and raises the overall level of violence within the polity.

Elites and Sufficient Consolidation: The Case of Spain

Spain in the period 1979–82 clearly reveals how and why our concept of consolidation provides a powerful explanation of the resilience of new democracies in the face of serious challenges, and why even partial consolidation can be crucial during times of stress. While most scholars would contend that the democratic regime in Spain became consolidated at the national level only after the trials of rebellious military officers in 1982 (in the course of which, the defendants thoroughly discredited themselves and the cause of antisystem opposition to the new democracy), substantial progress towards consolidation had been achieved with ratification of the constitution in 1978 and the autonomy statutes for the Basque and Catalan regions in 1979. Nonetheless, it cannot be argued that full consolidation had been achieved by that time. In the 1980 Basque regional election, the explicitly antisystem and separatist party, Herri Batasuna, received electoral support from more than one out of every seven voters; Euskadiko Ezkerra (at that time still tied to the violent separatist organization ETA *político-militar*) received another 10 percent of the vote; and the Partido Nacionalista Vasco (PNV, Basque Nationalist Party, which at that time maintained a semiloyal stance vis-à-vis the Spanish regime) was supported by nearly 40 percent of the voters. Clearly, within this region, the democratic regime was not consolidated at that time. The basic nature of politics within the region reflected this absence of a democratic consensus: violent clashes between ETA supporters and the police occurred with great frequency, acrimonious disputes erupted among political elites, terrorist violence (which by 1990 had claimed more than 700 lives) was at its peak, and a considerable polarization of politics and society had taken place. Thus, within this one region (containing just under 6 percent of the population of Spain) democratic politics and institutions were not consolidated at that time.

At the national level, however, the picture was quite different. Antisystem parties (such as the extreme right-wing Fuerza Nueva) attracted a negligible and declining level of electoral support. More importantly, the major parties, ranging from the communist PCE on the left to Alianza Popular (founded by prominent elites from the Franquist regime) on the right had entered into the politics of consensus, producing a democratic constitution that they all supported and which was ratified by an overwhelming margin in the December 1978 constitutional referendum. Moderation characterized political behavior at both the mass and the elite levels. But while party elites fully embraced the democratic consensus, military elites (who had been socialized in military academies under the Franco regime and who had not been included in the negotiations that forged the democratic consensus) did not. In short, there was a partial consolidation of the regime, with sectors of the military and some Basque nationalists maintaining antisystem or semiloyal stands but with leaders and supporters of the major nationwide parties firmly supportive of the institutions and procedural norms of the new democracy.

This partial consolidation, incomplete as it was, constituted an essential resource that enabled the regime to survive an extreme test—an attempted coup in February 1981, in which, at one point, virtually the entire Spanish party elite was held at gunpoint by rebellious military officials. The coup collapsed, in large measure because of two factors, both of which are central to our conception of democratic consolidation. The first was the legitimate authority of the king, whose orders to potentially rebellious military units to stand down were obeyed. The second involves the consensual unity established among national-level party leaders that led them to stand firm in unanimous support for the democratic regime. If the elite of any significant party had abandoned its support for the regime and participated in a military-civilian government (as was proposed by one of the conspirators, General Alfonso Armada), the outcome might have been quite different. Instead, the coup was opposed by all parties: of particular symbolic importance was the behavior of the leader of the right-wing Alianza Popular, Manuel Fraga, who melodramatically stood up in defense of the regime while being held at gunpoint by the rebels.[30] In short, over a year before consolidation of the regime had been substantially completed, a degree of consolidation was achieved that proved to be essential for regime survival. Since then, a considerable broadening and deepening of consolidation has taken place, but this earlier watershed must be regarded as of considerable theoretical and practical importance.

Indicators of Consolidation

How can the analyst determine if a regime is consolidated? One temptation might be to infer consolidation from the appearance of stability: the regime survived, ergo it must have been consolidated. This kind of argumentation would verge on tautology. It could also lead the analyst to confuse the concept of consolidation with the empirical test to which the regime is submitted. It is commonly argued that peaceful alternation in government between parties that were once bitter rivals constitutes such a test. We reject the use of this as a prerequisite for regarding a regime as consolidated, not only because we believe it reflects conceptual confusion, but also because it leads to some rather absurd applications to the real world: according to this criterion, the democratic regimes of Japan and Italy (both of which have survived and thrived but whose governments were dominated by a single party for over four decades) would not have been regarded as consolidated until the 1990s.[31] While the passing of a severe test (alternation in power between former rivals, continued widespread support and stability during times of extreme economic hardship, successful defeat and punishment of a handful of strategically placed rebels, or regime stability in the face of a radical restructuring of the party system) may constitute evidence that a regime is consolidated, that test should not be confused with the concept of consolidation itself.

Our conceptualization of democratic consolidation avoids the risk of being tautological by clearly separating the ultimate long-term product of consolidation (regime sustainability) from the concept of consolidation itself (which focuses on the extent of attitudinal support for the key representative institutions of the democratic regime and respect for its specific rules of the game), and by insisting on unequivocal empirical measures of the extent to which institutions are regarded as legitimate and the regime's specific behavioral norms are respected. Accordingly, evidence of consolidation or the lack thereof should not simply be derived from such behavioral manifestations as efforts (successful or otherwise) to topple a regime but rather from public statements by leaders of political parties, social movements, and large secondary organizations, by official documents and ideological declarations made by such groups, and by symbolic gestures and behavioral habits that reflect a denial of the legitimacy of a regime's representative institutions and its behavioral norms. The absence of sufficient regime consolidation may be *confirmed* by subsequent acts such as a military coup or mass-level protest and rebellion, but in order to avoid tautological argumentation these kinds of obvious behavioral manifestations should never be relied upon as the sole measure of a lack of consolidation.

One broad indicator of consolidation is the absence of a politically significant antisystem party or social movement. The concept of an antisystem party or movement, however, must be clarified at this point, given the abuses to which this term has been subjected. It has sometimes been used for polemical purposes to stigmatize a democratic party that has no real intention of overthrowing a regime: this is certainly true of the Italian Communist Party (PCI) of the early and middle 1970s, which, despite having embraced Eurocommunism and repeatedly demonstrated its commitment to democracy, was regularly accused by the Christian Democrats (DC) of being an untrustworthy and disloyal competitor. To be regarded as an indicator of the absence of democratic consolidation, an antisystem party or movement must be unequivocally opposed to the existing regime. Fortunately (from an analytical point of view, that is), most antisystem groups make no bones about their stance: they vote against constitutions or organize boycotts of constitutional referenda in a direct challenge to the legitimacy of the regime and its key institutions, they regularly condemn the regime and articulate their vision of the alternative regime they seek, and they often try to subvert existing institutions, even when elected to serve in them. Accordingly, the analyst can identify antisystem parties on the basis of their official ideological and programmatic declarations, speeches by their elites, or probing interviews with party leaders, in conjunction with certain behavioral manifestations.

The existence of a politically significant semiloyal organization also constitutes evidence that full, or perhaps even sufficient, consolidation has not been achieved. Semiloyal parties and groups can be identified using the same published or verbal declarations and behaviors. A semiloyal stance, however, is not as easy to identify as an antisystem orientation. Semiloyal elites and organizations do not overtly reject the institutions or norms of a political regime, but, rather, they maintain an ambiguous stance towards that regime. They may operate within its institutional channels and follow its rules, but this behavior does not reflect a full acknowledgment of their propriety or legitimacy. Instead, it reflects a conditional or instrumental acceptance of the regime's rules and institutions.

Again Spain provides a clear example of semiloyalty, in a party that is politically significant within the Basque region. The Basque Nationalist Party adopted a tortuously ambiguous stance vis-à-vis the Spanish state during and after the transition to democracy. Its delegation in the Congress of Deputies walked out of the parliament to avoid voting on the constitution, and the party recommended that its voters abstain from the December 1978 constitutional referendum. While it did not reject the constitution or directly challenge its legitimacy, neither did it endorse that document or the democratic regime it established. Instead, its official stance was one of *acatamiento*—obedience, submission, and (grudging) respect. It also maintained a highly ambiguous stand concerning its ultimate intentions, particularly concerning whether it regarded the self-government rights it enjoyed under its statute of autonomy as adequate or whether it would seek to form an independent Basque nation-state. This attitudinal ambiguity was accompanied by semiloyal behavior, including a PNV boycott of all sessions of the Spanish Cortes from January through September 1980, a "war of the flags" in 1983 (in which PNV-controlled municipalities refused to fly the Spanish flag), and a refusal, until the late 1980s, to condemn ETA's use of terrorist violence.

Semiloyalty can have a considerable impact on the performance of the political system, particularly insofar as other political elites may, in reaction, adopt a skeptical, suspicious, or outright hostile stance towards virtually everything the semiloyal party does or says. In the case of Basque-Spanish political interactions in the early 1980s, it led to tense, rancorous verbal exchanges—in contrast with the structural integration among rival Spanish elites that further enhanced the consolidation of regime at the national level.[32] Semiloyalty in the Basque region also contributed to frequent and serious impasses between the

Basque and Spanish governments over such issues as the transfer of governmental functions from the center to the regional level.

We have asserted that acknowledgment of the propriety and legitimacy of a regime's key institutions is central to our definition of consolidation. This assertion implies that fundamental and protracted disagreement among politically significant groups concerning the legitimacy of a particular set of institutions or rules of the game in a given democratic regime may well lead to the deconsolidation of that regime and set in motion an uncertain process which can result in any of three options. One possible outcome is the reequilibration of the same regime, following the negotiation and emergence of alternative and possibly new institutional rearrangements and rules of the game that are more acceptable to politically significant groups and to the public at large. A second possibility is the emergence of a qualitatively different, and hence new, democratic regime, whose key political institutions and rules of the game differ substantively from those of its predecessor. (This would appear to be the case in Italy, following the crises of 1992–94.) The third potential outcome of deconsolidation is the collapse of the democratic regime and eventual instauration of a nondemocratic alternative.

Thus conceived, our definition of democratic consolidation, which regards the absence of serious conflict among politically significant groups over the acceptability of the basic framework for political contestation as central for regime sustainability and democratic persistence, imposes more demanding criteria than do definitions based upon the simple notion that widespread support for democracy in the abstract is sufficient for regarding a regime as consolidated. To be sure, widespread support for democracy may be important, particularly insofar as it increases the chances that whatever new governmental system or regime may come into existence will be democratic. It also helps to channel pressures for change through established democratic institutions and to process them in accord with procedural norms that eschew violence or other potentially polarizing forms of behavior that could pose a threat to the maintenance of civil order. But insofar as widespread support for democracy undervalues or ignores the importance which the absence of fundamental disputes among politically significant groups over the acceptability of the basic framework for political contestation implies for democratic stability, predictability, and ultimately sustainability, its theoretical utility for the rigorous analysis of democratic consolidation remains limited.

Our focus on the basic institutions and procedures of a democratic regime leads inexorably to two important questions: Which political institutions are included in the category of basic institutions and procedures? And does this notion imply that there can be no criticism or reform of governmental institutions in a consolidated democracy? Clearly, the answer to the latter question is no. Huntington long ago pointed out that one important feature of stable and durable institutions is their adaptability.[33] On occasion, democratic regimes must modify the structure of governmental institutions in order, for example, to make their performance more efficient or to respond to popular demands for change. We believe that criticism of inefficacy and demands for basic institutional reform are perfectly compatible with a regime's status as a consolidated democracy, as long as such criticism or resulting institutional changes do not violate the basic tenets of democracy (as defined above) or lead a politically significant group or sector of the public to challenge the legitimacy of the regime itself. Indeed, as long as such groups consent to the reforms, the scope of institutional change may be quite extensive: in the Spanish case, negotiations over autonomy statutes for various regions in the aftermath of ratification of the 1978 constitution culminated in nothing less than a radical devolution of extensive policy making and executive authority from the center to new regional governments without threatening the legitimacy of the regime itself. It was not the scope of change or the identity of the specific institutions involved that determined the acceptability of these reforms, it was the fact that they were undertaken through decision-making procedures that established or maintained a broad consensus among all politically relevant groups. In short, the determination that an institutional arrangement or reform proposal is so unacceptable that it precludes acknowledgment of regime legitimacy is subjective, and can only be determined by the politically significant groups themselves, on a case by case basis, and not in accord with some standing a priori criteria. To be sure, those institutions whose alteration has led to social polarization and regime delegitimation in the past have most commonly been highly visible and important ones, such as monarchy versus republic, centralized versus federal or decentralized government, electoral laws, or the balance of power between executive and legislature. But this is not always the case. The Greek regime that came into existence in 1974 did away with the monarchy without trauma and without undermining its own legitimacy. Conversely, in the Spanish case, one significant challenge to regime legitimacy derived from a dispute over a largely symbolic, rather than substantive, matter. The PNV boycotted the parliamentary vote on the constitution, recommended that its electorate abstain from the referendum, and maintained a semiloyal stance for nearly a decade, not because they objected to the characteristics of any particular political institution or procedure established by the constitution,[34] but because of the symbolic importance of a six-word clause included within an "additional disposition" to the constitution.[35]

Bringing the Masses Back In

To this point, we have focused our attention on mobilized, active, and organized segments of a political system. This reflects our view that the stability and resilience of democratic regimes are most directly affected by the behavior of relatively powerful elites, who control organizations (such as political parties, trade unions, military units, or mass movements) with sufficient resources as to pose a threat to regime survival. But we also acknowledge the important role of the attitudes and norms of the mass public. While most ordinary citizens may not be politically active and may not possess significant political resources, their attitudes, values, and beliefs are potentially relevant to regime stability over the long term. A sizable segment of a population that is alienated from a regime may be mobilized at some point in the future, given the right circumstances, elite stimuli, or organizational opportunities. This is particularly relevant to polities emerging from decades of authoritarian rule, when the norms and values inculcated by state-dominated agents of socialization (schools, the media, and politicized secondary organizations) may have been hostile to democracy. Thus, if a significant portion of a population were to question the legitimacy of a regime and its key institutions, reject democratic rules of the game, or regard an authoritarian alternative as preferable to the current democratic regime, we would conclude that consolidation is incomplete, despite the absence of behavioral manifestations of this political alienation.[36]

Two caveats are in order at this point. The first is that we regard the most crucial aspect of mass-level political culture for regime stability as involving an overtly *negative* stance, challenging the legitimacy of the existing system and/or preferring an authoritarian alternative, rather than as necessarily involving positive affirmations of "civic" values. Those who mouth civics textbook clichés may just be repeating slogans disseminated by formal agents of political socialization, rather than expressing the norms and values that actually guide their behavior. Such apparent attitudes may not be central elements in those citizens' belief systems and may be quite easily altered by political circumstances. Such "attitudes," moreover, may be difficult or impossible to measure in cross-national comparative studies, since the content of formal political socialization varies substantially from one democratic regime to another. And finally, insofar as such attitudes are not linked to actual behavior, they may be irrelevant to system resilience and survival. Indeed, some studies of public opinion have concluded that the stability of the American system is not primarily the result of an attitudinal consensus at the mass level, and that support for such fundamental democratic norms as those reflected in the Bill of Rights is surprisingly weak.[37]

The second caveat involves the temporal dimension: insofar as alienated or disloyal segments of the mass public are not politically active and organized, they may not pose a threat to regime stability over the short and medium term. A democracy may be consolidated despite the existence of such pockets of potential opposition for some time. Nonetheless, the reduction of political alienation and the inculcation of democratic norms and values into a population significantly broadens the consolidation of a democracy and sinks its roots into the political culture, thereby reducing the potential for disruption over the long term. The political resocialization of a population may require more than a generation, as some scholars have argued.[38] Insofar as that process is successful, we conclude, the political system thereby moves progressively closer to complete conformity with all the criteria inherent in the ideal-type definition of democratic consolidation set forth here.

We contend, nonetheless, that new democratic regimes may be sufficiently consolidated in a relatively short period of time. As long as the active, organized sectors of a political system do not challenge the legitimacy of a new democracy's political institutions and consistently conform to its behavioral norms, the regime may be resilient and stable, despite the absence of a fully democratic mass-level political culture. At the same time, this focus on the mass-level attitudinal aspects of consolidation should sensitize us to the possibility of movement in the opposite direction—a previously stable regime may eventually become *de*consolidated. Indeed, while democracies may be sufficiently consolidated as to survive and thrive over considerable periods of time, we acknowledge that no democracy is immune from deconsolidation and possible breakdown over the long term.

Using this definition of democratic consolidation, we conclude that all four Southern European democracies were consolidated by the early to mid-1980s, despite certain features of each political system, particularly of their mass-level political cultures, where there remains considerable room for movement towards complete conformity with our ideal-type conceptualization of democratic consolidation. In Italy, however, following a period of stable and consolidated democratic politics from the late 1970s to the early 1990s, several important partial regimes (including the electoral system, the party system, and the structure of the state itself) were challenged, became deconsolidated, and entered into a significant process of restructuring beginning in 1991. Notwithstanding questions concerning the deepening and the quality of democracy in Italy, as well as about the Italian political crisis, democratic consolidation experiences in the Southern European region stand in sharp contrast with the other recent transitions from authoritarian rule. Very few Latin American democracies are consolidated—only Costa Rica and Uruguay, with Chile moving towards consolidation. Prior to the late 1980s, Venezuela could have been added to this list. Among the new regimes in Eastern Europe, it cannot be said that all have become fully democratic, and none can be regarded as consolidated.

Differing Consolidation Trajectories

A central theoretical concern of this and the other volumes in this series is the multifaceted impact on politics and society of the trajectories followed by each of these Southern European countries in its process of democratization. For this reason, familiarity with the historical sequences of events and key actors involved in the transition to and consolidation of these democratic regimes is necessary. The following descriptive account of these processes is intended to provide such an understanding. This section does not attempt to set forth an analytical or theoretical elaboration of findings derived from the study of these processes; that more challenging task is undertaken in the remaining chapters of this book.

The four Southern European democracies achieved consolidation via quite different routes. Indeed, our analyses of these and other cases reveal substantial variation in the manner in which democracies are consolidated. These variations, in turn, give rise to certain generalizations concerning democratic consolidation that should be tested in light of political developments elsewhere. First, consolidation processes may be fundamentally different from case to case; no single model can adequately capture the dynamics of these processes. Second, these processes may involve different institutions and sets of actors at various stages of each process (although political party elites are almost invariably central actors in successful consolidation processes). Third, the amount of time required for consolidation can vary considerably; restricting our attention to the Southern European cases, they ranged from just over five years in Spain to about three decades in Italy. Finally, it is important to note that progress towards consolidation is neither inevitable nor unilinear: in a single country there may be periods of rapid progress toward consolidation, followed by stagnation, crises, or setbacks. Indeed, as the cases of Venezuela and Colombia suggest, deconsolidation and potential breakdown are distinct possibilities.[39]

Two distinctly different types of consolidation process are described in a recently published study. Michael Burton, Richard Gunther, and John Higley set forth elite settlement and elite convergence models of consolidation processes, the end product of which is "elite consensual unity" in support of the institutions and rules of the game of democratic systems.[40] In an elite settlement, political leaders representing all politically relevant groups in a society meet face-to-face and behind closed doors to negotiate the ground rules for nonviolent institutionalized competition in the future. This process can lead to elite consensual unity in a relatively short period of time, although the broadening and deepening of the democratic consensus (extending it to their respective sets of followers and, ultimately, to unmobilized sectors of society) may require much longer. As we have argued, however, incorporation of all politically relevant *elites* within the democratic consensus is usually sufficient to guarantee the survival and resilience of the new democracy over the intermediate term. The concept of elite settlements shares some aspects with that of Lijphart's classic concept of consociational democracy, as well as with the elite pacts discussed and analyzed by Terry Karl, Philippe Schmitter, and Guillermo O'Donnell. In several ways, however, this concept is quite distinct from both pacts and consociationalism.[41]

Consolidation via elite convergence involves a series of deliberate tactical decisions by rival elites that have the cumulative effect, over perhaps a decade or more, of creating elite consensual unity. This process typically entails two distinct phases. In the first step, some elites establish a stable alliance and organizational base powerful enough to win governmental office and establish a position of electoral dominance that threatens to exclude its rivals with exclusion from office for the foreseeable future. This has the immediate effect of stabilizing political relations at one end of the political spectrum. More importantly, it triggers the second stage of this process, in which the opposition abandons its antisystem or semiloyal stance and usually (but not inevitably) moderates its stands on certain important issues as a means of making itself more attractive to larger numbers of voters in an effort to come to power via the regime's rules of the game. In the Burton, Gunther, and Higley formulation, the desire to secure electoral victory is the principal motivating force that, through this process, serves to consolidate democracy and legitimate its rules and institutions. This concept is similar (but not identical) to that of "negative integration," as advanced initially by Guenther Roth, in his exploration of the processes that culminated in the moderation of the German Social Democrats, and subsequently by Juan Linz and Leonardo Morlino, in their analyses of the moderation of the Italian Communist Party.[42]

These two different processes are neither mutually exclusive nor are they likely to be the only pathways to democratic consolidation, but they do capture important aspects of the dynamics of democratic consolidation in Spain and Italy. The cases of Portugal and Greece, however, resist easy categorization using this typology, although more limited hypotheses derived from these models provide insights into the dynamics of consolidation in both countries.

Spain

Democracy in Spain has been substantially consolidated since about 1982 or 1983. The continuing but gradually diminishing political violence in Euskadi and the antisystem stance of Herri Batasuna indicate that there is a significant regional exception to the full consolidation of Spanish politics. At the national level, however, this consolidation has been sufficient to guarantee the stability and resilience of the regime in the face of several severe tests, including more than seven hundred terrorist assassinations, unemployment rates that twice exceeded 20 percent of the labor force, collapse of the governing party, and radical restructuring of the party system.

The consolidation of Spanish democracy occurred largely as a product of elite settlement.[43] The most dramatic steps towards consolidation were taken in the process of drafting and ratifying a new democratic constitution during the period August 1977–September 1978. Inclusion within the politics of consensus of all nationwide parties—from the Communists, on the left, to their former Franquist enemies in Alianza Popular, on the right—not only led to overwhelming popular support for the new democracy, but also cemented patterns of mutually respectful and, indeed, cordial elite interactions that persist to this day.[44] This same co-optive process was employed in negotiations over regional autonomy statutes for Catalonia and Euskadi, but with only partial success in the latter case. Aside from Herri Batasuna (whose electoral support is restricted to Euskadi), no party is disqualified as an untrustworthy contender in politics, and, again with the exception of Herri Batasuna, no party or significant sector of the Spanish public denies the legitimacy of the regime or regularly violates its rules of the game. As explained earlier, only segments of the military departed initially from this democratic consensus. With the complete discrediting of antisystem options, and with careful integration of the military elite into collaboration with civilian politicians (particularly under Socialist defense minister Narcis Serra), it is widely believed that no significant sector of the Spanish military today holds out any hope for an antidemocratic alternative to the present regime.

Even in Euskadi there has been considerable movement towards greater consolidation. First, Euskadiko Ezkerra (EE) definitively severed its links with clandestine terrorist organizations and abandoned its antisystem stance by late 1981, becoming a loyal democratic party of the Basque nationalist left. (Further evidence of its abandonment of Basque-separatist aspirations was the EE's merger with the regional branch of the Spanish Socialist Party, the PSOE, in advance of the 1993 election.) By the late 1980s, the PNV, as well, moved towards more unambiguous support for the regime. This development may be the product of a confluence of factors: shifts within the party's leadership, a natural reaction as party-of-government against ETA terrorism (*Basque* police had become targets of attacks), and the gradual development of more collaborative interactions with the governing party of Spain, the PSOE, with which the PNV coalesced in the late 1980s to form a regional government. The consequence is that the PNV has de facto abandoned its semiloyal ambiguities.[45] Only persistent hostility towards the Spanish state by Herri Batasuna, its allies in ETA, and its electorate prevent democracy in this region from being regarded as fully consolidated.

In terms of some aspects of the quality of democracy, however, there is considerable room for improvement in Spain. Pervasive cynicism at the mass level and extraordinarily low levels of mass-level involvement with politics reflect the incomplete status of efforts to resocialize the Spanish public, some of whose members had been exposed to antiparty rhetoric and developed nonparticipatory patterns of behavior under four decades of authoritarian rule.[46]

Italy

The most difficult and protracted consolidation process was that of Italy. While the transition to democracy in Italy was completed in the 1940s (setting the Italian case apart from the other three in several important ways), one recent study has concluded that the democratic regime was not fully consolidated until the middle to late 1970s.[47] This is not to say that substantial but incomplete levels of consolidation were not achieved in earlier decades. Indeed, an exploration of those earlier stages reveals the complexity of consolidation processes, as well as the extent to which it is erroneous to assume that consolidation is secured through steady and linear progress towards full compliance with our ideal type.

Overall, the Italian case conforms most closely to the elite-convergence model. The first stage in this process unfolded in the late 1940s and early 1950s, when the Christian Democratic Party established its predominant position straddling the center-right segment of the political spectrum. Italian politics had become quite polarized in the aftermath of the breakup of the immediate postwar DC-Socialist-Communist coalition in 1947, triggered largely by the outbreak and intensification of the Cold War. A schism within the PSI (Italian Socialist Party, from which Social Democrats departed to form the PSDI), resulting from the PSI's "Unity of Action" pact with the Communists, ultimately led to a confrontation between left and right. During the first decade of this bipolar competition, the DC made impressive progress towards "the reorganization and consolidation of a powerful center."[48] Its first success in this regard was a smashing electoral victory in 1948, in which the DC (for the first and, to this point, only time in Italian postwar history) secured an absolute majority of seats in the Chamber of Deputies. Both Gianfranco Pasquino and Leonardo Morlino stress the importance for democratic consolidation of the initial efforts of the DC to strengthen its hold over social groups of the center and center-right. Morlino concludes that the DC played an especially important role in anchoring certain social groups in support of the new democracy: "Social groups in agriculture and industrial entrepreneurs who had supported fascism from the outset, and who had been accommodated by it to considerable political and economic advantage . . . emerged from the fascist experience in a defensive position, but nevertheless with enormous resources. . . . The problem then was of how to integrate these groups within the newly founded democratic regime."[49] He also points to the existence in Italy of a "Catholic cultural background quite unprepared for the new responsibilities and tasks of democracy."[50] This, too, was converted into a force supportive of the new regime through the establishment of DC "party government." Morlino argues that this DC-led dual process of partisan consolidation on the center-right and partial consolidation of democracy required about a decade. Quoting Pasquino, he concludes that "at the end of the fifties . . . party government was well established. . . . That is to say, the governing parties had 'occupied' the bureaucracy, and had expanded and colonized the public sector of the economy, and had penetrated civil society."[51] From this, Morlino concludes that an important requisite for successful democratic consolidation is that political parties be sufficiently well established and influential to effectively serve as "gatekeepers" or "access controllers," linking government and the state to the disparate interests and groups present in a society undergoing a transition from authoritarianism. (He further amplifies this point in Chapter 10 of this volume.)

Thus, by the end of the first stage in this protracted consolidation process, the DC had effectively established itself as a democratic gatekeeper for groups on the center and right and as the predominant force in the party system and essential member of every government. The Socialists and Communists were excluded from power at the national level. In accord with the elite-convergence model, the parties of the left gradually abandoned their polarized stands on several key issues and moved closer to the governing centrist majority. The first crucial step in this direction was the "opening to the left" which incorporated the PSI within the governing coalition for the first time in 1963. Again, this provoked a schism, culminating in the formation of a new Partito Socialista Italiano di Unitá Proletaria in 1964, which preferred to side with the still-excluded PCI. Nonetheless, broadening the governing coalition to include the center-left represented an important achievement on the road to full democratic consolidation. Still, the process was incomplete.

The creation of a new democracy during the most intense stage of the Cold War had given the consolidation process a characteristic not shared with the more recently reestablished Southern European democracies—the disqualification of the second-largest party in the country on the grounds that it was an untrustworthy antisystem party. While the PCI itself vigorously contested the appropriateness of that label, and through its behavior in the 1960s attempted to demonstrate that it was a trustworthy and loyal democratic competitor, other parties' perceptions of its intentions as antisystem gave partisan competition in Italy many of the same characteristics as if the PCI were actually opposed to the regime. As Maurizio Cotta describes it, "although by as early as the end of 1948 it had become sufficiently clear that a revolutionary insurrection was not an option for the Communist Party, and although the party itself repudiated that option, its strong links with a nondemocratic regime, the Soviet Union, and its regular claims about the superiority of Soviet-type regimes to bourgeois democracies regularly fueled suspicions about the PCI's 'real' intentions among its opponents.[52] It was not until the mid-1970s that the PCI succeeded in undermining the credibility of the antisystem label applied to it. This change entailed several steps: condemnation of the Soviet invasion of Czechoslovakia in 1968, parliamentary reforms in 1971 that gave Communist deputies a more central role in setting the parliamentary agenda, and negative integration in the trade union arena and in municipal governments, in which pragmatic, incremental policy advances increasingly prevailed over radical partisan rhetoric.[53]

Progress towards democratic consolidation, however, was neither unilinear nor irreversible. The social and political unrest of the late 1960s and 1970s assumed crisis proportions, culminating in mass mobilizations and serious outbreaks of terrorist violence by both the extreme left and the extreme right in the late 1970s. Paradoxically, this may have contributed indirectly to the completion of the consolidation process, insofar as it provided the PCI with a highly visible opportunity to demonstrate its commitment to democratic stability by closely collaborating with the parties of the center in the fight against terrorism. The most important and dramatic of developments at this time were the 1976 agreements that brought the Communists into the parliamentary majority supporting Christian Democratic minority governments. Although they were still excluded from cabinet posts, the agreements gave PCI elected officials other important posts from which they had previously been excluded (e.g., speaker of the chamber of deputies and the presidencies of some legislative committees). The agreements also included an exchange of programmatic and policy concessions that reflected a significant enhancement of the party's governmental role and, at the same time, formalized its commitment to more moderate stands on key issues. By the end of the 1970s, the PCI had demonstrated its reliability as a loyal democratic competitor, and democracy in Italy was by and large consolidated. At the level of organized parties and politically significant elites, the process could be regarded as largely complete—only the persistently anti-system stands of the neofascist Movimento Sociale Italiano and of the Red Brigades represented departures from full conformity with our ideal type.

An empirical analysis, in this volume, by Leonardo Morlino and José Ramón Montero of survey data collected in 1985, however, reveals that mass-level attitudinal support for the regime was not as enthusiastic or widespread as one might have expected. Many Italians harbored reservations about the efficacy of their democracy and were cynical towards political parties. These public opinion data, in retrospect, can be regarded as harbingers of developments that radically destabilized the Italian party system in the early 1990s. Antiparty movements began to attract a large electoral following, and support for established parties, especially the DC and PSI, began to collapse. Paradoxically, at the same time, the last politically significant antidemocratic party, the MSI, underwent a transformation from an antisystem fascist party to a heterogeneous but largely democratic party of the right—through processes that substantially accord with the logic of elite convergence. (These phenomena will be extensively analyzed in Volume 2 of this series.)

Several aspects of the Italian transition to democracy set it apart from the other Southern European transitions and are worthy of mention at this point. Some of these transitional elements have significantly affected the subsequent character of Italian politics, and all of them derive from the fact that the Italian transition unfolded in the mid-1940s, rather than the mid-1970s, as in the other three countries. Unlike the other transitions, Italian democracy was born in the aftermath of a protracted and violent struggle: the eighteen-month-long resistance campaign against the German-puppet regime in the north mobilized and organized important segments of Italian society. As Pasquino argues, "the resistance movement, the accelerated politicization of a new generation, the experiences and the memories of a profound moral renewal constituted one additional, probably unrepeatable phenomenon."[54] Perhaps even more important, in terms of the politicization of social cleavages and secondary associations, as well as the polarization of partisan politics, is the fact that the roots of the party system were being set down at the time the Cold War was entering its most intense early stages. Also, parties in Italy were created within a somewhat less modern social structure, a decidedly more impoverished economic environment, and at a lower level of international technological advancement than would be characteristic of the crucial party-building processes in the other Southern European systems three decades later. Among other things, television had not yet been commercially marketed, and geographic mobility was more restricted than would be true of Greece, Portugal, and Spain. We will systematically explore the political, cultural, social, and economic consequences of these and other transition characteristics at various points in this five-volume series.

Portugal

The consolidation of democracy in Portugal occurred through processes that can best be described as a series of partial settlements, which, between 1975 and 1989, progressively moved Portugal towards full conformity with our ideal type of democratic regime, as well as towards full consolidation. These partial settlements included two pacts between military leaders and political parties (in 1975 and 1976), endorsement of the constitution of April 2, 1976, and interparty accords concerning revisions of the constitution in 1982 and 1989. Unlike in an elite settlement, these agreements, as described by Lawrence Graham, "concentrated on the resolution of a significant issue dividing a particular set of political forces, excluded other significant actors, and set up transitory arrangements subject to redefinition once the key players had changed. It was not until the end of 1989 that all major actors in postauthoritarian Portugal accepted procedural democracy as the framework most appropriate to structuring and regulating Portuguese politics for the foreseeable future."[55]

The Portuguese transition to democracy was initiated by a military coup, and was accompanied by substantial mass mobilizations (particularly in the latifundist south and in the industrial center) oriented towards carrying out an economic and social revolution. Much of the consolidation process (not to mention the achievement of full conformity with our definition of democracy) involved undoing some of the excesses of this initial revolutionary period. This required extrication of the military from politics and the assertion of civilian supremacy (to be explored in much greater detail by Felipe Agüero, in this volume), as well as reversal of some of the "irreversible" economic conquests of the revolutionary period. This process took the form of five partial settlements. They have been analyzed by Graham, and all dealt with one or another aspect of undoing the excesses of the revolutionary period.

The first partial settlement was the pact of April 11, 1975, between the Armed Forces Movement (MFA, which had taken power following the coup that toppled the Salazar-Caetano regime) and political parties. This agreement took a partial and inadequate step towards establishing a governmental role for civilians by creating the Assembly of the Republic. At the same time, however, it attempted to institutionalize a substantial political role for the military through establishment of the Assembly of the Armed Forces Movement. While this reorganization of civil-military relations may have promised an expansion of the civilian role in government, and served to stabilize relations between military and party elites over the short term, such an arrangement would have fallen far short of compliance with our procedural definition of democracy. It was, in any event, short-lived.

The second civil-military pact, made on February 16, 1976, followed the November 1975 countercoup that brought more moderate (but still generally leftist) military officers to power. This agreement paved the way for establishment of a semipresidential system of government that was much closer to our definition of a democratic regime. This pact foresaw a somewhat reduced role for the military: the military's presence would be institutionalized in the Council of the Revolution (with judicial review powers), rather than an assembly, as envisioned earlier.

This arrangement was reflected in the 1976 constitution and remained in force for six years. Throughout this period, the military wielded much more power and influence than in other West European democracies, both because of the existence of the undemocratic Council of the Revolution and through military domination of the presidency of the republic: indeed, in the 1980 election, *all* of the candidates for president were acting or former military officers.

The civilian-military agreements that culminated in the constitutional revisions of 1982 and enactment of a new defense law represented a decisive step towards completion of the transition to democracy. These reforms abolished the Council of the Revolution (creating a constitutional tribunal to take over its judicial review functions), reduced the powers of the president, and took steps to assert civilian control over the military. They also contributed substantially to the consolidation of Portuguese democracy, in that they removed several objectionable features that rendered incomplete the full legitimation of the regime and its key institutions.

Even after these constitutional reforms, there remained two significant obstacles to full consolidation of the new regime. One was the existence of a Marxist-Leninist antisystem party with considerable electoral support, the Portuguese Communist Party (PCP). The other was inclusion within the constitution of clauses which (1) defined the objective of the new political institutions of the regime to be "the assurance of the transition toward socialism" (preamble of that document), (2) endorsed "the collective appropriation of the principal means of production" (Articles 9 and 10), and (3) flatly asserted that "all nationalizations effected since April 25, 1974, are irreversible conquests of the working classes" (Article 83). By removing important substantive policy issues from the everyday give and take of democratic politics, these clauses not only represented an infringement of popular sovereignty (and, hence, represented incomplete conformity with our ideal type of democracy), but they also precluded full, unconditional acceptance of the regime's basic charter by all political groups—thereby raising the real possibility of semiloyal behavior on the part of political groups that otherwise would be enthusiastic supporters of the regime. This last obstacle to unconditional commitment to the regime by those parties was removed through the May 1989 constitutional reform, which eliminated clauses guaranteeing the irreversibility of the nationalizations carried out during the revolutionary period. These constitutional changes were supported by all major parties except the PCP.

Finally, even the Portuguese Communist Party altered its ideological and programmatic orientations in such a fashion as to further contribute to full democratic consolidation. Following serious internal conflict which erupted in the aftermath of the party's 1987 electoral defeat, pitting the orthodox communist supporters of Cunhal against the much more moderate "critics" within the party, the PCP formally abandoned its revolutionary program and strategy and acknowledged the legitimacy of Portugal's democratic regime. Accordingly, we can regard Portuguese democracy as having been fully consolidated by the end of the 1980s.

Greece

Two dates can serve as logical end-points for the consolidation of democracy in Greece: 1977 and, alternatively, 1981. If one concludes that Greece was substantially consolidated in 1981, then important elements of the Greek democratization process fit well with the convergence model. If, on the other hand, one regards 1977 as the more persuasive date, then the mode of democratic consolidation only partially conforms to that model. The surprising swiftness of consolidation in Greece would raise questions concerning the applicability of the convergence model.[56]

One reason for regarding 1981 as the *terminus ad quem* for democratic consolidation in Greece is that the opposition socialist party, PASOK, came to power in that year. This represented an alternation in power which, although it is not synonymous with consolidation, could be regarded as a test whose successful passing confirmed that consolidation had occurred. This governmental turnover takes on additional significance in light of a long-term perspective on Greek political history: PASOK's victory brought to an end almost forty-five years of uninterrupted dominance of Greek political life by the Greek right, whether in its parliamentary or its authoritarian manifestations. The coming to power of the first left-of-center political force in modern Greek history seemed to bring to a close a long historical cycle whose salient characteristic had been the repeated failed attempts at incorporation of the rural and urban masses into the Greek political system. While the 1974 transition made possible the incorporation of the heretofore excluded rural and working class masses into the new political system (a decisive step towards the normalization of Greek politics), the 1981 change in government actually brought to power the party representing them. The fact that these formerly excluded groups could come to power in a manner which scrupulously adhered to both the letter and the spirit of democratic procedures, established in 1974 and 1975, with no significant actor challenging either those procedures or that outcome, strongly suggests that Greek democracy was consolidated in that year.

The case for using 1977 as the date signaling the end of consolidation rests on a somewhat different argument. The parliamentary elections in that year effectively doubled PASOK's electoral support (from 13.6 percent in 1975 to 25.3 percent in 1977), catapulted the party to the role of major opposition in Parliament, and brought about a marked change in its attitudes, behavior, and public persona. The clear prospect that political power was within the party's reach produced a significant moderation in its positions on a number of major issues of Greek politics. Most remarkable, for example, was the party's careful but clear distancing of itself from its erstwhile Third World orientations towards Greek foreign policy and, especially, NATO and the European Community, which, since 1974, had been consistently denounced as part of the same "syndicate" of Western forces seeking to dictate polity options to Greece. These and other verbal maximalisms or actions—which, in the period 1974–77, had led many to believe that PASOK was, at best, a semiloyal party whose presence clearly impeded democratic consolidation in the country—became decidedly muted and progressively eliminated from the party's public discourse from 1977 onwards.[57]

At a deeper, and probably more convincing level, this change in PASOK's attitudes could be attributed to the resolution of a fundamental cleavage internal to PASOK which, since the party's inception, had tended to play a dominant role in the debates and struggles relating to the design and formulation of policy. This was the divide between the maximalist and moderate wings of the party. The maximalists originated in the Panhellenic Resistance Movement (PAK), the resistance organization set up by Andreas Papandreou during his years in exile to combat the military regime and to pave the way for the creation of a new political formation in the future. Favoring the adoption of a strategy which emphasized ideological coherence and purity, they opted for a the "long road to power" and, as a result, resisted massive and indiscriminate expansion in party membership.

Conversely, the moderate wing of the party, dominated by parliamentarians of the old Center Union, who since 1974 had adhered to PASOK, and by moderate elements in other resistance organizations, favored a more electoralist strategy based on the logic of the "short road to power" and, as a result, encouraged massive expansion of party membership and the rapid conversion of PASOK into a catch-all party. It was Papandreou's decision to side with the latter group which, for all practical purposes, inexorably led to the marginalization and rapid eclipse of the maximalist wing and of the radical discourse and semiloyal stance towards the new political system which it most clearly represented.

Consistent with an "elite convergence" characterization of the party's behavior after 1977, the decision to adopt a strategy favoring the short road to power effectively implied PASOK's conversion to a catch-all party and commensurately necessitated first the abandonment of the radicalism that had served as the major underpinning of the party's perceived semiloyal profile, and second the formulation of a more moderate platform and a public image designed to maximize the party's appeal to as wide a segment as possible of the Greek electorate, especially the pivotal centrist voters, whom the radical discourse of the 1974–77 period had clearly kept away from the party.[58]

Seen in this light, 1977 can be said to constitute the moment in the Greek democratization process when, following PASOK's abandonment of its semiloyal utterances and practices, no significant groups in Greece contested the legitimacy of political institutions and rules of the game in the new Greek political system. Certainly the armed forces, chastened by their sobering experience with the exercise of power in 1967–74, especially the Cyprus debacle, were content to remain within the barracks and to abide by the principle of civilian control of the military. At the same time, the communist left—whether in its Eurocommunist version (Communist Party of Greece-Interior) or the more traditional and more powerful orthodox Marxist manifestation (Communist Party of Greece or KKE)—was most eager to enjoy the newfound freedom of expression and movement which derived from its ability to operate legally in Greece for the first time since 1947 and rested on acceptance of the rules of the game established by the new political system. Finally, the monarchy, which in the past had served as a major obstacle to the democratization of Greek politics, had been eliminated from the new system in 1975, in the wake of the fairest and most impeccable plebiscite in modern Greek history.[59]

Thus, depending on which particular criterion one chooses to adopt, it can safely be argued that Greek democracy had reached substantial consolidation as early as 1977 and certainly by 1981. Both of these possible dates are, to varying degrees, compatible with a convergence interpretation of democratic consolidation in Greece. The earlier date, however, would require some modification of the convergence model, given the surprising swiftness of the Greek consolidation process. At the same time, the absence of pacts precludes direct application of the elite settlements model to the case of Greece. As is more extensively discussed elsewhere in this volume, we believe that a satisfactory explanation must take into consideration two important and intertwined factors: time and political learning, as these relate to the fact that the Greek transition, in 1974, essentially involved both an *instauration* as well as a *restoration* of democracy.

Collectively, the consolidation trajectories of the four Southern European democracies point to the rich variation in empirical reality that can serve as primary material for theorizing. They also underscore the need for broadening our conceptual understanding of these phenomena by bringing more cases (derived from the Latin American, East European, and East Asian democratization experiences) into the framework of comparative analysis and by using the insights derived from these additional cases to test, confirm, modify, or reinterpret the lessons drawn from the consolidation of democratic regimes in Southern Europe.

2 The Political and Socioeconomic Contours of Southern European History

Edward Malefakis

There is no mystery about the increased interest in Southern Europe during the past two decades. It has been a fairly direct response to the myriad processes of parallel evolution that have taken place in Italy, Spain, Portugal, and Greece since the early 1950s. The two main processes, under which many lesser ones can be subsumed, were toward economic, social, and cultural modernization and toward a more stable democratic polity. The similarities first began to be noted in academic circles in the late 1960s. They became a major focus of concern, especially among political scientists, after the dramatic events of 1974 and 1975 when, within nineteen months, dictatorial regimes were replaced by democratic ones in Portugal, Greece, and Spain, while major changes were occurring in Italy as well.

Most of the chapters in this volume analyze the processes of democratic consolidation in Southern Europe since the mid-1970s. My task is different: to examine the background to these processes and the historical context in which they took place. In doing so, I will address the following questions: To what extent do the Southern European nations deserve comparative study prior to the 1960s and 1970s, for reasons other than their recent political and socioeconomic development? Do the similarities in the democratic consolidation of Italy, Spain, Portugal, and Greece represent something new, or do they continue older parallelisms? If the latter is the case, what fundamental features do these countries share on which the correspondences among them are based? Put differently, this chapter will try to examine the ways in which "Southern Europe" can be thought of as a regional concept, applicable generally and over a long period of time, rather than as a convenient term which helps us group together a few transitory—albeit important—recent phenomena.

Two sets of objections to this effort immediately spring to mind. First, for several reasons, Southern Europe cannot be thought of as a region in the same sense as Western or Eastern Europe: it has not firmly been recognized as such by any academic discipline, including until recently political science; its component parts are not geographically contiguous, as are those of Western and Eastern Europe, but are separated by hundreds—even thousands—of miles of sea; partly because of this lack of contiguity, the nations included in Southern Europe have not interacted with each other very much in recent centuries and their histories have differed greatly in many ways.

Second, to the extent that a regional concept of Southern Europe might be admissible, is not the one chosen either too narrow or too broad? Why should it be limited to these four countries and not include Southern France as well, not to speak of Turkey, Malta, and Cyprus? Indeed, why limit the concept to the European shores of the Mediterranean at all and not expand it to deal with the Mediterranean basin as a whole? Or perhaps our grouping is too inclusive? It may make sense to link together Portugal, Spain, and southern Italy, but northern Italy is so advanced that it corresponds more to France. And why not follow tradition by leaving Greece to the Balkans?

Both sets of objections carry some force, but not enough to invalidate our analysis. If it is true that Southern Europe is not a region in the same sense as Western or Eastern Europe, there are many other senses in which a regional concept can be viable. We must also remember that Eastern and Western Europe are themselves relatively recent constructs, which envelop disparate places and conceal many differences. These are complicated issues, which I will try to develop during the course of this chapter. But let me point out here that the predominant regional paradigm of Europe throughout most of its history was a south-north one; our present east-west bifurcation was rarely invoked prior to the eighteenth century and became the paramount mode of classification no earlier than 1918. It is also worth noting that if Britain, France, and Germany can properly be considered Western Europe's modern core, looked at in other ways they were radically different from each other, especially prior to the 1950s. The same might be said for Poland, Hungary, Romania, Serbia, and Bulgaria in Eastern Europe. In short, nations need not be identical in all their myriad aspects for an identity to exist among them; it suffices that they resemble one another in significant ways for such an identity to be valid.

But there are also dangers of the opposite kind, as the objections concerning the areas chosen for inclusion in Southern Europe show. These objections all suffer from excessive decontextualization and are based on the belief that because certain actors share a few traits, these are enough to make them comparable to each other. Southern France, Malta, Cyprus, large sectors of Turkey, the former Yugoslavia's Dalmatian coast, and the southern and eastern littorals of the Mediterranean as well, all have many geographic and climatic features in common with our four countries, as well as some economic and anthropological characteristics that stem from those features or date back to ancient times, when contacts of all kinds among the Mediterranean peoples were frequent. But are these commonalities sufficient? Do they have the density and range of those that link our four countries to one another?

The answer must be negative. For example, parts of Turkey and Italy may have geographic and climatic similarities, and their respective peasantry may share certain customs and beliefs. But how can Turkey *generally* be compared to Italy when the latter eagerly accepted the printing press in the fifteenth century while it was only grudgingly admitted to the former in the nineteenth century? Religion, intellectual life, economic and political practices were all radically different in Turkey from the Middle Ages until at least the 1920s, when Kemal Atatürk imposed his westernization policies. They continue very different now, as a glance at comparative birth rates, literacy rates, or occupational distributions will show. What is true for Turkey is even more true for North Africa, or the Mediterranean's eastern shore. To include these areas with Southern Europe in a single concept whose fundamental purpose is sociopolitical, not geographic, is to seriously misrepresent reality.

Southern France, however, shares not only geographic and climatic similarities with our four countries but a multitude of social, cultural, and historical features as well. Why is it not incorporated into the concept we are trying to develop? Because, since at least as early as Richelieu, it has lacked political autonomy. France has been governed neither from Marseilles nor from Toulouse but from Paris; southern France has not been free to develop in the directions in which its own physical and human resources might have led it, but in directions largely shaped for it from the center and north. Political sovereignty of a certain duration in modern times seems to me an indispensable condition for inclusion in our concept. This, together with their tiny size, is why Malta and Cyprus are excluded. It is also why we cannot deal only with southern Italy. Had Cavour's initial vision of Italy prevailed, and a unified northern state been created while the Kingdom of the Two Sicilies continued to encompass the south, then our choices might have been different. But it did not; Garibaldi knit the two parts of the peninsula together in an indissoluble union, which neither the north, much as it sometimes might secretly wish to, nor outside observers like ourselves, can any longer undo.

Why are Albania and the Adriatic coast of former Yugoslavia excluded and Greece included? The reason is partly topographic; for most of the stretch from Epirus to Croatia mountains shut off the interior from the sea rather than opening it up to maritime activity. And political sovereignty has been a rare phenomenon throughout the history of the region. This was true even in the short-lived Yugoslav state, dominated as it was by Serbia, an inland region with few of the historical traditions of our four countries and fewer still of the geographic and climatic features of the Mediterranean. As to Greece, it obviously does share physical traits with Italy and Iberia, as well as many social and historical characteristics. Had the Greek civil war ended differently and Greece fallen under communist rule, then these resemblances might not seem compelling enough to justify Greece's inclusion with Southern Europe rather than the Balkans. But as with Italy, we can only deal with what actually happened. Greece differs religiously from the Catholic nations, to be sure, and its geopolitical position guaranteed for centuries that its history and social development would chiefly be that of the Balkans. Nevertheless, as we will see, it retained many social and historical similarities with Italy, Spain, and Portugal even while it was part of the Ottoman Empire, and these commonalities were considerably fortified during the nineteenth and early twentieth centuries. Now that they have been further reinforced by the experiences of the past four decades, the balance has tipped; and, while recognizing that it is not the exclusive possession of either, Greece can more productively be thought of as part of South Europe than of the Balkans.

Common Traits

What traits do Italy, Spain, Greece, and Portugal have in common? The physical ones are the most obvious. All four have a Mediterranean climate,[1] with its very special blend of heat and water, over most of their territories. The four also have the mountainous topography typical of the Mediterranean; indeed, along with Switzerland, Austria, and Albania, they are the most mountainous countries in Europe. All four are on peninsulas, and hence have longer coastlines in relation to their size than is customary, but none possesses a truly navigable river. Less obviously, Southern Europe is poor in coal and iron deposits but relatively rich in nonferrous minerals.

Various human consequences stem from all this. First, agricultural patterns tend to be similar: a wider variety of crops is possible than in the rest of Europe; several of these (wine, olives, and fruit) are luxury crops which require marketing (and thus preclude subsistence farming); they also are labor intensive, and thus tend to resist modernization and retard the exodus of the rural population to the cities. Irrigation also assumes great significance. Unirrigated, agriculture in Southern Europe is much poorer than in the wetter climates of Western and Eastern Europe; irrigated, it can equal California, as first the Po Valley, then Valencia, and now several areas of Spain, Italy, and Greece have proven.

Second, the mountainous topography tends to encourage regionalism, and within each region to divide the population between often antagonistic highlanders and plains people, thus giving rise to the characteristically Southern European phenomenon of social banditry. The topography also creates communications problems, making road and especially railroad construction more costly; these problems are further aggravated by the impossibility of using rivers for transportation, or of building networks of canals.

By contrast, maritime activity is easier than in most of the rest of Europe, especially as the pull towards the sea exerted by long coastlines and many harbors is intensified by the presence of nearby islands. It is no accident that, among Europeans, the seas were first conquered by southerners. The Greeks pioneered, then the lead passed to various states of medieval Italy, then, in the early modern period, to Portugal and Spain. One of the major signs of Southern Europe's decline came precisely when the three Catholic countries lost their maritime superiority to the Dutch, British, and French in the seventeenth century. Since then, only the Greeks have been able fully to revive their maritime tradition. But this should not blind us to the ascendancy that the south long exercised on the seas.

Finally, the distribution of mineral resources influenced societal development both in the preindustrial age, when nonferrous ores and marble quarries were key economic assets, and in the nineteenth century, when industrialization gave a premium to coal and iron deposits. In the many centuries which stretch from the silver mines at Lavrion in ancient Athens to the mercury deposits at Almadén of imperial Spain, mining enriched and diversified southern society; but the lack of coal and iron, except in Spain, made the process of industrialization all the more difficult.

The geographical setting of the four countries is perhaps the physical feature that has most affected their social development and what economists would call their human capital. Greece and Italy were the earliest areas of Europe to establish complex, urban societies, partly because of the factors mentioned above—crop diversity, mining, proximity to the sea—but also because of their locations on the edges of the ancient Middle East, with easy access to complex civilizations that had been developing for millennia. Less generally remembered is that the Iberian peninsula was the earliest overseas conquest of the Romans, and during their six centuries of rule probably also became the colony most deeply imbued with Greco-Roman culture.[2] Urban, commercial societies thus emerged along the entire northern shore of the Mediterranean. They were disrupted when the Roman Empire collapsed, of course, but to a lesser extent than in the rest of Europe. Once again, Southern Europe's geographic situation proved of critical importance: the urban tradition in Greece and parts of Italy could be maintained by the Byzantine Empire; in most of the Iberian peninsula it was revitalized after 711 by the other great urban-oriented civilization of the early Middle Ages, the Islamic.

The extraordinary transformation of northwestern Europe in the eleventh and twelfth centuries finally created urban societies there on a par with those of Southern Europe. A rough parity continued over the next five centuries, although major decline occurred in southern Italy and Sicily after about 1300, in Catalonia after about 1350, and above all in Greece. In the last, a complicated process of reruralization occurred. It had begun with the displacement of the locus of Greek life from the peninsula to Anatolia under the Byzantine Empire, and was intensified first by the numerous Slavic and Frankish invasions of the peninsula from the seventh to the fourteenth centuries, then by the definitive Ottoman conquests of the fifteenth century. Paradoxically, the Greek peninsula, birthplace of the urban tradition in Europe, became in the modern era the place where that tradition was most severely disrupted. But, as we shall see, this did not mean that the Greeks as a nation had become a rural people or that Greek society entirely lost its complexity.

The decline of Southern Europe as a whole did not begin until the seventeenth century. It was a dramatic decline, for three reasons. It followed immediately upon the pinnacles of cultural, economic, and political power attained by central and northern Italy during the Renaissance and by Spain and Portugal during their golden ages. Its extent was magnified by the unusually rapid economic and technological change that occurred in England and France during the late seventeenth and eighteenth centuries, as well as by the gradual recovery of Germany from the disastrous effects of the Thirty Years War. Finally, the perception of decline was accentuated by the sudden appearance between the 1680s and 1740s of three major eastern powers—Austria, Russia, and Prussia. For the first time, a firm political dimension was added to the socioeconomic differences that had long since distinguished Eastern Europe from the rest of the continent, and that region became a permanent part of the state network which previously had included mainly Southern and Western Europe. Indeed, from the mid-eighteenth century on, the south-north axis which had predominated in European history was replaced by a west-east axis. This is especially evident in relation to warfare. Except in Napoleon's time (and then the personal idiosyncracies of this son of the Mediterranean were partially responsible), major wars since the mid-1700s have primarily pitted not south and north against each other, but east and west. To be sure, Italy and Greece did participate in both world wars (and Portugal in the first), but in each case their entry was delayed and they never became the central focus of the struggle.

Structural Differences with Eastern and Western Europe

At the end of the eighteenth century, on the eve of the contemporary era, several major differences distinguished Southern Europe from its western and eastern regional counterparts. These differences are well known in relation to Western Europe, so need not be elaborated here. There is a tendency, however, to meld Southern and Eastern Europe and to regard them as constituting a single "periphery" to a West European "core." This practice severely distorts historical reality. For several centuries, both south and east were indeed peripheries of the west, but they were peripheries of distinct kinds. The east had never known anything *except* a peripheral relationship to the west, whereas the south had long been the west's equal, and often its superior. Many other features also separated them. A brief summary of the most important of these dissimilarities will help establish the individuality of Southern Europe.

One can perhaps best sum up the differences by saying that, whereas Southern Europe tends toward social and economic heterogeneity, the complexity of Eastern Europe lies more in its ethnic and linguistic diversity. The socioeconomic contrast is based on the fact that the south is the portion of Europe which has the greatest variety of agricultural conditions as well as the oldest urban, commercial, and high-cultural traditions. The east is almost its obverse: both because of topography and climate, it has the narrowest range of agricultural patterns and possibilities; it is also the region where urban culture developed last and was least organically linked with society as a whole.

In regard to ethnic and linguistic factors, the contrast largely results from the different geographic positions of the two regions. Because Southern Europe lies far from the great Eurasian plain which was the chief route for the movement of peoples prior to the modern era, mass migrations to it ended almost as early as they did in Western Europe (the Moorish conquest of Iberia notwithstanding; indeed, the Slavic invasions of Greece are the only major exception). In Eastern Europe, on the other hand, they continued not only throughout the Middle Ages, but well into the eighteenth century, as an accompaniment of the huge political readjustments which occurred in that region, both in the Balkans during the ebb and flow of the Ottoman Empire and then as a consequence of the rise of the Austrian and Russian empires.

These broad differences manifested themselves in many specific ways. They can be observed in the settlement patterns that prevailed in each region. Not only were cities smaller and less frequent in Eastern than in Southern Europe, but their commercial and cultural elites, as well as their artisans, consisted largely of foreigners (Germans and Jews principally, but also Greeks in the Balkans) until the closing decades of the nineteenth century—a situation which would have been as unimaginable in Southern Europe as it was in Western Europe. Rural settlements were also smaller, often mere hamlets attached to local manors, with few counterparts to the "agropolis" pattern of rural settlement characteristic of much of Southern Europe. In turn, this difference partly reflected the more limited range of rural social structures in the east. The monotonous pattern of lord and serf which predominated throughout the northern reaches of Eastern Europe is well known; despite the emancipations of 1848 and 1861 and the "green revolutions" of the 1920s, it was not entirely broken until after World War II. It contrasts sharply with the highly varied land tenures of Southern Europe. If southwestern Spain and southern Italy were large-holding areas, it was not on the scale that prevailed north and east of the Danube; one might encounter a few landowners in the Alentejo, Andalusia, or Sicily whose property and power approached the levels customary among the great Russian, Polish, and Hungarian magnates, but they were rare and had almost no counterparts elsewhere in the south. Nor was there, outside of Serbia and Bulgaria, any place in Eastern Europe where small peasant proprietors were as prevalent as in Piedmont, Old Castile, or northern Portugal. Nor did the sharecroppers of Tuscany or the small tenant farmers of Valencia have counterparts of equal social weight in Eastern Europe.

Indeed, the south may even have surpassed the west in the complexity of its social structures during the nineteenth and twentieth centuries. With zones of large and small property so intermixed, rural society (except in Greece, for reasons to be discussed later) was more variegated than in France, western and southern Germany, England, or Prussia, where either small or large property prevailed. As to urban areas—since industrialization was less rapid and decisive in Southern than in Western Europe but did nevertheless slowly and sporadically take place—the traditional elites and artisans of the southern cities were mixed together with new groups thrust up by the new processes for much longer than was true in the west. It was as if the London of Dickens had survived alongside the London of Orwell. Spain above all became a kind of museum in which every tendency—social, economic, or political—that had ever existed in Europe could be found in some corner, because the old tendencies were not strong enough to exclude the new, nor the new strong enough to vanquish the old, at least not until the 1970s.

Much of the above discussion can be illustrated by statistics on the occupational distribution of the working population in different regions of Europe around 1930. In the west, if we leave aside that exceptionally early and profound industrializer, the United Kingdom (where only 6.2 percent of the population was engaged in agriculture), the average proportion of the active population working in agriculture was 24.2 percent. The range ran from 14.1 percent in Belgium to 31.0 percent in Sweden, though in most countries the proportion lay between Germany's 20.1 percent and France's 28.8 percent. In the east, the average was 65.5 percent, with the range running from Hungary's 51.5 percent to Albania's 79.8 percent, but with most countries falling between Poland's 60.3 percent and Yugoslavia's 76.3 percent. The 1930 southern average, 46.6 percent, was almost exactly equidistant between the two, and the range which that average encompassed was very narrow, from Italy's 43.6 percent to Spain's 50.3 percent.[3] No better representation of Europe's regional divisions in modern times can be asked for. An essentially industrial west contrasted with an essentially rural east. The south shared features of each but differed from both.

Historical Differences from Eastern and Western Europe

The history of each region closely reflects these structural differences. In Western Europe, except for during the two world wars, the main feature of the past two centuries has been fairly steady and successful sociopolitical as well as economic modernization. Although there have been many variations in the pace followed by the individual western countries, none has failed to modernize economically. In regard to political change, only imperial Germany intransigently disputed the trend from absolutistic to liberal to democratic rule for a long period of time, and this trend was successfully disrupted by domestic forces, acting without external aid, only in Nazi Germany. As to social conflicts, they have tended to be fairly well organized, both institutionally and ideologically, in the west since 1789, and have occurred almost entirely in urban areas, among industrial workers. The peasantry in the west usually remained politically quiescent—indeed, except in France on a few occasions, it constituted a bastion of conservatism.

By contrast, East European history, except for the four decades under communism, centers almost obsessively on the issue of nationalism. The primary struggle in the east throughout the nineteenth and early twentieth centuries was between the supranational Ottoman, Austro-Hungarian, and Russian empires and the ethnic groups under them that sought to create or expand nation-states. This was always accompanied by a secondary struggle among rival ethnic claimants to power, however; and once the old dominant powers had been overthrown and liberation achieved in 1918, this second struggle became paramount. With the energies of the eastern elites so absorbed by national and ethnic conflicts, the struggle for liberalism and democracy per se did not form as central a part of their experience as in Western Europe. Since parliamentary government did not really begin anywhere in the east until the 1860s, and its first feeble traces were not implanted in Poland and Russia until 1906, the elites also long lacked one of the critical arenas in which this struggle could be waged. Neither was economic modernization very successful, despite being more consciously pursued by the eastern state bureaucracies than perhaps anywhere else in Europe from the late nineteenth century onward. Finally, social conflicts in the east were also different, occurring mainly in the countryside, rather than the cities, and tending to be sporadic and spontaneous in nature, rather than relatively continuous and with a certain degree of organization. When violence occurred, it tended to be of the *jacquerie* rather than of the strike variety.[4]

The main features of southern history were more like those of Western than Eastern Europe, but were not so close as to deprive the south of its individuality. The struggle against absolutism and in favor of liberalism and democratization was mounted very early in Southern Europe and remained a major issue throughout the subsequent history of all four nations. It had a much rougher road to follow than in the west, being repeatedly challenged, especially from the right, but also from the left. In the west during the past two centuries, severe political retrogression occurred only once, in Nazi Germany. In the south, political involution happened much more frequently and continued to manifest itself throughout the entire period. It first took place in Spain and Italy in 1814 and was last witnessed in Greece in 1967. In the twentieth century the periods of retrogression sometimes were of long duration: over two decades in Italy under Mussolini, nearly four decades in Spain under Franco, almost half a century in Portugal under the Salazar-Caetano regime. But even these, in the end, did not reverse the southern trend that had manifested itself during the nineteenth century, of following—albeit at a distance and with great difficulty—the political evolution of Western Europe.

Something similar might be said for economic modernization. The indigenous urban elites of the *ancien régimes* in Spain, Italy, and Portugal did not display the same entrepreneurial spirit as their northern colleagues. They were also badly handicapped, first by the disruptions and dislocations caused by frequent political conflicts, especially in Spain, and then by Southern Europe's structural disadvantages in the industrial age that was dawning—its paucity of iron and coal resources, the greater difficulty of building railroads, and, perhaps above all, the much higher costs of modernizing its agricultural output because of the need for drainage and irrigation works. Nevertheless, the southern economies did develop, slowly and sporadically, and without as much state aid as those in Russia and Austria received. Although the southern economies were often deformed in comparison to Western Europe's, and major time lags always existed, similar trends were nevertheless being followed.

Social conflict was also different in Southern Europe. The urban proletariat became more active as industrialization proceeded and by the turn of the century had emerged as the principal source of revolutionary militancy in Italy and Spain, as shown by the *fatti di maggio* of Milan in 1898 and the *semana trágica* of Barcelona in 1909. Violent protest did not die out among the peasantry, however, as it had by the 1850s in France, England, and Germany. Instead, militancy continued to grow among them also, reaching its peak in Italy in 1919–20 and in Spain in 1932–37. This combination of urban and rural protest also manifested itself in Portugal, in mild form in 1910–11 and spectacularly so in 1974–75. It was a combination unknown in the rest of Europe except during the French and Russian revolutions. But in both those instances, the peasantry acted spontaneously, without ideological orientation or institutional organization, at a time when state power had essentially collapsed. This was not generally true of the Spanish and Italian peasant protest movements, in which rural militancy was as structural a part of social protest as urban militancy was. No major social sector remained entirely outside the struggle. This was an important reason behind the especially turbulent labor history of Italy and Spain in the nineteenth and early twentieth centuries. It also helps explain why the communists were neither the only nor the most aggressive revolutionary working class movement in the interwar period.

Why Greece Fits in with the South

Greece constitutes a special case within Southern Europe. Much of its history links it more to the Balkans than to the Italian and Iberian peninsulas. Although the Byzantine Empire started with pan-Mediterranean pretensions, its main areas of concern from the eighth century on were the Balkans and Asia Minor. This remained the predominant—at times almost the exclusive—orientation of Greeks for the next millennium. During this period the Greeks also diverged in other ways from the Southern European experience, which they had so intimately shared throughout ancient times. The most relevant divergence for our purposes was the gradual weakening of urban life throughout Byzantium and its nearly complete collapse on the Greek peninsula as that region became an economic backwater of the empire. Also important was the decline of governmental experience among the elites, due to the empire's increasing autocracy and because the Latin states erected after the Fourth Crusade brought foreign masters to most of peninsular Greece. Greek society became narrower and more restrictive during these long centuries of deterioration. Its commercial and maritime traditions were largely taken over by Venice and Genoa; its high culture began to resist innovation at precisely the time when the West was striking out in dramatic new directions. With the Ottoman conquest of 1453, the survival of an autonomous Greek society was seriously put into question.

But the Greek past was too strong to be wholly extinguished. The Orthodox Church provided one major refuge, as the Ottoman authorities, far from suppressing it, centralized many aspects of Christian life—civil as well as religious—under the Patriarchate of Constantinople. A large ecclesiastical bureaucracy, staffed by Greeks, thus obtained unprecedented administrative authority not only over its own people but over Bulgarian, Serbian, and other Balkan Christians as well. Vigorous and wealthy, the church could also keep alive its tradition of learning, albeit usually in very rigid form. The Western world, particularly the Italians, provided another source of salvation. This was true both in the continued presence of Venetian outposts in ethnically Greek areas until 1797 and in the intense interest in ancient Greece that the entire Western world displayed from the Renaissance onward. Commercial and cultural interaction with the West was thus never completely disrupted by the Ottoman conquest. The third indispensable element of salvation was the nature of the Ottoman Empire itself. Militarily oriented and land-based since its inception, it was also religiously devout and wary of non-Muslim cultures. Army service, some aspects of domestic administration, and the staffing of Muslim religious and cultural institutions were the professional outlets honored among Ottoman elites. Finance, commerce, maritime activity, and diplomacy were less esteemed, and tended to be left to the subject peoples.

Among the subject peoples, the Greeks benefited most from these Ottoman social preferences, in some fields dramatically so. From the 1660s onward Greeks monopolized both the highest diplomatic office of the empire and its top naval command; after about 1710, the governorships of the principalities of Moldavia and Wallachia were also exclusively theirs. In addition, many lesser posts became the private fiefs of Greek clans, both within the Ottoman administration and among the Western consulates then being established in the empire. The eighteenth century also witnessed a great increase in trade between the Ottoman Empire and the West. Much of this fell into Greek hands, whether on the seas (since Venice and Genoa had ceased being competitors), or along the land routes that traversed the southern Balkans, or along the Danube, the principal trade route in the northern Balkans. In Vienna, the western terminus of the trade, a sizable Greek colony grew up.

For all these reasons, the loss of independent statehood did not mean a total involution of Greek society. In subtle ways, and at first very precariously, Greek urban, commercial, and high religious culture survived. By the late eighteenth century Greek culture had become vigorous enough to establish direct links with the Enlightenment ideals that were sweeping Western Europe, thus adding a modern, secular dimension to its intellectual life. All these factors were strongest in Constantinople and Anatolia, of course, not in peninsular Greece. Yet there too new life was stirring. It was fanned for nearly two decades (1796–1814), during the French revolutionary and Napoleonic wars, because the peninsula's geographical proximity to Italy and the foreign-occupied Ionian Islands exposed Greece to influences from both sets of combatants. In 1821, what was intended to be an empirewide rising against Ottoman rule took hold only in the southern part of peninsular Greece. Greek elites from other areas (from Trieste, where the first major prophet of Greek independence had been arrested in 1797, to Odessa, where the secret society that prepared the 1821 revolt was founded among Greek merchants engaged in the Russian grain trade) came to the peninsula and helped restore it to what it had not been for many centuries—the center of life for a Greek nation whose peoples were widely dispersed over many lands.

By this point I hope I have established at least preliminary *bona fides* for the concept of Southern Europe and for Greece's right to be included within it. But does the credibility of the concept stand up when examined more specifically against what happened during the nineteenth and twentieth centuries? It is to this test that the rest of this chapter is devoted.

Patterns of Political Development

It would obviously be impossible here to go into every aspect of the history of our four nations during the past two centuries. I will be able to mention only a few of the more important factors that differentiated them from the rest of Europe (and, on occasion, from each other). My central theme will be the intermediacy of Southern Europe, both in relation to other major European regions and in the sense of its own incompleteness, of its having to take an especially long time to reach stability. In the political sphere, I will try to show how Southern Europe was characterized both by precocious development and kaleidoscopic politics: modern political movements arose early but were unable to establish their hegemony, so that illegitimacy, instability, and great flux became the customary pattern of political life. Certain types of political actors and issues also tended to have special importance—the army, the church, anticlericalism, inflexible but often opportunistic court circles, minimally organized but frequent labor protests, a revolutionary peasantry, feelings of national inferiority, strong regional consciousness. Finally, similar patterns prevailed in the socioeconomic sphere: southern society was neither especially urban nor especially rural; capitalism was accepted as the primary mode of economic organization from early on, but its legitimacy was always questioned; new technology also tended to be adopted quickly but was also unable to establish its predominance, with the result that "economic dualism"—the mixture of the new with the traditional—was more evident than in other parts of Europe.

The best way to proceed might be to divide the past two centuries into four broad periods: 1814–70s, 1870s–1914, 1915–49, and 1950–75. Within each period, I will discuss a few of the especially important characteristics which mark our four nations. I will not touch on the period of democratic consolidation after 1975, as it is the subject of the other chapters in this volume. The drift of my argument is reflected in the subheadings of the following discussion.[5] Accordingly, I have dubbed the period from 1814 to the 1870s one of "traumatic beginnings," the second era one of "defective consolidation," the period 1915–49 as one of "conflict and collapse," and 1950–92 as a season of "transcendence and redemption?" As the question mark suggests, Southern Europe's recent progress and stability might prove too fragile to warrant so strong a word as *redemption*. Yet, on the whole, I feel confident that the agonized development of the past has been definitively overcome and that the region has entered into a new and more favorable historical epoch.

Traumatic Beginnings (1814–1870s)

It is easier to distinguish common patterns during the early and middle portions of the nineteenth century between Portugal and Spain, on the one hand, and Italy and Greece, on the other, than to find such patterns in Southern Europe as a whole. The Iberian nations suffered grievously from the Napoleonic Wars, which ravaged their societies far more than others in Europe, while precipitating the loss of the South American colonies on which their economies so heavily relied. For decades afterwards theirs was a miserable history, characterized by intense internal violence that polarized rather than united them. By contrast, little fighting occurred in Italy during the Napoleonic period and the regimes the French installed there were enlightened and generally effective. Greece, still stateless, also benefited, because of the wartime stimulus to irregular forms of trade under which its merchants flourished. The ensuing decades are the most glorious in modern Greek and Italian history, as each nation freed itself from foreign oppression and established its unity or independence. On the basis of this period, then, from the early 1800s to roughly the 1870s, it might appear more logical to think of a bifurcated Mediterranean Europe, with quite distinct western and eastern halves, than of a single region.

Yet despite such differences, the period from 1814 to the 1870s witnessed as many parallel developments throughout Southern Europe as any of the subsequent ones. Notwithstanding the contrasting experiences of Italy and Iberia between 1796 and 1814, the restored absolutist regimes in both peninsulas were more precarious than in the rest of Europe. This insecurity was largely a consequence of the long absence and special ineptness of the restored rulers, the relative cohesion and self-confidence that local liberals had established while governing during the war, and the widespread disaffection that existed among army officers.

Another similarity is that attempted coups, and the growth of secret societies which united military and civilian rebels, characterized the immediate postwar period throughout Southern Europe. In March 1820, an army rising backed by widespread urban revolts finally succeeded in forcing the Spanish king to restore the Constitution of Cádiz, promulgated during the war by the liberals. Under the leadership of similar coalitions of military and civilian forces, Spain's example was followed, first in Naples, then Portugal, and finally, in March 1821, in Piedmont. In each case, the Cádiz constitution was also adopted as the provisional legal framework. In each case, however, the new regimes were unable to develop broad support among the populace and were easily crushed by foreign armies acting on behalf of the "Holy Alliance:" Austrian forces restored absolutism to Naples and Piedmont in 1821; a French army ousted the Spanish liberals in 1823; in Portugal no actual foreign intervention occurred, but the collapse in Spain enabled the absolutists there to overthrow the liberal regime also. In contrast to the rest of Europe, the Italian and Iberian peninsulas thus endured two absolutist restorations. The second was even more repressive than the first, partly because of the vigilante groups which had sprung up on the right during the revolutionary period. Each country's stock of human capital was significantly diminished as Spanish, Italian, and Portuguese middle-class liberal exiles became a common sight in London.

Portugal and Spain were the first to begin to transcend the liberal-absolutist dichotomy, because dynastic conflicts within the ruling families divided absolutist ranks and caused their less intransigent members to seek liberal support. This alliance was the basis for the liberal triumph in the ensuing civil wars against the absolutists. Long and bitter contests, the Miguelist war in Portugal (1831–34) and the first Carlist war in Spain (1833–40) greatly reinforced the political role played by the victorious armies. They also significantly diminished the secular power of the church, tarnished in both countries by its close identification with absolutism. Because the liberal-monarchical alliance was an uneasy one, however, intense political conflict continued after the defeat of the absolutist forces—primarily within liberal ranks, as progressives sought to implement a more radical program than moderates were willing to allow. The latter could usually rely on royal support against the former, but sometimes the situation was complicated by the appearance of neoabsolutist tendencies in court circles, which forced the moderates to rally together with the progressives to protect parliamentary rule. The result was especially chaotic in Portugal, where political change was brought about by extraconstitutional means on several occasions between 1836 and 1851, with the greatest violence occurring during the Maria da Fonte revolt of 1846 and the seven-month civil war known as the Patuleia in 1847. In Spain, the periods of conflict were more scattered (1835–44, 1852–54, 1856–57, 1866–68) but continued over a longer period of time. With two important exceptions in Portugal, the main leaders of the progressive and moderate sides in both nations were army officers who had risen to prominence in the civil wars of the 1830s.

In Italy, the liberal-absolutist struggle lasted much longer. Indeed, in Naples it worsened after the revolution of 1848 failed and the reigning Bourbon monarchy instituted its third, and most savage, repression within a generation. Nevertheless, elsewhere it showed signs of easing by the early 1840s, as the idea of ousting Austria from Lombardy and Venetia and achieving some sort of greater Italian unity permeated elites throughout the peninsula. The decisive moment came in the revolutionary year of 1848 when, with Europe turned upside down, Charles Albert of Piedmont decided to cast his lot with the liberals who were demanding war against Austria. Although his forces were soon defeated, the alliance between the Piedmontese monarchy and liberalism endured. The brilliant leadership of Cavour during the 1850s helped consolidate it, as did the drawing off of the political extremes by outside forces: the left by Mazzini's republicanism, the right by the increasing hostility of the papacy to Italian unity. But more fundamental to the alliance's stability was that the monarch needed the liberals if he was to expand his domains, and the liberals needed the crown if they were to achieve their dream of national unification. The identification of liberalism with nationalism served as a political adhesive and saved Italy from both the recurrent bouts of neoabsolutism and the intense conflict between progressive and moderate liberals which characterized the Iberian peninsula.

The stable alliance exacted its price, however, as Italian liberalism shed its progressive elements too readily in its identification with the Piedmontese monarchy. The cost first became evident with the unification of Italy. While the unification was achieved, in 1859–60, with almost miraculous ease, the aftermath was brutal, as centralized Piedmontese control was imposed in very disparate regions, with little regard for legal niceties, local conditions, or aspirations for limited degrees of regional autonomy. Italian liberalism had become too domesticated to demand a constitutional assembly that would create new rules of the game appropriate to the entire nation. The consequences were especially grievous in the south, where rebellion (the misnamed "brigandage") continued for six years, on occasion approaching the dimensions of a civil war. Tension was also severe in the Romagna and other areas.

The parallels between political developments in Greece and the other Southern European countries are less compelling in this period than they would later become, but a similar pattern of frequent political instability, considerable domestic violence, and long-lasting governmental illegitimacy prevailed. A secret society encompassing military men and civilians initiated the Greek War of Independence in March 1821.[6] Contemporaries of all political persuasions regarded it as of a piece with the 1820–23 revolutionary movements in Italy and Iberia. The damage done during the seven years of active hostilities (1821–28) was even more severe than that endured by Spain during its 1808–14 war against Napoleon. After the fighting stopped, Greece underwent a prolonged political crisis, which culminated in anarchic civil war from 1831 to 1833. The new, foreign-appointed monarchy restored order for some years but reneged on early promises to institute parliamentary rule, until 1843, when an army-led revolt in Athens forced the ruler, Otto of Bavaria, to accept a constitution. But the weak sociological basis for liberalism in what was still a quite primitive society, plus conflicts among the liberal factions, enabled the king to recover the initiative after 1847. Otto temporarily gained much popularity by playing on nationalist sentiments during the foreign policy crises of the early and middle 1850s, but renewed resentment against his excessive powers, and the ineptness with which he used them, led to his ouster by a new military-led insurrection in 1862. Chaos again briefly threatened during the interregnum before a new ruler could be chosen, but the crisis ended with the more liberal constitution of 1863 and with the conciliatory policies followed by the new king, George of Denmark.

Spain, which had enjoyed long periods of relative stability between 1844 and 1866, would be the last country to escape from the vicious cycle of internal conflict. As in Greece earlier, the crisis was provoked by the ineptness and autocratic tendencies of the monarch, Isabel II. A longer struggle, from 1866 to 1868, was necessary to overthrow her; and it also took longer for a new king, Amadeo of Italy, to be found. By the time he arrived in 1870, the coalition that had unseated Isabel had disintegrated. The dynastic liberals reverted to their past habits and fought so bitterly among themselves as to make effective government impossible. This encouraged both the reemergence of Carlism and the growth of the Federal Republican movement on the left. A new Carlist bid for power gained strength in 1873 as, first, Amadeo resigned, then the Cortes proclaimed a republic by default, and finally the republic fell apart as the radical fringe tried to impose an extreme version of federalism, forcing the moderates to use the armed forces against them. The second Carlist war would not end until 1876, and a rebellion in Cuba would simmer on until 1878. This decade of intense crisis, added to the civil war of the 1830s, the savage 1808–14 struggle against the French, and the many lesser conflicts in between, gave Spain the dubious distinction of being the European nation most ravaged by political conflict during the nineteenth century, with Portugal, Greece, and Italy immediately following it. Eastern and Western Europe lagged considerably behind all four of the southern nations in this regard.

Two factors were especially distinctive in Southern European politics during this era: the position of the army and of the church. The former was more often than not an instrument of progressive change, particularly from about 1810 to the 1830s. Why was this so? Professional grievances played an important part, as did personal opportunism; but in a sense the armed forces were also acting as a surrogate for the middle classes, still too weak in Southern Europe to lead the drive for modernization. As the middle classes grew in size and factions among them became allied with the monarchy (the 1830s and 1840s encompassed both processes), moderate conservatives began to predominate in the army. But at no point during this period would the army assume the role it customarily has had during the twentieth century as a primarily reactionary agency. Indeed, as late as 1862 in Greece and 1868 in Spain, the armed forces helped bring about liberal regime change. The army became least active politically in Italy after the 1830s, for several reasons. Because there were no prolonged civil wars, as in Spain and Portugal, nor a major war of independence, as in Greece, the Italian military never became inflated in size and no popular heroes (except the antiestablishment Garibaldi) emerged from its ranks. Moreover, the reduced political dissidence in Piedmont after 1848 (because of the bond created among the dynastic parties and the crown by the nationalist cause) afforded fewer opportunities and less justification for the army to intervene in politics.

The church also played an important political role, above all in the Latin nations. It contributed heavily to the reactionary nature of the 1814 and 1821–28 restorations, thus ensuring that anticlericalism would become a fundamental component of Southern European liberalism. The antagonism was reinforced in Portugal and Spain by clerical support for the Miguelist and Carlist causes in the 1830s. The church paid heavily for its choice in both nations, as most of its properties were seized and sold to private owners. This disentailment converted it from a rich institution into an economically dependent one. As to Italy, it briefly seemed in the mid-1840s that old enmities might be transcended, as Pius IX flirted with Italian nationalism. But in 1848 the papacy balked, and subsequently did everything possible to sabotage the nationalist cause, especially after the Papal States were incorporated into the new kingdom in 1860. This helped pave the way for Italian disentailment in 1866. More important, it caused anticlericalism to become perhaps more universal among Italian liberals than in Spain and Portugal, where it was primarily a progressive doctrine. Greece, because of the distinct ecclesiastical tradition of orthodoxy (combining weak hierarchical organization with a long acceptance of caesaropapism), differed from the Catholic nations. Besides, religion had helped to preserve Greek national identity under Ottoman rule and to mobilize the people during the War of Independence. Hence, anticlericalism barely existed in Greece.

The peasantry was politically more active in the south than elsewhere in Europe during this period. This was partly due to the mobilizing capacities of clerics, but it also reflected the slight degree to which the state, hindered by poor communications and its own weakness, penetrated the countryside. The major instances of rural mass mobilization occurred in northern Spain (during the guerrilla war against the French and the Carlist wars), in northern Portugal (the Miguelist war and Maria da Fonte revolt), in southern Italy (the "brigandage" of 1860–66), and in Greece (the War of Independence). There was little correlation between degree of mobilization and rural social structure; on the Iberian peninsula small-holding areas were more active, whereas in Italy rural restiveness mostly occurred in large-property regions. The peasantry usually supported antiliberal causes, an indication of the influence clerics still enjoyed at the local level. The only socially inspired rural risings, such as those which rallied to Garibaldi in Sicily and Calabria in 1860, or those of Andalusia in the 1860s and early 1870s, were short-lived and easily defeated. As to the urban working class, it played a less important political role in Southern Europe than in Western Europe, reflecting the lesser degree of southern industrialization.

Defective Consolidation (1870s–1914)

Parallels among the four countries are even stronger from the 1870s to 1914. The earlier phase of endemic internal conflict was followed by a long period of relative stability which, although it began at different times (Portugal in 1851, Greece in 1864, Italy in 1866, Spain in 1876), was at its peak throughout Mediterranean Europe from the 1870s to the 1890s. Crisis struck again during this latter decade, however, and helped release a new cycle of domestic conflict, with a new set of political actors. Divergences persisted among our four nations, of course, though they were less pronounced than between 1814 and 1870. The division between the western and eastern halves of Southern Europe no longer made much sense, but a distinction between the smaller countries (Portugal and Greece), which had a narrower range of social, economic, and political possibilities than did the larger ones (Spain and Italy), became increasingly compelling. Also, it was during this era that Italy began to diverge significantly from the others in its economic prowess. Greece moved closer to the rest as its society adopted European attitudes and structures more fully; nevertheless, it continued to differ, because its incompleteness (more Greeks lived outside the dwarf kingdom than within it) and its geographical position condemned it to a preoccupation with foreign affairs that was unmatched elsewhere.

During the period between the 1870s and 1914, the Southern European countries shared several major patterns. First, intra-elite conflict was greatly attenuated as the old liberal-absolutist struggle was superseded and intraliberal clashes declined. Court circles became more reconciled to their new status and stopped trying to sabotage the parliamentary regimes. The political role of the church was also transformed, by the material losses it suffered during the middle decades of the century and because its links with both the crown and a dissatisfied peasantry had weakened. Military intervention in politics also became rare, as the generation of war leaders from the 1830s passed away in Portugal and Spain and as the greater cohesion of the new polities reduced the opportunities available to ambitious officers. But the greatest change took place among the liberals themselves. As had occurred earlier in Italy, the range of liberalism in Portugal and Spain narrowed, and intransigence at both ends of the political spectrum became discredited. Conservative and progressive liberals were now willing to cooperate, rather than seeking a complete victory over each other. The change is most strikingly illustrated in Spain where, in the four decades between 1833 and 1874, there had been sixty-seven governments headed by forty-seven individuals, whereas only two persons governed Spain during the next quarter-century (until 1899), except for some brief caretaker cabinets. Greece remained an exception, as divisions over pressing foreign policy issues provided a basis for intraparty strife. Yet Greek rhetorical violence was not accompanied by physical coercion, and one man, Charilaos Trikoupis, dominated politics for most of the 1875–95 period, despite the attacks against him.

If society benefited by the diminishing of intra-elite conflict, the problem of illicit collaboration among politicians soon replaced it. Liberalism, won at such cost earlier in the century, became more corrupt in Southern Europe than elsewhere. Similar, smoothly functioning political practices existed in the three Latin countries: these were dubbed *rotativismo* in Portugal, *caciquismo* in Spain, and *trasformismo* in Italy. The Portuguese system had evolved gradually during the 1850s and 1860s, while the Spanish and Italian variants had been more consciously constructed after 1876. The heyday of the *cacique* system in all three countries was from the late 1870s through the 1890s, although in Spain the system continued to operate well into the twentieth century. Its essence was agreement on certain ends among the major factions of the dynastic parties in each country, and electoral manipulation on the local level in line with those agreements. On the Iberian peninsula, elections were managed so that the liberal and conservative parties would rotate in office. In Italy, where liberals and conservatives gradually melded into a diffuse centrist coalition after 1876, voting was arranged so that "governmental" candidates won. Another major difference was that the *cacique* system could continue to function in Spain despite the granting of universal male suffrage in 1890, whereas in Portugal and Italy suffrage remained severely limited. Radical, republican, socialist and regional parties outside the system were kept small, though this did not necessarily render them impotent. Because electoral corruption was well known and increasingly denounced after the 1890s, the opposition gained considerable moral force. Moreover, it became more difficult to control the vote in heavily urbanized areas, particularly where working-class organizations or regional sentiments were strong. Hence, a few islands of electoral freedom emerged, especially in northern Italy and Catalonia. The *cacique* system did not operate primarily for personal gain. Nor was government rendered ineffective by it, especially in Italy, where much was accomplished through state action. Indeed, one can argue that the precocious establishment of advanced liberal government in what were still economically and socially backward nations made the system a necessary evil. Yet it obviously kept many problems from being dealt with. And, since it violated the most fundamental liberal principles, it became the scapegoat for everything that went wrong, and thus ended by discrediting liberalism as a whole.

Political stability coincided with, and to some extent was buttressed by, a long period of economic growth. This was not the first time Southern Europe had been economically active. It had shared in the general European boom of the 1850s and 1860s, benefiting from sizable foreign investments (above all from France) and making important strides in building railway networks and other kinds of modern infrastructure. But, in contrast to most of the rest of Europe, where prosperity gave way to the long recession of the 1870s through 1890s, the southern economies remained vigorous for much longer. A major reason for the different course of events was the phylloxera disease which ravaged French vineyards around 1870. For two decades, wine had to be imported in huge quantities and at high prices from the Mediterranean nations, the only other significant producers. Additional factors contributed to continued prosperity in each nation, particularly in Spain, where spectacular growth in the mining industry (above all, of iron ore mining in the Basque country) coincided with a great expansion of Cuban sugar output and the flourishing of Catalan textiles to create boom conditions from about 1878 to 1892.

Once more in contrast to the general European pattern, good times were replaced by bad in the late 1880s and early 1890s. The factor that earlier had helped Mediterranean Europe now turned against it, as French vineyards recovered from phylloxera and wine prices fell sharply. In Italy the crisis was aggravated by the 1887–92 tariff war with France and by great banking scandals. Greece, especially dependent on its vineyards and in a precarious economic position due to its ambitious development programs of the 1880s, was forced to suspend payments on state debts in 1893. Portugal experienced a major fiscal crisis in 1890–92, while for Spain the really serious troubles began in 1895, when revolution reappeared in Cuba and disrupted the sugar industry. Yet the crises were surprisingly short-lived. A new common factor helped foster recovery—the massive emigration to both of the Americas that began in the 1890s and swelled to flood proportions in the 1900s. Southerners participated in this far more than other Europeans, and the remittances they sent home became one of the mainstays of the southern economies. Other factors also contributed to recovery in each country. This was especially so in Italy, which became the first Mediterranean nation to acquire, via hydroelectricity, a reasonably adequate supply of inexpensive energy. Fundamental restructuring of the banking system after the 1892–94 scandals also helped, as did the fact that huge land reclamation projects, started decades earlier, began to pay off. After 1896 the pace of Italian economic growth accelerated. Since Italians also soon proved able to pioneer in new industries with such firms as Fiat and Olivetti, Italy experienced her first "economic miracle," pulling decisively ahead of Spain for the first time. Yet Italy did not thereby escape from the Southern European orbit, not even in strictly economic terms, because only northern Italy benefited from the boom, while the *mezzogiorno* fell further behind.

Foreign policy disasters struck all four nations during the 1890s. Portugal's occurred first, in 1890, when its oldest ally, Britain, threatened war unless Portugal abandoned its efforts to link its coastal colonies, Angola and Mozambique, across the body of Africa. The Portuguese had to swallow their pride and comply. Italy's turn to be humiliated came next, in 1896, when Francesco Crispi's aggressive policies in Ethiopia led to the rout of an Italian army at Adowa, the first time Africans had been able utterly to defeat a major European force. Greece followed in 1897, marching bravely into Macedonia against the Ottoman Empire in April, and by May begging desperately for foreign intervention to prevent Turkish armies, already deep in Thessaly, from continuing south toward Athens. Disgrace also came quickly for Spain in its 1898 war with the United States: destruction of its Pacific fleet took but a week, the loss of Cuba and Puerto Rico only three months. Nothing mitigated any of these disasters; there were no heroes, no barely missed opportunities on which expiatory mythologies might be based, just unrelieved defeat and humiliation, which seriously undermined the already weak legitimacy of the existing regimes.

Political stability was also undermined by the growth of new antisystem forces. The most important in Italy and Spain were the worker movements, which only in the 1890s became a constant presence in national life. The movements resembled each other in that they included stronger anarchist components and won more support among agricultural workers than elsewhere in Europe. As a result, in addition to normal industrial strikes, Italy and Spain experienced unique phenomena: periodic protest in rural areas, occasionally involving entire provinces and requiring the dispatch of army units; two great urban risings of the sort that no longer were customary in Europe, in Milan in 1898 and Barcelona in 1909; and more frequent terrorist acts than anywhere except Russia. The Italian and Spanish labor movements tended to be more volatile than their European counterparts, fluctuating more violently between reformism and revolutionary intransigence, their membership oscillating wildly in size according to circumstances. The treatment they received from employers and the state also varied widely, though on the whole it was sufficiently brutal that a subculture of fierce conflict between capital and labor became deeply rooted. The sociological bases for these singular developments are hard to determine, but they include the high proportion of landless workers in such large-holding regions as Andalusia, Emilia-Romagna, and Apulia, and the small size and precarious condition of most industrial firms in cities like Barcelona and Milan. The smaller countries, Portugal and Greece, diverged from the large in that their labor movements remained minuscule, not yet able to play a major role in political life. Cities there were still too small, industry too embryonic, and rural property too widely distributed for workers to organize in large numbers.[7]

Other new destablizing forces emerged. In Spain, the most important was Catalan nationalism; born as a cultural movement in the 1840s, it began to take on political shape during the 1880s and consolidated itself as a major movement in the aftermath of the 1898 disaster. An intense, highly complex struggle between Barcelona and Madrid would henceforth mark Spanish politics. It also fueled other sources of discord, such as Basque nationalism (though this was as yet too modest a force to count for much) and the revival of the army's tradition of intervention into politics. In Italy, several new movements revealed the disenchantment of the elites. Most important were the Nationalists, who played on the theme of Italy as a "proletarian nation" which required stern policies, both domestic and international, for its salvation. By 1911, they had developed a corrosive power disproportionate to their small numbers. In Portugal, the Republican Party reaped most of the benefits of the 1890 humiliation, and during the next two decades was remarkably successful in becoming all things to all people, appealing strongly to intellectuals, businessmen, and nationalists, but also developing a considerable following among urban workers. In Greece, while there were many dissenting intellectuals and politicians, no single movement succeeded in organizing the opposition. Resentment and disillusion filled the air, but they lacked specific focus.

By the turn of the century, the disruption caused by foreign policy and fiscal crises and by the rapid growth of new political forces had made it obvious even to the political establishment that the corrupt liberalism of the 1870s–90s was no longer viable. "Regeneration" became the cry of the day. The conservatives tended to lead the way, advocating a Bismarckian-style "revolution from above," to be carried out by strong governments which would rely on the "vital forces" of the nation to revitalize it. The liberals appealed more directly to the people, with demands for more inclusive politics and greater democratization. In Spain, the Conservative Party itself led the drive for regeneration, especially under Antonio Maura in 1907–9. In Portugal, political parties were less responsive, so over their protests the king took the initiative in 1906 by allowing a dissident conservative, João Franco, to rule "dictatorially." Italy flirted with a return to some sort of royal semiabsolutism between 1896 and 1900. Only in Greece was there no swing to the right, as the major parties were too moribund for such initiatives and the king too insecure after the 1897 disaster to act in their stead.

Conservative regenerationism failed wherever it was tried. Maura's authoritarian reformism first alienated most of the rest of the political establishment then brought about his downfall when he overreacted to the 1909 uprising in Barcelona. In Portugal, both major parties bitterly denounced Franco and, after his royal protector was assassinated in 1908, forced him from office. In Italy, the struggle against the emasculation of parliamentary rule won a resounding victory in 1900, when both court decisions and elections went against the revisionists and the king was assassinated. With the neoconservatives routed, power passed to other forces. In Spain and Italy, these were the democratizing sectors of the liberal parties, lead by José Canalejas and Giovanni Giolitti, respectively. Both of these also failed. Canalejas's tenure (1910–12) was cut short by a bullet.[8] Giolitti, during his long era of predominance (1903–14), created a mixed legacy. On the one hand, he favored social legislation and sought to incorporate previously marginalized groups into politics, but he also continued to employ the corrupt tactics of *trasformismo* to achieve his ends. Thus, he ended up being bitterly attacked from both ends of the political spectrum.

Events took a different course in Portugal. Because both dynastic parties remained as incapable as ever of striking out in new directions after the king was slain and Franco fell, the Republican Party filled the vacuum. Several different urban middle- and upper-class groups flocked to it, as did many army and navy officers. In 1910 this broad coalition of forces rose in Southern Europe's first successful revolution since 1868. The old mold was broken: the monarchy was abolished and a republic (a radical polity by definition in pre-1914 Europe) was proclaimed. The new regime would prove a bitter disappointment, but for the moment slow-moving Portugal seemed once again to have anticipated the future course of its Southern European sisters. In 1831–34 it had witnessed the first break in the united absolutist front against the liberals; in the 1850s it had been the first to transcend intraliberal conflict by developing the rotativist system; now, with the apparent triumph of full democracy, it seemed a harbinger of developments that would come to Italy in 1919–21, to Greece in 1922–24, and to Spain in 1930–31.

Greece also struck out in new directions. Although there was no republican party to channel opinion as in Portugal, the disgust against "old-partyism" in the urban centers and among military men was so great that a limited revolution took place in 1909. The crown trembled for six months while a military league acted as political arbiter. But the crisis was resolved in 1910 when Eleftherios Venizelos, called to Athens from Crete by the league, convoked a constitutional assembly and used it both to authorize a program of democratizing reforms and to reconcile dissidents with the crown. Venizelos would soon have cause to regret the political and military prerogatives he left to the monarchy, but at the time his moderation seemed wildly successful. In the elections of December 1910, his party won the largest majority ever recorded. His triumph became complete two years later when he steered Greece through the Balkan wars of 1912–13. At one blow, many of Greece's long-frustrated irredentist dreams were suddenly realized. A dwarf state even after its 1864 and 1881 accretions, Greece now almost doubled in territory and population, adding Crete, Epirus, and above all Macedonia. It is no exaggeration to speak of an apotheosis of Venizelos by late 1913. Never before had anyone been so popular in Southern Europe; having gathered behind him the energies of nationalism, Venizelos appeared likely to be able to carry out that combination of democratization and modernization which had eluded Canalejas and Giolitti.

But what might be called the curse of Southern Europe would not be lifted so easily for Greece, any more than for Portugal, Italy, or Spain. The new era that was dawning would prove grim for them all. They had been incapable of using the relatively stable and prosperous 1870s and 1880s to make up for the decades lost in civic discord earlier in the century and to lay stronger foundations for the future. The liberal order and capitalism were consolidated, but in defective ways which left them weak in the face of the new challenges that began to appear in the 1890s, and would become overwhelming after the outbreak of World War I. The political realm had not been truly integrated with society but had stayed isolated from it, operating according to its own rules. It was during this period that the distinction between the "real" and the "official" country gained wide currency. The new order had gained neither the devotion of the people nor the respect of the intellectuals. It thus lacked ballast for the storms that lay ahead.

Conflict and Collapse (1915–1949)

Already quite different from either Western or Eastern Europe, the singularity of the south was further accentuated between 1915 and 1949. The broad pattern followed, during and immediately after World War I, was one of severe crisis, in which leftist forces were at first predominant. This in turn led to a regrouping of the right during the early 1920s and to the establishment of relatively mild dictatorial regimes which, since they were more prevalent than any other type of political system, might be considered a kind of Southern European "norm" for most of the interwar period. The model becomes complicated, however, during the following decade. The Spanish dictatorship collapsed in 1930 and was followed first by a highly democratic republic, then by a savage civil war, and finally by a new dictatorship so much harsher than its predecessor that it no longer fit into the norm I just referred to. In the middle and late 1930s, the Italian dictatorship underwent radical mutations which placed it in a different political orbit as well. On the other hand, Greece, which had earlier escaped authoritarian rule, fell under a 1920s-style Mediterranean dictatorship in 1936. It is hard to give coherence to all this, not to mention the different paths these countries followed during World War II. Because of the kaleidoscopic nature of the 1930s, this period might seem to be the one in which our four nations diverged the most. Nevertheless, the model does not break down; indeed, paradoxically, this may be the time when more significant interaction occurred within Southern Europe than ever before.

Also notable are the parallels between this era and the era of turmoil from 1814 to the 1870s. The military once more plays a major political role, anticlericalism again becomes a burning issue, the church revives its ties with the most extreme rightist forces, massive mobilizations occur among the peasantry (though now for revolutionary rather than conservative ends), and land reform looms large on the political agenda, as does the legitimacy of the monarchy. For all the "modernity" of fascism, communism, and other new forces of the era, some things had not changed.

Because they lay outside the main lines of action, none of our countries was forced precipitously into war in 1914. Almost alone in Europe, they could decide whether and when to enter. This apparent advantage was double-edged, however, because the agonizing decision as to whether to participate in what was soon recognized as unprecedented slaughter polarized southern society. The interventionist controversy in Italy from August 1914 to May 1915 was critical, because it further damaged the already-low prestige of parliament, and the violent tactics used by the interventionists set dangerous precedents for the future. The fascist coalition began to emerge in embryonic form. The crisis in Greece lasted longer and was of even greater intensity; indeed, in its latter stages it can be considered a low-grade civil war. It began in March 1915, when Venizelos wanted to join the Gallipoli campaign, and was not resolved until June 1917, when the Entente powers forced King Constantine into exile. The apparent unity which the triumphs of 1910–13 had brought to Greece crumbled as Venizelos was twice forced from office despite huge parliamentary majorities, the country was partitioned de facto as France and England occupied Salonica and Venizelos established a provisional government there, and the royalist portions of Greece were subjected to almost continuous blockade and occasional military incursions. In Portugal, the initial conflict was milder, but antiwar fervor revived as troops actually began to be sent to the Western Front in 1917, and it contributed to the establishment of Sidónio Pais's populist dictatorship in December of that year. Even in Spain, which did not enter the war for a variety of reasons, the interventionist crisis seriously exacerbated political conflict, adding still another source of dissension to the many that already characterized political discourse there.

Almost unique in their interventionist crises, the southern nations again displayed their distinctiveness at war's end. The immediate postwar period was conflictive throughout Europe, of course, but only in Russia and in the defeated countries was there more internal conflict than in Southern Europe. No other nation on the winning side would experience the kind of discord that shattered Greece, Italy, and Portugal, and no neutral country the turmoil that shook Spain. Because foreign policy issues so deeply conditioned what happened in Greece, I will leave that country for later discussion. In the other three, the specific mix of forces differed, but in the opening stages of the crises the left held the initiative. In Spain, the tension first openly erupted before the war ended, in the summer of 1917, when progressive parliamentarians tried to force the convening of a constituent assembly and the socialists launched a semirevolutionary general strike. In Portugal, the first blow was struck in December 1918, with the assassination of Pais and the disintegration of his year-old dictatorship. In Italy, the great 1919 socialist electoral victory (under a new voting system) triggered the crisis.

The left would remain predominant until 1921. In Spain and Italy, labor movements played the chief role, swelling to approximately seven times their 1910–14 size and launching an unprecedented number of strikes of equally unprecedented dimensions. The period was dubbed the "bolshevik triennium" in Spain, though it was the anarchosyndicalists who usually took the initiative. The Italian workers' movement was even more powerful, terrifying industrialists by the legendary "occupation of the factories" in September 1920, and northern landowners by imposing "labor dictatorships" in many rural areas. In Portugal, worker groups were also more active than before, although middle-class radicals continued to be most responsible for setting the pace.

Despite their ascendancy, the democratizing forces could not achieve hegemony. The strength and revolutionary rhetoric of the trade unions frightened middle-class progressives and prevented the formation of lasting alliances on the left. And, as the forces of the right recovered their confidence, a stalemate developed during which the left no longer could realistically hope to seize power but neither could it be entirely destroyed within the framework of liberalism. The period of instability lasted longest and was perhaps greatest in Portugal, where from 1918 to 1926 there were five presidents, thirty-three governments (one of which ended when the prime minister was assassinated), two large-scale insurrections, and many lesser acts. In Spain a multisided form of urban terrorism developed among police, anarchist "action groups," and company unions in Barcelona and other major cities; this had claimed hundreds of lives by 1923, among them a prime minister, an archbishop, and the top syndicalist leader. In Italy, the government was headed by democratizing liberals like Francesco Nitti and Giolitti, so repressive acts usually originated outside the regular state apparatus, even though they presupposed the connivance of the police, the army, and many state officials. This is how fascism made its first major advances, in the winter of 1920, when local elites in Emilia-Romagna and other northern rural areas turned to the fascist squads as extralegal means of destroying socialist power in their localities.

Because of the utter bankruptcy of its liberal forces and the cunning of Mussolini, who blended Mafia-like tactics involving the squads with traditional legitimate political maneuvres, Italy's stalemate ended in October 1922, when the king acquiesced to the March on Rome. The Italian example was followed eleven months later in Spain, when a military coup headed by Miguel Primo de Rivera was also welcomed by the crown. In Portugal, where there was no king to ease the transition to authoritarian rule, the task took longer, but in May 1926 an army conspiracy overthrew the republic. Since all this happened well before the economic collapse and Nazi successes of the 1930s had made dictatorship a general European phenomenon, the three Latin nations again proved the special weakness of their liberal regimes. In a sense, by being the first to lapse toward nondemocratic politics they were once more displaying their political precocity, as they had during the nineteenth century by their early acceptance of liberalism. The Italian dictatorship differed from the other two, of course, if only because of Mussolini and the Fascist Party. But the differences were as much apparent as real during this period: neither dictator nor party was all-powerful; key sectors of Italian society, including the church and army, retained their autonomy; the idea of a totalitarian state was widely trumpeted, but little was done to actually implement it. Moreover, if we stress the differences too much, we risk overlooking the similarities.

Among these was the fact that force had scarcely been necessary in any of the seizures of power. The parliamentary regimes had become so discredited that there was little opposition to, and considerable initial enthusiasm for, the new authoritarian rule. Corporatism emerged as the major organizing principle of all three dictatorships, in part because of the central role the concept had played in Catholic social thought since the 1890s. The residual power of the church, and its close identification with the new regimes, was another common feature, especially after António Salazar gained predominance in Portugal in 1928–30.

The pattern of relatively mild authoritarian regimes in the three Latin nations was broken when Primo de Rivera's lightly rooted dictatorship collapsed in 1930 and a republic was proclaimed in 1931. As defined by Manuel Azaña's coalition of 1931–33, the republic was unusually ambitious and idealistic, and for a while seemed capable of realizing the social and political reforms for which leftist forces throughout Southern Europe had long been struggling. But in the end, Spain's republic was destroyed by some of the same factors that had earlier undone Portugal's and were, simultaneously, contributing to the collapse of the Greek republic. Southern Europe's long tradition of factionalism on the left, which Spanish republicans had miraculously transcended in 1930, returned to plague them after 1933. Especially crucial was the falling out between the working and the progressive middle classes, as the difficulties which appeared reduced the zeal for reform among the latter and turned the workers toward revolutionary solutions. The abundance of unresolved problems inherited from the antecedent liberal regimes also helped overwhelm the new democracies, whether they tried seriously to address them, as in Spain, or tended to ignore them, as in Portugal. Anticlericalism proved counterproductive in the Iberian nations, by providing an issue around which enemies of the two republics could rally. It was impossible to create an atmosphere of mutual tolerance, or respect for due process, as the political culture of violence and corruption that had developed throughout Southern Europe during the previous century enabled most groups to feel justified in persecuting their opponents mercilessly whenever possible. Finally, as had also been true for nineteenth-century liberalism, the Spanish and Greek democracies were unfortunate in their timing; few periods in Europe's history were as ideologically conflictive or economically unstable as the 1930s.

Thus, what started in Spain as a triumph of the center-left degenerated from 1934 on into a renewal, on a larger scale, of the struggle for hegemony between right and left that had characterized the immediate postwar period. In July 1936 the struggle escalated into civil war, as an army rebellion seized control of half of Spain but was defeated in its other half by a revived coalition of working- and middle-class groups. Three years of fratricidal conflict followed, during which many of the pressures which had been building up for decades suddenly exploded, in a great social revolution among the workers and peasants and in an unprecedented wave of brutal repression on the part of the right. Uniquely Spanish, the civil war can nevertheless also be seen as a metaphor for the conflictive history of Mediterranean Europe as a whole during the previous two centuries. It also brought forth extensive interaction among the southern nations, as both Mussolini and Salazar sent large troop contingents to aid the nationalists, and many Italian antifascists (plus some three hundred Greeks) fought for the republic. With Francisco Franco's victory, most of the liberal gains of the previous century were wiped out. The church's deep involvement with authoritarian politics was resumed, and the army won unprecedented political power. Franco adopted many practices of the early Mussolini regime, from its corporatism to its Charter of Labor, from settling peasants on reclaimed lands to emasculating and bureaucratizing the Falange, Spain's fascist party, while paying it lip service. But because it had come to power through military victory in a savage civil war, the Franco regime was far harsher than the Italian dictatorship had been in its early stages. Political slayings in Italy numbered in the hundreds during the two decades from 1922 to 1941, but in Spain nearly 40,000 were executed in the first four years after the war. Certainly the Franco regime in its early stages could not be considered a mild dictatorship of the 1920s type, despite the many structural features it adopted from them.

The Italian dictatorship itself changed radically in the mid-1930s. The pragmatism that had earlier characterized it gave way to dangerous new initiatives in foreign policy, which tried to take advantage of the unstable international situation created by the rise of Nazi Germany. The Ethiopian war of 1935–36 came first, then intervention in Spain, then the seizure of Albania in 1939. Mussolini's sense of reality did not disappear entirely, so Italy initially stayed out of World War II; but when France collapsed, caution no longer seemed necessary. In September 1940, Italian forces in Libya were launched against the British in Egypt, and those in Albania struck at Greece a month later. Both campaigns resulted in defeats from which Italy had to be rescued by Germany. The defeat in Albania was especially humiliating, as Greece had only one-fifth Italy's population and an even smaller proportion of its economic prowess. Italy was effectively reduced to a German satellite, as would be proven by the ease with which Hitler's forces took over most of the country after Mussolini was overthrown in a palace coup in July 1943. Italy now entered its darkest era: fierce combat between Allied and German armies ravaged the peninsula for two years; in the south, the royal government proved utterly incompetent and its authority was sharply disputed; in the center and north, a civil war got under way as the resistance movements had to struggle not only against the Germans but also against the hard-core fascists, who had regrouped in a vicious new "social republic" headed by Mussolini.

As for Greece, the Great Schism of 1915–17 was not healed by Venizelos's extraordinary triumph at Versailles, when he convinced the victorious Entente to grant Greece not only Thrace but also Smyrna in Asia Minor. A "Greece of the five seas and two continents" was thus created, but this did not sway Greek voters, who, resentful both of the high-handed measures used to force Greece into the world war and of the continued mobilization required to make good her Asia Minor claims, returned the royalists to power in 1920. The Greek army was weakened as royalist officers who had sat out the war replaced Venizelists, and Greece lost foreign support because Constantine was still anathema to the Entente. More important, a Turkish resistance movement, led by Atatürk, sprang up in Anatolia and was harassing the Greek armies there. Conditions deteriorated steadily for two years, until August 1922, when Atatürk launched a great offensive and the Greek armies crumbled before it. Smyrna's large Greek population was abandoned to its fate, which meant first pillage, then expulsion. The same fate awaited Greeks throughout Asia Minor and in eastern Thrace, which Atatürk also reconquered. In one blow, a heritage that dated back nearly three thousand years was eradicated. Some 1.2 million refugees settled in Greece, a number equivalent to one-fourth of the previous population—perhaps the largest proportion of refugees any nation has ever been called upon to absorb.

It is not surprising that after so great a trauma Constantine was overthrown by a military coup and a republic was proclaimed. We cannot go into its history here. Until 1926, it was as chaotic as the Portuguese republic. After that time, the parallels came to be more with the Spanish republic, and ranged from an epoch of solid accomplishments under Venizelos in 1928–32 to the disintegration of republican legality in 1933–36, for which both Venizelists and royalists were responsible. Military leaders often intervened in politics (occasionally, like George Kondylis, switching sides), except during the 1928–32 period. Because of the refugee influx and rapid urbanization, workers, organized mainly by the communists, also played a key role, for the first time in Greek history. A final link between the two nations was the impact of the Spanish Civil War on Greece. The new king, George II, restored via an army coup in late 1935, had returned from exile in a remarkably conciliatory mood; but in August 1936, two weeks after the Spanish conflict began, he abruptly shifted course and authorized a conservative minister, Ioannis Metaxas, to disband parliament.

With the Metaxas dictatorship, Greece reenacted the history of the Latin countries in the 1920s. An authoritarian regime was created which adopted much of the paraphernalia of fascism but allowed a limited degree of pluralism. Its chief victims were the communists. The regime was less well received both among elites and the populace than the Latin dictatorships of 1922–26 had been, but neither was there much opposition to it. Indeed, when Mussolini attacked in 1940, the nation rallied to the war effort with unprecedented unanimity, enabling Metaxas to preside over what is perhaps Greece's proudest moment since its War of Independence. Yet the six-month triumph in Albania could not prevent a turn of the tide, first against the dictatorship, which disintegrated after Metaxas died during the war, and then against the monarchy that had sired it.

For the third time in a generation, Greece found itself severely divided. The new left-right cleavage had many of its roots in the old national schisms of 1915–24 and of 1933–36, but it involved different social alliances and became enmeshed in wider issues, as the communist-affiliated National Liberation Front (EAM) took command of the antimonarchist cause. The largest of the resistance groups, the EAM tried to impose its authority by force of arms both before the German withdrawal and—in a more confused and contradictory manner—via the bloody events of December 1944 in Athens. With the failure of the latter effort, a vicious cycle again came into being. Justifying their wartime actions as inspired by anticommunism, many collaborators slipped into the monarchist ranks; meanwhile, most progressives, alienated by the EAM's early aggressiveness, kept silent as royalist extremists began to persecute suspected leftists. Unrelieved repression in 1945 and early 1946 finally drove the EAM to take up arms once more, this time with the support of the new communist states that had arisen in the Balkans. A full-scale civil war followed; it lasted for three years and ranks in its destructiveness only after Spain and Russia among European civil wars of the twentieth century. Tens of thousands were killed, other tens of thousands imprisoned, and hundreds of thousands more were harassed for their political beliefs. And at war's end, in 1949, there were more exiles relative to the population even than in Spain.

As was mentioned earlier, internal strife was also rampant in Italy in 1943–45, and might also have developed into full scale civil war; but in contrast to Greece, Italy was occupied by huge Allied armies, which imposed restraint on all local groups. For this and other reasons, the Italian Communists were never tempted to make a bid for power and the monarchists were unable to become as hegemonic on the Italian right as they were among Greek conservatives. Yet Italy did not escape unscathed, as was shown by the postwar purge of collaborators, which took about fifteen thousand lives, and by the apocalyptic denunciations of communism with which the Christian Democrats filled the 1948 elections.

Spain, despite having avoided World War II, suffered terribly during the 1940s. Moral recovery from the civil war was slow. Although executions stopped after 1943 and the number of political prisoners fell, repression continued in milder form, especially during 1945–48, when (replicating in miniature contemporaneous events in Greece) guerrilla groups organized both locally and from France tried to oust Franco's dictatorship. Material recovery was also difficult, because of the shortages created by the world war, the international ostracism of Spain afterward, one of the worst droughts in Spanish history, and the regime's incompetence in the administration of economic affairs. The entire decade became known as the "years of hunger," and neither agricultural nor industrial production recovered their already-low 1931–36 levels until the early 1950s.

Transcendence and Redemption? (1950–1992)

Southern Europe thus reached a nadir at the close of the 1940s. This was especially true for Greece, which had been triply cursed: by an exceptionally brutal Axis occupation in 1941–44, by intense civil strife in 1944–46, and by full civil war in 1946–49. Spain, tormented and asphyxiated throughout the decade, was not much better off. Italy had avoided civil war but was impoverished and politically polarized. Only Portugal was an exception. That country had gone through continuous turmoil for two decades, from 1908 to 1928; but two decades of stability and peace had followed, during which Portugal had even managed to become relatively prosperous, due to Salazar's careful fiscal management and because it was one of the few neutral nations during World War II and benefited by trading with both sides.

All this would change during the next quarter-century. Dramatic transformations occurred not only within each of our nations but also in their position relative to one another other and to the rest of Europe.

By 1975, Southern Europe had converged so much with Western Europe that the line separating the two was becoming blurred, whereas communist predominance in the east had further magnified the contrasts between the two sectors of the so-called "European periphery." The rate and ubiquitousness of change was unprecedented. Unprecedented too was its generally positive direction. In contrast to the experience of Eastern Europe, this was an era of fulfillment for the South, a time when it finally seemed to find its way after nearly two centuries of wandering about in the dark.

International interaction increased so enormously after 1950 that it is pointless to deal any longer strictly with national histories; everything that happened locally was so profoundly conditioned by what was occurring in a wider arena as to be unintelligible without it. This commonplace is particularly applicable to Southern Europe and to the Western bloc of which it was part. Three factors which characterized the bloc as a whole had special relevance for the South. First was the unprecedented unanimity about democracy that derived from World War II and the Cold War. The democratic ideal was held more firmly in theory than in practice, of course, but its existence was overwhelmingly important to the southern nations, since they were the ones in noncommunist Europe where democracy either did not exist or was most fragile. Conspiracies against democracy, like those retroactively discovered in Italy, were handicapped, as antidemocratic discourse utterly lacked legitimacy for the first time in Europe's history. If a conspiracy succeeded, as in Greece in 1967, the new dictatorship was regarded as an anachronism and a pariah and so could not sink roots at home or abroad. As for the long-established Iberian dictatorships, they had to pay high costs of many kinds, especially their exclusion from the European Economic Community (EEC) and its antecedent European economic organizations.[9] In short, the interwar situation was reversed: in the 1930s, the international climate had favored dictatorship, but from the late 1940s on it clearly advantaged democracy, within Europe at least.

Second, the Western world experienced an unprecedentedly long and dynamic economic boom, from the early 1950s to the oil shock of 1973, and Southern Europe was the region that most benefited by it. Two of postwar Europe's three recognized "economic miracles" took place in Italy and Spain, but since Greece also underwent remarkable growth in the 1950s and 1960s, and even Portugal enjoyed a boom in 1966–73, one might well speak of an economic miracle for the region as a whole. The gap that formerly existed was either narrowed or, in the case of Italy, reversed with every West European nation except Germany. Once again, certain common factors help account for the southern boom. One, at the turn of the century, was huge remittances from abroad, as large-scale overseas migration revived and the *Gastarbeiter* phenomenon developed within Europe. The south once again sent proportionately more of its population abroad as migrant labor than did any other region. It also led the world in benefiting from the enormous new tourist industry that was developing; no other world region so combined sun, sea, culture, and convenience. Also fundamental to the boom were low labor costs, which made southern products cheaper abroad and attracted much foreign investment. Finally, the south was at long last able to overcome two major deficiencies that had earlier handicapped its development. As hydroelectricity advanced and coal was replaced by oil, it was at less of a disadvantage in terms of its energy supplies. Equally important, except in Portugal, Southern Europe experienced a major agricultural revolution, as irrigation works spread, self-sufficiency in all basic foodstuffs save meat was achieved, and demand abroad spiraled for specialized Mediterranean crops.

Third, this was a period of unprecedented social and cultural change throughout the West, but especially in Southern Europe. The growth of the mass communications media was partly responsible, of course; but in addition, several special factors contributed, among them Southern Europe's huge number of tourists and migrant workers. Although both groups were mostly ghettoized, the interchange of peoples on such a vast scale also helped transmit new attitudes of all kinds—political, social, economic, cultural, sexual. The exceptionally rapid urbanization of Southern Europe was also important. Never before had so high a proportion of Europe's rural population moved to the cities so quickly. In 1950 the southern nations were still basically agricultural, but by 1975 they had become heavily urbanized. Another factor that made the population more receptive to outside influences was the remarkable growth of southern educational systems, especially on the secondary and higher levels. Illiteracy was finally eliminated, and university enrollment reached West European dimensions. Finally, almost as a prerequisite to everything else, Southern Europe was one the very few developing regions in world history where rapid material growth was accompanied by slow demographic change. Economic gains were not compromised by excessive population growth nor, under the new circumstances that had arisen, could they be monopolized by those on top, so a great rise in real per capita income took place. This increased the size of the middle classes and altered the common man, making both more receptive to new ideas.

The above three factors combined to foster an extraordinarily rapid political, economic, and cultural modernization of Southern Europe. The involutions and frustrations which had dominated earlier periods continued to seem formidable, but under the surface they receded in importance as a new dynamic took hold. The pace differed in each nation, of course, for societies are not passive agents shaped solely by the environments in which they find themselves. History and politics have their own spheres of autonomy. Only Spain after 1950 developed more or less unilinearly in ways that might have been predicted on the basis of the structural factors mentioned above. In Greece, Italy, and Portugal, much happened that a structural approach alone cannot explain.

The effects of Greece's long trauma of the 1940s could not be eliminated overnight; they were manifest in the flawed democracy that governed the country. Among the flaws were these: neither king nor army truly accepted the supremacy of parliament; electoral fraud was common; and the state apparatus habitually discriminated against those suspected of sympathizing with the losing side in the Civil War. Nevertheless, democratic forms were preserved, and from 1953 to the mid-1960s, mostly under conservative governments led by Constantine Karamanlis, very rapid economic growth occurred, soon to be followed by a major cultural flourishing. Though still behind Italy in per capita income, by the mid-1960s Greece stood ahead of the Iberian nations. But unlike what would happen in Spain, Greek economic growth proved neither self-sustaining nor able to create favorable conditions for the full consolidation of democracy. Two factors interrupted the "virtuous cycle" that seemed to be developing. An external issue, Cyprus, was the first to emerge, assuming crisis proportions in 1955–60, in 1964, and in 1967, but also permeating Greek political life in quieter times. Cyprus undermined the mental attitudes necessary for modernization; concern with internal affairs, especially economic growth, once again began to take second place to irredentism of the kind that had distorted Greek life in the nineteenth and early twentieth centuries. The only good effect of the Asia Minor disaster of 1922 was that it seemed to have ended this obsession forever, especially as excellent Greco-Turkish relations had prevailed from 1930 to 1955. Now Greece became hostage to Cyprus, saddled with a military budget triple (proportionally) the size of Italy's or Spain's, and with every demagogue once again able to invoke the irredentist cause to suit his purposes.

A series of domestic conflicts, each having some of its roots in and echoing some of the themes of the old Venizelist-royalist schism, also helped reverse the tide in Greece. First, from 1961 to 1963, came the "unremitting" campaign of George Papandreou against Karamanlis's conservative hegemony. This was followed, in 1964–67, by even fiercer strife between Papandreou's center-left forces and the crown, which sought to exclude them from power. The conflict culminated in 1967 with an army coup. For six years Greece had undergone acute political crisis, and this was now followed by seven years of military dictatorship. So much discord inevitably disrupted the modernizing trends that seemed to have been taking hold. Yet the 1950s had not been entirely wasted. Due to the socioeconomic transformations that occurred then and Greece's deeper interaction with the West, the dictatorship could not take root. Politicians of all persuasions refused to serve under it, and its various attempts to gain legitimacy all failed. Its isolation was fully exposed in November 1973, when it bloodily suppressed a student demonstration in Athens. The colonels had imposed a dictatorship *on* Greek society but could no longer make it penetrate deeply *into* that society.

Italian democracy was also flawed, though to a lesser degree than Greek. *Trasformismo* had suffocated the Risorgimento, hence an idealistic political tradition had been lacking since unification. Fascism had penetrated Italian society deeply, and as there was no general purge of fascists in 1945, many antidemocrats remained in powerful positions, above all in the police and army. The permanent Christian Democratic domination of government, and the exclusion of the huge Communist Party from it, created unhealthy political conditions, as did the continued retrogression of the south, where corruption and intimidation abounded. The economic miracle of the 1950s and 1960s brought unprecedented prosperity to most Italians and created a solid base which would enable society to withstand the new difficulties about to beset it. But the miracle did not permit Italy to transcend the consequences of its many remaining defects. Social conflict and political instability abruptly reemerged in the autumn of 1969, which saw the beginnings of what would develop into perhaps the longest and most intense strike wave of postwar Europe. December 1969 witnessed the advent of urban terrorism, instigated by rightist groups which probably enjoyed tacit support in police circles, even though the leftist "brigades" assumed the initiative from 1975 to 1980. These two sets of crises continued for over a decade, until the early 1980s. Meanwhile, the political establishment was terrified by the dramatic rise in the Communist vote during the early and mid-1970s. And in 1981 there were two new tokens of the prevailing malaise: the discovery of an elite secret society that appeared to have been plotting the overthrow of Italian democracy, and the continued growth of the Mafia, which for the first time felt confident enough to assassinate a top state official.

Clearly, Italy had not become as different from the other southern countries as is usually thought. Despite its economic miracle and decades-long institutional integration into the new Europe, it had not fully transcended its old weaknesses, and it still needed to fortify its democracy.

Portugal did not go through the cycle of early promise and subsequent crisis that characterized Italy and Greece; rather, it followed a fairly uniform pattern of decline from the relative heights attained during World War II. To a considerable degree, this was due to Salazar's antipathy to the idea of modernization which gripped the rest of the Western world, including his fellow dictator, Franco. Aside from some bridges and roads, little effort was made to build up the nation's infrastructure or to attract investment from abroad. Irrigation works were especially neglected; tourism was left to develop on its own. Portugal stood still during the 1950s, and in so doing saw the advantages it briefly had over its Southern European neighbors disappear. This stagnation, however graceful, was an important factor in fostering the great political crisis that shook the regime in 1958–62, first with Humberto Delgado's campaign against Salazar, then with major symbolic acts of opposition, plus two important though unsuccessful military coups.

The regime's truly profound difficulties, however, began with the colonial revolts in Angola in 1961, which had spread to Portugal's other African possessions by 1964. Unimaginative in his domestic policies, Salazar was equally unable to grasp the new realities emerging abroad; with a fraction of the resources of England, France, or Belgium, he persevered in a policy these countries had abandoned as futile—the maintenance of colonial rule by force. The cost to Portugal was enormous, as almost half the state budget went to war operations after the mid-1960s and males were subjected to four years military service. Youth began to vote with its feet, by clandestinely leaving for France. With this emigration added to that of workers seeking opportunity abroad, the drain became so great that Portugal actually lost population over the decade. Paradoxically, these disasters forced the dictatorship to abandon its antiquated policies at home, and after 1966 it belatedly began to interest itself in economic development. The progress made, especially after 1968, when Salazar was incapacitated and replaced by Marcelo Caetano, was substantial, but it did not suffice to counteract the effects of the colonial war. To return to the metaphor I used earlier, a virtuous cycle of socioeconomic change got under way, but its effects were less evident in Portugal than elsewhere because it started so late and was eclipsed by the political costs engendered by the African wars.

I will discuss Spain at greater length, as it best illustrates the processes of indirect change brought about by the structural factors mentioned at the start of this section.[10] It is often forgotten that Spain's unusually smooth transition to democracy was preceded by an equally orderly transformation in the closing phases of the Franco regime. There were many crises, to be sure, but none on the scale of those of 1961–67 or 1973 in Greece, or of 1958–62 in Portugal. Paradoxically, politics, so dominant in the early Franco dictatorship, ceded its primacy to economic development. This was the unintended consequence of a dialectical process set in motion by the stabilization program of 1959–61. Although the Spanish boom started later than the Italian and Greek, once under way it proceeded more rapidly than those. Tourism played a greater role in it, contributing heavily to the attitudinal changes that occurred. It also forced the Franco regime to exercise political restraint: by far Spain's largest single source of foreign earnings during the entire development period, tourism could not be endangered by repressive policies. Worker migration to Western Europe had fewer political ramifications but was important in reducing the labor pool at home, thus creating labor scarcity, which in turn made possible the rise of a new workers movement. Still officially prohibited, trade unions reappeared on an ad hoc basis and became so active by the late 1960s that Spanish strike rates usually exceeded those of any European nation except Britain and Italy. Real income, pushed upward by labor scarcity, was raised further by direct worker action. Consequently, the boom tended to be especially beneficial for the working classes.

Prior to the 1960s, frequent strikes and pay hikes would have caused Spanish employers to plead for state intervention. This did not happen now: under boom conditions and with liberal capitalist attitudes being introduced from abroad, it was easier to accept union demands than risk interrupting production. No longer dependent on the dictatorship in labor relations, the economic elite began to realize that it was becoming a handicap to further growth, especially as its very existence precluded entry into the EEC. Other elite groups also drew away from the regime. This was especially true within the church after the Second Vatican Council, but it also characterized much of the state bureaucracy, sectors of the army, and many high-level administrators, for whom the regime was becoming increasingly anachronistic, given the prevailing trends in the Western world of which Spain more and more formed part. The dialectical processes of the 1960s and early 1970s profoundly affected not only the dictatorship but also its opponents. Having escaped poverty for the first time, and thus being able to participate in the consumerism which was sweeping the entire Western world, a kind of *embourgeoisement* transformed the Spanish working classes. Its moderating effects were reinforced by the greater political sophistication being bred among them by massive urbanization, the partial erosion of class barriers, higher educational levels, and the increasing influence of the media. The extent of the mutation would become evident after Franco's death, when workers rejected extremist tactics and played a moderating role in several crises.

To this dialectical process on the national level, an inverse one occurred in the Basque country, where state overreaction to small-scale ETA terrorism in 1969 initiated a vicious cycle which, by 1975, had led to political chaos and economic decline. By their counterexample, the Basque provinces show that Spain's relatively peaceful transformation was not inevitable. The regime might also have responded savagely to other crises, and thus set in motion a Basque-style involution for Spain as a whole. But this did not happen, because an invisible web of constraints had been spun by the economic, social, and attitudinal changes of the previous two decades. Even Luis Carrero Blanco's assassination in 1973, the hardest blow struck against the regime, produced not repression but its opposite, further liberalization. This was too much for regime intransigents, who banded together to force a return to the past, and for a few weeks in 1975 they seemed to have caught Franco's ear. Franco died soon after, but even had he lived, repression on a national scale could not long have been sustained, as it was too diametrically opposed to what the virtuous cycle of change begun in the late 1950s had made the chief interests and values of the bulk of society and its elites. A subtle process of protodemocratization had occurred which greatly facilitated the democratic transition now about to begin. Spanish civil society, factious and polarized since the late eighteenth century, would finally become healthy and strong.

With this account of the nearly simultaneous fall of the Iberian and Greek dictatorships in 1974–75, my task is nearing its end. But a few points should be made. There were many differences in the actual events. The Portuguese and Greek dictatorships collapsed dramatically, in the course of a few hours. In Spain there was no abrupt change; the regime was dismantled piecemeal by the very persons Franco had entrusted with its preservation. Greece also avoided a power vacuum, as the junta, always shallowly rooted, so utterly discredited itself during the 1974 Cyprus crisis that Karamanlis, recalled from exile, was able to put together a viable government almost overnight. By contrast, a power vacuum of spectacular proportions developed in Portugal, because the military rebels who ousted the dictatorship had no clear idea of what should replace it, and the great explosion of popular feelings that followed further confused the issue. For nineteen months the nation was gripped by a revolutionary situation on a scale not seen in Europe since Spain in 1936. Other differences also existed. Portugal's military forces, radicalized during the colonial wars, were primarily leftist, but in Spain and Greece the continued rightist orientation of the military constituted a major threat to the new democracies. Spain's king played an indispensable role in assuring a smooth transition to democracy; Greece's king was repudiated by popular referendum, and a republic was created. Foreign policy issues had no impact on domestic developments in Spain but were vital to them in Portugal and Greece. Spain's constitution was achieved via consensus and accepted by almost all groups, whereas Greece's was strenuously attacked by the leading opposition party, and Portugal's contained many nonviable provisions which the right had accepted only to appease the leftists.

Beyond all these differences, the transitions had one great point in common: their moderation. Few, if any, revolutions in world history have shed as little blood as Portugal's, and this was not because of any innate mildness of the people, as many gruesome events of the 1830s and 1840s and of 1908–28 show. The same was true in Greece. Only in Spain was there significant violence, but since Spain was otherwise so relatively stable and the transition was so well managed by Adolfo Suárez, it could not disrupt the process of reconciliation. Moderation was possible because most people supported it. A notable phenomenon in all three countries was the consistency with which the population rejected, electorally and in every other way, extremist solutions. This was true even in Portugal, where, despite tacit state support and predominance in the field of propaganda, the Communists were not able to win much of the vote. Moderation also usually characterized the political elites. From 1976 to 1979, Suárez proved masterful in domestic diplomacy, inducing the Franquist Cortes to disband and slowly winning over the democratic opposition, which also became infected with his enthusiasm for consensus politics. The decompressing of the Portuguese revolution in 1975–76 constituted another masterpiece of domestic diplomacy. Only in Greece did old-style politics of the rhetorically extreme kind reappear, due mostly to the populist demagogy of the new PASOK party under Andreas Papandreou.

This fundamental moderation, on both the popular and the elite levels, was indispensable not only to the transition period but also to the subsequent consolidation of democracy. It continues to characterize Southern Europe now, further evidence of how deeply rooted it became during the four decades of 1950–90. Many differences of detail exist, of course, above all in Greece, which cannot as easily divest itself of its foreign policy burdens as the others did and which, during the

1980s, under Papandreou, fell behind the fast pace that Portugal and Spain set. Nevertheless, all three nations now find themselves politically more on a par with Italy than before, since the latter's repeated failure to undertake genuine political reform during the 1970s and 1980s, together with other factors, finally brought about a profound crisis of its political system in the early 1990s. Economically and culturally Portugal, Spain, and Greece still lag significantly behind Italy, of course, but fundamental divergences within Southern Europe are fewer than perhaps ever before, and Southern Europe as a whole is closer to the European core than it has been for centuries.

But these are issues whose ramifications my colleagues will explore in this and subsequent volumes. My own task is finished. I hope to have shown that the parallelisms of recent decades are not new phenomena and that our four nations have long followed a common pattern of historical development, which justifies grouping them together under the regional concept of Southern Europe. One decidedly nonscientific way of briefly summarizing this common pattern might be as follows: The decades from the 1790s to the 1870s witnessed the agonizing birth of a new and seriously deformed Southern Europe. From the 1870s until around 1914 many of the birth defects seemed to be disappearing, but the victory over them proved more apparent than real, especially as new deformities began to emerge. From 1915 to 1949, because of a unique mix of external and domestic factors, Southern Europe was plunged into a new prolonged agony, crueler than ever before and in several ways distinct from the agony the rest of Europe was enduring during the same period. Again because of a unique mix of external and internal factors, the quarter-century between 1950 and 1975 witnessed an astonishing reinvigoration of Southern Europe, one which carried it well beyond the thresholds of sickness around which it had hovered for the preceding two centuries and one which seemed to assure it a more or less normal future.

3 Democratic Transition and Consolidation in Southern Europe, with Reflections on Latin America and Eastern Europe

Juan J. Linz, Alfred Stepan, and Richard Gunther

All three of the recently redemocratized countries of Southern Europe—Spain, Portugal, and Greece—have not only completed transitions to democracy but they have also consolidated their new democratic regimes. They therefore stand in sharp contrast with the great majority of recently redemocratized countries of Latin America, which remain largely unconsolidated. The contrast is even greater with new regimes that have emerged since 1989 in Eastern Europe and the former Soviet Union—which are not only unconsolidated but in some instances not fully democratic.

These Southern European successes have given rise to temptations to extrapolate from these experiences and generate models for emulation elsewhere; this is particularly true of the highly successful Spanish transition and consolidation processes. Such academic and practical exercises, however, should be undertaken with great care. Before any Southern European models are exported to other parts of the world, it is important that the complex processes of transition and consolidation in these cases be fully understood. We have, over the past decade and a half, systematically examined these processes and have compared and contrasted them with the transition trajectories followed in four South American countries (Argentina, Brazil, Chile, and Uruguay) and seven postcommunist countries (Bulgaria, Czechoslovakia, Estonia, Hungary, Poland, Romania, and Russia).[1]

The weight of evidence amassed in the course of this research has led us to the conclusion that there are multiple factors that contribute to success and failure in democratic consolidation, several of which had not previously been examined in the literature on redemocratization. Among the more important explanatory variables is the basic nature of the outgoing nondemocratic regime. In attempting to hypothesize about the impact of such variables on transition and consolidation processes, we found that much of the vocabulary and even some key concepts used in comparative politics for decades were not fully adequate. One such formulation was the tripartite conceptualization of political regimes—as democratic, totalitarian, or authoritarian—set forth by Juan Linz in the 1960s and 1970s. Although Linz, stimulated by Max Weber's description of sultanism as a type of patrimonial regime, had already characterized certain regimes as "sultanistic" and distinct from authoritarian regimes, this distinction was rarely acknowledged. There was also a growing consensus that "classical" totalitarianism was no longer an appropriate description of the post-Stalin Soviet Union, but there was no consensus concerning how to characterize the Soviet system: it was neither totalitarian nor authoritarian. Thus, it became useful to set forth a "posttotalitarian" regime type. Before entering into a systematic comparative assessment of democratic consolidation in Spain, Portugal, and Greece, it is necessary to briefly define (or redefine) some of our concepts.

Democratic Consolidation

One of the most crucial distinctions in studies of redemocratization is between transition and consolidation. Democratic transitions relate to the creation of democratic regimes in which there is open contestation for the right to win control of the government, and this in turn requires free elections, the results of which determine who governs. Democratic transitions clearly relate to democratization, not merely to liberalization. Liberalization is characterized by a mix of policy and social changes, such as less censorship of the media, greater freedom to organize autonomous group activities, the introduction of legal safeguards for individuals (such as *habeas corpus*), release of political prisoners, the return of political exiles, and, most importantly, toleration of political opposition (while excluding it from competition for power).

Regardless of when and how a democratic transition begins, we can say that it has been successfully completed when the following criteria are met: a government comes to power that is the direct result of a free and popular vote; this government has full authority to generate new policies; and the executive, legislative, and judicial power generated by the new democracy does not have to share power with other bodies de jure. It should be noted that this definition builds upon Linz's 1975 description of democratic regimes by adding the notion that the authority of democratically elected leaders should not be constrained by reserve powers held by any group or institution that is not democratically responsible.

Democratic consolidation, in our view, involves three distinct dimensions:

- Structural: This overlaps somewhat with our definition of democracy. It posits that no significant reserve domains of power should exist that preclude important public policies from being determined by the laws, procedures, and institutions that have been sanctioned by the new democratic process.
- Attitudinal: When a strong majority of public opinion acknowledges that the regime's democratic procedures and institutions are appropriate and legitimate, and where support for antisystem alternatives is quite low or isolated from the prodemocratic forces.
- Behavioral: When no significant national, social, economic, political, or institutional actor spends significant resources attempting to achieve its objectives by challenging the regime's institutions or rules with appeals for a military coup or revolutionary activities, and when the prodemocratic forces abide by its rules and do not engage in semiloyal politics.

On the basis of these criteria, we regard all three of our Southern European cases as both fully democratic and consolidated. Among the four South American cases we have analyzed there is considerable variation. The only Southern Cone regime that is a consolidated democracy is Uruguay, despite its continuing problems of economic stagnation and government inefficacy. In Chile, despite very favorable economic conditions, widespread support for democracy, and high levels of structural integration and procedural consensus among party elites, military prerogatives are so great that the regime falls somewhat short of being fully democratic according to our definition; until various authoritarian enclaves are removed or greatly diminished, the Chilean transition cannot be regarded as complete. There is even evidence that this structural impediment had by 1993 begun to weaken attitudinal support for democracy in Chile. Argentina underwent a dangerous state of regime decomposition and military recomposition during the final years of the first democratically elected government of Raúl Alfonsín. While the practices of President Carlos Menem leave much to be desired from the point of view of the quality of the nation's democracy, his efficacy in dealing with economic matters and the extent of control he has secured over the destabilizing actions of the military and the trade unions have put the country on the road to consolidation. Brazil has clearly been the least consolidated of the four South American cases we have analyzed: indeed, it was less consolidated in 1993 than it was in 1985, when military rule ended. Popular support for democracy is lower in Brazil than in any of the South American or Southern European cases for which we have comparable attitudinal data. However, the election of Fernando Henrique Cardoso as president in 1994 might initiate a reversal of those trends.

Of the postcommunist European regimes, Hungary, whose transition most closely resembles that of Spain, comes the closest to meeting our criteria. As in Hungary, the Polish regime is fully democratic, but the long period of constitutional incertitude and high levels of governmental instability and inefficacy have delayed the consolidation process. Similarly, the Czech Republic is fully democratic. Questions were initially raised as to whether the new Bulgarian regime could be better characterized as a liberalizing authoritarian regime than as democratic: pluralism was supported by weak legal guarantees, the Turkish minority population was regularly subjected to authoritarian measures, and the outcome of the first election was significantly influenced by mobilization of the former Communist Party's traditional resources. The holding of a second election, however, as well as formation of a coalition government that includes representatives of the Turkish minority, suggest that democratic procedures and institutions are becoming routinized. In Romania a segment of the former Ceauşescu regime's elite has availed itself of vast state resources, while it has denied such resources to opposition forces. It has also occasionally mobilized its supporters to engage in political violence against the emerging opposition. While the holding of a second election is an encouraging sign, the governing elite's lack of respect for democratic procedures represents a significant departure from the democratic ideal type. The case of the Baltic republics poses particular problems. "Titular nationality" in 1989 was shared by only 52 percent of the population in Latvia, 61.5 percent in Estonia, and 79.6 percent in Lithuania (with the Russian component of these populations being 34 percent, 30.3 percent, and 9.4 percent, respectively.[2] For ethnic Estonians, the regime is fully democratic. Citizenship, however, has been so narrowly defined as to exclude 40 percent of the population. Insofar as Russian-speakers (even those born in Estonia) are excluded from the democratic political process, we must conclude, this regime does not meet all of our criteria of democracy. Finally, the most important of the postcommunist transitions is also the most problematic. Not only did the multinational Soviet Union fragment (in some areas, violently) along ethnic and cultural lines, but the largest of the states to emerge from this process, Russia, can still not be regarded as fully democratic. The initial elections to the congress were marked by undemocratic practices designed to maintain the dominant position of the Communist Party. Moreover, as the ongoing (and sometimes violent) struggle between president and congress has clearly revealed, there is no consensus concerning the rights, functions, and jurisdictions of the regime's central representative institutions. Overall, one cannot yet speak of a completed transition to democracy in Russia but rather of an uncertain transition.

Variables Affecting Transition and Consolidation

We shall argue that prospects for success or failure in attempts to consolidate new democracies are greatly affected by several specific variables. It is beyond the scope of this chapter to present a complete summary of our theoretical propositions concerning the determinants of success or failure in democratic consolidation (for that the reader is invited to consult Linz and Stepan's book-length treatment of these themes cited in the endnotes to this chapter); instead, we will restrict our attention to those variables that are relevant to comparisons between Southern Europe and the two other regions in our study. They include:

- the nature of the previous nondemocratic regime;
- the added complexities inherent in simultaneously undertaking radical economic, social, legal, and bureaucratic reforms at the time of a regime transition;
- the question of stateness;
- the strength of the hierarchical or nonhierarchical military in the outgoing nondemocratic regime;
- the question of who starts the transition;
- various international influences; and
- the style of constitution making.

Before moving on to an examination of the Spanish, Portuguese, and Greek transition and consolidation processes, let us briefly introduce some new terminology and concepts relating to these variables.

The Nature of the Previous Nondemocratic Regime

For over a quarter of a century, the dominant conceptual framework among analysts interested in classifying political systems has been the distinction among "democratic," "authoritarian," and "totalitarian" regimes.[3] While the very large number of cases in the authoritarian category was always problematic, this tripartite typology retained considerable descriptive and analytical utility for some time and represented an advance over the temptation to view the world in bipolar terms of democracy versus totalitarianism or to consider other forms as transitional or tutelary rather than distinctive. Our study of the dynamics of democratization, however, has demonstrated that this tripartite distinction has limited predictive or explanatory power in dealing with questions involving democratic transition and consolidation processes. We therefore concluded that it was necessary to disaggregate the overpopulated authoritarian category into distinct regime types, thereby creating a five-part typology of political regimes: *democratic, totalitarian, authoritarian, sultanistic, and posttotalitarian*. While the democratic and totalitarian ideal types remain intact, the sultanistic category needed further elaboration; and we needed to articulate a new and particularly relevant ideal type, the posttotalitarian regime.

One of the key distinctions between authoritarian and posttotalitarian regimes concerns the extent and type of institutionalized pluralism present in civil society. In an authoritarian regime, there is limited political pluralism and often quite extensive economic and social pluralism; in a totalitarian regime, there is virtually no pluralism. Posttotalitarian systems stand somewhere between these two regime types. There is much more social pluralism than in a totalitarian system, and there is often much discussion of a "second culture" or "parallel culture" which features a robust underground literature (although many of its authors and leaders are often imprisoned). This social and economic pluralism, however, is different in degree and kind from that found in an authoritarian regime. Authoritarian systems have a much more autonomous private sector, often greater religious freedom, and a greater amount of above-ground cultural activity. If there is a growing institutional pluralism in a posttotalitarian regime, it should be understood as a kind of pluralism that emerges *out of* the previous totalitarian system. Overall, it should be stressed, there are important limits to pluralism in posttotalitarian societies—in contrast with the better developed civil societies found in authoritarian regimes, posttotalitarianism may be described in organizational terms as a "flattened landscape," with few and very poorly developed secondary organizations. Another important difference is that elites who emerge as potential political leaders in posttotalitarian systems are often recruited from the ranks of the formerly totalitarian regime's single party; in most authoritarian regimes, in sharp contrast, leaders emerge from groups that have some power, presence, legitimacy, and autonomy. Indeed, authoritarian regimes will sometimes attempt to co-opt leaders of nonregime organizations into leadership positions. Posttotalitarian and authoritarian regimes also differ insofar as in the former there is an important ideological legacy that cannot be ignored and cannot be officially questioned; most authoritarian regimes do not have the highly articulated ideologies (concerning the leading role of the party, interest groups, religion, and the state) that are seen in posttotalitarian systems. As we shall see, all three of the Southern European transitions began with the breakdown of former *authoritarian* regimes. The dynamics of transitions in most of Eastern Europe, on the other hand, were greatly affected by the fact that liberalization and democratization were being attempted within posttotalitarian societies.

Sultanism was originally described by Weber as a special type of patrimonialism. On that basis, Linz distinguished a type of contemporary regime that did not fit well into the authoritarian regime type that he termed sultanistic. This concept will not be discussed extensively here, since such regimes do not exist in either Southern Europe or the Southern Cone.[4] Suffice it to say that such systems are characterized by a high fusion of public and private possessions of the ruler, the absence of the rule of law, and low institutionalization. All individuals, groups, and institutions in sultanistic regimes are permanently subject to the unpredictable and despotic intervention of the ruler. The critical difference between the type of pluralism in authoritarian and sultanistic regimes has immense implications for subsequent regime transitions. A transition-by-transaction or by negotiated political pact, for example, is possible in an authoritarian regime; in a regime with strong sultanistic tendencies, however, neither regime reformers nor a viable democratic opposition can emerge—both of which are necessary for consensual transitions. Many of the unique characteristics of democratization in Romania should be seen as consequences of political transformation of the Ceausescu regime, with its strong sultanistic tendencies combined with totalitarianism.

The Problem of Simultaneity

The interconnected and mutually reinforcing dimensions of the polity imply that processes of democratic consolidation will be complex, and may be multidimensional. The following political, economic, legal, social, and economic objectives must be achieved in order for a regime to be regarded as a consolidated democracy:

1. the organizational and associational life of civil society—protected by law and with some base in the economy—must have a reasonably high degree of autonomy;

2. the specific procedures and institutions of political society (parties, electoral systems, legislatures, etc.) must be valued in themselves, and have a sufficient degree of autonomy to function adequately;
3. the institutions of democracy, individual rights, and the rights of minorities must be embedded in—and guided and protected by—constitutionalism and the rule of law;
4. the state bureaucracies whose task it is to implement the laws, procedures, and policies decided upon by political society must operate within the confines of democratic mandates, constitutionalism, and professional norms; and the vast majority of the bureaucracy, both civil and military, must respect the authority of any democratically elected government; and
5. there should be a certain degree of market autonomy and ownership diversity (government regulation of economic relations and mixed patterns of public and private ownership notwithstanding), so that sufficient pluralism can exist to permit the autonomous group activity necessary for a modern democracy.

Given these five distinct dimensions of a democratic polity, it should be clear that the character of the previous nondemocratic regime can have profound implications for the magnitude of the tasks countries face when they enter into the democratic consolidation process. In some instances, most of these objectives will have been attained prior to the transition to democracy. An authoritarian regime in its late stages, for example, might have a robust and democratic civil society, a state bureaucracy that operates within professional norms, a high degree of market autonomy and a plurality of capital ownership, a rule of law in most realms of society and administration, and sometimes "constitutional" rules to which the state apparatus and even the political class and the ruler might feel bound. For such a polity, the only necessary item on the initial agenda would be to establish the autonomy, authority, power, and legitimacy of democratic institutions. A transition from a communist posttotalitarian regime, however, poses the question of simultaneity in its starkest form. Not only is it necessary to transform political relations, but it may also be necessary to undertake radical reforms of the economy, the legal and judicial system, the state bureaucracy, and civil society itself. The tasks of regime transition (let alone democratic consolidation) are therefore much more daunting. For this reason, the transformation of a totalitarian regime to a consolidated democracy has been fastest when it was managed by foreign military occupation, as in Germany. Transitions from sultanistic regimes, as in Haiti, are also highly complicated and problematic: here, too, it is necessary to construct an autonomous civil society, establish constitutionalism and the rule of law, and instill professional norms within the military and the bureaucracy, apart from the always difficult task of creating legitimate democratic political institutions.

The Question of Stateness

The processes of democratic consolidation can also be greatly complicated if the breakdown of the former nondemocratic regime is accompanied by a crisis of legitimacy of the state. Under these circumstances, the goal of those challenging the regime might not be the democratization of the state but the disintegration of the state. The emerging literature on democratic transitions has not evidenced much thought on this problem. To be sure, questions regarding stateness are irrelevant to political transitions that occur within established nation-states or state-nations, but this variable is of fundamental importance in the case of states containing populations that regard themselves as belonging to different nations. If a significant group of people deny the legitimacy of a state and its institutions because they demand creation of their own nation-state, it may be difficult or impossible to consolidate a single democracy within that territorial unit. Such groups may support anti-system parties, and overt conflict may break out over attempts at secession or resolution of irredentist disputes. These outcomes would be detrimental to prospects for democratic consolidation in the original state or the new states.[5]

The Hierarchical versus Nonhierarchical Military

Whenever a nondemocratic regime is led by military officers, another important variable becomes relevant—whether that governing military elite is hierarchical or nonhierarchical. All hierarchical military regimes (i.e., where the government is composed of or controlled by the highest-ranking military officers) share one characteristic that is potentially favorable to democratic transition. The officer corps, taken as a whole, sees itself as a permanent part of the state apparatus, with enduring interests and permanent functions that transcend the interests of the government of the day. Thus, it is possible that, if the hierarchical leaders of the military come to believe that the costs of direct involvement in nondemocratic rule are greater than the costs of extrication, they may conclude that the interests of the military-as-institution would best be served by abandoning governmental authority and allowing civilian elites to come to power. Democratic elections are thus often a part of the extrication strategy of military organizations threatened by their prominent role in nondemocratic regimes.

However, hierarchical military regimes also have certain characteristics that can seriously complicate or hinder processes of democratic consolidation. Precisely because the military is a permanent part of the state apparatus, with privileged access to coercive resources, it will be an integral part of the machinery that a new democratic government will have to manage. The more extensive the governmental role of the military prior to the transition, the more salient will be the issue of successfully managing the military under democratic control. Indeed, hierarchical military regimes may be in a position to impose very confining conditions on the transition or to retain nondemocratic prerogatives under the new regime, thereby undercutting its democratic quality and greatly complicating the consolidation process. The more hierarchically led the outgoing military regime, the less its extrication from government is forced by internal contradictions; and the weaker the coalition pushing it from office, the more likely this less-than-fully democratic outcome will be. More than other organizational bases of nondemocratic regimes, the hierarchical military poses the threat of having the power to impose "reserve domains" on the newly elected government, and this, by definition, precludes democratic consolidation.

A nonhierarchical military regime, on the other hand, has some characteristics that make it less of a potential obstacle to democratic transition and consolidation. If a nonhierarchical military regime (i.e., one led by lower-ranking officers, such as colonels) enters into political difficulty, there would be an incentive for the senior officers, acting in defense of the military-as-institution, to reestablish hierarchy by supporting an extrication coup against the military-as-government. Under these circumstances, the military-as-institution would be much more willing to tolerate punishment and trials for the outgoing nondemocratic government—a group within the military that had violated hierarchical norms—than they would if the military hierarchy itself were being held accountable. And if the colonels had established parastate intelligence operations that were perceived as threats even to the organizational military, the hierarchical military would be even more likely to acquiesce (or even insist) that their reserve domains of power be eliminated. Clearly, this would facilitate democratic consolidation.

Who Initiates and Who Controls the Transition?

Our study of regime transitions in Southern Europe, South America, and postcommunist Europe suggests that the question of who initiates the transition has an important bearing on the initial course that the transition will take. Transitions initiated by an uprising of civil society, an armed revolution, or a nonhierarchically led military coup tend toward the establishment of provisional governments. Conversely, transitions initiated by reformers within the state or nondemocratic regime do not. The establishment of provisional governments can pose special problems for democratic transitions. If the provisional government quickly sets a date for elections and rules as a neutral caretaker, then this can be a rapid and efficacious route toward democracy. However, if the provisional government claims that its actions in overthrowing the government gave it a legitimate mandate to make fundamental changes defined as preconditions for democratic elections, the provisional government can set into motion a dangerous dynamic in which a whole series of problems can place the democratic transition at peril.[6] The most dangerous course of action is the postponement of elections *sine die*.

Spain

There is growing consensus that the Spanish transition is in many ways the paradigmatic case for the study of transitions, almost as the breakdown of the Weimar Republic has been for the study of the fall of democracies. Indeed, much of the vocabulary of the theory of regime transition is based on the Spanish case. A number of factors help to explain why the Spanish model of *reforma pactada/ruptura pactada* (negotiated reform/negotiated rupture) has held such special status in the comparative study of transitions.[7] Foremost among these is the fact that it was one of the first in a series of nonviolent transitions. It therefore influenced the thinking of many who later would undertake similar difficult tasks. In contrast with many transitions, it was not triggered by defeat or near defeat in war, as occurred in Portugal and Greece. Likewise, its rulers did not confront a deep economic crisis, as did their counterparts in Latin America and the former communist countries of Eastern Europe and the Soviet Union. Neither was it a case in which an external factor—such as withdrawal of support by a hegemonic power—influenced vulnerable authoritarian rulers.

Another reason the Spanish model has been widely admired is that, to outsiders, memories of its civil war gave it the appearance of a highly conflictual and potentially violent society. The outsider's vision, however, did not correspond to the reality of Spanish society in the 1970s. Inside Spain, the "cultural work" of political and civil society before and during the transition had transformed historical memories of the civil war into a positive factor that aided the transition.[8] (The contrast with the historical meaning of the Croatian-Serbian civil wars of the 1940s could not be more dramatic.) To this it should be added that Spain's was the first transition in which problems arising from multilingualism and multinationalism emerged at the same time as the regime transition process was being initiated.

Another aspect of the Spanish transition, the Moncloa Pacts, has also become a standard reference in discussions of the role of pacts in stabilizing transition processes. All too often, however, it is forgotten that this agreement was not a *social* pact between trade unions and employers' organizations but, rather, a *political* pact. Adolfo Suárez called the Moncloa meetings because he wanted to involve political society (and, in particular, all the parties that had representatives in the Spanish legislature after the first free elections) in negotiations among themselves. During the Moncloa meetings, the parties consulted with their key constituents in civil society. Suárez considered this link between political society and civil society particularly crucial in the case of the Communist Party and the trade unions. Only after these extensive negotiations was the Moncloa political pact approved, in a solemn session of the Cortes.[9]

Another circumstance that makes the Spanish case particularly interesting is that the authoritarian regime had lasted thirty-six years and had created a complex institutional structure. It was not possible, therefore, to think of retaining existing institutions and simply filling them with democratic content, or of proceeding to a restoration of predictatorship democratic institutions, as has occurred in some Latin American cases. Finally, a unique feature further complicated the transition—Franco's installation of a monarchy, whose low historical legitimacy could easily have been contested by many democrats. Nowadays, the king is often referred to as "*el piloto del cambio*" (the pilot of change), or at least the facilitator of the process of change. One must recall, however, that through his actions the king legitimated the monarchy, more than the monarchy legitimated the king.[10]

The relatively smooth process of the Spanish transition has led many, *a posteriori,* to consider the Spanish model of political engineering as an overdetermined success. Indeed, if we reduce the messy historical process, with all its complexities, frustrations, delays, and doubts, to a theoretical model, it appears as an elegant process susceptible even to a game-theoretical analysis.[11] In fact, the comparison between *post hoc* theoretical modeling and the inevitably more complex real-life experience of the process should be a warning to those who analyze similar changes while they are still unfolding. It is well to remember that even the "easiest" and most successful transition was lived as a precarious process, beset with numerous uncertainties and constantly requiring innovative political action.[12] While it is now largely forgotten, Spanish public opinion in the late 1970s and early 1980s was characterized by a widespread *desencanto*—disenchantment—with the process and its leaders, particularly prime minister Adolfo Suárez, a development which has occurred subsequently in many other countries undergoing regime transition. More importantly, the potential threat to the new regime posed by high levels of Basque terrorist violence and the military coup attempted on February 23, 1981, should not be underestimated.[13] Observers should avoid falling into the trap of believing that Spain's successful transition was overdetermined or that the political engineers at all times followed a rational model. Such opinions not only misinterpret the actual process of democratic consolidation in Spain but also fail to appreciate the serious obstacles to democratic consolidation that Spain had to surmount in the late 1970s and early 1980s.

To be sure, Spain entered into the transition in a comparatively privileged position with respect to several of the variables discussed earlier in this chapter. Unlike many of the recent East European transitions, the *only* task that had to be confronted immediately following Franco's death in November 1975 was the creation of new democratic political institutions with autonomy and support. Thanks to changes that predated the transition by at least a decade, it was not necessary at that time to establish a *civil society* with a reasonably autonomous organizational and associational life protected by law and with some base in the economy. Even the exposure to West European political life and the political pluralism in the alegal and illegal opposition made the articulation of political society before the election that much easier. The *rule of law* was reasonably well established by the final years of the former authoritarian regime. Established professional norms within the *state bureaucracy* were compatible with democratic control of public administration. And an advanced *market economy*—regulated by government and with mixed patterns of public and private ownership, but with sufficient autonomy from the state—had given rise to the pluralism upon which democratic systems depend.

The Spanish transition to a democratic regime, however, was greatly complicated by the existence of a serious stateness problem. At the same time that an authoritarian system was being dismantled and a new democratic regime established, it was necessary to initiate a profound decentralization of the state itself, so as to accommodate the aspirations to autonomy of peripheral nationalist movements. Thus, when Spain began its transition, questions concerning stateness posed a serious threat to political stability and democratization. Unlike in Yugoslavia and the Soviet Union, however, the challenge was handled quite well in Spain. The Spanish case therefore has important theoretical implications for transitions in heterogeneous states with important regional, cultural, and national differences, such as Yugoslavia, the Soviet Union, Czechoslovakia, and Indonesia.

The best indicator of the danger inherent in the stateness problem is that, while not one army officer was killed during the Basque insurgency between 1968 and 1977, thirty-seven army officers died due to Basque nationalist violence between 1978 and 1983, following the restoration of democracy.[14] Surprisingly, despite the deaths of military officers and the inevitable difficulties of creating a quasi-federal state in Spain, none of the important statewide interest groups or parties engaged in system blame. Adversity was not deliberately used to delegitimate either the fledgling democratic regime or the new constitutional structures that departed from Spain's traditional unitary state organization.

The Timing of Elections

One important factor underpinning Spain's success in dealing with the stateness problem involves the timing of statewide elections. This matter has not been analyzed in earlier studies of the Spanish transition, but our exploration of the USSR and Yugoslavia has brought it to our attention. Elections, especially founding elections, help create agendas, actors, organizations, and, most importantly, legitimacy and power. In a country facing a stateness problem, it makes a critical difference whether the first elections are statewide or regional. In Spain, a series of statewide elections preceded regional elections by several years. The first was a referendum, in which 77.4 percent of the electorate participated, on a "law for political reform," approved by 94.2 percent of the voters, which unequivocally initiated a process of democratization, not just liberalization.[15] The second key vote, held on June 15, 1977, was a statewide general election to select deputies to draft a new constitution. In the course of this election, five statewide parties conducted a statewide campaign around statewide themes, and won 325 of the 350 seats.[16] Just as importantly, the statewide parties campaigned very hard in areas where the potential for secession was greatest and the history of antisystem sentiment was most deeply rooted—the Catalan and Basque regions. While strong Catalan and Basque nationalist parties did emerge, four statewide parties and their regional affiliates won 67.7 percent of the vote in Catalonia and 51.4 percent of the vote in the

Basque Country.[17] Representative elites recruited through this statewide election then engaged in prolonged public and private negotiations over the constitution and over how to proceed on the stateness issue. A consensual constitution was finally supported in the parliament by the four major parties and the major Catalan nationalist party. It was subsequently approved in a referendum (Spain's third consecutive statewide election) by 87.8 percent of the voters, with 67.7 percent voting—a level of participation that should be considered high, since no significant statewide party opposed the constitution and a positive outcome was a foregone conclusion. In Catalonia, the constitution was approved by 90.4 percent of the voters, with a 67 percent turnout. In the Basque country, 68.8 percent of those who voted approved the constitution, but voter turnout was only 45.5 percent, well below the Spanish and Catalan rates of participation.[18] On the basis of this new constitution, parliamentary elections were held in early 1979, which largely confirmed the alignment of partisan forces that had first emerged in 1977.

Strengthened and legitimated by these four elections, the statewide government and parliament entered into negotiations with Basque and Catalan representatives (whose legitimacy as spokespersons for their respective regions stemmed largely from the mandate they received from the 1979 statewide election) over the devolution of power to new Basque and Catalan regional governments. Surrounded by intense controversy, the negotiators eventually crafted a system by which Spain would exchange its historically centralized state structure for a new decentralized one characterized by an unprecedented devolution of power to the peripheral nationalist constituencies. These negotiated agreements over regional autonomy (the Statutes of Autonomy) were submitted to Basque and Catalan voters in October 1979. The Catalan statute was approved by 87.9 percent and the Basque statute by 90.3 percent of those who voted in the regions.[19] The largest and oldest Basque nationalist party, the Partido Nacionalista Vasco (PNV), which had urged a boycott of the constitutional referendum, adjusted to the new political situation and urged approval of the Statute of Autonomy.[20]

We believe that if the first elections in Spain had been regional, rather than statewide, the incentives for the creation of statewide parties and a statewide agenda would have been greatly reduced. Consequently, the statewide parties and their affiliates would have received fewer votes; even when stateness issues are not salient, regional parties in Spain tend to poll 15–25 percent better in regional elections than they do in statewide elections. We also believe that if the first elections had been on the regional level, ethnic issues would have assumed a much more substantial and divisive role in the electoral campaign than they actually did and that the nationalist parties and their affiliates would have been more extreme. Strengthened nationalist parties would have gravely complicated the stateness problem in Spain. Relations between the military and the democratizing forces of the central government would almost certainly have been subjected to greater strain. In a context of heightened conflict over stateness, the 1981 coup coalition—defeated by the king's personal intervention on February 23—would probably have emerged earlier and with greater force, against a divided and less legitimate government, and would have represented a much more serious threat to democracy. The democratic transition in Spain certainly began under favorable conditions, but the severity of the challenge posed by the stateness problem could have been sufficient to abort the democratization process. Instead, the clear commitment to democratization and statewide elections strengthened the legitimacy of the central government, helped forge links between political society and civil society, and contributed to a new, constitutionally sanctioned, relationship between Spain's peripheral nationalisms and the central government.

Most importantly, the timing of elections affected a transition variable that is extremely significant for polities with stateness problems—the nature of national political identities. We contend that such identities are less primordial and fixed than is often assumed. Instead, they are contingent and changing, and they are amenable to being constructed or eroded by political institutions and political choices. In the Spanish case, the timing of elections helped to restructure identities in ways that were supportive of democracy in Spain. Specifically, they contributed to the emergence of complementary multiple identities. We can see this most clearly in the case of Catalonia. Catalans now have political and cultural control over education, television, and radio, and indeed over most of the arenas in which Catalan nationalism had been most repressed in the past. They also participate as a supranational regional group in the European Community, a body which in some important respects is a community of regions as much as a community of states. This has helped make Catalans feel more content with their status and, to a greater extent than ever before, accept their identity as members of the Spanish state. A recent survey revealed that the overwhelming majority of Catalans are proud of being both Catalan and Spanish: 82 percent of those interviewed in Catalonia said they were "proud to be Catalan;" at the same time, 73 percent also said that they were "proud to be Spanish," a figure which is not far from the 85 percent level of agreement throughout all of Spain. An even higher percentage of Catalan respondents (83 percent) stated that they were in favor of "unification of Europe under the European Community," as compared with 76 percent of statewide Spanish respondents. We contend that the sequence of elections in Spain helped constitute these mutually supportive legal and affective memberships in substate (Catalan), state (Spanish), and suprastate (European Community) polities.[21] The Basque Country presents a more difficult political situation. Routine separatist violence in the Basque Country continues, and in the survey cited above only 44 percent said they were proud to be Spanish as compared with 69 percent who said they were proud to be Basque. But here, as well, we believe the overall political situation has been ameliorated by the sequence of elections, which helped to restructure identities and delegitimize certain types of antistate violence.

How are national identities affected by political processes? A comparative overview of political developments in Spain and the former Soviet Union and Yugoslavia provides some answers. Between 1977 and 1979 the most heated question in Spanish politics concerned the relationship of peripheral nationalisms to the unitary Spanish state. In this two-year period the percentage of the population in the Basque region who said they wanted to be independent more than doubled, to represent about a third of the entire population. In Catalonia, starting from a smaller base, proindependence sentiment *tripled* during the same period, to 15 percent. Obviously, if these trends had continued for a few more years there would have been a severe crisis of stateness in Spain. Instead, following referenda on regional autonomy statutes and the establishment in 1980 of regional governments with Basque and Catalan nationalist parties in office, proindependence sentiments declined steadily: by 1982 only about one out of five Basques favored independence, while over that same three-year period support for Catalan independence dropped to just seven percent.[22] Assassinations, kidnapping, and terrorism by proindependence groups in the Basque Country still continued after the referendum, but their political significance changed dramatically. Before the 1979 autonomy referendum, only 5 percent of Basque interview respondents labeled terrorists criminals and only 8 percent called them deranged. Three years after the referendum, however, the general population assigned much more pejorative identities to terrorists, and by so doing began to marginalize them politically: 29 percent now called them criminals, and 29 percent said they were deranged. Above all, the same "identity delegitimation" occurred among those who voted for the largest Basque nationalist political group, the PNV. In 1979, only 6 percent of PNV supporters had called terrorists criminals and only 12 percent said they were deranged. By 1983, the percentages had increased to 27 percent and 30 percent, respectively.[23] Although Basque political killings continue, they no longer threaten to bring down the democratic government. The crisis of Spanish stateness has been contained, largely due to the choice of electoral sequence. Political decentralization processes and the development of political identities have been stabilized and constrained because the constitution of a new Spanish state was legitimated democratically before deliberations over regional autonomy were permitted to begin.

By way of comparison, while stateness problems in the Soviet Union and Yugoslavia may have been initially more difficult to handle than in Spain, we contend that political structures, institutions, incentives, and choices had an important impact. Indeed, we believe that policies selected in the Soviet Union at crucial stages in its political evolution were optimal for the disintegration of the state, heightening ethnic conflict, and creating long-term obstacles to the forging of democratic polities. Certain aspects of the former Soviet regime had previously served to deepen potentially divisive national identities,[24] but the processes of political change in the late 1980s and early 1990s greatly exacerbated these latent tendencies. *Perestroika* and *glasnost* involved liberalization but not democratization of the posttotalitarian central power structures. Gorbachev never at any time from 1985 to 1991 unequivocally committed himself, the party-state, or the central government to democratization as defined above. His reforms reduced the party-state's ideological, coercive, and economic control capacities but did nothing to create new democratically legitimated state and federal structures. Statewide elections were held in 1989, but they did nothing to give democratic legitimacy to the president himself, and important aspects of the elections to the Congress of Peoples' Deputies were clearly undemocratic.[25] Instead, *the first multiparty competitive elections were held at the republic level, rather than statewide.*

This sequence of elections provided rational incentives for republican elites to play ethnic politics, to build constituencies by creating ethnic agendas, and, in general, to make ethnicity the center of politics. The ethnic regional elites' control over cultural organizations, university, and state personnel policies, moreover, had given them access to organizational resources. In the flattened landscape of the posttotalitarian regime (within which detotalitarianization had clearly not gone as far as in countries like Hungary), the absence of autonomous organizations in civil society made ethnicity and the organized power bases of republican leaders the only effective means of mobilizing voters. Accordingly, in no republic in the USSR or Yugoslavia did a new statewide political organization emerge from the elections that was in any sense a counterweight to local nationalism. And in the course of these elections, political identities in the USSR and Yugoslavia became more narrow, compounding, exclusive, and unsupportive of participation in a multinational democratic entity. In Spain, during and after the electoral processes political identities became more multiple, cross-cutting, inclusive, and supportive of participation in a reconstituted Spanish democratic state. In short, the regime-transformation initiated by Gorbachev directly mobilized ethnicity and inadvertently undermined his own bargaining position: the nationalist regional forces could make a stronger claim to democratic legitimacy than could the unelected Gorbachev.

Thus, the sequence of elections, in combination with certain characteristics of the pre-Gorbachev regime, helped establish centrifugal drives that eventually blew the Soviet Union apart: the articulation of disintegrative ethnic themes during the republican elections encouraged the development of exclusionary and separatist national political identities and exacerbated relations among ethnic groups; and the democratic legitimation of leaders of the republics coupled with the relative lack of legitimacy of the president of the Soviet "Union," created an extremely unbalanced dialogue over the course of the transition in the aftermath of the abortive 1991 coup. The fear of further disintegration of the state has weakened support for democratic rule inside and outside the Russian government. Some highly placed officials and advisors go so far as to argue that some form of an authoritarian state is necessary to avoid a collapse. Russia's stateness problem has thus served to legitimize the public articulation of nondemocratic solutions to a degree not found in any East European country except Yugoslavia.

Democratic Consolidation

The Spanish transition began with the death of Franco on November 20, 1975, and was completed on October 25, 1979, when the Basque and Catalan regional autonomy referenda were held. With the ratification of the Basque and Catalan regional autonomy formulas, Spain met our three requirements for a completed transition: a government was installed in office as the result of a free and popular vote; that government had sovereign authority to formulate and implement policies; and it did not have to share power with other bodies. Until this point, there had been some doubt as to whether the military might successfully challenge the government's sovereign right to negotiate and generate new policies in the highly controversial area of regional politics. Furthermore, if a democratically elected government had not solved these problems of regionalization, its legitimacy might have been questioned, because the government could have been seen as displaying excessive continuity with the Franquist regime.[26]

There is broad scholarly consensus that Spanish democracy was consolidated no later than the peaceful transfer of power to the Socialist opposition following the October 1982 general elections. We accept that date, although we believe that a case could also be made that Spanish democracy was consolidated even earlier, with the completion of the successful trials and imprisonment of the military leaders involved in the February 23, 1981, coup attempt. For us, it is very significant (and a startling contrast with Argentina) that the two major leaders of the coup attempt, Colonel Tejero and General Milans del Bosch, were sent to jail without any politically significant movement in the military or in civil society to grant them clemency.

In our discussion of democratic consolidation we distinguished the *attitudes* of mass publics from the *actions* of nationally significant groups, and the *structural* reality of whether or not the democratic government was sovereign in the policy-making sphere. In the Spanish case, the first component to become fully congruent with consolidation was public opinion. Spanish public opinion was already strongly democratic by 1976 and has remained so ever since (see Table 3.1 for examples). Not only was Spanish public opinion strongly prodemocratic in the abstract sense, it also firmly rejected the major possible alternative to democracy, a military government. A public opinion survey undertaken by DATA, S.A., in the immediate aftermath of the February 1981 putsch attempt, revealed that only 5 percent of Spaniards favored the formation of a civil-military coalition government and that just 2 percent wanted to see a military government come to power. Ten years after the death of Franco, moreover, 76 percent of the population felt pride in the transition, and only 9 percent said the transition was not a source of pride. This sense of pride was particularly strong on the left, where 82 percent of those who said they would vote Communist and 88 percent of those who said they would vote Socialist expressed pride in the transition.[27]

In terms of the *actions* of nationally significant groups, until the failed coup of February 1981 parts of the military spent significant resources attempting to condition democratically elected governments, by pressure and, if necessary, by military force. Paul Preston argues that some party activists were in sufficient contact with coup conspirators to count as a semiloyal opposition.[28] The overwhelmingly negative reaction the coup received from the king, the public, trade unions, business organi-

Table 3.1 Spaniards' Survey Response to "Democracy Is the Best Political System for a Country Like Ours" (percentages of respondents)

	1978	1980	1981	1982/3	1983
Yes	77	69	81	7	85
No	15	20	13	6	10
Other	8	11	6	7	5
N	5,898	[a]	1,703	5,463	3,952

Source: Juan Linz and Alfred Stepan, "Political Crafting of Democratic Consolidation or Destruction: European and South American Comparisons," in Robert Pastor, ed., *Democracy in the Americas: Stopping the Pendulum* (New York: Holmes and Meier, 1989), p. 44. Reprinted by permission.
[a] Datum not available.

zations, and party leaders, however, helped to establish very clearly that "the only game in town" after February 1981 was a democratic game.

The final criterion of democratic consolidation to be met was the successful exercise by the democratic government of its right to formulate and implement policies unconstrained by nondemocratic institutions. This was clearly achieved with the trials and imprisonment of rebellious military officers in 1982. These trials helped to consolidate democracy by showing how divided and without an agenda the military "alternative" really was. The most important hardliners were defeated, disgraced, and jailed. As Felipe Agüero argues, after the trials there was a "steady realization among large numbers of officers that democracy was there to stay and that the military ought to accommodate itself within it." Faced with the solid parliamentary majority achieved by the Socialists in the October 1982 elections, moreover, "military contestation shifted from politics to more strictly corporate concerns, and from resistance to accommodation." From December 1982 until March 1991, the Socialist defense minister, Narcis Serra designed and implemented an imaginative and sweeping restructuring of the military. When he left office "the once feared *poder militar* was now, in many respects, one more branch of the state administration."[29] In terms of civil-military theory, a democratic pattern of civil-military relations is one in which there is low contestation by the military of the policies of the democratically elected government and where the military accepts that they have few prerogatives or reserve domains.[30] This has been characteristic of Spain since about 1983.

Facilitating Conditions

A review of the basic background variables that can facilitate or impede a democratic consolidation shows that Spain—with the important exception of the stateness variable—began its transformation under favorable conditions. The organizational base of the authoritarian regime consisted of civilians or civilianized proregime officials. Some may think of the Franco regime as a military regime, since Franco was a general and came to power largely on the basis of support from the military. Studies of decision making in the last twenty-five years of the Franco regime, however, support Agüero's conclusions that, "although the military in Spain was highly present in the Franquist structures, it did not delineate or monitor government policy or control its leader," and that it "did not participate in the elite nucleus that made the core decisions for the transition."[31] There was no constitutional basis in the Franco regime for the military to participate or even be consulted as an institution in the transition process. In our judgment, it is appropriate to regard Spain in the late 1960s and early 1970s as having a civilianized authoritarian regime. We contend that regimes of this kind present fewer potential obstacles to democratic transition and consolidation than posttotalitarian, sultanistic, military, or even strong-party authoritarian regimes.

The transition in Spain was initiated by the outgoing regime's political leaders, especially Adolfo Suárez, who introduced and secured passage of the Law for Political Reform and who presided over the process of writing a new democratic constitution. Social and political pressures for change were exerted when Franco died, but these popular pressures served primarily to establish the dialectic captured by the famous Spanish phrase *reforma pactada/ruptura pactada,* and to help keep the transition going forward. Since the Franquist regime's elites played such key roles at all stages of the transition, it is appropriate to call Spain a case of transacted transition which, consistent with our argument, is a format that avoids most of the problems of a provisional government.

Other characteristics of Spain in the late stages of its authoritarian regime—the status of its civil society, its constitutionalism and rule of law, the state bureaucracy, and the economy—were also quite supportive of a democratic transition. In the words of Víctor Pérez-Díaz, "by the time we get to the mid-1970s the economic, social and cultural institutions of Spain were already quite close to those of Western Europe, and the cultural beliefs, normative orientation and attitudes that go with the workings of these institutions were also close to European ones. This is one of the reasons why the political change to democracy worked so swiftly." He further notes that, by the mid-1970s, "Spain's economy was a modern economy, ranking tenth among capitalist economies throughout the world, with a large industrial sector, a booming service sector and its agriculture undergoing rapid transformation."[32] Indeed the Spanish economy had benefited from the overall development of Western Europe, and from 1955 to 1975 it had an average annual growth rate of close to 8 percent, one of the highest in the world.[33]

The character of the previous authoritarian regime thus meant that the new democratic regime would inherit a civil society already reasonably differentiated, a political society in the making, an economy that functioned well, a state apparatus tainted with authoritarianism but adaptable to control by a democratically elected government (indeed, many members of the first democratic government had been recruited from the ranks of the administration), and a reasonably strong recent tradition of rule of law. The only immediately salient item on the transition agenda was political—the creation of new democratic institutions.

Given this situation, international influence, we feel, was not critical for Spain's transition and consolidation (as it was for Portugal), but it certainly was systematically supportive. Democracy in Spain was already consolidated before Spain entered the European Community in 1986. However, the fact that the EC was solidly democratic and had "set up a stable pattern of rewards and disincentives for would-be members" was helpful for Spain's consolidation.[34] As the former Socialist minister José M. Maravall has noted, "Adolfo Suárez presented Spain's request for membership to the EEC in 1977 and the totality of parliamentary parties supported him. It was widely believed that international isolation and the dictatorship had been closely connected in recent Spanish history. The European Community was seen as a symbol of democracy and development; this symbol had been very important in the struggle against Franquism. Joining the EC was believed to be a decisive step for the consolidation of democracy."[35] Foreign policy towards Spain, and the prevailing *Zeitgeist* in Western Europe, were thus very supportive of democratic consolidation.

One must recall, however, that the economic situation of Spain deteriorated sharply during the transition and did not improve until three years *after* consolidation in 1982. Spanish unemployment rates in the early 1970s under Franco were among the lowest in Europe, hovering around 3 percent. With the advent of democracy, unemployment rose dramatically. Spain's 20 percent unemployment rate in the mid-1980s was the highest in Western Europe. Economic growth rates, which averaged over 7 percent from 1960 to 1974 and were among the highest in the world, averaged only 1.7 percent between 1975 and 1985.[36] The hypothesis of a tightly coupled relationship between economic efficiency and political legitimacy would lead us to predict a corresponding decline in the legitimacy of democracy. Public opinion polls during this period did show a sharp decline in the belief in the socioeconomic efficiency of the regime, but at the same time there was a significant *increase* in the number of citizens who answered affirmatively to the question "Is democracy the best political system for a country like ours?"[37] Despite economic decline, the Spanish in the 1980s (like the Dutch in the middle 1930s) struggled harder to make the democratic regime work because no alternative seemed more appropriate. Helped by the fact that they started with a reasonably healthy economy, the sequence of reforms following the death of Franco began with political change, which was followed by social reforms. Only after consolidation of the new democratic regime was economic restructuring attempted. In Eastern Europe, given the simultaneity problem that all posttotalitarian regimes face and the collapse of many East European economies, the option of this sequencing was largely unavailable. Even in many Latin American countries, the choice has been to address serious debt-related economic problems and political problems simultaneously.

Our final conditioning variable is the formula by which the constitution is adopted. In Spain, in our view, the absence of a sultanistic background or an armed conflict within the state precluded imposition of a constitution by a provisional government. Similarly, the relative absence of the military from the day-to-day governance of the old authoritarian regime, and the fact that the transition was led by the regime's civilian leaders, meant that the military would not attempt to impose authoritarian prerogatives or confining conditions on the constituent assembly. Finally, the civil war legacy, the great socioeconomic changes since the 1930s, and the fact that the Franco government had been in power for forty years, virtually precluded a restoration of the Second Republic and its constitution. These factors plus the constant pressure of the democratic opposition led the regime's leaders to adopt a free constitution-making formula. Within this formula, Spain elected the consensual as opposed to the majoritarian style of constitution making.[38]

The result of the consensual approach to constitution drafting was that the constitution was approved in the lower house by a margin of 325 to 6, with 8 abstentions. To further legitimize the new constitution, Spanish political elites chose to have their collective work submitted to a constitutional referendum where it obtained about 88 percent approval. Probably the most significant consequence of this consensual constituent process is that, ten years after the death of Franco, 65 percent of those polled felt that the constitution "was an accord among almost all political parties," whereas only 10 percent felt it was an "imposition by one party on the other." Fifty-seven percent further believed that the ideas of "everyone" had prevailed, only 7 percent thought that the ideas of the "center" had prevailed, and fewer thought that the constitution represented a victory for the left or right.[39] The constitution, therefore, was and is an element of popular consensus in the new democracy.

Again, we caution against the temptation to regard the Spanish transition as overdetermined by our variables. The stateness question was serious, and the events of February 1981 posed a severe threat to the new democracy. The skill and imagination of party leaders and the king were indispensable for success. Nevertheless, in comparative terms, Spain began the transition under quite favorable conditions—far more favorable than if it had begun the transition from a totalitarian, post-totalitarian, or sultanistic base. And, as we shall see in the following analysis of Portugal, a transition that begins with a coup by a non-hierarchical military confronts vastly more complicated circumstances, even though it shares the same typological origin as an authoritarian regime.

Portugal

The transition to democracy in Portugal was different in several important ways from the Spanish transition. It was initiated by what we refer to as the nonhierarchical military. This led to rule by provisional governments and a constitution-making process heavily conditioned by nondemocratic pressures, resulting in reserve domains of political authority that for some time precluded not only democratic consolidation but also a completed democratic transition. In short, the manner in which regime change began in Portugal complicated both the processes of democratic transition and consolidation.

The natures of the previous regimes did not determine the great differences between the Portuguese and Spanish transitions, because the Salazar regime was not significantly different from that of Franco. The epithet "totalitarian" was sometimes used to describe the Salazar regime, but the bulk of modern scholarship concurs that the regime never was totalitarian, even during its most repressive period.[40] Indeed, since the Franco regime exhibited totalitarian tendencies in its early phase, the Portuguese regime was even farther from the totalitarian model than the Spanish. The Salazar regime did, of course, have a fascist-styled structure for mass organizations; but these structures were actually less important than in Spain, and the official party was not well organized. The regime had a nondemocratic constitutional system with strong corporatist features, but (more than in Spain) it also had certain institutions of a liberal origin, such as regular elections to a parliament, and even a short period of tolerated political contestation prior to elections.[41] For a while, there was even a direct election of the president; the election results in 1958 were, in fact, surprisingly close.

Despite its military origin, Portugal's was not a military regime. Military conspiracies and unrest were frequent, however, and both the regime and the opposition attempted to bolster themselves by having military officers as their presidential standard bearers. In fact, all presidents of Portugal from 1926 to 1986 came from the military.[42] But overall it must be regarded as a civilianized authoritarian regime with a weak party (as in Spain), rather than a military regime (as in Chile). Antônio Salazar was a university professor who was surrounded by academics, and his successor as head of government, Marcelo Caetano, was a distinguished university professor. Until his death, Salazar, like Franco, was committed to sustaining the nondemocratic regime he had created.

With such similar regimes in Portugal and Spain, what explains why Portugal had a revolutionary rupture while Spain had a transition-by-transaction? This, obviously, is not a question that occupies a central place in the literature on the Portuguese revolution and transition. Writing today about the transition, we tend to see it in the framework set by later transition processes, forgetting that in 1974 it was the first of the transitions in the Mediterranean. There was no Spanish model of the sort that was so much discussed by government and opposition elites alike in Hungary, Brazil, Uruguay, and South Korea. Portugal, as the first transition, was not helped by a diffusion effect. The model of *reforma pactada/ruptura pactada* had not been invented. Indeed, the Portuguese upheavals (occurring as Franco died) served for many in Spain as a lesson in how *not* to make a transition.

Under what circumstances might a transition-by-transaction have taken place in Portugal? Theorists of transitions-by-transaction, such as Scott Mainwaring and Donald Share, generalizing from Spain and Brazil, have posited that such a transition is most likely if there is a reasonably well established regime, a low subversive threat, a cooperative opposition, low mobilization, and innovative leadership.[43] With the exception of its small, orthodox Communist Party and radical groups, Portugal at the death of Salazar in 1970 shared great similarities with Spain and Brazil on the first four of these conditions. What Portugal lacked was an innovative leader to play a major role in initiating a transition.[44] In the end, the military, whose hierarchy and morale were being destroyed and whose junior officers were being radicalized by the colonial wars in Africa that the regime would not end, terminated the regime.[45] It was a *ruptura* by *golpe*—by *coup*.

In our analytical framework, the most important variables relevant to the dynamics of transition and consolidation in the Portuguese case concern who initiated the transition, the role of mobilization, international influences, and the constitution-making process.

The transition in Portugal was, by and large, initiated by army captains. Unlike the Spanish and Greek cases, the Portuguese transition was not initiated by the regime. This made for a crisis of normal military structures, as well as a general crisis of the state. Consistent with our analytical framework, this opened up a period of provisional governments in which the possibilities for full democratic transition, not to speak of democratic consolidation, were very much in doubt. The junior military, pulled along by extensive mass mobilization in Lisbon and in southern Portugal, were for some time effectively in alliance with an orthodox Marxist-Leninist party and radical groups in an effort to transform society.[46] Between 1974 and 1976, the country lived through a turbulent period of provisional governments and a nearly disintegrating state. Indeed, Kenneth Maxwell suggests that Portugal's situation was closer in several ways to that of Nicaragua during this period than to any Southern European or South American transition.[47]

The military became deeply involved in all phases of political activity. After April 1974, the Junta of National Salvation, headed by seven officers, assumed sovereign power, elected a new president from among its members, and appointed the government. Another revolutionary organ of the new regime, the Council of State (only five of whose 21 members were civilians, and even they were appointed by the military), exercised legislative power until the election of the Constituent Assembly. The last five provisional governments were all headed by military officers. Forty of ninety cabinet positions were held by members of the military. In addition, the military's jurisdiction in 1974–75 extended to all counterrevolutionary "crimes," including those committed by the mass media. The military reserved for itself the power to arrest, carry out police investigations of, and submit to military justice those civilians accused of crimes involving the military. The military also assumed unilateral control of key foreign policy issues. In the words of one of the most radical military leaders of the provisional government, Vasco Gonçalves, "the MFA [Armed Forces Movement] was the only, and exclusive, group in charge of decolonialization."[48] Finally, the military played an important role in the mass media: their *Bulletin of the MFA* had a circulation of 100,000, and the MFA (through the unit called Dinamização Cultural) carried out extensive political mobilization efforts in support of the revolutionary process. Even the winner of the competition to participate in the first Eurovision Music Festival was a military officer.[49]

How did Portugal simultaneously complete its democratic transition and its consolidation on August 12, 1982, despite the significant impediments of the extraordinary political involvement of the nonhierarchical military, the Moscow-line Communist Party, and popular revolutionary actions? We believe that the provisional government's commitment to free elections, with a set date, exerted the strongest countervailing force in favor of democratization. Elections can create new democratic political actors, fill the newly opened political space with institutions associated with democracy, give a claim of democratic legitimacy to forces that have not necessarily played a role in the destruction of the authoritarian regime, and provide the first opportunity for all the citizens of the country to render a positive or negative judgement on the provisional government. The case of Portugal illustrates this.

For reasons that are still unclear, the initial program of the Armed Forces Movement included an explicit commitment to hold elections to a constituent assembly within a year, as well as to convene presidential and parliamentary elections one year later, in accord with the provisions of the new constitution. In the constituent assembly elections of April 25, 1975, a center-left party, a center-right party, and a conservative party—all of which were in favor of procedural democracy—won 72 percent of the vote. In 1976, in the first free parliamentary elections since the 1920s, these same three parties won 75 percent of the vote and 222 of the 263 seats in the assembly.[50] The crucial analytical point is that provisional governments formed by groups who destroyed an authoritarian regime can always make the claim that they legitimately represent the wishes and needs of the people. Such claims are virtually impossible to verify or dispute in the absence of free, democratic elections. Elections, however, create new democratic claimants. The monopolistic claims of a provisional government are thus contested, and an important part of the newly created political space is occupied by actors recruited through democratic procedures.

This does not mean that the struggle over the democratic or nondemocratic direction of the transition is over. In a highly fluid environment, it means only that a democratic discourse and democratic power resources have been created which may be used to contest those of the forces associated with the provisional government. The preferences and political objectives of various groups may be radically divergent, even following elections, as was made strikingly clear by the leader of the Portuguese Communist Party, Alvaro Cunhal, in an interview with the Italian journalist Oriana Fallacci in 1975: "If you think the Socialist Party with its 40 percent and the Popular Democrats with its 27 percent constitute the majority . . . you're the victim of a misunderstanding. . . . I'm telling you that elections have nothing or very little to do with the dynamics of a revolution. . . . I promise you there will be no parliament in Portugal."[51]

Why then was a parliament successfully established in 1976? One important factor relates to the origins of the revolution among the nonhierarchical military. We contend that a nonhierarchically led military regime perpetually risks being checked by the assertion of control by the officers associated with the military hierarchy. Here we differ somewhat from the important work of Felipe Agüero. He asserts that if the previous authoritarian regime is civilianized and the transition is begun by a military coup, the relative power position of the military will be strong.[52] We believe that this is correct only when the coup is led by a hierarchical military. When the coup is led by the nonhierarchical military, they are, as we argued, always vulnerable to a hierarchical countercoup.

In Portugal, politics under the provisional governments increasingly threatened the military chain of command. In some cases, parallel operational command units were set up that refused to comply with orders from their nominal superiors. Mixed groups of officers and enlisted men occasionally met in debating forums. Eventually, the solidarity of the self-proclaimed "motor of the revolution" cracked, and this generated sharp intramilitary conflicts about future policy directions and alliance strategies. As Lawrence S. Graham has noted, by late 1975, the political involvement of the Portuguese military had reached a point where the political alignments on the left, the right, and the center all represented different constellations of civilian and military leaders. Seen in organizational terms, by this point the military had largely ceased to exist as an identifiable institution distinct from civilian society. The prerevolutionary divisions between the services and, within them, between officers and enlisted men had disintegrated further into warring factions.[53] A group of senior officers concerned about institutional unity and discipline began to form around Colonel Ramalho Eanes. On November 25, 1975, what appeared to be a leftist putsch, involving an officerless group of paratroopers, was put down by Colonel Eanes, backed by a strong political coalition of national and international forces. This began a long process in which hierarchical control was progressively reasserted. Respecting electoral results became a part of the military hierarchy's own depoliticization strategy. As Maxwell says, "the army, which in 1975 talked of itself as a 'revolutionary vanguard' and a 'movement of national liberation,' by 1976 praised 'hierarchy' and 'discipline.'"[54]

The interlude of provisional governments and extremely high involvement of the military in politics, however, had left its legacy. In terms of democratic theory and democratic institutions, this meant that (unlike in Spain) the constituent assembly was neither fully sovereign nor unconstrained in drafting a constitution. In order to allow the 1975 constituent assembly election to go forward, political parties bowed to revolutionary military power and signed a formal written pact with the MFA, agreeing to a supervisory role for the MFA even after the election.[55] A second pact was signed on February 26, 1976, while the Constituent Assembly was in process.[56]

As a result of these pacts, the 1976 constitution contained some clearly nondemocratic features. The predominantly military Council of the Revolution was given the power to enact its own legislation and to judge the constitutionality of all laws passed by the Assembly. Accordingly, Article 149 of the 1976 Portuguese constitution flatly asserted, "Decree-laws of the Council of the Revolution shall have the same validity as laws of the Assembly of the Republic." Article 148 stated that the Council of the Revolution would have the authority to "make laws concerning the organizational functioning, and discipline of the Armed Forces. . . ." and that these powers "shall be vested in the Council of the Revolution alone." As long as the constitution gave these de jure prerogatives to an institution whose power did not derive from democratic procedures, Portugal did not meet our criteria of a completed democratic transition. The Council of the Revolution, moreover, often exercised these powers. According to Thomas Bruneau and Alex Macleod, "the Council adopted an activist stance which upset many civilian politicians, rejecting no fewer than thirty-five of the seventy-four bills that were submitted to it."[57] In the end, it required six years of pressure from the democratic political parties, and the acquiescence and at times active support of President Eanes, before constitutional revisions could be enacted that abolished the Council of the Revolution and established a legal framework for democratic control of the military.[58] In that same year, 1982, a national defense law was passed which specified the institutional details of civilian control.

Democratic transition and consolidation are not necessarily separate and temporally sequential processes. Under some circumstances, such as in Portugal on August 12, 1982, they can occur simultaneously. Concerning the *attitudinal* dimension of democratic consolidation, we regard the surprisingly strong and stable support for prodemocratic, proregime parties throughout the period from 1975 to 1985 as reflecting a pervasive preference for procedural democracy. Bruneau and Macleod assert that "party loyalty was defined early, in 1975, and continued with very little movement of the voters from one party to another between 1976 and 1983."[59] The founding election of 1975 is particularly illustrative in this respect. The 1975 election became a contest between a revolutionary military that campaigned openly for abstention or a null vote, and the democratic political parties who urged a high turnout. The military's campaign had virtually no effect. Participation was over 90 percent—an extraordinarily high rate of turnout, even for a founding election—and the percentage of null ballots was only 2 percent higher than would be recorded in the 1976 elections, when no one campaigned for null votes.[60]

Even in the absence of conclusive public opinion data from the pre-1982 period, this voting pattern supports the argument that, attitudinally, Portugal had crossed our threshold for democratic consolidation by 1982. A survey administered in 1988 reveals a public opinion profile not unlike that of other consolidated democracies. In that poll, 90.2 percent of the population generally favored democracy; of this total, 38.9 percent actively supported democracy and another 51.3 passively accepted democracy. Significantly, of the 24.6 percent of the population polled who said they were "dissatisfied" with how democracy had functioned in the previous ten years, only 5.1 answered that they were against democracy, while 19.1 percent said they favored democracy.[61] By 1990, prodemocratic sentiment in Portugal was above the West European norm. In answer to the standard Eurobarometer question "How satisfied are you with the way democracy works?" an average of 62 percent of EC respondents answered "very satisfied" or "satisfied," while in Portugal the figure was 71 percent.[62]

Behaviorally, it is important to note that by 1982 no organization or movement of national importance was spending significant resources to attempt to achieve its goals by nondemocratic means. The authors of an important comparative article on the new Southern European democracies give Portugal the same regime support rating they give to the consolidated democracies of France, Italy, and Finland.[63]

Finally, according to the *structural* dimension of democratic consolidation, the reserve domains of nonaccountable power held by the Council of the Revolution were still so great in the first half of 1982 that Portugal could not be regarded as fully democratic. With military acceptance of the constitutional changes of August 12, 1982, however, not only was the transition complete, but, attitudinally, behaviorally, and structurally, democracy was consolidated in Portugal.

Of our variables, the most important in the Portuguese transition and consolidation processes is "Who initiates the transition?" Because the transition began with a liberation by a nonhierarchical *golpe,* a dynamic of provisional governments developed in which revolution was as much an option as parliamentary democracy. The second and third most important of our variables in this case are closely related to the first: the extraordinarily powerful role played by the nonhierarchical military (backed by the Communist Party and by impressive societal mobilization in the capital and its southern environs) in turn led to a tightly constrained constitution-making process.

None of the other variables were as pertinent in the case of Portugal. Unlike in Spain (and, even more so, in the Soviet Union and Yugoslavia), stateness was not a problem, because Portugal, more than any other country in Europe, is a nation-state. Portugal is a monolingual nation-state whose borders have been fixed for hundreds of years. The only possible *irredenta* is a town of 25,000 bordering Spain. And the only potential stateness problem was separatism in the Azores if the country had become communist, but this never actually became a salient issue.

Other nations were actively supportive, and in two respects played a more critical role in Portugal's transition to democracy than in the Spanish case. There is some evidence that the United States was so worried about the revolutionary dynamic in Portugal that it considered a range of covert and even paramilitary operations.[64] Given the degree of Portuguese mobilization in 1975, it is most unlikely that U.S. covert military operations (as in Guatemala in 1954) would have created an atmosphere conducive to democratic consolidation. Instead, the European Community urged the United States to follow a political and not a military strategy. Moreover, European socialist parties (especially the West German Social Democratic Party) contributed funds, organizational links, and moral support to bolster the most important democratic party in Portugal, the Socialists, led by Mário Soares. The same was true for the Christian Democrats. The European Community was a valuable and steady pole of attraction for Portuguese democratic governments.[65]

Mobilization also played an important role, but a more complicated one. There was no significant mass mobilization before the "liberation by *golpe*," but the outpouring of support in the streets that immediately greeted the revolution certainly helped reduce the chances of a successful counterattack by the supporters of the Salazar-Caetano regime. Within a few days, members of the dreaded security forces were in disorganized flight, the state was dissolving, and the most extensive purges found in any of these countries (including those in postcommunist Europe) were under way.[66] A very different kind of mobilization, however, did play a critical role in the transition to democracy, if we can broadly define as mobilization a phenomenon in which millions of people by their own actions play a role in dictating events. Millions of Portuguese citizens refused to answer the call for a null vote in the 1975 election, an extremely significant demonstration of the overwhelming preference of Portuguese citizens for procedural democracy. In addition, large numbers of people marched in support of democracy at critical junctures.

What role did the economy play in the Portuguese transition? Between the incapacitation of Salazar in 1968 and the revolution by *golpe* in 1974, the Portuguese economy averaged 6.5 percent annual economic growth.[67] Thus, economic crisis per se cannot be said to have contributed to the start of the transition. What did contribute to the start of the transition was that a key component of the coercive apparatus, the military, became convinced that the regime could not end the colonial wars and that this would create a profound crisis for them, moving them to adopt an antiregime stance. Further, many of the regime-associated politicians who in the 1960s had urged liberalization had by 1974 become convinced that a transition would not be led by reformers within the regime. They were thus available to support the antiregime actions of the military. Politics, not economics, caused the breakdown of the regime and started the transition.

But what of the role of the economy in democratic consolidation? We have argued that democracy was consolidated in Portugal in October 1982. It is important to stress that due to the oil shocks, the recession in Europe, the return of an overseas population proportionately five times greater than France absorbed after Algerian decolonization, and the economic disarray in the aftermath of the abortive 1974–75 revolution, the Portuguese economy was in dire straits until well after democratic consolidation.[68] The stabilization plan of 1983–84 further increased economic hardships for most people. Surveys undertaken by Thomas Bruneau, however, revealed that very few Portuguese blamed the democratic regime for this economic decline: 93 percent of those interviewed in a 1984 poll said that there was an economic crisis, but, as Bruneau noted, "respondents saw little relationship between it and any particular government; rather it was due to the world economic crisis. . . . [there was no indication] of serious alienation from the present regime."[69] Between 1989 and 1991 Portugal did have one of the fastest-growing economies in Europe, but since this economic boom occurred after democracy was consolidated it is more accurate to say that economic growth *deepened* the consolidation of democracy, rather than that it contributed to its initiation. In Portugal, democracy was consolidated during a period of deep economic hardship but not of political despair or system blame.

Greece

A strong case can be made that the Greek transition began on July 21, 1974, and was concluded on December 9, 1974. This 142-day transition is by far the most rapid in our Southern European and South American sample. What accounts for the rapidity of the Greek transition?

The institutional base of the Greek authoritarian regime takes us a long way towards answering this question. The 1967 military takeover in Greece was a nonhierarchical colonels' coup led by George Papadopoulos. The nonhierarchical nature of the coup is underscored by the fact that the junior officers in the army purged approximately 400 of their senior officers in 1967.[70] They also staged the coup without the active support of the navy or the air force. Of all the nondemocratic regimes whose transition we are studying, the Greek junta had the narrowest base within the state. As Nikiforos Diamandouros states, the king's opposition was "latent from the start, open during the ill-planned and ill-executed countercoup of 13 December 1967, and muted but continuous after that." This "clash between crown and colonels resulted in a sharp split within the Greek officer corps, pitting the vast majority of the navy officers and a large number of the air force counterparts against their army colleagues." The junta also lacked support from parties of the right. Indeed, Diamandouros refers to the "quasi-unanimous refusal of the parliamentary right to cooperate with the military."[71] This contrasts markedly with the military regimes in Brazil and Chile, which for many years received the very strong support of the traditional parliamentary right. Finally, the growing mobilization of civil society had been one of the reasons for the 1967 coup. These mobilizations began to pick up again in 1973 and culminated in the student uprisings at the National Polytechnic in November. The fact that the army colonels had such a narrow base in the state and political society meant that student uprisings received widespread national and international support, which further isolated and divided the military and contributed to a hard line coup by Brigadier General Ioannides, supported by the military police and the lower ranks of the army. But this only led to deeper divisions and purges in the officer corps and further accentuated the nonhierarchical base of the regime.

This hostile political context and military fragmentation made the Greek junta operationally incapable of responding adequately to Turkey in the Cyprus crisis of July 20, 1974. Under these conditions, as described by Diamandouros, "the Joint Chiefs, invoking the threat of war, reasserted the hierarchical lines of command within the armed forces and effectively neutralized the power base sustaining Ioannides and the hard-liners. This move signaled the distancing of the armed forces from the disintegrating regime and made easier the search for a transfer-of-power formula under their initial aegis."[72]

Four key institutional dimensions of the Greek transition directly relate to our conceptual framework, and go a long way towards explaining why in Greece in 1975 many officers were convicted of crimes and the sentences were not resisted by the military-as-institution. First, the transfer of power was made by the military hierarchy acting more as part of the state than of the regime. Within seventy-two hours of the Turkish invasion of Cyprus, the hierarchical military had deposed the nonhierarchical military and negotiated the swearing in of the conservative civilian political leader, Constantine Karamanlis, as prime minister. Second, because of the military urgency of immediate extrication from government, the military-as-institution was not able to impose any confining conditions on civilians as a precondition for extrication. Indeed, Thanos Veremis argues that the military's incapacity in the face of war increased Karamanlis's bargaining power. The hierarchical military wanted him to assume power immediately, but "a condition of Karamanlis' acceptance of office was a pledge that the armed forces should return to their former military duties, and desist from further interference in government."[73] Third, the hierarchical military, after having been purged by the nonhierarchical military, were called back to active duty and assigned to the top positions in the military chain of command of the new civilian government. Constantine Danopoulos estimated (in a conversation with one of the authors) that approximately 75 percent of the senior officers purged in 1967–68 were returned to key positions in 1974. Finally, this transfer of power by a state institution to a caretaker government precluded a revolutionary provisional government. This clearly distinguishes the Greek transition from those in Spain and Portugal. In the Spanish case, there were strong initiatives within the regime that contributed to the democratization process, and the regime was able to carry the state with it. In Portugal, by contrast, the regime showed weak will and little capacity to transform itself; a nonhierarchical military revolution, immediately supported by mobilization in civil society, destroyed the regime and much of the state. In Greece, the outcome was more controlled, because part of the state (the hierarchical military) overthrew the regime and transferred power immediately to a conservative but prodemocratic government.[74]

Other factors played less important roles in explaining the rapid collapse of the colonels' regime and the consolidation of a new democratic regime. The fact that the colonels' regime was of such short duration, and was so widely disliked, meant that it was capable of posing few obstacles to democratization. International influence made a positive contribution; the EC pushed for democratization through the use of both sticks (shelving Greece's application for membership after the 1967 coup) and carrots (acting very quickly on the Karamanlis government's membership request by admitting Greece in 1981). A stateness problem was presented by the Cyprus issue, but this was obviously less of a crisis for the democracy than it had been for the authoritarian regime; in addition, it was not a case of secessionist demands, but rather less problematic irredentist desires. Finally, democratic consolidation in Greece was not aided by favorable economic conditions: indeed, as in the rest of Europe, the 1975–81 period was one of stagnation and periodic economic crisis.

In our view, the Greek transition was completed on December 9, 1974, when, following free elections and a referendum that abolished the monarchy, Parliament opened and Prime Minister Karamanlis became accountable to Parliament. In the 142-day period between the military step-down and the opening of Parliament, a number of impediments to full democratization were removed. Karamanlis, who had been actively complicitous in the exclusionary legislation that had marred Greek politics ever since the civil war, "put an end to Law 509/1948, the last major piece of civil war discriminatory legislation."[75] He announced that an elected parliament would revise the constitution, he restored many civil liberties that had been absent since the civil war, and most significantly, he ended the proscription of the Communist Party. Thus, the Greek transition was complete.

The question of when Greek democracy became consolidated is more difficult, although we would argue that the electoral victory and assumption of power by the Socialist opposition in 1981 represented a test whose uneventful passing indicated that Greek democracy was consolidated by that time. *Structurally,* the hierarchical military neither insisted on reserve domains nor contested the first elected (New Democracy) government's decision to go forward with widespread military trials. Successful conclusion of the trials (in which many officers were convicted) within a year of elections made a positive contribution politically and militarily to democratic consolidation. As Veremis observes: "No doubt the trials and imprisonment of leading members of the dictatorship, and some of their henchmen, left much to be desired in terms of a clean sweep of the armed forces from Junta sympathizers. Yet governments since 1975 felt no threat from the army nor were they in any way obstructed by it. . . . Officers . . . possibly shaken by the disastrous outcome of military rule, choose to abide by the rules of professionalism which had been the hallmark of officer corps in the West."[76]

A series of constitutional and legislative reforms was enacted following the trials that restricted military authority to areas within democratic boundaries. Before the end of 1975, a new constitution had been installed (democratically, but over strong opposition, as we shall see); and there were no laws, procedures, or prerogatives that constrained the sovereignty of democratic politics and procedures. In complete contrast to Portugal, in Greece, structures were the first dimension of democracy to be consolidated.

Behaviorally, the institutions and values of Greek democracy had become the only game in town by the 1981 election, especially in terms of all major players accepting each other's right to compete, and if victorious, to exercise power. Between the civil war and the 1967 breakdown, two important groups maintained semiloyal or even nondemocratic stands: rightist groups, who were almost continually committed to a "controlled democracy" that denied citizenship rights to those on the left whom they deemed not "nationally minded"; and the communist parties (especially the pro-Moscow KKE), who intermittently committed themselves to nondemocratic oppositional tactics.[77] Even the Panhellenic Socialist Movement (PASOK) founded by Andreas Papandreou in September 1974—on the basis of the Panhellenic Liberation Movement he had helped to create in 1968 after his release from prison—had antisystem overtones. During the 1974 elections the leading group within PASOK was former members of the resistance organizations. This wing of PASOK was more maximalist than the communists. They deeply distrusted the right, and, in turn, were deeply distrusted by the right.[78]

Some important aspects of the new political system were not readily accepted by PASOK and the main communist party, the KKE. The electoral system was sharply criticized by the major parties of the left, who argued that it was constructed to overrepresent the largest party in the hastily convened first election and to underrepresent the opposition. Indeed, in the 1974 election the New Democracy Party, created by Karamanlis and supported by most conservatives, won 54.4 percent of the vote but 73.3 percent of the seats, while PASOK and the Electoral Alliance of the United Left won 23.1 percent of the vote but only 6.7 percent of the seats.[79] New Democracy, having an overwhelming majority, was thus able to structure the constitution in 1975 in accord with its preferences. In striking contrast with the nonmajoritarian government in Spain, the New Democracy government devoted little effort to securing a constitutional consensus. The opposition objected, in particular, to strong presidential emergency powers. According to Nikos Alivizatos, the "debate led to a major clash, all opposition parties finally withdrawing from the Assembly in May 1975, denouncing the new constitution as authoritarian. As a consequence, at the final vote on 9 June 1975, the constitution was approved only by the New Democracy deputies."[80]

Over the next five years, however, all the major players made substantial adjustments towards accepting democratic practices and the specific institutions of Greek democracy. PASOK advanced a less maximalist program in the 1977 election campaign and emerged as the major opposition party. New Democracy, in turn, did not continue to abuse majoritarian prerogatives. And each of the two major parties entered the 1981 election accepting the democratic loyalty of the other, and arrived at a series of tacit understandings over how the parliamentary game would be played.[81] PASOK grew to accept most of the specific electoral and constitutional provisions and was able to secure parliamentary support for constitutional reforms in 1986. Both communist parties increasingly eschewed antisystem behavior and attempted to achieve their goals within the framework of a democratic regime. Behaviorally, then, one could argue that democracy was consolidated in 1981, at the latest. Indeed some specialists believe that an argument could even be made that behaviorally it was consolidated in 1977.

In terms of our *attitudinal* criterion for democratic consolidation, we are on less solid ground. Systematic public opinion polls of attitudes relevant for assessing democratic consolidation were conducted for the first time in the mid-1980s. Lacking survey data before then, we can only infer that Karamanlis's creation of a new conservative party (called, significantly, New Democracy), the legalization and participation of the communist parties, and the evolutionary change of PASOK all helped create attitudes supportive of democratic consolidation within these critical party groupings and among their mass followings. By 1985, when the relevant public opinion data first become available (as part of a cross-national survey of Southern European electorates), two conditions clearly existed. First, Greeks had a much more negative opinion about their military dictatorship than the Spanish had of the Franco period, or the Portuguese had of the Salazar period. Second, Greeks were much more likely to express preferences for democracy over authoritarianism, perhaps because of the intensity of their rejection of their authoritarian past. (These data are presented by Leonardo Morlino and José Ramón Montero in Table 7.1 in this volume.) These and other attitudinal data support our conclusion that Greece had become a consolidated democracy by the time the government changed in 1981.

In Greece the historical memory of the civil war now plays a role similar to that in Spain (and completely unlike that in Croatia and Serbia). In one recent public opinion survey, for example, a plurality (41 percent of those interviewed) blamed *both* the communists and government forces for the civil war, and the next largest group of respondents (32 percent) did not even offer an opinion on the subject.[82] Despite the acrimonious partisanship of public debate, moreover, citizens have revealed an increasing propensity to say that they would consider voting for a party of the opposite camp in the future. This suggests that there is less cultural difference between the parties and that the realm of democratically acceptable alternatives is broadening.

Perhaps the most dramatic evidence of change can be seen in party responses to the problem of government formation in a hung parliament. Following the indecisive election of June 1989, the two descendants of the warring sides of the 1946–49 civil war, the pro-Moscow Communist Party and New Democracy, formed a coalition government. This coalition would have been unthinkable at the start of the transition in 1974. Indeed, if 1949 can be seen as marking the military end of the Greek civil war and the election of 1974 as demonstrating the political end, then the 1989 Communist–New Democracy coalition of June–November 1989 was the cultural end of the civil war. When the November 1989 elections again failed to produce a winner, extensive inter- and intraparty negotiations produced an all-party government that ruled until the April 1990 elections produced a slender majority for New Democracy.

Some observers have raised questions about the quality of democracy in Greece. We believe that among democratic regimes that are consolidated it is possible to identify some in which democratic consolidation deepens over time, as well as to separate democracies that are of low quality from those of high quality. We consider Greek democracy to be of relatively low quality, as reflected in accusations of corruption against high-ranking government leaders (including Prime Minister Andreas Papandreou), huge and seemingly uncontrollable budget deficits, and a dangerously acrimonious style of political discourse. Low-quality democracies have fewer degrees of freedom than those of high quality and can break down more easily. However, despite its relatively poor performance in terms of policy outputs and economic indicators, Greek democracy has weathered serious political crises, and there has been no sign of breakdown. In fact, old enemies have been able to cooperate. We believe that if democracy ever breaks down in Greece it will not be because Greek democracy was never consolidated. Instead, any fundamental crisis of Greek democracy will have less to do with the theory and praxis of transition and consolidation than with the theory and praxis of breakdown.[83]

Concluding Observations

All three of the recently redemocratized Southern European countries are democratically consolidated, no consolidation took longer than eight years, and the new Southern European democracies are becoming increasingly comparable in their political patterns to other West European parliamentary democracies. How can we account for the much greater success in achieving democratic consolidation in Southern Europe than in South American and East European cases we have studied?

The most important explanatory variable to emerge from this analysis is the nature of the outgoing nondemocratic regime. In all three of the Southern European cases, democratization followed the breakdown of an authoritarian regime. Secondly, in none of these three cases was this regime dominated by the hierarchical military. By way of contrast, all of the outgoing authoritarian regimes in South America had been dominated by the hierarchical military, and, in accord with our hypotheses, this meant that the military intervened heavily in the transition and consolidation processes. In Chile, the Pinochet regime was able to impose such extensive reserve domains on the incoming civilian democratic elite that it is difficult to regard the Chilean transition to democracy as complete, in its structural dimension. While the strength and unity of the outgoing hierarchical military elite is an important variable in accounting for the imposition of undemocratic constraints on the transition and consolidation processes, we have seen that this factor must be weighed against the strength of the prodemocratic forces pushing the military from power. Looking at both sides of this equation, we can partially account for differences among the South American cases. Uruguay has been most successful in consolidating its democracy (despite severe economic problems and an inefficacious government) in large part because of the strength of its democratic parties and the lack of support in civil society for military involvement in politics. To be sure, the lack of a serious threat (after the 1989 referendum) that military officers might be prosecuted for their crimes under the former regime also helped to guarantee military acquiescence in Uruguay. In Argentina, there were frequent military rebellions under the Alfonsín government, but since most such outbursts were increasingly led by lower-ranking military officers, the military hierarchy eventually cooperated with the much more efficacious Menem government in maintaining the order and discipline necessary for continued progress towards consolidation. The unconsolidated regime in Brazil, meanwhile, has been negatively affected by incertitude about the final constitutional structure, by extremely inefficacious government under three weak presidents, by extremely weak political parties, and by the lowest level of socioeconomic modernization among the South American countries we have studied.

Only one of the former communist cases, Poland, could be characterized as undergoing a transition from an authoritarian regime. The important role played by military officials in Poland, however, bore a striking resemblance to the South American cases. Accordingly, the "pacted transition" initiated by the regime in Poland was comparable in its confining conditions to those we have seen in Chile, Uruguay, and Brazil. In both Chile and Poland, this has meant that democracy started with the old regime's constitution, and with the old regime still retaining strong positions in the legislature and in the state apparatus. Only one of the other postcommunist transitions, Hungary's, resembled the Southern European (particularly the Spanish) patterns of regime change. While Hungary can be classified as having evolved from a posttotalitarian society, its detotalitarianization began earlier and reached a greater extent than has been the case in any of the other countries in the Soviet Union's "outer empire." Thus, the extent of pluralism and rule of law in Hungary came closer to Southern European levels than elsewhere in the Eastern bloc. Because of this, and because Hungary had a negotiated transition and lacked an acute stateness problem, it faced less severe obstacles on the path towards democratic consolidation than did any other Eastern bloc country.

None of the other East European countries we have examined had been as detotalitarianized prior to the breakdown of its nondemocratic regime. Czechoslovakia, was a case of mature posttotalitarianism only in the cultural sphere, certainly not in economics or politics. Bulgaria and Russia were examples of very early posttotalitarian regimes whose leaders had vastly more power than the incipient civil society opposition to initiate and control a reformulation of the political system. The relative absence of organized pluralism in Czechoslovakia, Bulgaria, and Russia precluded the kind of pacted transition that contributed so substantially to democratic consolidation in Spain.

Romania in the late 1980s had a regime that exhibited strong sultanistic and totalitarian tendencies. The Romanian regime had experienced brief and weak detotalitarianization from 1965 to 1971, but from 1974 to 1989 the regime had become increasingly sultanistic. Ceauşescu was clearly unbounded by rational legal constraints or by any ideological principles not elaborated by himself, and his rule was highly personalistic and arbitrary, exhibiting pronounced dynastic tendencies. Ceauşescu's habit of arbitrary intervention prevented groups and institutions from developing any significant degree of autonomy. Coercion, clientelistic methods of control, and periodic violence by parastate groups were used to disrupt the development of civil society. Similarly, no reform-oriented elites could emerge within the regime itself. This precluded any possibility of a pacted reform. The highly personalistic nature of a sultanistic regime also makes possible the "capture" of a revolution by nonrevolutionary forces, insofar as new, nondemocratic leaders can advance the claim that the leader was responsible for all the evil in the country and gain popular support by playing a prominent role in his overthrow. These aspects of the initial stages of regime transformation may delay if not impede subsequent processes of full democratization and consolidation.

A third major explanatory variable concerns the sequence among the multidimensional changes that may be required to consolidate a new democracy, and the presence or absence of a simultaneity problem. The Southern European countries were structurally able, and consciously chose, to concentrate first on politics, secondly on social welfare policies, and only later on structural economic reforms, except in Portugal, where the nationalizations and collectivizations of the revolutionary period made subsequent economic restructuring even more difficult. We consider this the optimal sequence if it is at all possible. Democracy in any given country entails understandings concerning decision-rules, the creation of institutional arrangements, the removal of barriers to participation, the indispensable element of elections, and the creation of political society. Ideally, socioeconomic policies are produced by, and flow out of, this setting. When such profound political changes are accompanied by equally profound changes in society and economy, the agenda for change may be overloaded, impeding successful achievement of each one of these ambitious objectives. Moreover, the social strains that accompany radical economic change (such as the stabilization plans that followed in the aftermath of the South American debt crisis) may substantially polarize politics and jeopardize the transition to democracy. In some of the postcommunist countries, a "shock therapy" strategy of economic change was given priority over the full institutionalization of democracy—which ultimately made *both*

Table 3.2 Tax Revenues, Total Public Expenditures, and Public Employment Expenditures (percentages of GDP)

	Spain			Portugal			Greece		
	1976	1984	1988	1976	1984	1988	1976	1984	1988
Tax revenues	25.0	33.2	36.7	31.0	34.6	36.6	29.2	34.2	35.9
Total public expenditures	26.0	38.7	41.7	37.3	41.6	43.7	20.9	44.2	51.3
Public employment expenditures	8.5	12.8	13.8	8.8	13.3	13.8	8.5	9.4	10.1

Source: J. M. Maravall, "Economic Reforms in New Democracies: The Southern European Experience," *East-South System Transformations,* working paper no. 3, October 1990, Department of Political Science, University of Chicago, p. 25.

economic and political transitions more complex and difficult.

This comparative study has highlighted one important characteristic that clearly distinguishes patterns of economic change in Southern Europe from economic policy changes elsewhere. In an era when "state shrinking" is advanced as an imperative for the struggling new democracies of Latin America and Eastern Europe, it is important to note that all three of the new Southern European democracies strengthened their states by *increasing tax revenues* during the transition and consolidation processes. All three Southern European states used this revenue to significantly *increase social welfare expenditures and state employment.* These patterns are clearly revealed in Table 3.2. All three Southern European countries also became consolidated *before* their economies improved, and even before economic restructuring began. Spain did not begin major structural economic reform until 1982, Portugal until 1985, and Greece's first unsuccessful effort was in 1985–87. In *none* of the Southern European countries, during the critical period between the elected governments' assuming office and democratic consolidation of the regimes, were issues concerning the design or functioning of the economy as salient as debates about the design and functioning of political power.

International factors also played a role in the Southern European transition and consolidation processes, although they were by no means as important as they were in Eastern Europe. The announcement of what has been dubbed the "Sinatra doctrine" by the once hegemonic Soviet Union was decisive in triggering the collapse of nondemocratic Eastern bloc regimes. Similarly, once the first East European transitions were set in motion, a powerful diffusion effect gave rise to mass mobilizations in favor of political change elsewhere in the region. In Greece, the transition to democracy was triggered by the threat of a disastrous military confrontation with Turkey over Cyprus, and in Portugal the military rebellion that toppled the Salazar/Caetano regime was a long-term product of debilitating colonial wars in Africa. In Spain, international factors did not play a significant role in the transition, except insofar as the tumultuous Portuguese revolution presented Spaniards with an example of how *not* to undertake a political transformation. International affairs might have exerted greater influence if the Spanish army had not stepped aside and abandoned the Spanish Sahara in the face of the Moroccan Green Wave in late 1975, but, fortunately, the possibility of entanglement in a colonial war dissipated quickly. In all three countries, the impact of the European Community can be seen as more subtle and indirect in encouraging democratization. We agree with Laurence Whitehead's conclusion that the EC (which had a deep and abiding concern with consolidating democracy in the region) contributed to this process by setting up a stable pattern of rewards and incentives, and that the prospect of membership in the European Community "produced a substantial long-term pressure for democratization."[84] But by no means was this impact as direct or dramatic as in the Eastern European countries.

International factors may have been more significant in the longer-term processes of democratic consolidation. Since Geoffrey Pridham explores this factor at greater length in this volume, we shall only briefly summarize a few key points here. First, the European Community represented a positive political and economic network to which Spain, Greece, and Portugal could aspire. EC membership also offered some financial incentives for democratic consolidation: integration with the EC held out the positive transfer of close to 5 percent of GNP. No comparable positive economic or political network exists for the Southern Cone. Indeed, the market-economy democratic countries, led by the United States, were, in the mid-1980s, seen primarily as sources of foreign indebtedness. Continued market integration for the Southern Cone countries meant debt payments of close to 5 percent of GNP for Brazil, Argentina, and Uruguay. Second, NATO membership has played a positive role in democratic consolidation in Southern Europe insofar as it helped ease the militaries' transition to democracy by giving support to missions and identities based on enhanced military professionalism. NATO membership has also meant that the tension-fraught question, "Why do we need a military in a democracy?" was not a major source of civil-military conflict. The Southern Cone countries have no NATO-like roles. The major international role that the United States has encouraged the Latin American militaries to perform is in the politically explosive area of joint anti–drug trafficking operations.[85]

A more potentially powerful explanatory variable involves what we have called stateness. This variable was irrelevant to all of our South American cases, however, and among our Southern European cases, only in Spain did stateness problems potentially complicate the transition and consolidation processes. The infrequency of stateness problems among our sample countries is, in fact, a statistical oddity. Empirically there are very few polities in the world that are simultaneously a state, a nation, and a democracy. There are almost two hundred states in the world, but, according to a standard homogeneity index, less than twenty of these approximate the ideal of a homogeneous nation-state. Since democracy implies rights of minorities, some reconciliation is necessary. This is so because throughout most of the globe there is such an overlapping and intermixing of different cultural nations that the possibility of clear territorial boundaries that are congruent with even a very small nation-state cannot be obtained short of "ethnic cleansing" and mass migrations. It is important to note that in many circumstances, nation-state, democracy, and state are competing—and at times mutually destructive—logics precisely because all three concepts entail some legitimate values which are worth aspiring to but which can be reconciled only if there is an effort to mitigate the competing logics. Our case studies suggest that in multinational or multicultural societies the prospects of democratic consolidation can be greatly enhanced through the fostering of complementary multiple political identities, such as those in Catalonia, rather than exclusionary identities, such as those in Estonia and many of the former states of the Soviet Union and Yugoslavia. In Estonia (as well as in Latvia and several other post-Soviet republics), the logic of the nation-state in a territory that is de facto multinational has weakened democracy in three critical ways: it has decreased the diffuse loyalty towards the institutions of the new state among the minority population; it has made the roles of many of the important, proindependence, prodemocracy leaders of the Russian minority marginal or indifferent; and it has stimulated extreme irridentist nationalists in Russia to claim that the Russian "homeland" must protect its fellow nationals in Estonia. And the manner in which the violent dissolution of Yugoslavia and parts of the Soviet Union has precluded democratization, let alone democratic consolidation, need not be elaborated upon here.

The structuring of political institutions and the sequence of elections have a pronounced impact on the development of national political identities. Despite the frequently used language about "fixed" and "primordial" identities, the identities of individuals and peoples can be multiple and they frequently change. It is the possibility of such multiple identities that makes life in a multinational democracy possible. A political and legal structure that gives some guarantees to the state's different nationalities helps to foster such orientations, as do institutional arrangements (perhaps of a consociational nature) that allow cultural minorities to express themselves and to feel at home in the state.

Apart from their impact on stateness problems, we believe that political institutions can have an important independent impact on the courses of transition and consolidation. This is particularly true with regard to the choice of presidential versus parliamentary or semipresidential forms of government as metainstitutional frameworks. We have argued elsewhere that the parliamentary organizational form gives the political system significant advantages over presidentialism in terms of three capacities useful for democratic consolidation: efficacy, consensus creation, and the ability to terminate a crisis of government without its becoming a crisis of the regime.[86] That the new democracies in Southern Europe did not choose U.S.-style presidentialism in our judgment increased their degrees of freedom in confronting crises. In Spain, parliamentarism allowed Suárez, when he had exhausted his support, to step down; it allowed his successor, Calvo Sotelo, to lead the efforts to jail the coup makers; and it allowed the early calling of elections, which led to the Socialists assuming power. In Greece, the parliamentary framework allowed the formal coalition of New Democracy and the communists. In Portugal, the semipresidential framework allowed a military president and an increasingly powerful civilian prime minister to coexist. None of this would have been possible in a pure presidential system.

Conversely, all Southern Cone countries have adopted presidential systems. And in all cases, this has created problems. In Brazil, the "accidental" president, José Sarney, served five years and helped block the constituent assembly's choice of parliamentarism; he often relied upon military power. In Argentina, the presidential format blocked any possibility in 1984–85 for the then-popular President Alfonsín to win a majority; and it later "forced" an unpopular President Alfonsín to continue ruling in 1987–88, after he had been defeated in congressional elections. In Uruguay, the first two civilian presidents have been minority presidents. The weak incentives in presidentialism for coalitions make effective coalition government difficult. In Chile, the effective coalition of the opposition in 1988–89 would have been threatened by the run-up to presidential elections in 1993 were it not for the renewal of the *Concertación* agreement. This, however, deprives supporters of the various allied parties of the choice of the candidate closest to them.

Similarly, none of the European postcommunist cases except Hungary (which progressed the fastest towards democratic consolidation) initially adopted a purely parliamentary form of government. Poland opted for semipresidentialism, but democratic consolidation in Poland was initially impeded by adoption of an electoral law that led to an extremely fragmented party system (leading in turn to high levels of cabinet instability and a collapse of public support for political parties). This gave rise to great uncertainty and political conflict, since the government was effectively controlled neither by the legislature (given its partisan fragmentation) nor the president (given his occasionally aggressive interventions in governmental decision making combined with his absence of party ties). This odd version of semipresidentialism has contributed to both governmental deadlock and periodic constitutional crises which delay democratic consolidation. The 1993 shift to an electoral law with a high threshold for parliamentary representation (5 percent for individual parties and 8 percent for electoral coalitions) might have eliminated this deadlock, but since it was not accompanied by a change in behavior by most parties, it led to an unusual and unanticipated situation—the two postcommunist parties, which received 35 percent of the popular vote, won two-thirds of the parliamentary seats.

We believe that these institutional features, which have been given scant attention in the literature on democratic transtions, are deserving of further analysis.

4 Democratic Consolidation and the Military in Southern Europe and South America

Felipe Agüero

With the inauguration of Chilean president Patricio Aylwin in March 1990, all acting presidents and most of the legislatures in South America had been elected in open, competitive elections—a remarkable accomplishment for the region. Although these transitions were hailed with little of the international glamour and recognition that initially accompanied the dismantling of the communist regimes in Eastern Europe, the South American countries nonetheless enthusiastically went along with the seemingly unstoppable wave of democratization which had started in Southern Europe in the 1970s.

Democratization, however, advanced unevenly. Whereas the new Southern European democracies became consolidated, many of the new regimes in Latin America are not fully democratic. Critical among the factors that have influenced this unequal development are the differences in limits to democratization set by the militaries and the variation in powers and capabilities which democratizing elites have exhibited to overcome those limits.[1] This chapter addresses the military component in the processes of political democratization, comparing the consolidation of democracy in Southern Europe and the uncertainties facing the postmilitary regimes of South America in their attempts to reach democratic consolidation. This comparison will identify the nature and manifestation of the military problem in these processes and the ways in which it has influenced various outcomes.

This chapter first examines the differences in the extent to which the military in these countries has retreated from political involvement and submitted itself to civilian control. It then explains these differences, focusing on the initial conditions surrounding the transitions to democracy. I argue that whether the outgoing authoritarian regime was militarized or civilianized affects the ability of the military to influence the transition and subsequently to create advantageous conditions for itself, erecting obstacles for the advancement of civilian supremacy. A classification of democratic transitions, based on the previous distinctions, is offered to help differentiate transition trajectories. Lastly, the chapter highlights the notion of a posttransition process and identifies several factors within it which affect the prospects for attaining civilian supremacy, such as the level of support for successor governments, international variables, and the timing and pace of implementation of military reforms. It is necessary to start, however, with a consideration of the way in which the military dimension ought to be included in the concept of democratic consolidation.

The Quest for Civilian Supremacy

In fully consolidated democracies the military is socialized, along with the entire polity, to accept the superiority of democratic institutions and procedures. In new democracies, where militaries only yesterday were the backbone of authoritarianism, no such socialization takes place and the military tends to hold on to an ideological identification with the past.[2] This absence of conversion may make democratization a more strenuous process, but it is not an insurmountable obstacle. Changes in the content of socialization are helpful and indeed critical for democratic persistence in the long run, but they are not really essential for the consolidation of nascent democracies. Early demands for democratic indoctrination place the cart before the horse and may in fact trouble the military's practical acquiescence to democratization by unnecessarily sparking conflict with its prevailing ideological tenets and world views.

The case of Spain exemplifies well the possibility of democratic advancement without prior changes in the military's socialization. Democracy in Spain has been consolidated despite the fact that, were one to judge from the profusion of pictures of Franco hanging prominently on walls in army facilities across the country, there was until recently much nostalgia for the values and norms of the authoritarian past. But, insofar as the military remained within well-bounded spheres of competence and did not interfere with political decisions by civilian officials, Franquist nostalgia among the armed forces was not a forbidding impediment to democratization. Here as elsewhere, the "presence or absence of preferable alternatives" seems to have played a more important role in the military's acquiescence to democratization than subjective agreement with democratic norms.[3]

Critical to the military's perception of alternatives to democratization is the behavior of influential elites. If important segments of these elites signal that they would still welcome some kind of military participation in politics, full military acquiescence to democratization will be discouraged; but if all major political elites ostensibly renounce the use of violence and reject the possibility of appealing to the military to pursue their interests, the military is not only relieved from hard-to-bear outside pressure but it is also deprived of the conditions which would justify a counter-democratization stratagem. Thus, elite unity in support of democracy is an important factor in the promotion of military acquiescence to democratization.[4]

However, even if this unity helps to discourage contestation from within the ranks, it cannot fully guarantee military acquiescence. In post-1976 Spain and Portugal and in post-1959 Venezuela, for example, unity among civilian elites was not sufficient to prevent significant military challenges to democratization.[5] As long as the military continues to challenge democratization, democracy cannot be deemed to be fully consolidated, even if the crucial proviso of elite unity among civilians places it within short reach of that goal. This unity has to be supplemented with provisions that specifically apply to the military and which, I submit, refer to the attainment of *civilian supremacy*. This is the point at which, in regard to the military, and using Di Palma's expression, democrats can really begin to relax.[6]

Civilian supremacy is reached through a process consisting, first, of the removal of the military from powerful positions outside the defense area and, second, of the appointment and acknowledgment of civilian political superiors in the defense and military areas. Civilian supremacy is finally attained when the military does not interfere with the ability of a civilian, democratically elected government to conduct general policy, and actually accepts it as a prerogative of this government to define the goals and general organization of national defense, to formulate and conduct defense policy, and to monitor the implementation of military policy. In short, as the military withdraws from policy areas not related to defense, civilian officials gain authority in all policy areas, including defense. Obviously, as the very definition of the boundaries between strictly military and nonmilitary areas is controversial, the assertion of civilian supremacy entails the acceptance of spheres of competence as defined by legitimate civilian authorities, and which in practice involve a reduction, but by no means an elimination, of the military's sphere of autonomous action.[7]

This definition, in fact, is little more than a specification for a particular domain of widely accepted, minimal procedural definitions of democracy. It helps to highlight a critical area of government policy which definitions of democracy submit to democratic accountability only implicitly by, for instance, postulating that "institutions for making government policies depend on votes or other expressions of preference."[8] In democracies, elected individuals fill major political offices and exercise the powers assigned to those offices. Armed forces, which hold the monopoly of a society's coercive power, form the core of the state's security apparatus and, as a major bureaucracy, constitute a substantial part of the state's administration. It would thus be untenable for a working procedural definition of democracy not to explicitly include the military as subject to the policies formulated by elected individuals holding the highest state offices. Our definition of civilian supremacy highlights the critical position of the military in facilitating or hindering movement toward a situation where the standards of procedural democracy are met.

Civilian supremacy involves the restriction of military roles to assistance in the formulation and implementation of national defense policy. It also involves acceptance of government decisions in areas which, although customary in long-established democracies, are rather sensitive in new democracies, because they entail a new delineation of prerogatives. These decisions may, for instance, affect areas as critical as the defense budget and the size of armed forces, or the promotion of officers to the most senior grades and posts. The transfer of prerogatives in these areas takes place more or less gradually during or, more often, after the transition. Civilian supremacy is unlikely to be asserted in one blow and does not necessarily come by civilian imposition; it may well develop through a process in which the military confines itself to a role more restricted to professional matters. Decisions leading to civilian supremacy generally involve more or less overt civil-military negotiations or a tacit bargaining process, before the extent and shape of military participation under the new arrangements are more permanently defined. It should be underscored that, in successful cases, these arrangements balance the expansion of civilian prerogatives with the establishment of appropriate avenues for the expression of professional concerns by the military, and instill confidence in the military that its core institutional interests are being reasonably accommodated.

In successful new democracies, these changes develop gradually into a situation in which the level of attainment of civilian supremacy is roughly comparable to that found in older, long-established democracies. Although this situation is not attained overnight but rather gradually, the analyst should still be able to determine the point at which the new situation has emerged. Useful indicators of this condition include the formalization of the new allocation of prerogatives in the constitution, in major pieces of legislation, and in adequate decision-making structures, *and* the absence of overt challenges by the military to the repeated exercise of civilian prerogatives in both general and defense-related policy areas.[9] Before undertaking a review of the extent to which civilian supremacy has been attained in the new democracies of Southern Europe and South America, it is important to briefly introduce these cases in the context of the transition paths they followed toward democratization.

Transition Paths

It should be recalled that the rather abrupt end of the authoritarian regimes of Portugal, Greece, and Argentina placed these countries in the distinct category of transition triggered by collapse.[10] In Portugal, a coup staged by junior officers in 1974 ended with the long-lasting Salazar-Caetano regime and inaugurated a revolutionary military government which, not without significant tensions, opened the way to a government of moderate, democratically elected civilians. In Greece, the shorter-lived colonels' regime collapsed in embarrassment, also in 1974, under the weight of the fiasco of its Cyprus adventure, leading overnight to the transfer of power to civilians and the prompt restoration of democratic politics with the election of parliament and the approval of a new constitution. In Argentina, the military junta inaugurated in 1976 collapsed in 1982 in the face of disarray among its own forces and the anger of a mobilized public after military defeat by England in the Falklands/Malvinas War. The military transferred power to elected civilians in 1983.

The other cases followed a more gradual process, and they differed with regard to the pace at which the transition proceeded and the extent to which its dynamics came more from elites within the regime or from the interaction between those elites and mass mobilization. In all of them, however, the transition was made possible through more or less explicit agreements for the transfer of power between ruling and opposition elites. For instance, the Spanish transition, described as "reforma-ruptura pactada" or "transition through transaction,"[11] stood out for the success with which reforms initiated by Franquist elites culminated in a clean break with the authoritarian past, leading to the unequivocal inauguration of democratic institutions with the approval of the Constitution in 1978, three years after Franco's death.

In South America, with the exception of Argentina, the transitions also were regime-led and, to varying degrees, negotiated. Brazil's military-authoritarian regime, established in 1964, initiated a protracted liberalization under Geisel's administration in 1975 which, overcoming numerous roadblocks and following intense elite negotiation, resulted in the indirect election of an opposition figure to the presidency in 1985. The death of President-elect Tancredo Neves, however, left the government in the hands of old allies of the preceding authoritarian regime. Only in 1990, and under a new constitution, was the presidency transferred to a democratically elected civilian. In Uruguay, the military regime installed in 1973 attempted in 1980 to institutionalize itself by submitting to referendum a constitution which would have established a *democradura*. Defeat at the polls led to the protracted planning of military extrication, facilitated by a civil-military pact and the subsequent holding of elections in 1984. In Peru, the revolutionary government of the armed forces, headed by General Velasco Alvarado since the coup of 1968, changed leadership and course in 1975 to face mounting opposition and worsening economic conditions. Widespread popular discontent led the new government of General Morales Bermúdez to initiate a gradual extrication process which included the election of a constituent assembly in 1978. In agreement with the Alianza Popular Revolucionaria Americana (APRA), the military oversaw the constituent process, which ended in 1980 with the passing of a new constitution and the election of a civilian president. A similar process took place in Ecuador, where a renewed military junta, first established in 1972, initiated a negotiated transition in 1977. This process included a plebiscite for a new constitution in 1978 before power was turned over to elected civilians in 1979. In Chile, elites from the regime and the opposition negotiated partial reforms of the authoritarian constitution of 1980, following Pinochet's defeat in the 1988 plebiscite that frustrated his attempt to institutionalize a *democradura*. These negotiations allowed for the successful holding of competitive elections for president and Congress in 1989 and the ascent to government of civilian, democratically elected authorities in 1990. In Paraguay, the authoritarian party (the Colorado Party) remained in control after the ouster of General Alfredo Stroessner in 1989 and, under the leadership of successor president General Andrés Rodríguez, commanded a substantial majority in the freely elected constitutional convention of 1992. As we shall elaborate below, the South American cases distinguish themselves for the tremendous influence wielded by the military during the negotiated transitions.[12]

Civilian Supremacy and the Military in South American and Southern European Democracies

The new Southern European democracies have clearly been the most successful. Greece has faced no challenges from its military since consolidation of its democratic regime in the early 1980s, and Portugal, whose democracy remained incomplete as a result of military tutelage until the constitutional reforms of 1982, has since achieved civilian supremacy. In Spain, military contestation remained a threat until 1982, but a relatively tranquil context has since prevailed, allowing for the promotion of significant military reforms by civilian officials. These cases stand in sharp contrast with the difficulties which faced civilian governments in the new Latin American democracies, caused by militaries inimical to the assertion of civilian power.

Greece, Portugal, and Spain

In Greece, the collapse of the colonels' regime allowed the new Karamanlis government to swiftly establish a firm grip over the armed forces. This control was further facilitated by the substantial electoral support obtained by the governing party in 1974, by the referendum that same year against the reinstatement of the monarchy (which in the past had played an active and mostly deleterious role in civil-military relations), and by the subsequent enactment of a new constitution. Although the military contested the government's legalization of the Communist Party, its redeployment of large regiments away from Athens, and the reincorporation into the army of officers who had been dismissed by the junta, the Karamanlis government prevailed. The government also had to face subversive plots by army officers in 1975, which led it to dismiss several hundred officers and to transfer several others to different posts. Also in 1975, the former junta chiefs, whom the government had taken to court with charges of insurrection and high treason, were sentenced to life imprisonment. Although manifestations of discontent would still surface at later stages, no major domestic military challenges took place in Greece beyond this year.[13]

A decisive step towards civilian supremacy was a government act passed in 1977 which reorganized the command structure of the armed forces by eliminating the post of chief of the armed forces, conceived by the junta as a permanent buffer between the military and a future civilian government. The Supreme Council of National Defense was created to assume responsibility for defense policy and for the top appointments in the military. With the creation of the council, consisting of the prime minister and five cabinet members in addition to the chief of defense staff, the government affirmed the direct subordination of the armed services to civilian authority.[14]

Socialist leader Andreas Papandreou, with whom the military had a history of hostilities prior to the dictatorship, was elected to head the government in 1981. Papandreou decided to deflect any military concerns by directly assuming the defense portfolio and promoting a foreign policy with nationalist overtones which would give him support in the armed forces. This government promoted reforms which challenged the lack of pluralism and the strong anticommunist rhetoric in military academies, which had persisted since the civil war of the late 1940s. In the same vein, the government granted general amnesty to individuals who had fought on the side of the Communists in the civil war, and it eliminated the requirement of background investigations for eligibility to enter the military. These policies provided an opportunity for the expression of dissent and opposition from military circles, but the government prevailed in carrying out the policies, proving its supremacy.[15]

In Portugal, the constitutional revisions of 1982 eliminated the tutelage which the military had held over democratic politics since the overthrow of Caetano, and the principles of civilian control were unequivocally asserted in the Armed Forces and National Defense Law. Both the Council of the Revolution, with its broad prerogatives, and the Armed Forces Movement were dismantled; and the powers of the president, the assembly, and the government were clearly defined. The new High National Defense Council, with a majority of civilians (including the president, the prime minister, and representatives of Congress), was charged with the final approval of military promotions. In order to prevent partisanship in the military and to guarantee its control by civilian powers, the armed forces were placed under the supreme command of the president and the government was given political authority over military and defense policy. The president and the prime minister were, in practice, left to share in the power of appointment of the chiefs of staff, but the cabinet's leading role was enhanced by the incorporation of the armed services into the structure of the Ministry of Defense.[16]

Although the constitutional changes and legislation of 1982 ended military tutelage and provided the formal framework for the advancement of civilian supremacy, effective implementation was quite slow.

The chiefs of staff of the armed services maintained substantial leverage while the effective leadership of the ministry was hardly visible. Also, military officers in Portugal remained much more outspoken about internal political matters than officers anywhere else in Southern Europe. It has been only very recently, a decade after the 1982 reforms, that the defense ministry has started significantly to promote its institutional strengthening, along lines similar to those developed earlier in Spain, and to enhance its capacity to formulate policy and effectively advance military reform and modernization.[17]

In Spain, the first major challenge by the military to civilian authority concerned legalization of the Communist Party in 1977. The government successfully overcame this challenge, but numerous episodes of army undiscipline and protest, aimed especially at government policies on terrorism and the *autonomías,* continued to cloud the army's allegiance to the nascent democracy. The most spectacular episode was, of course, the coup attempt of February 1981, which failed, as a result of the king's resolute stance, the bickering and divisions among the rebels and discontented militaries, and its rejection by all major political sectors. A year and a half later, the putsch that had been uncovered just before the 1982 general elections that brought the Socialists to power was the last visible expression of forceful military opposition in Spain. Military discontent, of which there has been much, has since been channeled through regular procedures and has concentrated around internal military issues rather than broader political concerns. In the past few years, discontent has surfaced only in reaction to the perseverance of military reforms that undermined previous individual and institutional privileges.

These reforms were made possible by the empowerment of civilian authorities with well-defined prerogatives in the conduct of defense and military policy. A special organic law enacted in 1984 ended the ambiguity of previous legislation and significantly empowered the minister of defense and the ministry's agencies to formulate, implement, and monitor policy. The restructuring of the ministry in 1977 and the 1989 law on professional military personnel further expanded civilian prerogatives, streamlined force structures, and modernized the general organization of defense. The government was able gradually to overcome corporate military resistance, which has consisted only of the bureaucratic infighting not uncharacteristic of advanced democracies with large military establishments. The last major issue which pitted the army against the government was smoothly resolved with the 1986 decision to grant former members of the Unión Militar Democrática, the clandestine organization of junior army officers that functioned during the end of Franquism, the option to reenter active service. The government's success in modernizing the central organization and forces of defense, as well as in redefining the mission of the armed services, was made easier by the cooperation it was able to obtain from the most professionally oriented segments in the military.[18]

All the Southern European democracies have secured civilian supremacy. Greece had the least difficulty doing so, whereas Portugal was the slowest to attain this status. Spain achieved a cleaner democratic break with the past and settled its military problem earlier and more thoroughly than did Portugal. Spain thus stood closer to Greece, albeit from quite a different transition trajectory.[19] The connections between outcomes and initial transition paths will be analyzed below.

South America

The regimes which emerged in South America after the demise of authoritarianism have been less successful in the promotion of civilian supremacy.[20] Under a combination of legally formalized and de facto arrangements which vary across countries, the military has entrenched itself to secure the protection of prerogatives acquired during authoritarian rule, and continues to exert undue influence over civilian institutions and the political process. The resulting situation, varying from place to place, has civilian authorities formally reigning over government and the administration but actually facing significant constraints in many policy areas as a result of overlapping prerogatives, or the more or less overt fear of military retaliation.

The situation in Argentina following the resumption of democracy in 1983 is a good example of a government that empowered itself with prerogatives from the preauthoritarian order and with new ones but which in practice failed in numerous instances to impose its authority over an unyielding military. The administration of President Raúl Alfonsín (1983–89) passed legislation that redefined the military mission, reassigned prerogatives, restructured the central organization of defense, and increased the number of civilians in charge of defense agencies. These reforms were enacted, along with initially impressive attempts to substantially reduce military expenditures and force levels and to hold the military accountable for past crimes—leading to the incarceration of former junta leaders, a feat unprecedented in Latin America. Halfway through the Alfonsín administration, however, the military gradually reasserted its power by reacting against budget cuts, organizational reform, the "hostile media," and legal actions against hundreds of officers for human rights offenses, all of which were seen as part of a concerted "attack." In retaliation, middle-level officers staged a series of revolts against both government policy and "weak" senior military leaders. President Alfonsín yielded to demands of the rebels by submitting a bill—*ley de punto final*—which set a deadline for the initiation of judicial action against military officers, limiting the number of such actions, and then another bill—*ley de obediencia debida*—which restricted responsibility for human rights crimes to only senior officers, relieving hundreds of officers from court action.[21]

The partial success of the revolts weakened government leadership and encouraged army factions to seek further concessions. In fact, President Carlos Menem, seeking to appease military discontent, started his term in 1989 by granting pardons to all officers who had participated in military revolts during the Alfonsín administration, as well as to senior officers prosecuted for human rights offenses. Then, in 1990, and against the wishes of public opinion, Menem went much further, to pardon the former junta members sentenced during Alfonsín's term. But in December 1990 the government was surprised by a bloody uprising of several hundred army men, most of them noncommissioned officers. This uprising, however, received no support among commissioned officers, who felt satisfied with the government's recent concessions, and the rebels were swiftly repressed by the army leadership. The failure of this uprising significantly strengthened the government and substantially reduced the chances of a new rebel plot. However, the concessions which led to this situation, the reversal of legislation on military roles in internal security which had been advanced under Alfonsín, and the persistence of numerous internal military problems all imply that Argentina still falls short of the goal of full-fledged civilian supremacy.[22]

In Brazil, the accession of a civilian to the presidency in 1985, for the first time in two decades, did not lead to a reduction of the military's political power. During the five-year term of President José Sarney, the military participated in the administration by having six active-duty officers in the cabinet, controlled their own services and the national intelligence and defense systems, and held an expanded presence in the presidential and general government bureaucracy.[23] The military continued to act on its own initiative in social and political affairs: it mobilized against workers on strike, for example, without any prior instruction from the appropriate civilian officials. The armed forces also organized the country's largest and most efficient lobbying team, with officers assigned full-time to the Congress, in an effort to influence the debate on the new constitution that would replace the authoritarian document of 1967. The team successfully influenced the assembly's deliberations over several important matters: they helped oppose legislation on agrarian reform and played a critical role in defeating proposals in favor of a parliamentary form of government and a move to shorten Sarney's presidential term.[24] Although the 1988 constitution made some progress on clauses dealing with the military, the military remained largely autonomous.

President Fernando Collor de Mello, upon assuming the presidency in 1990, implemented his campaign promise to reduce the number of military ministers. He also appointed a civilian to head National Intelligence and disciplined officers who verbally challenged his authority. Collor also took other steps which would have been unthinkable a few years earlier: he denounced a secret military program to build a nuclear bomb, worked with Argentina to set up a system of international safeguards, and created a reserve in the Amazon for imperiled Yanomami Indians. Despite the visible relative decline in military influence (and budget), however, the military still challenged decisions by elected officials, prevented the substitution of a defense minister for the separate armed services' ministers, and managed to prevent civilian officials from effectively controlling intelligence, nuclear sector planning, and other strategic domains.[25]

In Chile, democratically elected authorities assumed office under a constitution that had originally been devised to perpetuate Pinochet and his authoritarian regime in power. These intentions were thwarted by Pinochet's defeat in the 1988 plebiscite, which led to partial reform of the constitution (agreed upon by the government and the opposition) and paved the way to a viable transition. Before leaving the presidency, however, Pinochet used his constitutional powers to appoint members to the partially elected senate and to other official agencies. The designated senators have played a critical role in hindering reforms in Congress and precluding any chances of major constitutional revisions. The constitution also grants the military a diffuse oversight capacity through the National Security Council, and limits the president's powers to appoint and dismiss military chiefs. General Pinochet, for instance, remains commander in chief of the army and may choose to keep the post until 1998, and the president has no power to remove him. Legislation passed during the final days of the Pinochet regime placed limits on the power of government to significantly affect the military budget or to appoint senior officers and kept military officers immune from judicial action for human rights crimes. The inauguration of elected authorities was also accompanied by a massive transfer to the army of state facilities and resources, in particular, those associated with intelligence activities, greatly empowering the army and withdrawing resources from the new government. During the first years of democratic government, however, officials were able to affirm some civilian prerogatives and to fend off disgruntled noncompliance by Pinochet, although significant reforms remained conditioned by the requirement of securing, as demanded by the constitution, a large congressional majority, which the government simply has not been able to do.[26]

In Peru, democracy was officially established by a new constitution, approved in 1980 by an assembly which, although under military supervision, had been freely elected in 1978. The cohesion of APRA and the plurality it held in the assembly led the military to reconcile with its old foe. It entered into agreements that secured a smooth transfer of power following the two-year coexistence of a military government with an elected assembly whose jurisdiction was restricted to constitution making. Under the skillful leadership of the octogenarian APRA helmsman, Víctor Raúl Haya de la Torre, the assembly managed to resist many pressures from the military, maintain its independence, and produce a democratic constitution, while simultaneously letting the military govern.[27]

The 1980 presidential elections favored Fernando Belaúnde, the former president whom the military had overthrown in 1968. This time he made sure that he would preside over a peaceful coexistence, by keeping the military appeased, respecting its ample sphere of autonomy, and rewarding it with a generous increase in military expenditures. Civil-military relations were clouded, however, by the dramatic escalation of violence by the subversive Sendero Luminoso. The role assumed by the army in countersubversion highlighted the significant emergency powers that the military had secured through laws passed in the final days of the military government. These powers were further expanded in 1985 with the creation of political-military commands in geographical areas placed under states of emergency. In these areas, the military's control was total and was not politically accountable. Violations of human rights skyrocketed during this period; in contrast to the other South American cases, in Peru they became pervasive and highly visible only after the termination of military-authoritarian rule.[28]

President Alan García (1985–90) attempted to restrain military autonomy and enforce presidential prerogatives over the armed forces. His strategy included creating a ministry of defense—a move supported by the army but strongly opposed by the air force, whose chiefs staged a mutinous mobilization when, after several postponements, the ministry was actually created. Confirming the fears of the air force, the new ministry was placed under the control of an army general instead of a civilian. The escalation of Sendero Luminoso's war, entangled with the problems of narcotics traffic, massive violations of human rights, and the loss of legitimacy of the national government, rendered ineffectual the efforts to enhance civilian control.[29] Finally, President Fujimori's unconstitutional coup against Congress and the parties in February, 1992, supported by the military, moved this country further away from the chances of building a stable democratic regime.

Uruguay has been more successful in restoring traditional civilian prerogatives but had first to overcome major roadblocks. During the civil-military negotiations of the Naval Club Pact, which opened the way to the first democratic elections in 1984, the military demanded that special prerogatives be incorporated in the constitution. After the inauguration of democracy, however, these demands were given no serious consideration, and President Julio María Sanguinetti (1985–90) succeeded in bringing civil-military relations closer to traditional patterns of civilian control in Uruguay. Then, in an event rare in Latin America, President Luis Alberto Lacalle (1990–) appointed new service commanders in the navy and the air force against the preferences of top military commanders.[30] The military, nonetheless, retained autonomy in most internal matters and succeeded in removing defense intelligence from the direct control of the new civilian minister of defense. Later, with the appointment of former junta chief General Hugo Medina as defense minister, the ministry itself became more of a buffer between military and civilian authorities than the government's instrument for the conduct of military policy.

The most sensitive issue facing the ministry involved past human rights violations. In dealing with these matters, Minister Medina overtly assumed the role of protector of the armed forces and, in open defiance of judicial authority, instructed military officers not to appear in court in the case of crimes committed during the dictatorship. The situation forced President Sanguinetti to urge Congress to approve the Ley de Caducidad, which in practice granted amnesty to human rights violators. Opponents of the amnesty, invoking a clause in the constitution, succeeded in collecting the required number of signatures (one fourth of the electorate) to call a national referendum. They were defeated, however, in the referendum held in 1989, and the Ley de Caducidad was upheld. The dark spots related to human rights violations, military pressures for the law that exempted officers from legal responsibility, and military concern with domestic political dynamics separate this case from the successful European cases. However, the referendum may well have laid to rest the most touchy issue in civil-military relations and opened the way for a normalization and gradual progress in civilian control.[31]

Explaining the Differences

In Greece, Spain, and Portugal, the military is confined to its specific professional duties in national defense, and defense and military policy are conducted and monitored by the civilians in charge of defense ministries. In the new South American democracies, in contrast, the military, often under the guise of civilian leadership, conducts its own business with little or no outside civilian monitoring and intrudes into the domains of politicians, judges, and elected officials, exerting undue influence in policy areas outside of defense. Can these differences be attributed to the fact that the Southern European transitions started earlier than those in South America and that they have therefore had more time to develop the conditions and instruments of civilian control? Could one speculate that the South American cases will be able to achieve similar levels of success after comparable periods of time?

Democracies obviously take time to consolidate. One could not argue, for instance, that civilian supremacy and democratic consolidation had been attained in Spain by 1981, in the midst of military turmoil and rebellion, six years after Franco's death. It is true, as Gunther has argued, that, with the exception of Basque nationalists, all major civilian elites fully supported the regime and that high levels of elite consensus had developed through intense negotiations between 1977 and 1979. Substantial progress had thus been made toward democratic consolidation.[32] The 1981 coup attempt and other important episodes in the following months, however, revealed that a substantial portion of the military remained outside this elite consensus and still sought alternatives to the existing democratic regime. It was not until after the failure of the coup attempt and the subsequent public discrediting of the plotters that the military began to give unambiguous allegiance to the democratic regime. The critical turning point, in my view, did not in fact come until 1982, when the military as a whole came to realize, gradually but steadily, that there were absolutely no possibilities for the advancement of personal, professional, or institutional interests outside the democratic regime.

If democratic consolidation was not achieved in Spain until approximately seven years after the death of Franco, and if in Portugal the critical turning point did not occur until the constitutional reforms of

1982, then it is certainly not inconceivable that the South American cases which initiated the transition later may succeed in due time. This is especially so in regard to civilian supremacy, the effective implementation of which in Spain and Portugal took even longer than consolidation.[33] The hope that time will bring success also in South America should be tempered by recognition that the oldest new democracies in South America (Argentina, and Peru before the recent constitutional breakdown) have had elected governments for at least eight consecutive years—as much time as the Southern European countries required to achieve consolidation. Yet, it is not time differences per se which shape the likelihood of civilian supremacy and democratic consolidation but, rather, the particular conditions surrounding the processes of democratization in these two regions.

Differences in initial conditions, such as the extent of military control of the transition, affect the subsequent power relations between civilians and the armed forces, greatly influencing the chances of the successful advancement of democratization and civilian supremacy after the transition to democracy is completed. The extent of military control of the transition is, in turn, largely determined by the previous position of the military in the outgoing authoritarian regime and by the specific nature of the transition path. Relative civilian-military empowerment, and the chances of civilian officials' advancing their control, are also affected by a diverse set of variables, such as international factors, the legitimacy of successor governments, and policies and strategies in the area of civil-military relations in the posttransition process.

The unity of civilian elites in support of democracy, as noted above, also is a critical factor. In the Southern European cases, such unity made it easier for civilian governments to overcome military obstacles to democratization. In the new South American democracies, with the exception of Uruguay, elite unification has thus far remained rather elusive.[34] Another factor that critically affects the prospects for civilian supremacy is the extent of vertical and horizontal unity of the armed forces. A military strongly unified around a well-defined counter-democratization scheme will enhance its ability to influence the transition agenda and will impede the work of civilian democratizers. In most cases, however, the military is likely to be riven by various vertical or horizontal fissures which, depending on their nature and depth, may favorably or negatively affect the chances of promoting civilian supremacy. A systematic analysis of these different conditions for consolidation is beyond the scope of this chapter, however, and they will be touched upon only in the context of specific arguments.

Civilian versus Military Control of the Transition

Transition to democracy opens up an uncertain future to all participants. They will strive to reduce this uncertainty by trying to influence the amount and direction of change and—the military in particular—by protecting their own corporate interests and boundaries from "outside intrusion." The capacity of the military to exert effective influence and to maintain its prerogatives throughout the transition is affected by the position it held in the outgoing regime.

In cases where the military occupied the core leadership positions of the exiting authoritarian regime (i.e., in militarized regimes) the military was in a better position to set or significantly influence the transition agenda and to impose protective preconditions. Conversely, where the outgoing authoritarian regime was led by civilians, the military found it harder to significantly influence the agenda and to steer change in directions closer to its own preferences. In the latter case, moves toward democratization could be pursued swiftly and more thoroughly by civilian democratizing elites. What were the consequences for the unfolding of transition of variations in the position of the military in the departing authoritarian regimes under consideration here?[35]

Franco's authoritarian regime in Spain was clearly civilianized. Although the military participated in the council of ministers and other institutions of Franquism, such as the Cortes and the Council of the Realm, this participation was restricted and did not represent the military-as-institution. Franco had been appointed chief of the government by a collective body of army generals at the beginning of the civil war, but, with the exception of an attempt in 1943 to remind him of the origins of his power, no major government policy decisions during Franquism were undertaken by an ensemble of generals. Rather, critical and ordinary policy decisions were adopted by Franco personally or by civilian appointees.[36] Franco's power and Franquist institutions were eventually formalized in the Leyes Fundamentales, which gave the military no prerogatives in legislation or in the critical issue of succession, which Franco reserved for himself.

The military's position was quite different in the militarized authoritarian regimes of South America. Despite important differences in the extent and mechanisms through which it appeared, military participation reached high levels in all these regimes. These high levels were not necessarily related to, or derived from, military predominance in the most visible government positions. In Uruguay, for instance, all but one cabinet position were assigned to civilians, including the defense portfolio. In contrast, Peru had an all-military cabinet during the 1968–75 period, and only two civilians served as ministers (of foreign affairs and the economy) between 1975 and 1980. These differences notwithstanding, both the Uruguayan and Peruvian regimes were held under equally tight military control. In Peru, General Velasco Alvarado relied on a small clique of army generals, while his successor, General Morales Bermúdez, brought the junta more actively into the government. In Uruguay, behind the civilian cabinet, the military developed an elaborate mechanism for collegial participation via a military assembly and an advisory committee for political affairs. In these cases, as in Argentina, the military junta retained ultimate power over legislation, the constitution, and the appointment and removal of the president.

The Brazilian authoritarian regime was also militarized, although the mechanisms for military participation were less formalized and the legislative role was performed by a limited but functioning congress. Beginning with the Geisel presidency, the executive became more independent of the military, but the army still decisively influenced the selection of the president, who was, until 1985, recruited from a group of presidential hopefuls within the army. The military also influenced policy decisively, through its pervasive presence in state bureaucracy and its control of powerful intelligence agencies.

In Chile, power was extremely personalized around the figure of General Pinochet, who simultaneously held the positions of president of the nation and commander in chief of the army during the entire authoritarian period. This, however, did not preclude high levels of military participation, especially by the army, in critical regional and central administrative posts and, particularly, in the presidential staff. And no matter how much Pinochet tried to eclipse the powers of the military junta, the latter maintained legislative and constitutional powers until the very end—powers which it exercised effectively.

The peculiarities of each case notwithstanding, the level of military participation in all the authoritarian regimes of South America was consistently high. This high level of military participation led to significant levels of control or influence over the pace and agenda of the transitions. In Ecuador and Uruguay, for instance, the military conditioned the election of new authorities by preventing popular leaders from running as candidates; and in Brazil, the military resolutely opposed holding direct presidential elections. In Ecuador the military also controlled the submission of constitutions to referendum, and in Peru the government of General Morales closely monitored the constitutional assembly. In Chile, the transition proceeded according to the amended authoritarian constitution of Augusto Pinochet and by party and electoral laws drafted by the junta. Aside from these schemes to influence the general political outcomes of the transitions, the militaries also were able in all these cases to formalize extended prerogatives and protective preconditions for themselves. Even the Argentine military, collapsed from defeat and protest, managed to preside over a year-long transition, to grant itself amnesty and to engage in deals with Peronists in the expectation that they would win the presidential election. Often, the results of these machinations were far from what the militaries had worked for, a situation which illustrates the limits of political engineering by discredited authoritarian regimes.[37] The militaries did succeed, nonetheless, in establishing prerogatives for themselves and restraining legacies to the successor democracies.

In Spain, on the contrary, the transition was conceived and its core aspects implemented without direct military input and often without prior knowledge by the military.[38] And, while military officers held important positions in the first governments of the monarchy, the military was not part of the core group of decision makers. Many reform decisions made by the government and later by the constituent assembly were offered to the military as *faits accomplis*. The military resented many of the reforms carried out during the transition but was unable to oppose them effectively, or even to steer them in directions closer to its preferences. It could not prevent strongly undesired outcomes such as the negotiations with representatives of "the nationalities" or the inclusion of the Communists in the political system.[39]

The difference between the Spanish and the South American cases is not primarily about degrees of subjective military acquiescence to reforms. In both regions the military was concerned about and feared the uncertainties of the transition; the Spanish military was less prepared to step in and directly influence it than were the South American militaries. The critical difference was the ability of the military to influence the transition, which in turn was influenced by the position of the military in the power structure of the outgoing regime.

Civilian technocrats and policy makers occupied critical positions in the authoritarian regimes of both regions, and the term *militarized regime*, used to characterize the South American authoritarian regimes, does not ignore the participation of this civilian cadre. Rather, the term points to the centrality of the military in the definition of major policy orientations, in the powers of appointment for major posts in the administration, and in executive and legislative roles. The performance of these roles enabled the military to develop the appropriate structures for the managing of expanded responsibilities; these structures included policy advisory committees, communication and information agencies, legislative boards, and other supporting councils, all of which helped to enhance military control when the transition started. In civilianized authoritarian regimes, the military had not developed these structures; so when those transitions started, the military was already habituated to a structure in which policy initiatives came from civilian decision-making units.[40]

The different starting points in which civilians and militaries found themselves in these cases led to different results. In Spain, despite occasionally strong opposition from the military, civilian democratic reformers moved swiftly to accomplish a clean, thorough break with authoritarianism and to inaugurate democratically elected authorities under a new constitution. None of the South American countries managed to confidently inaugurate a fully unencumbered democracy, as the Spaniards did.

The early stages of transitions create new sets of rules, in which the burdens and costs of political action are unevenly distributed. The costs of political action are higher for those who must change the rules in order to participate actively in politics than they are for those who can participate effectively without having to redefine their roles in politics. In Spain, for instance, the military felt uneasy in the new democratic situation, which was far more pluralistic than the military had anticipated. This pluralism opened the way for the development of the national-regional *autonomías* that the military overtly disliked. However, the constitutional and popular legitimacy of the new regime made it very costly for the military to attempt to reverse its subordinate position vis-à-vis civilian authorities in order to limit the extent of the transition.

In South America, on the contrary, the heaviest burdens and highest costs fell on civilian democratic elites, who sought to restrict formal and de facto military prerogatives and thereby, in the process of establishing a new regime, to redefine the political role of the military. In Peru, for instance, it took several years and the crushing of a mutiny by the air force to create a ministry of defense, as the government attempted to reform the structure of military participation inherited from the transition—an attempt which met with only limited success. The Brazilian government's plans for the creation of a ministry of defense were aborted by the military even before they could be debated. In Chile, attempts to empower the government vis-à-vis the military were limited by the requirements of constitutional reform. As these examples indicate, once the transition to democracy has been completed with a particular set of institutional arrangements in place, it becomes onerous for any group to introduce substantial changes. A military which remains in a subordinate position finds it harder to react against the achievements of the transition. Similarly, democratic authorities facing a military which manages to retain substantial prerogatives find it harder to promote new measures to subordinate the military to government control.

The connection established here between position in the previous regime and control of the transition does not hold for transitions triggered by sudden, unanticipated events that drastically alter power relations. These "transitions by collapse," such as those in Greece and Portugal, bring about the abrupt replacement of governing elites.

Like Franco's Spain, Portugal's authoritarian regime was civilianized. Although the Portuguese military had been more restless under the Salazar/Caetano regime than the Spanish military had been under Franco, it had been even less visible in state institutions. This situation was drastically altered by the military coup that swept away the authoritarian regime of Caetano in 1974. The new government was completely dominated by the military, and military presence remained quite high even after the first elections and ratification of the new constitution. This was, in fact, the only case among these Southern European and South American transitions in which democracy was inaugurated with a general (António Ramalho Eanes) elected president who simultaneously maintained the position of chief of the army. Although General Eanes used his position to help gradually subordinate the army, the military in Portugal, as in South America, maintained high levels of control over the transition. But, as the military-controlled transition got started as a result of a coup staged by only a faction within the armed forces, the army was much more divided than in most of the South American transitions—a situation which weakened its political position.

In Greece, the authoritarian regime was distinctly a *colonels'* regime rather than the institutional expression of the armed services' higher leadership. It was—this caveat notwithstanding—a militarized regime like the South American ones. However, the swift removal of its leaders following the Cyprus fiasco facilitated the surrender of power to civilian elites. Once Karamanlis assumed office, the military, as in the case of Spain, held no formal powers to control the ensuing democratization. As noted earlier, Karamanlis faced resistance, opposition and even assassination attempts, but his government set the course and prevailed in all instances. As in Spain, albeit via a very different path, the inauguration of democracy in Greece was more unambiguous and unbridled than in the other cases, to a large extent due to the subordinate position of the military.

Classifying Transitions from Authoritarian Regimes

The most useful typologies of transitions to democracy are described in terms of the forces which initiate or control the transition. Guillermo O'Donnell and Philippe Schmitter, for instance, distinguish between transitions initiated by successful, self-confident regimes, which control the rhythm and scope of liberalization, and transitions initiated by the opposition, which generally occur where the regime has failed.[41] Along similar lines, Alfred Stepan distinguishes transitions "initiated by the wielders of authoritarian power" from those in which "oppositional forces play the major role," and he explicitly distinguishes civilian-led from military-led transitions.[42] Scott Mainwaring, in turn, proposes a typology which focuses on the extent to which the transition process is influenced by the authoritarian regime. At one extreme he places transitions that come about through defeat of an authoritarian regime, in which case ruling elites have little choice but to relinquish office. At the other extreme he places transitions through transaction, in which "the authoritarian government initiates the process of liberalization and remains a decisive actor throughout the transition." Finally, an intermediate category—transition through extrication—comprises situations in which "an authoritarian government . . . is able to negotiate crucial features of the transition, though in a position of less strength than in cases of transition through transaction."[43]

These typologies make useful distinctions, but because they are each based on a single dimension, they generally fail to incorporate critical distinctions such as those emphasized here, and thus they prompt misleading classifications. For instance, focusing only on whether transitions were initiated by successful, self-confident authoritarian governments places the Spanish and Brazilian cases in the same category, which, as Stepan rightly points out, fails to acknowledge the critical differences in the position of military and civilian elites in the authoritarian regimes of these countries.[44] On the other hand, when the role of military institutions in initiating transitions is underscored, cases such as Greece, Portugal, and Peru fall into the same category, which ignores important differences in the role of those militaries during the course of the transition itself.[45]

The classification presented in Table 4.1 combines two dimensions: Mainwaring's distinction of the extent to which elites in the outgoing

Table 4.1 Transitions from Authoritarian Regimes

Nature of Dominant Elite	Extent of Influence by Outgoing Regime, and Type of Transition: Very Low (Collapse)	Intermediate (Extrication)	High (Transaction)
Civilian	Czechoslovakia East Germany Greece Venezuela	Hungary Poland[a]	Bulgaria Romania Soviet Union Spain
Military	Argentina Portugal	Ecuador Peru Uruguay	Brazil Chile Paraguay

Note: This typology and the analysis which accompanies it focus upon that period of the transition between the collapse of the nondemocratic predecessor regime and the inauguration of democratically elected officials.

[a] As Przeworski points out, "except in Poland, the Communist systems of Eastern Europe produced civilian regimes" (Adam Przeworski, *Democracy and the Market: Political and Economic Reforms in Eastern Europe and Latin America* [Cambridge: Cambridge University Press, 1991], p. 74). I nonetheless place Poland among the civilianized regimes, because the military's presence in government and core party agencies had declined towards the regime's end and because the influence of the generals was still exercised within the party. The army's leading organs did not substitute for the party. See Paul G. Lewis, "The Long Goodbye: Party Rule and Political Change in Poland Since Martial Law," *The Journal of Communist Studies* 6, March 1990.

authoritarian regime influence the transition, and the military or civilian character of the elites actually in control during the transition. This classification captures differences which are critical, especially in regard to the military problems of democratic consolidation.

In the cases of collapse, authoritarian rulers were ousted and replaced with new elites, who swiftly initiated the transition. In the cases of transaction, the transition was conducted under the auspices of the authoritarian constitution, enabling authoritarian elites to command high levels of influence over the transition. In the cases in the intermediate category, the authoritarian elites either failed to pass a new authoritarian constitution (Uruguay) or let an elected convention create a new one (Peru; in Ecuador voters were given a choice of two documents). They were thus forced to negotiate with the opposition before the actual transfer of power to a larger extent, or on more substantive issues, than was the case in Spain, Brazil, Chile, or Paraguay. This classification scheme makes it possible to capture important aspects of the elites in control during the transition. There is a crucial difference in this respect between Spain, on one hand, and Brazil and Chile, on the other.

Whereas, in the intermediate cases, the military nature of the elites in control during the transition needs no further elaboration, the classification of cases of collapse does. In Greece and Venezuela (1958–59), military authoritarian rulers were ousted by military coup and new civilian elites took over to guide the transition. In Portugal, a military elite ousted a civilianized authoritarian regime and thus controlled the transition. Argentina was a less clear-cut case. The government was not overthrown, but the military was in such a state of disarray after defeat in the Falklands/Malvinas that the junta virtually ceased to exist for a few months during the transition under President Bignone, a retired army general appointed by the junta. It may be argued that the leaders of the major political parties largely dictated the terms of the transition. However, the fact is that military elites, although severely wounded, remained in power for over a year after the conclusion of the war, conducting initiatives which had enormous consequences for the subsequent resumption of democracy when power was transferred to democratically elected President Alfonsín.[46] Thus, Argentina belongs with Portugal in the category of military-controlled transitions.

This classification improves upon the traditional clustering of Argentina and Greece as cases of collapse simply because of the similarities in the military fiascos—Cyprus and Falklands/Malvinas—that led to the fall of their military regimes. However, while the Greek military swiftly extricated itself from power, giving way to a civilian elite, the Argentine military stayed on for over a year and attempted to create favorable conditions for its withdrawal by granting itself amnesty and trying to strike deals with the Peronists.[47] Admittedly, the military failed on both counts, since the Peronists did not win the presidency as expected and Alfonsín swiftly repealed the self-granted military amnesty. However, by staying in power during the transition and trying to block the future government's actions, the military created a confrontational scenario that demanded costly civilian mobilization by the new administration. Such a confrontational scenario was avoided in Greece by the rapid removal of the colonels from power by the military itself. But in Argentina, actions against military officers for human rights offenses helped the military recover much of its lost power, because the charges aroused internal solidarity against what the military perceived as unfair treatment for its "victory in the countersubversive war." This recovery ultimately forced the government to limit its actions against criminal offenders in the military and even to pardon the former junta chiefs. In Greece, on the contrary, the political clout of the military was systematically weakened, and the junta leaders who were sentenced to prison terms for the crimes of high treason and insurrection remain behind bars. It makes sense, therefore, to place these two cases in different categories.

The table highlights differences among these cases which have affected the transitions' aftermath. The usefulness of this typology is confirmed by the fact that the Southern European and South American cases in the civilian category tended to be more successful in achieving democratic consolidation. This way of viewing transition trajectories suggests that whenever the military secures an important position in government policy making—either as a result of the militarization of the outgoing authoritarian regime or, as in Portugal, as a by-product of the transition, it will complicate the transition to and the consolidation of new democratic regimes. The Portuguese transition, for instance, required eight years (1974–82) before the military was removed from tutelary positions, and then several more for the consolidation of civilian supremacy (1989). In Greece and Spain, the military was put in a position in which it could only react to policies initiated in civilian quarters, and the consolidation of those new regimes underwent a much cleaner process.[48]

So far, we have been concerned with the initial conditions of democratization. However important the early impact of these conditions in shaping the posttransition situation, it is certainly not the sole determinant of success or failure of democratic consolidation. Other actors and background factors become significant as the posttransition process begins to unfold.

The Impact of the Posttransition Process

More often than not, the "military problem" has not been resolved by the time the transition ends. The end of the transition gives birth to a new phase, in which, varying from case to case, the military attempts to maintain initially strong positions, recover from previous losses, redress grievances, resist civilian encroachments, and seek the best possible terms of accommodation in the new situation. Civilian governments, in turn, under varying constraints and with differing abilities, seek to establish new patterns of interaction with the military. The patterns which ultimately take shape could not have been predicted solely on the basis of the initial conditions examined above. Uruguay's progress in reasserting the traditional, preauthoritarian pattern of civil-military relations could not, for instance, have been predicted from the initially powerful position of the military in the transition. In Argentina, the high levels of military contestation of the new democratic administration could hardly have been foreseen from the state of military disarray following the Falklands/Malvinas defeat. In Spain, military contestation following the transition contrasted somewhat surprisingly with the discipline which Franco had successfully inculcated during his reign. These examples point to the presence of other factors and events which appeared later in the process to influence the evolution of civil-military relations.

The new regimes faced unequal burdens in dealing with the military during democratization—burdens which were determined by the features of the first postauthoritarian arrangement institutionalized (or quasi-institutionalized) by the end of the transition. These burdens were heavier in those cases where the military claimed a role in politics that went beyond its responsibility for national defense and where it had managed during the transition to secure these claims with more or less well defined prerogatives (Portugal and most of the South American cases). The burden was relatively lighter in cases where a restricted military role was immediately redefined and enforced (Greece) or where a pattern of military subordination had been previously internalized (Spain). In the former cases, the magnitude of the effort demanded of civilian elites was evidently larger.

The weight of the burden also depended on the legacy inherited from the previous authoritarian regime. A legacy of human rights violations forced many successor governments to adopt mechanisms and policies to redress the claims of victims and their families and to take offenders to court. These issues troubled the relationsbetween governments and the military in Argentina, Chile, and Uruguay, where repression had been especially harsh. In these countries, the government, the judiciary, or civilian nongovernmental organizations were pitted against militaries which refused to acknowledge responsibility for human rights crimes and which felt institutionally threatened by legal actions against individual officers. This situation created animosities and perceptions that embittered civil-military relations and raised the stakes of reforms aimed at the advancement of civilian prerogatives and democratization.

Democratization in Southern Europe was spared these difficulties. Repression under Salazar-Caetano or under the last two decades of Franquism never reached the level of the systematic detention and torture of large numbers of political prisoners which characterized all the South American military regimes with the exception of Peru and Ecuador, or the assassination and disappearance of opponents which took place in Chile and, especially, in Argentina. Spanish memories of atrocities during the civil war and of extreme repression in its aftermath had faded with time and never became an issue during the transition. In Greece, an isolated group of military leaders was swiftly tried for sedition and for the repression of students that had taken place in a specific incident during their tenure, and this helped lay to rest the question of human rights violations. In South America, repression of massive proportions, which had reached its climax only a few years before the transitions to democracy began, made human rights an inevitable and highly emotional political, judicial, and moral issue. With militaries in Argentina, Chile, and Uruguay well entrenched in their corporate defense and unwilling to cooperate by providing information or minimally acknowledging responsibility, the treatment of prior human rights violations inevitably became a major stumbling block in the normalization of relations between civilians and the military.

A Brief Note on the Role of Pacts

Given these burdens, legacies, and grievances, it is relevant to ask whether civilian-military pacts were or could have been helpful. It should first be noted that all-inclusive, purely civilian pacts, as mentioned earlier, contributed to democratic consolidation by making explicit the consensual unity among civilian elites. They also provided predictability for the posttransition scenario. In addition, when pacts succeed in foreclosing the recourse to violence, they have the effect of isolating adventurous military groups from potential civilian allies, as the earlier experience of Venezuela and Colombia has suggested. In Venezuela, all major political forces converged in a general agreement about the transition and government platform—the Pact of Punto Fijo—before the end of authoritarian rule in 1958–59. Pacts of this kind, however, have not taken place in the more recent wave of democratic transitions.

In the absence of broadly based civilian pacts, narrower civil-military pacts have been made, with consequences for democratic consolidation that are much harder to predict. In Uruguay, part of the opposition and the military reached the Naval Club Pact, thereby opening the way for a peaceful transition without subsequently hindering the prospects for further democratic progress. In Peru, there were understandings between APRA and the military which never reached the scope and openness of a pact but which achieved a necessary and difficult military-APRA reconciliation that facilitated the management of the constituent assembly under very strenuous circumstances. In Portugal, agreement between the Armed Forces Movement (MFA) and political parties facilitated the first democratic elections, which led to the new constitution as well as the later revision of the excessive prerogatives which it granted the military.

In Brazil and Chile, military and civilian elites undertook negotiations mediated by third parties, brokered by moderate civilian allies of the military. In these cases, however, the militaries were in positions of strength and consented to little in the way of transfer of prerogatives. In the absence of genuine long-term commitments to commonly defined rules, agreements were conceived with short duration and narrow scope. In Argentina, agreements were rejected by the military because the cost for entering them was deemed too high. For instance, Alfonsín's initial attempt to have top military chiefs tried by their own military courts amounted to the offer of a pact, but the military was unwilling to take it up and opted for a confrontational stance.

In the most successful cases, Spain and Greece, there were no civil-military pacts, and the governments were left with no formal constraints on their subsequent initiatives toward the military. In Spain, for instance, the constituent assembly agreed to a few general statements concerning the military, one of the most important being the postponement of more substantial definitions for subsequent treatment in organic laws. This left future initiatives entirely in the hands of elected civilian representatives. Such was also the case in Greece.

Burdens, legacies, and pacts provided different starting points for the new democracies, which were subsequently affected by a number of other factors in ways more or less favorable for democratic advancement. Below I address some of these factors: the degree of popular support and legitimacy secured by successor governments, the pace and strategies followed in pursuit of military reforms, and international factors.

Legitimacy: Problems of Government Support

The capacity of governments to advance democratic policies regarding the military is strongly affected by their ability to maintain high levels of public support.[49] A military will find it harder to push for nondemocratic prerogatives and to resist government policies when the government is visibly backed by a wide array of electorally strong political forces. Thus, it is critical to the advancement of civilian supremacy that the government, because of popular backing and the unity of the forces supporting it, be able to persuade the military to desist from further opposition.

An important determinant in whether governments can maintain high levels of public support is their success in handling the economy. All the cases considered here were put to severe tests by difficult economic conditions, especially those faced at the time of regime change and during the first years of democratic government. The Southern European democracies, particularly Spain, suffered the consequences of the oil shock in the mid-1970s, declining rates of growth combined with unemployment, increasing social mobilization, and strike activities. The South American democracies suffered the constraints imposed by the debt crisis, which consumed much of their foreign currency earnings and drastically shrank the availability of badly needed external resources. It was often necessary, moreover, to impose highly unpopular stabilization policies to counter internal economic imbalances. Overall, governments in Southern Europe were able to face these difficulties in relatively better conditions.[50] In South America, social demands which had accumulated over time in the context of greater inequality presented stiffer challenges to governments facing much more severe economic constraints.

Juan Linz and Alfred Stepan have pointed out, however, that new democracies are not evaluated solely on the basis of socioeconomic efficacy. They argue, based on the analysis of opinion polls in post-Franco Spain, that democracy can be valued as the best political system even if its socioeconomic efficacy is negatively assessed: "The political perception of desired alternatives has a greater impact on the survival of democratic regimes than economic or social problems *per se*."[51] Memories of atrocities and the lack of liberties under the previous authoritarian regime—they maintain—provide new democracies with the additional capital of public confidence and support.[52] However, it is unclear to what extent this system- or regime-tied capital is actually transferred without losses to specific administrations, especially in the face of extreme economic distress and the perception of government policy failure.

The new Southern European democracies never reached the levels of economic disruption displayed by most of the new South American democracies, where inflation skyrocketed to three-digit levels. Such economic hardship and uncertainty nurture the feeling that governments are not really in control, that they lack a sense of direction, and, essentially, that they cannot be trusted. While the public may still prefer democracy over a return to military rule, extreme economic hardship may lead the public to withdraw its support from the government, leaving it in a weak position vis-à-vis the military. Lacking popular support, incumbents in the presidential systems of South America have been left to sit out the rest of their terms merely awaiting the inevitable electoral defeat that will throw them out of office. In this scenario, governments become incapable of meeting the great challenges posed by the military.[53] The parliamentary systems of government in Southern Europe—which in most cases assure that the government will enjoy majority support in parliament—can avoid the lame duck phenomenon that often afflicts South American presidents.[54]

The cases of Argentina and Peru are quite illustrative of the problems created by weak government support. President Alan García (1985–90), in the second postmilitary administration, started out his term with immense popularity and far-reaching plans. Reversing his predecessor's passive style in military affairs, he pursued reforms to strengthen civilian control and reduced the levels of military spending which Belaúnde (1980–85) had substantially raised. By 1987, however, the situation had dramatically changed. Challenged from within his party and from the left, he embarked on erratic policies which included a nationalization of all major banks, provoking a reaction from the right and further increasing his isolation. The gross domestic product fell abruptly, inflation skyrocketed to over 1,000 percent, and the president's approval rating fell from over 70 percent in June 1987 to below 30 percent in October of that same year, and then to under 10 percent in 1989.[55] Paralyzed by these economic difficulties and lack of popular support, the initially activist president quickly turned into a lame duck, which inhibited the government's ability to solidify civilian control.

In Argentina, President Alfonsín also started out with tremendous popularity and even more far-reaching plans. The government set out to implement unprecedented policies that would subject the military to civilian control, to restructure labor relations, to promote broad constitutional reforms, and even to create a new capital city. The government's initial strength and popular support were ratified later in midterm congressional elections and in a referendum convoked by the president concerning resolution of the Beagle dispute with Chile. However, failure in the battle against inflation and a sharp decline in the standard of living of most Argentines led to electoral defeat in the 1987 congressional elections and further failures in economic policy.[56] Optimistic initial plans had to be shelved, and severe military challenges to presidential authority (which a strongly supported government could eventually have overcome) acquired self-sustained impetus for increased military assertiveness.

In both of these cases, significant sectors of the public found ways to express their preference for democracy whenever a serious threat from the armed forces emerged to challenge it. The calculations made by the military, however, considered not the general regime preferences of the public as much as its own assessment of the strengths and weaknesses of a specific administration and its leader.[57] Leaders and governments with waning support among the elites, the public, and the congress find it difficult to appease discontented militaries or maintain ascendancy over them in conflict-laden posttransition situations.

In Spain, Adolfo Suárez's visible loss of popularity and the steady weakening of his government during 1980 strongly contributed to the arousal of authoritarian illusions among military hardliners, despite the fact that the public expressed a general preference for democracy. The military mood that led to the coup attempt of February 1981 was certainly aided by the declining support for the Suárez government as it confronted high unemployment and terrorist activities and Suárez faced an increasing personal isolation in the power struggle inside his party and a severely stiffened opposition from the Socialists.[58] In Spain, this trend toward weak government was starkly reversed, a result of the failure of the coup attempt and of the 1982 elections, which gave the Socialists a solid majority in Congress. The defeat of the coup led to the imprisonment of the military conspirators and to the reawakening of the public's rejection of a military alternative. The election of the Socialists, in turn, provided a homogeneous and stable government majority and a credible institutional vehicle for the affirmation of democracy, thus making it possible for the new government to confidently approach significant reforms in the military and the general organization of defense.

Postmilitary governments in Greece never had to face decay of popular support. Large electoral pluralities for the major parties and the system of reinforced proportional representation assured sturdy parliamentary majorities, which were further strengthened by the firm leadership of both party and government under Karamanlis and Papandreou.[59]

Portugal, on the other hand, experienced frequent government turnover and all kinds of government—presidentially appointed, coalition, and minority—until the elections of 1987. This very instability, although far from the ideal of any executive, at least precluded paralysis, by providing for expedient removal of ineffective governments. In any case, the fundamental features of civil-military relations during the period prior to 1982 were somewhat paradoxical: on the one hand, there was the constitutionally affirmed military tutelage; and, on the other hand, there was President Ramalho Eanes, a moderate general reasserting discipline within and government authority over the armed forces. However, it was not until the 1987 elections (which produced an unprecedented parliamentary majority and stable government) that government officials were decisively able to promote military reforms and enhance civilian supremacy.[60]

In sum, threats to government support were better overcome in the new Southern European democracies, where the electoral and governmental systems adopted were parliamentary or semipresidential and tended to facilitate the formation of working government majorities. The early Unión de Centro Democrático and the Socialist governments in Spain, and the Conservative and the Socialist governments in Greece, for instance, were incomparable with the awkward position in which Alan García, Raúl Alfonsín, and José Sarney were placed as lame duck chief executives in the presidential systems of their countries. With the loss of support in congress, either because of midterm elections or shifting loyalties of undisciplined party members, presidents were unable to implement their policies or recover popularity and were forced to wait out the rest of their terms in minority status, while retaining only formally the powers granted the executive branch. These institutional rigidities only compound government weaknesses in dealing with the military.

In addition to the impact of institutional features and government performance on government support in the Southern European and South American cases, the role of parties of the right must also be highlighted. In Southern Europe, parties of the right in the successor democracies included elites who had either participated in the previous authoritarian regime (Spain and Portugal) or supported restricted forms of democracy in the past (Greece). These elites, however, later gave wholehearted support to democratization. In Portugal, this was the consequence of their alienation from authoritarianism in its later stages, and especially of the nature of the military, which controlled the transition. The Portuguese right had a special stake in removing the military from politics. In Greece, the power usurpation of the colonels and their alienation of monarchic sectors also helped place the right strongly in the opposition to the authoritarian regime. When the right returned to power, it pursued full-fledged democratization. In Spain, Franquist elites facilitated the transition, and substantial parts of them contributed to the establishment of a consensus in support of the democratic constitution. In the South American countries, where parties of the right are significant, a previously successful association with the military in power, such as in Brazil, Chile, and Paraguay, made the elites' transfer of allegiance to the new democracies much less unequivocal than was the case in Southern Europe.

The Timing and Pace of Reforms

The extrication of the military from politics, or the assurance that it will not interfere, is a necessary first step in the road from authoritarianism to democracy. For democratic consolidation, however, a second and distinct step is required, the promotion of reforms actually aimed at establishing the preeminence of civilian government officials in the defense sector. In all the Southern European cases, these reforms were not carried out until after some time had elapsed following the installation of democracy. Among the South American cases, only in Argentina was there an attempt to promote such reforms, and they were swiftly implemented at the very inauguration of democracy, although with somewhat limited results. On the basis of this admittedly limited set of cases, one may conclude that reforms which were appropriately timed and gradually pursued obtain better results than comprehensive reforms, promptly enacted at the onset of the postauthoritarian period.

Gradual reforms generally seem more sensible from the viewpoint of civilian decision makers. The initiation of democratic government places numerous burdens on new and often inexperienced civilian officials. If military nonintervention is reasonably guaranteed, these officials will be free to deal with the many policy issues before them, postponing sensitive military and defense reforms until later. Postponement of these difficult issues allows time for the development of trust between civilian and military officials, assuaging military fears that civilians will act precipitously and with revenge, hitting at core military institutional concerns. In addition, it allows time for civilians to acquire expertise in defense and military affairs. The passage of time can thereby prepare the ground for more solid reforms later on, preventing an early military backlash based on a corporate reaction to "civilian interference." Excessive delay on the part of civilian officials who are satisfied with a situation of peaceful coexistence with the military, on the other hand, may culminate in failure to seize opportunities for the expansion of democratic prerogatives. Determining the right time, pace, and sequence of reforms is thus a leadership factor which plays an important role in achieving civilian supremacy. This role, however, is embedded within a set of opportunities and constraints largely established by the specific mode of transition. Indeed, in the cases considered here, seldom were civilian officials entirely free, or even able enough, to decide at the outset on a sequence of stages for the pursuit of military reform. More often, reforms were either postponed because there was little alternative or swiftly pursued because there was no apparent incentive to delay.

In Portugal, for instance, the military's bargaining power during the transition in 1974–75 led to civil-military agreements that postponed any consideration of the role of the military until 1982. Even after that date, it took much time and effort to gradually transfer effective authority over defense policy from the general staff to the civilian-led defense ministry. In Greece, the collapse of the colonels' regime in 1974 enhanced the leadership role of civilian officials in balancing the demands for punishment of the military against the threats of military resistance and the need to maintain an efficient military force against Turkey. Even in this case of collapse, substantial reforms were not enacted until 1977, and they were facilitated by the discreditable legacy of the colonels' regime within the military itself.

In Spain, a case of civilian-controlled transition from a civilianized authoritarian regime, substantial military reforms did not start in earnest until 1984, nine years after Franco's death. Democracy was installed outright in a relatively short period of time, but the promotion of reforms in the military was a slower, more gradual, and more selective process. Concern about military opposition and actual military resistance and about civilian inability in the earlier stages either persuaded or compelled civilians to take a slower path. When reforms were eventually implemented, however, success in establishing the primacy of civilian authority over defense became evident.

Because of the civilianized nature of the previous regime and the secondary position of the military in the transition, the military in Spain was less prepared to prevent the advance of democracy, although it was not by any means indifferent to it. Following the transition, the army maintained important prerogatives and corporate autonomy, and was still essentially the same Franquist body, led by generals who had fought "the Reds" and who considered themselves true carriers of the everlasting principles of the *cruzada*. The promotion of civilian supremacy thus posed numerous difficulties. Just as the military had faced many constraints in its opposition to full democratization, so did civilian authorities in their attempt to promote changes in the military.

The initial reforms were only inevitable steps demanded by the break with the Franquist Fundamental Laws of the State and the installation of democracy. Reforms in military ordinances and the code of military justice, and separation of the civil guard from the armed forces (in order to remove police functions from the military), for example, were all necessary in order to adapt military structures and practices to the precepts of the new constitution. From the defense ministry (created in 1977 to replace separate ministries for each of the armed services), General Manuel Gutiérrez Mellado initiated the gradual implementation of a few reforms. Much of his attention, however, was demanded by an increasingly restive military, which, severely hit by ETA's Basque-separatist terrorism, gave more and more signs of mounting discontent. Eventually, this discontent was released in the attempted coup of February 1981.

The failure of the coup provided a splendid opportunity to weaken military opposition by the imprisonment of rebel leaders, which was done during Calvo Sotelo's government in 1981–82, effectively accomplishing the first step of guaranteeing military removal from political concerns. But reforms in the defense sector, the second step in the attainment of civilian supremacy, were not given a decisive impulse until the Socialists were catapulted into control of the government by an absolute majority in the 1982 elections. With the confidence provided by such a majority and with the stability assured by party discipline and team homogeneity, the government initiated a gradual but persistent process of military reform.

Even this new government prudently waited for a year before it produced a coherent policy on the military and defense and proposed its first set of important reforms. The Socialists had first to overcome the distrust with which they were greeted in military circles. Once peaceful coexistence with the military had dispelled any major fears, the government set out to reform and modernize the defense sector and the army. The 1984 reform of the organic law on defense vastly enhanced the prerogatives of the ministry of defense. In 1989, the Ley Reguladora del Régimen del Personal Militar Profesional delineated career patterns and further specified the allocation of powers for civilian and military officials, completing a complex and gradual reform process. Reforms were appropriately timed and paced, as a result of both objective constraints and moderate civilian strategies, and were implemented through a process which combined persuasion and rewards with authoritative use of enhanced prerogatives.

In Argentina, the installation of democracy also was accomplished in a short period of time—more quickly than in Spain—as it only entailed reinstatement of the previously suspended constitution and the election of civilians to government and legislative positions. The military reforms conceived by Argentine civilian leaders were almost as thorough as the Spanish reforms, but their implementation was anything but gradual. Government officials faced challenges which they confronted immediately and simultaneously. Given that the new democracy had come about as a result of a military defeat, it was especially tempting to swiftly redress authority patterns in favor of civilians by weakening military prerogatives and political power.

The government promptly reorganized the top command (placing it under the direct authority of the minister of defense and turning over key positions in the ministry and military enterprises to civilians), and dramatically reduced the defense budget. The government also initiated prosecution of top leaders of the former regime for human rights violations. Government officials had expected a quick, surgical solution to the human rights problem by pursuing exemplary punishment of the highest-ranking former chiefs by the military's own high court. However, after the high military court decided not to handle the cases, thereby greatly delaying the process, civilian courts were ushered in. At the same time, individuals, human rights groups, and local courts initiated hundreds of legal actions against hundreds of middle-level officers. As resolution of these accusations dragged on, the government was kept from moving on to other issues and appeasing the military.

Middle- and lower-level military officers soon became demoralized by their low salaries, which led them to search for outside jobs, and professionally paralyzed as expenditure reductions halted operations. In addition, they felt unjustifiably blamed for the loss of the Falklands/-Malvinas War and for having staged what they thought was a legitimate war against subversion, the so-called dirty war. The rebellions that these officers subsequently led forced concessions from the government which drastically limited the number of officers that could be tried for human rights violations. By climbing "from the depths of their professional despair to discover a new resolve," the armed forces placed the government on the defensive.[61] Actions out of weakness, many of the positive measures initially taken for civilian control lost much of their significance.

This turn of the tide within the military reflected a civilian misjudgment of the implications of the human rights prosecutions and of the capacity of the military to recover from its initial weakness and paralysis. The Argentine civilian government also misjudged the diverse effects their internal reorganization reforms would have. While empowering civilians with greater formal authority, these reforms also added to the growing military resentment and ultimately helped in sparking its recovery. Civilians miscalculated as well their own ability to handle the expanded responsibilities which would result from reforms occurring simultaneously on various fronts. These reforms demanded a definition of new missions, a task for which civilians found themselves ill-equipped.[62]

Attempting to define a new military mission, the government introduced a national defense bill in 1984, finally passed in 1988, which replaced an old national security law and was intended to eliminate the legal foundation of the national security doctrine. The new bill explicitly confined the armed forces to an exclusive concern with external threats, but it showed little sensitivity to military concerns and to the long-term need for a stable structure for civil-military relations. It created a national defense council whose regular membership was composed exclusively of civilians, with the military included only at the discretionary invitation of the defense minister.[63] The military was thus denied an adequate mechanism for the expression of professional concerns and expert advice. Nearly unanimously criticized by the military, the bill unnecessarily created a new area of civil-military confrontation while providing very few practical benefits for the government. Also, the law's most important advance was swept away by an internal security decree, issued by Alfonsín in 1989, which allowed for armed forces participation against internal subversive attacks. The decree, passed in response to an armed guerrilla-type attack on a military garrison, squarely contradicted central tenets of the national defense law.

During his tenure, President Alfonsín faced nearly unsurmountable constraints, imposed by a recalcitrant military that recovered quickly from the state of collapse in which the transition had left it. Alfonsín's policy failures in other realms, coupled with the boomerang effect of the human rights litigation against the military weakened irretrievably the military's regard for his government. Given the magnitude of the effort involved in the human rights actions, and their potential to mire relations with the military, it now seems that the administration stepped in too hurriedly to pursue an excessive number of reforms. In the zero-sum scenario created by the civil-military confrontations, Alfonsín's weaknesses instantly became sources of strength for the military. Under these circumstances, it is quite remarkable, indeed a historical landmark in Argentina, that he succeeded in transferring power peacefully to another democratically elected civilian.

Many of the military measures taken by the Alfonsín's government were forced upon it by the circumstances of the transition. But many were not, and one must wonder, especially in light of the Spanish experience, whether a less activist administration in Argentina might not have been more effective in the long run.

International Factors

External factors were critical, in several cases, in triggering or encouraging transition to democracy and in supporting processes of democratic consolidation later on. For instance, actual or anticipated external defeat played a decisive role in the erosion of support for and the ultimate collapse of the authoritarian regimes of Portugal, Greece, and Argentina. Southern European democratic transitions were also encouraged, and the subsequent consolidation strengthened, by a regional environment that was strongly democratic and by the benefits of further economic integration. This type of international influence—"democratization through convergence"[64]—is distinctively Southern European and clearly different from the international conditions facing South America. What stands out as we look at the effect of international factors on the military aspects of democratization is the differing impact of regional military alliances in these two areas.

International conditions in the aftermath of the Southern European transitions made it possible for civilian governments to redirect the military to missions away from domestic politics, with a convenient accompanying restructuring of military forces and defense organization that enhanced the leading role of civilians. Although the presence of NATO was generally beneficial for the purposes of accommodating the military during democratization, it certainly was not a panacea. It will be recalled that NATO had unquestioningly accommodated authoritarian Greece and Portugal, and that Secretary of State Alexander Haig, former NATO commander, had dismissed the 1981 coup attempt in Spain as merely "an internal affair." Nevertheless, in very specific ways for each of the three Southern European cases, NATO provided an opportunity for redirecting military missions to external professional concerns, and this certainly aided democratization.

This effect was especially visible in Spain, the only Southern European country which was not a NATO member at the time of its transition. At this time, the structure of the Spanish military, particularly the army, placed its primary roles in domestic affairs and in its North African concerns. During the transition, the importance of the latter was lessened, following the army's hasty withdrawal from the western Sahara to avoid an armed confrontation with Morocco. The military's domestic concerns diminished gradually during the posttransition years. The prospects of joining NATO provided a substitute for the old defense concerns. In addition, the internal and occasionally bitter debate among badly divided political forces over the issue of NATO membership unexpectedly broadened the debate over military mission well beyond the narrow confines of small military circles and anchored it firmly within civilian political domains. The protracted debate, beginning under the Suárez government and intensified with Calvo Sotelo's government decision to join NATO in 1982, finally ended with the 1986 referendum, under Socialist sponsorship, that ratified membership, although under new terms.[65]

Implementation of the decision to enter NATO, which occurred during the Socialist administration, played a critical role in strengthening civilian supremacy. Not only did NATO membership contribute in redirecting Spain's military mission away from previous domestic concerns, it also accelerated military modernization, including participation in supranational technological development projects. In both areas, civilian authorities were the critical link in the internalization of the benefits of membership; this made them indispensable for the goals of military modernization and therefore significantly empowered them in the view of the armed forces.

Although Portugal had been a longstanding NATO member at the time of its transition, the Portuguese military was not engaged in the East-West concerns of the Atlantic Alliance as much as it was in holding on to its African dependencies. The ousting of the Caetano regime, however, brought a swift end to the colonial struggle, and with it thousands of troops were returned to Europe. The extraordinary power which the radical faction of the military held during most of the transition to democracy intensified foreign involvement in support of the moderate groups. Among a number of foreign initiatives undertaken to influence the course of the transition, veiled NATO pressures were brought to bear on the radicals, who were forced to reassure the allies. When the moderates took control of the transition, after the November 1975 showdown with the radicals, General Eanes moved the military closer to NATO perspectives and simultaneously arranged for a swift reduction of military forces from over 190,000 to a little over 40,000 in the course of a few years. The reorientation of the military's mission from colonial and domestic concerns to those more in accordance with NATO's outlook started at this point. Goal reorientation, effective modernization, and command reorganization evolved only very slowly and gradually, but in directions compatible with democratization and civilian control. Regardless of the pace with which these goals were attained, however, civilian officials had NATO to rely upon as a reference point for future reforms.[66]

Greece was also a NATO member at the time of transition, but membership played a different role in its case. The successor civilian officials in fact reduced the country's NATO participation as a result of NATO's inability to prevent Turkey's maneuvers in Cyprus. A visible shift occurred in Greek foreign policy at this time; greater autonomy for Greece within the alliance was claimed, especially in regard to the United States, mustering the consensus of all major Greek political forces. Persistent disputes with Turkey, coupled with the problematic implications of this conflict over Greece's military role in NATO, were sufficient to redefine the mission of the armed forces to one outside internal politics. The "Turkish factor" thus provided the civilian leadership with an opportunity to convincingly redirect military concerns strictly to external defense.[67]

In South America, international condemnation of the military regimes and support for the democratic opposition, especially from West European sources and, more erratically, U.S. administrations, certainly played important roles, which have been the subject of careful analysis.[68] On the whole, however, the international context of democratization in South America was much less auspicious than it was in Southern Europe, especially in regard to the military dimension. Within the region, the Interamerican Treaty of Reciprocal Assistance (ITRA) was the equivalent, or rather the poor relation, of NATO. The ITRA—established in 1947—had long before lost its initial dynamism and was perceived by most of its members as moribund.[69] It therefore did not provide the kind of framework for military renovation that NATO provided for the Southern European democratic governments.

In addition, many features of the military component of the interamerican system were much less unequivocally supportive of the goals of civilian supremacy than NATO was. NATO had a clear and integrated structure of political and military participation, with preeminence of the political aspect, whereas in the interamerican system the political and military components functioned separately. Thus, military participation in interamerican military activities did not lead to strengthening civilian political supremacy. For instance, interamerican army conferences often ended with statements on policy orientations that had great relevance to domestic affairs but little to do with the stated goals of the national governments. Also, despite the gradually more supportive stance towards democratization which U.S. administrations took after President Reagan's second term, U.S. security concerns in the hemisphere led to an emphasis on domestic issues in the Latin American countries, which did not facilitate mission reorientation away from domestic politics. In sum, civilians in Southern Europe could utilize international structures to their own advantage in ways which were not available to civilians in South America.

Concluding Observations

In his analysis of democratization in Brazil, Alfred Stepan noted that the military dimension has often been neglected in studies of regime change. He attributed this neglect largely to what he viewed as a "normative disdain for the military as a topic." This disdain was part of a "liberal bias," which preferred to focus on developments within civil society and the advent of new social movements. It also occurred because the prevailing theoretical approaches ignored the often autonomous role played by military organizations.[70] Indeed, one may go further to observe that the focus on elites which has dominated recent analyses of democratization has often defined the concept of elites as meaning purely civilian elites, with the result that the nature of the roles played by military elites in these processes has gone unnoticed, or has been simply taken for granted. That the roles of the military were often crucial in the Southern European and South American transitions makes this neglect especially unacceptable.

Indeed, the various transition trajectories and consolidation processes described in this volume strongly suggest that the role of the military must be explicitly taken into consideration. The editors' middle-range notion of democratic consolidation has been conceived in such a way as to specifically include the attitudes, strategies, and behavior of military elites within its explanatory framework. Other recent works on democratization and consolidation have also explicitly referred to the military dimension of regime change. Terry Lynn Karl's very definition of democracy, for example, has expanded to explicitly include civilian control of the military; previously, this factor had remained only implicit in definitions of democracy, behind Dahlian assumptions.[71] Samuel Valenzuela's notion of consolidation has the military in mind when it refers to the impact of authoritarian enclaves or reserve domains as standing in the way of progress towards democratization.[72] Students of civil-military relations who address problems of democratization (e.g., Fitch, O'Donnell, Stepan, and others) have certainly contributed to bringing the military dimension more fully into the study of democratic consolidation.

Assessments of the long-term outcomes of democratization processes require thoroughly considering the military dimension. To some extent, doing so leads to an understanding of significant differences among the three recently redemocratized Southern European countries. As I have argued in greater detail elsewhere, military discontent with democratization in Spain postponed the attainment of democratic consolidation until the aftermath of the defeated coup attempt of February 1981 had revealed to the military that there were no feasible alternatives to full compliance with the democratic regime.[73] Had it not been for this delay in securing military compliance, democracy could have been deemed consolidated much earlier, in 1978–79, when significant elite consensus on the constitution and the organization of the national state had been reached.[74] In Portugal, as well, the persistence of tutelary roles for the military postponed a consolidation which would otherwise have been attained earlier. In Greece, on the contrary, democratic consolidation was not delayed by the military, but rather by the persistence of elite disunity.

This factor assumes even greater importance in contrasting Southern Europe with South America: indeed, the role played by the military is the single most important factor distinguishing the transition and consolidation experiences of Southern European democracies from those of South America. Obstacles to consolidation which the latter have encountered have been so substantial that they have prompted attempts to conceptualize regime types that may endure as postauthoritarian and yet not fully democratic.[75] The persistence of unconsolidated democracies constrained by military influence is a real prospect for South American postauthoritarian regimes.[76]

The nature of the preceding regimes and the characteristics of their transitions have made it harder for democratizing elites in South America than for those in Southern Europe to overcome the institutional arrangements inherited from the transition, but these circumstances do not foreclose the possibility of success in the future. In fact, some of these democracies, such as Uruguay and Argentina, have been more successful in resisting unfavorable conditions than initially anticipated.

The resilient nature of military influence in democratization requires a long-term view of the consolidation process. In the terminology employed by Geoffrey Pridham in the next chapter, one might say that civilian elites must shift from a "negative" to "positive" form of consolidation. "Negative consolidation" may be taken to mean elite satisfaction with the creation of conditions which prevent military rebellion against democratization. "Positive consolidation" refers, instead, to conscious, long-term efforts by civilian elites to devise policies and strategies aimed at a positive reincorporation of the military into the goals and institutions of the new democratic regime. A positive reincorporation is one which, while securing indisputable civilian supremacy, grants the military enough institutional autonomy for the efficient pursuit of its mission. Civilian leadership in developing the framework for such a positive reincorporation, in which the military feels its institutional interests are guaranteed, is what may ultimately facilitate the expansion of attitudinal change among members of the armed forces in support of a democratic regime. This kind of civilian leadership, then, emerges as a key factor differentiating the Southern European from the South American cases.

5 The International Context of Democratic Consolidation: Southern Europe in Comparative Perspective

Geoffrey Pridham

In an increasingly interdependent world, the argument for incorporating the international context in studies of democratic consolidation becomes compelling. It has long been noted that the United States has historically played a considerable and sometimes decisive part in conditioning—sometimes aborting—democratization in Latin America; and dramatic international developments like the Turkish invasion of Cyprus and Portugal's colonial wars are regarded as having led directly to the fall of authoritarian regimes in Southern Europe. But two recent developments have made questions regarding the impact of international factors on democratization of even greater importance in the European context. The democratization of Eastern Europe, especially the crucial role of Gorbachev's Moscow and the subsequent withdrawal of the Soviet hegemon, has highlighted more dramatically the impact of international influences in system change. Also, the earlier entry of the new Southern European democracies into the European Community (EC), and the subsequent widening and deepening of the integration process among member states of the Community, has played an important role in securing the consolidation of these new democracies.

Analyzing the real impact or influence of the international context on democratic transition, either theoretically or empirically, is no easy task.[1] We are looking not merely at the significance of outside actors, of which hegemons are the most visible, but at the way in which different international agents and influences—some less visible than others—interact with domestic system change. In a review of literature on the subject, Gabriel Almond came to the view that "the penetration of domestic politics by the international environment is not only a matter of dramatic events but is a constant process at medium and lower levels of visibility, affecting political, economic and social stability in both positive and negative ways."[2] It is also an intrinsically complex area of investigation, given the interactions among variables in the domestic and international arenas. For several reasons, these various problems are magnified in the related and subsequent process of democratic consolidation.

First, while different theories of regime or democratic transition are to some extent viable for comparative studies,[3] democratic consolidation as a concept and analytical framework has so far suffered from a poverty of theory; and, compared with regime transition, it is a much more nebulous phenomenon, and there is considerable uncertainty about its point of termination.[4] In turning to the international dimension, therefore, one must start theoretical construction virtually anew. Second, consolidation is qualitatively different from transition in that it is both a broader and a deeper process. While transition may revolve essentially around questions of political or strategic choice, when it comes to consolidation attention is much more concerned with structural conditions and constraints, such as those deriving from membership of international organizations.[5] Hence, the consolidation process is rather more complex and multilayered than that of transition, all the more when we are relating it to the external environment.

Consolidation is, furthermore, a lengthier process than transition, which leads us to the third reason why its analysis is problematic. Since the time frame for full consolidation is said to range from one decade to as much as a generation, the three Southern European states that embarked on their transitions in the mid-1970s may conceivably not yet have reached the final stage of consolidation. However, incorporating postwar Italy into the sample provides a useful cross-time basis for our comparison, since Italy's parliamentary system was consolidated earlier, although that took virtually a generation.[6] This study inclines towards the longer-term definition of democratic consolidation, while arguing that its achievement is cross-nationally variable in this respect. The first decade of consolidation, however, is regarded as the crucial phase, after which the successful outcome of this process becomes more and more predictable.

In the absence of a widely accepted theory of democratic consolidation, there is a particular need to define clearly the two key concepts in the title of this study, distinguishing between transitions to democracy and consolidation of new democratic regimes. Consolidation is a qualitatively different process, requiring that a different set of questions be specifically addressed. For instance, what legacies or problems remain in the aftermath of a democratic transition, and how do these affect the consolidation process? Do the processes of transition and consolidation relate to the internal and external arenas in different ways? Special account must also be taken of the differing roles of international organizations in each region and, therefore, of their capacity for affecting the consolidation process. The European Community's capacity for "penetrating" member states' systems, for example, may set it apart from other international influences on new democracies; and the Community certainly requires special attention, since it operates both within and between member states.

One final factor which can complicate comparative studies of international influences on democratic consolidation is that these processes unfolded in different countries at sometimes greatly different times. Italy's consolidation occurred in the 1950s and 1960s, and the other three Southern European countries underwent the process in the 1980s and beyond. In some respects, this nonsimultaneity may facilitate analysis, by introducing considerable variance into the comparisons: the international environment during the Italian consolidation process was markedly different from that during the three later cases. But this historical approach also poses analytical risks if it treats the consolidation process too mechanically as time-bound. Democratic consolidation involves meeting certain principal conditions, and the time required for their achievement varies cross nationally. While consolidation is conceptually distinct from and temporally more protracted than transition, some of its key phases may overlap with or commence during the transition process. This introductory section will therefore elaborate further on these approaches and present the conceptual framework adopted in this study.

Defining Democratic Consolidation

Democratic consolidation is a process that diminishes the probability of reversal of democratization. In essence, basic political structures and procedures established during transition become institutionalized, "internalized," and eventually legitimated. The rhythm and dynamics of politics in the new democracy become and remain more system promoting than system destructive, so that "the conditions necessary to keep the intervening process on track" are established.[7] An initial distinction may be made between "negative consolidation," involving the effective or final removal of the prospects for nondemocratic system alternatives, and "positive consolidation," whereby the democratic system becomes operationally settled and gains credibility. Negative consolidation implies the achievement of a significant or partial degree of consolidation, but it is positive consolidation which ultimately completes the process.

Negative consolidation includes the solution of any problems remaining from the transition process and, in general, the containment or reduction, if not removal, of any serious challenges to democratization. The latter usually take the form of groups or individuals characterized as antisystem. Negative consolidation is achieved when their presence or impact becomes numerically or politically insignificant, for example, they either become neutralized and opt out of the political game or they may become converted to democratic politics. Clearly, this dimension of consolidation relates particularly to elites and their behavior during regime consolidation. Obviously, too, problems of negative consolidation are most likely to exist in the first phase of the overall consolidation.

Positive consolidation places more emphasis on attitudinal patterns, and it refers especially to wider or deeper levels of the overall process. It includes the inculcation of democratic values at both elite and mass levels, and, therefore, it involves some remaking of the political culture in a direction that is system-supportive for a new democracy. *Positive consolidation* refers to longer-term change, while negative consolidation may be achieved in a shorter time span.

Such a distinction is useful, insofar as it indicates that new democracies may still be somewhat fragile at the outset and that progress is not necessarily linear. These different dimensions of consolidation may proceed at different rates and involve different sets of actors. For instance, while transition and negative consolidation may largely involve elite behavior and decisions, positive consolidation places more emphasis on the relationship between the new political system and society.[8] Hence, influences or pressures emanating from the latter may well create opportunities for or constraints on elite actions.

The international context could simply be viewed as a component of this process, but to do so would risk missing the full range and complexity of its potential importance for systemic change. What matters generally in examining the consolidation process is not merely identifying its different levels, but also seeing how far and in what way these interact (the dynamics of consolidation leading to a successful, delayed, or aborted outcome). And, in any case, the approach taken here, in line with the linkage politics school, is to unscramble the domestic and international arenas.

The international context may hypothetically affect the consolidation process in both negative and positive ways. International developments may help to disrupt the early stage of consolidation when the new system is still vulnerable to internal challenges, particularly if the country in question is sensitive to such events (e.g., they involve a neighboring state or one with a traditionally close link, or, for reasons of political culture, they have a poignant impact). Clearly, too much instability in the world or the surrounding region can undermine regime consolidation. Conversely, regional international organizations may afford some protection to new democracies, just as they may also constrain the degree or even the course of internal system change.

The external environment can impose a set of confining conditions for internal regime consolidation, deriving from either multilateral linkages (membership in international or regional organizations) or bilateral linkages with other states (be they contiguous, regional, or superpower). The state of the regional or international political economy, or systemic attitudes or trends that spill over boundaries, can also influence internal political developments. The prevalence of liberal democratic norms in a region like Western Europe, for instance, can reinforce the democratic option in postauthoritarian states, thereby contributing to positive consolidation. Also, positive consolidation will probably be encouraged by effective government performance in foreign policy or defense policy arenas, depending on national cultural predispositions towards external relations and issues. Conceivably, too, policy efficacy may firm up the achievement of negative consolidation by convincing antiregime groups or individuals to reconcile themselves with a new democracy.

Democratic consolidation may be close to achievement when government performance is no longer systemically crucial and merely reflects on the standing of the party in power. This is equivalent to Easton's thesis of diffuse support, whereby a new system takes hold and becomes operationally settled despite occasional crises in performance, although too many crises in the early stages of consolidation might prove detrimental.[9] An indication of diffuse support is the establishment of basic policy orientations, whether external or domestic, as a matter of explicit or implicit consensus among the main political actors, notably parties. In other words, distinction should be drawn between key external allegiances, such as membership in international organizations with systemic implications (like the EC and NATO) and differences of outlook and priority, which reflect the pluralism of viewpoints characteristic of liberal democracies but do not challenge the former. Clearly, any persistent or remaining problem of basic policy orientation will overload any alternation in power, itself widely regarded as evidence of democratic consolidation underway, or perhaps even inhibit its occurrence.

Democratic consolidation may be said to have been completed when there is evidence that the political culture is being remade in a system-supportive direction, thus removing the last of the uncertainties remaining in the aftermath of the transition. Here, external developments or issues may or may not play a significant part, depending upon either long-term historical experiences (where history is a principal aspect of political culture) or more recent external transition events having some persistent impact on political attitudes in new democracies. Accordingly, some countries may be termed "penetrated systems" for reasons of national history (Greece) or postwar development (Italy), making them particularly open to external influences. Questions may justifiably be asked as to whether such a high degree of international penetration is unhealthy for new democracies to the extent that it may delay consolidation (postwar Italy?), or whether rejection of such a condition is a sign of an acquired democratic maturity (post-1974 Greece?). There are other ways in which the remaking of political culture may be affected by the external environment, especially the "Europeanization" of political perspectives that derives from EC membership.

Altogether, the achievement of democratic consolidation is essentially a qualitative occurrence and not one easily subject to a strict time-bound explanation. For this reason, the process of consolidation is best discussed by means of an approach that differentiates between the levels of that process.

The other key concept requiring clarification is *international context* itself. The term refers to a variety of outside actors—international organizations, foreign governments, transnational nongovernmental actors—and external influences of a less concrete kind, such as those referred to earlier in this discussion.

It is important to note that the relationship between the consolidation process and the international context is two-directional: linkages may be either inner-directed (where the international system has an impact on domestic structures) or outer-directed (vice versa). For instance, external actors or events may be either a source of or an outlet for internal tensions, with significance for the course of democratic consolidation. Thus, analysis of the dynamics of this process should focus on how different aspects of consolidation interact with one or several components of the external environment.

This method is known as unscrambling the domestic and external arenas; it drew originally on ideas from the linkage politics literature. The framework applied in this study is similar to that utilized in earlier research on the international context of democratic transitions.[10] In summary, it incorporates a number of significant background variables (geopolitical location and historical and cultural factors, including the legacies of transition) and elaborates linkages in two different directions: inner-directed, which refer primarily to conjunctural factors (international trends, the international economy, socioeconomic modernization pressures) and to international organizations and foreign governments; and outer-directed, which involve sets of linkage actors (especially party-political, economic, military, and other elites) and the domestic environment (governmental structures, public opinion, cleavages, social actors, and overall stability).

This framework focuses our attention on the principal agents and variables for comparing similar and largely parallel processes, while allowing sufficient flexibility for both cross-national variation and differing time contexts, such as with regard to postwar Italy. While adapted from work on democratic transition—thus signifying a continuity of problems between the two processes—it stresses the qualitative differences between transition and consolidation by highlighting the roles played by certain variables, such as transnational modernization pressures and the impact of the domestic environment. Above all, the increasing penetration of European integration will come into play much more during consolidation. Since the new democracies are now EC member states, and since the Community itself has developed considerably as a political and socioeconomic entity in recent years, there exists greater potential for the EC to influence domestic politics in a variety of ways during the process of consolidation.

Moving towards Consolidation: Historical and Environmental Perspectives

Greece, Italy, Portugal, and Spain have a common Mediterranean environment that entails similarities of culture, climate, and concern over a variety of common transboundary problems, such as pollution and tourism. Their international strategic concerns have also been broadly similar in recent times: they have faced the strong military and naval presence of the United States (the resident superpower), and the Mediterranean region acquired greater strategic importance during the 1970s. At the same time, however, there are important differences among these states.

Of these three recent cases of consolidation, Greece has probably been the most vulnerable in terms of the East-West struggle. Being on the edge of the Middle East, moreover, it has been particularly concerned about developments there and, above all, about relations with

Turkey. The Iberian states are more distant from the pull of these unsettling regional problems, although Spain's international impact and historical interest in Arab matters dictates a special involvement. Portugal, on the other hand, because of a traditional Atlantic vocation and a recent colonial past in western and southern Africa, has tended to look away from the Mediterranean. Indeed, we must recall the familiar refrain about Portugal's not being Mediterranean at all.

But geopolitical location is not an unconditional or even consistent determinant of a country's external orientation. Some enduring problems may have long historical roots (e.g., the Greek-Turkish conflict), but conjunctural conditions invariably evolve over time and sometimes change abruptly (e.g., the radical change in Soviet domestic and foreign policies in the late 1980s). These can affect the course of democratic consolidation, as did the reorientation in East-West relations and the radical change in fortunes of national communist parties during an important phase of the Southern European consolidations. While Spain, Greece, and Portugal experienced their transitions and consolidations in roughly the same international environment, the case of postwar Italy illustrates how much a different time context matters in shaping the consolidation process.

Italy achieved transition and embarked on consolidation from the early 1950s, at the height of the Cold War, which contrasts with the period of détente which was the setting of the Southern European transitions in the later 1970s. Italy was deeply affected by this external environment—witness the decisive impact of East-West confrontation in the crucial transition election of 1948,[11] after which Italy became a client state in the U.S. sphere of influence. Consolidation in Italy thus occurred in the shadow of American tutelage. This lent Italy's parliamentary system a very specific orientation in her external relations (Atlanticism and Europeanism as inextricably linked in defense of Western democratic values) and imprinted itself on domestic political patterns. Although the strong left-right polarization drew on subcultural roots (Marxist versus Catholic) that predated fascism, it was undoubtedly driven powerfully by superpower hostility during these first postwar decades and by the allegiance owed by the two main political parties to Moscow and Washington respectively. The ruling Christian Democrats (DC) and other center-right government parties benefited significantly from U.S. financial, political, and moral support.

While the special and rather subordinate relationship with the United States may be seen as peculiar to the type of liberal democracy consolidated in postwar Italy, it is also very arguable that this link was not conducive to easy consolidation: American influence was significant in discouraging any alternation in power to the left, although this does not really resolve the issue of whether the Italian Communist Party (PCI) was an antisystem party. It also leaves open the question whether this problem was first and foremost a consequence of the international conjuncture during consolidation[12] or whether the loosening of the American grip on Italian political attitudes from the 1970s reflected not only a new national confidence in Italy but also the achievement of consolidation.

Clearly, the Italian case exemplifies a kind of legacy from democratic transition that very much involves the international context. In the normal course of events, transition legacies entail policy uncertainty which, once consolidation occurs, is replaced by a revised policy orientation or, perhaps, confirmation of some pre-existing policy patterns. Regime change can call into question policy continuity or assumptions, for a new set of political actors is usually installed with different views of the world. How much change in policy direction occurs may be influenced by the speed and extent of system transition, but it is almost certainly determined or constrained by socioeconomic conditions on the domestic front and standing external policy commitments. Such determinants and constraints tend to come into play once the phase of democratization shifts from transition to consolidation.

The international context can well have a bearing on the new system's legitimacy, particularly if the transition has been contested at home or abroad. An external policy reorientation, however, may serve to reinforce the systemic choice by helping to resolve the historical quandary that often accompanies transition, namely how to accommodate the usually discredited past. The classic instance of this was postwar Italy's and West Germany's espousal of European unity as an escape from the evils associated with the nation-state under fascism. The European option had not such traumatic motives in the Greek and Iberian cases, but it performed a similar function as the most obvious policy departure.[13]

Policy Reorientation and the Symbolic Dimension

The extent to which the international context can have a symbolic effect on consolidation, redefining national self-image or even national identity, is worth pursuing briefly. The international context has been especially significant in the Greek and Spanish cases. In both countries, the EC's identification with liberal democracy in the eyes of political elites and at the public level (rather more in Spain than Greece) meant that regime consolidation would be a subtheme of EC entry. In fact, negotiations for membership virtually coincided with successful democratic transitions and with the commencement of the consolidation process in both cases. Actual entry represented international acceptance of these countries' new democratic credentials and was regarded as offering a form of guarantee against a return to the authoritarian past. This was not merely a pious hope: a formula of democratic conditionality had been applied to the applicant states, requiring free elections, liberal-democratic constitutions, the institutionalization of political pluralism, and reasonably stable government.[14] By the time entry actually took place (Greece in 1981, Spain and Portugal in 1986) these criteria had largely been satisfied.

In Greece, historical experience of foreign intervention made a cause célèbre of rejecting the past and embracing wholeheartedly a new democratic future. The discredited pre-1967 system was widely and rightly regarded as subjecting Greece to direct American interference; then the national disgrace of the Turkish invasion of the northern half of Cyprus in 1974 both brought about the fall of the hated colonels and provided the occasion for dismissing the client relationship with the United States, eliminating the latter as the preeminent actor in Greek foreign policy.[15] Anti-Americanism affected all political tendencies, as did negative orientations towards NATO, especially given its close identification with the United States and its uncritical position on the military junta (somewhat in contrast with attitudes of the European Community). Karamanlis, within weeks of his return, responded to this mood and signaled an external-policy reorientation by withdrawing Greece from the military wing of NATO. This action was combined with abolition of the controversial monarchy and the underlining of political pluralism through legalization of the Communist Party, thus allowing those vanquished in the civil war to re-enter the political process.[16] Karamanlis's apparent intention was that this policy reorientation should involve a shift from a bilateral and subordinate relationship to a multilateral and equal one through EC membership.[17] This was eventually achieved, but not without an uncertain phase, during which an anti-West tendency seemed to challenge this policy course, given the hostility of the opposition socialist party, PASOK, to EC entry.

For some time, Papandreou's nationalistic attacks on foreign powers produced a neutralist and Third Worldist orientation as an alternative.[18] His stance may actually have contributed to the consolidation process by providing a cathartic outlet for Greek historical resentments. As Nikiforos Diamandouros has eloquently put it, PASOK offered itself as an attractive instrument for "reductionist yet powerful conceptualizations" in the postauthoritarian period:

> This was a time when accumulated resentments and collective feelings of inadequacy born of unrealized national dreams, of long and conspicuous foreign interference in Greek politics, and of the inability effectively to affect larger processes directly affecting the nation (Cyprus crisis, threat of war with Turkey, role of the United States and of NATO allies) made it easier to bring to the surface deep and fundamental ambivalences concerning Greek identity and the country's relationship with the West. In so doing, they inevitably helped to foster a greater sense of affinity for "radical" alternatives posed by the "periphery" rather than the "center" of the world system and, however naively, to enhance the appeal of the cathartic benefits to be derived from a break with unwanted elements of the national past.[19]

During the 1980s, a consensus emerged over EC membership, with PASOK shifting its policy on Europe and abandoning its systemic objections to the Community. The Greek Communist Party also later revised its position in a similar manner.[20] As Verney has argued, the lengthy debate over the EC fulfilled an important need at the subjective level through the public airing of Greece's role in the world.[21] This exercise and the subsequent cross-party acceptance of the country's new European vocation contributed meaningfully to the consolidation process. In this sense, it is possible to say that Papandreou's nationalist approach in external relations during the 1980s performed a certain transitional function, as a bridge on the road towards final achievement of democratic consolidation.

With postwar Italy, the situation was somewhat different. Italy's flight into client status with the United States was dictated by postwar circumstances, and in any case it suited the economic and political interests of the ruling Italian elites.[22] At the symbolic level, the country's escape from the fascist period was still painfully apparent in national defeat. National self-awareness was consequently affected by the discredit now cast upon the Italian nation-state itself. Clearly, Papandreou's brand of nationalism would have been inconceivable in postwar Italy. Nor was anti-Americanism a popular phenomenon there, although it was present in the communist movement, as an ideological rather than a nationalistic attitude. Interestingly, anti-Americanism began to appear at the public level in the 1980s, at a time when Italy under Craxi and Andreotti began to assume a line somewhat more independent of the United States in international affairs, especially in the Mediterranean. National pride even became a topic of discussion then, suggesting some kind of link with the achievement of system consolidation.

The case of post-Franco Spain is similar to that of Greece insofar as abandonment of the status of client to an outside power made a political and symbolic contribution to the consolidation process. It was, however, less poignant and less generic than the case of Greece, and focused specifically on the defense treaty with the United States originally signed by Franco in 1953 and indelibly associated with the latter's regime. The existence of the treaty did much to explain the emotive quality of the debate surrounding the NATO referendum of 1986 and the subsequent thorny negotiations with Washington over defense arrangements. In effect, Spain reordered its defense commitments to create a more equal relationship with the United States within NATO, in the process breaking symbolically with the authoritarian past. Anti-Americanism was thus a powerful force at both elite and mass levels in Greece and Spain.

There is an evident link, therefore, between recasting the national self-image and opening the way for consolidating a new democracy. It is partly symbolic, psychological, and attitudinal, and partly political in that abandonment of client status increases the scope for a new democracy's autonomous role in international affairs. The implications for system legitimation are obvious, given the benefits for national pride and self-image.

In Spain, the question of national self-image was most evident in the debate over entry to the EC. This had an undoubted symbolic and political value for consolidation, because of the widespread Spanish association of Europe with democracy. In the words of a Spanish economist,

> The dictatorship of General Franco accentuated the sensation of isolation of the Spanish. In this situation, the democratic Spain, the Spain that fought against the dictator and dreamed of the restoration of a democratic regime, saw that the historical moment was in its favor. . . . since 1956 this democratic dream was identified with the EEC. The feeling was that the EEC could convert Spain into a democracy, although formally this was impossible, since under the conditions of the Treaty of Rome the chain of causality must run in the opposite direction. The Treaty requires all candidate countries to have democratic governments for entrance. In spite of this, the Spanish dreamed and idealized in the hope that EEC membership would convert it into a democracy.[23]

Thus, a link was forged between democratization and escape from Franquism, on the one hand, and EC entry and emergence from international isolation, on the other. This was all the more important since Spain was in the process of emerging from a long authoritarian period. Prime Minister Felipe González explained in 1987,

> Looking at our history since the 19th century . . . I can pick out some conclusions that also lead to the idea of participating in the European institutions.

> Throughout that period, we Spaniards lived in political and cultural isolation. That was a breeding ground for authoritarianism and exaggerated nationalism, and explains the fragility of our democratic experiments. Political isolation was accompanied by an economic isolation—let us call it hyperprotectionism—that fitted in consistently with nationalist thinking. The result was comparatively less development than our European neighbors. That process of political isolationism and economic protectionism was negative for Spain. Opening the political frontiers and becoming part of broader areas is the consistent response for those of us who seek a better, democratically stable and economically developed Spain. Here is the real foundation for our wish to join the Communities.[24]

Here we have the outline of a consolidation strategy with a distinctly historical and international dimension. Successful conclusion of membership negotiations in spring 1985 was hailed as a great historical moment for Spain.[25] Entry into the European Community the following January brought a sense of completion of democratic transition, although this had already essentially been achieved. Acceptance into the EC provided a form of external validation of Spain's new democracy: "The impact of entry for Spain is mainly psychological. . . . Achieving membership was the political equivalent of a doctor's certificate—a sign of acceptance and recognition of Spain as a 'normal' country."[26]

Compared with Spain, in post-1974 Portugal there was much less sense of historical mission in Europe, and distinctly less popular enthusiasm on the occasion of EC entry. Yet, the link between EC entry and democratization had been made by Portuguese government leaders in the mid-1970s in an effort to protect the emerging liberal democracy from internal challenge on the extreme left.[27] The Portuguese national identity was complicated in that it suffered from a sense of being a peripheral country and a fear of Spanish dominance.[28] Relations between these neighboring countries, which had remained largely separate during their authoritarian periods, now, with common EC membership, opened up, leading to regular consultation at the official level and the growth of tourism and trade.[29] There has been some debate in recent years over Portugal's national identity within Europe,[30] but the link between the two has been less intensely felt than in Spain. In cultural terms, this opening up of Portuguese society has probably been beneficial for democratic consolidation.

It goes without saying that national identity, which normally comprises an ethnic definition, shared cultural characteristics, and a form of self-image, includes a significant international dimension. This may be through a certain distinctiveness vis-à-vis other countries, but it can also involve views of one's own country, including the standing and reputation of its regime.

Regime change usually involves some form of confrontation with national history. Invariably, this is uncomfortable and painful, since the process requires not merely rejecting the preceding regime but also confronting a slice of national history which may have deeper roots. There arises from this controntation a desire to escape this national experience and a need to accommodate the past—the authoritarian legacies for democratization. This conflict may be resolved by means of reinterpreting national history, which may be less tendentious in democratic than authoritarian hands. It is clearly a fundamental and sensitive problem, in which political leaders have a role to play through key decisions they take and through the symbolism that surrounds the politics of regime change.

Successful handling of this problem certainly promotes the chances of democratic consolidation, both by reconciling public attitudes with the new system and by freeing elites to concentrate more effectively on its operation. This is, of course, a process that begins with the transition. Nevertheless, the relationship between this symbolism and political and socioeconomic reality can be difficult in these early stages of the consolidation process. There is a potential risk that expectations of the international context (e.g., Spain's high hopes regarding Europe) might be disappointed, thereby posing some potential risk for consolidation.

We have to remember, however, that the consolidation process consists of different, albeit interconnected, dimensions. Thus, symbolic questions, notwithstanding the importance they are lent in the sometimes emotive situation of regime change, cannot be viewed in isolation. It is these complexities in the relationship between the international context and democratic consolidation that will emerge from our focus on inner- and outer-directed linkages and interactions between them.

Inner-directed Linkages: Democratic Consolidation in the Age of European Integration

European integration has had much greater importance for Southern European democratic consolidations than for transitions, for although it provided some direction for postauthoritarian external policy during the latter process, EC entry during transition was more a matter of promise than of reality.[31] Clearly, the effect of integration on a new member state is gradual and rather long-term. Nonetheless, despite the recentness of both democratic transitions and EC membership for the Iberian countries, it is possible to make a preliminary assessment of the impact of membership on Spain, Portugal, and Greece, and on the consolidation of their democratic regimes. Inclusion of the Italian case will again provide some parallel with an already consolidated democracy. It is difficult to isolate the independent effects of EC membership, given the growing penetration of national politics by the Community, but a number of political and economic issues can be explored to assess their relative influence.[32]

Political Effects of EC Membership

Entry into the European Community encourages and in certain ways compels the opening up of systems to new institutionalized forms of external cooperation. It requires governmental and administrative structures to adapt to regular procedures at the European level. Political leaders (notably cabinet ministers) are drawn into the functioning of the different versions of the council of ministers; national officials from a wide range of ministries are involved in the EC's routinized form of diplomacy; and new and old member states alike take their turns in managing the EC presidency, which involves an intense effort in political initiative and statecraft as well as an administrative burden. The pressures on political elites to adopt a "European" approach are considerable, especially during service in the EC presidency. Greece has assumed this responsibility three times, in 1983 and 1988 and again in 1994. Spain and Portugal have held the post once each, in 1989 and 1992, respectively. Italy, as one of the founder states of the EC, has occupied the presidency on numerous occasions. The importance attached to holding the EC presidency is particularly strong in new democracies, since it represents a very visible form of external validation.[33]

Even though Greek performance in the first presidency was not distinguished, the prestige of holding that position was not forgotten by Andreas Papandreou when Greece's turn appeared again in the summer of 1988, just prior to another round of national parliamentary elections. Papandreou was aware of the possible electoral payoffs to be derived from this prestigious international role, as well as the extent to which EC funds had aided PASOK's electoral fortunes in rural areas in the 1985 election, providing the means to implement long-neglected public works projects.[34]

The Spanish presidency of 1989 was inaugurated with considerable fanfare. It provided Spain with an opportunity to demonstrate its international importance and to push for policy harmonization in a variety of areas, such as monetary integration and social policy. It also gave Felipe González an opportunity to shine as a European statesman.[35] While the EC presidency offered Spain and Greece a vehicle for demonstrating executive or diplomatic skills at the European level, thus reinforcing the legitimacy and authority of national leaders, it also promoted public awareness of the EC itself. For example, Eurobarometer data reveal that in 1989 72 percent of Spaniards were aware of the Spanish EC presidency, 78 percent considered it important, and 21 percent regarded it as very important. Similarly, a 1988 Eurobarometer poll of Greece revealed that 74 percent of citizens were aware of Greek incumbency in the EC presidency, while 73 percent and 44 percent, respectively, regarded it as important or very important.[36]

Government leaders can also benefit from the political expediency of EC membership. Decisions taken collectively in Brussels have allowed governments to impose unpopular measures at home under the umbrella of the Single Market and for the sake of economic restructuring as a consequence of EC entry. Papandreou, who returned to power as a result of the October 1993 election in Greece, has often highlighted an external threat or crisis as a diversion from domestic difficulties. Moreover, the strict conditions attached to the huge (£1.5 billion) EC loan to Greece in early 1991 would, it was noted at the time, "help Mitsotakis to introduce harsh economic measures which are certain to trigger a strong public reaction, but which are widely seen as vital to restoring any kind of economic health."[37]

This instrumental use of EC membership has been even more systematic in the case of Spain. Introduction of the value added tax (VAT) in 1986 caused anguish among business circles, but the domestic political consequences of this unpopular tax could be softened by labeling it a "European tax" imposed as a condition of EC entry. At the same time, the new tax represented a significant fiscal reform, since VAT replaced a thicket of twenty-five Spanish taxes that were easier to avoid paying and "left tax inspectors in the dark about real levels of economic activity."[38] The Spanish tax structure as it has developed in the past half-decade has undergone a greater degree of change that can be associated with EC membership than has Greece's tax system. Simplification of the Spanish tax structure and the marked increase in direct taxes appears to have significantly improved the administrative capacity and political authority of the Spanish government.[39] This reference to system performance implies a link with the consolidation process, although it is difficult to draw any firm conclusions yet on this point.

Italy's overriding concern with political stability helped to overcome economic reservations about entry into the European Coal and Steel

Community (ECSC) and the European Economic Community (EEC) in the 1950s.[40] Whether political stability was facilitated by membership is debatable, however, since for some time Italy often proved less effective than other major member-states when pushing for its national interests. There also emerged a tendency for Italian governmental leaders to conceptualize or rationalize in European terms for reasons of convenience. After interviewing Prime Minister Colombo in 1971, a British journalist commented: "The Prime Minister did not say so in so many words, but he gave me the impression that at the root of the importance Italy attaches to the political unification of Europe is a desire to escape from her own politics, to break out of the constricting structures which cannot contain the economic miracle."[41] Italian leaders have quite regularly used the "Brussels card" to justify their policy decisions, a tactic which may have some credibility in a country with such a strongly pro-European consciousness. But this approach can also have its down side. As Giorgio Galli, the well-known Italian political commentator, remarked sarcastically, during the Italian economic crisis of the 1970s, there was a new element of "*deresponsabilizzazione*" (shelving one's own responsibility) among government leaders, who took the view that it was up to Italy's EC partners to solve the country's problems.[42]

It is difficult to determine the extent to which longstanding EC membership has had the effect of opening up the Italian system in the manner suggested above, as this requires measuring the separate effects of the EC system after decades of membership. Instead, it is better to focus on specific problems to gain some comparative insights from our four countries. As Sidjanski has shown, for instance, national interest groups in the three new Southern European democracies benefited considerably from their insertion into the EC network, from which they acquired new habits of consultation, dialogue, and information to a degree not practiced in their home countries. The legitimation of interest groups through EC involvement has helped to reaffirm their representative function and has thereby contributed to the growth of pluralism in the new member states.[43]

Furthermore, the EC has provided an extra layer to the guarantees of civil rights and electoral competition previously provided for in the national constitutions and other treaty obligations, notably the Council of Europe,[44] which the new Mediterranean democracies had (re-)joined soon after embarking on transition in the mid-1970s. The Greek constitution of 1975 placed detailed emphasis on securing civil rights, a sensitive issue in the aftermath of the abuses of the junta period, when Greece had been forced to withdraw from the Council of Europe. In Portugal, a consensus developed in the mid-1980s around the need for further constitutional revisions to facilitate economic modernization and restructuring. Earlier moves to open up the state sector to private capital were considered inadequate preparation for Community membership. A link was forged in the public mind between EC membership, on the one hand, and economic modernization and political stability, on the other.[45]

It is significant that EC circles long ago dispensed with talk about democratic conditionality regarding Southern Europe, simply because the requirements had been met. It is also noteworthy that, whatever the economic and social strains of adapting to EC membership, European integration did not encourage antisystem disaffection. On the contrary, the initial consensus over membership has been strengthened both among the general public and (especially in Greece) among political parties. The increased political weight recently acquired by the European Community offers still greater possibilities for EC membership to contribute to democratic consolidation.

Economic Effects of EC Membership

Let us briefly examine the direct economic benefits of membership in the European Community and its impact on economic restructuring then assess how the Southern European economies have developed in the light of EC entry. Again, the short-term perspective of half a decade necessarily makes this exercise somewhat tentative, but the initial impact can be examined, and some insight can be gained concerning the extent to which the Community has begun to act as a framework for economic modernization.

The potential benefits include loans from the EC, resources derived from the structural funds and the newly established integrated programs for Mediterranean Europe, stimulation to investment, and pressures for economic growth. For these countries, which have been described as semiperipheral in relation to the rest of Western Europe,[46] such benefits had a particular appeal.

Spain, for example, benefited from net annual transfers that rose from 13.7 billion pesetas in 1986 to an estimated 160 billion in 1988. The doubling of structural funds in 1988 was expected to increase infrastructural investments by 8 percent in the following year, with more to come.[47] Spain thus overtook Italy as the largest recipient of regional development funds, and reform of the structural funds helped Spain to develop a real regional development policy.[48] Portugal, once Europe's poorest country, found that it could develop more easily with EC status. Net financial transfers from the EC amounted to 188.1 billion escudos ($1,065 million) in 1986–88, and in 1989 transfers of structural funds were 148 billion escudos, representing 11 percent of total domestic investment. Visible infrastructural effects included new roads and better railways, which helped to reduce regional imbalances, and newly established factories.[49] The decision late in 1991 to establish the EC Cohesion Fund had as its objective a further improvement in the southern members' infrastructural modernization, although it is far from sufficient for overcoming their problems of economic convergence with Northern Europe.

A similar story unfolded in Greece, where new roads proved a real boon to this very mountainous country. Other material benefits included those derived from agricultural price supports, as well as the prompt emergency loan from the EC Commission in 1985 that averted a balance of payments crisis.[50] These visible benefits have helped to push Greek attitudes towards the EC in a positive direction.

At the same time, EC entry produced shock effects for Southern Europe resulting from increased exposure to European trade and the prospect of the Single Market coming into operation in half a decade. In the long run, these changes in the economic environment would stimulate socioeconomic modernization. The immediate outlook, however, was dominated by major difficulties of adjustment for these economies, which were less advanced compared with the rest in the Community. Business and industry were understandably cautious, if not fearful, of what they faced in the years ahead.

Much in the future of these economies depended on the general economic climate of the time, but also influential was how governments seized the opportunity to promote economic change that might cause short-term unpopularity. In this, Spain proved more adept at this juncture than Greece and perhaps than Portugal. Felipe González enjoyed greater room for maneuver, partly because he headed a strong and stable government and because EC entry was supported by a strong consensus in Spain. This allowed him to ride out the problems of adjustment. By the time Spain entered the EC, government leaders were largely free from the political legacies of democratic transition, such as fundamental disputes over the constitution (aside from Basque disaffection over devolution). This enabled them to devote sustained attention to the economy and problems of modernization. Spain's economic miracle of the 1960s had unfolded within traditional economic structures. By the mid-1970s its economy still had many characteristics of a developing country, such as a high proportion of small businesses, almost nonexistent long-term credit facilities, and a large, mostly inefficient, parastate sector.[51] Concerned over the high expectations of most

Spaniards, González warned them, in a midnight speech at the time of Spain's entry into the EC, not to expect miracles from Community membership.[52] In fact, the years that followed coincided with recovery in the Spanish economy, and rapid growth eased some of the transitional problems. The lack of competitiveness of industry was quickly exposed, as imports soared and the country's trade surplus disappeared. On the other hand, there was an unprecedented inflow of investment from EC countries, leading to widespread changes in the industrial sector and takeovers of Spanish companies.[53] It was in this context that the Socialist (PSOE) government implemented a series of structural reforms, including mergers to create larger enterprises, some privatization, investment in hydroelectric and nuclear energy to cut the high dependence on foreign energy sources, and various liberalization measures in the banking system.[54]

While Spanish preparation for the Single Market has been reasonably successful, the situation of Greece and Portugal is less clear, partly because their economies were less dynamic than that of Spain but also because they experienced less initial national consensus over EC entry. In Portugal, moreover, government instability was endemic from the beginning of the transition until the mid-1980s. Portuguese policy making was further complicated by disputes over economic principles set forth in the constitution. The election of one-party majority governments in 1987 and 1991 was seen as a hopeful departure from previous governmental instability, as were the constitutional reforms of 1989. In Greece, Papandreou's government could be said to have represented strong leadership in a traditional charismatic sense, but his ideological preconceptions and initial antagonism to the EC, not to mention his somewhat erratic style, did not encourage European confidence in Greek economic performance. Mitsotakis, by contrast, adopted a more moderate approach to the EC.

Portugal's response to the first period of EC membership turned out to be rather better than expected. Within a few years, the economy had begun to flourish, helped by the effects of the tough International Monetary Fund adjustment program of 1983–85 and a flood of investments.[55] One can even say that a radical transformation began, aided by a special EC program for modernizing Portuguese industry and by rapid development of tourism. The Cavaco Silva governments embarked on a policy of economic restructuring with an ambitious reprivatization program (once constitutional revision permitted this in 1989), reform of the tax and financial systems and of labor practices, and other measures designed to open up the economy.[56] Despite an impressive start, serious difficulties were anticipated concerning Portugal's overall ability to adapt to the Single Market, not least because some key areas remained largely untouched by restructuring (agriculture is still notably inefficient, and traditional industries like textiles have changed little) and because many social structures were antiquated.[57]

Greece's performance on the economic front has been the least encouraging among the new member states of the 1980s. Economic management was not given high priority, and there is evidence that EC funds have been used more for clientelistic purposes than for economic restructuring.[58] Greece's economic record, the worst in the European Community, was such that in 1990 Brussels lost patience: EC Commission president Jacques Delors was moved to fire off a letter to the Greek government warning that the country's deteriorating economic situation (a rapidly rising public debt and other economic imbalances) threatened the EC's move to monetary integration and the Single Market. Greece had failed to abide by the requirements of the 1985 loan from the commission, so stringent conditions were imposed by the EC as part of a three-year effort to bring down inflation. These requirements included cuts in government borrowing, reductions in public sector employment, and broadening the tax base.[59] This was a clear case of European pressure for national policy change—an example of an inner-directed linkage. Whether Greece can cope with the Single Market remains to be seen; of the three new democracies it is least in step with the policy momentum of the European Community.

EC membership has undoubtedly created pressures for economic modernization, but for political and economic reasons the response has been varied among the three cases. It was to be expected that the new member states would face the greatest difficulty in meeting the challenge of socioeconomic cohesion ultimately presented by the Single Market. Since they joined the EC at a time of greatly accelerated progress towards political and economic integration, the demands for economic convergence with established members were all the more severe. These demands became particularly acute with the move towards monetary union and the concern that the Southern European states (including Italy), burdened by high inflation and heavy public debt, would be unable to participate fully. There was even talk of these countries forming a second rank among member states. This was particularly galling to Spain, which had ambitions of becoming a leading partner in the EC.[60] It is significant, however, that these pressures and tensions deriving from the Community have not essentially undermined the consolidation process in the new Southern European democracies.

Our discussion of inner-directed linkages has been dominated by issues related to the EC, for the Southern European countries' ability to respond to the international economy and to international trends and events is very much conditioned by their Community membership. Spain, for example, has sought a more active role as an international actor (especially in the Mediterranean and in relation to Latin America), but this desire is very much based on Spain's status as a larger member state of the EC.

The Europeanization that came with EC membership also meant that the most important bilateral links of Spain, Greece, and Portugal with other national governments in Europe have been subsumed within the Community networks: their closest economic and political partners are other EC states. In effect, multilateral links have replaced separate bilateral links and, since traditionally the latter had tended to involve client subordination to the regional superpower, the change was probably conducive to a healthy democratization process. At least it removed the risk of old-fashioned penetration by external actors and the consequent destabilizing effect.

This last problem is well illustrated by the different way in which matters evolved in postwar Italy. First, Italy embarked on democratic consolidation when European integration was at its inception. Although De Gasperi clearly viewed Italy's role as a founding member state of the ECSC and other European organizations as supportive of her new and fragile parliamentary democracy, the real possibilities for interpenetration were very limited and the European federalist ideas that attracted Italian government leaders in the late 1940s were unrealizable. Projects for political integration in the 1950s and 1960s proved to be premature. Nevertheless, European integration eventually fostered the country's industrial development, although this development was highly uneven and economic benefits varied greatly among sectors.

Unlike the three new democracies of the 1980s, moreover, Italy saw the European framework as a complement rather than as an alternative to its client relationship with Washington; it was part of a dual response to the Cold War environment prevalent in the 1950s and 1960s.[61] Against the background of domestic uncertainty and party-political polarization, this opened the way for the United States to exert a powerful influence over Italy's government leaders and political life, including political parties and trade union organizations. American interference in Italian politics took different forms—diplomatic, economic (through aid), financial or subventional (above all, the funding of center-right parties)—and was usually covert; public forms of pressure were sometimes used, especially at election time.[62] Dictated by international strategic concerns, U.S. policy was directed towards limiting, if not undermining, the political prospects of the left, above all the PCI, in

Italy's domestic life. Thus, in the Italian case we see a different form of penetration at work, for while Italy became integrated into the European economic framework and the Western defense networks, the subordinate link with Washington remained influential for some time.

Significantly, the United States took a rather more relaxed approach towards the Southern European transitions from the mid-1970s and was prepared to let the EC supervise their democratization from close by.[63] But, then, this was a period when superpower tensions had declined. The international context was very different from that in which the Italian republic was established.

Outer-directed Linkages: Domestic Actors, the Consolidation Process, and External Relations

Emphasizing European integration reminds us that disaggregating internal and external factors is a complex enterprise. James Rosenau used the term *fused linkages* to describe the kind of long-term interweaving of policy-making procedures typical of the European Community.[64] In reality, inner-directed and outer-directed linkages interact. One might hypothesize that the intensity of such interactions is related to the process of democratic consolidation: a close or intense interaction may reflect a point of crisis in the consolidation process, and the opposite might indicate that political patterns, including external policy concerns, have begun to settle into the normality of established democratic politics and that, indeed, consolidation is on track. But we cannot be absolutely sure of this hypothesis, and it is the purpose of this section to examine and if necessary question it.

Policy Consensus and System Consolidation

An important benchmark for the consolidation process is the point when sufficient consensus underpins external policies that disputes over policies cease to have systemic implications or consequences. While there may continue to be an international dimension to the domestic strategies of political elites, at this point they cease to look for external actors to buttress their demands regarding fundamental characteristics of the political regime. This need for external support was a salient concern in the Portuguese and particularly the Italian transitions.[65] Foreign policy issues continued to be the source of domestic conflict in both Greece and Spain well into the mid-1980s, when both countries were well on the way to achieving consolidation. External policy patterns have already been discussed, but it is important for us to reexamine them from the standpoint of domestic pressures.

Political change in Portugal reveals a shift from extra-European to Eurocentric concerns with the abandonment of colonial responsibilities. The strong association between this shift and support for liberal democracy found its counterpart among opponents of this option, who also preferred neutralism, links with the Third World, or alliance with the Soviet bloc.[66] The "Europeans" triumphed at an early stage in Portugal's lengthy transition, establishing policy continuity in support of EC entry and continued membership in NATO. The only exception has been the persistent opposition to both objectives on the part of the Portuguese Communist Party (PCP). As we shall see, this impediment has been effectively neutralized by the domestic isolation and decline that the PCP has subsequently experienced. The modernization strategy of the Cavaco Silva governments has included a distinctly European dimension. Compared with the domestic upheavals during the transition process, external policies have remained remarkably stable throughout consolidation. This relative calm has facilitated the latter process and has helped to offset strains resulting from the country's economic difficulties, adjustment to EC membership, and the legacy of political fragmentation.

For Italy, the basic external policy choices were made between 1947 and 1950. Its policy commitments combined the Atlanticist and the European options, Italy being a founding member of both NATO and the ECSC. Both options were contested on the left, however, well into (if not throughout) the consolidation process. The cleavage over external allegiances was deep and had important systemic implications. The protracted controversy over the nature of the postwar transition was reinforced by an international dimension, due to the main parties' traditional links with the opposed superpowers.[67] A basic consensus was not established until after the PCI had accepted the EC (in the 1960s) and NATO (in 1974). Insofar as Italian parties geared their foreign policy preferences to domestic strategies, it follows that the establishment of this consensus was an important element in the achievement of consolidation. Indeed, the PCI consciously used the European policy area as a channel for its own legitimation.[68]

In Greece, there was some fluctuation in external policy in the 1980s, and this was linked to polarization between the two main political parties. Alternation in power in 1981 opened the way for PASOK to implement its alternative to New Democracy's emphasis on a European strategy, with attention given to links with the Arab world and a somewhat independent stance in East-West relations. As we have seen, this alternative position was expressed in hostility towards the American defense relationship and the EC. External constraints combined with economic interest and domestic considerations (such as the pro-NATO attitude of the Greek military), however, to induce Papandreou to modify his policies.[69] At the same time, his nationalistic approach to relations with Turkey helped to reassure the military, while the military and public opinion reduced Papandreou's room for maneuver in seeking rapprochement with Ankara in the late 1980s.[70] Again, the eventual consensus over the EC may be seen as contributing to the consolidation process.

Government leaders did not always act deliberately to promote democratic consolidation, for often this motive was embedded in other considerations, such as partisan self-interest. The PSOE's foreign policy after its election to power in 1982, for example, was consciously influenced by the need to strengthen the new Spanish democracy—indeed, the word *consolidation* appeared in some of González's speeches on this and other subjects.[71] It was also a primary reason for the PSOE government's change of position on Spain's membership in NATO, this being closely linked to its military-reform policy. Even so, it was difficult to secure consensus on the NATO issue. Only with his surprising victory in the 1986 referendum was González able to appeal more convincingly to all political forces for establishing a permanent national consensus on foreign and defense policies.[72] Such a consensus regarding the EC had been achieved years earlier.

A variety of questions arises from this exploration of the linkages between democratic consolidation and government management of external relations. Do policy decisions and the manner in which they are taken serve to promote the legitimacy of democratic politics? What is the effect of external policy on the outlooks and interests of political and other actors whose attachment to the new regime might vary? How much does government performance in the external field encourage the development of diffuse support, so that systemic risks gradually diminish?

Government Structures and Policy Performance

Since government structures change significantly with regime transition, an initial concern is whether the constitutionally determined institutions with responsibility in external relations function effectively or satisfactorily. As Theodore Couloumbis has noted, in Greece foreign policy, decision-making practices changed dramatically after 1974. Previously, a wide variety of actors, including the throne, the military (especially during the junta period), the diplomatic service, and even the United States government played key decision-making roles. Following the restoration of democracy, however, it was the cabinet and especially the prime minister who carried responsibility for external relations.[73] This clearer concentration of authority made for potentially effective leadership. At the same time, Papandreou's monocratic exercise of his role as prime minister during 1981–89 was controversial because it led to abuses of power. Nonetheless, PASOK consistently received better evaluations by voters for its foreign policy than for most of its other policies, since it was seen as enhancing Greece's international position.[74]

Recent research on the opinion-policy nexus in the new Mediterranean democracies has shown that in all three cases public opinion was more consistent with foreign policy than with domestic policy during the period 1978–86.[75] Whether or not this was due primarily to a counterfeit consensus process—in which the low level of public knowledge of foreign issues enables a government to control more effectively the flow of information—the outcome was on balance likely to have been beneficial for democratic consolidation. Undoubtedly, the citizens of these countries felt gratification over being treated as equals by international partners. By and large, we may say that external policy practice has confirmed the credibility of the democratic decision-making structures. For example, despite the fact that King Juan Carlos has operated as a kind of grand ambassador for Spain—making some key speeches during visits to Washington, Latin America, EC capitals and institutions, and Eastern Europe—in no way has this conflicted with parliamentary government. Instead, he is widely regarded as a significant force for democratic consolidation (not least for his crucial role in the coup attempt of 1981).

Government performance cannot be divorced from wider aspects of state structure. The establishment of regional governments in Spain, for example, introduced an extra element of complexity into the country's European policy, even though Madrid has remained officially responsible to Brussels for its regions. European involvement in the regions is partly a consequence of the growth of EC aid programs, such as the structural funds, which have stimulated interest among the regions; but it also results from certain regions' strategies to "play the European card" in struggles with the central government over constitutional powers. Both the Basque and the Catalan governments have exploited links with EC institutions in a way that has informally bypassed Madrid. Some of the regions have set up offices in Brussels to lobby for their interests. Catalonia has been especially active in this respect; under Jordi Pujol, the regional president since 1980, it has developed something of an individual European profile, including cooperation with regions in some other EC states, in a deliberate attempt to outmatch Madrid.[76] The Basque Country's forays into European affairs have provoked prickly clashes with the central government, such as those over the issue of separate representation in Brussels. In many instances, domestic tensions have been extrapolated onto the European stage. In some respects, however, EC ties have facilitated the handling of a domestic issue clearly threatening to the new democratic system. Spain's efforts to deal with problems created by the Basque terrorist organization ETA have been greatly facilitated by a 1984 agreement with France regarding the extradition of terrorists.[77] This is a good example of Spain's "transnationalization" of a problem that is primarily internal, although it also has some transnational aspects, given Basque ethnic links with southwestern France and frequent use of the Pyrenees as an escape route for ETA activists on the run.

EC membership has also exerted pressure towards reform of national bureaucracies. At first glance, bureaucratic reform might not appear to be related to democratic consolidation, except that under authoritarian rule the bureaucracy had acted as a mediating structure and tended to consist of personnel who might use their influence to check democratic reforms.[78] A more widespread problem, perhaps, has been the persistence of the clientelistic practices and inefficiency that have served as an obstacle to effective government, especially regarding economic policy and development. Such obstacles can relate to consolidation insofar as they impede development of diffuse support for the system.

Membership in the European Community created pressures for greater policy coordination at home as well as in Brussels. In the first half-decade of Greek, Portuguese, and Spanish membership, this pressure did have some effect on their public administrations, but it also ran up against deeply rooted habits. Portugal has faced basic policy coordination problems, because her bureaucracy has simply not been adequate for EC membership: it was so unwieldy and its personnel so lacking in technical skills that Portugal declined her first opportunity to assume the Community presidency in 1987.[79] Greece did not decline the presidency for reasons of prestige, but her administration was hardly able to do the job. Greek governments have responded to EC and other pressures with some proposals for reform, but real change has been difficult, because clientelistic practices are so ingrained and, since 1974, have been entwined with governing party interest.[80] A 1991 EC loan included among its strict conditions a 10 percent reduction in the civil service, which, by the end of 1993, did not seem to have been realized.[81] Concern about Greece's administrative capacity has remained conspicuous in anticipation of the Single Market.

Spain has evidenced the greatest adaptability to EC administrative procedures. Serious reform efforts have produced results, especially at the level of interministerial coordination in Madrid, and this has improved the formulation of Spanish positions on EC affairs.[82] The greatest challenge has been felt by the diplomatic service, because of the general expansion of Spain's world role in addition to her active part as an EC state. Involvement in EC institutions and close cooperation between foreign ministry personnel and their EC counterparts have tended to improve efficiency and have increased pressures for more democratic or open procedures in the Spanish bureaucracy.[83]

This examination of government structures and policy performance has suggested that there are two consequences for democratic consolidation. First, the routinized involvement of national bureaucrats in the work of the EC and other European organizations has opened up channels for their Europeanization, thus increasing their exposure to influences likely to promote a democratic outlook. Second, EC membership has exerted extra pressure for administrative reform. It would be premature to assess the ultimate outcome, but even if its success is limited, it can only contribute to effective system performance. This improved effectiveness, in turn, will surely increase the credibility if not the legitimacy of democratic politics. A brief look at postwar Italy shows, however, that these two phenomena do not necessarily go hand in hand. Italy has undoubtedly become known for the pro-European ideology of her ruling elites, but unlike post-Franco Spain this has not acted as a stimulus to her playing a consistently active role on the European stage. On the contrary, inept administrative backing for Italian policy positions has tended to detract from the country's impact as a member state.[84]

Linkage Actors and Elite Groups

Actors under consideration here include both political and nonpolitical elites, with the latter referring primarily to military and economic leaders. Parties are the key political linkage actors that look outward when formulating positions on external relations and engaging in transnational activity through cooperation with like-minded parties in other European states. Collectively, they control debate about external issues in a way that might have some implications for the consolidation process. Parties can, for example, create or acerbate international cleavages in domestic politics, and can influence public opinion on external issues. This is true of both opposition as well as government parties—particularly the former, where antisystem forces are present.

In Spain, the broad consensus over EC membership among all major political parties was consistent with pro-European tendencies at the mass level. The Communist Party (PCE) acted as a decidedly prosystem party in constitutional negotiations during the transition,[85] and it agreed with the other parties on the European option. On the brittle issue of NATO membership, however, the PCE (as chief component of the new United Left alliance) sought to mobilize negative opinion and revive its political fortunes after its collapse in the earlier 1980s.[86] It is difficult, however, to see this as an antisystem move, for it genuinely hoped to exploit growing disaffection with the PSOE as governing party, a legitimate tactic in democratic politics.

On the transnational front, which has usually been a matter of limited importance for Spanish domestic politics, two developments are nevertheless worth mention. On the right, the renamed Popular Party (PP, successor to Manuel Fraga's Popular Alliance) decided in 1989 to leave the European conservative group and to join the Christian Democrats at Strasbourg. While this was motivated by basic differences with the British Conservatives over European integration, the change of allegiance also suited José María Aznar's strategy to convert the PP into an unambiguously center-right party and to shake off remaining doubts arising from its Franquist roots.[87] Aznar even declared the following year that the PP was Christian Democratic in its values and principles.[88] In other words, he had added a European dimension to his party strategy. On the left, the PCE chose also in 1989 to join with the Italian Communist Party (PCI) in a separate group breaking with the French and Portuguese Communist parties. This was no surprise, given the PCE's Eurocommunist approach of the 1970s. The PSOE felt sufficiently threatened by the PCE's new moves on the European front to exclude it from a summit in Madrid of the European left (that included the PCI) in 1990. Thus, in different ways the parties projected their domestic rivalry outward. By this time, however, the sudden collapse of communist regimes in Eastern Europe had thrown the PCE (and other Southern European communist parties) into renewed crisis.

In Portugal the PCP is an obvious case of an antisystem force, because of its strict adherence to the traditional Moscow line. It had resisted democratization, benefiting for a while from the instabilities of the transition. Its view of parliamentary democracy as transient, however, was a fundamental misjudgment.[89] The PCP has begun to modify its original hostility to the EC (in 1986, at the time of entry, the PCP argued that Portuguese membership would undermine the gains of the

Revolution of 1974), and revisionists in the party have capitalized on this issue.[90] Overall, however, the PCP was highly embarrassed by the changes in Eastern Europe after 1989. Those events provoked a further crisis over party strategy, not to mention the withdrawal of financial aid from the East.[91] However, party leader Alvaro Cunhal continued to show no real interest in this debate and has, for instance, resisted moves for PCP involvement in a European left formation at the transnational level.

While Greek parties have traditionally viewed external relations with systemic eyes and thus regarded the EC as a system-defining choice,[92] the only serious antisystem party in the conventional sense has been the orthodox pro-Moscow KKE. PASOK, for all its radical positions, nevertheless performed an important consolidation function by channeling longstanding Greek resentments and reconciling "left" and "nation."[93] The KKE shared many traits with the PCP, although it eventually adopted a more flexible stand on the EC. Having failed to broaden its support over earlier public disquiet over EC entry (probably because PASOK acted as tribune on this matter), by the late 1980s the KKE had generally moderated its tone on the Community, as part of its rapprochement with other forces on the left.[94] This stance was also influenced by the shift in the Soviet position on the EC under Gorbachev.[95] However, the KKE reverted to a more rigid stance on the subject of Maastricht.

Thus, in Spain, Portugal, and Greece we can detect a connection between external policy positions and system support. Where serious cleavages have existed, these have tended to diminish during the past decade, particularly those on the central question of European integration. It is difficult to determine whether this change was autonomous or was closely linked with the process of consolidation itself, but it has tended to have positive effects. The disappearance of communist regimes in Eastern Europe has further weakened what remained of antisystem inclinations on the extreme left.

Postwar Italy is a more difficult case. There political parties were a considerable force for mobilizing and determining opinion on external as well as domestic issues, and for a long time an international cleavage marked that country's politics. It was significant, however, that one of the main reasons for the PCI's change of position on the EC was the beneficial effects of membership for Italian economic expansion and the growth of living standards among the working class.[96] In other words, European integration had a system-reinforcing effect.

Matters were further complicated by the susceptibility of Italian political elites, especially those in government, to penetration by external actors. This no doubt explains why they held no ideological reservations towards European unity on grounds of national sovereignty. But at the same time, it accounts for the leverage enjoyed by Washington in Rome. Commenting on the regular trips made by Italian politicians to the U.S. capital, one former Italian ambassador to the United States said, "In the Italian case, one tends to attribute to the meeting with American figures the value of political recognition, of the opening up of credit; and this reduces the independence of our foreign policy."[97]

Among nonpolitical actors, the military must feature prominently in any discussion of postauthoritarian democratization. Transition should lay the basis for civilian supremacy over national defense and withdrawal of the military from a political role, while consolidation essentially deepens this relationship through the operation of the new system. Legacies from the transition might remain, however, in the form of organizational procedures inadequate to support the shift to civilian control, a lack of personnel turnover, or the persistence of antidemocratic political sympathies which could be mobilized into active disaffection over certain issues. The military's retention of a role in the governmental structure of Portugal, through the Revolutionary Council (abolished in the constitutional revision of 1982), is an example of a legacy from the transition, although it was not one which occasioned any serious problem for the new system. Spain presents us with a potentially more serious situation, in which there was insufficient diffusion of support for the regime among the military in the early 1980s. This was complicated by military discontent over such issues as government performance vis-à-vis terrorism. Military reform in the decade that followed, however, was successful in dealing with these problems.

It is worth noting that this problem of the military illustrates a straightforward version of an outer-directed linkage. Governments in these new democracies took the view that one effective way of keeping the military out of domestic politics was to reinforce their external orientation. This might involve longstanding issues, such as Papandreou's using the continuing tensions with Turkey over the Aegean and Cyprus to distract popular (and military) attention from internal affairs, entailing high military expenditures.[98] The intensity of popular concern with external issues usually fluctuates over time, but relations with Turkey had long held considerable and more-or-less constant potential for arousing Greek feelings.

A more stable way for these governments to internationalize the military role was through integration in a European organization such as NATO. Involvement with NATO served to institutionalize the military's concentration on national or external defense and away from matters of civil order—a responsibility often accorded them under authoritarianism. NATO facilities, training programs, and sources of information all provided opportunities for officers to rub shoulders with their opposite numbers from established democracies and increasingly exposed them to influences outside special national preoccupations. As Gregory Treverton notes, NATO membership also provided government leaders with arguments and incentives for streamlining and professionalizing the military. It was therefore a useful component of military reform in Spain.[99] The PSOE government's change of position on NATO membership was, from this perspective, an instance of a conscious consolidation strategy.[100]

The military's reconciliation with liberal democracy was influenced by the behavior of other elite groups, and especially by elite unity around the new system. This includes attitudinal patterns—the military or business may be reassured by an overwhelming preference among political elites for liberal democracy—but at least as important is how the behavior of one group impacts on another. Political leaders are invariably the pacesetters in the consolidation process, which a look at business and economic leaders makes evident. We saw earlier that initial concern among some sectors about EC membership was overcome by the dramatic rise in investment and other benefits that derived from it. Problems of adaptation arose, however, especially as business and industry had grown up in the greenhouse of protectionism and were now forced into a much more competitive environment. But, politically, such problems did not have any apparent systemic repercussions, in part because EC entry came to be seen widely as an important achievement and, above all, as providing a definite direction and purpose for national economic policy.

Direct links between economic and political leaders also assist adaptation by business to political change. These links may be semi-institutional, through some organizational or financial relationship (party collateral and party financing), like business interests' links with the Italian DC or the Spanish Popular Alliance. In such cases, the party's own attitudes toward liberal democracy are likely to rub off on the economic elites. Government intervention in the economy is also likely to have some systemic effects during the course of consolidation. The case of Portugal is particularly illustrative, given the economic disruptions of the period after the 1974 Revolution and the significant element of state control. Some large businesses had enjoyed a close relationship with the Salazar regime, but there has been no temptation on their part to engage in risky politics even during the protracted and difficult transition. The emphasis on free enterprise by the Social Democratic (PSD) governments since the mid-1980s has been attractive to business, and, as Ken Gladdish argues, its leaders have little incentive to endorse any return to authoritarian rule in a modernizing EC member country.[101]

The Domestic Environment: Mass-level and Political-Cultural Influences

The nature of public opinion and, where present, social movements is usually of some importance to the consolidation process. Of particular significance are trends relevant to change in political culture and movement towards system legitimation. As an ideal type, full legitimacy cannot ever be attained. What is important is that political culture moves in the right direction and makes any reversal of democratization more and more improbable. Elite groups, and especially parties, have a special potential for influencing public opinion in ways that may reinforce the new system. But how much does the international context matter?

Postwar Italy has long ranked high if not first among EC member states in her degree of public support for European integration. Any skepticism concerning this orientation is due to the fact that this attitude is more abstract or impressionistic than tangible in the sense of penetrating political mentalities: levels of informedness on EC questions have been low, and Italian life has continued to be marked by a strong localism.[102] At the same time, the material advantages of EC membership have always tended to make a positive impression and, as in Greece (another strongly clientelistic country), to give a particular twist to support for the Community. Strong partisan affiliation or subcultural allegiance in these countries has strengthened the ability of the various parties to influence public views of the international context. In this light, attitudes towards the EC on the part of party elites (especially on the left) acquire much importance.

Portugal has often displayed a weaker awareness of, if not a certain indifference towards, external issues.[103] The intensification of the importance of external issues through dramatic events can obviously alter this situation. The manner in which the transition crisis of 1975 tempted international pressures could have had such an effect on Portugal, but the consolidation process there has not witnessed any such consequence, and matters have tended to be relatively calm on the international front for Portugal.[104] Available evidence suggests that political culture in Portugal is still in a transient stage, and according to José Magone, the emergence of democratic values has been constrained by the country's semiperipheral status.[105] There are substantial urban-rural differences, with urban areas more marked by the shift to modernization and, presumably, more open to international considerations. Thomas Bruneau has observed a new orientation toward Europe, in contrast with centuries of colonial attachments—a tendency likely to continue with growing European investment and tourism in Portugal.[106] Survey evidence has supported this judgement: pro-EC attitudes have been relatively strong and have been paralleled by satisfaction with liberal democracy.[107]

Greece, by contrast, has demonstrated a strong inclination to mobilize on foreign issues. This propensity is a product of the country's historical penetration by outside actors and, no doubt, of Greece's geopolitical location. An important version of this mobilization was the anti-Americanism that surfaced with the transition of 1974 and continued to mark Greek attitudes for some time. Recently, however, there has been some decline in this feeling, as well as of interest in foreign issues, although the country's stance in the Balkan crisis of the early 1990s constituted evidence of a partial resurgence of such feelings.[108] The relationship between parties and public on external relations is obviously two-directional. On the one hand, parties have a strong influence on public attitudes in Greece, and conceivably any decline of interest may well be due to a convergence of party positions, as on the EC. At the same time, Greek voters habitually get excited over foreign issues. This can place constraints on politicians, as Papandreou discovered at the time he sought a rapprochement with Turkey following the near-war in the Aegean in 1987. Clearly, he underestimated the degree of basic mistrust between Greeks and Turks.[109] But such problems have now ceased to have any systemic consequences, since Greece's new democracy has become consolidated.

For Spain, the foreign issue of some relevance to consolidation was NATO membership. One can even argue that the high moment of this issue, the 1986 NATO referendum, was one of those decisive events in securing Spain's democratic consolidation. The NATO issue was particularly salient because Spain's link with the Western alliance, based on the 1953 treaty with the United States, was distinctly associated with the authoritarian past. Conflict over this issue may have been exacerbated by the domestic political environment of the early 1980s. Although the 1981 decision to join the alliance may have been motivated by proper concerns over consolidation in the aftermath of the February coup attempt,[110] the government did not prepare opinion for this decision. Instead, this policy was made by a governing party on the defensive domestically (the Union of the Democratic Center was on the verge of disintegration), against strong opposition from the left and in defiance of public opinion.

The election of a strong PSOE government in 1982 did not help to resolve this issue, as the new governing party was divided over it. González had to maneuver between these party pressures, against a background of continuing public disquiet over NATO and pressures from external commitments and bilateral links with partner countries. Defense Minister Serra had to make much effort to reassure the NATO defense establishment over his government's intentions in the period before the referendum.[111] The relationship between the government and the public threatened at times to deteriorate. Public confusion and alienation over the government's change of position on NATO membership gave rise to a credibility problem, which was magnified by the lack of explanation of the change to the public by government figures.[112] Difficulties also arose as the emergence of a peace movement both challenged the government's control over debate and further undercut its credibility, forcibly presenting the argument that the decision to join NATO had not been democratic.[113] From another viewpoint, however, the peace movement was a healthy sign of participatory politics in a new democracy that had previously evidenced a low level of involvement in political affairs.

The positive outcome for the government—a yes vote of 52 percent against a 39 percent no vote, but with a high abstention rate of 40 percent—was a surprise. It owed much to González's intensive campaigning, in which he put his government's credibility on the line, as well as to tactical mistakes by the opposition. The Popular Alliance's advice to voters to abstain from voting had further strained the credibility of politicians, coming as it did from a right-wing party committed to NATO. The outcome of the referendum, however, put this issue to rest and allowed the government to escape from a situation that might have had negative repercussions not merely for itself but also for the system. Above all, it cemented the Spanish military's role in NATO, thereby confirming their outward reorientation away from domestic politics.

As a whole, the crisis over Spain's NATO membership was one of those points in the consolidation process when a major international issue seems to have had played a significant role. At other phases of consolidation, it is more difficult to measure the exact impact of external relations and even to separate the external from the domestic—particularly following entry into the European Community. Unscrambling the domestic arena, however, provides a useful way of identifying how outer-directed linkages have been present to a greater or lesser degree. The overall picture is that these new democracies are displaying signs of normality, and are dealing with such issues in a routine fashion. It is already possible to distinguish between this situation and the tendency in unconsolidated democracies for "high politics" issues—whether external or internal—to have an unsettling effect.

Conclusion: Comparing Consolidation Processes in Southern Europe

This survey of inner-directed and outer-directed linkages suggests that the international context has tended to reinforce and promote the consolidation process in Southern Europe, although such linkages have also been a source of tension at times. The overall contribution of the international context has been to provide scope and opportunities for reasonably effective government performance at a time when attachments to these new democracies were still malleable. The credibility that has been accorded the EC in these countries has clearly helped Southern European governments, or at least enhanced respect for their management of policy issues. In this broad sense, the international context has contributed significantly to keeping Southern Europe's new democracies on track towards achieving consolidation.

At the same time, the gradual emergence of basic consensus on external issues—an outcome of the 1980s—has created a situation in which political debate can now be exercised without this necessarily entailing systemic risks. Furthermore, the external environment has had some influence on the formation of postauthoritarian political attitudes: the Europeanization of perspectives has tended to promote liberal democratic values. In this sense, the dominant European values of today stand in contrast with those of earlier periods of twentieth-century history, notably the 1930s. What the European Community and, to some lesser extent, other European organizations have done is to institutionalize linkages in a way that strengthens the permanence of external influences. Juxtaposing the case of postwar Italy has of course underlined how much different time contexts matter and that founding a new democracy during the Cold War period was more complicated than doing so afterward and involved different kinds of external linkages. One may infer from the above discussion of Italy that the international context had much to do with the extended consolidation process in that country.

It is possible therefore to conclude that developments in Southern Europe have encouraged the emergence of diffuse support, with the new democratic systems gaining in legitimacy and becoming more able to cope with the strains and challenges that confront established democracies. At least system alternatives have receded from the forefront of politics. While this development was to some extent achieved in transition, international factors have contributed in certain ways to negative consolidation, for instance by opening an external outlet for the military as a profession and by weakening antisystem forces on the left, against the background of a general tendency towards basic consensus on external policy options or allegiances. All these tendencies point towards the achievement of democratic consolidation in Greece, Spain, and Portugal in that order. However, in the short term, difficulties arising from the speed of change are likely to continue. This study has identified a number of ways in which patterns of modernization exact a painful price in terms of social and political stability. This is particularly true of these countries' problems in keeping pace with European integration.

The importance of the international context for positive consolidation has many dimensions. These include the symbolic or historical, the state or governmental, different intermediary or elite structures, and the mass-level or cultural. Furthermore, a distinction is necessary between short-term impacts of external events and the long-term influences of organizational linkages, whether bilateral or multilateral. It would therefore be inappropriate to regard international factors as simply secondary to domestic ones in the consolidation process. This is especially true in the interdependent world of the 1980s and 1990s and particularly among member states of the European Community (now the European Union), where internal and external factors progressively interweave. We may conclude, therefore, that the EC illustrates the strongest external linkages to the consolidation process.

Interactions between different sets of linkages may produce fluctuations in the intensity of international influences at different points in the consolidation process. Clearly, this is a problem that merits further research. Such interactions also give rise to significant cross-national variation regarding specific forms in which the international context influences democratization. There is a much greater potential for public mobilization over external issues in Greece and Spain, for instance, than in Portugal and possibly Italy. On the other hand, in Italy the ruling elites have revealed a greater tendency to be affected by external influences and pressures in decision making, including in the choice of government coalitions. And in Portugal, European influences were important in various ways, including revision of the constitution and, more broadly, in solving the main legacy from the difficult transition in that country.

The European Community can provide no firm guarantee against the accidents of domestic politics. Indeed, its impact in overcoming the uncertainties of these countries' transitions to democracy was rather limited. However, the effect of European integration on the consolidation process has steadily increased. New democracies undergoing their consolidations in the age of European integration have a distinct advantage.

6 Mass Mobilization and Regime Change: Pacts, Reform, and Popular Power in Italy (1918–1922) and Spain (1975–1978)

Sidney Tarrow

There was a time not long ago when students of democracy felt obliged to present a full-fledged model of the social structural preconditions of democracy. "Be macro-oriented, focus on objective conditions, and speak in the language of determination"—this approach, in Adam Przeworski's summary, was part of the 1960s' urge to compare "most different systems" across huge territories.[1] This sociological determinism, however, has given way to a more process-oriented emphasis on contingent choice. As Dankwart Rustow wrote when he launched a new strand of research in 1970, "decision means choice, and while the choice of democracy does not arise until the background and preparatory conditions are in hand, it is a genuine choice and does not flow automatically from these two conditions."[2]

This emphasis on choice has been refreshing for a field that had become weary of debates about the correlates of democracy based on multivariate analysis of aggregate (and often not very good) data. But as often occurs when there is a paradigm shift, the new approach emphasizes newly discovered factors at the cost of established regularities, and its practitioners sometimes evidence a certain disregard for, and even stereotyping of, previous findings. As Terry Karl writes, "this understanding of democracy has the danger of descending into excessive voluntarism if it is not explicitly placed within a framework of structural-historical constraints."[3]

To a generation of scholars jaded by sociological determinism, the logic of this position is attractive: if countries passively "received" democracy from social or economic determinants, then the number of successful transitions would increase proportionally as countries reached the "appropriate" socioeconomic thresholds—which the checkered history of democracy shows us has not always been the case. Therefore, the proper emphasis is on choice and not on determination, on politics and political culture and not on social and economic structure.

From Choice to Elitism

But who makes the choice of successful "crafting" of new democracies? Does it revolve only around transactions among political elites, captains of industry and labor, and international systemic forces? Or can it also include those for whose benefit democracy was first invented—the mass public? In their "tentative conclusions," Guillermo O'Donnell and Philippe Schmitter are nearly categorical: "Elite dispositions, calculations, and pacts," they write, "*largely determine* whether or not an opening will occur at all" (emphasis added).[4] The mass public rumbles in the wings; the actors on the stage are the elites.

Although Rustow is often credited with initiating this new approach, the emphasis on elites actually dates not from his work directly but from the study of democratic breakdowns pioneered by Juan Linz and Alfred Stepan.[5] It was their important book on the collapse of democracy in interwar Europe and Latin America that located the major causes of democratic breakdown in elite dissensus and disagreement. Both the focus on elites and the narrative method that they and their collaborators employed have been carried over from the study of breakdown to the more recent study of transitions to democracy.

There are three problems inherent in any attempt to directly transfer this heavy, if not exclusive, emphasis on elites from democratic breakdown to democratic transitions: First, it is questionable to assume that democratization can be seen as the mirror image of its opposite. Second, in its focus on processes that can be observed in the process of democratization, the elite approach seems to be based on the assumption that because we *see* them making decisions affecting the prospect of democracy, elite transactions must be given *causal* primacy.[6] Third, a direct leap from the socioeconomic "zone of transition" of the old approaches to elite transaction in the new one leaves out much of the infinitely varied and highly problematic politics of the transition process, in which elites and masses, institutions and newly formed organizations interact in the context of social and institutional structures. Events are contingent and subject to choice; but contingency, writes Terry Karl, is also subject to structural constraints.[7]

All three points are illustrated in the period that initiated the democratization of the British competitive oligarchy—that of the first Reform Act of 1832. If it was a the result of elite transaction, it was also much more than that: across the Channel, a constitutional monarchy had just been challenged in the streets; in English society, a growing middle class was feeling the imbalance between its social weight and its lack of political clout. Within the political elite, Whigs and Tories jockeyed for position; in the streets there was a wave of popular collective action that produced a major national cycle of protest and reform.[8] These movements and reforms included Catholic emancipation and the anti-Catholic reaction to it, the "Swing" movement in the countryside, and even Church and Poor Law reform. They produced well-organized reform associations and led to the first modern social movement organization, the Chartists. The centerpiece of the government's policy was the electoral reform of 1832, which was certainly *carried out by* elite transaction; but a historian would be bold indeed to disconnect that reaction from the international situation, the growth of the middle class, splits within the ruling elite, and the swelling wave of mobilization in the country demanding reform. In fact, if we looked only at British elites in 1832, it would be difficult to understand the reasons for their passing the Reform Act and for the entire future pattern of British politics.[9] British transition was the result of mobilization and reform.

Choice and the Mass Public

This analysis begins with the premise that, in all processes of collective action, political choices are made at the mass level as well as the elite level. These choices are not mere dependent variables of social structure—as the old "conditions of democracy" approaches seemed to imply—nor are they always a danger to the successful conclusion of the democratization process—as the successful transition to democracy in Spain will demonstrate. Ordinary people rush into the streets or stay at home in response to the political opportunities they perceive and the values they think will be gained by collective action, which may be democratic, antidemocratic, or merely self-interested but may advance the cause of other, more system-regarding actors. Most important, collective action is best seen, not as an automatic reflex that needs to be controlled, but as a factor which varies in size and timing, and in terms of whether it is activated in the direction of democracy or against it.[10]

I will apply this approach in the context of the development of studies of democratic transitions. The much-criticized "preconditions" literature of the 1960s tried to accomplish two things, which it sometimes conflated: first, it focused on exogenous social forces' correlations with the existence or nonexistence (or the stability or instability) of democratic politics; second, it looked upon those forces as *objective* determinants of democracy, often neglecting the fact that, if a new democracy is to be generated, someone must transform structural factors into action through political choice.

In contrast, an exclusive focus on elites in democratization reverses both of these procedures and conflates their reciprocals: by focusing on choice instead of determination, and on elites rather than on social structures, it operationalizes choice mainly through elite decision making, ignoring the important and sometimes decisive role played by mass mobilizations and reform in support of regime change. In the long-term evolution of studies of democratization, then, there has been a shift from a structural and largely deterministic analysis of society to an emphasis on elites that does not take into account the possibility that actors other than elites can choose democratization (or its opposite) or follow paths of collective action that enhance the possibility of either one.

To be more specific, what remains largely absent from the new tradition of studying democratization are two basic problems: first, the strategic choices that mass publics make in inducing elites to move either towards democracy or in some other direction, and second, how the solution of this problem conditions the nature of the emerging democratic system and its consolidation. Although I will focus here on the first problem, its solution has obvious implications for the second.

Rustow was well aware of the shifting and intersecting arenas of conflict and transaction. In his treatment of democratic transitions, he delineated three stages in full democratization. In his view, the crafting of democratic arrangements comes only at the end of a long historical process. The first prerequisite is the achievement of national unity. Then comes a period of prolonged political struggle. During this struggle, social and political groups interact, form alliances, and struggle for supremacy. Only then does a small circle of leaders negotiate a successful transition.[11]

At some phases of the process of democratization—particularly with regard to the consolidation of newly emerging democratic regimes—elite choices appear to predominate. For example, Michael Burton, Richard Gunther, and John Higley show that "a key to the stability and survival of democratic regimes is . . . the establishment of substantial consensus among elites concerning rules of the democratic political game and the worth of democratic institutions." In fact, they contend that the deliberate demobilization of activists by opposition leaders may be necessary for consolidation to occur.[12] But at earlier stages in the democratization process, during what Rustow calls "prolonged struggle," critical choices are made among the mass public and in its interaction with elites. What these choices are and how they intersect with elite transactions are largely responsible for the differences in outcome, as I will attempt to show in the comparison that follows. If Rustow is correct, then a sole emphasis on elite decision making may draw our attention to the most overt phase of institution building and away from others, and towards only the culmination of a longer and broader-based process which is the necessary foundation on which the terms are set for these negotiations. Moreover, it may make elite "pact making" the master process of democratization and give insufficient attention to other types of transition, such as reform, imposition, and revolution.[13]

In summary, if prolonged struggle is an essential stage in preparing the way for elites to craft democracy, then the nature of the actors in the struggle and their relations with each other are critical and it will be necessary to pay attention to them in order to understand the outcome of the process. If nothing else, the period of prolonged struggle before the transition becomes overt gives elites important signals in predicting how different sectors of the mass public are likely to respond to various moves on their part.[14] In particular cases the struggle may be less prolonged and less critical than in others, while international, political, and institutional factors may combine to place greater emphasis on the decisions and negotiations of elites. Such a situation is often said to have been true of Spain in the middle to late 1970s—the paradigmatic case of elite transaction. But a look at the period only a few years earlier shows a much richer and broader-based process.[15]

If this is true of Spain, how much more may it be the case in transitions which are less managed and less well prepared than the Spanish one? The recent transitions in Eastern Europe are a case in point: in some, like Hungary, mass mobilization appears to have been slight; in others, like Poland, democratization began at the base of society; and in others, like East Germany, a true cycle of protest brought on the collapse of the regime.[16] I will use the contrasting case of Italy after World War I to show how the structure of conflict in civil society intersected with elite politics to produce a still-born democracy and twenty years of fascism.

An Interactive Approach to Transition

To begin, we need a framework that will draw our attention to both elite and mass levels and to the interactions between them in the democratization process. Let us begin by assuming that every democratic episode, whether successful or not, can be seen as a cycle of mobilization and

Table 6.1 A Framework for the Analysis of Democratic Episodes

Level of Society	Level of Analysis	
	Civil Society	Political Society
Elite	Social coalition formation	Institutional pacts and transactions
Mass	Mass collective action	Oppositional organization and strategy

strategic interaction, in which actors at both the elite and mass levels take advantage of new and expanded opportunities in both political and civil society. Opportunities not only present themselves exogenously (e.g., from war, international pressure, or economic change), but develop endogenously, in response to actions taken by other actors in the system—elite and mass, institutional and extrainstitutional. Collective action by the mass public may be either present or absent, democratic-leaning or inimical to the construction of democracy. Table 6.1 proposes a framework for the further elaboration of this idea.

This typology can help us to analyze the interaction of elites and mass publics in democratization processes in three ways. First, on the assumption that different actors in the system are conscious of one another's moves, it can help us to map their strategic interaction. Second, it expands the usual dichotomy of elite and mass by drawing attention to the fact that the actions of each result from characteristics of both politics and civil society.[17] Third, the typology can help us move through time over the various stages of a democratic episode without reducing the analysis to a story of heroes and villains, failures and successes.

I will proceed by comparing two polar cases: one of bitter failure and the other of triumphant success; the first of elite dissensus and the second of elite negotiation; the first occurring in a context of international and economic crisis and the second in one of economic growth and international stability. The failed case is that of Italy from 1919 to 1922, but it is *not* a failure of pact making, since the strategy of change was one of reform and not transaction. The outcome reflected alignments within the opposition, and the jumbled lines of contact between mass and elite politics as well as the incapacity of elites to reach agreement. The success story is that of Spain in the late 1970s, which was clearly a success of pact making that occurred because of the breaches in the old system that opened up during the "prolonged struggle" of the preceding years and through the interactions between elite and mass politics.

Italy, 1918–1922: The Failure of Reform and Mobilization

The trauma of the interwar period left many European observers with a nightmare image of what had happened in Italy when uncontrolled masses were let loose, an image that was reinforced by the greater horrors of national socialism and genocide. Seymour Martin Lipset has distilled this trauma into more analytical language in his classic essay, "'Fascism'—Left, Right and Center," in which he argues that "the real question to answer is: which strata are most 'displaced' in each country? In some, it is the new working class . . . ; in others, it is the small businessmen and other relatively independent entrepreneurs. . . . In still others, it is the conservative and traditionalist elements who seek to preserve the old society from the values of socialism and liberalism. Fascist ideology in Italy . . . arose out of an opportunistic movement which sought at various times to appeal to all three groups."[18]

The new literature on the collapse of democracy would place far more emphasis on the mistakes of, and conflicts among, elites during 1918–22 than Lipset did on the unprepared masses. Had the elites had the courage and wisdom to oppose Mussolini's blackshirts and adapt to the challenge of mass politics, this argument goes, Giolitti and Turati, Sturzo and Victor Emmanuel could have stopped Italy's slide into dictatorship.[19] The willingness to compromise and to provide guarantees to minorities that led to a successful transition in post–World War II Italy might have saved the country from dictatorship after World War I.

But the 1918–22 period was radically different in many ways from the situation that would prevail after the Second World War. First, after the defeat of the Central Powers, there was no American occupying army to press for democracy, nor was there any equivalent of the Marshall Plan to reconstruct an economy dislocated by war. Nor had Italy much experience with real dictatorship to react to—although, for the lower classes, the so-called "Liberal" state had been far from benevolent. So new was Italy's encounter with mass democracy in 1918–22 that it is difficult to consider it a case of democratic breakdown at all.[20] It can more usefully be seen as a case of the failure of democratization through reform, as is argued by Paolo Farneti, whose analysis of this period remains the most synthetic and penetrating. "Fascism," he concludes, "was finally able to exploit the confused reaction to the process of democratization of Italian society." Farneti's argument reveals the importance of all four quadrants in Table 6.1: elite transactions, opposition politics, social coalitions, and mass collective action, as well as the strategic interaction among elites and mass publics.[21]

The Absence of Transaction and the Results of Reform

With their small numbers and ridiculous pomp, how could the Fascists have so easily undermined Italian democracy? At the most surface level, they were able to destroy democracy because of the failure of the party system to produce an alternative to the old Liberal-led coalitions that would reflect the new conditions of the expanded suffrage and proportional representation installed in 1919. But this was not just a failure of elite will or wisdom; it was mainly due to the overlapping of three sets of political cleavages in the parliamentary elite—between left and right, interventionists and neutralists, clericals and anticlericals—which structurally constrained the possibilities for reform.

The suffrage reform of 1912 had produced a Chamber of Deputies that, while different, still left the old center-right group of Liberals and Democrats with a comfortable majority.[22] But the bitter experience of the war, its difficult economic aftermath, and the 1919 reform, which extended the vote to all males over 21 years of age and to all veterans over 18, produced a divided Chamber in which the old center-right alignment was shattered without giving way to a new majority.

The left emerged from the 1919 reform much strengthened, with 275 seats, as opposed to its earlier 169. The right, internally divided between neutralists and interventionists, was much weakened, with 129, down from 339 seats. And a new Catholic party, the Partito Popolare, came from nowhere to win almost 100 seats, reflecting both the expansion of the suffrage and the end of the Vatican's ban on Catholic participation in national politics.

When faced by the extraparliamentary challenges of, first, militant socialism and extreme nationalism, and then fascism, none of the traditional political formulae could produce a stable majority. A coalition of the left was out of the question and the Popolari, closely linked to the Vatican, would not unite with either the anticlerical Socialists or Giolitti and the Liberals. The bitter rivalries between Giolitti and the right-wing Liberals—not to mention the latter's sharply reduced parliamentary strength—made it impossible for a traditional Liberal majority to emerge. Farneti shows that it was the numerical difficulty of producing a workable majority from the electoral reform and structural realignment of 1919, and *not* a failed transaction among elites, that "reduced the political arena and created a power vacuum that made the possibility of a government 'imposed by the streets' more and more feasible."[23] We see this most clearly in the divisions within the opposition.

An Opposition Divided

Every transitional situation to some extent produces similar problems of adaptation to the presence of new actors in the political game. But in Italy, deep ideological cleavages and searing political conflicts divided the parliamentary elite, making compromise difficult to fashion. This can be seen both in the relations among the opposition parties and within the largest of them, the Socialists, and in the wild card of Catholic participation for the first time since the Risorgimento deprived the church of its temporal domains.

Contagion to the Left. The biggest winners in the 1919 elections were the various leftist parties—Socialists, the Social Reformists, and, after 1921, the Communists. The reform socialists of Bissolati had already been expelled in 1912, and remained to the right of these groups through the postwar period. But after the war, the socialists faced a wider set of constraints, the first resulting from internal divisions, and the second from contradictions within the largest left-wing party, the "official" Unified Socialist Party (PSU). These constraints were the result of deep fissures in the electorate and not the outcome of elite decisions or mistakes.

From the point of view of interparty divisions, the data are clear. In the elections of 1921, the PSU gained 123 seats in the Chamber, the Social Reformists 25, and the Communists 13. By 1922, under the external influence of the Comintern, the PSU fragmented still further, into a reformist group around Turati with 83 seats and a maximalist one around Serrati with 40. "Here we get to the heart of the matter," writes historian Edward Malefakis: the working-class organizations moved leftward *regardless* of organizational form.[24]

Behind this contagion to the left there lay the dream of an Italian October and the unwillingness of socialist politicians to dissociate themselves from it, but there also lay the uneven structural development of Italian society.[25] The most important structural factor was the imbrication of urban-industrial conflict with continuing traditions of agrarian revolt in a country in which close to half the working population (in 1930) remained in agriculture. The strains placed upon the fragile Italian economy by total war and the postwar collapse of production also contributed to this development, as did the false expectations raised among socialist leaders by the dramatic increases in votes and membership that they enjoyed after the war.

Divisions among the Socialists. Faced by these problems, the Italian socialists were unable to resolve two fundamental cleavages—between parliamentary reformism and revolutionary politics, and (within the unions) between maximalism and syndicalism, which by 1919 was no longer revolutionary. By 1919, the Italian labor movement was divided both transversely and vertically by these splits. While the secretariat of the Socialist Party was in the hands of the maximalists, the majority of the parliamentary group was reformist, and the unions were led by moderate syndicalists, like Buozzi, opposed by a radical maximalist wing.[26] These splits, and the readiness of the maximalists—sustained by militancy at the base—to take advantage of any hint of reformist moderation, led to both verbal revolutionism and paralysis.

As a result, between 1919 and 1921, the Socialists were incapable both of entering the government—*any* government—and of leading a revolution like the one that swept Spain in 1934. Had they done so, the split between reformists and maximalists in Parliament would have become irreparable and the reformists might have lost to their competitors in the unions. Giolitti's prewar strategy of buying off the left with reform bills could no longer work either, as there were few resources with which to carry out these reforms.[27] Besides, after the schism at Livorno, cooperation with the right would have given the newly formed Communist Party a chance to expose the socialists as the running dogs of capital, just as Lenin was simultaneously condemning Kautsky.

Exploitation from the Right. These divisions in the country's largest opposition party and the realignment in the country that they represented were all the more tragic because they left the party paralyzed just as the supposed threat of socialism began to serve as the pretext for the growth of extraparliamentary fascism. There had been an extreme right in Parliament in 1919—the Nationalists—but they were a "respectable" right, rejecting the practice of violence and supporting king and army.[28] And there was already an extraparliamentary fringe in the country, which fed on Italy's failure to make significant gains from the war, expressed in d'Annunzio's comic opera march on Fiume.

What Mussolini did was combine the two and add to them his skills as a showman and a journalist. His strategy was simple and contradictory—to foment violence in the country while calling in Parliament for law and order against the left.[29] How could he get away with so grotesque a contradiction in so sophisticated a political community? The reason cannot be understood without coming to grips with fascism's strategic interaction with the other forces in play. Among the socialists, the verbal revolutionism of the maximalists and the only slightly more credible threat of the communists helped make the threat of an Italian October seem real. At the same time, the inability of any of the moderate political groupings to form a majority provided Mussolini with the political space in which to develop. His victory, however, was not the result of strategy alone. Its basic causes came from the economic catastrophe of the war, the collapse of the left's mobilization wave, and the realignment that was taking shape in Italian society as a result of the entry of the Catholics into active politics, the expansion of the suffrage, and postwar manpower demobilization. These aggravated the desperation of the lower classes, as they put pressure on small landholders and the urban middle class. This combination of factors led to simultaneous urban middle class and rural landholder alarm and produced what Farneti calls "a coalition of property and acquisition."

A Coalition of Property and Acquisition

Italian society in the immediate postwar years was undergoing a tremendous realignment of class forces. On the one hand, if the war created strains that permitted poor peasants and workers to mobilize "in a way unprecedented in the country's history," this also had the perverse result of allying the middle and upper classes against the fear of an Italian October. On the other hand, during the war there had been an enormous increase in the number of small landowning peasants, who rose from 18 percent to 32 percent of the farm population in just ten years.[30] These rural groups were badly hit by the postwar collapse in farm prices and demobilization of troops, many of whom came home only to find themselves unemployed. Many new landowners could not make the payments on their mortgages, at precisely the time when farm workers were demanding to be paid wages at wartime levels. Squeezed between the banks and the demands of agricultural labor, who were backed by the Socialists and the unions, a mass of small farmers, tenants, and even sharecroppers turned to agrarian fascism.

The agrarian crisis was not the only source of fascism's political support. The economic dislocations of the war and the labor agitation that followed produced such widespread fear among urban propertied groups that the traditional cleavages of country and city, industry and agriculture, were temporarily bridged. "Salaried [agricultural] workers, small peasants and industrial workers were aligned on one side, small and large property and business owners on the other."[31] Much of the growth in union membership after the war came from the countryside of the Po valley, coinciding with the occupation of the factories in the north and with sporadic land occupations in the south and center of the country. Even in Tuscany, writes Malefakis, landowners "were shocked to discover that the *mezzadri* saw things so differently as to join forces with the peasant leagues in the immediate post-War era."[32]

The postwar crisis, the fear of socialism and the climate of social turbulence could not fail to have an effect on a state which had never been neutral in the struggle between property and labor. The march on Fiume gave the signal that those who carried the banner of irredentism could enjoy the neutrality of the state; the coming together of an urban-rural coalition of property and acquisition gave the fascist movement the social and political bases it needed to take advantage of this situation; and the forces of order turned a blind eye to attacks against Socialist militants and headquarters. Although the army had a plan to round up the Fascists, it was loyal only to the monarchy, and the king never gave the order to move against Mussolini.

The Collapse of Popular Collective Action

The defeat of interwar European democracy is often linked to the simultaneous development of the extremes and their "objective" collaboration to bring down democracy. However true this might have been in Weimar Germany in the 1930s—and we must not forget that the Nazis rose to power *despite* the German Social Democrats' consistent defense of democracy—it was certainly *not* the case in Italy in 1918–22. In that country, the upsurge of fascist strength came only in mid-1921, when mobilization from the left had already begun to collapse. Mussolini exploited the left-wing danger, but the fact that mass mobilization from the left was already declining in 1922 left the socialists without the resource of popular support to confront him and allowed the political class to waver when faced by reaction.[33]

There are many reasons for this sudden collapse of left-wing militancy. Rural collective action had a major share in postwar mobilization. Rural workers, as Malefakis reminds us, flock to labor organizations in times of "generalized hope." But because they are exposed to far greater danger of retribution than the urban proletariat, they tend to abandon these movements rapidly as events confirm their fundamental pessimism. This is the reason why CGL membership declined to less than one-fifth of its 1920 size just before Mussolini took power and to one-tenth of that figure by 1923.[34] Cycles of rural mobilization characteristically contain high peaks followed by precipitous declines. The left was deserted by its rural base just as its most ferocious enemies were taking the field.

But in the cities, also, the mobilization wave had collapsed by the time the fascists began their heavy depredations on left-wing unions and parties. The decline in industrial employment in 1921 and the conversion from a war to a peacetime economy rocked the labor movement and sent hundreds of thousands of workers into unemployment. The reduced pressure on employment had an immediate effect on the strike rate, which declined from over 900,000 strikers in 1919 to 858,000 in 1920 to under 600,000 in 1921. By the time the fascist *squadre* went seriously to work, the workers' movement was in disarray and could barely defend itself.[35]

The early school of democratic breakdown theorists saw the revolt of the masses—of left and right—as a main factor in the collapse of Italian democracy. But it is worth underscoring that it was when the left was *no longer able* to put up a solid front against reaction—and not as the result of simultaneous left- and right-wing mobilization—that Italian democracy failed. We may even speculate that *had* the working class been in the field in 1922, which it assuredly was not, politicians of left and moderate right might have had the incentive to oppose fascism more forcefully.

The Italian case of 1919–22 shows that there are alternative paths towards democratic transition beyond pact making and transaction. Pacts were never on the agenda in Italy, which was attempting a transition through reform that, for structural and political reasons, it was unable to complete. The strategy of the opposition, the shape and structure of mass mobilization, the weakness of a coalition for reform, and the miscalculations of elites contributed to this failure, but so did the divisions, outbidding, and paralysis on the left, the realignment in the country, and the absence of a social coalition favoring democracy. Let us turn to a contrasting episode of democratization to sketch how the same variables take shape under very different circumstances.

Spain: Pacts in the Presence of Mobilization

The Spanish case is often regarded as the archetype of a new wave of democratization which began in the 1970s. Even though other cases in the same decade lend themselves more easily to other models of transition, politicians outside Spain and many scholars have come to regard Spain's "transition through transaction" as the model to follow. Since Spain's transition was so self-evidently successful, the pact making that it pursued has come to be seen by many, especially in Eastern Europe, as the master process of democratization.[36]

There are various versions of this model, and they differ in the degree of autonomy they assign to elites and masses, institutions and social coalitions, constraint and voluntarism. Some assign primary responsibility to elites; others regard elite transaction as only one of a typology of routes of democratization; while for others, the democratization process is the result of the interplay between elite strategies and mass mobilization and opinion.[37] José Maravall regards the transition in Spain as "the result of two driving forces: one providing impetus for reform, negotiation and agreement 'from above,' and the other emerging 'from below' in the form of pressures and demands."[38]

Transition through Transaction

The story of Spain's transition through transaction has been told in many versions. The most "elitist" among them has the following components: Influenced by the repugnance for the regime that had grown up among broad sectors of the public and by the country's economic backwardness, small groups of "seceding" elites took advantage of a liberalizing process within an eroding dictatorship, which was unable to stop the logic of liberalization once it had begun. These seceding groups built bridges to moderate groups in the opposition, convincing them—by involving them progressively in agreements and pacts—that they could well afford the risk of playing the democratic game. Their participation, and the concessions they were willing to make for it, convinced reactionary elites—the well-known "bunker" of the Spanish regime—that they had nothing to fear by going along with the choice of a new regime.[39]

The ability of Spanish elites to create the institutional arrangements that eventually led to representative government contrasts vividly with the apparent blindness and inadequacy of the Italian political class of 1918–22, and with that of the Spanish one of the 1930s.[40] Aided by the presence of a far-sighted constitutional monarch and a gifted negotiator in the person of Adolfo Suárez, Spanish elites avoided the mistakes of their predecessors, preempted revolution by co-opting elements of the opposition, and avoided mobilization from the extremes.

Once begun, the process accelerated as various groups from both inside and outside the regime saw their best interests served by participation in the constitutional negotiations and brought their followers to compromise in order to advance the democratic project. The period from the preconstitutional negotiations of July 1976, when Suárez was appointed, to June 1977, when the first general elections were held, was the most critical phase of the process, during which confidence and structural integration were built among formerly divided elites. The keystone Moncloa Pacts pledged all of the major actors to cooperation, while the participation of the Communists and Socialists in the process assured that the workers over whom they had influence refrained from excessive strike activity and limited their demands.[41]

The success of the process was proven by the self-liquidation of the Cortes in November 1976, and its passage of the Law for Political Reform. Military intervention was sidestepped by careful preemption of key issues by Suárez and by the fact that no significant faction came forward to urge the military to intervene.[42] The process culminated with the alternation in power from the Union de Centro Democratico to the now-moderate Partido Socialista Obrero Español (PSOE) and the failure of the one major challenge to the process, the coup which almost toppled the government.

This rendering of the story leaves out a great deal, though. First, it focuses mainly on what happened during the crucial years 1976 and 1977, ignoring the earlier period of "prolonged struggle." Second, in emphasizing regime liberalization, it ignores the considerable back-peddling towards repression during the 1969–73 period and the question of why the regime liberalized when it did. Third, it leaves out the infighting in the Franquist establishment and the conflicts between it and important social forces.[43] In turning to these questions, the transformation of Spanish society during the decade of the 1960s is the obligatory starting point.

A Coalition for Productivity and Reform

The basic changes in Spanish society in the postwar years are too well known to delay us for very long. By the 1970s, "Spain had become a major industrial power and its gross national product per capita had risen to a level comparable to those of other Western European countries."[44] These changes can be gleaned in summary form from a set of indices constructed by Tatu Vanhanen in his study *The Emergence of Democracy*. Vanhanen has constructed what he calls an "index of power resources" (IPR), which combines an index of occupational diversification (IOD)—the arithmetic mean of the percentage of population living in cities and the percentage in nonagricultural pursuits—with the percentage of literates in the population (index of knowledge distribution, IKD), and with the proportion of agricultural acreage that is in family farms (FF).[45] These data from Vanhanen are summarized in Table 6.2.

As the table indicates, progress in two of the three indicators was slow and steady until the 1960s when Spain experienced an economic breakthrough. At that time, it was, as one observer puts it, "as if the Spanish nation entered a crucible at the end of the fifties and emerged a decade later in a different form."[46] Both the new working class, whose emergence is documented by Sebastian Balfour, and a new and more cosmopolitan industrial elite were important social products of this transition. But perhaps more important still was massive urbanization, interregional migration, and the Europeanization of the Spanish economy.

An important aspect of Spain's economic spurt in the postwar period

Table 6.2 Indices of Democratization in Spain, 1930–1979

	IOD	IKD	FF	IPR
1930–39	38.5	39.5	22	03.3
1940–49	42.0	46.0	22	04.3
1950–59	45.5	48.5	22	04.9
1960–69	51.5	52.5	24	06.5
1970–79	58.0	57.5	24	08.0

Sources: Table constructed from data in Tatu Vanhanen, *The Emergence of Democracy: A Comparative Study of 119 States, 1850–1979* (Helsinki: Finnish Society of Sciences and Letters, 1984), p. 147; definitions of indices from Tatu Vanhanen, ed., *Strategies of Democratization* (Washington, D.C.: Crane Russak, 1992), p. 22.

Note: Explanation of column heads:

IOD = index of occupational diversification: mean of percentage of population living in cities plus percentage of population in nonagricultural occupations

IKD = index of knowledge distribution: percentage of population that is literate

FF = family farms: percentage of total farm acreage that is in family farms

IPR = index of power resources: combines preceding three indices plus number per 100,000 of population attending degree-granting institutions and a measure of the decentralization of nonagricultural resources

was its increased involvement in international exchange. Spain joined the International Monetary Fund, the World Bank, and the Organization for Economic Co-operation and Development in the 1950s, and the government began negotiations with the European Economic Community in 1962.[47] This not only increased the pressure on Spanish elites to become more "European" but forced upon them the need for the economy to become more competitive. The stabilization plan of 1959 was one product of this realization; changes in the composition of the cabinet to include more "technocrats" (and exclude some old Franco loyalists) was another.

These changes created new opportunities for increased differentiation within the regime and for the development of an effective coalition for reform outside of it, and these two trends interacted. For example, if Spanish industry was to become European and competitive, it would have to allow workers both to negotiate on their own and to produce grassroots leaders with the autonomy to back up the contracts they had signed. For purely economic reasons, some managerial groups had been pressing for this type of change since the late 1950s. By the 1960s, many were dealing secretly with the Workers' Commissions, rather than with the state-controlled *Sindicatos*.[48]

Alongside the new industrial elite there was also an enlarged professional middle class among whom the idea of a Spain outside of Europe was no longer conceivable.[49] Few of these groups could be comfortable in a regime whose military-clerical-agrarian social origins had left it with a stifling cultural parochialism. Even under full authoritarianism, polls carried out by the Instituto de la Opinión Pública were, as early as 1966, showing that a large plurality favored a government elected by the people over government by a single leader.[50] It was a clear sign of the political bankruptcy of the regime that a large proportion of future student radicals would come from among the children of high-status Spanish families.[51]

The formation of new social coalitions is not as visible as are politicians declaring the signature of pacts at well-publicized news conferences, but by the late 1960s there was growing impatience in much of the Spanish upper and middle classes with Spain's self-exclusion from Europe,[52] and a visible revulsion in those sectors of the population with access to public opinion at the outrages being perpetrated by the regime. These changes could be seen in the replacement within governing circles of loyalists by technocrats and in the evolution of both the press and the Roman Catholic Church.

The breakup of the old coalitional equilibrium was first signaled in the late 1950s, when Catholic Opus Dei technocrats "entered the political scene as the main protagonists of the new economic policy."[53] The story of the role of Opus Dei in the transition of the Spanish political economy to advanced industrial status is too well known to need elaboration here. Its importance lay in the dedication of its representatives to Spain's integration into Western capitalism and in the dialectic of conflict that it helped to trigger within the regime. Such conflicts, however subtle and guarded, could not be kept from the rest of Spanish society. Although Opus Dei was hardly radical, intra-elite conflicts widened the political opportunities for other actors and demonstrated the vulnerability of the regime to political change.

The evolution of the press during the same decade was a palpable sign that the regime's unity was cracking. In moderate journals like *ABC*, *Ya*, and *Cuadernos para el Diálogo*, which brought constitutional monarchists, Christian Democrats and moderate socialists together, the government found itself subjected to increasingly vocal criticism from inside the establishment.[54] Although it was eventually closed down after the Burgos trial, the daily *Madrid* had, by the end of the decade, evolved towards a constitutional monarchist position.

Also important in providing opportunities for the opposition was the evolution of the Catholic Church. The defection of churchmen from unconditional support for the regime began among younger clergy living in substandard housing estates at the parish level and extended to the hierarchy when the Second Vatican Council legitimized pulling away from the regime. Most startling to Spaniards in the late 1960s were the dramatic changes in the attitude of the hierarchy, the liberal appointments to high positions in the church, and the attacks on liberal priests by right-wing thugs under apparent police protection. By the early 1970s, the church—or at least its most visible segments—could be counted among the opposition. The shift was made official in 1971 when the Catholic Church acknowledged its errors for taking sides in the civil war.[55]

These shifts within the regime and among social and institutional elites make it difficult to understand the Spanish transition in terms of either elite or mass-level decisions taken on their own. What was really happening was the growth of *a coalition for productivity and reform* in Spanish society and a consequent pluralization of the political game, as segments of the elite distanced themselves from the regime and began to imagine alternative scenarios to the "organic democracy" of its *ultra* supporters. The signs of this could be found in mass culture, in art and literature, but it became publicly manifest in response to critical events in the economy and society and, in particular, in response to collective action.

Protest as a Resource[56]

Elite fractionation was not simply the result of the liberalization of an authoritarian regime unraveling from within. On the contrary, the regime went through a viciously repressive phase from 1969 to 1973 which attempted to roll back the changes of the mid-1960s. But by then it was too late to stop the unraveling of the regime's unity from within and the attacks on it from without. These two processes were closely interrelated: for key elite sectors, especially in the church and the press and among intellectuals, the turning points in their shift towards acceptance of political change came in response to the mobilization from below that surged during the 1960s and early 1970s and especially in reaction to the state repression that was organized against it after 1969.

While the events that produced the successful calendar of elite transition were limited to the mid-1970s, mass collective action had developed much earlier and played a key role in the defections outlined above as well as in the development of the opposition. This could be seen in the workers' movement, in the student movement, and in the repression and radicalization of protest in the Basque country, especially in the Burgos trial.

The Workers' Movement. From the mid-1960s on, the Spanish working class sustained a level of strikes "that fell well within the broad Western European pattern even though such industrial conflict [in Spain] was illegal."[57] The scope and intensity of strike activity, moreover, in-

Table 6.3 Working Hours Lost through Strikes in Spain

Year	Millions of Hours
1966	1.5
1970	8.7
1975	14.5
1976	150.0
1977	110.0
1978	68.0

Source: Maravall, *The Transition to Democracy,* pp. 33, 37.

creased dramatically as the transition to a post-Franco democracy began (see Table 6.3). Perhaps equally important, these strikes took on an increasingly political tone. Maravall estimates that between 1963 and 1967 only 4 percent of all workers' demands were political in nature (the overwhelming majority being purely economic) and that during the period 1967 to 1974 nearly half (45 percent) were solidarity or political demands.[58] In the mid-1970s, the pattern of strikes and demonstrations was closely calibrated with the political program of the political opposition, giving it a powerful tool with which to back up its demands.

The origins of the workers' movement were largely spontaneous, local, and work related, but deliberate labor organization was clearly evident by the mid-1960s. In the last decade of the Franco regime, a new type of action, the *huelga general local* (local general strike), combined economic and political demands. Several such protests took place in 1973—in Pamplona, Catalonia (Sardanyola and Ripollet), the Basque country, and Madrid. This type of strike showed both opponents and potential allies that the workers had a high level of organization and capacity for mobilization on a mass basis.[59]

Mass collective action was widely diffused across industrial areas and showed the unity of the working class through increasing solidarity and political strikes, which rose from 4 percent of all strikes in the mid-sixties to more than 45 percent after 1966. Solidarity strikes became more and more common in the early 1970s, particularly in the key sectors of coal in Asturias, metal working in the Basque country, Catalonia, and Madrid, and even in new industrial areas.[60]

How could working-class collective action contribute to a democratic outcome, when so many observers feared it would polarize the situation and lead to reaction? Since the breakdown of democracy in Spain in the 1930s had been so closely related to labor strife, the question is of more than academic importance. There are four key contrasts between Spanish collective action in the 1970s and Italy's after World War I that will help us to understand this key difference.

First, where the Italian wave of popular collective action had peaked by 1921, leaving the political elite to respond to the growing threat from the right, the wave of strikes in Spain progressively grew, then swelled enormously immediately following the death of Franco—a crucial period when hopes for democratization were high but were frustrated by the lack of progress towards democracy under the government of Carlos Arias Navarro. The magnitude of this increase in strike activity can be seen in the data presented in Table 6.3. These strikes not only helped to isolate the Franco regime from key industrialists—who would have liked to quickly settle their industrial disputes on economic terms—but in the mid-1970s, the threat of popular militancy held the governing elite's feet to the fire and gave the opposition a political resource with which to bargain.[61]

Second, and again in contrast to Italy in 1918–21, the labor movement avoided the "contagion to the left" and the outbidding that so often accompanies competitive situations. This was in part because communists and socialists, having experienced decades of exile and persecution, had learned the strategic virtues of unity. The disappearance of the anarchists from the panoply of left-wing organizations in the years since the civil war and the organizational preponderance of the Comisiones Obreras (CCOO) simplified the problem of common action. Labor leaders did not have to look over their shoulders to worry that competitors to their left were criticizing them for the moderation of their goals. As a result, they were able to employ tactical moderation during key phases of the transition process—for example, after the signing of the Pacts of Moncloa. Support for strikers by influential sectors of the public and the church made it difficult to see them as sequels to the anarchy of the 1930s.[62]

The third reason for the effectiveness of collective action during the transition was that it was accompanied and constrained by a democratic vocation on the part of the working class and its representatives. This was as true of factory-level militants as it was of ordinary voters. Fishman has produced evidence that suggests that the bulk of the labor movement was not advancing radical sectoral goals at the cost of democratization. And the relatively moderate views of working-class voters when they participated in the first democratic elections in post-Franco Spain indicate that there was no antidemocratic thrust in the strike wave of the mid-1970s.[63] Indeed, in retrospect we can see that the character of working-class mobilization fit well with the exigencies of the political transition. Politicized strike activity reached a peak during the first few months of 1976; these waves of protest contributed to the dismissal of the do-nothing Arias Navarro government and its replacement by the decisively prodemocratic government of Adolfo Suárez. These strikes also helped Suárez to neutralize the "bunker," making it possible for him to point to the most likely alternative to his proposed reforms. Following the first democratic election of 1977, however, and especially following the signing of the Pacts of Moncloa, there was not only a lessening of strike activity but strike demands were largely devoid of political content, focusing instead on economic grievances. Thus, during the 1977–78 period, when elites were negotiating the shape of the new democracy, proponents of democratization could point to the substantially more tranquil political atmosphere (except, obviously, in the Basque country) as a preferable alternative to the polarization and social instability of the final days of the former authoritarian system. Fishman adds that, after the new democratic constitution came into effect and the Pacts of Moncloa expired (January 1, 1979), workers remobilized and mounted the greatest campaign of strike activity of the post-Franco period, but restricted their demands to economic issues.[64]

The fourth reason has to do not so much with the behavior of any particular group during the transition but with a "dog that didn't bark"—the agrarian sector. Much of the labor violence in Italy in 1919–21, as in Spain in 1934–36, had been rural—on the part of the agricultural proletariat. When violence explodes in the countryside, it is often more ferocious and widespread than in the cities, as in Córdoba in 1918–19 and Badajoz and Málaga in the spring of 1936. "When this occurred," writes Malefakis, "the very bases of society must have seemed to be collapsing to the urban as well as rural middle classes."[65]

But in the intervening decades, Spanish class structure had evolved in ways very similar to Italy's and France's. By 1976, only 9 percent of active Spanish population still worked in agriculture, and there were twice as many small proprietors as farm workers.[66] The numerical decline of the agricultural sector and the widespread migration to the cities meant that labor conflict in the late 1960s and early 1970s fell into patterns that, but for the government's repressive policies, would have resembled the simultaneous strike waves elsewhere in Europe. There was no equivalent of the class war in the countryside that had turned Spanish conservatives into reactionaries and provided a mass base for General Franco's coup d'état.

The Student Movement. As its children grew to college age, the new Spanish middle class produced a large-scale expansion of university enrollment. The first student protest dates to 1956, but until the end of the 1950s, political activities within the universities were rare and mobilization was almost nonexistent. The oldest national-level secret student organization (FUDE) dates from the early 1960s, but by 1967–68, an illegal democratic student union, the SDE, controlled by the Communist Party, was operating in all Spanish universities. By 1968, "the gravity of the situation had been acknowledged by a feeble gesture consisting of the introduction of an Opus Dei member, José Luis Villar Palasí, as Minister of Education,"[67] but "the universities slowly began to become arenas of discussion, and university magazines . . . were sometimes used as platforms of nonorthodox or reformist political and cultural views."[68]

While much weaker than in Western Europe, the pattern of student mobilization would have been familiar to any student of Italy or France in the 1960s: "It was a period of permanent assemblies and sit-ins against repression. The claims were for a democratic student union and for general freedoms, of association, reunion, and expression. These freedoms were established within the Faculties, which became 'liberated territories,' and we had to defend them day by day."[69]

A large majority of the sample of student radicals studied by Maravall had traveled abroad, and they attributed their radicalization in part to foreign influence. But in Spain, the movement had a special importance, for when sons and daughters of the middle and upper classes were brutalized by the police for protesting, it demonstrated the regime's peculiar anachronism and weakness. However weak, the student movement showed that the workers were far from isolated, and it eventually produced the cadres of a new political class.[70]

Burgos and the Basques. Finally, Basque militancy both began to destroy the myth of the invulnerability of the regime and brought a number of people across the line from tepid support of the regime to opposition. Following more than two decades of terrorism by Euzkadi ta Askatasuna (ETA), it is perhaps difficult today to recall the electrifying effect of the Basque movement on public opinion before the violent wing took control of the movement. Both the popularity of the movement (its terrorist phase began later) and the repressive phase of the regime culminated in the Burgos trial of 1970.[71]

Why was the trial such a turning point? There was the involvement of the church: because several priests were among the accused, Catholic officials insisted that the trial be held in public, and they helped to publicize its outrages. Also, the trial gave the opposition its first opportunity to unify around a popular cause, particularly at the spectacular Abbey of Monserrat assembly.[72] Finally, it gained tremendous international attention, especially after a section of ETA kidnapped the West German consul and threatened to kill him unless the accused received clemency. The trial helped to unify the opposition, produced a countermovement of regime supporters, and caused many former supporters of the regime to cross the Rubicon into the opposition.

A Growing Opposition

Each of these movements against the regime—among workers, students, and the Basques—produced defections among sectors of the elite and helped to unify the opposition around a few key goals. These effects could first be seen in 1970, at a dramatic meeting of Catalan artists, writers, and intellectuals to protest the Burgos trial at the Abbey of Monserrat, and more dramatically still at the Assembly of Catalonia in 1971, inspired by the earlier event. The example was soon followed elsewhere, especially in Madrid and Seville. Both the defections from the regime, which snowballed after the Burgos trial, and the regrouping of the opposition were directly related to the growth of collective action.[73]

Internal groups had begun to organize in parts of Spain as early as the 1950s, well before liberalization began.[74] But it was in the late 1960s that a national opposition began to form. The diffusion of the CCOO in the early 1960s, their adoption as major internal factory structures by the Communists, and the reorganization of the Socialist Party were the first organized signs that such a resurgence was taking place.

Although opposition activity accelerated with the liberalization of the 1960s, much more than liberalization was at work. First, the international situation that had kept the PCE in a ghetto became, in the new climate of Eurocommunism, far less of a constraint. Second, as we have seen, working-class leaders at the base linked their economic demands to democratization. Third, despite tactical differences between the two main sectors of the opposition, mass mobilization and opposition organization worked together to weaken the regime and to induce it to negotiate. Not only was "every arrest of a leader, every abuse or provocation" used by the opposition "as an occasion for joint actions and for massive demonstrations," after demanding nothing less than a *ruptura democrática,* the opposition was able to combine around a *ruptura pactada,* forcing the government to take an intermediate position between the advocates of change and those of continuity.[75] As Robert Fishman concludes, "the ability of the left to pressure *and* negotiate with the post-Franco . . . successor governments contributed crucially to the rapid move in the second half of 1976 towards a full political opening."[76]

Conclusions and Implications for Consolidation

I have tried to show that elite unity in Spain and disunity in Italy were the efficient—but not the solitary—causes of the success of democracy in the former and its failure in the latter. Both elite disunity in Italy and elite integration in Spain operated within social, cultural, and especially political contexts that placed constraints upon and offered opportunities to leaders and their opponents. If elite unity produced successful democratic pacts in Spain, it was made possible by congeries of structural factors and by the choice of the mass public for democracy that was nowhere evident in Italy.

The timing of mass mobilization was the first important difference we found. In Italy, mobilization from the left had essentially collapsed when the liberal regime faced its greatest crisis in 1922, providing neither socialists nor Catholics with the support they needed to oppose the fascists and to stiffen the backbones of politicians. Rural collective action both heightened tensions among landowners and rendered the left prey to fascist depredations in the countryside after mobilization collapsed—which it did quite rapidly in 1921.

In Spain, by contrast, mass mobilization never ceased to increase during the 1970s—when it was a resource for the left, focusing the attention of the regime on the need for change. At times it was coordinated with the opposition's political project and at times it revolved around mainly economic demands. But in either case, it concentrated the minds of elites on the need for an accommodation and played a crucial part in the transition.[77] The fact that the unions were relatively united in their demands and did not suffer from competition from their left helped them gain the neutrality—if not the support—of the urban middle class.

The second contrast between these two cases was the significant difference in the composition of mass mobilization. The Italian worker's movement of 1919–21 was accompanied by rebellion in the countryside, and the two together fed the fear of Italy's urban and rural propertied classes that an Italian October was at hand and drove them to coalesce around Mussolini. The contagion from the left and the divisions in the opposition parties paralyzed the left and transfixed the center just as the country faced an economic crisis and a major political realignment.

In Spain, on the other hand, the agricultural proletariat that had terrorized rural elites in the 1930s had largely disappeared by the 1970s, and Spanish workers were joined by movements in the universities, in the church, and in the Basque country, and by at least passive acquiescence from business. This broad coalition made it impossible for the regime to isolate the workers through an anticommunist campaign and draw on a "coalition of property and acquisition" like the one that Farneti wrote about in Italy. International factors, which had fed illusions of revolution in 1919–20 in Italy, here played a moderating role. The PCE struggled under the banner of Eurocommunism, and the PSOE, despite its Marxist rhetoric, was linked to Northern European social democrats who were hardly interested in fomenting revolution.

Finally, it is not enough to register the *fact* of mass mobilization in assessing its role in democratization: like elite political action, mass movements have a *content* that results from the choices of the mass public, just as the actions of elites result from their choices. Italy in 1918–22 was a politically backward country in which most of the workers had been excluded from participation until quite recently, while the Catholics, under Vatican injunction, had excluded themselves until not long before 1921. Since there was no democratic vocation at the grassroots of Italian society, it is not surprising that there was little pressure on political elites to resolve the country's crisis within the framework of parliamentary institutions.

That the Spanish transition was effected by creative negotiations among elites who put aside their differences to craft an agreement that most Spaniards could live with has been amply demonstrated by the "new" (and now established) literature on democratization. But it, too, had a set of preconditions: it was facilitated not only by the economic, social, and cultural development of the country after the 1940s, but also by the choice of democracy among the bulk of the population and by the social movements that had been stirring in Spanish society since the 1960s.

Implications for Consolidation

In an interesting passage on the Spanish left, Richard Gunther provides the germ of a hypothesis for understanding much of what has happened in Spain since 1977—and especially after 1981: "the emergence of two large opposition parties in the final days of the Franquist regime greatly facilitated the bargaining processes that followed, *making it possible to demobilize activists in order to stabilize the political environment*" (italics added).[78]

Gunther is correct in the sense that mass protest was deliberately moderated by the opposition parties during the key phase of pact making in 1977, in order to calm defenders of the regime and obviate the possibility of a reactionary inversion. This tactical moderation is, however, very different from the spontaneous demobilization in city and countryside that occurred in Italy in 1921–22. Whereas the Italian demobilization came from the base and left the field open to Mussolini's *squadre* and to parliamentary vacillation, the tactical demobilization of the Spanish left in 1977–78 came from opposition leaders, and left no doubt in the elite's mind that mass mobilization was still a powerful potential force for change—as it remains today.

But the pattern of pact making and demobilization from above had important implications for how Spain would be governed during its first decade and a half of stable democracy. In her analysis of democratization in Latin America, Terry Karl hypothesizes that "pacted transitions are likely to produce corporatist or consociational democracies in which party competition is regulated to varying degrees determined, in part, by the nature of foundational bargains."[79] It is not clear how "regulated" Spanish party competition has become, or if Spain can be considered a "corporatist" system, but it is a tenable hypothesis that the success of pact making in installing democracy in Spain led, at least at first, to attempts to continue to govern through elite transaction and consociational bargains.

From the initial foundational bargain and its adumbrations through a series of additional social and economic pacts, there followed Spain's rapid adjustment to EC membership through the concerted industrial policy that this required, and a remarkably successful consociational bargain with the regions. But, as in corporatism in general, something else followed as well—both a disturbingly low frequency of political involvement and increasingly frequent strikes and mass labor demonstrations, sometimes of an extremely violent nature.[80] The coincidence of these two trends hints that all is not perfect in a democracy that was born through elite pacts imposed—in the name of democracy—on a previous process of mass mobilization.

If Italy after World War II was an imperfect bipartyism, the Spanish transition produced an imperfect corporatism. The unity of organized labor on which all successful corporatist bargains are fashioned has eluded Spanish workers and so has the unity of the left-wing parties. Rather than acting as tribune for the organized working class, when it came to power, the PSOE fell over itself to represent the "productivity" part of the coalition for reform and productivity—not to mention its embrace of NATO and the EC. And the managed demobilization in 1977–78 was based on the discipline of the communists and on the democratic proclivities of the mass base and not on a spontaneous deference of the working class for its leaders. That difference has made of Spain both a competitive democracy and an increasingly difficult one, like Italy, in its phase of consolidation.[81]

So here, at last, our analysis of Spain and Italy finds an area of convergence: both are generally agreed to be consolidated democracies; both have mixed economies in which the private sector is rapidly gaining ground; but both are increasingly competitive systems trying to contain potentially explosive collective action. In both countries, collective action is often crude, interest-based, and intolerant of the rights of others; but if it concentrates the attention of elites on the job of representation, it will be a healthy reminder to them—and to students of elite politics—that the power of democracy comes from the people.

7 Legitimacy and Democracy in Southern Europe

Leonardo Morlino and José R. Montero

In this chapter we address two questions: To what extent were democracies in Southern Europe regarded as legitimate during the 1980s and early 1990s? And what are the distinctive characteristics of this legitimacy? These questions are relevant not only for countries such as Portugal, Spain, and Greece, which underwent processes of consolidation during that period, but particularly for Italy's older democracy, whose consolidation underwent an important test in the early 1990s. Greece, Portugal, and Spain were confronted with especially serious problems, which arose because their transitions from authoritarian rule coincided with the severe economic crises that began in the mid-1970s. Legacies from the authoritarian past also had to be overcome. Thus, most scholars dealing with the period following the reestablishment of democracy in these countries regard the establishment of legitimacy for the new regimes as one of the central aspects of the consolidation process.[1] Scholars who have not placed legitimacy in the foreground of their analysis have nonetheless dealt with very similar or closely related concepts, such as "contingent consent."[2]

In the case of Italy, also, the problem of legitimacy has been a recurring topic of research. During the 1970s, Italy underwent a series of crises which we regard as deeper than those most commonly analyzed in the substantial literature on crises of ungovernability or overload in Western Europe.[3] Italy's dramatic scandals and governmental crises of the early 1990s, culminating in a complete restructuring of its party system in 1994, further tested the degree of consolidation achieved by Italian democracy.

This chapter begins with a discussion of the concept of legitimacy, offering a theoretical basis for the subsequent analysis. We then survey the distribution in Southern Europe of orientations towards democracy as a regime, attitudes towards past authoritarian experiences, and satisfaction with the actual performance of democracy, as well as some possible explanations of these survey findings. The analysis is then broadened to include an exploration of related orientations, especially towards politics in general. Finally, since we are focusing our attention on *democratic* legitimacy, we examine the different conceptions of democracy held by Southern Europeans. Most of the empirical analysis undertaken in this chapter is based upon data collected by the Four Nation Survey, conducted in Portugal, Spain, Italy, and Greece during the mid-1980s.[4] These data have been supplemented at relevant points by more recent Eurobarometer survey results.

Legitimacy and Other Positive Attitudes

Legitimacy is defined here as a set of positive attitudes of a society towards its democratic institutions, which are considered as the most appropriate form of government.[5] While there are several alternative definitions of this concept, this conceptualization would be shared by Lipset, Almond, and Verba, by Linz, and by a large number of other authors familiar with it.[6] The development of positive attitudes towards democracy is an important aspect of democratic consolidation, since it generally brings about loyal and obedient behavior. Even elite-oriented approaches to the study of democratic consolidation acknowledge the importance of this mass-level development, which, as argued in the Introduction to this volume, represents a broadening and deepening of consolidation, which further enhances a regime's prospects for stability over the long term. Geoffrey Pridham (also in this volume) refers to this as "positive consolidation."

Our Southern European survey data, collected in the mid-1980s, are the principal basis of this analysis. These data suggest that in three of the four countries under consideration, supportive popular attitudes had begun to develop in the aftermath of the installation of new democratic regimes. In earlier stages of democratization we should not expect to find that system-supportive attitudes of this kind, or the behaviors associated with them, are well-rooted in civil society. While vaguely prodemocratic orientations may be widespread, support for a particular democratic regime and its key institutions will not have had a chance to develop. These attitudes are formed and strengthened during the process of consolidation. Accordingly, scholars who consider the establishment of legitimacy as paramount regard a democratic regime as fully consolidated only when a high degree of legitimacy is achieved. We anticipate that the period of time required for the establishment of such system-supportive attitudes will vary from one case to another. In some cases, positive attitudes develop quickly, while in others the process of legitimation is a longer one: it may take years, it may be interrupted by crises, and its content may be profoundly transformed by political changes carried out under the regime. Most authors would suggest that Italy falls into this last category.

How should legitimacy be measured? This classic question has been addressed by scholars in many different, and sometimes contentious ways. For some, legitimacy is a value-loaded concept whose very nature precludes analysis using conventional indicators; for others it is regarded as virtually impossible to detect empirically.[7] Problems of measurement and operationalization are further complicated when its multidimensionality is taken into consideration.[8] The literature on legitimacy and related concepts is characterized by a remarkable gap between the relatively high level of theoretical and conceptual development, on the one hand, and, on the other, the weakness of the many empirical indicators that have been used to date.[9] Analysis of this concept is further complicated by the fact that a regime is never perfectly legitimate for everyone, nor does it enjoy the same degree of legitimacy or support from all sectors of a society.

Faced with these daunting complexities, we have adopted a rather minimalist and relative notion of legitimacy. Accordingly, legitimacy is defined by the belief that, in spite of shortcomings and failures, existing political institutions are better than any others that might be established; or by the belief that a political regime is judged the "least bad" of all possible forms of government. As Linz has written, "ultimately, democratic legitimacy is based on the belief that for that particular country at that particular juncture no other type of regime could assure a more successful pursuit of collective goals."[10]

Our approach entails empirical analysis of two separate dimensions of legitimacy and a third set of attitudes which is empirically and theoretically related to, but conceptually distinct from, the first two. First, we consider the most general and abstract attitudes relevant to a democratic regime: Is democracy preferable to any other kind of regime? We may call general attitudes of this kind "diffuse legitimacy."[11] Since these attitudes involve an opinion of democracy as a type of regime, their salience is greater in those countries which have experienced other types of regime (authoritarian or totalitarian). This is true of all four countries of Southern Europe, whose citizens have experienced antidemocratic regimes either personally or through the collective memory embedded in the culture of the society.[12] Thus, these citizens' responses to survey questions relating to this dimension are much more self-conscious than responses given by citizens in countries that do not have recent histories of authoritarian or totalitarian rule.[13]

The second dimension of democratic legitimacy that we examine involves the extent to which citizens under a democratic regime conceive of preferable alternatives to that system. This is more important in cases, such as Spain and (to a lesser extent) Portugal, where a long authoritarian past is associated with important processes of economic growth and social and economic modernization. It may also be relevant to cases, such as Italy and Spain, in which collective memories of war and other kinds of suffering relevant to politics may be fading with the passing of time, and where, among older people, memories of an authoritarian past may be inextricably intertwined with pleasant recollections of their own youth. If alternatives to the new democratic regime are not viewed positively, despite evaluations of an authoritarian past that may not necessarily be negative, attitudes of diffuse legitimacy may be reinforced and given added salience, and support for the democratic regime may thus be strengthened. We label this second dimension "legitimacy by default." In some cases, this dimension may take the form of legitimacy by reaction against the past.[14]

When considering positive attitudes towards an existing democracy it is also relevant to take into consideration the perceived efficacy of that regime. It is reasonable to assume that the satisfaction of basic demands through specific governmental actions can induce people to form, maintain, or strengthen their positive attitudes towards the democratic regime. Popular perceptions of the capability of a political system to solve problems are particularly important to the success of new democracies where the system-supportive attitudes described above may not have been deeply rooted in society. Thus, the perceived efficacy of a regime is among those attitudes which are fundamentally related to democratic legitimacy and perception of its political institutions as the most appropriate means of government.[15]

Considered by itself in behavioral terms, efficacy may or may not influence legitimacy. This issue was first raised by Seymour Martin Lipset and by Juan J. Linz.[16] However, some scholars have also raised doubts about the possibility of distinguishing between legitimacy and efficacy in empirical analysis.[17] The high correlations that often result suggest an undetermined causal structure linking the two concepts.[18] In this vein, opinions about the legitimacy of a regime are linked to judgments of the merits of incumbent authorities, perceptions of governmental performance, and/or the gap between respondents' ideals and political reality.[19]

For several reasons, we believe that it is possible to distinguish analytically between legitimacy and efficacy. The first and most important is based on the nondemocratic experiences of Southern Europeans, even though these occurred at different times and with different durations and intensities. These personal experiences with various types of regimes help us to distinguish empirically between legitimacy and efficacy, since Greeks, Portuguese, Spaniards, and Italians have clear frames of reference when asked about political alternatives to democracy, the desirability of democracy in the abstract, and regime performance. Because of their personal experiences or collective memories, Southern Europeans are culturally and attitudinally equipped to separate the legitimacy of a regime from perceptions of its efficacy, although we suspect that the ability to make these distinctions will gradually decline as the passage of time makes the authoritarian experience more and more irrelevant to the collective memory of each country. In the 1980s, however, that memory was still vivid, although to a lesser degree in Italy than in the other three cases. In contrast, when respondents in well-established democracies lacking a nondemocratic past are polled, their lack of any similar experience makes questions about political alternatives to democracy highly abstract and unrealistic to them. Lacking a meaningful conception of political alternatives, they are likely to recall efficacy or performance when asked to evaluate legitimacy.[20]

Levels of Legitimacy and Efficacy

The Four Nation Survey included three items that dealt directly with the legitimacy and efficacy of political regimes in Southern Europe.[21] Table 7.1 presents the distributions of attitudes in the four countries relating to these concepts. High levels of support for democracy are shown in all four countries: specifically, two out of three people expressed a preference for democracy, whereas one out of ten would have preferred an authoritarian regime in some cases; two-thirds of all respondents believed that democracy works; and only a very small minority evaluated the past authoritarian experience positively.[22] More interestingly, some differences emerge among the four cases. In Italy, criticisms of democracy's efficacy were more widespread; the highest percentage of positive attitudes is found in Greece's responses; the highest number of "no answers" may be seen in Portugal (a feature which is consistent throughout the survey); and in Portugal and Italy, the level of perceived efficacy was lower than in Spain and Greece.

With regard to the authoritarian past, Greeks were consistently more critical in their evaluations than were Portuguese, Spanish, and Italian respondents, who expressed some degree of ambiguity or ambivalence. Added to these mixed opinions are higher percentages of positive eval-

Table 7.1 Attitudes towards Democracy in Southern Europe, 1985 (vertical percentages)

	Portugal	Spain	Italy	Greece
Diffuse Legitimacy				
Democracy always preferable	61	70	70	87
Authoritarianism preferable in some cases	9	10	13	5
All the same	7	9	10	6
"Don't know" or no answer	23	11	7	2
Opinions on the Past				
Bad	30	28	37	59
Part good, part bad	42	44	43	31
Good	13	17	6	6
"Don't know" or no answer	15	11	14	4
Perceived Efficacy				
Our democracy works well	5	8	4	35
Many defects, but it works	63	60	61	46
Getting worse and will not work at all	11	20	28	14
"Don't know" or no answer	21	11	6	4
N	2000	2488	2074	1998

Source: Four Nation Survey, 1985 (see note 4).

uations of the past in Portugal and Spain (13% and 17%, respectively). These higher percentages, however, come as no surprise if we consider the duration of Salazarism (almost half a century) and Franquism (about forty years) and the inevitable attachment to a regime of such duration, particularly among the older generations.

A comparison of proauthoritarian responses to the first two questions reveals an interesting pattern. In Italy, 6 percent evaluated the authoritarian past as positive, while 13 percent stated that in the abstract "an authoritarian regime, a dictatorship, is preferable" in some cases. If we regard the former group as "old authoritarians" and the latter as "neoauthoritarians," we might infer that proauthoritarian attitudes in Italy derive from more than fond recollections of the Mussolini regime. The reverse appears to have been true of Spain and Portugal, where fewer respondents found an authoritarian regime preferable in the abstract (9% and 10%, respectively) than favorably evaluated the previous authoritarian regimes (13% and 17%). This would suggest that some nostalgic supporters of the past in Spain and Portugal converted to prodemocratic commitments.[23] These findings accord with those of other studies, showing that most of those who had positive attitudes towards Franco and were ideologically identified with Francoism acknowledged the legitimacy of the new regime: only 4 percent of respondents interviewed by DATA in 1981 totally identified with Francoism and maintained clearly antidemocratic positions.[24]

The overall conclusion we derive from an examination of these data is that in Southern Europe today there are no alternatives to the present democratic arrangements: not only is the historical past (with its array of dictators, military intervention in politics, and one-party systems) definitely over, but there are also no longer any serious challenges to the democratic regime from either authoritarians or neoauthoritarians.[25] This conclusion is largely confirmed by an examination of recent data on the support for democracy over authoritarian forms of government among citizens of European Community countries. Despite the economic crises that have beset all of the Southern European countries at some point during the 1980s or early 1990s, support for democracy has strengthened in all four countries (as can be seen from Table 7.2). Between 1985 and 1992, the percentages of those polled in EC countries who stated that they preferred democracy increased from 70 to 73 in Italy, from 87 to 90 in Greece, from 70 to 78 in Spain, and from 61 to 83 in Portugal. Support for democracy in 1992 equaled or exceeded the average for the European Community in three of the four Southern European countries, and Italy's score of 73 percent was not below the European average (78%) by a very wide margin. Perhaps most significantly, support for Italian democracy has remained firm despite the dramatic political upheavals of 1992–94. These findings provide strong evidence that the support for and the stability of a democracy may persist despite the deconsolidation of its party system and the possible restructuring of its core political institutions. The passing of such a severe test in Italy, moreover, clearly demonstrates that democratic consolidation had been achieved by the early 1990s.

Another way of viewing democratic legitimacy, suggested by Lipset and slightly modified by Linz and others working on the Spanish case, is to leave aside the dimension concerning the past (and the existence of perceived alternatives) and consider only the two main dimensions, diffuse legitimacy and perceived efficacy.[26] Using these two dimensions, we can establish a typology, consisting of "full democrats," (who both acknowledge the unconditional legitimacy of democracy and regard their democratic regime as efficacious), "critics" (who prefer democracy over authoritarianism but regard their own regime as inefficacious), the "satisfied" (who regard their democratic regime as efficacious but would prefer an authoritarian system under some circumstances), and "antidemocrats" (who are furthest from full democrats).[27] The data (from 1985) presented in Table 7.3 reveal even

Table 7.2 Preferences for Democracy over Authoritarianism (Diffuse Legitimacy) in EC Countries, 1992 (horizontal percentages)

	Prefer Democracy	Prefer Authoritarianism	"They're All the Same"	"Don't Know," No Answer
Denmark	92	4	2	1
Greece	90	4	3	2
Portugal	83	9	4	4
Luxembourg	82	2	6	9
Germany	81	8	7	3
(West Germany	83	8	5	2)
Netherlands	81	9	5	5
Spain	78	9	7	6
France	78	7	11	5
United Kingdom	76	6	11	6
Italy	73	14	6	7
Belgium	70	10	10	10
Ireland	63	10	21	6
EC average	78	9	8	5

Source: Eurobarometer, 37, spring 1992.

more clearly how few Southern Europeans hold negative attitudes towards their present democratic regimes. Antidemocrats, who are negative both with regard to diffuse legitimacy and perceived efficacy, represent a tiny minority in all four countries. At the opposite extreme, three out of four Portuguese, Spaniards, and Greeks, and two out of three Italians can be categorized as full democrats. All four democratic regimes enjoy a high level of legitimacy.

Table 7.4 presents data from these Southern European countries in comparison with the European Community average with regard to feelings of satisfaction "with the way democracy works" applied to the period 1985 to 1993. These time-series data suggest that this indicator of perceived efficacy is sensitive to short-term economic and other conditions and is therefore much more volatile than are attitudes of diffuse legitimacy, but they also reveal that throughout most of the late 1980s and early 1990s Greeks, Portuguese, and Spaniards were roughly comparable with other Western Europeans in terms of their levels of satisfaction with the performance of their governments. Only Italians were significantly and persistently below the EC average in their opinion of the efficacy of their governments.[28] (We shall discuss these findings and their implications later in this chapter.)

Data concerning the two main behavioral indicators of legitimacy—civil order and the absence of electorally significant antisystem or semi-

Table 7.3 Legitimacy and Perceived Efficacy in Southern Europe (percentage of all respondents)

Diffuse Legitimacy		Perceived Efficacy +	Perceived Efficacy −
		Full Democrats	Critics
+	Portugal	77	9
+	Spain	75	12
+	Italy	65	19
+	Greece	84	11
		Satisfied	Antidemocrats
−	Portugal	10	5
−	Spain	7	6
−	Italy	7	9
−	Greece	3	2

Source: Data from the Four Nation Survey, 1985 (excludes missing data).

Table 7.4 Satisfaction with How Democracy Works

	1985	1987	1989	1991	1993
Portugal	34	70	60	70	54
Spain	51	55	60	61	39
Italy	28	26	27	33	32
Greece	51	49	52	37	45
European Community	58	57	66	57	41

Source: Eurobarometer, 39, June 1993, A14.
Note: Percentages of respondents who were "very satisfied" or "fairly satisfied with the way democracy works."

loyal parties—also reflect relatively high levels of support for democracy in all four countries in the mid-1980s, a period of sustained economic growth, when these countries were fully consolidated. The problems of terrorism and civil violence, still present in Italy, Spain, and Greece at the beginning of the 1980s, were slowly fading away, although at different rates. Antidemocratic stands were also virtually absent at the national level in Spain; such extreme positions were only to be found on the issue of regionalism.[29] In Italy, antisystem attitudes were disappearing as a result of the crisis of the right (mainly the neofascist Italian Social Movement [MSI]), as well as the profound transformation of the Communist Party which began in the early 1970s, its decisive role in supporting democracy during the worst terrorist attacks at the end of the seventies, and its de facto parliamentary support of the cabinets of the 1976–79 period. Only very small minorities at either end of the political spectrum could be considered antiregime (rather than antidemocratic). Higher levels of support for antiregime parties were present in Greece and in Portugal (mainly on the communist left, which in the previous election had received 12 percent of the vote in Greece and 15 percent in Portugal), but these groups were declining in electoral support in both countries.[30]

It is clear from Table 7.3 that Italy and Spain have the highest percentages of antidemocrats and critics. To this must be added our finding from Table 7.1 that support for authoritarianism is also highest in these two countries (particularly in Italy). In addition, Italy has the lowest percentage of full democrats, and Spain has the highest scores for a positive evaluation of the past, Franquism in this case. At the same time, however, these two countries in the mid-1980s had only small extremist groups, and their two communist parties were fully integrated with and supportive of the regime. Portugal and Greece, in contrast, with fewer antidemocrats and lower levels of support for authoritarianism, had more extremist communist parties than those of Italy and Spain. How can we account for such a contradiction?

First of all, these findings are consistent with the common observation regarding the general gap between attitudes and behavior, as well as the specific gap between attitudes present in a society and the extent to which they are politically translated as a result of the actions of groups and leaders. But there is a second explanation for this contradiction; it emerges from a cross-tabulation of the four groups of Table 7.3 and respondents' left-right self-placement (see Table 7.5). Those on the left have more positive attitudes towards democracy than do the rightists. This fact challenges common assertions during the 1980s, when the survey was conducted, concerning the alleged antidemocratic stance of the left. These data also leave room for speculation about the prominence of the ideological factor in explaining the level and characteristics of democratic legitimacy.

Let us briefly turn our attention to two unusual findings concerning Portugal and Greece. The Portuguese data reveal an unusually high percentage of "no answer" responses to questionnaire items. In most of the surveys used to support this chapter, and other published studies,[31] more than twice as many subjects in Portugal declined to respond to questions than in the other three Southern European countries. Without entering into a full discussion of the meaning or methodological problems associated with such abstentions in survey analysis, let us simply suggest that in this instance a high rate of "no answer" should not be regarded as implying a lack of fundamental support for the democratic regime.[32] One interpretation of this finding is related to certain characteristics of the Portuguese population. Compared with

Table 7.5 Legitimacy and Efficacy, by Left-Right Self-placement (horizontal percentages)

	Full Democrats	Critics	Satisfied	Antidemocrats	*N*
Portugal					
Left	74	9	12	5	107
Center-left	79	12	7	2	225
Center	81	7	7	4	520
Center-right	71	8	14	8	171
Right	63	12	13	12	57
Total	77	9	10	4	
Spain					
Left	77	15	3	5	137
Center-left	86	9	4	1	665
Center	74	11	9	6	546
Center-right	53	22	8	17	190
Right	44	18	16	22	45
Total	75	12	7	6	
Italy					
Left	53	32	5	10	285
Center-left	64	22	5	8	307
Center	76	12	8	4	566
Center-right	60	11	15	14	128
Right	51	17	9	23	96
Total	65	19	7	9	
Greece					
Left	89	9	2	—	306
Center-left	95	3	2	—	419
Center	87	9	3	1	612
Center-right	67	20	6	6	160
Right	54	27	7	12	182
Total	84	11	3	2	

Source: The Four Nation Survey, 1985.

the other three Southern European countries, Portugal in the mid-1980s was characterized by lower levels of social modernization, as reflected in its level of education, urbanization, labor-force structure, and development of communications media.[33] These factors are conducive to low response rates in public opinion interviews. Another possible interpretation would portray these nonresponses as reflecting certain short-term aspects of Portuguese politics: the survey was carried out in a period of political change in Portugal, when uncertainty was so widespread that it may have extended to attitudes towards democracy. It should be remembered that in the elections of 1985 a new party (the Democratic Renewal Party of President António Ramalho Eanes) appeared and surged to 18 percent of popular votes cast. The extent of electoral volatility experienced in that election was the highest since the founding of Portuguese democracy. Over the following two years, moreover, the Social Democratic Party (PSD) emerged as the dominant actor in the political arena.[34] Portugal had been under authoritarian rule longer than any country in Western Europe, and virtually none of its citizens had democratic experience of any kind. Portuguese political culture during this period has been characterized in terms of political cynicism and ignorance.[35] The governmental instability and economic difficulties of the period immediately preceding the 1985 survey had a direct and significant impact on satisfaction with democracy and may have led, as well, to higher levels of uncertainty concerning fundamental democratic orientations. Prima facie evidence consistent with this "authentic uncertainty" hypothesis can be seen in Table 7.4: levels of satisfaction with Portuguese democracy were, indeed, quite low in 1985. Some years later, however, they had risen to a level substantially above the European Community average. We shall return to this authentic uncertainty hypothesis later in this chapter.

The second anomaly worthy of discussion at this point involves Greece's high percentage of positive attitudes in every dimension of legitimacy (Table 7.1) and largest percentage of full democrats (Table 7.3). The figures are so high that one is tempted to doubt the representativeness of the Greek survey sample.[36] Sampling considerations notwithstanding, there are several respects in which these data present an accurate portrayal of Greek political culture. First, the interviews were conducted during the most intense days of the electoral campaign of that year, when declarations of support for the democracy were probably at a high point. Second, Eurobarometer data tend to corroborate these findings. As Table 7.4 reveals, satisfaction with democracy in Greece in 1985 was much higher than the levels reported for Italy and Portugal. Third, several scholars, including Diamandouros, Dimitras, and Papacosma, have characterized Greek political culture as highly politicized, with high levels of popular involvement in politics, intensely held political attitudes, large radicalized groups (especially among the young), and positive attitudes towards politics in general.[37]

These two anomalies regarding Portugal and Greece suggest that the analytical tool we have adopted is very sensitive to changes in public attitudes resulting from political events or short-term circumstances.[38] Such trends, however, require panel survey designs or repeated cross-sectional data, such as those generated by Eurobarometer surveys. Most of our analysis is based upon a single cross-sectional survey for

Table 7.6 Correlations (Pearson's r) among Diffuse Legitimacy, Perceived Efficacy, and Opinions on the Past

	Our Democracy Works Well	Evaluation of Past Authoritarian Regime
Democracy is Preferable		
Portugal	.16	.25
Spain	.29	.33
Italy	.24	.26
Greece	.21	.34
Our Democracy Works Well		
Portugal	—	.09
Spain	—	.19
Italy	—	.00
Greece	—	.26

Source: The Four Nation Survey, 1985.

each country, so we will not focus extensively on changes in these attitudes over time.

The principal conclusion to be derived from these data is that, by the mid-1980s, the process of democratic consolidation was largely complete in Southern Europe. Previously, levels of satisfaction and perceived efficacy were much lower, especially given that these political contexts were characterized by rising expectations and economic crisis. Accordingly, frustration, disillusionment, and disenchantment were widespread during those first years.[39] Nonetheless, negative perceptions of democratic efficacy did not affect the level of legitimacy to the same extent. This phenomenon is consistent with Linz's argument concerning the relative autonomy of democratic legitimacy from perceived efficacy. Although such autonomy was lower during the first phases of regime change, it helped the new Southern European democracies to cope with problems arising from the gap between social expectations and the attempted solution of serious economic and social problems.[40] As the data presented in Table 7.6 clearly reveal, the correlations between preferences for democracy over authoritarianism (diffuse legitimacy), on the one hand, and satisfaction with the working of the respondent's democratic regime (perceived efficacy), on the other, are rather low. In no case do the correlations (Pearson's r) reach .30. Thus, according to one crude statistical indicator, we can conclude that efficacy "explains" less than 10 percent of the variance in the diffuse legitimacy variable. The questions involving regime preference and satisfaction appear to be tapping different dimensions, although theoretically related ones. In line with our hypothesis, Southern Europeans were

Table 7.7 Evolution of System Support in Spain, 1978–1989 (vertical percentages)

	1978	1980	1985	1989
Full democrats	74	46	75	76
Critics	11	32	12	11
Satisfied	3	4	7	6
Antidemocrats	12	18	6	7
N	1190	4784	1926	2472

Sources: For 1978 and 1980, Linz et al., *Informe sociológico*, p. 628; for 1985 and 1989, data from Centro de Investigaciones Sociológicas, Madrid.

able to distinguish between legitimacy and efficacy, such that dissatisfaction with the working of their democracies was not mirrored by a decrease in the general preference for a democratic regime.[41]

A more detailed examination of the Spanish case lends more persuasive support to this conclusion. The four surveys conducted by Samuel H. Barnes, Peter McDonough, and Antonio López Pina—in 1978, 1980, 1984, and 1990—included similar items measuring legitimacy and efficacy. Their data confirm both of the conclusions stated above. First, they indicate that the autonomy of legitimacy from efficacy increased with time, as the new regime became consolidated: Pearson's r correlations between indicators of positive orientation towards democratic government and satisfaction with "the way democracy is working in Spain" were .81 in 1978, .68 in 1980, .57 in 1984, and .59 in 1990.[42] Second, despite an accumulation of unsolved problems during the 1980–81 period (including an upsurge of Basque terrorism, a divisive debate over regional autonomy, the deep crisis of the incumbent party [the UCD], and even an attempted coup d'état in February 1981), the basic legitimacy of the new Spanish democracy remained largely unshaken. Table 7.7 shows that the number of critics (loyal democrats dissatisfied with the performance of the government) increased almost threefold and that these negative evaluations only improved after the PSOE came to power in 1982. Nonetheless, the basic legitimacy of democracy was not eroded by economic discontent or political pessimism, and the number of respondents expressing antidemocratic sentiments remained acceptably low. In short, Spaniards were able to distinguish between governmental performance and the democratic regime, and they did not blame democracy for their problems. While the increase in the number of critics eventually contributed to a profound electoral realignment, this was not accompanied by a meaningful increase in support for antidemocratic solutions.[43] It should be noted that this finding also holds with regard to Italy, with its low levels of perceived efficacy. Thus, all four Southern European countries clearly display a lack of linear and transitive relationships between legitimacy and (perceived) efficacy.

This initial examination of survey data suggests two broad and important conclusions. The first is that the level of legitimacy is high in all four countries (especially Greece), some Portuguese anomalies notwithstanding. Secondly, the relationship between regime legitimacy and perceptions of government efficacy is rather loose. This finding holds up despite considerable cross-national variance regarding perceived efficacy: perceptions of efficacy were low in the early 1980s in Spain and Portugal but have increased substantially since, but the trends are quite different in Italy (where levels of satisfaction remained consistently low) and Greece (where perceived efficacy declined somewhat in 1990). In neither of these latter two cases, however, has there been a decline in the level of diffuse legitimacy.[44]

Some Reasons for High Levels of Legitimacy

The first, most obvious explanation of the high levels of legitimacy accorded these democratic regimes involves the lack of a clearly perceived alternative to democracy: in all four countries, to varying degrees, there has been a fundamental delegitimation of the authoritarian past. What is most striking about the extent of legitimacy of these regimes is that, with some interesting exceptions, such sentiments of diffuse support are evenly distributed throughout all sectors of these societies.[45] An extensive analysis of possible relationships between diffuse legitimacy, legitimacy-by-default, and perceived efficacy, on the one hand, and on the other the most commonly analyzed socioeconomic variables (such as income, occupational status, social class, education, age, and religious practice), produced low or very low correlations. In other words, there is no specific social group or demographic group which is differentiated from the rest of society by higher or lower levels of support for democracy.[46]

In contrast, correlations with an important political variable, self-placement on the left-right continuum, are much more substantial. Earlier in this chapter we noted that this variable was significantly related to separate measures of support for democracy. To take this analysis one step further, we constructed an index of positive attitudes towards democracy, by combining respondents' answers to the three central questions of this study. This produced three categories of respondents: "strong support" consists of respondents who gave the most positive answers to the diffuse legitimacy and perceived efficacy ques-

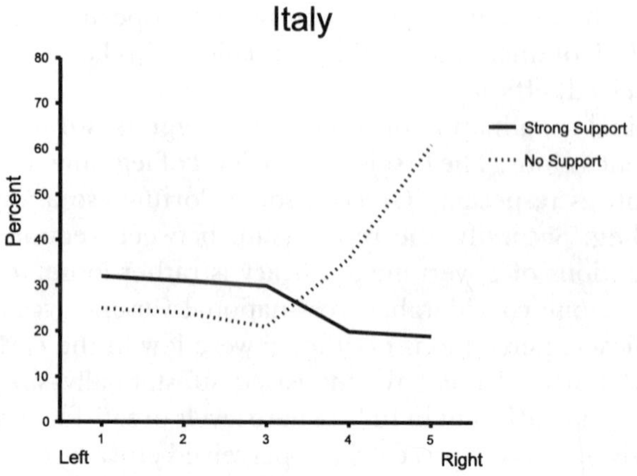

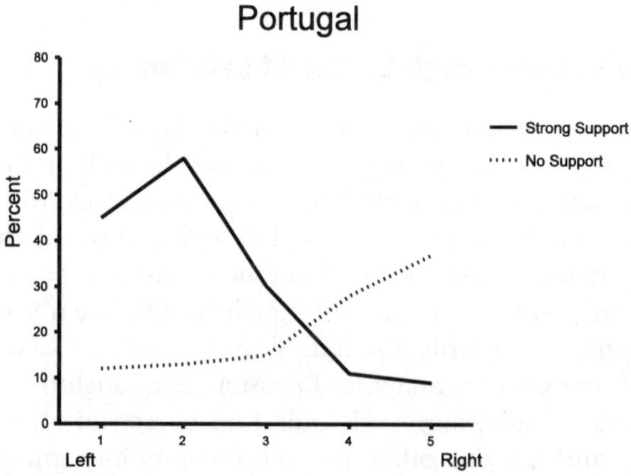

Figure 7.1 Support for Democracy, by Left-Right Self-placement (percentage of respondents)

tions and the most negative assessment of the authoritarian past; "no support" consists of respondents who gave negative or indifferent responses to the diffuse legitimacy and perceived efficacy questions and positive or mixed evaluations of the authoritarian past; and "weak support" consists of respondents who set forth mixed evaluations or selected intermediate response categories.[47] There are significant cross-national differences concerning the link between this index and the left-right continuum. This relationship is strongest in Spain and Greece, with correlations of .45 and .47, respectively. With regard to

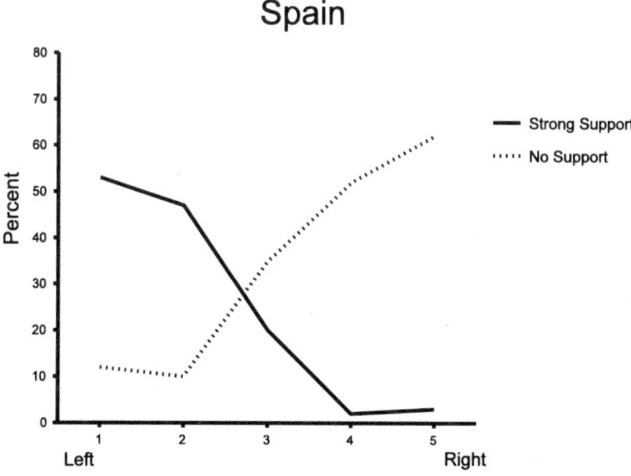

Figure 7.1 *Continued*

the other two countries, the correlations are much lower: .16 for Italy and .23 for Portugal.

Figure 7.1 depicts the cross-tabulation of left-right self-designation and this index of positive attitudes towards democracy (for the sake of clarity, the intermediate weak support category is not presented). The strength of the relationship between left-right self- designation and this cluster of attitudes in each country can be seen clearly. This graphic depiction, moreover, corrects one error of interpretation that might have been made on the basis of correlation coefficients alone: the correlation in Portugal between the left-right variable and this index of support is depressed somewhat by a curvilinear relationship linking the two.

Separate correlations between left-right self-placement and the individual components of this index reveal patterns that might help to interpret these findings. The relationship between evaluation of the authoritarian past and left-right self-designation shows that there is more left-right polarization of such opinions in Spain (Pearson's r is .53) than in Greece (.46), Portugal (.33), and Italy (.31). Perceptions of governmental efficacy are also less strongly associated with left-right self-placement in Italy (Pearson's r -.11) and Portugal (.05) than they are in Spain (.22) and Greece (.26).

How shall we interpret these findings? The literature on the left-right dimension suggests that this variable includes both an ideological and a partisan component. This would suggest that some of these findings are affected by partisan orientations.[48] Accordingly, the performance of parties in government (clearly relevant to the perceived efficacy dimension) and the positions taken by parties and their leaders on the issue of diffuse legitimacy greatly affect the attitudes of partisan respondents. This interpretation of variance in system support acquires some credibility when the partisan preferences of respondents are introduced as a control, as shown in Table 7.8. Partisanship has a particularly strong effect on perceptions of efficacy. This influence is not particularly surprising, since, in essence, respondents are being asked to evaluate the efficacy of a democratic government that is under the control of a particular party or coalition: thus, PSOE voters more favorably assessed the performance of democracy under the PSOE government in 1985 than did supporters of other parties; PASOK voters gave even higher marks to Greek democracy under PASOK leadership; and supporters of parties in the 1985 Italian coalition government (the PSI, PSDI, PRI, PLI, and DC) more favorably evaluated their government's democratic performance than did supporters of parties occupying the opposition benches. The only significant exceptions to this pattern were Portuguese Socialist voters, whose party was involved in the collapsing government coalition and which was on the verge of a long period as part of the opposition.

Other aspects of the data presented in Table 7.8, however, clearly indicate that factors other than partisanship were also responsible for these patterns. First, in all countries, voters for parties of the right gave the least supportive responses to the diffuse legitimacy and perceived efficacy questions and most favorably evaluated the authoritarian past. Second, despite the opposition status of the Portuguese, Spanish, and

Table 7.8 Opinions on Regime Legitimacy, the Authoritarian Past, and Efficacy, by Partisan Group (percentages of respondents)

	Democracy Is Preferable	Past Was Only Bad	Our Democracy Works Well
Portugal			
PCP	77	64	82
PS	67	32	75
PSD	64	17	80
CDS	56	8	65
Other	75	44	75
Spain			
PCE	89	71	73
PSOE	86	42	84
CDS	68	12	67
AP	53	1	53
Other	80	42	74
Italy			
PCI	70	61	50
PSI	77	36	71
PSDI	88	42	73
PRI	71	36	84
DC	80	32	83
PLI	67	29	62
MSI	30	3	39
Other	69	47	62
Greece			
KKE	96	86	86
PASOK	93	74	95
ND	75	26	58
Other	87	77	78

Source: The Four Nation Survey, 1985.

Greek communists, their supporters expressed more strongly the diffuse legitimacy of democracy than did socialists, whose party was either the only or the dominant party in the government. In general, respondents on the left were significantly and consistently more supportive of democracy than those on the right. This is particularly apparent when we control for incumbency (such as by combining the "full democrats" and "critics" presented in Table 7.5). Moreover, in the case of Spain (where time-series data are readily available), it is noteworthy that respondents on the left were even more supportive of democracy than those on the right in 1978, when the center-right Unión de Centro Democrático was in government. To these observations we may add that in Italy and, to a lesser extent, Greece parties are more important and visible in society than in the other countries. This conclusion is based on analysis of several indicators (described in Chapter 10 in this volume), but at this point let us restrict ourselves to a consideration of just one: party identification.[49] Significantly fewer Spaniards and Portuguese (43% and 48%, respectively) identify with a party than do Italians (57%) and Greeks (72%).[50] While Italy ranks high in terms of the portion of its population identifying with political parties, it should be recalled that the correlation between left-right self-placement and democratic support was significantly lower than in the other Southern European countries. Conversely, Spain had the fewest party identifiers and the highest correlation between legitimacy and the left-right continuum. This would suggest that the ideological component of the left-right continuum becomes more relevant if partisan attachments are not particularly widespread, intense, or salient. Furthermore, both the ideological and partisan components are relevant if there is a strong, widespread presence of parties in society. This latter condition appears to apply to Italy and Greece, while the former most clearly applies to Spain; Portugal is near the middle on this continuum.

Left-right self-placement, therefore, consistently and significantly affects the propensity of citizens to acknowledge regime legitimacy and to perceive its performance as efficacious. The two components of this factor are relevant in different ways in the four countries. In Greece, the two aspects appear to mutually strengthen each other. While there is a stronger ideological component and greater polarization in Portugal, more frequent turnover of parties in government is reflected in a low correlation between left-right self-placement and democratic legitimacy. In Italy, parties have been dominant for a long time, and polarization largely decreased during the early 1980s. Spain seems to be the case in which the left-right component is strongest. In all of these countries, the left-right dimension appears to function as an orientation device, a compass to simplify the political universe and make it more understandable. In general, then, left-right self-placement has an autonomous meaning and political attitudinal content, including orientations regarding regime legitimacy. These attitudes may be associated with but are certainly not equivalent to specific partisan loyalties.[51]

Attitudes towards Politics

The data presented to this point clearly indicate that democracy occupies a central position in the political culture of Southern Europe, as it does throughout the Western world. By the mid-1980s, the existing democratic regimes were regarded as legitimate by all sectors of society,

Table 7.9 Feelings towards Politics (vertical percentages)

	Portugal	Spain	Italy	Greece
Positive				
Interest, commitment, enthusiasm, passion	20	29	25	65
Indifference, diffidence, boredom	52	54	47	26
Negative				
Irritation, disgust	16	10	27	8
"Don't know" or no answer	12	7	1	1

Source: The Four Nation Survey, 1985.

and there was no significant support for nondemocratic alternatives. Some supportive attitudes (particularly perceptions of efficacy) were somewhat weaker than they are in some other West European democracies, but, overall, these regimes could be regarded as well on their way towards full consolidation.

These attitudes towards political regimes are paralleled by more general orientations towards politics. Respondents in the Four Nation Survey were asked to select (from a closed list) a term which best described their feelings about politics. The results are presented in Table 7.9. Country-by-country comparisons of these responses lead to many of the same conclusions reached in our exploration of the support for democracy. The most positive attitudes towards politics (interest, commitment, enthusiasm, and passion) were held by Greeks. Portuguese respondents, once again, had the highest percentage of nonresponse, along with a large number of responses reflecting noninvolvement with politics. Spanish respondents also expressed high levels of indifference towards politics, but their attitudes were, on balance, somewhat more positive than those of the Portuguese. Italy stands out as having both high levels of negative attitudes towards politics and low levels of involvement with politics. Nearly three out of every four Italians were either not involved in politics or had negative feelings about politics. These findings closely parallel the figures reported above concerning perceived efficacy and satisfaction with the workings of democracy. When we introduced left-right self-placement as a control variable, the same basic pattern discussed above could be observed: respondents on the left were more positive in their feelings about politics while those on the right were more negative, and centrist and center-right respondents were less involved with politics.

The data presented here suggest that, in one important respect,

Table 7.10 Index of Political Alienation (vertical percentages)

	Portugal	Spain	Italy	Greece
Strongly alienated	57	43	57	32
Somewhat alienated	17	19	21	25
Neutral	6	12	9	20
No alienation	3	8	4	15
"Don't know" or no answer	16	18	8	7

Source: The Four Nation Survey, 1985.

there may be a variety of Southern European exceptionalism regarding political culture. Two-thirds or more of the Italians, Portuguese, and Spaniards interviewed in the Four Nation Survey expressed negative feelings towards or noninvolvement with politics. Our overall conclusions concerning widespread democratic legitimacy notwithstanding, these findings distinguish citizens of these three countries from their Northern European counterparts.

To what extent are these largely affective evaluations accompanied by parallel cognitive orientations? Are these attitudes related to perceptions of *personal* efficacy, that is, to respondents' assessments of their own capabilities for influencing politics? To address these issues, we constructed an "index of political alienation," combining responses to three questionnaire items dealing with "internal" and "external" efficacy.[52] The resulting data, presented in Table 7.10, reveal the extent of alienation from and negative attitudes towards politics and political elites in this population. Again, the case of Greece is a notable exception.

The findings presented in our index of alienation are consistent with those of several other studies. *The Civic Culture,* for example, thirty years ago described an alienated political culture as characteristic of Italy in the late 1950s. Two decades later (in a somewhat different historical context), Sani described that political culture as "reticent." José María Maravall and, more recently, Joan Botella similarly have described Spain's political culture as one characterized by a lack of popular interest, perceptions of inefficacy, a critical skepticism, and a lack of confidence in political elites. Maravall referred to this combination of attitudes as "democratic cynicism," while Botella described them as "cynical democratism." Maravall further argues that a cynical view of politics has long been a central trait of Southern European political culture and that this trait could even be a rational judgment based on a long experience of politics as the abuse of power. Both authors stressed the apparent contradiction between negative attitudes towards politics and basic acceptance of the regime.[53] Our data also clearly reflect this apparent contradiction between acceptance of the regime and several negative attitudes.

Thus, legitimacy of democratic regimes in Southern Europe may be high, but the political climates in which they exist are characterized by largely negative affective and cognitive attitudes, again with the exception of Greece. This combination of conditions would suggest that the present level of democratic legitimacy has its origins not so much in a cluster of positive attitudes but rather in the intensity of the rejection of the authoritarian past[54]—a hypothesis consistent with the exceptional status of Greece among the four countries. The Greek military regime existed for the shortest period of time and was never consolidated; the violent and repressive phase of establishing that regime was more recent (hence, more vivid in the historical memories of Greeks), and accordingly, as our data revealed, its repudiation by the general public was more widespread and extreme than was true in the other three Southern European cases.

Conceptions of Democracy

While our data indicate that there is widespread attitudinal support for democracy in Southern Europe and that nondemocratic alternatives are not favored by significant numbers of citizens in any of these four countries, one important question remains to be addressed: how do these individuals define democracy, and what kinds of regimes would they like to see consolidated? In the introductory chapter of this book, democratic consolidation is defined as involving acknowledgment of the legitimacy of a particular regime, not merely an endorsement of the principle of democracy in the abstract. Not only do citizens express attitudes *towards* democracy but they also maintain conceptions *of* democracy, although these are often poorly structured and more or less consistent with their own basic political orientations. An exploration of these conceptions is useful for better understanding the attitudinal maps of Southern Europeans. Putnam's research on British and Italian political elites suggests that a knowledge of the "cognitive predispositions" and "operational ideals" of Southern European citizens is particularly important in understanding to what extent the political realities in those countries differ from what the citizens believe they should be.[55]

This aspect of our study is based upon two different (and classic) survey questions. The first, about the extent of personal involvement in political decision making, asked respondents to choose between direct participation in the resolution of problems and passive acceptance of the decisions of authorities.[56] The second question posed a choice between fast and efficient processes of decision making and ones that place greater emphasis on extensive consultations and representative institutions.[57] By combining the answers to the two, we can develop a four-part typology of basic conceptions of democracy. "Decisive democracy" conceives of a regime in which the authorities have full responsibility for running the country effectively. In this type of democracy, the structures of intermediation have only a limited place and civil society plays a passive role in decision making. A "representative democracy," by contrast, is one in which the role of intermediational structures is fully recognized, although decision-making responsibility rests with the authorities. This conception is the closest to the basic notion of representative government, in which decisions are made by elected representatives while citizens play a relatively passive and acquiescent role. In a "populist democracy" there is no room for the role of associations, groups, or any type of intermediational structure. Direct—but unorganized—participation and an emphasis on efficient decision making are the two most relevant features of this conception. The underlying objective of this model is to maximize personal efficacy and political identity while at the same time maintaining an authoritarian component. "Participatory democracy" is characterized by the active role of society in both the decision-making process and in the way demands are formulated by groups and associations, as well as by demonstrations and other forms of direct participation. The main concern of this model is to guarantee societal involvement in the decision-making process, even at the expense of efficiency. This four-part typology is intended to present fairly simple notions or images that can be used to capture mass-level perceptions; there is no pretense here of posing alternatives to more sophisticated theories of democracy that have been set forth in a very rich and extensive literature.[58]

Table 7.11 presents the percentages of respondents in each country falling into one or another of these categories. The most striking conclusion is that substantial majorities in all four countries acknowledged the prominent decision-making role of authorities. Most Southern Europeans express a preference for an efficiently functioning regime, not stalemated by conflicts among groups. At the same time, the role of citizens, through groups and associations, and the usual forms of representation are accepted as well: what we have labeled "representative democracy" was supported by about half of the population in all four countries. In this instance, Greece was not an exception; about as many Greeks as other Southern Europeans selected this option. Significant cross-national differences can be observed, however, in which option

Table 7.11 Conceptions of Democratic Decision Making (percentages of respondents)

	Decide Quickly without Consultation		Consult Citizens or Associations	
	Decisive Democracy		Representative Democracy	
Rely on Authorities	Portugal	36	Portugal	51
	Spain	22	Spain	51
	Italy	29	Italy	45
	Greece	7	Greece	53
	Populist Democracy		Participatory Democracy	
Involve Society	Portugal	4	Portugal	10
	Spain	6	Spain	21
	Italy	8	Italy	18
	Greece	2	Greece	38

Note: See notes 56 and 57 for questionnaire items used as basis for this typology. Table excludes missing data.

claimed the second largest bloc of adherents in each country. In both Portugal and Italy (two countries which, until 1985, were characterized by high levels of cabinet instability) there was a strong preference for decisive democracy. In Greece, on the other hand, there was an extraordinarily high level of support for participatory democracy. Spanish and Italian preferences were more evenly divided between the decisive and participatory options. This division of opinion between two diametrically opposite conceptions of democracy is significant, particularly insofar as it could give rise to political conflict in the future. There was one uniformity across all four countries, however: in none of these countries was there any significant support for the populist democracy option. This implies that the consultative role of intermediation structures was highly valued throughout all of Southern Europe.

These differing conceptions of democracy are closely related to broader clusters of ideological and partisan preferences, as reflected in the left-right continuum. The data in Table 7.12 reveal that leftists are most strongly in favor of participatory democracy. The notion of popular participation in both consultations over policy and in decision-making processes receives much lower levels of support among respondents of the center and right. The opposite conceptualization, decisive democracy, receives greatest support from those on the right, and (except in Portugal) is endorsed by very few respondents on the left. Rep-

Table 7.12 Conceptions of Democracy, by Left-Right Self-placement (vertical percentages)

	Left	Center-Left	Center	Center-Right	Right
Decisive Democracy					
Portugal	19	26	36	46	41
Spain	10	15	26	38	19
Italy	14	27	34	33	35
Greece	2	4	8	9	13
Representative Democracy					
Portugal	51	54	54	44	52
Spain	35	50	53	45	70
Italy	44	41	44	43	49
Greece	37	47	57	57	65
Populist Democracy					
Portugal	6	5	3	4	1
Spain	9	9	6	4	2
Italy	9	9	8	8	6
Greece	2	2	2	2	4
Participatory Democracy					
Portugal	23	14	7	7	6
Spain	46	26	14	12	9
Italy	33	24	13	16	10
Greece	59	46	34	31	18

Note: See notes 56 and 57 for the questionnaire items used as the basis of this typology.

resentative democracy, however, receives widespread support from all portions of the left-right continuum in all countries. Only Greek and Spanish leftists do not select this as the most preferred form of democracy.

How do political parties fit into these conceptualizations of democracy? In order to explore the preferred role of parties, we constructed an "index of party legitimacy" by combining responses to a series of questions tapping positive or negative evaluations of the political parties.[59] The distributions of respondents in each country on the resulting scale can be seen in Table 7.13. As expected, the legitimacy of parties is high in all four countries, but it is particularly high in Greece, where positive attitudes were expressed by 76 percent of those polled. At the other extreme is Portugal, where slightly more respondents adopted a neutral stance towards parties than were positive. The opinions of Italians were also less than uniformly supportive, although positive evaluations significantly outnumbered neutral and, especially, negative attitudes. Thus, the lowest levels of attitudinal support for political parties were found in two countries, Italy and Portugal, whose governments had

Table 7.13 Index of Party Legitimacy (vertical percentages)

	Portugal	Spain	Italy	Greece
Strongly Positive	18	38	30	44
Positive	24	18	24	32
Neutral	44	30	32	18
Negative	7	8	11	3
"Don't know" or no answer	7	6	2	3

Source: The Four Nation Survey, 1985.

Table 7.14 Correlations (Pearson's r) of Party Legitimacy with Democratic Legitimacy and Political Alienation

	Democratic Legitimacy	Political Alienation
Portugal	.29	−.35
Spain	.45	−.41
Italy	.28	−.30
Greece	.34	−.20

Source: The Four Nation Survey, 1985.

been formed by relatively unstable multiparty coalitions and where longings for "decisive democracy" were strongest.

It is important to note that, although parties are favorably regarded in all four countries, the levels of legitimacy accorded parties are somewhat below the legitimacy invested in the democratic regime per se. The relationship between the legitimacy of parties and of the democratic regime is measured by correlations between the two indices. The results of this analysis are presented in Table 7.14, which also reports the correlations between the Index of Party Legitimacy and the Political Alienation Index (which, we should recall, primarily involves the perceived efficacy of individual citizens). These data reveal that support for parties is most strongly related to democratic legitimacy in Spain. Spain is also the country where the negative relationship between political alienation and attitudes towards parties is the strongest.

The most plausible explanation of this finding is that it was in Spain that parties played the most important role in the transition to democracy, a highly successful transition. In addition, the strong party government of the Socialists was still quite popular, and was widely regarded as contributing decisively to the consolidation of the new regime in the aftermath of the 1981 coup attempt. In contrast, Portuguese and Italians see parties as much less associated with democracy and more with conflict, instability, and poor performance. The key

Table 7.15 Weighted Mean of Sympathy for Various Groups

	Portugal	Spain	Italy	Greece
Parties	4.4	4.2	4.1	4.9
Unions	4.5	4.3	4.5	7.9
Interest groups	5.3	5.7	5.6	5.4
Church	7.0	5.4	6.7	7.3
Institutions	6.0	5.4	6.3	6.9
Police	5.8	6.1	7.1	—
Military	6.3	5.2	6.4	6.7
Judiciary	5.8	4.9	5.5	7.1

Source: The Four Nation Survey, 1985.
Note: Lowest score (representing extreme hostility towards group) is 1; highest score (reflecting greatest sympathy or positive affect) is 10.

question, therefore, is why the much less positive evaluation of parties in these countries has not had a negative impact on the legitimacy of democracy.

The low correlations between regime and party legitimacy suggest that there is a relatively weak linkage between the two and that the underpinnings of democratic legitimacy are based on institutions other than parties. From the standpoint of regime legitimacy, this may be fortunate, since parties are less positively evaluated than other important social and political institutions. When asked to evaluate parties on a ten-point "feeling thermometer," only 2 percent of Spaniards and 4 percent of Italians awarded parties the highest scores; while negative feelings (1 to 4 on the scale) were expressed by 36 percent of Spaniards and 45 percent of Italians. Parties received relatively low marks even in Greece, where support for democracy is extraordinarily high. The mean feeling thermometer scores for parties and other institutions are presented in Table 7.15.

How can we explain this ambiguity towards parties? A full answer to this question is well beyond the scope of this chapter, since it would entail a far-reaching analysis of a broad array of relevant data. An inventory of promising factors worthy of such exploration would include the following: (1) the divisive and polarizing role played by parties in these countries in the past; (2) the antiparty propaganda of the former authoritarian regimes; (3) scandals involving corruption in government under party leaders; (4) divisive, opportunistic behavior of party elites, now of greater visibility (if not intrusiveness) in the television age; and (5) party occupation of the state and various sectors of the society, which, at least in Italy, does little to generate feelings of sympathy. In a nutshell, citizens of these countries may have adopted the stance that "we know we need parties, but we don't like them;" or "we need parties, but because we know too much about them, we don't like them."[60]

Concluding Observations

Given the "success" of democratic arrangements and their increasing embeddedness in the political cultures of these four countries, political alternatives and antiregime oppositions are virtually nonexistent. Attitudes supporting democracy are widespread among all social groups, and only self-placement on the left-right continuum differentiates systematically among Southern Europeans in their attitudes towards democracy, their evaluation of the past, and their perception of the efficacy of government institutions. From this perspective, the democratic regimes of Southern Europe were legitimate and consolidated in the mid-1980s.

Our surveys conducted during the mid-1980s, however, revealed considerable differences among Southern Europeans in their conceptions of democracy. Particularly significant was the gap between those on the right, who preferred decisive government, and those on the left, who expressed a preference for widespread consultation with social groups and direct popular participation in governmental decision-making processes. In any case, overwhelming majorities of Southern Europeans acknowledged the importance of the roles played by political parties, and the preferred government in all countries was some form of representative democracy. Despite this acknowledgment, parties seem to be regarded as an unavoidable necessity, rather than as institutions supported by high levels of popular sympathy.

This overview of the attitudinal underpinnings of support for democracy, therefore, produces a somewhat mixed picture. On the one hand, in all four countries we find a realistic political culture, where support for democracy is high, where there are no viable alternatives to democracy, and where the authoritarian past is regarded with nostalgia only by small minorities. At the same time, we also find pervasive feelings of political alienation and cynicism, an intense distrust of elites, and limited legitimacy of parties, together with a low level of sympathy for them, in spite of the acknowledgment of their role in politics.

These conclusions raise a new set of questions, answers to which would require additional and, ideally, time-series data to confirm the results of this single cross-sectional survey. In our opinion, the most important of these issues include the following.

First, we have seen that widespread positive attitudes towards democracy in these four countries are accompanied by weak support for parties. Does this weak attitudinal support imply that these party systems are weakly institutionalized or not institutionalized? If so, does the inconsistency between support for democracy and support for parties suggest that democratic regimes can be perfectly consolidated while their party systems are still fluid? Additional data and analysis are required before a tentative answer to the latter question can be set forth.[61]

Second, it is important to recollect that these surveys were conducted in the mid-1980s. Our Italian data reveal strikingly low levels of satisfaction, perceived efficacy, and support for existing parties. These indicate that Italy at that time was in a phase of potentially high electoral volatility and possible realignment. This mass-level development (combined with dramatic elite-level "stimuli" and a change in Italy's electoral law) culminated in substantial party-system change in the elections of 1987, 1990, 1992, and, especially, 1994. Among the most notable transformations were the decline and then disappearance of the communist PCI (1987–91) and the Christian Democratic Party (1992–94), the resounding success of antiestablishment and antiparty movements (1987–92), and the reconfiguration and restructuring of all of the political families represented in the Italian party system (1993–94). Our 1985 data suggest a reinterpretation of the electoral earthquakes of 1992 and 1994: rather than a sudden or unpredictable event, this electoral change was the product of long-term developments whose roots can be traced back to the preceding decade.

Third, we believe that this study has demonstrated the importance of further research in this area, which will require additional data collection and analysis. Our tentative findings concerning conceptualizations of democracy, for instance, open up a broad array of new questions. To cite one example, we have seen that leftists tend to conceive of democracy as involving extensive popular participation, while those on the right place much greater emphasis on the efficiency and decisiveness of the decision-making process. Are there other important dimensions of these differing conceptualizations of democracy that more detailed and probing questionnaire items might uncover? How closely is the economic dimension related to politics in the minds of Southern Europeans? How do these conceptions of democracy compare with those emerging in Eastern Europe or other countries currently undergoing regime transition? These are among the many new issues which have emerged from our preliminary analysis and that we regard as worthy of further study.

8 Executive-Legislative Relations in Southern Europe

Gianfranco Pasquino

The construction and consolidation of a viable democratic regime requires the crafting of democratic institutions and structural mechanisms capable of providing for system stability and decision-making efficacy. It is not just a matter of constitution building, although this is, undoubtedly, involved. It is fundamentally a question of institution building—that is, the crafting of the basic form of government, specific institutions, and the relationships among these institutions. Understandably, sociologists and economists have not paid much attention to these problems. Less understandably (but consistent with the postwar behavioral revolution), neither have political scientists devoted much effort to exploring these issues. This is particularly true for European political scientists, who have neglected one of the strongest aspects of their scholarly tradition. The somewhat misplaced and misleading attempt to "bring the State back in" has not sufficed to reorient the attention and the analysis towards concrete institutional structures and mechanisms. Finally, and perhaps even more importantly from the perspective of this essay, constitutional lawyers have so far been unable, and/or unwilling, to formulate precise, nonformal analyses of Southern European constitutions and institutions. Collaboration between them and political scientists has been almost nonexistent. The ultimate product has been a remarkable gap in the literature, which makes the task of describing and, even more, of analyzing executive-legislative relations formidable. Given the scarcity of relevant studies, this essay must be considered a preliminary effort. It will have achieved some of its goals if it succeeds in raising the right questions and providing some meaningful answers—or, at least, some clues as to how and where answers can be found.

The Problem Defined

Our exploration of executive-legislative relations will be limited to the relationship between government and parliament: between the executive, strictly defined, and the elective-representative assembly or assemblies, and between the parliamentary majority and opposition parties. The existing literature on executive-legislative relations reveals several deficiencies. There are several good monographic studies of a single institution in a single country, and some studies compare either executives or legislatures cross-nationally, but there are very few nonformalistic comparative studies of executive-legislative relations and the role of parties. The most notable exception is the classic work of Karl Loewenstein.[1] Among recent publications, however, only one study has undertaken a comparative examination of relationships between executives and legislatures in established democracies.[2] Since that article deals with Great Britain, France, and the Federal Republic of Germany, however, its analytical framework and inferences cannot easily be utilized in exploring, analyzing, and assessing the contributions to democratic consolidation made by certain types of executive-legislative relationships in Southern Europe. These relationships are of great, if not decisive, importance in explaining not only the dynamics of a specific form of government but also the political performance of that specific democratic regime,[3] although we must at the outset acknowledge that political science has been rather weak in evaluating the performance of democratic regimes.[4] An important initial contribution to this overall effort is the volume of original essays edited by Ulrike Liebert and Maurizio Cotta, in which the various authors highlight and explain differences in relationships between parliament and government as they are affected not only by formal structures and rules but also by informal rules and political dynamics.[5]

My intention in this chapter is not to determine whether Southern European democracies conform to "a Mediterranean model of democracy"[6] but, rather, to examine the dynamics of several interinstitutional relationships. I deal not so much with how executives and legislatures are formed, or how they operate in their respective arenas (although we are interested in the specific structures and mechanisms which make up executives and legislatures and the underlying party system) but with the interactions *between* executives and legislatures. This specific theme helps to limit the potential scope of this survey and focus our attention on a few paramount factors.

According to Loewenstein, legislative-executive relations may be characterized either by coordination or by subordination. Coordination, however, is difficult and rare. As Loewenstein pointed out, "the alternatives are either a strong government superior to the parliament, at the expense of responsiveness to public opinion, or a government continually dependent on the whims of parliamentary parties. The controlling viewpoint is the avoidance of cabinet crises occasioned by the lack of stability of the party coalition supporting the government."[7] There are, of course, basic structural arrangements which may provide either for a strong executive—a presidential or semipresidential system—or for a strong representative assembly, in a pure type of parliamentary system. There are also some political factors which may influence the distribution of power among the different actors within each basic form of government. In particular, the executive may still be able to dominate the legislature in a parliamentary system if the executive is cohesive and disciplined. This is usually the case when the executive is formed of representatives of a single party. Conversely, the legislature may play an important role in a presidential or semipresidential system if a single party enjoys a solid majority in the legislature in opposition to the executive. And, in a parliamentary system, the executive may be somewhat shielded against the legislature by certain mechanisms such as the constructive vote of no-confidence. Many of these relationships are greatly affected by the nature of the party system; the number of politically relevant parties, the existence or absence of a dominant party, the cohesion of the governmental coalition, and the extent of fragmentation of the party alignment all significantly affect executive-legislative relations.

Between Westminster-style and consensus democracies there lies a broad political and institutional space filled by various institutional and political relationships.[8] Indeed, the majority of parliamentary forms of government fall between these two poles, such that parties with majorities will try neither to crush the opposition nor to engage in extensive bargaining with the opposition as is done, for instance, in Scandinavian democracies. Semipresidential systems also represent intermediate options between the Westminster and consensus models. As defined by Maurice Duverger, they combine three elements: "(1) the president of the republic is elected by universal suffrage; (2) he possesses quite considerable powers; (3) he has opposite him, however, a prime minister and ministers who possess executive and governmental power and who can stay in office only if the parliament does not show its opposition to them."[9] One can speak of a "semiparliamentary" situation whenever power shifts more towards parliament in such a system. Thus, a wide variety of institutional relationships can affect the consolidation and subsequent performance of democratic regimes.

In principle, one can hypothesize that the *concentration of power in the executive* contributes to political stability but prevents the accommodation of new demands, which can ultimately produce widespread disenchantment with politics. Conversely, the *dispersion of power* opens channels of communication between the legislature and the executive, but it makes substantial policy changes and alternation in government very difficult, if not impossible. Thus, concentration and dispersion have differing implications and consequences, depending on the problem at hand. Our concern is with the contributions of executive-legislative relationships to the consolidation of democracy. Therefore, we are interested more in political stability than in change in and rotation of power; we are interested more in governance than in representation. The reason for this preference springs from the very logic of democratic consolidation's being that facet of the democratization process in which the rules and regulations of the democratic game worked out during the transition become institutionalized. Assuming (as does the working definition of democratic consolidation adopted in this series) that no significant political elites or organizations actively contest the authority of the government to make binding decisions, it follows that, other things being equal, cabinet stability will create conditions favoring institutionalization of rules and regulations devised during the transition. Conversely, cabinet instability and continuing uncertainty over the prospects and capacity of the government to act authoritatively and to make binding decisions will impede the institutionalization of these rules. In so doing, such instability may impede the consolidation process, consequences of which might be a political system mired in uncertainty and unpredictability and prone to stagnation, erratic decision making, and a stalemate between government and opposition. Stability and governance will be the standards applied to the evaluation of these complex relationships.

Executives and Legislatures in Southern Europe

Explanations of patterns of executive-legislative relations in Southern Europe are hindered by a lack of precise accounts of why and how specific institutional arrangements were chosen and crafted. Some studies have addressed these issues in the context of founding democratic regimes in Italy and France.[10] Comparable studies for the other Southern European democracies would be extremely helpful, particularly insofar as they might shed some light on the nature of the constitutional and political constraints these countries had to overcome, and the confining conditions with which they were confronted.[11] A considerable literature exists concerning the contexts within which these institutions were created (e.g., concerning the nature of the previous regimes, the breakdown or the survival and transformation of some elements of the previous regime, the configuration of forces moving towards a democratic outcome),[12] and some partial studies of constitution- and institution-building processes have also been published.[13]

These studies suggest that certain aspects of the historical and political contexts within which basic institutional relationships were forged constrained the options that were available. In Italy, the breakdown of fascism and the disrepute of the monarchy (which had been instrumental in the ascent to power of fascism) made it necessary to write an entirely new, democratic, parliamentary constitution. In Portugal, the collapse of the authoritarian regime facilitated the drafting of a brand new constitution, but the Armed Forces Movement made it very difficult to precisely define the powers of new institutions and actors. Constitutional revisions were necessary before these relationships could be clarified and their contributions to consolidation addressed. The breakdown of the Greek military junta in the wake of a turbulent seven years' rule made it easier to wipe out all of its constitutional "innovations," including a presidential form of government. Nonetheless, this did not open the way to a return to the past. The monarchy was terminally discredited, and the memory of the (fraudulent and manipulated) break-up in 1964–65 of a government supported by a parliamentary majority had not faded away. Thus, there was great concern that the new parliamentary system would be characterized by a very close, supportive relationship between the government and its parliamentary majority.[14] The Spanish transition was also constrained by (but also successfully exploited) its institutional and political contexts. Previous arrangements and the balance of political power favored creation of a constitutional monarchy. In order to divide political power and provide for diversified political representation, the transition opted to retain an upper house (which the Portuguese did without); and it had to adopt a proportional representation system to safeguard all significant political actors and guarantee representation of regional minorities.[15]

Other institutional features and the dynamics of institutional interactions were left to be determined by specific clauses of the respective constitutions or through the free play of parties and voters, coalitions and executive leaders. It is to these features and to their interplay that one must look in order to appreciate the relationships between the executive and the legislature, hence the functioning of the forms of government in Greece, Italy, Portugal, and Spain.

It is important to note at the outset that all four Southern European countries have adopted parliamentary forms of government, albeit with significant differences among them. If Walter Opello is right, Portugal moved from the semipresidential form of government initially adopted in the 1976 constitution to a semiparliamentary form following constitutional revisions promulgated in 1982. Opello argues that "the key change in this regard is Article 194, which makes it clear that the prime minister is responsible politically to parliament and not the president, to whom he is only 'institutionally' responsible."[16]

These varieties of parliamentary government are differentiated from each other by the nature and roles of their respective heads of state. In Spain, a constitutional monarchy, the head of state is a hereditary position. The head of state in Portugal is popularly elected and (as in Finland and France) performs the important roles of appointing and dismissing the prime minister. He or she will obviously appoint as a prime minister the leader of a parliamentary majority, if there is one, and otherwise someone who is capable of mustering a reliable parliamentary majority. And the head of state would not dismiss a prime minister who continued to enjoy the support of a parliamentary majority. Still, the Portuguese president of the republic possesses a popular legitimacy competitive with that of the prime minister. The term of the Portuguese president lasts five years, and reelection to one additional term is permitted. The most noteworthy characteristic of Portuguese presidents is that (as in all semipresidential systems) they have often had to confront the problems of *cohabitation* with a relatively hostile prime minister, who belonged to a different party and was supported by a different political coalition. In Italy, the head of state is elected by a joint session of the Chamber of Deputies and the Senate, plus representatives of the regional councils—a total of slightly more than one thousand electors. A two-thirds majority is required for election on the first two ballots; an absolute majority is required from the third ballot on. Therefore, rarely does the head of state represent a purely political or governmental majority. While the president's appeal and functional role transcend the boundaries of any governmental majority, the lack of a clear definition of the role has subjected presidential activities to severe scrutiny and criticism. Moreover, due to the resilience and pervasiveness of *partitocrazia,* rarely, if ever, can the head of state exercise the power to appoint the president of the Council of Ministers autonomously. Instead, appointment of this head of government is usually the product of an agreement among the parties making up the intended governmental coalition.

In Greece, the head of state is elected by parliament (the Vouli). The Greek president's term lasts five years, and reelection can be only for one additional term. The president must be elected by a qualified majority, defined as two-thirds of the deputies on the first two ballots and three-fifths of the deputies on subsequent votes. A vouli unable to elect a president is automatically dissolved. The new vouli can then elect a president with a three-fifths majority of all deputies; failing that, an absolute majority will suffice on subsequent ballots. If, after all of these possibilities have been exhausted, no candidate reaches the absolute majority, there will be a run-off between the two best-placed candidates. These elaborate procedures reflect a deliberate attempt to elect a president who will enjoy broader support than from a purely political majority. In order to succeed, the president must build a national majority. Perhaps because of this, the constitution originally attributed executive powers to the president, to be exercised jointly with the government. Thus, the Greek constitution initially created a reinforced form of parliamentary government. The 1986 constitutional revision, however, eliminated most of these presidential prerogatives.

Appointing a Prime Minister

This exploration of the nature of executive-legislative relations and their contributions to democratic consolidation requires an understanding of three specific aspects. The first involves the formation of the government and the appointment and dismissal of the prime minister. The second relates to the balance of power between the executive and the legislative branches. And the third derives from the ties existing between the government and its majority.

Differing constitutional formulae notwithstanding, in all four countries the power of appointment of the prime minister is in the hands of the head of state. This power is duly restricted and circumscribed, however, in order to prevent the formation of minority governments without parliamentary support ("president's governments," in the Italian jargon), except under extraordinary and temporary circumstances. The essence of the parliamentary form of government is, after all, support for the executive from the parliamentary base.

In the Spanish case, the role played by the head of state in appointing a government and its prime minister is exceptionally constrained by the constitution. Indeed, the monarch has no authority to approve an official document unless it is countersigned by the relevant government or parliamentary official. In the appointment of a premier (as well as the dissolution of the Cortes) this *refrendo* provision requires a countersignature of the president of the Congress of Deputies. Apart from this restriction, the monarch's role is comparable to that of heads of state in other parliamentary democracies: a candidate is first designated by the king, following consultation with representatives of the various parliamentary groups. This is followed by a positive vote cast by an absolute majority of deputies or, if necessary, after forty-eight hours, by a relative majority or plurality. The final appointment is then made by the king. The head of state, however, will have designated a candidate who is deemed capable of mustering a majority of parliamentary votes. Thus, the king's candidate will almost inevitably be the leader of the party having the largest number of seats in the Congress of Deputies. Ministers are then appointed and dismissed by the king at the prime minister's proposal. (Felipe González has used extensively his powers in this realm, producing some substantial reshuffling.) If, within two months after the election, no majority has emerged in support of a prime-ministerial candidate, the king, with the approval of the speaker of Congress, will dissolve parliament and call new elections.

More important for our purposes are institutional factors which contribute to governmental stability. The considerable stability of governments in Spain has been greatly facilitated by two factors in particular. The first is the constitutional provision regarding removal of a prime minister who has lost majority support in parliament. Under these circumstances, the prime minister can be forced from office only by parliament through a constructive vote of no-confidence—that is, one in which the motion of censure simultaneously replaces the old prime minister with a new one. The UCD minority governments of Adolfo Suárez (July 1977–Jan. 1981) and Leopoldo Calvo Sotelo (Feb. 1981–Oct. 1982) were capable of remaining in office at least in part because of the virtual impossibility of assembling an absolute majority of deputies behind the motion. In the first two legislatures, this would have required a voting alliance among nearly all the opposition parties, from the right-wing Alianza Popular to the communist PCE. This procedure was initiated by Socialist opposition leader Felipe González against Adolfo Suárez in May 1980. It failed by a vote of 152 in favor versus 166 votes against (with 21 abstentions). While the action was unsuccessful in replacing Suárez as prime minister at that time, it did contribute to his downfall over the long term, by highlighting the weakness of the Suárez government and undermining his support in parliament and within his own party. It also made more visible the opposition role of the PSOE, its program and governmental ambitions, and the personality of its leader.[17] This procedure was also initiated by the newly elected leader of Alianza Popular, Antonio Hernández Mancha, against the Socialist government of Felipe González in March 1987. Like the *moción de censura* of 1980, it failed to receive majority support in the Cortes. Unlike in that earlier vote, however, this *moción de censura* did not significantly undermine support for González, since opposition leader Hernández Mancha failed to unify the parliamentary opposition and to present himself as a credible alternative to the sitting prime minister.

Some scholars question the extent to which the constructive vote of no confidence contributes to governmental stability. They argue that it may play the role of a deterrent against frequent governmental crises in Germany as well as in Spain but that it cannot create stable governments. Others stress that the constructive vote of no confidence may effectively function as a dike against governmental instability, and, in the case of Spain, may have held down the number of damaging attacks on Suárez and his weak minority government during crucial stages of the transition. Some further argue that it helped make the transition from Suárez to Leopoldo Calvo Sotelo in February 1981 smoother and less traumatic, not accompanied by a major governmental crisis (since the opposition knew it did not have enough parliamentary votes to challenge this outcome). In the end, however, it remains to be seen whether the constructive vote of no confidence will be viable and effective if and when more drastic choices may be called for.

Certain features of the Spanish party system have also significantly affected the nature of executive-legislative relations in a manner that contributed to democratic consolidation. Spain has been fortunate in that each of its parliamentary elections has produced one large party which, at a minimum, needed only a few additional votes to form a government and to pass legislation (the UCD governments), or which by itself controlled a majority of seats in the Congress (the first three PSOE governments, 1982–93). Spain has also experienced one significant alternation in the government. From the point of view of executive-legislative relations, this has implied a rather clear subordination, though by no means total submission, of the legislature to the executive, of the Cortes to the government, especially under the socialist governments.[18] To a large extent, the Spanish prime minister, who is also the leader of his party, enjoys a very powerful position. He cannot be dismissed by the king, only defeated through a constructive vote of no confidence. He dominates his party, and therefore his parliamentary majority, through well-enforced party discipline: as former vice premier Alfonso Guerra has been quoted as saying, "He who moves is out of the picture." Overall, these elements would characterize the Spanish form of government as a successful variant of chancellor-democracy.

Greece has also enjoyed about fifteen years of cabinet stability and single-party parliamentary majorities. This political-electoral situation subordinated the parliament to the government, the legislature to the executive or, better, the parliamentary majority to its government. An interesting procedure for the appointment of the prime minister is set forth in the Greek constitution. The president is obliged to appoint the leader of the majority party and, on the latter's proposal, the ministers. He has practically no discretion in this appointment, since Article 37 indicates all the steps to be taken when there is no majority-party leader: under these circumstances, a leader must be elected by the parliamentary caucus; when there is no majority party, the leader of the party with the largest parliamentary delegation must be appointed, at least for an exploratory mission. Finally, one outside personality may be appointed as *extrema ratio*, if there are reasonable prospects that he will win a vote of confidence. If not, the last appointed prime minister may dissolve parliament. Obviously, these detailed procedures are meant to preclude misguided interference by the head of state, as had occurred in the period 1965–67 and doomed Greek democracy.

As the long crisis of 1989–90 revealed, when the dominant party declines and a situation of three-party competition emerges, the president will have greater discretionary powers.[19] Even under these circumstances, however, intervention by the head of state is controversial and is regarded as of questionable democratic legitimacy. Until recently, the political game in Greece had been played by strong and popular personalities, such as Constantine Karamanlis and Andreas Papandreou. Accordingly, constitutional prerogatives tended towards a semipresidential form of government in an early period, and then, following the 1986 amendments, towards near omnipotence of the prime minister. Despite the prime minister's significant constitutional powers, however, actual political success depends on his or her ability to muster a cohesive parliamentary majority, especially a single-party majority.

The transition to and consolidation of democracy in Portugal was plagued, until 1987, by a problem with which it had previous historical experience—governmental instability and frequent parliamentary elections. Until a substantial departure from this pattern occurred in 1987, the only political stability which could be offered came from the head of state and from that position's semipresidential powers. Manifestations of this instability included the following: (1) Between 1974 and 1986 there were sixteen different governments (six provisional and ten "constitutional"). (2) Of the ten constitutional administrations, only five enjoyed majority support in parliament, and then only on the basis of often fragile coalition arrangements. (3) The average government survived for only about eleven months, and the high rate of ministerial turnover (281 ministers between 1974 and 1986) created discontinuity in the government's senior echelons. (4) The frequency of elections generated a public mood of disillusionment and voter apathy, as reflected in abstention rates which rose steadily from 16 percent in 1980 to 28 percent in 1987. (5) In a four-month period between October 1985 and February 1986, the electorate was called upon to participate in no fewer than four elections (parliamentary, municipal, and presidential).[20]

This instability created opportunities for active interpretation of the role of president of the republic. Indeed, Gen. Ramalho Eanes effectively operated to counter political instability, up to the point of creating what may correctly be defined as "governments of the president" or "presidential cabinets." There were three cabinets of this type, led, respectively, by Alfredo Nobre da Costa, Carlos Mota Pinto, and María Lourdes de Pintassilgo—the third, fourth, and fifth governments of Portugal, spanning the period from August 1978 through August 1979. These governments lacked a preexisting and solid parliamentary base, as did the coalition governments that followed, each of which had a short and troubled life.

All of this changed following the unexpected landslide victory in July 1987 of the Social Democrats, led by Anibal Cavaco Silva, who secured an equally impressive electoral triumph in 1992. This electoral change has produced solid parliamentary majorities (148 seats out of 250 in 1987 and 132 out of 230 in 1991) and cabinet stability. With the surprising electoral victory of the socialist Mário Soares in the February 1986 presidential elections, and his reelection in 1991, it also produced a case of "cohabitation," beginning more or less at the same time as the more famous French experience. Cohabitation seems not only to have been quite successful, but rumors suggest that Soares and Cavaco Silva established a positive working relationship: "Indeed," one observer noted, "by calling a snap election rather than asking the opposition to form a government, Soares, who made a number of references to the need for stability, appeared to do Cavaco a political favor. Some commentators surmised that the president hoped to be reelected in 1991 with PSD votes."[21] It is supportive of such speculation that Soares was, indeed, reelected with a large majority of popular votes, unchallenged by Cavaco Silva's party.

All in all, the Portuguese form of government has appeared to have shifted from semipresidentialism to a semiparliamentary system. From a constitutional perspective, the semipresidential variant was already significantly curtailed after the 1982 revisions. Politically, however, a strong president could still be in a powerful position if the party spectrum becomes fragmented again and no viable parliamentary majority emerges. Thus, in the Portuguese case, there is some (or, perhaps, ample) room for oscillation within the boundaries of the constitution.

The regime that first emerged in postwar Italy was, and still is, characterized by a weak form of parliamentary government, in which all institutional actors—the president of the republic, the parliament, the government and the president of the Council of Ministers (*not* a prime minister)—stand in an uneasy equilibrium in which no institution really has propulsive powers, and in which political parties emerge, by default, as dominant actors.[22] In effect, this is reflective of the existence of two types of constitution in Italy, one formal (i.e., the written text) and one material (embodied in the patterns of behavior of political actors, implemented and indeed enforced by the political parties).

The constitution, for example, clearly assigns the appointment of the Council of Ministers and its president to the president of the republic. In practice, however, the president of the republic simply appoints the candidates nominated by the secretaries of the parties making up the governing coalition. In general, this power of appointment is largely *pro forma*. To date, there has been only one exception to this pattern—a government appointed by the president in 1960 without prior and explicit parliamentary support—and this created a serious political crisis. In addition, there was one similar but unsuccessful attempt by President Pertini in March 1979. In all but a few cases, the party secretaries have submitted only one name for president of the Council of Ministers. In those few cases, the Christian Democrats submitted a small roster of DC names only to the president of the republic. In actual practice, then, one could conclude that the president of the republic has little or no discretion in the appointment of the government. Indeed, a departure from this pattern would probably be reflective of an existing or impending political crisis. The appointment in April 1993 of the governor of the Bank of Italy, Carlo Azeglio Ciampi, the only nonparliamentarian until that point ever to hold this office, is a case in point. Following an important (through very complex and somewhat contradictory) reform of the electoral law, the entire political system has entered a major transition leading to a reduction of the role and power of political parties.

Italy has the longest record of unstable coalition governments—fifty-two as of March 1994—though this governmental instability has been accompanied by extreme continuity (stagnation, perhaps) of ministerial personnel and of the parties making up the governmental coalitions. Almost all of Italy's governments have been coalitions, and several have been short-lived Christian Democratic minority governments supported by centrist parties. With one significant exception (1948–53), the largest party has never had more than 40 percent of the seats. In comparison, Greece has had only two transitional coalition governments (1989–90). Except for this brief period, one party has been able to form a single-party government backed by an absolute majority in parliament: New Democracy, 1974–81 and again 1990–93, and PASOK, 1981–89 and since 1993. From 1977 until June 1993, Spain had no coalition governments. Portugal has had two minority governments (Mar. 1977–Jan. 1978 and Nov. 1985–Apr. 1987), several coalition governments, and three presidential cabinets. Since 1987, however, it has had one-party majority governments only.[23]

Overall, the variants of the parliamentary form of government adopted in Greece, Portugal, and Spain are all stronger than that in Italy. The role of the prime minister in these three countries has been designed in such a way as to allow that person to exercise real power. The government as a whole, moreover, has been given enough constitutional and political resources to protect it against an unruly legislature and to implement its program. The structure of the parliamentary party system appears to be a crucial variable in this regard: in Greece (except for the 1989–90 "catharsis government") and in Portugal (since 1987), governments have been supported by single-party parliamentary majorities, as they were in Spain from 1982 to June 1993. Lacking single-party majorities, some systems reinforce the stability and authority of governments through various constitutional devices: the UCD minority governments in Spain were capable of governing for five uninterrupted years at least in part because of the constructive vote of no confidence; and in Portugal prior to 1987, some stability was derived from the semipresidential system, with several governments pivoting first on the Socialist Party, later on the Social Democratic Party. Italian governments, in contrast, have usually been at the mercy of their parliamentary majorities: the combination of a fragmented multiparty system and the absence of presidential authority comparable to that found in a semipresidential system has culminated in a weak parliamentary system.

It would appear that Greece, Portugal, and Spain learned, *ex adverso,* from the Italian experience of governmental instability. Among other things, they have avoided the Italian variant of proportional representation. This is no place to provide a detailed comparative analysis of the electoral systems used in Southern Europe. Suffice it to say that Greece has resorted to a reinforced or "corrected" proportional system, that Spain and Portugal utilize the d'Hondt system in (compared with Italy) relatively small constituencies (the obvious exceptions being Madrid,

Barcelona, and Lisbon), and that all elect a small number of representatives (from 250 to 350) to a single chamber. In contrast, Italy has a bicameral parliament, with 630 deputies and 315 elected senators. Until 1992, the electoral system was a relatively pure form of proportional representation with large electoral districts. Following the 1993 reform of the electoral law, 75 percent of senators and deputies are now elected in single-member districts with a first-past-the-post system. The remaining 25 percent are elected with a proportional representation system. For the Chamber of Deputies, only parties and lists polling 4 percent of the national vote will receive any of these PR seats.

These different institutional arrangements have affected the style of dialogue between government and opposition. Apart from a few exceptional moments and decisions, the Italian style has been consensual, even exaggeratedly so. Some interactions between government coalitions and the Communist opposition have verged on consociationalism. In Greece and in Spain since 1982, the style of governance has been majoritarian, even excessively so, producing some tensions, perhaps "at the expense of responsiveness to public opinion," as anticipated and criticized by Loewenstein. In Portugal, the political situation prior to 1987 seemed to require a consensual style, but President Eanes was not inclined to play this kind of game. Most of the time, when the parliamentary numbers allowed it, the style of dialogue between government and opposition was majoritarian. Following the Social Democratic victory in 1987, majoritarianism became numerically possible and has become the dominant practice, mitigated somewhat by the relationship between the Social Democratic (moderately conservative) prime minister and the Socialist (moderately progressive) president of the republic.

Executives versus Legislatures

Whatever their crucial components, successful democratic consolidations must entail some stability of the executive. Indeed, one could argue that excessive cabinet instability and the fragmentation of governing coalitions can help bring about the breakdown of democratic regimes.[24] In any democratic regime, however, parliamentary support for the government must be balanced against the possibility for parliament to censure the government and to oust it from power. On the one hand, confidence and cabinet stability are necessary for reasons of political efficacy. At the same time, however, individual ministers and the cabinet as a collectivity must be held accountable, if the system is to be regarded as democratic, and censure may be the only weapon the parliament possesses to achieve that objective. It is also the most important weapon which both the opposition and dissenting members of the majority can wield in order to bring about a debate or to propose a policy change.

These considerations notwithstanding, a successful vote of censure against the government is a rare occurrence in established parliamentary systems. Indeed, most governmental crises are extraparliamentary crises—that is, the majority coalition breaks down for reasons other than a vote of censure.[25] Moreover, most governing coalitions try to avoid motions of censure, in order not to bring out into the open their internal problems, rifts, and weaknesses, thereby risking the potentially negative reaction of informed public opinion.

Unfortunately, there exists no accurate in-depth analysis of the nature, dynamics, and resolution of governmental crises in Greece, Italy, and Portugal (Spain has basically been spared these experiences). Despite this gap in the literature, some general observations can be set forth. First, as has often been argued, the instability of executive-legislative relations has hindered or, at least, delayed the Portuguese consolidation process. Indeed, one can closely link the consolidation of Portuguese democracy with the stabilization of political relations through the constitutional reforms of 1982 and the emergence of a single-party parliamentary majority in 1987. Democratic consolidation in Italy and Greece was facilitated by large, cohesive, and stable governmental majorities: a centrist coalition dominated by the Christian Democrats ruled from 1947 to 1963 in Italy; New Democracy's sizable one-party majority was in control of developments in Greece from 1974 to 1981.[26] The very different transition in Spain, the salient feature of which was the absence of a clean and sharp break with the past, required and luckily found a heterogeneous majority (the governing UCD was composed of Christian Democrats, Social Democrats, liberals, and reformist elements of the former authoritarian regime), which proved willing to engage in bargaining over a peaceful transition to a new democratic system.

Given the lack of behavioral studies of the nature and development of governmental crises in the four Southern European countries, we must base our remaining comments on the formal provisions of their respective constitutions. Needless to say, constitution makers in new democracies must concern themselves with the problem of securing political stability for the government. Given their previous experiments with what admittedly had been limited democracy, and the syndrome of fragmentation and governmental instability typical of the political forces in their respective countries, the preoccupations of Southern European constituent elites were well founded.[27] One way of successfully confronting these problems was to devise an appropriate electoral system—that is, to work on the input side of the equation and to seek to influence the articulation and aggregation of interests by devising electoral systems capable of providing for proportional representation of public opinion and at the same time avoiding political fragmentation. This strategy was implemented successfully in Greece and Spain, less successfully in Portugal, and, because of historical memories and political reasons, not at all in Italy.

The problem was also approached from the decision-making side, working on executive-legislative relations. Governmental or executive stability can provide for broader political stability.[28] To a great extent, a stable executive shapes politics and political alignments in such a way as to enforce and maintain political stability among institutions and actors, and perhaps even in electoral behavior. While this kind of stability is largely dependent on the success of the electoral system in producing a one-party majority or in providing incentives for cohesive coalitions, some institutional mechanisms can indeed be devised as buffers against challenges coming from fragmented and fractious parliaments.

Given the dynamics of Italian politics after liberation, it would have been easy to predict that Italian governments would be unstable, and to conclude that some mechanisms of this kind might be necessary. Still, no such provisions were included in the Italian constitution. What emerged, instead, was a decidedly weak variant of the parliamentary form of government. This weakness derived, above all, from the institutional and political debility of the governing coalitions, which often led to the fall of governments under circumstances clearly not envisaged by the constitution. More specifically, the constitution identifies only two instances when the government must resign: if it does not receive a vote of confidence at its inauguration, and when a motion of no confidence is approved by a majority of at least one chamber. This narrow constitutional delineation notwithstanding, Italian governments have submitted their resignations on many other occasions. Even in a case where the constitution clearly denies this obligation—that is, when a governmental bill is rejected by one or by both chambers (Article 94)—Italian governments have often seized the opportunity to resign and to produce a reshuffling. At the same time that these governments were unstable, however, the components of their governing coalitions were stable. The same four centrist parties, their most important leaders, and the president of the Council of Ministers himself—the Christian Democrat Alcide De Gasperi, who occupied the post uninterruptedly from December 1945 until May 1953—served as the bases of this stability throughout the period of democratic consolidation.

In search of buffers against governmental instability, the framers of the Spanish constitution borrowed the constructive vote of no confidence from the German Grundgesetz. So far this has proved an effective deterrent and a stabilizing mechanism. Spain was blessed (though in the eyes of some observers it might seem a mixed blessing) with one-party governments for sixteen years (June 1977–June 1993). During this period, only three persons served as prime minister (one of them for over a decade), governments were durable, and, particularly under the Socialist governments of 1982–93, there was considerable policy continuity.

The Portuguese constitution (in Article 198) identifies three causes implying the resignation of the government: (1) the rejection of its program (approval requires an absolute majority of the deputies), which amounts to a vote of no confidence, (2) the failure to adopt a motion of confidence submitted by the government, and (3) the approval of a motion of censure. It is important to stress, however, that Article 198 does not authorize the president of the republic to dissolve the Assembly unless three consecutive motions of censure have been voted.[29] At that point, it would have be taken for granted that no government would enjoy the confidence of the Assembly, and new elections would have to be held. It is also important to stress that once a motion of censure has been defeated, no other such motion can be introduced in the same parliamentary session. In practice, due to the varying strength of the many and different parties, Portuguese governmental coalitions prior to 1987 were weak and unstable. Together with the role played by the military, this weakness effectively postponed the process of democratic consolidation until the second half of the eighties, when a civilian, Mario Soares, was elected to the presidency of the republic and a single party succeeded in securing a comfortable and absolute parliamentary majority. One additional point should be stressed. According to Article 40, which closely follows a similar "Gaullist" clause in the constitution of the Fifth French Republic, no Portuguese government and, for that matter, no president can dissolve a new parliament in the year immediately following a dissolution, except when that parliament has censured two governments. And parliament cannot be dissolved twice for the same reason. Finally, Article 194 in the revised constitution introduces a key change in the relationship between the president and the prime minister, effectively shifting the form of government from semipresidential to semiparliamentary. According to Opello, "Article 194 will effectively prevent the president from dismissing the prime minister and the government except when it is necessary to assure the regular functioning of democratic institutions and after consultation with the Council of State. Thus, the president can no longer dismiss governments which enjoy the confidence of parliament."[30]

We have already seen that the Greek parliament can be dissolved if it is unable to elect a president with a qualified majority. According to Article 84, all Greek governments must enjoy the explicitly voted confidence of the parliament. The motion of censure must be signed by at least one-sixth of the deputies. It is adopted only if it is approved by an absolute majority of deputies. On the other hand, a vote of confidence requires only a simple majority of the deputies, provided they represent at least two-fifths of the total. Unless signed by the absolute majority of deputies, no motion of censure can be reintroduced until six months after the previous submission. The net effect of such a provision, in this case, is that the motion of censure comes close to serving as the functional equivalent of a vote of no confidence. In the Greek case, too, it is evident that the underlying party system is the necessary and sufficient cause of political stability and instability. The executive has enjoyed stability as long as it has been supported and led by one-party majorities. Following the decline of PASOK in the late 1980s, it has become more and more difficult to secure absolute parliamentary majorities. (It took three elections within a year, in 1989–90, to produce a one-seat majority for a new government under Nea Democratia.) By that time, however, the consolidation of democracy had already taken place. Absolute parliamentary majorities and relatively strong executives had already accomplished their task.

Finally, there is the very thorny and complex but most important question of the relations between a government and its own parliamentary majority. The contemporary forms of parliamentary government are rooted not in the confrontation between the executive and the legislature—a characteristic more typical of presidential forms of government—but rather in the juxtaposition between the government and its parliamentary majority, on the one hand, and the opposition as a parliamentary minority, on the other.[31]

The particular make-up of this set of relationships, its viability or nonviability, its functionality or dysfunctionality, vary from country to country. It can be argued that the cohesion of the government and the discipline of its parliamentary majority constitute excellent resources for democratic consolidation. They were distinct features of the Greek and, to a lesser extent, of the Italian and the Spanish consolidation experiences. The hidden costs of such "assets," however, lie in the often excessive constraints which they impose on opposition parties and majority-party backbenchers. Stalemate and sterile confrontation may be the downside of cohesion and discipline, in the absence of institutional mechanisms that would allow members of the majority party to fulfill, at least partially, their role of legislators and grant the opposition some influence over the legislative process. Standing parliamentary committees might serve as the suitable institutional locus of such mechanisms. To be sure, party discipline will inevitably be a factor in all such arrangements, but the more informal and relaxed atmosphere, and the freer exchange of opinions, ideas, and information typical of such smaller settings may enhance the capacity of both majority and opposition deputies to act more freely and to contribute more substantially to the legislative process. In the case of Italy, because of both the long tenure of the governing coalitions and the discipline of the major opposition party, the government-opposition relationship has, indeed, been characterized by "exchange," bargaining, and compromise. The structure of political opportunities made all this well nigh indispensable for the smooth functioning of the regime. As is well known, the structure of political opportunities in the Italian case has been characterized by multiparty governments, with factionalized parties, a bicameral parliament whose two houses have the same powers and functions, and a rather powerful, cohesive, disciplined opposition, representative of important interests, to be taken into account in the decision-making process. These institutional features are absent from the other three countries. There is no guarantee that some of them will not appear, but so far this has not been the case.

The four Southern European cases suggest that part of the price to be paid for prompt and successful democratic consolidation may be a contraction of the role of individual deputies, whether in the majority or in the opposition. In Greece and Spain, where the process took less time to complete and where cohesion and discipline were most clearly visible, a streamlined style of decision making and the quiescence of legislatures has been a salient feature of politics. In the Italian and the Portuguese cases, where democratic consolidation required more time, cohesion and discipline were less observable, less contraction of the role of deputies has occurred, and a more difficult and less streamlined process of decision making has emerged.

The functionality of specific patterns of executive-legislative relations appears to vary depending upon whether democratic consolidation has been achieved. A high concentration of power in the government and its parliamentary majority contributes to political stability and effective decision making and to the consolidation process itself. Once a regime has been consolidated, however, an excessive concentration of power may generate certain liabilities for democracy. At that point, the quality of the democratic game may be enhanced by a greater dispersion of power (or, to use Loewenstein's terms, more coordination and less subordination) and greater flexibility in the relationship between government and opposition, as well as within the parliamentary majority itself. Apparently, neither the PSOE in Spain nor PASOK in Greece has been able or willing to allow for that flexibility and provide greater political space for its own parliamentarians and those of the opposition. The differing consolidation trajectories followed by Italy and Portugal, and the different political and institutional arrangements these have implied (composite governing coalitions, less streamlined parliamentary mechanisms and procedures), have culminated in greater institutional flexibility and discretion for parliamentarians belonging to the majority and opposition parties alike.

The implications of this difference in consolidation trajectories are perhaps worth drawing out. From the standpoint of electoral politics, a disciplined and cohesive party might be perceived by voters as trustworthy and efficacious, and rewarded. This is especially likely when such a party is in the government, but the same perception can also prove beneficial to an opposition party's chances of coming to power. From the standpoint of representativeness, openness, and the quality of democracy, however, a government led by such a party may run the risk of becoming relatively introverted and unwilling to look for agreements with other political, economic, and social actors, while an opposition headed by this type of party may be adamant and uncompromising. A party with the opposite characteristics may possess a different cluster of assets and liabilities. Electorally, a party divided by sharp internal dissent may be seen as an unconvincing option for many voters. At the same time, the need to search for compromise might render such a party flexible and open to different points of view in government. In short, governing and electoral imperatives are likely to be conflicting. The PSOE and PASOK governments of the 1980s clearly conformed to the first of these two models of executive-legislative relations, while the UCD governments of 1979–82 clearly revealed the advantages (in terms of securing broad interparty consensus in support of the new regime) and drawbacks (internal instability and ultimate electoral collapse) inherent in the latter. The Italian Christian Democrats, the governing party in Europe *par excellence*—whose governing experience was based on shifting coalitions, less discipline, and more openness, but also less effectiveness in the government—also falls into the latter category.

This implies that different stages in the democratization process may require different arrangements for their successful completion. What is good for the transition to a new democratic regime may not be good for consolidation, and what makes a positive contribution to the consolidation process may be disadvantageous in some respects over the long term. Specifically, some flexibility and adaptability in executive-legislative relations are likely to be extremely functional in the transition from authoritarianism. A flexible and adaptable arrangement can facilitate the participation of many groups in the process and encourage their involvement in the shaping of the political and institutional structures designed to enhance democratization. A greater level of stability and executive authority, however, may be beneficial for democratic consolidation, whose distinguishing feature is the need for players to abide by rules already set and to learn how to live with them. Once consolidation has been achieved, some relaxation of party discipline and some curtailment of the power of the executive might be salutary for the smooth functioning of the democratic regime, provided, of course, that (as Loewenstein was not tired of stressing) this relaxation does not lead to frequent "cabinet crises occasioned by the lack of stability of the party coalition supporting the government."[32] But since we should not tinker frequently with institutions and mechanisms, a particular set of institutional relationships adopted to meet the demands of one period may persist and have dysfunctional consequences over the long term. Every institutional arrangement has a cost. Thus, to be properly understood and evaluated, the alternatives must be considered in historical context, compared, and analyzed in terms of the contributions they can make to democratic transition, consolidation, and postconsolidation political normalcy.

A Few Tentative Conclusions

At least three of the constitutions analyzed in this chapter contain tangible evidence of valiant attempts to reach a stable and working equilibrium between government and parliament.[33] To be sure, it would not be correct to attribute all the political stability of these regimes exclusively to the above-mentioned structures and mechanisms. Neither would it be fair to infer that these or other processes of successful consolidation are to be attributed solely to those structures and mechanisms. This having been said, it still remains the case that these structures and mechanisms have served as constraints or incentives affecting the behavior of parliamentarians, ministers, prime ministers, and heads of state.

Much could be learned by examining systematically the impacts of executive-legislative relations on democratic consolidation processes.

At this point, our limited knowledge suggests that executive-legislative relations in the three newer democracies have derived clear benefits from the imperative of party discipline and from the existence of real competition among parties. There are also good reasons to believe that parliamentary regulations were, generally speaking, designed in such a way as to streamline parliamentary debates and foster the ascendancy of the executive branch over the legislature—in the process, tipping the balance in favor of the decision-making and somewhat against the representation function. The overall outcome seems to have been a complementary relationship positive for, even conducive to, democratic consolidation.

These patterns of executive-legislative relations seem to have been affected by learning from past experiences. Perhaps the most important lesson, drawn from the brief and unstable previous democratic experiments in the region, was that the stability of democratic regimes during consolidation processes is greatly facilitated by executive stability. Consequently, the balance between the powers of the executive and those of the legislature has been knowingly and deliberately shifted towards the former. Less representation and more decisional efficacy seem to have been the goals set and attained by the politico-constitutional arrangements constructed in the new Southern European democracies.

In many respects, the Italian case is very different. There, the fear associated with the potential emergence of a new tyrant tended to privilege representation over decision-making capabilities. Revealing, in this context, is the recent emergence of major conflict and debate over the merits and demerits of stronger decision-making capabilities in the executive branch of government. This has gone so far as to place the direct election of the prime minister on the political and institutional agenda, together with the need to provide that office with a working parliamentary majority (by means of giving the victorious prime minister a bonus of several parliamentary seats).

The agenda for future research should include an assessment of how electoral and party systems contributed to or affected these politico-constitutional arrangements. No doubt, the impact has been very significant, but we need to know the extent and direction of such influence. The same holds true of parliamentary committees and their actual functions and folkways. Here, too, there is an important difference between the Italian case and the rest of Southern Europe, in that standing committees in Italy enjoy potential law-making powers, which they can exercise once a decision of the pertinent chamber turns them into *deliberanti* or deciding committees. A final item to pursue in detail concerns changes in the constitutional arrangements introduced in the four countries during the various phases of democratization—transition from authoritarianism, democratic consolidation, and normal politics in consolidated democracies. Essentially, this would entail analyzing and explaining the motivations, rationale, and goals pursued by the protagonists in this process.

Let me conclude with one central point: a well-conceived strategy for executive-legislative relations conducive to system stability and flexibility entails the creation of a relatively strong executive. Armed with the democratic authority it derives from the electoral mandate, and subtly invoking the threat of defeat implicit in a new electoral contest, such an executive will be in a position to utilize its powers to convince, and, if necessary, to secure the submission of its legislative counterpart. On the whole, executives in the new Southern Europe have proved adept in protecting and sheltering themselves against the challenges of unruly or, more simply, fragmented parliaments. Indeed, experience shows that they have also proven capable of affirming their authority even during crisis situations. Above all, they have managed to govern. And this, undeniably, constitutes their most positive contribution to the process of democratic consolidation and to its successful completion.

9 Organized Interests and Democratic Consolidation in Southern Europe

Philippe C. Schmitter

The transitions from authoritarian rule to democracy in Portugal, Spain, Greece, and Italy have, by now, been examined from many perspectives. Given the absence of prior attention to the dynamics of democratization, it is not surprising that the attention of analysts was initially focused on the most visible, the most "standard," institutions of already established democracies, namely, parties, elections, public opinion, and political culture.[1] This proved in retrospect to be a wise choice, even if it was rarely guided by explicit theoretical priorities. The sheer mechanics of such regime changes seem to privilege the channels of territorial representation and partisan competition. Not only are freely contested elections of uncertain outcome the most salient events—indeed, the hallmarks—of democratization for the population as a whole, but also the presence of a uniform set of rules and a singular competitive mechanism makes institutionalization in the territorial-cum-partisan realm a relatively easy task. Moreover, the event that is most frequently cited as "proving" that democracy has been successfully consolidated—namely, the eventual rotation in power of competing political parties—depends critically on the success of these rules and this mechanism.

All of which is no reason for ignoring the second generic channel of access to political authority in modern democracies, that of the direct representation of class, sectoral, and professional interests through specialized, permanently administered associations. For one thing, these organizations may have the capacity to disrupt, circumvent, or nullify actions taken in the territorial-cum-partisan realm of representation. Governments and parliaments may pass laws and regulations which never get implemented because of the resistance of organized interests. A given regime may appear quite consolidated in many regards: for example, party identification may be high in the general public, recruitment of militants and candidates may be handled regularly, voter preferences may vary within predictable margins, regional differences in electoral outcomes may have diminished, and defections from one party to another may have become rare. Yet such a regime may continue to experience a great deal of volatility in other regards: the membership of trade unions and business associations may remain erratic and their behavior unpredictable; groups may be constantly forming, splitting up, and merging; bargaining arrangements for such key areas as industrial relations, macroeconomic management, and social policy may vary from issue to issue and moment to moment; local and regional peculiarities may fail to converge toward a national norm.

Interest associations, even if they do not (or cannot) directly disrupt the territorial channel, may still have an indirect but lasting impact upon democratization. Their policy role has increased greatly in recent decades, largely due to the expansion in state activities and the need for specific information to implement chosen policies. The conditions of participation, access, responsiveness, and accountability that surround these exchanges between specialized associations and administrative agencies have become a significant element in how citizens evaluate the performance of the political order. Not only are these functional channels more continuous than the traditional ones of party loyalty, machine politics, clientelistic patronage, and the like, but more and more of the deliberate effort at legitimation expended by the contemporary regulatory-cum-welfare state flows through them.

Put simply, interest associations may be important (if subsidiary) sites at which the legitimacy of democracy is accorded. We are used to thinking of political parties as the only places from which popular consent is extracted—from which a winning majority is produced through the free and competitive expression of voter preferences that can plausibly claim to rule "in the name of the people" and to which a losing minority will defer in return for its being allowed eventually to form a government once it has assembled an alternative majority.[2] But to the extent that citizens interact more frequently with and receive more benefits through their interest representatives of various provenance, attitudes toward public authority may be formed outside the partisan channel, and therefore the long-term viability of a given democratic regime may come to depend on the configuration and behavior of such groups.[3]

The major implication of the above discussion is that it is not democracy as such that is consolidated in the aftermath of the demise of an authoritarian regime. Rather, it is a bundle of diverse institutions or "partial regimes" that link citizens to public authorities, thereby rendering these authorities accountable.[4] Not all of these institutions are organized according to the same principles, nor are they necessarily closely related to each other. One reason for this is the "compromised" way in which most modern democracies emerge.[5] As I have argued elsewhere,

> democrats usually have very different institutional arrangements and political practices in mind in their struggle against authoritarian rule. These desired arrangements and practices tend to correspond—not incidentally—to the structure of power that democratizing actors consider will best guarantee the defense of their established interests or the acquisition of their coveted ones. In short, actors in the transition do not choose democracy *toute court,* but some type of democracy—and the version that eventually emerges may well be a compromised hybrid that resembles none of their first preferences.[6]

To cope with this requisite (if unintended) variety, what is needed is a middle-level approach to regime change that focuses on and maps out the independent structuration of different partial regimes—without presuming that these must all conform to some consistent configuration, least of all, to some existing model of democracy.[7] Hence, it is useful to conceive of political parties, interest associations, and social movements as competing sites at which the primary units of society (individuals, families, firms, localities, etc.) can use different strategies and resources to forge links with state authority in efforts to capture office or otherwise influence policy. Around each of these entities and between them can develop partial regimes—relatively stable sets of structures and rules, each with its own logic of action and principles of evaluation.

Constitutions are formal efforts to establish a single, overarching set of "meta-rules" that will assign specific competencies to each of the partial regimes and govern possible conflicts among them. Their elaboration and ratification no doubt represent a most significant moment in the process of consolidation.[8] However, constitutions are rarely successful in formalizing all the relationships and in rendering them consistent.[9] And it is precisely in the interstices between different types of organized intermediaries that constitutional norms are most vague and least prescriptive. For example, very little can be deduced from even the most detailed of constitutions (and they are tending to become more detailed) about how political parties, interest associations, and social movements will interact to structure the channels of representation.

Organized Interests in the Structuration of Partial Regimes

We now turn to the specificities of Southern Europe, dealing, of course, with the four countries that serve as the primary geographical focus of this volume—Greece, Italy, Portugal, and Spain—but examining, as well, two other cases that, arguably, may be considered Southern European in some respects—France and Turkey. The preceding discussion suggests that we can assume the following:

1. Democratic consolidation is a process that involves the structuration of several partial regimes, each linking different institutions and their respective publics, clients, members, or voters.
2. Despite their common *appellation non-controllée* of "democratic," these partial regimes are likely to be organized around different principles or decision rules with respect to their domains and resources.
3. The timing of such partial structurations is also likely to vary from case to case; moreover, those institutions that are consolidated in their domains and resources earlier in the course of a regime transition are likely to have a significant impact on later-emerging ones.
4. The overall type of democracy that ensues will be defined by the permutation (and, hence, by the sequence) of partial regimes that form during consolidation.

Interest associations, even those representing important class, sectoral, or professional interests, can rarely be expected to play a leading and early role in the consolidation process. The experience of Portugal, Spain, Italy, and Greece clearly confirms this. In no case did such associations determine the advent or timing of regime change, or its immediate outcome.[10] So-called "peak" organizations, which aggregate interests at a relatively high and encompassing level, were even less of a factor. More specialized associations—especially, local ones with direct membership—played some role in the earliest phase of the transition when working-class, professional, and even business groups succeeded in discrediting and challenging the indispensability of authoritarian rule. Human rights and civic associations can help to undermine a regime's legitimacy, although they were relatively inactive in the Southern Europe countries, at least, by comparison with Latin American transitions. Once liberalization began, associations of all types tended to get swept up in what Guillermo O'Donnell and I have labeled "the resurgence of civil society."[11] Nowhere was this more evident than in Portugal, where the rapidity and unexpectedness of the collapse of the *ancien régime* left a vacuum into which were drawn a variety of trade unions, neighborhood associations, and social movements. Some observers were so impressed by these groups' capacity for spontaneous mobilization and radicalization of demands that they predicted the emergence of a new form of political domination based on *poder popular*.[12] Once elections were convoked and held in Portugal, and once the last group of radical military officers was suppressed, these inflated expectations faded fast.[13]

Interest associations in Southern Europe seem to have had a good deal of initial difficulty in adapting to the emergent, "democratic" rules of the game for several reasons. First, they were displaced from the center of political life and public visibility by the political parties, which organized (or reorganized) to structure competition for the new positions of representation that were to be filled in the forthcoming elections—once these elections were announced and it seemed safe to run for office. Early on, parties drew some of their resources and personnel from preexisting interest associations (especially in Spain where the latter had been less persecuted by the outgoing regime), but the dynamics of future recruitment and competition soon compelled party strategists to appeal to wider and more heterogeneous publics. They were even led to deny their dependence upon the very "special interests" that helped them get started, although the peculiar radicalization of the Portuguese transition tended to obscure this for a longer time than in the other cases. Eventually, however, territorial constituencies everywhere tended to impose a different logic of competition and coalescence than functional ones. Interest associations tried as best they could to penetrate, even to colonize, these partisan units, but the imperative of assembling numbers and the rhetoric of appealing to the public interest worked against their success—at least until longer-run needs for financial resources and specialized information began to assert themselves.[14]

Instead, the inverse occurred in Southern Europe during the transition and early consolidation periods. Political parties sought with considerable success to penetrate and colonize interest associations. They were especially successful in the domains of working-class and agrarian interests, where, as we shall see, they managed to produce (or reproduce) a set of associations split internally into competing units of party-cum-ideological faction (as in Greece) or of representation (as in the other countries). In either case, the result was a working-class or agrarian movement which had fewer members and financial resources than one might have expected, had class, sectoral, and professional associations been able to retain their organizational unity and, hence, monopolistic location in the general system of interest bargaining. To the extent that capitalists and professionals were able to avoid comparable partisan or ideological splits, their influence over the process of consolidation has been correspondingly greater—*vide* Italy and Spain.

The above-noted tendency toward fragmentation and competitiveness has been further exacerbated by the emergent challenge of responding to the resurgence of regionally based or locally based identities. The highly centralized nature of most autocratic regimes typically left an accumulated heritage of frustration in peripheral areas—all the more so when these were ethnically, linguistically, or culturally distinctive. Especially in Spain the transition towards a new configuration of public offices brought out strong demands for a new configuration of territorial authority. Even in Italy and Portugal, the issue of reform of territorial political and administrative units emerged *pari passu* with democratization.[15] Admittedly, these tensions also affected the unity of political parties, but the creation of subnational representative bodies with their own party systems tended to absorb much of this impact relatively easily. Regionalism brought little more than symbolic satisfactions to most class, sectoral, and professional interests, since the core issues of economic management and social policy that most affect them tended to remain firmly in the hands of central authorities. Effective influence over outcomes in these macropolicy areas depended crucially on having the organizational capacity to respond and negotiate at the national level, but associations found it hard to ignore (and difficult to gauge) the strength of these resurgent regional identities during the relative uncertainty of the transition.

Finally, interest associations in Southern Europe faced rather special problems of "resource extraction" following the change in regime. The new basis for both joining and contributing was (presumably) *voluntarist,* although we shall discover occasional pockets of resilient corporatist compulsion. Invariably, all the new constitutions enshrined freedom of association among the fundamental rights they protected. The Spanish one (alone) guaranteed its citizens *negative Koalitionsfreiheit,* or freedom from having to join a given association. This presumably implied an end to the collective obligation of each group to contribute and to exclusive state recognition. Individuals from different social classes, economic sectors, and professional categories would have to agree voluntarily to support their respective associations. One does not have to be a strict devotee of Mancur Olson's *Logic of Collective Action* to recognize that, once the "uncalculated" enthusiasm of participating in the mobilizational aspect of regime change was over, the temptation to choose to freeride on the effort of others would tend to settle in.[16]

The cases of Southern Europe seem to confirm the hypothesis that the more the outgoing regime was characterized by pervasive state corporatism, the greater was the difficulty in adjusting to privatistic voluntarism and official indifference. Admittedly, when one looks in detail at specific cases, one tends to find ample evidence that it is possible to grant informally what constitutionally granted freedom of association formally denies. The complex provisions of a labor code, social security, and labor court systems, the operation of assorted advisory commissions, the complexities of setting agricultural price levels—not to mention the (often surreptitious) concession of outright subsidies—can help to overcome the limitations of voluntarism. In several instances, the initial resource problem centered on the ownership of certain physical assets and the control over certain monopolistic services that associations had acquired under authoritarian auspices. Spain, again, was an extreme case in which the patrimony from the defunct corporatist regime became a major focus of group struggle, pitting factions within the same class, sector, or profession against each other. Once the issue was resolved, the distributed assets and compensations were an important initial determinant of the resources available to newly "liberated" interest associations.

In all countries—and the Southern European ones are definitely no exception—one of the murkiest areas of associability is finance. This is all the more the case during regime transition. Regardless of the formula that was eventually applied—retention of monopolistic privileges, distribution of patrimony, subsidization by the government in power (or by other *inconfessable* sources, domestic or foreign)—the adjustment to new conditions of affiliation and support rarely conformed to liberal democratic principles. In virtually all cases, the business, labor, and agricultural associations that emerged depended on precarious, highly unequal, and generally inadequate sources of financial support, thereby weakening not only their capacity for collective action but their legitimacy in the eyes of their members and the public at large.

The gist of the above is that one should not expect interest associations to have been a major factor in determining whether democracy as a general mode of domination in Southern Europe would succeed autocracy and whether it would persist into the foreseeable future. Rather, their (delayed) impact should have been more significant in determining what *type* of democracy would eventually be consolidated. The longer-term implication is that the postauthoritarian pattern of associability will effect the distribution of benefits that is likely to set in, the formula of legitimation that is likely to be employed, and the level of citizen satisfaction that is likely to prevail. In a nutshell, organized class, sectoral, and professional interests do have an impact on the consolidation process, but it will take some time and a great deal of scrutiny before their qualitative contribution becomes evident.

The Emergent Individual Properties of Interest Associations

The place to begin our empirical inquiry is with the description and analysis of certain emergent properties of individual associations. Some of these may not differ that much from what they were under the *ancien régime*; others will represent original (and even desperate) efforts to cope with the new conditions of competitive uncertainty, citizen empowerment, legal freedom, and so forth, that come with democratization. What are the characteristics of individual, direct, and specialized membership organizations representing the interests of business, labor, and agriculture that are most likely to have an impact upon the eventual type of democracy?[17]

Number of Associations

Theoretically, the number of associations should be unlimited under the twin freedoms of association and petition, although several factors may emerge that can either raise the threshold for group formation or restrict the access to bargaining arenas or policy processes of those that do form. Linked to this basic condition are subsidiary questions of whether the associations are new or merely rebaptized versions of previous ones, whether their formation is spontaneous or sponsored (and, if so, by whom), and whether they tend to emerge early or late in the process of transition.

There are no comparative data on the sheer number of interest associations and movements that have either persisted from the respective *anciens régimes* or emerged since their demise in Southern Europe. It is even difficult to obtain reliable census-type data on single countries. Carlos Gaspar and Manuel Lucena have demonstrated that the total number of trade unions in Portugal increased only modestly with democratization—from 325 in 1969 to 354 in 1985—although this masks a much more substantial shift from local and provincial unions towards national ones (36 under state corporatist constraints to 109 under pluralist rules). Business associations (including those in agriculture) took a nose-dive with the *revolução*, falling from 551 to 246 in a single year (1974–75) and then gradually increasing to 365.[18]

Table 9.1 gives some idea of the numerical development of Spanish interest associations during the transition. The *sindicalismo vertical* of the Franco regime had grouped employers and employees in the same organizations (of which there were a total of 14,424) and had severely limited the number of national organizations (30 in 1972). Most of the

Table 9.1 Development of Class Associability in Spain, 1977–1984

	Total in 1977	Additional Associations Registered during Each Year						Total by 1984
		1978	1979	1980	1981	1982	1983	
Business associations	3,845	1,846	826	703	568	483	513	9,030
Trade unions	2,814	1,239	939	770	396	225	199	6,676
Total associations[a]	6,659							15,706

Sources: Carlos Iglesias Selgas, *El sindicalismo español* (Madrid: Doncel, 1974), pp. 51, 87; José María Zufiaur, "El sindicalismo español en la transición y la crisis," *Papeles de economía española,* no. 22, 1985, p. 207.

[a]Under the *sindicalismo vertical* of the Franco regime, employers and workers were grouped in sections of the same organization. In 1972, there were 14,424 such associations.

system consisted of local units (12,789, of which 8,791 represented agrarian interests). With the new law of free associability in 1977, a large number of organizations immediately legalized their status by registering, and the process continued at a diminishing pace through 1984. By that time, the total number (15,706) was astonishingly close to the number of *sindicatos verticales* under the previous system of state corporatism (14,424), although one suspects that their territorial distribution, especially the quantity of national organizations, differs considerably from what it was in the past. It is also worth noting that business associations in Spain now handily outnumber trade unions, but by less of a margin than in other well-established European democracies.[19] In Portugal, the totals were much closer: 365 for business and 355 for labor (in 1985).

Turkey offers a dramatically different perspective. Due to the forced closure of a major left-wing labor confederation, DISK, and repressive legislation regulating associability *after* the advent of an elected government (1983), the number of trade union confederations and sectoral organizations there declined significantly with democratization—from 10 confederations in 1975 to 3 in 1984, and from 366 sectoral unions to 117. The number of purely local unions mushroomed from 155 to 798. Paradoxically, despite this decline in numbers (and in membership and level of activity) among nationally organized workers, the formation of national "unions" within the employers' association, TISK, has accelerated since 1980.

Greece exhibited yet another pattern. Unlike Spain and Portugal, which substantially liberalized their respective legislations with regard to associability, or Turkey, which tightened measures that were already restrictive, the New Greek Democracy of Karamanlis did the most it could to restore pre-1967 practices—corporatist arrangements for trade unions, agricultural cooperatives, and even chambers of commerce and industry that went back to 1914. In the workers' movement, monopolized by the GSEE, the number of regional labor centers declined slightly (from 70 in 1966 to 65 in 1983). The number of national sectoral federations increased from 42 to 64, but the number of primary, local unions barely changed: 1,304 in 1966 and 1,415 in 1983. The major developments regarding business seem to have involved frustrated efforts at fusion among existing associations, rather than actual changes in the total number of associations.

Membership Density

The quantity and proportion of those eligible to join and contribute to this form of collective action who actually do so is, in principle, determined only by the rational and independent calculation of individual capitalists, workers, and agriculturists. In fact, the usual social and economic filtering mechanisms are often supplemented by deliberate policies of political parties and state agencies. This leads to the murky area of outside sponsorship, statutory obligations (*vide* chamber systems for capitalists and agriculturists, closed shops and union taxes for workers), subtle forms such as fiscal discrimination, licensing, export certification, subsidized services, and even outright coercion—all of which tend to bind various social and economic categories to their respective units of representation in ways they do not freely choose.

Table 9.2 displays the available data on trade union membership for five countries. The variation is, again, impressive. Italy has, by far, the two largest labor confederations in the area, the CGIL, with over five million (reported) members, and the CISL, with over three million. It also has the highest density of membership—39.6 percent of the economically active population are reported to belong to unions—although it should be pointed out that these data are from 1989, long after Italy's democratic institutions were consolidated. According to Marco Maraffi, the density of Italian union membership (excluding pensioners and unemployed) was even higher in 1950–52, when it was 43 to 45 percent. Greece, with its state corporatist system of monopolistic representation (GSEE) and compulsory contributions from employers and employees (administered through a public agency, the Labor Home, which has existed since 1931), comes in a close second in terms of density at 35 percent. This is, however, dispersed over a large num-

Table 9.2 Reported Membership in Trade Unions, 1989

Union	Membership	Density[a]
Italy		
CGIL	5,026,851	
CISL	3,379,028	
UIL	1,439,216	
Total	9,845,095	39.6
Spain		
CCOO	477,000	
UGT	490,000	
USO	35,000	
CGT	16,000	
Independent	50,000	
Total	1,068,000	9.3
Portugal		
CGTP	550,000	
UGT-P	350,000	
Independent	100,000	
Total	1,000,000	28.6
Greece		
GSEE	564,000	
ADEDY	100,000	
Total	664,000	35.0
Turkey		
TURK-IS	1,493,100	
DISK	186,000	
HAK-IS	200,000	
YURT-IS	150,000	
Independent	242,000	
Total	2,271,000	19.7

Sources: Jelle Visser, "In Search of Inclusive Unionism," *Bulletin of Comparative Labour Relations,* 18, 1990, pp. 173–74, and "Southern Europe: The State of the Unions," University of Amsterdam, Sociology of Organizations Research Unit, unpublished paper, 1993.

[a] Percentage of economically active population.

ber of federations and unions, each with a relatively small individual membership. Portugal's density of 28.6 percent and Turkey's of 19.7 percent place them well within the middle ranks of European unionization. The former is roughly equivalent to the level in the Netherlands and Switzerland; the latter is slightly higher than that of France.[20]

The truly astonishing data come from Spain. Its 9.3 percent rate is the lowest in Western Europe—perhaps even lower than what has emerged so far in Eastern Europe, where the association of previous unions with the Communist Party and state had severely discredited this form of collective action. Spain, on the other hand, has had a long tradition of union struggles. Unlike the other cases, autonomous worker self-organization and protest preceded regime change by more than a decade and contributed significantly to ensuring that it would not be followed by *franquismo sin Franco* or some other authoritarian outcome. What makes this all the more surprising is that Spanish unions may have few members (and, therefore, precarious finances), but they exercise impressive power. They negotiate collective contracts that cover a very substantial proportion of the workforce;[21] they regularly win most of the elections held for representatives at the enterprise level;[22] and they have succeeded in mobilizing workers to strike—including a massive general strike on December 14, 1988![23]

Data on membership density for other social categories are much more difficult to come by. Business associations seem to be most successful, usually recruiting between 50 and 80 percent of their potential members. The Spanish peak association for business, the CEOE, claims 75 percent of firms and an even higher proportion of total production.[24] Italy's Confindustria was a bit less successful in its early years. Its member firms employed 68.9 percent of the industrial workforce in 1950; this figure declined to 48.1 by 1960.[25] The most prestigious business peak association, the SEB, of Greece has had a mixed membership of associations, firms, and individuals, which makes its representativeness particularly difficult to assess. In 1979, it changed its basis of membership and its name from the Federation of Greek Industrialists to the Federation of Greek Industries. By 1987, it had only 300 firms as members, hardly enough to justify its claim to represent all of Greek industry. Moreover, a substantial number of industrial associations for specific sectors (32 out of 73) are not members of the SEB. In Portugal, 44 of 120 industrial associations in the mid-1980s were not affiliated with the national peak association, the CIP.

In each of these Southern European countries except Portugal, merchants, manufacturers, artisans, and small shopkeepers are grouped by statute into obligatory "chambers" of varying configuration and autonomy from the state. In Portugal, the chambers were extinguished by the *revolução*. The Italian *Camere* do not seem to play any role as interest intermediaries, while the Turkish TOB and the Greek EESE are reputed to be important in the representation of provincial and local businesses. The Spanish Consejo Superior de las Cámaras Oficiales de Comercio, Industria y Navegación managed to survive the transition to democracy but has been completely overshadowed by the CEOE.[26]

Almost everywhere in the region, agriculturists are weakly associated and, as we shall see, frequently divided into competing organizations linked to rival political parties or ideological camps. The remarkable exception is Italy, where the Christian Democratic Party built a formidable machine around the Confederazione Nazionale Coltivatori Diretti (Coldiretti) in the aftermath of fascism. According to Maraffi's data, the Coldiretti grew from its foundation in 1944 to have over 12,000 branches throughout the country covering over 7,000,000 members and their families by 1954—easily the largest interest association in postwar Italy.[27] In Greece, cooperatives form the basis of the largest agrarian interest association, PASEGES. More a product of state than partisan sponsorship (although very much subject to partisan dispute), it also grew rapidly to become the most extensive interest association in the country, with 7,500 cooperatives and over 700,000 individual members. Were its density to be measured, it might, due to multiple memberships and double counting, even exceed 100 percent—surely a record for Greece and elsewhere![28]

Domains of Representation

According to the usual canons of liberal democracy, associations (old or new) should be able to determine by themselves whom they wish to represent. They should set the limits on the persons or firms they attempt to recruit as members and the category of interests they purport to speak for. Rarely, however, is this the case. Under state-corporatist auspices—the usual Southern European inheritance from authoritarian rule—these domains are specified by law or administrative regulation. Interests must be organized by economic sector or professional specialization, must adopt a given territorial format, must restrict themselves to a certain level of interaction, and must perform a prescribed set of tasks. Conversely, certain domains and activities are proscribed, as are specific political, ideological, or cultural affiliations. These are organizational "habits" that may decay slowly, even though the original measures may have been revoked.[29]

Whatever their inheritance or habits, countries are likely to vary considerably in the way interest domains are defined. Two dimensions seem especially crucial for future democratic practice: (1) the degree of specialization into separate domains based upon function (e.g., product, sector, or class), territory (e.g., local, provincial, or national), and task domains (e.g., trade versus employer associations, unions oriented towards political action versus those oriented towards the provision of services); and (2) the extent of discrimination based on the characteristics of individual members, such as size of firm, level of skills, public or private status, religious belief, ethnicity, or party affiliation.

No convenient and reliable indicator exists for measuring the degree of specialization attained by the interest-association systems of Southern Europe. To some extent, however, it can be inferred from data on the total number of affiliates of the respective confederations of capital, labor, and agriculture. Italy, Spain, and Turkey follow the general European pattern in which capitalists have more specialized units of representation than does labor.[30] In Italy, the largest trade union confederation, the CGIL, is made up of 19 separate associations. This is substantially fewer than the 204 affiliates that make up Confindustria (of which 106 are territorial and 98 functional); the smaller number implies much less specialization than is inherent in the agricultural confederation, Coldiretti, which has 6,898 member associations. Similarly, TOB, the Turkish business confederation (with 273 affiliates, all of which are territorially based), appears to be far more specialized than the trade union confederation TURK-IS (with only 31). As in Italy, in Turkey the agricultural association, TUCA, has the largest number of affiliates (330). In Spain, the gap between business and labor organizations is not quite so extreme: the CEOE is composed of 133 business associations (of which 39 are territorial and 92 functional), while the CC.OO. has 41 affiliates (17 territorial and 24 functional). At first glance, Greece and Portugal would appear to depart significantly from this pattern. Greece's SEB appears to be exceptionally compact, with only 48 member associations, and seemingly less specialized than the GSEE, with its 122 associations. These figures are somewhat misleading, however, since the SEB is not a pure confederation and relies heavily on the direct membership of some 300 firms. No such ambiguity surrounds the Greek peak association for agriculture, PASEGES, which has 147 member associations. Similarly, the unusually high number of trade unions affiliated with the Portuguese CGTP-IN (215) is due to the fact that it is not a pure confederation, having some 153 local unions as direct members. If one excludes the latter and counts only the association's 18 regional federations and 44 sectoral ones, Portugal would conform to the standard pattern, since the industrial and agricultural confederations, CIP and CAP, are made up of 74 and 72 associations, respectively.[31]

If one tries to summarize this information by rank-ordering the respective confederal structures of representation from the most to the least fragmented, a curious pattern emerges: capital and labor are almost perfectly and inversely correlated. Where business and agricultural confederations are organized into relatively specialized units (the most extreme cases being Turkey and Italy), trade unions are relatively more encompassing in their domains, and vice versa. Agriculture shows a clear tendency to replicate the structure of business associability. Whether this finding would hold up for the established democracies of Northern Europe remains to be tested, but my impression is that the latter tend to have more congruent confederal structures across classes—perhaps because they have had more time to work them out.

In yet another aspect, the Southern European neodemocracies demonstrate little divergence. One characteristic of Germany, Austria, Switzerland, and all of Scandinavia is for capitalists to create and support parallel systems, one representing their interests as producers (trade associations) and the other their interests as employers (employer associations). Only Turkey adopted this form of organizational specialization. Indeed, it has three peak associations: TOB, TISK, and TUSAID, each with different functions and memberships. Elsewhere, except for Portugal, there is only one and it looks out for both trade and employer interests. The rivalry between the Associação Industrial Portuguesa and the Confederação Industrial Portuguesa is of a slightly different nature: the former is a pure trade association; the latter claims to exercise both trade and employer functions.

The extent to which discrimination within a given class by size, status, religion, ethnicity, or ideology leads to the formation of different associations varies considerably across the five neodemocracies. Spanish capitalists easily stand out as the greatest success. Their CEOE combines virtually all sectors of industry, commerce, finance, and even agriculture. It includes firms of all sizes and covers the entire national territory.[32] Its only competitors, the semipublic Chambers of Commerce, Industry, and Navigation, play an insignificant role in interest representation. The Greek bourgeoisie emerged from authoritarian rule at the other extreme. It is severely fragmented by size of enterprise, by sector, and by region, with no uncontested representative for the class as a whole. The other countries lie between these extremes. Italy and Turkey have institutionalized major cleavages between large- and small-scale enterprises, and in the latter case its artisans are further divided by party affiliation. Portuguese capitalists are fragmented by sector—industry versus commerce—and, as we have noted above, by functional rivalry—AIP versus CIP. These patterns can be seen in Table 9.3.

Everywhere in Southern Europe (except Greece) the working class became organizationally fragmented by ideological and partisan cleavages. Initially, a single, dominant confederation was formed—usually under communist control—only to give way quite rapidly to rival organizational efforts. Italy, with its tripartite structure, represents the classic case: CGIL (communist) founded in 1945, CISL (Catholic) in 1950,

Table 9.3 Peak Associations of Capital in Southern Europe

	Date of Creation	Affiliated Associations	Affilliated Firms	Size of Budget (ECUs)
Italy				
Confindustria	1944	189 (1950)	75,076	
Confapi	1947	13		
Confartianato	1946			
CNA	1946			
CASA	1958			
Intersind	1960			
Spain				
CEOE	1977	133	1,300,000	3,602,177
Portugal				
AIP	1860	4	1,440[a]	5,567,440
CIP	1975	74	40,020[a]	604,000
CCP	1976	126		94,000
Greece				
SEB	1907	48	300[a]	862,089
SBBE	1915		225[a]	81,086
GSEBE	1919	85	400,000	2,237,304
EEE	1924	0	1,949[a]	693,420
EBEA	1919	48	35,000[a]	5,652,825
ESA	1902	0	1,300[a]	
SELPE	1974		23[a]	
SESME	1975?			
POEKE	1981	14		
EESE	1986	36		
EISP	1984		7,000[a]	
Turkey				
TOB	1925	273	470,000	
TISK	1962	12		
TUSIAD	1971		216[a]	
ESNAF		2,093		

Sources for Tables 9.3, 9.4, and 9.5: Economic and Social Committee of the European Communities, *The Economic and Social Interest Groups of Greece* (Brussels: Editions Delta, 1981); Comité Economique et Social des Communautés Européennes, *Les Organisations Socio-professionnelles du Portugal,* and *Les Organisations Socio-professionnelles d'Espagne* (Brussels: Editions Delta, 1984); Bertrand Hervieu and Rose-Marie Lagrave, eds., *Les Syndicats Agricoles en Europe* (Paris: L'Harmattan, 1992); and various communications with Manuel Lucena, Marco Maraffi, George Mavrogordatos, and Ilkay Sunar.
Note: Empty cells in table indicate that those data were not available.
[a]Directly affiliated member firms (or ships, in the case of the Greek EEE).

and UIL (social democratic) also in 1950. Portugal's CGTP-IN (communist) gained an initial monopoly in 1974, only to lose it four years later to the UGT-P (socialist). The same pattern unfolded in Spain. The communist-dominated Comisiones Obreras (CC.OO.) took the lead in the immediate aftermath of the transition, but it subsequently declined,

Table 9.4 Peak Associations of Labor in Southern Europe

	Date of Creation	Affiliated Associations	Total Membership	Size of Budget (ECUs)
Italy (ca. 1950)[a]				
CGIL	1944	19	4,313,774	
CISL	1950	38	1,094,406	
UIL	1950	28		
Spain (ca. 1980)				
CCOO	1977	22	2,000,000	1,696,594
UGT	1888	15	1,400,000	1,313,201
USO	1960	22	644,476	1,403,087
ELA/STV	1911	32	110,000	
INTG	1980		58,000	
Portugal (ca. 1983)				
CGTP-IN	1974	215	1,347,240	1,306,900
UGT-P	1978	49	981,000	710,770
Greece (ca. 1981)				
GSEE	1918	130	623,159	1,184,166
ADEDY	1945	65	60,000	41,934
Turkey (ca. 1981)				
TURK-IS	1952	31	1,450,000	
HAK-IS		n.a.	200,000	
MISK		n.a.	150,000	
DISK[b]	1967	28		

Sources: See note to Table 9.3.
Note: Empty cells in table indicate that those data were not available.
[a] Date indicates when data were gathered.
[b] Disbanded. Some members seem to have joined TURK-IS.

relative to the Socialist Unión General de Trabajadores (UGT), during the 1980s. The Spanish panorama is further complicated by the presence of a minor independent federation (the USO) and by regionally powerful organizations in the Basque Country (ELA/STV) and in Galicia (the INTG). Turkey would fit the general pattern better were it not for the banning of the socialist-communist DISK in 1980 and the presence of two small federations: HAK-IS, linked to the extreme right, and MISK, linked to pro-Islamic circles.

Farmers form another category that has emerged from the transition with a very fragmented structure. In addition to the usual associations based on splits between large- and small-scale agriculture, several countries have specialized associations for the representation of the interests of cooperatives. Spain has a particularly puzzling and complex variety of agrarian groups, including one just for younger farmers, which

Table 9.5 Peak Associations of Agriculture in Southern Europe

	Date of Creation	Affiliated Associations	Affilliated Firms	Size of Budget (ECUs)
Italy				
Coldiretti	1945	6,898	1,502,947	
Confida	1945			
ANCD	1944		158,000	
Federconsorzi				
CIC				
Spain				
COAG	1976	27		71,251
CNAG	1977	27		554,180
UFADE	1978	26		70,420
CNJA	1977	9	98,090	252,162
OPAs	1977			
CONCA	1980	50		
ASAJA	1989			
Portugal				
CAP	1975	72		85,980
CNA	1978	492		
CONFAGRI	1985	25		560,000
Greece				
PASEGES	1935	147	636,014	1,238,045
GEGASE	1977		102,000	
SYDASE	1985	25	70,000	
Turkey				
TUCA	1957	330	2,644,918	
ACC		16	1,500,000	
ATA	1946		15,000	

Sources: See note to Table 9.3.
Note: Empty cells in table indicate that those data were not available.

contrasts with that country's neat and compact structure of business associability (see Table 9.5).

Summarizing this bundle of characteristics relative to individual associations, the emergent property that seems to make the most difference could be called "strategic capacity."[33] The question is whether these new or renovated organizations of interest representation are sufficiently resourceful and autonomous to be able to define and sustain over the long run a course of action that is neither linked exclusively to the immediate preferences of their members nor dependent upon the policies of political parties and state agencies external to their domain. When and where they do acquire this property, we can be reasonably confident that organized interests will play a significant role—not only in regime consolidation, but also in the selection of the particular type of democracy.

A definitive evaluation of the strategic capacity of Southern European interest associations would require much better data than I have been able to amass here, especially data relating to the structure and behavior of specific organizations. If, however, we assume that small numbers, high membership density, and broadly encompassing domains of representation are jointly conducive to increasing this property, then all five countries come off poorly. In general, Italy is most impressive for its relatively high levels of membership and comprehensive interest categories. Spain has developed an exceptionally compact and encompassing set of associations for the representation of business interests, but its trade unions are fragmented into competing partisan and ideological groups and practically devoid of members. In Portugal, both trade associations and unions are more fragmented and narrow in scope, even if the latter have higher membership densities. In Greece, the problem is less a matter of emerging organizational structures (indeed, they have changed astonishingly little) than of partisan and governmental intromission in the affairs of individual associations. Finally, Turkey has the worst of both worlds—weak and dispersed structures of interest representation, and strong and concentrated policies of state intervention.

The Emergent Collective Properties of Interest Associations

The second set of characteristics that is likely to have an impact upon consolidation and, hence, upon the eventual type of democracy refers to what one may loosely term, the system of interest intermediation. The role of organized interests cannot be assessed by merely compiling arithmetically the associations present in a given polity. It also hinges on properties that emerge from their interaction. To keep the discussion focused, let us again concentrate on just the three most salient dimensions.

The first is *coverage*. Which social groups are organized into wider networks of collective action, which operate strictly on their own, and which are completely left out? The decision to privilege class and sectoral associations already implies that these, among all the varied types of interest groups, are the ones most likely to make the crucial decisions with regard to partial regime structuration and, eventually, type of democracy. In the narrow sense, the issue is whether identifiable seg-

Table 9.6 Coverage of Collective Bargaining

	Percentage of Workers Covered	Percentage Adjusted for Excluded Categories
Spain		
1983	58	67
1990	68	68
Portugal		
1981	59	70
1985	61	75
1990	62	79
France		
1985	92	92

Source: Frank Traxler, "The Level and Coverage of Collective Bargaining: A Cross-national Study in Patterns and Trends," unpublished paper, Universität Wien, 1993.

ments or factions of classes or sectors ("potential groups" in the pluralist jargon) do or do not organize themselves—or do so to a lesser degree than would appear possible. Is this due to repressive measures held over from the *ancien régime*, or to a strategic calculation that interests would be better promoted through other means of collective action, or to a structural incapacity to act under the new conditions of voluntarism and competitiveness?

Strictly in the domain of class relations, there is one indicator of coverage which can indirectly provide some idea of how extensively the actions of employer associations and trade unions are affecting their actual and potential members: that indicator is data on the total proportion of employees and workers in the economically active labor force who are covered by collectively negotiated agreements. Unfortunately, these data are available for only two of our five subject countries. In Table 9.6, Spain and Portugal are compared to France. What is most astonishing is the extent of coverage of collective contracts, especially when compared to the best estimates of the density of trade union membership. By 1980, 68 percent of the Spanish working class was covered, but only 9 percent was unionized. The figures for Portugal are a bit more consistent—62 percent and 29 percent—but still far apart. France, with a much more established system of industrial relations, had higher coverage (92 percent) but a middling rate of union density (14 percent). What this suggests for Southern Europe is the importance of legal extension of collective contracts to include nonmembers as well as members of the associations that negotiate them, and the corollary that trade unions are much more representative than their membership figures would indicate. This point could also be substantiated by data on so-called "social" elections for representatives at the plant level, where union candidates regularly win a very high percentage of the posts. Presumably, the same would be true of collective negotiations over agricultural prices, credits, and subsidies. Whether or not farmers are members of one of the participating associations, they are bound by the decisions made by these negotiations; and to the extent that they accept them, their interests are being implicitly or vicariously represented. This sort of "free riding" is certainly not unique to the neodemocracies of Southern Europe, but it may be more massively practiced there.

The problem of evaluating associational coverage is exacerbated when one shifts from this narrow class and sectoral focus to the much broader question of "other" interests—for example, people who are aged, sick, unemployed, homeless, illiterate, dwelling in slums, suffering from pollution, subjected to ethnic, cultural, linguistic, or sexual discrimination, or otherwise deprived of something they desire. Here, there can be no initial presumption that collective action will take the rather limited and specialized form of interest associability. These demands may be better addressed via political parties (if those involved are voters), religious institutions (if they are believers), or state agencies (if they are clients). They can also form their own social movements, with both an agenda and a means of action that may not be compatible with the more specialized and narrowly constrained scope of class and sectoral organizations. No empirical study can feasibly cover all forms of actual and potential interest and their corresponding organizations. In the case of Southern Europe, it can be argued that functionally based interest associations will be more significant in the consolidation process than, say, social movements based on territorial cleavages and, subsequently, will contribute more to defining the type of regime that will emerge.[34] This cannot, however, become a license to ignore completely the role of organizations and institutions representing those other interests, if only because they will affect to some degree the number, member density, and domains, as well as the coverage, of class, sectoral, and professional associations.

Table 9.7 presents data from the European Values Study which enable us to compare membership in and unpaid volunteer work for trade unions, professional associations, and political parties in Italy, Spain, Portugal, and France. These further enable us to observe how these membership and activity levels changed during the course of the 1980s (except in Portugal). Several aspects of these data are worthy of note. First, when reported by individuals in surveys, the densities of

Table 9.7 Membership in and Unpaid Workers for Associations (percentage of population over 16 years old)

	Trade Unions	Professional Associations	Political Parties
Italy			
1981	8.3 (4.0)[a]	3.0 (1.4)	6.3 (4.4)
1990	6.0 (2.5)	3.6 (1.1)	5.2 (3.5)
Spain			
1981	6.1 (2.3)	5.2 (2.3)	2.8 (2.2)
1990	2.8 (1.2)	2.7 (1.0)	1.4 (0.9)
Portugal			
1990	4.7 (1.4)	4.3 (0.9)	4.7 (3.1)
France			
1981	9.6 (3.1)	4.3 (1.8)	2.5 (1.7)
1990	5.2 (2.4)	5.0 (3.1)	2.7 (1.6)

Sources: Marginals from the European Values Study, furnished by Leok Halman, Instituut voor Sociaal-Wetenschappelijk Onderzoek, Universiteit Brabant.

[a]Percentage outside parentheses is membership; percentage within parentheses is volunteer workers.

union membership are far inferior to those claimed by the respective organizations: 6.0 percent of Italian survey respondents stated in 1990 that they belonged to trade unions, as compared with a 39.6 percent membership rate reported in published aggregate data; and the reported densities were 2.8 percent versus 9.3 percent for Spain, and 4.7 percent versus 28.6 percent for Portugal. The same held true for France, however—5.2 percent versus 14.5 percent. These differences hold up even when we correct for the fact that the denominator used in calculating the survey percentage is the total population over age 16, while that used in estimating trade union membership rates based on aggregate data is the economically active population. (In the case of Spain, for example, if we were to adjust the survey-based figure for this factor, we would still find a significant difference, on the order of 5.6 percent versus 9.3 percent.) One suspects that these persisting inconsistencies reflect differences between subjective and objective notions of membership. Second, these survey data indicate that membership in trade unions is decreasing, while levels of affiliation with professional associations are increasing (except in Spain). Except in Portugal, there are more people in interest associations than in political parties, which are also losing members (except in France).[35] Third, unpaid work (the figures in parentheses in Table 9.7) is always inferior in volume to membership and seems to be declining in unions, associations, and parties—again with the marginal exception of professionals in France.

Fourth, membership in other associations (charitable, religious, educational and artistic, community-based, environmental, youth, developmental, sporting, women's, health, peace, human and animal rights, etc.) far exceeds that of functional associations and political parties, and seems to be increasing, except in Spain. (Because multiple and overlapping memberships in these other associations make these data not easily comparable with those for trade unions, professional associations, and parties, they are not presented in the table.) Sports associations have the largest memberships of any category, except in Spain where they are slightly outnumbered by religious groups. Overall, it should be noted, emergent patterns in the two newer democracies are not that divergent from those in the two longer-established democracies in this survey. France, in particular, provides an interesting template. The Socialist government has made a special effort since 1981 to encourage *la vie associative,* and it shows up in the 1990 data (except for the fall in unionization). Despite having provided its citizens a much longer and more consistent freedom to form and join associations, however, France in 1981 had proportionately fewer people in professional associations, political parties, and other associations than did Spain. This changed significantly in the ensuing nine years, with a steep decline in Spain and sharp rise in France.

If one simply adds all the memberships reported by respondents in the European Values Study—admittedly a distortion, given the aforementioned problems of multiple and overlapping memberships—France in 1990 takes the prize with 73.5 percent, followed by Portugal's 63.7 percent, Italy's 57.9 percent, and Spain's 36.8 percent. The latter is particularly puzzling, because, as we shall see by other indicators, Spaniards have emerged with a system of interest intermediation most favorable for playing an important role in the consolidation of democracy. Its main problem would appear to be that this system has so few members!

The second emergent collective property is *monopoly*. The advent of democracy makes possible competition among associations for members, for resources, and for recognition by and access to authorities. It does not, however, make it necessary or even likely. The usual assumption is that the previous authoritarian regime—if it did not suppress associability altogether for specific groups—compelled them to act within a singular, monopolistic, state-recognized (and often state-controlled) organization. Whether this situation will persist after that regime has fallen seems to be contingent on political factors that assert themselves during the transition and that can have a lasting effect. By far the most salient, especially with regard to trade unions, is the structure of competition among political parties. Rivalry between Communists and Socialists and, occasionally, with Christian Democrats over worker affiliation often antedates the demise of authoritarian rule, but it may be only after electoral politics has been restored that it can become sufficiently salient to split more-or-less unitary workers' movements, as has happened in Italy, Spain, and Portugal.[36] Business associations have historically been less organizationally affected by partisan divisions—even when their members voted for competing parties—but they have sometimes been fragmented by linguistic or religious differences. Far more divisive for them has been the conflict of interest between small and medium, and medium and large enterprises, which is analogous to the difficulties of containing white-collar and blue-collar workers within the same peak association or of working out nonraiding agreements among unions representing differing skill levels. As mentioned above, regionalism and micronationalism have also led to situations of competition for members or for access.

Returning to Table 9.4, it should be immediately apparent that relatively few class interests in Southern Europe are represented by monopolistic institutions. The major exceptions on the side of labor—GSEE in Greece and TURK-IS in Turkey—are the products of deliberate policies of state corporatism that carried over relatively unchanged into the nascent democracy. Even then, at least in the Greek case, this organizational unity is a political illusion. Parties, especially PASOK after it took over in 1981, have made concerted efforts to penetrate and capture leadership positions in GSEE. As George Mavrogordatos shows in considerable detail, the Papandreou government blatantly manipulated the internal structure of the organization by imposing proportional representation in order to ensure the election of PASOK candidates. Similar struggles occurred behind the unitary organizational façades of GSEBE, representing small businesses, and PASEGES, representing agricultural cooperatives. The idea was even entertained to extend this tactic to the big business association, SEB![37]

Elsewhere, the standard pattern is for competing trade union confederations, each closely affiliated with a different political party or parties. For example, the executive committee of CC.OO. has 42 members, of which all but five are members of the Spanish Communist Party. The UGT executive tends to have more heterogeneous composition, but all members of the Spanish Socialist Party (PSOE) are supposed to join one or another of the UGT affiliated unions.[38] Spain is unusual insofar as it is the only country in the region where the Socialists have managed to displace the Communists as the dominant force, taking advantage of regularly conducted "social elections" at the plant level and of PSOE's position in the government. In both Italy and Portugal the Communist Party–affiliated confederations organized first and have remained the largest. In Greece, government intervention in internal elections makes it more difficult to assess the competitive situation. In Turkey, state control and repressive public policies are intended to enforce a strict separation between union and party politics.

Agriculture is another arena in which the mixture of partisan action and state intervention has produced a fragmented or pluralist outcome throughout Southern Europe, even if at any given moment in time the government in power may choose to privilege a specific interlocutor. This sector is also strongly affected by the Common Agricultural Policy of the European Community. Authorities in Brussels seem to prefer corporatist-type arrangements, in which they need deal with only one bona fide and certified association on a given issue.[39]

It is capitalists who have been most successful as associational monopolists.[40] Confindustria, for example, was able to draw extensively from its fascist organizational legacy and to provide a relatively unified voice for Italian industry during the uncertain postwar period. Even so, it was rapidly challenged by separate party-linked associations representing small business and artisans and was, eventually, compelled by legislation to divest itself of public enterprises.[41] By far the greatest success has been Spain's CEOE. Not only did it manage to include a very wide spectrum of sectoral interests—industry, commerce, insurance, banking, and even agriculture—within its organizational embrace, but it also succeeded in 1983 in incorporating a major association representing small- and medium-size enterprises, the CEPYME. Even the country's deeply rooted regional identities with their own systems of business associability, especially in Catalonia, Galicia, and the Basque Country, have been brought under the CEOE rubric.[42] The predemocratic Chambers of Commerce, Industry, and Navigation (established in 1922) survived the regime change and remained outside the CEOE, but they play little or no role in the articulation of business interests.

No other Southern European business association comes close to having attained such prominence. In Portugal, commerce and industry are separately organized, and the latter is divided by organizational rivalries. In Greece, not only do these cleavages apply, but small businesses have their own numerous and extensive network of associations. Regional organizations, like the Association of Industrialists of Northern Greece (SBBE), act independently, as do various sectors, such as the shipowners and bankers. Turkey's capitalists seem mainly divided between a chamber system (TOB) and two voluntary ones (TISK and TUSAID), and there is a very large, state-sponsored system of artisans' associations (ESNAF).

The third collective property is *coordination*. Single associations tend to have a limited span of control and capacity for managing interest diversity. The age-old quest for "one big union" has gone unfulfilled for workers, although capitalists and farmers have sometimes come closer to that goal. In order to represent more comprehensive categories, the usual technique has been to create associations of associations. These peak organizations (*Spitzenverbände* is the incomparable German term) may attempt to coordinate the behavior of entities within a single sector (e.g., the entire chemical industry), a whole branch of production (e.g., all of industry), or a class as a whole (all capitalists, workers, or farmers irrespective of branch or sector). They may cover a locality, a province or region, a national state, or even a supranational unit such as the European Community. Their success in effectively incorporating all relevant groups and forging a unity of action among them has also varied, from very incomplete and loose confederal arrangements, in which members retain their financial and political autonomy and are moved to common action only by exhortation or the personal authority of leaders, to highly centralized and hierarchic bodies with superior resources and even a capacity to discipline all class or sectoral interests that refuse to follow an agreed-upon policy line.

The attainment of such a high coordinative capacity is not without struggle or, at least, never without significant threats to the interests at stake. It is obviously easier to achieve where the scope is purely local and the sector quite narrow, for at these levels the mutual effects of small numbers and close social interaction can be brought to bear. To accomplish such feats on a national and class basis requires much greater effort. Normally, it comes only after the building blocks—the direct-membership local and sectoral associations—have been created, but this tends to make the subsequent subordination of the latter more difficult.

The heritage of centralization from the immediately preceding state-corporatist experience may have facilitated such an outcome in Southern Europe. Confindustria certainly owed much of its postwar prominence to such a legacy, although the even more extraordinary success of the CEOE at the peak of Spanish business interests does not seem to be related so closely to the previous experience with *sindicalismo vertical*. That the CEOE was formed *before* many of its sectoral federations *and* was able to attract such pre-Franco regional associations as the Fomento de Trabajo Nacional *and* had to face a militant and (initially) better organized trade union movement seems to have made the difference.[43] Next door in Portugal, the radical expropriation of industry and financial institutions disoriented the initial response of capitalists and fragmented them by sectors. The two competing national industrial associations which did eventually emerge (the AIP and the CIP) have little or no power to coordinate the behavior of their members, much less to speak for those (numerous) sectors of business that fall outside the purview of either. In both Greece and Turkey, democratization brought little or no change to the organizational structure. State tutelage, especially over small business associations, remained constant, although the Greek SEB's capacity for autonomous action was demonstrated by its resistance to the PASOK government.

Peak associations of labor in these latter two countries are also so dependent upon state authorities that their capacity for the autonomous coordination of class interests is dubious, to say the least. Confederations in Italy, Spain, and Portugal, however, have been repeatedly successful in organizing broad, intersectoral responses to government actions or capitalist resistance, but the issue for them is whether the coordination function is being performed by the respective associations or by the political parties to which they are affiliated. One way of testing for this capacity is to examine the internal distribution of affiliates. Where one or two sectoral unions compose a high percentage of all members, it presumably should be easier to coordinate actions at the class level. Historically, in the workers' movements of the northern democracies, this vanguard function was performed by metal workers. As can be seen from Table 9.8, among Southern European countries, only in Spain are metal workers the largest affiliate of both the CC.OO. and the UGT; otherwise, the biggest union consists of retirees (Italy), public employees (Portugal), construction workers (Greece), or textile workers (Turkey). As for intraorganizational concentration, Italy and Spain are comparable to Sweden and Germany, while Portugal, Greece, and Turkey have a much greater dispersion than is the European norm, suggesting that they will have a more difficult time in coordinating large-scale collective action.

In all Southern European countries, moreover, there exist independent unions or syndicates that have refused to affiliate with any central organization, just as there are sectoral or regional business associations that act on their own. In Italy, this problem of the *autonomi* emerged only long after consolidation. In Portugal and to a lesser extent Spain, these independents have weakened the coordinating capacity of confederations but have been of only minor importance. In Greece and

Table 9.8 Concentration of Trade Union Affiliates in European Labor Confederations

	Two Largest Sectors	Combined Percentage of Confederation Membership
Italy		
CGIL	Retirees, metal workers	53.2
CISL	Retirees, public employees	42.4
UIL	Retirees, construction workers	25.0
Spain		
CCOO	Metal workers, construction workers	41.1
UGT	Metal workers, construction workers	32.9
Portugal		
CGTP	Public employees, metal workers	6.4[a]
UGT-P	Bankers, ?[b]	13.1
Greece		
GSEE	Construction workers, bankers	12.9
Turkey		
TURK-IS	Textile workers, municipal workers	12.5
Germany		
DGB	Metal workers, public employees	48.4
Sweden		
LO	Public employees, metal workers	48.2
Great Britain		
TUC	General workers, metal workers	27.5

Sources: Jelle Visser, "In Search of Inclusive Unionism," pp. 173–74; and "Southern Europe: The State of the Unions," unpublished paper, Sociology of Organizations Research Unit, University of Amsterdam, 1993.

[a] Metal workers only; membership data for public employees not available.

[b] Not determined which is second most numerous sector of UGT-P.

Turkey, the "official" corporatist controls inherited from the *ancien régime* tend to mask or repress such behaviors.

Agricultural *Spitzenverbände* have rarely acted in such an aggregative fashion, given regional and product differences, so that it is especially difficult to determine what their capabilities are. With the impending, across-the-board reforms in the EC's Common Agricultural Policy, that capability may well be tested in the coming years.

The two system properties that may emerge from the above collective characteristics of coverage, monopoly, and coordination are capacity for class governance and congruence. The first asks whether the new (or renewed) interest associations are able to commit a comprehensive social category—for example, all private owners of productive property or workers in all industrial sectors—to a common and long-term course of action and to ensure that those bound by such a policy will in fact comply with it. The second focuses on the question of whether the organizational characteristics and capabilities of one class, sector, or profession resemble those of other classes, sectors, and professions—especially those whose interests regularly and predictably conflict with it.

As was the case with the characteristics of individual associations, it is impossible simply to infer from the data presented on coverage, monopoly, and coordination what the collective capacity for class governance and congruence will be. Hypothetically, we can speculate that class governance is enhanced by high degrees of intra- and interorganizational coordination and monopoly, although high member densities and low numbers of individual associations probably help somewhat. It is the distribution of all the structural traits—individual and collective—across different class, sectoral, and professional categories that should determine the extent of congruence in a given system of interest representation, especially whether it can be expected to operate according to pluralist or corporatist principles.

Not only are our data incomplete (and, even where they exist, they may not adequately indicate the characteristic we are looking for), but also class governance and congruence (as well as strategic capacity) are relational in nature. They emerge not just from rational choices rooted in the fixed preferences of associations but from the complex interactions of these organizations with such things as constitutional norms, provisions of the civil or criminal code, programs and ideologies of political parties, electoral imperatives of particular candidates, standard operating procedures of state agencies, and unintended consequences of specific public policies. To analyze these properties properly requires a rich monographic literature, such as exists for only a few of the well-established northern democracies and for none of the newly installed Southern European ones. All we can do is to advance some tentative assessments.

The strategic capacity of Southern European interest associations is generally weak, and its coverage quite uneven. Only Spanish business in general and Italian industrialists in particular seem to have developed an autonomous and consistent ability to govern the behavior of their respective categories. Episodically, the labor movements of these two countries (and of Portugal) have been able to mobilize and commit their followers to a common course of action, although in the Italian and Portuguese cases an important element in the coordination of interests was often provided by "affiliated" political parties. In Spain during the transition, and in Portugal during the consolidation, organizations of capital and labor were able to enter into comprehensive socioeconomic pacts which made a major contribution to determining the type of democracy that emerged. The equivalent Italian peak associations, minus the communist CGIL, engaged in a comparable practice for only a short period, and then only long after democracy was consolidated. No such behavior came from the class associations of Greece and Turkey, nor was it demanded of them.[44]

All the Southern European systems are incongruent, with capitalists having more associations at the national level, more specialized domains of representation, broader coverage, higher densities of membership, and a greater tendency towards associational monopoly. Workers and agriculturalists are more likely to be fragmented into competing organizations, to have proportionately (but not absolutely) fewer members, fewer units at the national level (and more at the local level) and broader domains. Their confederations, however, seem to have a greater potential capacity for coordination and, hence, for class governance, both by leaving fewer units outside their hierarchic embrace and by having more capability to control member behavior.

Instead of an Adequate Conclusion

I propose to go beyond the confines of the empirical and quantitative material I have assembled above and to advance some more exploratory and qualitative generalizations about the role that organized interests have played in the consolidation of democracies in Southern Europe.

1. Spain, Portugal, and Italy—in that order—have experienced the most change in their interest associative systems as the result of democratization. Greece and Turkey show the greatest continuity; indeed, many of their respective structural and behavioral traits antedate their most recent authoritarian experiences.
2. Spain, Portugal, and Italy—again in that order—have developed systems of interest intermediation that most resemble modern neocorporatism, although they are all far removed in organizational structure and behavior from the extreme cases of this tendency in Northern and Central Europe. Agricultural and workers' organizations tend to be more pluralist than capitalists' organizations. Greece and, especially, Turkey still have the characteristics of older, predemocratic systems of state corporatism and have yet to be fully affected by the usual norms of associational freedom, voluntary contract, and collective bargaining.
3. Political parties have clearly played a more important role in the transition and early consolidation phases in four of the five countries (Turkey

is the possible exception). Moreover, they have made extensive efforts to penetrate interest associations and they have been particularly successful with regard to both labor and agriculture. Only in the cases of Spain and Italy is there any evidence that capitalist associations have tried independently to suborn parties and to influence the outcome of elections.

4. In Spain (from 1976 to 1986), Portugal (from 1986 to 1992), and Italy (only for a short period in the late 1970s and again in the mid-1980s), the peak associations of capital and labor were strong and confident enough to engage in tripartite bargaining with the government of the time. While it is debatable how effective these agreements were in reducing inflation or enhancing competitiveness, and rivalry between worker confederations linked to different political parties made them difficult to sustain, the efforts were nonetheless significant and established precedents for future corporatist solutions.
5. In all five countries, the system of interest intermediation had become relatively consolidated within eight to ten years after the change in regime—although in Greece and Turkey the outcome depended more on public policy and coercion than upon the autonomous choices of associational actors and, hence, remains intrinsically unstable. This is not to say that further changes in both structural and behavioral attributes are not occurring in Southern Europe, but these are being driven more by the processes of international competition and European integration than by the consolidation of national democracy.

10 Political Parties and Democratic Consolidation in Southern Europe

Leonardo Morlino

Most definitions of democratic regimes make explicit or implicit reference to political parties and party systems, placing them at the center of democratic institutions and processes.[1] As intermediary institutions, which are at the same time vote-seeking, office-seeking and policy-making institutions,[2] parties and the party system perform a variety of functions. These include the attraction of mass-level support in elections; recruitment to key governmental, parliamentary, and local government posts; formulation of alternative public policy options; and elite-level intermediation with the bureaucracy, the military, and the judiciary.[3] From a societal perspective, parties may be regarded as transmission belts for social demands, and as delegates or representatives of civil society.

Given the many crucial functions performed by political parties, their relevance to the consolidation of democracy is obvious. Indeed, one recent study enumerates twenty specific aspects of party-state, inter-party, and party-society relationships that should be taken into consideration in analyzing democratic consolidation.[4] If consolidation is conceived as a *process*, moreover, not merely as the *result* of a process, the main protagonists in that process—parties, party leaders, and other politically relevant elites, including those leading political movements—must be placed at the center of our analysis. Party organizations and elites are in a position to most powerfully facilitate consolidation or, conversely, to bring about a regime crisis. They are the social actors most capable of forming, maintaining, expressing, and deepening attitudes relating to regime legitimacy or illegitimacy. As argued in one classic study, within a society, a particular set of values, mass belief systems, or ideologies may be present, but partisan organizations play an essential role in structuring, maintaining, and strengthening them.[5]

This chapter is divided into two distinct parts. It begins with an exploration of the parties and party systems of the Southern European democracies, that is, of processes by which these parties and party systems became established and took on their distinctive characteristics. This exploration includes a comparative examination of varying levels of electoral volatility, critical elections, rules which govern competition within these party systems, and the extent of stabilization of the political class during the first years following each respective democratic instauration. This first part of the chapter concludes with a discussion of two factors relevant to the electoral stabilization of party systems: the development of party organizations and the establishment of stable relationships among parties, on the one hand, and interest groups and the rest of civil society, on the other. I shall refer to these two factors as the "structuring" of the party system.

Building on the findings of the first part, the second part of this chapter links parties and party systems to the processes of democratic consolidation. Several important questions can be derived from the definitions of consolidation set forth in the Introduction to this volume and in one of my other works.[6] One of the most salient and controversial questions involves the extent to which the consolidation of a democratic regime requires the electoral stabilization of its party system and the successful structuring of party organizations and their relationships with civil society. Earlier experiences with democratization suggest a strong relationship between regime consolidation and the stabilization and structuring of parties and party systems. The more recent Southern European experience, however, calls this relationship into question and seems to imply that it may have been spurious. After examining this question, I shall set forth my own hypotheses linking regime consolidation with party system stabilization and structuring. Regime legitimation, a crucial dimension of consolidation, will then be explored as a subprocess in which parties and party systems play a key role. The chapter concludes with an overview of patterns of consolidation, some additional observations suggested by these differing patterns, and a synthetic analysis of developments that have transpired following consolidation of these four Southern European democracies, with special emphasis on the Italian political crisis and party-system transformation in the early 1990s.

Two general points may be obvious but are worthy of mention nonetheless. First, while the empirical basis of this analysis will be data from the four Southern European countries—Greece, Italy, Portugal, and Spain—the issues raised here are also relevant for Latin American and Eastern European countries, where consolidation is an issue of great current or future concern. Second, while the processes of consolidation in Portugal, Spain, and Greece took place in the late 1970s and 1980s, in Italy the core of this process occurred in a completely different historical period, that is, at the end of the 1940s and during the 1950s, when ideological extremism and the Cold War were key aspects of the historical context within which that process developed. Thus, the strategy of comparing most-similar systems is complemented by that of comparing most-dissimilar systems. This facilitates our analysis by broadening the range of the phenomena under examination, with similarities reinforced and emphasized by differences, thereby highlighting the differing roles played by party systems in consolidation processes.

The point of departure for our analysis will be the moment when the instauration of the new democracy has largely been completed, with adoption of a new constitution signaling that moment. Accordingly, the relevant starting dates are 1947 for Italy, 1975 for Greece, 1976 for Portugal, and 1978 for Spain. It is more difficult to establish a date for termination of the consolidation process, so our end-point will be more approximate. In general, we shall focus on the first decade following the instauration as the core period of consolidation, recognizing, however, that some aspects of consolidation may be completed while others remain unresolved over a protracted period of time. This source of uncertainty notwithstanding, the point of arrival for most of our analysis of Italy is the end of the 1950s, while in Greece, Portugal, and Spain our analysis ends with the 1980s.

The Stabilization of Electoral Behavior

Electoral stabilization involves the stabilization of relationships between parties and the public and among the parties themselves. It is a multifaceted process that relates to the stabilization of electoral behavior and patterns of partisan competition, as well as of party leadership. Following the initial phase of democratic installation, which is most commonly accompanied by considerable electoral fluidity, mass behavior begins to follow more predictable and recurring patterns. Our key indicators of relevant voting behavior are electoral volatility[7] and critical elections.[8] As the process of stabilization proceeds, we should expect to find that volatility decreases (i.e., that there will be a progressive shift from high electoral fluidity and uncertainty to more predictable patterns of voting behavior) and that critical elections, which substantially realign voting patterns, no longer occur. These two developments indicate that party-voter relationships have become more stable, that parties have established and solidified specific images, that the range of effective electoral competition is restricted to only some sectors of the

Table 10.1 Trends in Total Electoral Volatility

	Italy		Italy	Spain	Portugal	Greece
1946	(42.9)[a]	1971				
1947		1972	4.9			
1948	22.8	1973				
1949		1974				
1950		1975				
1951		1976	8.2		11.3	
1952		1977				22.3
1953	13.3	1978				
1954		1979	5.3	10.8	10.5	
1955		1980			4.6	
1956		1981				26.7
1957		1982		42.3		
1958	4.5	1983	8.5		11.2	
1959		1984				
1960		1985			22.5	6.3
1961		1986		11.9		
1962		1987	8.4		23.2	
1963	7.9	1988				
1964		1989		8.8		6.9/4.3[b]
1965		1990				3.3
1966		1991			9.5	
1967		1992	16.2			
1968	3.4	1993		10.6		17.7
1969		1994	41.9			
1970						

Note: Total volatility is the sum of the absolute value of all changes in the percentages of votes cast for each party since the previous election, divided by two.

[a] This figure is an estimate of the change in vote since the last prefascist election.

[b] Two elections were held in 1989, one in June and the other in November.

electorate, and that party-system crises are unlikely. In other words, they indicate that a stable party system has emerged.

Electoral Volatility

The data presented in Table 10.1 clearly differentiate between periods of high electoral volatility and the point at which voting instability begins to decline. The most puzzling case, in this regard, is Portugal—the only Southern European country with no previous experience of mass democracy. The average total volatility score for Portugal between 1975 and 1983 was only 11 percent, even after excluding the 1980 election, held only a few months after that of 1979. If the 1980 election had been included in these calculations, average volatility would have been even lower, but with a less consistent trend. With the elections of

1985 and 1987, however, there was a substantial increase in total volatility, and a subsequent restructuring of the party system. To place these figures in comparative perspective, we should note that the average total volatility for all Western European democracies over the past decade was 9.2. Accordingly, the Portuguese figures were close to the European average over the course of the first eight years of electoral competition. The other three Southern European cases reveal different patterns. Italy shows the clearest declining trend. In both Greece and Spain, the highest level of volatility was manifested in the third election, in 1981 and 1982, respectively, with Spain's volatility score in that year being exceptionally high.

Critical Elections

The total volatility figures presented in Table 10.1 suggest that critical elections occurred in Italy in 1948, Greece in 1981, and Spain in 1982. These realignments are reflected in peak total volatility scores in those years, followed by a marked decline. In Portugal, an electoral realignment occurred quite late, in 1987. The dominant position achieved by the Social Democrats in that election was solidified by an equally impressive victory in 1991.

A second way of identifying critical elections is to analyze interbloc or area volatility. If we take for granted the salience of the left-right cleavage in all four countries, then a good way to evaluate the extent of electoral change is to count the number of voters shifting across the divide between the left or center-left and the right or center-right portions of the political spectrum. Table 10.2 presents data relating to this kind of change. It appears to confirm that realigning or critical elections occurred in Italy in 1948, Greece in 1981, Spain in 1982, and Portugal in 1987, particularly insofar as the highest interbloc volatility scores, by far, were produced in the same years as the peak total volatility scores.

The extent to which the 1987 election had a lasting impact in realigning the Portuguese party system is confirmed by the extraordinarily low interbloc volatility score produced by the next election, four years later.[9] Prior to that critical election, Portuguese electoral politics was dominated by a few parties that managed to maintain their relative positions with the electorate despite high levels of governmental instability, frequent changes in party leadership, and even changes in some basic aspects of the democratic regime itself, including significant revisions in the constitution (the longest such document in the world). When President Eanes created the Democratic Renewal Party (PRD) in 1985,

Table 10.2 Trends in Interbloc Volatility

	Italy		Italy	Spain	Portugal	Greece
1946		1971				
1947		1972	1.1			
1948	12.9	1973				
1949		1974				
1950		1975				
1951		1976	5.4		6.6	
1952		1977				13.7
1953	4.6	1978				
1954		1979	0.7	1.0	3.2	
1955		1980			1.7	
1956		1981				23.5
1957		1982		7.4		
1958	1.0	1983	0.3		7.8	
1959		1984				
1960		1985			0.5	3.4
1961		1986		2.6		
1962		1987	1.1		15.5	
1963	1.3	1988				
1964		1989		1.7		4.7/0.5[a]
1965		1990				2.2
1966		1991			1.2	
1967		1992	5.2			
1968	1.4	1993		1.7		4.2
1969		1994	5.8			
1970						

Note: Interbloc volatility, or area volatility, is the sum of the absolute value of the difference between the percentages of votes cast for the right and center (as one bloc) and the left, divided by two.
[a] Two elections were held in 1989, one in June and the other in November.

the electorate responded by giving it a surprising 18.5 percent of the vote: latent discontent and protest had found a voice. It is most noteworthy, however, that in that year of high total volatility, there was virtually no interbloc volatility. But the PRD proved to be a "flash party." Its electoral support fell to 5 percent in 1987 and to .6 percent in 1991. A more lasting and significant change occurred in 1987 with the unprecedented electoral triumph of the Social Democratic Party (PSD). Given the extremely high level of interbloc volatility in 1987 (15.45%, most of it from the center-left to the center-right), we can regard this as a basic realignment of the party system.

The Portuguese case suggests that adaptation is a key aspect of the processes under examination here. Significant changes in the regime itself took place between the time of the first elections and the consolidation of democracy in the mid-1980s. Until the second major constitutional revision in early August 1989, partial crises and adaptation recurred in Portugal. Indeed, in the end, the regime that was consolidated was not the same as that which had first emerged in the aftermath of the revolution. The party system also underwent considerable change during this period, evolving from a four-party to a predominant-party system. In this regard, it is interesting to note that in the early years of relatively low electoral volatility, parties were not very salient: the game of politics was also played in other arenas, and neutralization of the military had not yet taken place. The stabilization of voting behavior should be seen in the context of these crises and regime consolidation. Adaptation to altered political circumstances was essential.

The case of Spain is noteworthy insofar as its electorate has exhibited high levels of total volatility (with the electoral change of 1982 representing an enormous redistribution of voters among parties) but extraordinarily low levels of interbloc volatility: even in the party-system realignment of 1982, there were far fewer voters who crossed the divide between left and right (7.4%) than in any of the other critical elections examined here (12.9% in Italy, 15.5% in Portugal, and 23.5% in Greece). Spanish voters may be prone to shifting their allegiances from one party to another, but such shifts occur almost exclusively within the boundaries of the various blocs.

The opposite pattern emerges from an examination of comparable data for Greece. Virtually all of the total volatility manifested in the 1981 critical election was in the form of interbloc volatility: 23.5 percent of the total of 26.7 percent of votes shifted across the left-right divide. This is largely explained by the paucity of parties: given that most Greek voters cast their ballots for one of two parties, any substantial shifts must, almost inevitably, involve moves from left to right, or vice versa. In the other countries, a shift of voting may take place within the right or left camps, without necessarily involving interbloc volatility.

Our overall conclusion is that electoral stabilization has occurred in all four countries: in every case, following a critical election, volatility declined and voting behavior became more stable and predictable.

Party Systems and Patterns of Partisan Competition

The establishment of a party system with specific characteristics and with stable patterns of partisan competition is the second development we shall examine. In exploring this aspect of party-system stabilization, we shall rely upon two indicators of differing patterns of competition among parties: these are the index of party fractionalization and the number of effective parties. We should expect to find that these indicators will become stable and remain stable over time during the period of democratic consolidation. Indeed, perhaps the most telling indicator of the stabilization of a party system is the absence of new parties or movements.

The appearance of new parties or movements may be a frequent occurrence prior to regime consolidation. Indeed, during installation of a new democratic regime, a large number of new parties can be expected to present lists for the first one or two elections. At a certain point, however, the regime's electoral law should begin to contribute to party-system stabilization: the threshold level for parliamentary representation which it establishes will begin to work, effectively precluding the birth and establishment of new parties. To be sure, the differing electoral systems adopted by new regimes will have varying impacts on the prospects for viability of new parties. These differences notwithstanding, we should expect to find a clear difference between the first one or two elections, when hundreds of party lists are presented, and subsequent electoral contests, when a process of natural selection will have begun, contributing to the stabilization of party leadership, organization, identity, image, and programmatic commitments. Once this process has begun, party schisms or the fusion of formerly independent parties should decrease markedly in frequency. The crucial variable affecting the extent of stabilization is the level of the threshold set by each system's electoral law.

The threshold set by the Italian electoral law is quite low. Accordingly, the party system that first took shape in the second general election of 1948 was highly fragmented. The attempt by the Christian Democratic (DC) leadership in 1952–53 to strengthen its position and win a majority of seats, by changing the electoral law and imposing a much higher threshold, produced a strong mobilization by new parties attempting to enter the electoral arena. The DC's plan failed. The Christian Democrats, however, adopted a new strategy for strengthening their position. This new effort (to be analyzed later in this chapter) involved the attainment of autonomy through party organization and the management of public sector enterprises.

The new party system of Portugal in the 1970s and early 1980s was characterized by limited multipartyism, with a fairly large but gradually declining Communist Party. In the mid-1980s, however, a basic restructuring of the party system took place. This change was initiated by an attempt to build a new party, the PRD, under the former president Ramalho Eanes. The failure of this attempt contributed to the triumph of the PSD in the 1987 elections: the absolute majority of parliamentary seats won by the PSD marked a shift to a predominant party system in Portugal.

The party systems of Spain and Greece took shape quickly; they adopted a logic of competition, pitting one large party of the right against one large party of the left. The party system in each case was dominated by relatively few parties, and the entry of new political forces was largely prevented. In Greece, there was the early stabilization (by 1977) of a bipolar pattern of competition between Nea Democratia (ND) and the socialist PASOK. There were some problems in Spain, however, particularly concerning the structuring of the right and internal divisions within the Communist Party. These problems remained partially unresolved even after the critical election of 1982.

On the whole, the initial impact of the electoral threshold was to allow a few parties to dominate the electoral and political arenas and to prevent the entrance of new forces. Each of the four party systems adopted a clear structure of partisan competition and achieved some degree of stabilization. More serious problems remain at an intraparty level in each country, above all in Spain. Although some considerable stabilization has occurred, the histories of these four party systems indicate that actions by party leaders can interrupt and even reverse the process. In Portugal and Italy, this was manifested in the appearance of newcomers, while in Spain it took the form of a critical election in 1982, a radical restructuring of the nationwide parties to the right of center, the fragmentation of the communist PCE into three different parties, and continuing uncertainty as to the role of regional parties.

An implicit rank ordering in terms of stabilization of the party system is reflected in the index of vote fractionalization. As can be seen from Table 10.3, the index for Greece has been relatively frozen between .60 and .63 ever since the 1977 election. Following a temporary decline in fragmentation in 1948, the configuration of the Italian party system was stable throughout the 1950s and early 1960s: the index remained stable (ranging between .74 and .76) throughout this period. Spain and Portugal have had ups and downs, in this respect, but both appear to have stabilized in the late 1980s.

An analysis of the number of effective parties suggests a similar picture. Thanks in part to the strong representational biases in Greece's reinforced electoral law, a small number of parties has dominated a party system that has largely been stabilized since 1981. In Italy a somewhat less pronounced freezing of the party system occurred following 1948. The party systems of Spain and Portugal, meanwhile, appear to have stabilized only in the mid- to late 1980s.

This measure of effective parties, however, is not so useful in terms of

Table 10.3 Index of Vote Fractionalization

	Italy		Italy	Spain	Portugal	Greece
1946	.79	1971				
1947		1972	.76			
1948	.66	1973				
1949		1974				.64
1950		1975			.73	
1951		1976	.72		.75	
1952		1977		.77		.73
1953	.76	1978				
1954		1979	.74	.76	.69	
1955		1980			.68	
1956		1981				.63
1957		1982		.66		
1958	.74	1983	.78		.73	
1959		1984				
1960		1985			.79	.61
1961		1986		.72		
1962		1987	.78		.66	
1963	.76	1988				
1964		1989		.75		.63/.60[a]
1965		1990				.62
1966		1991			.64	
1967		1992	.85			
1968	.75	1993		.71		.62
1969		1994	.87			
1970						

Note: The index of vote fractionalization was calculated using Rae's formula,

$$F = 1 - \sum_{i=1}^{n} p_i^2,$$

where *p* denotes the share of vote attained by each party in the election.
[a]Two elections were held in 1989, one in June and the other in November.

its implications for patterns of partisan interaction. The number of effective parties in Portugal, Spain, and Greece appears to be quite similar, despite real differences in partisan competition in these countries which are masked by this indicator. By other rules for counting, more useful for an analysis of this aspect of party systems, Italy is distinctly different from the other countries. Throughout the 1950s and 1960s, Italy had at least seven relevant parties—one with a plurality, but by no means a majority of votes (Christian Democrats), but also at least six other parties, some with coalition potential (Liberals, Republicans, and Social Democrats), or on the way to acquiring coalition potential (Socialists), or with blackmail potential (neofascists and Communists).[10] In Spain, in contrast, for a decade and a half following the 1982 elections there was only one main incumbent party (PSOE), which faced only one significant electoral rival (the Partido Popular), less substantial opposition from the left (Izquierda Unida), a centrist rival that vanished altogether in 1993 (Centro Democrático y Social), and several regional parties. Similarly, in Portugal after 1987 there was only one main incumbent party (Social Democrats) supported by a single-party parliamentary majority, which faced smaller opponents on the right (Centro Democrata Social) and left (Socialists and Communists). In Greece, the main incumbent party as of 1974 was Nea Democratia, with opposition from socialists, communists and, between 1974 and 1977, the fading center (EDIK). Following the PASOK victory in the 1981 elections, there was an alternation in power and the situation was reversed: Nea Democratia became the main opposition party.

In terms of sheer numbers, Greece had three parties during the period under investigation, Portugal had four, Spain had four nationwide parties and several regional parties complicating the picture, while Italy had a seven-party system. When we take into consideration the size of parties and the dynamics of partisan competition, clearer distinctions between Italy and the other three countries emerge. Greece was close to a two-party system throughout this period, with a predominant party throughout the consolidation process, and a tripolar structure of partisan competition.[11] Spain (after 1982) and Portugal (after 1987) acquired systems with one main party (the PSOE and the PSD, respectively) at the center of the political arena. In spite of being a multiparty system, Italy also had a predominant party (the DC) during the most important phase of consolidation; but Italy also had a centrifugal structure of competition, while the other three party systems exhibited centripetal patterns of competition, despite the presence of leftist or isolated regional forces and, in the Greek case, a high (although declining) degree of polarization.

If we examine the level of competition, as measured by the difference between the strongest electoral party and the others, it is Greece which stands apart from the rest. The level of competition became very low in Italy and Portugal, and low in Spain. Only in Greece was there a high level of competition and, therefore, a strong possibility of alternation, as shown by the return to government of ND in 1990 and PASOK in 1993. The other three cases are characterized by the predominant role of one party. (Later we shall examine the possible relationship between the existence of a predominant party and the way consolidation took place, as well as the special meaning of predominant parties in countries with previous experience with nondemocratic government.)

A different way of exploring the patterns of competition is to see if

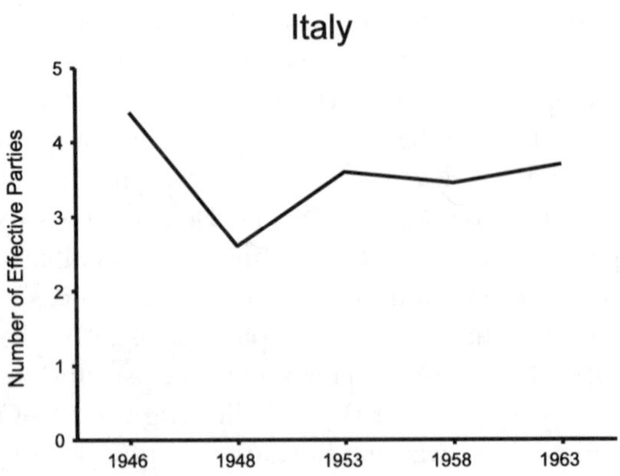

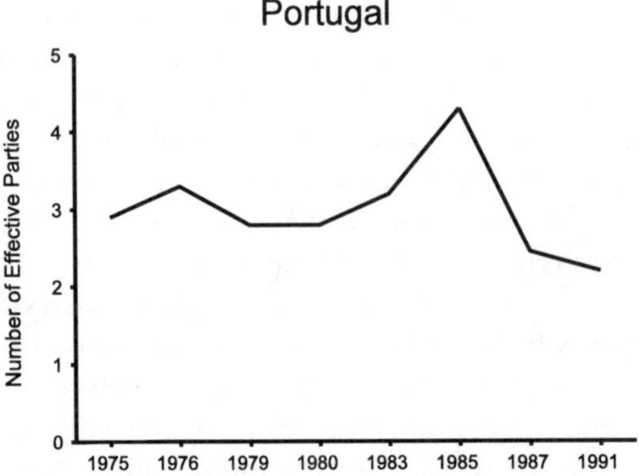

Figure 10.1 Number of Effective Parties

Note: This is based on the formula suggested by Laasko and Taagepera:

$$N = 1/\sum_{i=1}^{n} P_i^2$$

where P_i is the proportion of seats of the *i*-th party. (See Markku Laakso and Rein Taagepera, "'Effective' Number of Parties: A Measure with Application to West Europe," *Comparative Political Studies* 12, 1979, pp. 3–27.)

there has been a stabilization of cleavages. If we divide parties into two camps in accord with the left-right cleavage (the one common denominator for all four countries) and then use the interbloc volatility data presented in Table 10.2, we can see clear evidence that stabilization has occurred in all four countries: it occurred after 1948 in Italy, in Spain

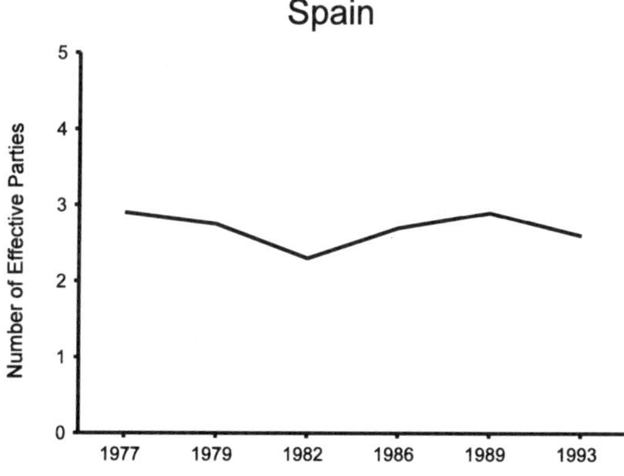

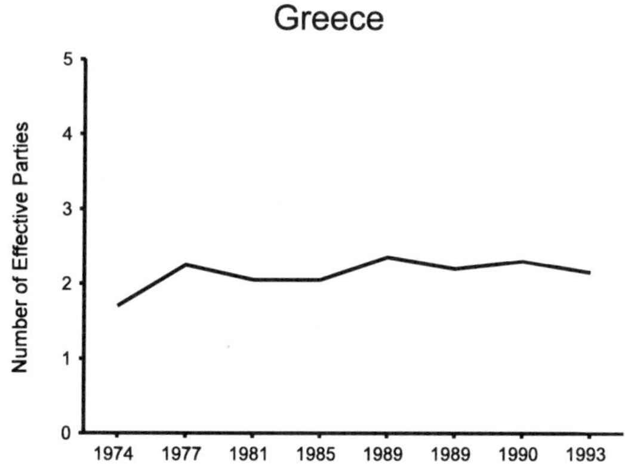

Figure 10.1 *Continued*

following the 1982 realignment, after the Portuguese Social Democrats' victory in 1987, and after the 1981 alternation in Greece. In each country, stabilization followed a critical election that involved high electoral instability and change. Once stabilization occurred, high total volatility of electoral change could still take place, but interbloc volatility was low. At first glance, it might appear as if the party system were still fluid and changing; but the low interbloc volatility characteristic of electoral behavior indicates, instead, that voting behavior has actually been structured by this cleavage. This further suggests that interbloc volatility is a better indicator of party-system stabilization than is total volatility. The marked stabilization of the Spanish party system following 1982 is clearly reflected in these interbloc volatility figures: following the 7.4 score for 1982, interbloc volatility figures have remained consistently low (2.6 in 1986, 1.7 in 1989, and 1.9 in 1993)—lower even than such scores for Greece (3.4 in 1985, the first election following the 1981 alternation in power, 4.7 in 1989, and 2.2 in 1990.

In the case of Spain, an additional cleavage is highly significant—that between center and periphery. Here, too, we can see evidence of stabilization following the 1982 election. The share of the total vote received by regional parties nearly doubled between 1977 and 1979, increasing from 6.2 percent to 11.1 percent, only to fall to 7.4 percent in 1982. Following that election, however, their share of the vote became more predictable. Regional parties received 9.5 percent of the total vote in 1986, 10.8 percent in 1989, and 12.0 percent in 1993.[12]

The Roots of Stability

To this point, we have examined data indicating that the party systems of all four Southern European countries have become stabilized and that this occurred in Italy after 1948 (and especially after 1953), in Greece after 1981, in Spain after 1982, and in Portugal after 1987. Let us now go beyond a simple description of the four party systems in order to explore some of the differences among them and to explain how stabilization came about.

Electoral Systems

There is no doubt that electoral laws can contribute significantly to stabilization, particularly if we take into account the passage of a certain period of time following the initial appearance of political parties and the progressive adaptation of voters to the representational biases inherent in the electoral system. The cumulative impact of the strong biases inherent in the reinforced proportional representation system can be seen in the steady narrowing of the gap between the index of vote fractionalization and the index of "seat fractionalization." At the time of the Greece's first democratic election, in 1974, the two indices differed by fully 18 percent. The progressive narrowing of this gap—to 16 percent in 1977, 11 percent in 1981, 8 percent in 1985, and 4 percent in each of the three elections held in 1989–90—clearly reflects that voters became increasingly aware of the representational biases of the electoral system and, wishing to avoid casting "wasted" votes, shifted their support from small parties to those with real prospects for winning seats in parliament. The Greek party system had become so stabilized by 1989 that even adoption of a more proportional and less biased electoral system in that year failed to bring about any significant change.[13]

A much purer form of proportional representation inherent in the pre-1993 Italian electoral law, not surprisingly, had a more limited impact on the party system: prior to the local elections of 1993, voters were much less prone to shift their votes from small parties to large parties. Portuguese electoral districts are somewhat smaller than those of Italy, while those of Spain are much smaller. In general, the fewer the number of deputies elected from each constituency, the greater the pressure towards reduction of the number of parties in the party system.[14] In Spain, however, the electoral law strongly discourages fragmentation among parties with nationwide bases of support but fairly represents parties with geographically concentrated support.[15] Thus, it is not surprising to find that the only fractionalization of the Spanish party system that has taken place resulted from the emergence of regional parties.

One indicator of proportionality assigns the electoral system of Italy a score of 95, as compared with 93 for that of Portugal, 88 for Greece, and 84 for Spain.[16] A somewhat different index produces the same rank ordering. Accordingly, Italy receives a nonproportionality score of 2.2, Portugal's score is 3.3, and Spain and Greece receive nonproportionality scores of 7.6.[17]

Party Leadership and the Political Class

Our exploration of the stabilization of electoral behavior and patterns of partisan competition has so far focused on the mass level. Elite-level factors are also highly relevant, especially the stabilization of party leadership and, more generally, of the political class.

In the Italian case, stabilization of the top party leadership was almost immediate, with minor changes in subsequent years. In the other three cases, however, some parties had very serious internal problems, with high levels of conflict, including splits and the formation of new parties. These three cases also reflect differences, Greece (where party leadership is further reinforced by certain provisions of the electoral law) most closely resembling Italy. Instability in party leadership was at times a serious problem in Portugal (primarily among the center and center-right parties following the death of PSD leader Francisco Sá Carneiro in 1980); it was sometimes very serious in Spain.[18] Some differences among these countries with regard to stabilization of the parliamentary political class can be seen in Table 10.4, which presents

Table 10.4 Stabilization of Political Class in Parliaments after Authoritarian Regimes' Demise

	1st	2nd	3rd	4th	5th
New Members (% of all MPs)					
Italy	—	56	37	36	35
Spain	—	45	60	43	
Portugal	—	52	25	46	40
Greece	61	38	41	13	
Reelected Members (% of all MPs)					
Italy	—	31	41	40	40
Spain	—	55	40	56	
Portugal	—	48	70	47	53
Greece	39	61	59	87	

Sources: For Italy, Maurizio Cotta, *Classe politica e parlamento in Italia, 1946–1976* (Bologna: Il Mulino, 1979); for Spain, Paloma Morán Marugán, *El Partido Socialista Obrero Español en la transición española: Organización y ideología (1975–1982)* (Madrid: Departamento de Ciencia Política y de la Administración, 1987, pp. 77, 79; for Portugal, Manuel Braga da Cruz, "Sobre o parlamento portugues: Partidarizaçao parlamentar e parlamentarizaçao partidaria," *Analise Social* 24, 1988, pp. 113–15; and for Greece, see Nikos Alivizatos, "The Difficulties of 'Rationalization' in a Polarized Political System: The Greek Chamber of Deputies," in Ulrike Liebert and Maurizio Cotta, eds., *Parliament and Democratic Consolidation in Southern Europe* (London: Pinter, 1990), p. 139.

the percentages of newly elected members and of senior members in the first legislatures following the reestablishment of democracy in each country. Italy and Greece show the clearest decline in newcomers and growth of seniority among members of parliament. Although an anomaly distorts the results for Portugal (i.e., the 1980 elections to the third legislature occurred only a short time after the 1979 elections to the second parliament), the same trend is apparent. The results for Spain, however, are inconclusive.

Overall, these data suggest that party-elite stabilization is greatest in Italy and Greece. Portugal's political leaders appear to have achieved some stabilization by the late 1980s, while Spain lagged behind, largely due to continued instability among party leaders on both the left and the right flanks of the PSOE, as well as within some regional parties. These patterns deviate somewhat from those observed in our analysis of electoral stabilization, where Spain exhibited signs of much greater stabilization.

Party Organization and Civil Society

The development of a network of relationships between parties and civil society is another important facet of the stabilization of party sys-

Table 10.5 Identification with a Political Party (percentage of survey respondents)

	1958	1985	1989
Portugal	—	48.9	49
Spain	—	47.5	30
Greece	—	69.6	57
Italy	76.0	52.0	63

Sources: For Italy in 1958, the Doxa Survey, in *Bollettino Doxa, 1958;* for 1985, *Four Nation Survey;* for 1989, *Eurobarometer Survey,* in Hermann Schmitt, "On Party Attachment in Western Europe and the Utility of Eurobarometer Data," *West European Politics* 12, 1989, pp. 183–84.

tems. The development of party organizations and of relationships among parties, interest groups, and individual citizens are two significant modalities for controlling civil society (which, I will argue, played an important role in consolidating Italian democracy), but they are also important bases for the stabilization of the party systems themselves. Thus, the extent to which parties develop their own organizational networks and establish close relationships with civil society emerges as an important aspect of political change. The extent of these changes depends in part on the development of widespread party identification among the electorate.

The main purpose of organizational structuring and of establishing party identification is to maintain and expand a stable electorate that shares the ideology, values, and programs of parties. As Barnes observed long ago, organizational development is best achieved when the ideological dimension is a relevant feature of political conflict in the country.[19] At the same time, its main thrust also comes from the logic of party competition, which induces parties to create organizational resources to win over and retain a larger share of the voters in the electorate.

The data on party identification presented in Table 10.5 reveal that party identification was widespread in Italy by the late 1950s: 76 percent of Italians interviewed by Doxa identified with a party. These data are consistent with a regional survey conducted in Emilia and Romagna shortly thereafter (indicating that 75.5% identified with a party),[20] and they are close to levels of party identification about that same time in Germany (76.5% in 1961) and the United States (72.5% in 1956). They are higher than levels of party identification found in surveys of France (53.0% in 1958, when the Fourth Republic collapsed) and even Norway (66.0% in 1957).[21] It is interesting to note that much lower levels of party identification were found in later surveys of Italy: by 1985 they had fallen to 52 percent; they had recovered somewhat, to 63 percent,

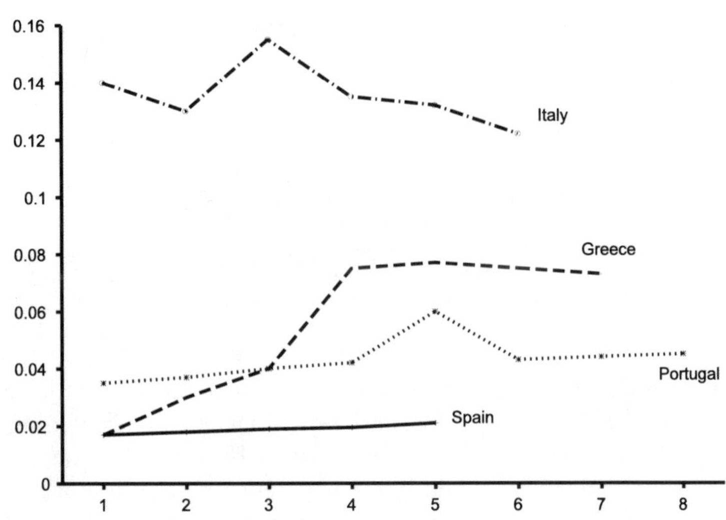

Figure 10.2 Rate of Membership in Political Parties
Note: Membership rate is the estimated membership of each party divided by the vote that party received in the previous election. The numbers on the horizontal axis correspond to the first through the eighth election following the restoration of democracy. Thus, for Italy 1 and 2 indicate the 1946 and 1948 elections, for Spain 1 is 1977 and 2 is 1979, etc.

by 1989. As the data in Table 10.5 show, only Greece has levels of party identification similar to those found in Italy. A 1985 survey found that levels of party identification in Portugal and Spain were roughly equal, but many other surveys have shown that Spain is definitely the country with the lowest party identification in Western Europe.[22]

The extent to which parties are capable of establishing supportive organizational structures is another factor related to the stabilization of party systems. One measure of organizational development is the membership rate of the political party—that is, the ratio between the estimated membership of the party and the number of votes it received in the previous election.[23] These figures may be regarded as measuring the extent of party penetration into society or, from the opposite perspective, the extent of "partisan associability" of society. As can be seen in Figure 10.2, Greece and, especially, Italy are the two countries with the highest membership rates, while Spain lags very far behind. In some respects, these data do not fit well with our rank ordering of party systems in terms of stabilization. As we have seen, the Spanish party system and (more recently) that of Portugal have become stabilized, and yet their party-membership rates are quite low. Another hint of the weak relationship between membership rate and stabilization can be seen in changes over time regarding Italy. Italian membership rates were clearly declining at the same time that the Italian party system was becoming more stable, both electorally and in terms of party leadership.

These data suggest that the development of party organizations, as measured by membership rate, is only part of an overall explanation of stabilization. We should note, however, that in some respects these data may be misleading. In the Italian case, for example, we must be aware that the early period was one of demobilization following the Resistance and the turmoil near the end of the war. The aggregate figures presented in Figure 10.2 conceal the fact that individual parties were undergoing distinctly different processes of change: specifically, the Christian Democrats were developing an impressive organizational structure and penetration into Italian society, while at the same time the communist PCI was experiencing a long-term process of membership decline. These mixed patterns can be seen better in Figure 10.3, which breaks down total membership levels by party. The decline of the Communist Party was perhaps inevitable, given that the PCI emerged from the Resistance as by far the largest party and was bound to decline in membership as mass mobilization subsided in the 1950s and early 1960s.

These data on party membership levels in Italy stand in stark contrast with similar data from Spain, as can be seen by comparing Figure 10.3 with Figure 10.4. The installation of democratic regimes in these two countries differed markedly in one key element: the degree of mass mobilization which characterized the two transition and consolidation processes. The transition and consolidation periods in Italy were accompanied by extremely high levels of mass mobilization, as suggested by high levels of party membership. Spain stands at the opposite end of the continuum. During the first five years following the death of Francisco Franco, all parties except the communist PCE had extraordinarily low levels of membership compared with Italy. Even the Communist Party of Spain should be regarded as poorly developed organizationally, insofar as its peak membership in the first years of the democratic era was only one-tenth that of the PCI during a comparable period. Following the collapse of the PCE, after about 1980, the party had only a minimal organizational presence in Spanish society. It is interesting to note that the low level of party membership in Spain also parallels the relatively low levels of voter turnout characteristic of most Spanish elections.[24] Clearly, these data are indicative of the much lower levels of ideological mobilization and polarization that characterized the Spanish transition to democracy. This sharply distinguishes the

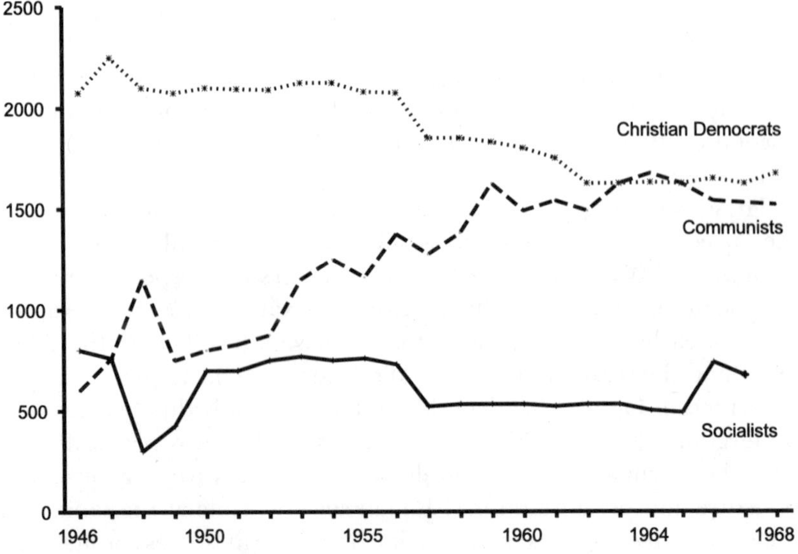

Figure 10.3 Membership of Main Mass Parties: Italy (in thousands)
Sources: For Communists, Celso Ghini, "Gli iscritti al partito e alla FGCI 1943–1979," in Massimo Ilardi and Aris Accornero, eds., *Il Partito Comunista Italiano: Struttura e storia del' organizzazione* (Milan: Feltrinelli, 1982), p. 237: for Christian Democrats, Maurizio Rossi, "Un partito di anime morte? Il tesseramento democristiano tra mito e realità," in Arturo Parisi, ed., *Democristiani* (Bologna: Il Mulino, 1979), p. 27; for Socialists, Valdo Spini e Sergio Mattana, *I quadri del PSI* (Florence: Nuova Guaraldi, 1981), p. 56.

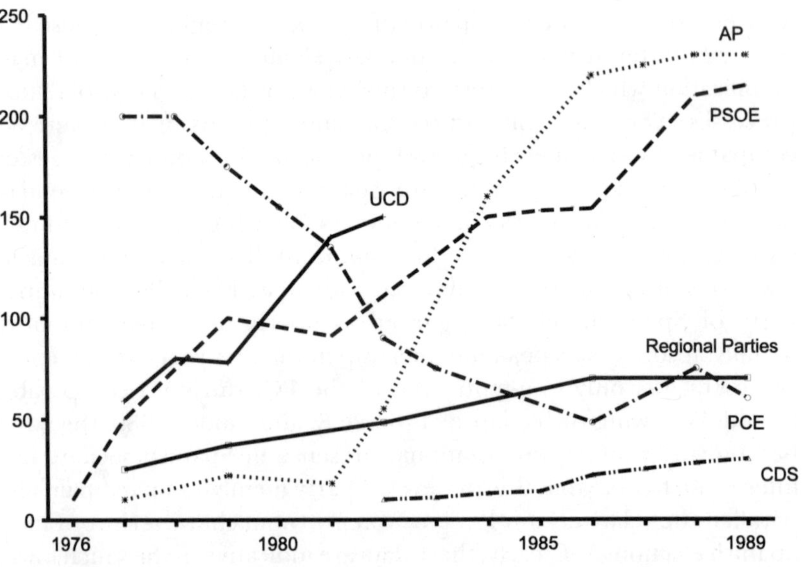

Figure 10.4 Membership of Main Mass Parties: Spain (in thousands)
Sources: Various party sources.

Table 10.6 Membership Rate of Main Parties: Italy

	1946	1948	1953	1958	1963	1969
DC	7.5	8.8	10.5	11.3	13.7	13.7
PSI	18.1	a	22.7	11.5	11.5	a
PCI	47.5	a	34.9	27.1	20.8	17.6

Sources: For Communists, Ghini, "Gli iscritti," p. 237; for Christian Democrats, Rossi, "Un partito di anime morte?" p. 27; for Socialists, Spini and Mattana, *I quadri del PSI,* p. 56

Note: The membership rate is the number of party members as a percentage of the total number of votes cast for that party.

[a] Data for individual parties not available for these years.

Table 10.7 Membership Rate of Main Parties: Spain

	1977	1979	1982	1986
AP	—	2.0	3.0	4.2
PSOE	1.0	1.8	1.1	1.9
PCE	11.8	8.0	10.0	7.8

Note: The membership rate is the number of party members as a percentage of the votes cast for that party.

Spanish case from that of Italy. Even after a decade and a half of organizational development, the two largest parties in Spain were able to attract only about one-eighth as many members as did their Italian counterparts. And, as Tables 10.6 and 10.7 reveal, membership rates in Italy have consistently remained vastly higher than those in Spain.

These data further suggest that there is a connection between incumbency and the growth of membership. In Italy, the Christian Democrats were the incumbent party from the very beginning of the transition to democracy in 1944–46. The DC's problems in establishing an adequate organizational network became particularly acute following the party's electoral victory in 1948. Indeed, that triumph was largely the result of extensive efforts by various organizations of the Catholic Church. Clearly, from the standpoint of party building, it was necessary for the DC to build its own autonomous structures, particularly in order to counteract the extensive communist organization. Under these circumstances, incumbency significantly facilitated the party's organizational growth, but it does not alone explain the growth. The DC became an incumbent party as early as 1944, but the most acute problems of organizational development came during the later phase of consolidation and competition with the PCI. In contrast with the successful efforts of the DC, the Socialist Party experienced no growth in party membership—neither in the short term nor over the long term. Instead, it largely accepted a position secondary to the Communists, until the Hungarian uprising of 1956.

Incumbency was also relevant to party membership growth in Spain. Indeed, it appears that membership growth tends to follow rather than precede electoral success. The Unión de Centro Democrático (UCD) had virtually no organizational structure when it came to power in 1977. Its position of incumbency, however, greatly facilitated the construction of a significant mass-membership base over the following five years. Similarly, the most substantial period of membership growth by the PSOE occurred after, not before, its electoral triumph in 1982.

While it is clear that electoral success greatly facilitates the growth of mass affiliation with parties, to what extent does a large base of party members improve prospects for electoral success? The Spanish data are indicative of a very weak relationship, if any. The governing UCD and the PCE were the two parties with the largest membership base in the period preceding the 1982 election, but both were devastated in that contest. Conversely, the AP (Alianza Popular, renamed the Partido Popular in 1989) had virtually no mass membership base prior to 1982, but in the election of that year it surged from 9 seats in the Congress of Deputies to 106! Its spectacular increase in party membership followed, rather than preceded, the 1982 election; by 1985, its membership base had quintupled.

Data concerning the organizational development of Portuguese parties (see Table 10.8) also undermine the notion that a mass-membership base is a key element for electoral success (some reservations concerning the reliability of these membership data notwithstanding). This is most clear with regard to the Portuguese Communist Party (PCP). Not only had the PCP experienced substantial membership growth between the first elections and the mid-1980s, but throughout this period it was the largest party, sometimes by a very wide margin over its rivals. Nonetheless, the PCP experienced a substantial electoral decline throughout the 1980s: its share of total votes cast fell from 18.9 percent in 1983, to 16 percent in 1985, to 12.5 percent in 1987, and to 9 percent in 1991. Data regarding the Socialists (PS) and the centrist Social Democrats suggest a correlation between mass membership and electoral success, but doubts concerning the proper direction of causality call into question the value of a mass-membership base as a significant electoral asset. To be sure, the PS suffered a substantial decrease in affiliation (most likely due to a leadership crisis and a reaction by militants to the austerity policies of 1983–85) preceding its 1987 electoral defeat, but it is clear that the greatest growth in membership experienced by the PSD occurred after its unprecedented electoral triumph in

Table 10.8 Membership of Main Parties: Portugal

	CDS	PSD	PS	PCP
1974		10,875	35,971	14,593
1975		20,445	81,654	100,000
1976		25,011	91,562	115,000
1978			96,563	142,000
1979		32,687		164,713
1980	6,732			187,018
1982	15,479			
1983	40,000?	85,217?	130,181?	200,753
1984	20,789	67,324	139,000?	
1986		89,899	46,655	
1987		101,454		
1988	25,696			199,275
1989			62,117	
1990		125,386		
1991	26,801	139,253	69,351	
1992	27,092	143,075	70,000	163,506

Sources: Maria José Stock, "O centrismo politico em Portugal: Evolução do sistema de partidos, genese do 'Bloco Central' e analise dos dois parceiros da coligação," *Analise Social* 21, 1985, pp. 60, 85; *Os partidos do poder dez anos depois de '25 April'* (Evora: Universidade de Evora, 1986), pp. 26–28, 137, 177; João Carlos Espada and Rui Perdigao, "O que sao e como funcionam os maiores partidos portugueses," *Expresso Revista,* April, 23, 1983, p. 38; Vinicio Alves da Costa e Sousa, "O Partido Comunista Portugues (subsdio para um estudo sobre os seus adeptos)," *Estudos Politicos e Sociais* 11, 1983, p. 497; and *Expresso,* July 4, 1992, pp. 20–21.

that year and coincided with its status as the sole party of government.

Similar conclusions can be drawn from an examination of Greek data on membership in PASOK.[25] Party membership experienced its most rapid rate of growth following PASOK's 1981 election victory. Between 1977 and 1981 (a period of Nea Democratia government), PASOK had between 50,000 and 100,000 members. In the two years following the party's 1981 election victory, however, affiliation with PASOK nearly doubled, from 110,000 to 200,000. Following several scandals, poor economic performance under the PASOK government, public reaction against an excessive personalism in public affairs, and the party's electoral defeat in 1989, however, it was not capable of maintaining this level of affiliation, which fell to 100,000 by 1990. Mass-membership patterns relating to other Greek parties depart somewhat from those observed above. Nea Democratia started from a very low membership base during its initial period of predominance (20,000 in 1977 and 150,000 in 1979) but experienced substantial growth in the late 1980s: ND membership increased from 220,000 to 400,000 between 1983 and 1991.[26] With regard to the communist KKE, the most noteworthy aspect of mass membership is its extremely low level. In contrast with most other West European communist parties (which relied heavily on the development of a large membership base), the KKE was remarkably unsuccessful: in 1983, it had only 12,000 members, increasing to 14,000 in the following year.

When we array Southern European parties in terms of their levels of affiliation, we find that Italy stands at one end of the continuum—with parties whose levels of mass membership reflect substantial organizational development—Spain is at the opposite extreme, and Greece and Portugal are somewhere in the middle. We can gain some idea of the order of magnitude of these differences by comparing membership rates of the largest party on the left of center in each party system about a decade after the first democratic election of the new regime. The range is quite extreme: the Italian PCI had a membership rate of 27.1 in 1958, PASOK had a score of 8.9 and the Portuguese PS 8.6 in the mid-1980s, while Spain's PSOE had a membership rate of just 1.9 in 1986.

Distinguishing Features of Southern European Parties

To this point, we have said nothing about the different types of parties that performed central roles in the consolidation processes in these countries. Let us briefly turn our attention to a qualitative examination of party organizations during the relevant periods of democratic transition—that is, the 1940s in Italy and the 1970s in the other three countries.

Italy

In Italy during the late 1940s and 1950s, the three main mass parties developed in accord with at least two different models. The Christian Democrats emerged as a confessional or denominational party, already very close to the catch-all party model.[27] The communist PCI, in contrast, was the classic party of mass integration, and the Socialists attempted to imitate the Communist model, albeit with limited success. A similar model of mass party was adopted in the formation of the neofascist Movimento Sociale Italiano (MSI), which had abandoned the more traditional pattern of a hierarchically organized party with militias.[28] The Liberals and Republicans, meanwhile, could be regarded as opinion parties and, at the same time, elite parties. In spite of their recurring references to the socialist model, the Social Democrats, led by their founder, Giuseppe Saragat, occupied an intermediate position between the mass party and the party of notables.[29] Finally, the small traditional parties, which participated in cabinets as junior partners of the Christian Democrats, had very limited organizational structures.

A closer look at the DC reveals that, despite the structures provided for by party statutes, most of the Christian Democrat organization remained on paper.[30] To be sure, there was a steady growth in membership after 1948, but basically the electoral strength of the party was derived from the support of Catholic organizations. Thus, the DC was dependent on external organizations and its own organization was fairly weak. Indeed, throughout the first decade of Italian postwar democracy, the party was defined by its closeness to various religious organizations, the Italian church hierarchy and the Vatican. Accordingly, the core areas of DC electoral strength were located in those areas of northern Italy where the Catholic subculture was strongest. An additional aspect of the DC during these years was the development of organized fractions. The six fractions that emerged initially had their own de facto structures, including their own press agencies or supportive media.[31] Closely associated with this organized factionalism was an extensive network of notables.

The organizational characteristics of the Communist Party were profoundly different.[32] Its dominant feature was the classic Leninist-Gramscian "democratic centralism," in which decisions were made by leaders following the cultivation of a supportive consensus, recruitment was through co-optation from above, and autonomous factions were strictly forbidden. Party activists—ideologically motivated militants—played a much more important role than in the DC: they were a key asset, working for the party, running its electoral campaigns at a local level, and disseminating propaganda without monetary compensation.[33] Unlike the DC, which counted very much on Catholic parishes, the Communists had a capillary organizational network at a local level, based on cells and sections, which were organized according to functional and territorial principles, respectively. Over time, workplace cells gave way to territorial units and sections.[34] In essence, a Leninist party organization designed for revolutionary and extra-parliamentary action (e.g., strikes, demonstrations, riots) was organizationally transformed to fit better with the requisites of peaceful democratic competition, such as in electoral campaigns or in representing the interests of peasants and workers in the parliamentary arena. The party thus abandoned its most characteristic Leninist aspects.

During the 1950s, the Socialists, a party theoretically very close to the Communists, actually became profoundly different. The party's *nuclei di aziendali socialisti,* which corresponded to Communist cells, never really developed during the 1950s. Instead, the principal organizational unit was the provincial federation. Given the low level of grassroots participation, these federations became bases for creating and maintaining the power of local notables. Thus, what was ostensibly structured as a mass party was also a party of notables, within which factions flourished and, after 1957, became autonomously organized, each with its own structure. The Socialist PSI had a small but stable membership, following a sharp decline between 1955 and 1957, as well as a stable membership rate. Its organization was much weaker than those of the DC and PCI, and its members were much less active: while the Communist Party had a ratio between militants and members of 1:18, and the DC's ratio was 1:23, the ratio between militants and members of the PSI was 1:50.[35]

Among the smaller parties, the neofascist Movimento Sociale Italiano was unique. Not only did it not participate in cabinets with the Christian Democrats (as did the Liberals, Republicans, and Social Democrats throughout the 1950s), but its organizational characteristics were also different. Indeed, if we ignore the association of the party with violent fascist extremist groups, its organizational model would be similar to that of mass-based socialist parties: the section was the primary local unit; provincial federations and the central committee were important; but the secretariat and the national executive had the greatest political power.

Finally, the Liberals, Republicans, and Social Democrats—all of which received less than 10 percent of the vote throughout the 1950s—may be regarded as elite or opinion parties, with a middle-class electoral appeal. Compared with the other Italian parties, they had few members and no real intermediate organizations or diffuse mass presence.[36] Instead, they were best characterized by domination by a few leaders and continuous governmental incumbency for almost the whole decade.

Overall, as we have seen, Italy was the Southern European country with the most highly developed party organization during the most decisive stage of democratic consolidation. Why? A considerable volume of research on Italian parties indicates that key explanatory factors include the fascist legacy, a wide network of Catholic structures, a large public sector, and, last but not least, polarization.[37] These factors interacted to create a complex system with several different kinds of parties and a number of related ancillary organizations with numerous links with civil society. The development of this party organizational framework contributed decisively to the stabilization of electoral behavior and represents one of the most important characteristics of democratic consolidation in Italy.

Spain

By comparison, party organization is rather poorly developed in Spain, although the growth of party membership during the 1980s was indicative of a certain institutionalization of parties. These parties were not, however, organized along the lines of the traditional integration or mass organizations typical of Italy in the 1950s, but were catch-all parties, in which leaders play extremely important roles while the significance of members and organizations is relatively slight. The low level of party organizational development in Spain has been attributed to the country's multifaceted modern social structure, and its "de-ideologized" political culture following many years of antiparty franquist propaganda.

The PSOE, the dominant force in the party system after 1982, is an excellent example of the weakness of party organizational development. On paper, the party's organizational model is similar to that of other European Socialist parties, with a great prominence given to membership, to the section as the main basic organizational unit, and to different organizational levels. In actual practice, however, the PSOE underwent a considerable transformation, from a radical, divided leftist party to an unified, centrist electoral organization dominated by strong leadership.[38] The party has a federal structure. The *agrupación local* is the primary local unit and is integrated, in turn, into provincial, regional, and national organizational structures.[39] In fact, however, a strong centralism tends to prevail over local autonomy. The internal dynamics of the PSOE were further complicated between 1977 and 1979 by mergers with several socialist formations, which sometimes contributed to internal conflict. The response to the considerable internal instability that erupted in 1979 (largely triggered by Felipe González's ultimately successful attempt to moderate the party's ideology) was to enforce greater internal discipline, perceived as lacking in the party.[40] At the same September 1979 extraordinary congress at which the party's ideology was formally modified (a development of great relevance for subsequent democratic legitimation), rule changes were enacted to inhibit the growth of factionalism and reinforce party discipline.[41] This substantially contributed to the PSOE's largely successful effort to become a cohesive party. After the party came to power in 1982, party congresses were increasingly dominated by elected or appointed public officials, as were the intermediate structures of the party.[42] Accompanying this conversion of the PSOE into a body whose overriding function was to win elections and form governments, party officials in charge of information, propaganda, party image, and relations with the press increased in importance.

Paradoxically, the stabilization of the Spanish party system with a predominant PSOE was facilitated by the weakness and instability of several of the other parties. By far the most dramatic example of this was the disintegration and collapse of the governing Unión de Centro Democrático, in 1982, which paved the way for the PSOE's accession to power as the predominant party. Indeed, the highly visible struggles between UCD leaders throughout the two years preceding that election (which contrasted starkly with the new-found cohesion within the PSOE) was the principal cause of the PSOE's smashing victory.[43]

Following the disappearance of the UCD, the right-wing Alianza Popular became the principal challenger to the right of the PSOE. From the time of its founding until the immediate aftermath of the 1989 elections, the AP was also beset with problems of elite-level instability. Born in 1976 as a coalition of seven small groups headed by former high-ranking officials of the previous regime, Alianza Popular initially established a centralized organization under the charismatic Manuel Fraga Iribarne. Local organizations were designated as the basic territorial unit, but the province was to serve as the principal level of party organization for such matters as elections to party congresses.[44] The AP was also a catch-all party, with no *classe gardée* and, by the late 1980s, had the highest membership among the Spanish parties.[45]

The AP entered into a series of unstable alliances in successive elections. It formed Coalición Democrática with two other small parties in 1979 and Coalición Popular with other political groups in 1982. While it later abandoned this practice of forming unstable alliances with small clusters of conservative elites and transformed itself into the unified Partido Popular, over the course of the first six national elections the party presented itself to the voters under four different names. These earlier alliances with other small conservative groups and the successive incorporations (especially numerous following the collapse of the UCD in 1982) of new conservative elites into the party also gave rise to a series of destabilizing and highly public conflicts, culminating most dramatically in the resignation of Fraga in 1986. This was followed by an unstable period of unsuccessful party leadership under Antonio Hernández-Mancha, and eventually to the return of Fraga following the 1989 election. It was only after Fraga's retirement from the presidency and the orderly transfer of party leadership to José María Aznar that elite relations within the party were stabilized, a change that contributed to the party's significant advance in the 1993 election.

Another challenger to the PSOE was the tiny Centro Democrático y Social (CDS), founded by Adolfo Suárez in 1982 following his withdrawal from the party that he had created, the UCD. The CDS was initially dominated by its strong president, Suárez. Unlike the UCD, the party had a small homogeneous elite and a strongly personalized leadership. After achieving some moderate success in the 1986 and 1989 elections, however, the CDS was totally destroyed in 1993, failing to elect a single deputy in that contest.

Fragmentation and crisis in both organization and leadership are the most distinctive facets of the lack of institutionalization in the PCE, which recently attempted a rebirth by forming the electoral coalition Izquierda Unida (United Left) with a few other leftist groups. This strategy obviously raises one crucial question: what happens when a typical, very organized communist party decides to renounce its traditional identity? This transformation had its origins in the period immediately preceding the transition to democracy in Spain. Under the leadership of Santiago Carrillo, for example, the party in 1976 shifted its basic unit of party organization from the functionally defined cell to the more open, territorially based *agrupación local* party. Accompanying this formal organizational shift was a broader attempt to transform a Leninist party into a more open mass mobilization party with a Eurocommunist ideology. While this may have fit better with the dynamics of competitive politics in the new democracy, the uneven transformation of the party, coupled with the complete lack of consensus over the future role of "democratic centralism" and the emergence of a center-periphery conflict (especially regarding the status of the Communist Party in Euskadi), contributed to substantial and ultimately debilitating conflict within its ranks that culminated in a series of schisms, massive defections of party militants, and a devastating electoral defeat in 1982.[46] By the mid-1980s, the PCE was splintered: fragments of the once unified party could be found within the Basque Euskadiko Ezkerra, the Catalan PCC, and two other tiny "parties" founded in the mid-1980s, one of them by none other than Santiago Carrillo himself. The United Left coalition strategy was part of an effort to overcome this fragmentation, but fluidity and instability persisted in that segment of the political continuum to the left of the PSOE. Even in the 1993 election, held at a time when registered unemployment exceeded 21 percent of the labor force and the governing PSOE was racked by a variety of scandals, Izquierda Unida failed to make any significant electoral advance at the Socialists' expense.

An overview of the Spanish party system would be incomplete without at least passing reference to several important regional or regional-nationalist parties. The most important of these are the Catalan Convergència i Unió (CiU) and the Basque Partido Nacionalista Vasco

(PNV), Euskadiko Ezkerra (EE), and Herri Batasuna (HB). The CiU is actually an electoral alliance of two distinct formations (Convergència Democràtica de Catalunya and Unió Democràtica de Catalunya), which joined in 1978. The CDC was a moderate, center-right Catalan nationalist party with a fairly developed organization but catch-all characteristics and dominance by its prominent leaders. The UDC was a much smaller party, whose programmatic stance and organizational characteristics were typical of Christian Democratic parties: it had a longer tradition than the CDC and ancillary organizations for women and young people, as well as an allied trade union; by way of comparison, the CDC had only a youth organization. This electoral alliance worked very well, making CiU the third largest parliamentary group in the Cortes in 1982, 1989, and 1993. It has also become the dominant party in Catalan regional politics.

In the Basque region, the situation is very different. The Basque regional party system is characterized by extreme instability and increasing fragmentation. Prior to 1978, there were only two significant Basque nationalist parties: the historic PNV and the left-wing Euskadiko Ezkerra. During the constitution-writing phase of the Spanish democratic transition, however, the EE split, and a more radical organization, Herri Batasuna, emerged to more clearly articulate demands for revolutionary change and Basque independence from Spain. HB is not even a party; it is an antisystem coalition of political groups and movements and is close to the terrorist organization ETA. The EE, meanwhile, absorbed much of the Eurocommunist elite that was defecting from the PCE within the Basque country. In 1992, it was itself absorbed within the regional federation of the PSOE. The PNV split as well, and from it emerged, in 1985, a new party, Eusko Alkartasuna (EA), under the leadership of the former PNV Basque regional government president, Carlos Garaikoetxea. The PNV remained a conservative, Catholic party, with deep roots in the region (except in the province of Guipúzcoa), a decentralized structure, and a strong preference for provincial- and municipal-level autonomy within the Basque regional government. The EA staked out a more social-democratic stance, favoring a strong regional government vis-à-vis local levels of government, and a more dogmatic defense of Basque national interests than was being articulated by the PNV (which, in the late 1980s, had begun to cooperate with the PSOE at both the regional and the national level). Thus, the Basque regional party system stands in sharp contrast with that of Catalonia: unlike the Catalan party system, characterized by stabilization and the emergence of a regionally predominant party, the party system in Euskadi has exhibited great instability, fragmentation, and polarization.[47]

An important characteristic of Spanish parties, in general, is the increasing role played by both media and party leaders and the personalization of political life. Electoral success is highly dependent on the ability to establish intraparty stability and cohesion, under a strong leader, as was typified by the PSOE beginning in the late 1970s. A key explanatory factor which differentiated the party politics of Spain from that of Italy was the low ideologization of political conflict and the correspondingly low polarization of partisan politics at the national level. In contrast with Italy, where the mass party with a strong organizational network was the prevailing type (be it a denominational party or a mass integration party with roots in the class structure), in Spain the predominantly electoral party of professional politicians has become the dominant reality. Relatively little development of organizational networks has taken place. Stabilization of the Spanish party system appears to be grounded, instead, on the relative dominance and cohesion of a party that has strong leadership, PSOE, and at the same time on the weakness, division, and instability of other parties. Significant change could occur if one of these two key elements were to change (as suggested by the marked electoral advance of the Partido Popular (PP) in the 1993 elections, following its recent internal stabilization and organizational growth).

Portugal

Among Portuguese parties, the communist PCP was the most organizationally developed from the very beginning of the transition. It had a classical communist organizational structure (largely rooted in its tradition of underground opposition), a strong leader, a significant base of militants, and tight party discipline. This structure seemed well suited to coping with the demands of the "revolutionary" situation that followed the collapse of the Salazar-Caetano regime. Following the end of the revolutionary phase of the Portuguese transition, however, and particularly during the regime consolidation that took place during the 1980s, the party experienced both electoral decline and organizational decay.[48]

In terms of both ideology and organizational characteristics, the party that stands at the opposite end of the continuum is the conservative Centro Democrático Social. The CDS is a loosely structured coalition of independent politicians and local notables, founded in mid-1974 by officials of the previous authoritarian regime.[49] In many ways, it resembles the small Italian opinion parties, except for one important difference: the CDS was not continuously in government, as those parties were. In addition, the CDS has not successfully undergone a process of organizational structuring.

The two most important parties in Portuguese democracy to date are the Socialists, the PS, and the Social Democrats, the PSD. On paper, both would appear to be mass parties with a highly organized structure; in actual practice, however, they are catch-all parties with internal factions. Both the PS and the PSD have also experienced considerable internal conflict and instability; both have suffered schisms on one or two occasions; and both have experienced a turnover in leadership, although for different reasons (the Social Democrat Francisco Sá Carneiro died in a plane accident in December 1980, while the Socialist Mário Soares was elected president of the republic in 1986). The two parties differ, however, in some important ways.

The PSD had a hybrid organizational structure that included local strongholds, regional leaders, and notables; a more formal organizational structure, based upon the eighteen electoral districts; the usual national committees; and ancillary organizations, such as youth and women's branches. The party was also riven by factions and internal divisions, which were especially disruptive in the immediate aftermath of Sá Carneiro's death. This situation changed substantially after 1985, under the strong leadership of Anibal Cavaco Silva. His electoral successes and extended period in government greatly reduced the internal divisions and contributed to the stabilization of internal organizational structures.[50]

The Socialists had a much older tradition, but following reestablishment of the party in 1974 the party had weaker local and intermediate organizational structures. It also had a different type of organization, closer to the classical workers' parties: its organizational features included both territorially based and professional or interest-group units, provincial or district federations, a national committee, a secretariat, and a secretary general (who is the party leader), as well as a youth group (but no women's organization). Even under the leadership of Mário Soares, internal factions continued to flourish, and the party's leader was really only able to consolidate his position 1983.[51] With his election as head of the state in 1986, the party lost its founding father; none of the other party elites was subsequently able to secure and consolidate a strong leadership position.[52]

In general, it can be said that only the PSD among Portuguese parties has successfully institutionalized itself. The PSD became the dominant party in the country after 1987, while, for one reason or another, the other three parties have continued to undergo changes and have continued to suffer from instability and organizational deficiencies.[53]

Greece

A profound transformation of the Greek party system also occurred following its reemergence in the mid-1970s. In short, the system evolved from a predominant party configuration to a polarized two-party system. This has involved two alternations in power between the major parties, Nea Democratia and the socialist PASOK, the decline and virtual marginalization of the communist parties—the KKE (which, until the end of the 1980s, was close to the Soviet Union) and the Eurocommunist KKE-Interior[54]—and the disappearance of smaller political groups, such as the EDIK.[55]

Nea Democratia was created in 1974 as a conservative party of notables, relying on its charismatic leader, Constantine Karamanlis, and on "MPs and their clientelistic networks for communicating with the electorate and rallying mass support."[56] Organizationally it was very weak.

PASOK, on the other hand, established a well-structured mass organization. Its distinguishing features included a populist program, a charismatic leader, and an authoritarian style of leadership.[57] Its main decision-making bodies at the national level were the president (Andreas Papandreou), the eight-member executive bureau, and the central committee, and at the local level prefectoral committees or local federations. The party's militants and elite were divided into five different ideologically defined factions: social democrats, Marxists, a Third World group, self-management socialists, and a nonideological group.[58] Overall, PASOK resembled other European socialist parties organizationally, although in practice the role of Papandreou was very dominant, while the middle-level party elite was quite weak and dependent on the upper echelons.[59] Indeed, party cadres drew their legitimacy from the party's leader rather than from party members and sympathizers.[60] The party's most fundamental strategic choice—to convert itself into a catch-all party with a mass base—was a decision made by its charismatic leader.

The elections of 1981 initiated the institutionalization of a different party system. In that election ND was replaced in government by PASOK. Upon the election of Karamanlis as president of the republic ND also lost its leader. PASOK, meanwhile, strengthened its position and that of

Papandreou, given its position as the new incumbent party. Finally, a clear bipolarization of the party system emerged following the disappearance of other center and rightist formations.

These two elements—alternation in power and the establishment of a new pattern of competition—had a great impact on the organizations of both major parties. The grassroots organizations of PASOK became much weaker, and conflicts often arose between the government and local party sections. These conflicts were often resolved through cooptation into the state apparatus, which further undermined the autonomy of local party organs.[61]

Nea Democratia also gradually changed its organization, largely in response to the loss of its charismatic leader as well as its loss of governmental power. Karamanlis's successors, Rallis, Averoff, and Mitsotakis, made great efforts to reorganize the party at a local level. This was an obvious response by party leaders who lacked their predecessor's charisma and had to develop other resources to overcome the resistance of local-level party bosses. ND's organizational reforms were also a response to the strong bipolar competition from PASOK. The success of these efforts can be seen in the increase in ND membership from 97,000 in 1979, to 200,000 in 1986, and to 400,000 in 1991. The ND also succeeded in attracting votes from a broader array of groups and social strata in all parts of the country.

Organization, Stabilization, and Democratic Consolidation

This qualitative exploration of Southern European parties complements the quantitative data on party organization examined in the preceding section, but it still does not provide a complete explanation of the bases of party-system stabilization. As we have seen, high party organizational development appears to have been conducive to stabilization. In Spain, both party organization and stabilization were low. But the case of Greece suggests that organization is not the only factor relevant to stabilization; as in Italy, stability was high but party organizations were substantially less developed. Despite ND's efforts, the most distinguishing feature of the consolidation phase does not seem to be the development of party organizational networks but rather the takeover of the state by the incumbent party, which was PASOK for much of the 1980s. Thus, in the following section we will turn our attention to an additional factor, the nature of the relationships between parties and interests. As we shall see, this perspective enables us to gain new insights into stabilization in both Greece and Portugal.

A second conclusion to be drawn from this analysis is that well-developed party organizations and a stabilized party system do *not* appear to be necessary prerequisites for successful democratic consolidation. The case of Spain is most revealing in this regard: virtually all observers agree that Spanish democracy was consolidated by the mid-1980s, and yet we have seen that political parties are weakly organized in Spain, at least compared to other Southern European countries, and that the most decisive phase of the consolidation process coincided with a period of considerable party-system instability. One may argue, however, that the organizational characteristics of parties may be of some importance in determining what specific kind of democratic regime becomes consolidated, as well as what particular pattern the consolidation process will follow. It is with this set of questions in mind that we turn our attention to an analysis of the relationships between parties and civil society.

Finally, the extent of ideological polarization among parties can be seen as having a significant influence on the stabilization of both parties and the party system and on the process of democratic consolidation. Indeed, in this respect it must be regarded as a double-edged sword. On the one hand, it can help to promote the organizational development of parties, as well as widespread party identification among their supporters. From this perspective, it can contribute to the stabilization of parties and electoral behavior. On the other hand, partisan polarization can intensify conflict within new democracies, which in turn may bring about a further radicalization over time and a greater likelihood that parties, their leaders, and their supporters might be moved to break some of the fundamental rules of peaceful democratic competition. This can obviously be detrimental to the prospects for regime consolidation. Conversely, responsible, moderate behavior by political parties may contribute decisively to consolidation of the new democracy, but such moderation can also undermine the solidarities among elites and supporters of political parties, thereby impeding party-system stabilization.

Parties, Interests, and the State

The classical view of political parties is one in which stable linkages with different sectors of civil society are secured through the organizational development of parties themselves and through their respective ancillary organizations. In this view, the key variables include an organizational network with central, intermediate, and local structures, activists and militants who give life to these institutions, and strong ideologies or, at least, a well-articulated set of partisan values. Furthermore, according to this perspective, linkages between parties and specific sectors of society can be strengthened through the logic of partisan competition itself. Our cases, however, suggest that this is not the only way by which parties establish connections with and seek to control civil society.

A second way by which parties establish stable relationships with more or less organized interest groups or sectors of society involves the processes through which public policies are made and the resources of the state are distributed. In these processes, links with sectors of civil society are not grounded on ideology and party organization but on economic interests and the manner in which they are affected by the activities of the public sector.

In performing their representative function, parties serve as institutions which channel interests into decisional arenas. In performing this function, parties should be in some way independent of interest groups. From a normative point of view, this should enable them to combine the specific interests of groups with the general interests of civil society, and thus be better able to attain the kind of efficacy that is also necessary to secure a higher degree of legitimacy. In his classic discussion of institutionalization, Samuel Huntington emphasizes the need for parties to maintain their autonomy from a particular group and the desirability of aggregating the interests of several groups.[62]

One way of looking at relationships between parties, on the one hand, and between interest groups or individuals, on the other, is to see whether parties and the party system as a whole are able to perform a gatekeeping role for the groups, or whether interests depend on parties for their satisfaction. I define gatekeeping as the role performed by the incumbent and nonincumbent parties in controlling access by interest groups to the decisional arena. Accordingly, party intermediation is the best way for groups to protect their interests. Gatekeeping may play an important role in democratic consolidation, since it induces the most relevant sectors of civil society to accept the role of parties and their position of dominance. It should be noted, however, that such a notion of gatekeeping concerns only the party system, not the judiciary, the bureaucracy, or the army. More importantly, we should note that gatekeeping is not the only role that parties may perform vis-à-vis interest groups.

At least three distinct scenarios for party-group relationships may be sketched out. The first, dominance or, in a stronger form, occupation, envisages a situation in which the party system largely dominates civil society in general and interest groups in particular. From the beginning, or very early on, parties relegate groups to the status of ancillary organizations, which have very solid autonomous sources of power in terms of ideology, internal organization, and full control of a large public sector. In a case of party occupation or dominance there is a growing presence and control by parties over civil society and, specifically, over their relationships with all interest groups. With regard to the public sector of the economy, not only is it very large, but all positions in that sector are filled by party appointment.[63]

The second scenario, neutrality, entails no definite links between groups and parties. Parties have their own autonomous power bases and control of the decision-making process, which are largely inherent in the rules of the democratic regime. In essence, they perform a gatekeeping role. More or less organized groups and individuals are compelled to appeal to parties and party leaders to promote and protect their interests, but their appeal is mainly a multiparty appeal, in which no strong or special relationship is established between a group and a particular party. This means that groups are in a more independent position vis-à-vis parties. They are not ancillary organizations and they enjoy a measure of autonomy in civil society.

In the third model, direct access, parties (and party elites) are bypassed in the actual performance of the representation function. Interest groups outbid parties through personal relationships with members of parliament, ministries, and the bureaucracy, or in other ways. In this scenario, parties have weak autonomous bases and sources of power and perform no gatekeeping role.[64]

These varying relationships between parties and interests must be explored in three specific domains: relationships between parties and entrepreneurs or organizations of propertied interests, relationships between parties and unions, and particularistic relationships and policies towards individuals or interest groups regarding the distribution of public sector resources. Spain and Italy emerge from this analysis as very different from each other, and Greece and Portugal are seen to more closely resemble Italy than they do Spain.

Italy

In Italy, the 1950s was a period of party dominance vis-à-vis civil society. In the words of Farneti, this was a "decade of political society," that is, of parties.[65] In the agricultural sector in the immediate postwar period, the association of landowners, the Confagricoltura, constrained by the need to defend the interests of its members in the new democratic context and to seek the support of the parties and their leaders, opted for neutrality and a multiparty appeal. In the 1950s, however, this association changed its strategy and established a privileged relationship with the governing DC and other rightist parties (especially the Liberal PLI and, in the south, the MSI and Monarchists).

A distinctly different kind of linkage was established between the DC and the association of small landowners, the Coldiretti. Its exclusive political relationship with the DC was more like that between a party and its affiliated trade union: the symbiotic relationship established between the DC and the Coldiretti was characterized by a coincidence of values in two different spheres of action, a relationship of equal standing with the delivery of electoral support in exchange for favorable decisions. In some respects, however, this relationship could be better understood as one of dominance of the interest group by the party. The strength of this relationship was manifested in many ways: in the delegation of the management of agricultural policy by the DC to the Coldiretti; in the presence of Coldiretti representatives in the Ministry of Agriculture (even at the level of under-secretary), in Parliament, and in parliamentary commissions; in the presence of numerous party members within provincial- and local-level Coldiretti executives; in political exploitation of land allocations during the implementation of the agrarian reform; and in both party and governmental policy making.

In the industrial sector the situation was not substantially different. In this sector, too, there was the dominance of the DC through a penetration of public agencies, and the marginalization and isolation of the organized groups of the left. Party control over access to the decision-making arena was not challenged either by the industrial entrepreneurs' association, Confindustria, or by the trade unions. DC dominance over the industrialists evolved in the course of three different periods. The first coincided with the democratic transition and installation of a new regime (1943–47) and was characterized by great hostility between the government and business elites: until the exit of the left from the governing majority (May 1947), the influence of Confindustria was very limited and mainly channeled through the PLI. The second phase began after May 1947 and featured a situation of *duopolio*: the DC was strong politically but needed an industrial sector committed to economic reconstruction. It was thus forced to concede to Confindustria (which had maintained its privileged relationship with the bureaucracy from the outset) decision-making influence in the management of public policy—particularly concerning implementation of the Marshall Plan—and in the attempt to solve the most pressing sectoral problems.[66] In the policy-making process, however, the influence of Confindustria was not direct but was primarily channeled through the ministers of economics, led by the Liberals. In fact, throughout this period the peak business association established a particularly symbiotic relationship with the PLI: in addition to nonoverlapping leadership, there was a coincidence of political values and policy proposals between Liberals and industrialists. The third phase of party dominance came after the break-up of the *duopolio,* when, as of 1953, Confindustria suffered a decline in both membership and political initiative. At this point the DC was weaker in terms of parliamentary seats but considerably stronger in terms of party organization and of its role in the expansion of the public sector and credit facilities managed by the public banks. In addition, the demobilization and fragmentation of the business elite as a social group had occurred following the departure of managers of public enterprises from Confindustria and their formation of a new association, Intersind, and the creation of a small businessmen's association.

The relationships between parties and trade unions also changed over time. In the first period of transition and installation, party dominance was clear-cut: ideological divisions affected all aspects of activity, and there was extensive electoral mobilization of the trade unions. But these relationships were complicated by a previous decision (in 1944) to create a unitary trade union. With the split in the trade unions in 1949–50, a second phase began. Parties became even more dominant, partly because of the fragmentation, demobilization, and membership decline experienced by trade unions. A further confirmation of party dominance over labor is the fact that during this period trade unions never adopted a clearly autonomous position in the area of industrial relations. Only in the early 1960s did a clearer differentiation of their respective roles appear; thereafter, trade unions often took their own initiatives, separately from parties, and assumed a somewhat greater degree of autonomy.

There was also some penetration of the DC by the Catholic trade union, the CISL, in parliament. Representatives of the CISL organized their own faction within the party, although the DC maintained its autonomy and refused to passively submit to the policy proposals of the CISL. The influence of the parties of the left in the Italian General Confederation of Workers (CGIL), or of the Republicans in the Italian Union of Workers (UIL), hardly requires explanation: there was a common understanding of party–trade union relations in which the party played the predominant role in the formulation of political options. Within the context of the "negative integration" of the left,[67] trade unions sought to retain their respective clienteles by maintaining high visibility in parliamentary activity. For this, they needed the support and collaboration of parties. Thus, trade unions largely accepted this dominance, since their relations with parties gave them a role in drawing up electoral lists and access to the parliamentary arena in general. Given the more developed ideologies of parties of the left, there was a greater coincidence of values which reinforced party dependence. Finally, one should recall that participation in trade union activity was one of the main channels of leftist party activism.

The expansion of the public sector played an important role in these party–interest group relationships. In the agricultural sector, the Federconsorzi, agrarian reform agencies, public pension agencies, and the Cassa per il Mezzogiorno conditioned all relations between the main incumbent party, the DC, and interest group associations. The same was true of the industrial sector. The role played by the Institute of Industrial Reconstruction (IRI) in economic reconstruction, the creation of the National Agency for Oil (ENI) in 1953 and the Ministry for State Investments in 1956, the laws on hydrocarbons (1957), the activity of the Cassa per il Mezzogiorno in the industrial sector, the presence of the public banks, and the creation of a series of public agencies—all controlled by the parties in government—profoundly affected the relationships between government parties, on the one hand, and entrepreneurs and trade unions, on the other.[68] For ideological reasons, the left supported the expansion of the public sector, not understanding until it was too late that such public intervention would have important political side-effects. Thus, in the 1950s, the enlargement of the public sector, the creation of the Cassa per il Mezzogiorno, and other parliamentary initiatives culminated in the establishment of a clientelistic system which would function as the core of particularistic ties between civil society and parties such as DC, PLI, and PSDI in some parts of the south.[69]

Spain

The Spanish picture is the very opposite of the Italian one. A different authoritarian tradition, a society and economy developed along different lines at the time of regime change, and an altered international situation largely explain the differences between the two cases. The several associations established in the agricultural sector mirror the diversities in Spanish agriculture. None of these associations, moreover, achieved either high political salience or a link with a specific party.[70] The problem of legitimation, which existed in Italy during the 1940s, was not present there during the 1970s and later. Thus, there was no sense that a rightist, perhaps ambiguously democratic, political force would become the monopolistic representative of an agricultural group. The political neutrality of these associations and the differentiation in voting behavior of their members contrast sharply with the Italian situation.[71]

The organizational structure in the industrial sector is different, but with regard to relationships with parties, Spanish industrial associations are similarly autonomous. Indeed, the association of industrial entrepreneurs, the CEOE, has maintained a manifest position of neutrality vis-à-vis parties and the party system as a whole, although there is a clear distinction between the periods before and after 1982. A clear distance was always maintained between the interest group and the political class.[72]

Unlike its counterpart in Italy, the CEOE was able to absorb, in 1980, the association of medium and small entrepreneurs (CEPYME). Also unlike the Italian case, the business association established no ties to the governing party, the centrist UCD. On the contrary, the relationship was characterized by periods of tension: in the 1977–78 period, entrepreneurs protested against the Moncloa Pacts and governmental economic policy in general; and in 1981, an attempt was made to create an allied party out of parts of the UCD (which was then in the process of breaking up) and the Alianza Popular.[73] Paradoxically, the election of a Socialist government in 1982 was followed by better relations with the government party: given the moderate, pragmatic policies of the PSOE government, a stance of sympathetic neutrality was adopted. (At this same time, the CEOE was undergoing an impressive process of growth and organizational development.) The quasi-corporatist economic agreements of this decade further contributed to the autonomy and independent identity of employers.[74]

During the emergence of Spain's new democratic regime, the main trade unions were the Comisiones Obreras (CC.OO.)—which was close to the Communist Party and already well organized in several economic sectors—and the UGT, which was allied with Socialists. There were also minor independent unions (such as USO) and regional bodies, like ELA-STV in the Basque country. From our point of view, what is most important to stress is that since at least 1980, in a context of worker moderation, unions and union leaders behaved as moderate collective-bargaining organizations which rejected the notion that they were "transmission belts" for political parties.[75] Spanish trade union associations evolved in a manner quite different from those in Italy: (1) the level of union fragmentation declined; (2) the more moderate UGT grew at the expense of the CCOO; (3) since, unlike in Italy, the entire left was not excluded from the political arena, CCOO did not depend upon the party for representation; (4) strikes were depoliticized; (5) the increasingly centrist (if not center-right) economic policies of the PSOE government led to a complete breakdown of relations between the Socialist Party and trade unions, culminating in the UGT's participation in the antigovernment and, consequently, antisocialist strike of December 1990; and (6) the unions achieved greater autonomy through several economic agreements with government and entrepreneurs during the late 1970s and 1980s.[76]

Spain also differs from Italy with regard to the evolution of its public sector. In contrast with Italy (whose public sector expanded considerably during the 1950s), the Spanish public sector was substantially reduced in size as the product of the Socialist Party's "industrial reconversion" policies of the 1980s; indeed, the Organization for Economic Cooperation and Development reported in 1989 that 30 percent of workers employed in public sector economic enterprises were dismissed over the course of this reform program.[77]

Spain and Italy are alike, however, insofar as party patronage was widespread in both systems. The spoils system or *sottogoverno* led to the partisan appointment of thousands of officials to posts in public enterprises, as well as national and local government.[78] Pérez Díaz also points out that a substantial enlargement of the political class resulted from the establishment of seventeen autonomous regional governments, complete with parliaments, cabinets, and administrative structures.[79] This same phenomenon occurred in Italy, when the process of regionalization led to the establishment of fifteen new governmental systems; it differs from Spain insofar as this development occurred between ten and fifteen years after the main phase of consolidation.

The nature of the relationship between party and civil society in Spain closely approximates our gatekeeping model. This development was facilitated by several factors that differentiate the Spanish from the Italian case. These factors include control of the decision-making agenda by a dominant government party, the mediation of relationships between individuals and the state by thousands of professionals in the administration and the public sector, a strong vested interest in maintaining the existing democracy by a large stratum of society, and, finally, the predominant status of the strong and unified Socialist Party (in turn, facilitated by the electoral law and various parliamentary regulations). Under these circumstances, there was no real need to build a large party organization. Indeed, the environment for the consolidation process, which had facilitated the development of strong parties in Italy (especially ideological polarization and the Cold War), was greatly different in the case of Spain. In the aggregate, this led parties to maintain a more neutral stance vis-à-vis organized social groups. At the same time, however, a partisan penetration of the state made it possible for the predominant party to control large sectors of society.

Greece and Portugal

Portugal and Greece are closer to the Italian model than to the Spanish. The point of departure for Portugal is the attempt to install a radical, socialist regime following the coup which toppled the Salazar-Caetano regime. The constitution of 1976 and legislation enacted in 1977 created a very large public sector. This established a state monopoly in banking, insurance, and virtually all the basic and infrastructural industries. The mass communications media were also placed largely under public ownership, and in the agricultural sector, agrarian reforms established large cooperatives.[80] Although legislation enacted in 1983 loosened the state's monopolistic control of these economic sectors, it was only with the constitutional revision of August 1989 that this situation was fully reversed.

All this led to a situation very different from that in Spain. The Portuguese business elite had been delegitimated by their previous support for the Salazar regime, and their organizations remained very weak. It was not possible for them to establish any kind of autonomous or neutral role.[81]

Trade unions quickly established and maintained close links with political parties. The powerful CGTP-Intersindical Nacional was closely allied with the Communists. Indeed, for many years this union federation came closer than most contemporary Western European unions to being a transmission belt for the Communist Party; only after the collapse of communism in Eastern Europe in 1989 did this relationship begin to change.[82] The second largest union, the UGT, was connected to the Socialists and the Social Democrats. These links were so strong as to induce the unions to adopt strategies in accord with partisan goals, thereby politicizing labor relations. This situation began to change only in the late 1980s.[83]

The Portuguese party system assumed its gatekeeping role through a nonlinear process, with several moments of crisis and considerable governmental instability. As late as the second half of the 1980s, the tripartite Council, formed by representatives of business, labor, landowners, and the government, was entirely dominated by the government. The key point is that this governmental dominance emerged because of the resources provided by a large public sector. Indeed, in the case of Portugal, state resources were proportionately larger (and the private sector, consequently, was less significant) than in Italy. This factor conducive to party dominance was offset, however, by the weaker development of party organization in Portugal. As in the cases of Italy and Spain, there was also a significant number of patronage appointments to the administration, contributing to an overall expansion of the bureaucracy.[84] It is likely that all this helped pave the way to a further key development in the party system: its transformation from four-party pluralism to a predominant-party system.

As in Portugal, the Greek business elite and its representative associations had been delegitimated because of their close relationships with the military regime. This contributed to their weak organizational development. In terms of relations with political parties, they were initially not close to Nea Democratia and were openly hostile to the radical PASOK. Between 1983 and 1985, however, their previously conflictual relationship with the Socialists changed; this is not surprising given PASOK's abandonment of its earlier radicalism and its more moderate economic policies. However, in the late 1980s and especially in the early 1990s, the industrialists' organization, SEB, showed an increasingly activist face, keeping its distance from both of the main parties.

Trade unions, in contrast, were closely connected with political parties—the Communists more than the Socialists—but at the same time they were fully dependent on funds from the Ministry of Labor. During the 1980s, however, an important change in party-union relations took place: as Mavrogordatos has argued, parties used internal union elections to deeply penetrate the unions and to establish solid links of dependency.[85] Mavrogordatos further argues that this party dominance (if not outright occupation of the unions) was paralleled by party penetration into cooperatives and a number of other associations in the agricultural sector.

As in Portugal, the weak positions of the business elite, dependent unions, and other penetrated associations were compounded by a large public sector in Greece. During the first PASOK government, this sector was further expanded: numerous industrial enterprises, banks, and insurance companies were added to the public sector. The end product is that almost 90 percent of financial institutions were state-controlled, subsequent government efforts to privatize notwithstanding.

PASOK governments, moreover, enacted an impressive volume of legislation regarding the public administrative structure that enabled the party to totally subordinate the state bureaucracy. Party occupation of secondary associations and the state during the PASOK decade appeared to be so widespread and penetrating that some Socialist supporters expressed concern about the weakening of the party's own organization.[86] Indeed, party appointments to the public sector were so numerous after 1981 that PASOK's organization was largely depleted of activists.

Although the Greek case is the only one where alternation was a real possibility—it actually took place three times (1981, 1990, and 1993)—the dominance of the Socialists is again the key to understanding party-society relationships during their decade in office. On the whole, developments in Greece paralleled those in Portugal, though differences in the processes of regime transition and the installation of a new democracy, as well as differences between the structure of the two party systems (a system with two parties dominating in Greece and a single-party-dominant system in Portugal) mainly account for these differences during the years of consolidation.

From Stabilization to Democratic Consolidation

To this point, we have focused our attention on the patterns and processes of party-system stabilization. Let us now broaden our focus by linking this analysis with processes of democratic consolidation. It will become clear that the relationship between stabilization and consolidation is complex and multifaceted. As I have argued, party stabilization may be encouraged by a polarization of public opinion and organizations; but while polarization may facilitate party stabilization, excessive polarization may culminate in radicalization of the polity and widespread antidemocratic attitudes, thereby undermining prospects for the consolidation of democracy.[87] Similarly, we have seen that the process of party stabilization can benefit from the organizational development of political parties. While, under certain circumstances (to be discussed below), this may contribute to democratic consolidation, under other circumstances it might be antithetical to consolidation: if a party opposed to the democratic regime becomes well organized, for example, it may use its organizational resources to mount a protracted struggle against the system, with possibly disruptive consequences. These speculative remarks suggest that the stabilization of parties may be neither necessary nor sufficient for the consolidation of a democratic regime. This is consistent with the cases of Spain and Italy: the democratic regime in Spain succeeded in becoming comparatively more consolidated than that of Italy, even though its parties were less structured than those of Italy.

The achievement of regime legitimacy, in contrast, is central to the process of democratic consolidation. But what, then, is the nature of the relationships between consolidation and legitimation and between party structuring and stabilization? A careful examination of this question sheds new light on the processes of democratic consolidation alluded to in the introduction to this volume. Since party leaders and institutions are widely regarded as playing important roles in transition and consolidation processes, it is important for us to attempt to determine what kinds of party-related features of the political system facilitate consolidation. Specifically, what kinds of relationships between parties and civil society, and which modalities of party control of civil society, are most conducive to consolidation? This "top-down" perspective must be complemented by a "bottom-up" examination of those institutions and processes that build consensual support for the democratic regime. In essence, we start with the notions that consolidation involves an interweaving of consensus and control in each country and that these interactive processes will vary from case to case—always involving the same basic factors but with varying degrees of rigidity and institutional control and of flexibility and societal consensus.

Before entering into this analysis, we must define two distinctly different dimensions that are relevant to processes of democratic consolidation. The first dimension, control, involves two different possibilities: (1) firm control over civil society may be achieved through party, state institutions, or both; or (2) a more active, autonomous civil society (regarding state institutions) may exist, given the low development of party organizations. We shall refer to the first situation as dominance and the second as neutrality. A democratic regime may be consolidated under either circumstance, but with distinctly different characteristics and through different processes. The second dimension involves the bottom-up consensual relationship linking individuals with institutions through the fostering of regime legitimacy (i.e., growing acceptance of and support for existing democratic institutions). Two different outcomes are possible in this dimension: an incomplete, limited legitimation, and a full legitimation of institutions, largely through the activities of parties and party elites. We shall refer to these alternatives as exclusive legitimation and inclusive legitimation, respectively.

Four different outcomes result from the combination of these two dimensions, creating a typology of consolidation processes. This typology may be seen in Figure 10.5. The right-hand column reflects situations in which there is widespread democratic legitimacy from the beginning, or a successful subprocess of legitimation (to be discussed below) develops, to the extent that antiregime and disloyal groups or parties are or become a tiny, unimportant minority—that is, situations where inclusive legitimation has been achieved. Under these conditions, democratic consolidation may occur in the absence of dominant

		CONSENSUAL LEGITIMACY **Exclusive**	**Inclusive**
CONTROL		Party Consolidation	State Consolidation
	Dominance	ITALY	PORTUGAL GREECE
		Maintenance	Elite Consolidation
	Neutrality		SPAIN

Figure 10.5 Models and Cases of Democratic Consolidation

or even well-structured parties. The presence or absence of well-structured parties, however, may have an important impact on the particular process of consolidation followed, as well as on certain features of the consolidated democracy that emerges. A period immediately following the installation of a new democratic regime characterized by inclusive legitimation in combination with control of civil society through a large public sector and parties with substantial penetration into civil society we shall regard as a process of state-based consolidation, or, more simply, state consolidation. Greece and Portugal are cases that conform to this state consolidation model. In the second possible outcome in this column, inclusive legitimation has been achieved but well-structured parties with the ability to control civil society are lacking. As I have argued, even under these circumstances party elites may play an essential role in fostering the legitimacy of the new democratic institutions and in supporting the process of democratic consolidation. Accordingly, this elite-based consolidation I have refered to as elite consolidation.

What of those situations in which acknowledgment of the legitimacy of democratic institutions and practices is not initially widespread? I contend that under conditions of limited or exclusive legitimation, a dominant partisan control of society may be the only route to consolidation. In other words, in the absence of an inclusive legitimation of the new regime, substantial levels of elite stabilization, party organization, or party control of organized and unorganized groups may be necessary if the system is to become sufficiently consolidated. Under these circumstances, party structures organize and, at the same time, encapsulate internal divisions in society. They constrain the behavior of individuals and groups in civil society, channeling that behavior into democratic institutionalized arenas with the capacity to contain conflict. Over an extended period of time, habitual conformity with democratic rules of the game can lead to widespread internalization of key democratic behavioral norms. Control of civil society by governing parties can also prevent sectors of society from defecting to antisystem extremist alternatives, insofar as they can provide incentives to groups to work within the system and deny rewards to those who overtly challenge its legitimacy. Over time, moreover, antisystem parties and movements may tire of their exclusion from power and may seek to adapt to the prevailing democratic norms and institutions in order to gain access to the benefits of governmental incumbency. Several years under this kind of party control can culminate in what I call party-based consolidation or party consolidation of democracy. I regard Italy as an example of where this process culminated in a relatively weak consolidation of democracy by the late 1950s. Over the following decade and a half, however, the legitimacy of Italian democracy spread such that a nearly inclusive legitimation of democracy (i.e., one that excluded only the neofascist MSI) was achieved by the 1970s.

In the absence of both widespread legitimacy in the immediate aftermath of a democratic instauration and strong party control of civil society, consolidation is unlikely to occur. Both attitudinal and institutional support for the new regime are weak or absent altogether, and crises may frequently erupt. Under these circumstances, the regime is potentially unstable and is likely to survive only in an international context highly favorable to democracy. I refer to this outcome as *maintenance*.[88] It should be noted that there are no Southern European cases that fill this fourth cell in our typology.

Before examining these varying scenarios in detail, let us briefly turn our attention to a description of the subprocess of legitimation.

Legitimation, Proregime Parties, and Antiregime Parties

If we regard legitimation as a crucial subprocess in the consolidation of democratic regimes, then it is not sufficient to examine mass-level attitudes towards democratic institutions;[89] it is also necessary to analyze the roles of parties and party elites as translators of popular sentiments into overt actions for or against the existing democratic institutions. The articulation of fundamental attitudes by parties, movements, or other political groups, and their manifestation in programs, ideologies, and behavior in parliament and other democratic arenas can have a significant impact on democratic consolidation. Not only do system-supportive attitudes and behaviors, and the absence of antisystem parties, show that there are no alternatives to the existing regime, but they also demonstrate the breadth of support for democratic institutions. Indicators of such supportive positions include the stands taken by parties on specific issues and in ideological or programmatic declarations, behavioral conformity with the democratic rules of the game and the eschewing of violence as a political tool, and availability of the party for inclusion within a government coalition with other parties.[90]

Although a detailed analysis of the relevant data cannot be undertaken here, a few key indicators linking parties with the legitimation process should illustrate the extent to which legitimation has taken place in Southern Europe. First, extreme right-wing parties have virtually disappeared from three of these four party systems. In Spain, the high-water mark for parties of the far right was 1979, when they received 3 percent of the total vote and elected one deputy; they subsequently vanished, receiving less than .05 percent of the vote in 1993. In Greece and Portugal, except in the Greek election of 1977, right-wing political groups did not achieve a parliamentary presence of any sort. That year a group of ultraconservatives who had splintered from Nea Democratia received 6.8 percent of the vote, but they then disappeared in the 1981 elections. Thus, in Greece and Portugal, the authoritarian alternative, which had ruled for 7 and 48 years, respectively, was fully delegitimated and became politically extinct.[91] While not fully delegitimated, the Spanish authoritarian right was also nonviable: anti-Franco sentiments were not terribly strong or widespread, but in a modernized and more European society parties with an authoritarian appeal had no chance of success.[92] In addition, none of these former authoritarian regimes had maintained a mass-mobilization capacity or socialized their respective populations in a manner that would have perpetuated the authoritarian option.

From this perspective, the Italian case is quite different: an extreme right-wing neofascist party (Movimento Sociale Italiano) consistently received 5 percent of the vote throughout the 1950s and has remained viable until the recent past.[93] The mobilizational characteristics of fascism—the rejuvenated mobilization of fascist "black shirts" during the Repubblica Sociale Italiana (RSI), 1943–45—helped by a highly proportional electoral law, largely account for the birth of this antisystem party, which has maintained an ambiguous relationship with violent terrorist groups.[94]

A more interesting trend is found among parties of the nonextremist right. Nea Democratia played a key role in the founding of Greek democracy, but both the Portuguese Centro Democrático Social and the Spanish Alianza Popular (AP) began by adopting relatively ambiguous positions towards the authoritarian past and the new democratic regime then subsequently integrated themselves fully into the framework of democratic competition. In Portugal, the right, some of whose leaders were survivors from the Caetano period, had political and organizational difficulties at the very beginning, in part because of the leftist leanings of the coup d'état which had established the new regime.[95] Despite their organizational weakness, rightist groups made clear their reservations about the new regime: in 1976, the CDS was the only party to vote against the constitution. Within a few years, however, thanks to the gradual, but profound change in the nature of the regime itself, the trend towards legitimation was complete: the CDS participated in coalition cabinets and played a role in supporting the new democratic system.

In Spain, Alianza Popular underwent a similar transformation. The AP had leaders whose origins were rooted in the Franco regime, and many of its voters maintained favorable attitudes towards Franco.[96] But in the aftermath of a schism, triggered by parliamentary ratification of the constitution in 1978, the party adopted an unequivocally prosystem stance. Party leader Manuel Fraga's unwavering support for the constitution that he had helped write, as well as the party's opposition to the attempted coup of February 1981, underscored its shift from initial ambiguity to a declared loyalty to the democratic regime. In addition, the party consciously sought to moderate its ideology and adopt a more centrist stance.[97]

The next important development was the general moderation in the initial stands of Southern European socialist parties, their full acceptance of their respective democratic regimes, and their successful attainment of government posts in all four countries. In the Italian case, the socialists' embrace of the existing democracy was slow to occur and can be dated mainly to after the Soviet invasion of Hungary in 1956. Socialists moved from a semiloyal stand to one of full loyalty following their detachment from the communists. In the early 1960s, they joined the DC in the governing coalition. The Spanish PSOE was, from the very beginning, a democratic party. The party's transformation therefore involved moderation of the economic proposals and programs of the party. This change closely paralleled the programmatic reforms adopted by the German Social Democratic Party at its 1958 Bad Godesberg conference. At its Extraordinary Congress in September 1979, the PSOE, under the leadership of Felipe González, abandoned all Marxist elements in its ideology. As in the case of the German SPD, this was an important turning point for the party and paved the way for its transformation from an opposition party to a governmental one.[98]

The Greek Socialist Party, PASOK, followed a parallel road. In 1974, PASOK emerged as a prodemocratic, but radical, anticapitalist, and fiercely confrontational party with a Marxist vocabulary. During the second half of the decade, however, the party became increasingly moderate and centrist. Specifically, a dogmatic and sectarian conception of socialism was gradually watered down, becoming a more generic commitment to change, characterized by greater moderation and pragmatism as well as by a fervent nationalism. At this point a "viable legitimate governmental alternative identified with noncommunist left" had been built.[99]

The same process of moderation can be seen in the evolution of the Portuguese Socialist and Social Democratic parties, although with some variations on this theme. The basic difference distinguishes between parties whose first experiences under the new democracy were ones of opposition to conservative governments and those socialist parties which were at the core of the democratic process from the very beginning. The PSOE and PASOK are good examples of the first pattern: in order to enhance their electoral acceptability and come to power, they were motivated to adopt more moderate, centrist programmatic stands and to accept a market, capitalist economic structure. The Portuguese socialists were characteristic of the second group of parties. They had first adopted Marxist positions but then quickly and completely embraced democratic pluralism, emerging as the staunchest defenders of pluralist representative democracy. They were at the core of the Portuguese consolidation process beginning in the "hot summer" of 1975 and continued to moderate their stands until the formation of the central bloc in 1983.[100]

With the exception of the Portuguese Communist Party, the same phenomenon can be observed farther towards the left end of the political continuum. The manner in which the Italian Communist Party changed its stands between the installation of the new regime and consolidation of democracy is most outstanding. The PCI had been very active and important in both the Resistance and the founding of a new democracy. It voted in favor of the constitution (December 1947) and even (in March 1947) in favor of its famous Article 7, which acknowledged the treaty (Concordato) between the Catholic Church and the Italian state, signed by Mussolini in 1929. After 1947–48, however, when the economic and ideological choices of the Christian Democrats and other democratic parties became clear, and when the outbreak of the Cold War contributed to the strong bipolarization of the party system, the Communists became an antiregime force. During the following decade, no process of legitimation occurred. On the contrary, the Communists were frozen out of power at the national level, a development which was only partly offset by their presence in local governments and in the parliamentary arena. In time, the Communists underwent a process of negative integration into the system. Communist legitimation advanced very slowly, through a series of landmark events: in 1963, the Socialists formed a new cabinet with the Christian Democrats; in 1973–75, the Communist leader, Enrico Berlinguer, proposed the so-called "historical compromise" and launched the idea of Eurocommunism; in 1978–79, the Communists entered a parliamentary majority, which supported a cabinet led by Giulio Andreotti; and in 1989–91, the party made the decision to change its name to the Democratic Party of the Left.[101]

The Spanish Communist Party, partly as a reaction to the dramatic experience of the Spanish Civil War and partly in exchange for its legalization in April 1977 (shortly before the first democratic election), became a loyal force from the very beginning of democratic inauguration.[102] Accordingly, the party played an active role in the politics of consensus during the democratic installation: it accepted the monarchy, it participated in the framing and approval of the constitution, and it negotiated and helped to implement the Pactos de la Moncloa. PCE leaders openly declared that the consolidation of Spanish democracy was one of the main objectives of the party.[103] Since the PCE was a proregime party from the very beginning, there was no process of legitimation at all. In this respect, the evolution of the Communist Party in Spain was very different from that of the party in Italy, and also in Portugal and Greece.

In Greece, the KKE (the larger of the two Greek communist parties) shifted from a semiloyal stance in 1974 to a position of full loyalty towards the regime. At the moment of democratic inauguration, the KKE was an orthodox communist party, close to the Soviet Union and maintaining the traditional conceptions of dictatorship of the proletariat and democratic centralism.[104] It attracted 10 percent of the vote in the first election, mainly concentrated in urban constituencies. Since it attracted nearly four times as many voters as its Eurocommunist rival, the KKE-Interior, its position of superiority was established very early on. In the 1980s, however, competition from PASOK led to an erosion of its electoral support.[105] But two key events, one international and one domestic, pushed the party towards integration: the disintegration of the Soviet Union meant that the party completely lost its international reference point, and a domestic crisis caused by scandals and by the bad economic performance of the PASOK government opened the way to a new and unprecedented role for the party in government. The culmination of this process was its participation in a coalition government with Nea Democratia in 1989–90. The party's subsequent behavior reaffirms its complete integration within the regime, its leaders' wild Marxist rhetoric and verbal nostalgia for the past notwithstanding.

The evolution of the Portuguese Communist Party bears a striking resemblance to that of Italy's. In both cases, Communists participated in the founding of the new regime and held government posts, but when the regime subsequently became more and more similar to the other European pluralist democracies, the Communist Party turned into an antiregime force, ostracized by the other, proregime, parties.[106] In a third phase, which in the case of the PCP began in the mid-1980s, the party tried to break its isolation by supporting the election of the Socialist Mário Soares as president of the republic (in the second round of balloting), as well as through its behavior in parliament. The ideological positions of the party, however, were adjusted only marginally to fit with the dramatically altered international situation after 1989: the term *advanced democracy* gradually replaced *revolution* in the party program. The party stated its opposition to the process of democratization in Eastern Europe, was critical of Gorbachev, and favored the authoritarian Chinese leadership. This resistance to change, coupled with the outbreak of intraparty conflicts, contributed to the party's electoral decline: in 1991, the PCP received only 9 percent of the vote—less than half the level of electoral support it had enjoyed in the late 1970s and early 1980s. Several observers have concluded that, as in the case of the French Communist Party, substantial changes are most unlikely for as long as the current leadership remains in control of the party.[107]

This picture would be incomplete without a brief overview of regional nationalist parties, particularly in Spain. The legitimation processes involving these parties had a broad array of implications—not only for the democratic regime, but for the stability of the state and civil society itself—since they directly pertained to acceptance and acknowledgment of the unity of the country, with all its administrative, judicial, and military aspects. Here, too, a process of legitimation took place. The Basque PNV did not vote for the constitution in 1978; however, in spite of ambiguities still present in the mid-1980s, it can be considered a party that accepts both the Spanish state and its democratic regime. By the end of the decade, moreover, the PNV had become an incumbent party at the regional level, in coalition with the PSOE. In fact, the coalition agreement signed by the PNV and PSOE included commitments at the national level, as well as those pertaining to the formation of a Basque regional government.[108]

Catalan groups and parties have always been more moderate than Basque parties and have been unequivocally committed to democratic values. Center-periphery conflicts have become much less tense, moreover, since enactment of regional autonomy statutes and rejection by the Constitutional Court of the most potentially explosive elements of the 1983 Ley Orgánica para la Armonización del Proceso Autonómico, and also as a result of habituation to and acceptance of the status quo.[109] Finally, the more radical, antisystem separatist party, Herri Batasuna, which has long been considered the legal façade of the Basque terrorist organization, ETA, was not able to win more than 1 percent of the national vote throughout the 1980s, while the somewhat less radical Euskadiko Ezkerra (Basque Left) abruptly adopted a prosystem stance after 1981 and became increasingly moderate, eventually merging with the PSOE in advance of the 1993 election. Terrorist violence itself, after peaking in 1980, declined sharply.[110]

Thus, the political parties of all four Southern European countries have been transformed through the processes of legitimation, although at different speeds and with somewhat different features. The process was very slow in Italy: it began in the late 1940s and, even by the early 1960s, the regime enjoyed only a limited legitimacy, with antisystem forces on both the right (the neofascist MSI) and the left (the PCI) that regularly won a combined total of about 30 percent of the vote. By the early 1960s, the previously semi-proregime forces, such as the Socialists (with 13–14% of the vote), had been integrated. This meant that during the first fifteen years after 1948 the proregime forces were basically limited to those participating in the unstable government coalitions formed by Christian Democrats, Liberals, Republicans, and Social Democrats. In other words, there was an internal party system that excluded the parties at both ends of the political spectrum, Socialists included. The broader party system, with its more radical patterns of competition, has been characterized by Giovanni Sartori as "polarized pluralism."[111]

The Spanish case is very different from the Italian. By the time of the 1982 election, the extreme right had virtually disappeared from the party system, as had several tiny parties of the extreme left; Alianza Popular had shifted to an unequivocally proregime party and had successfully integrated itself, becoming a central player in the democratic game of politics; the Communist Party, its own internal crises and schisms notwithstanding, had played a crucial moderating role at key stages of the transition and consolidation processes; and the socialist PSOE had transformed itself into a stable, centrist political force. Only in the case of the Basque regional party system was the legitimation process slower in developing.

In Greece and Portugal, regime legitimation processes have important differences between them, but they are both closer to those of Spain than to Italy's. In Greece, the right was very supportive of the installed regime, which, after all, had been created by Karamanlis and Nea Democratia. Even PASOK, which initially had adopted a rather semiloyal stance towards the regime, moderated both its rhetoric and its behavior and adopted a fully loyal stance by the early 1980s. The Greek communists have also been integrated into the regime. Their integration stemmed from the weakness of the two communist parties, which were subordinated following the electoral success of PASOK in 1981. While the KKE's rhetoric is consistently hard-line and Marxist in tone, the party's participation in a coalition government with Nea Democratia in 1989–90 marks the end of the process of legitimation. The Portuguese right also came to support the regime, but only after several years and two significant revisions of the constitution. The Portuguese Communist Party, meanwhile, despite the transformations of all communist parties in Western and Eastern Europe, remained under the control of an orthodox communist leadership and maintained a semiloyal stance towards the democratic regime—thereby consigning itself to a process of electoral decline.

When we array these four systems on a continuum measuring the legitimacy of the democratic regime, we find Italy located closest to the low end of the scale; Italy's is a case of partial, limited, and exclusive legitimacy. Portuguese democracy is also somewhat limited, given the continuing semiloyalty and orthodox communism of the PCP. Greece is at the opposite end, especially in light of the dramatic entry of formerly mortal enemies, the Communists and the conservatives of Nea Democratia, into a coalition government. A largely inclusive legitimacy was also achieved by Spain, where, by the end of the 1980s, regional antiregime forces such as Herri Batasuna were becoming increasingly irrelevant. If we regard legitimacy as the sole criterion for consolidation, we would categorize the Italian case in the late 1950s as one of exclusive consolidation, Spain and Greece in the 1980s as examples of inclusive consolidation, and Portugal in the 1980s as a case of quasi-inclusive consolidation.

It is important to note that in three out of four countries the legitimation process has not been linear. In Italy, it was basically frozen during the most intense years of the Cold War, between 1948 and 1956. In Spain, a period of difficulties followed substantial initial progress: between 1979 and 1981 this was manifested at the mass level in the so-called *desencanto* (disillusionment) and at the elite level in the breakdown of the Unión de Centro Democrático, which had governed Spain throughout the installation of the new democracy. These were also the peak years of Basque terrorism, accompanied by increases in electoral support for separatist parties. In Portugal, until the first important constitutional revision in 1982, there was a long phase during which it was even unclear what kind of democracy should be installed and considered legitimate, a radical socialist regime or a pluralist democracy, closer to European models. Only in Greece was the process basically linear: in fact, the legitimation process was really only relevant to the Communists, and there were no significant periods of backsliding.

Prerequisites and Determinants of Legitimation

I have argued that legitimation is a central component of the consolidation process and that legitimation has occurred in all four Southern European democracies. We have also seen, however, that there are important variations among these countries in how the processes unfolded, as well as the ultimate configuration of partisan forces in the new democracy. We have already explored several of the factors that led to important variations, but with regard to differences between Italy and the other three cases one previously unexplored variable should be mentioned. The presence of an extremist, nondemocratic right appears to be a function, at least in part, of the type of authoritarian regime that existed in each country prior to the transition to democracy. Italy, which has had a significant extreme right-wing party for decades, had a "mobilizing authoritarian" regime, while the authoritarian systems of the other three countries were nonmobilizing. The presence of a nondemocratic right was also facilitated by such developments during its protracted post-Mussolini transition as the establishment of the fascist RSI and the civil war. In Spain, some ambiguity towards democracy among those on the right resulted from the long duration of Franquism and the economic growth that occurred in the final phase of authoritarian regime, while in Portugal this was partly a residual reaction against the radical leftist aspects of the Revolution of the Carnations.

Cross-national differences on the far left are also largely explained by historical events that occurred at the time of democratic transition. The reestablishment of party politics in Italy in the mid-1940s was affected by the fascination of Socialists and Communists with a leftist alternative to the existing order, strengthened by the experience of the Resistance, and supported by the USSR. The transitions of the mid-1970s, however, occurred after Eurocommunism had already developed as an alternative perspective and ideological stance. The communist alternative subsequently entered into a period of decline until, in 1989, the collapse of communism in Eastern Europe and the Soviet Union closed off an important historical era.

A more fundamental set of questions involving legitimation processes focuses on possible prerequisites for successful legitimation and consolidation. While all four Southern European democracies have been legitimated and consolidated, it is clear that not all contemporary or historical examples of transition to democracy have been so fortunate. What kinds of factors were conducive to legitimation and consolidation in Southern Europe? If the passage of time is important in helping new democratic systems to put down strong roots, what initial factors help to explain how these processes are initially set in motion and maintained? One clue emerges from research on the roles of party elites in this process. Some studies have focused on processes of elite convergence or elite settlement as the specific mechanisms involved in establishing regime legitimacy. Despite some definitional differences, these processes are highly compatible with my conceptualization of legitimation, although the latter is broader than these elite studies insofar as it pays much greater attention to the collective dimension of regime support.[112] Let us examine each of the Southern European cases in search of factors conducive to legitimation.

In the Italian case, such key factors include the negative memory of earlier fascist experience and of the war, the appearance of a democratic Catholic option, and the alliance of the Christian Democrats with other smaller centrist parties (Republicans, Liberals, and Social Democrats). All these factors, together with certain policies introduced by De Gasperi helped to prime the legitimation process.[113] In Spain, whose transition unfolded in a different historical period and within a developed and complex society, factors conducive to the triggering and continued progress of legitimation and consolidation included the moderating effect of the collective memory of civil war, the political and economic appeal of other European countries, widespread (but vague and amorphous) mass preferences for democracy, and the deliberate decisions of elites.[114] Recurring social pacts linking the government, unions, and business associations, as well as the pacts for autonomy concluded by government and local elites, also contributed to the legitimation process.[115] A general effect of these pacts was unavoidably to confer legitimacy on the existing regime and to integrate the social groups and their representatives into that democracy. In Portugal as well, the appeal of the European model of a pluralist democracy and the refusal to consider the radical left alternative proposed by the "Revolution" and by those political groups who persistently tried to implement it, were at the heart of support for the kind of regime which eventually was consolidated by Socialists, Social Democrats, and the CDS. Indeed, this large core of support for a pluralist democracy was a vital prerequisite to a fundamental step in the consolidation (if not the establishment) of a democratic regime—the 1982 constitutional reforms, which politically neutralized the military and eliminated its odd (and undemocratic) "protection" of the new regime and the achievements of the revolution. In Greece, the previous negative experience of the military regime, widespread democratic attitudes, the shift of the Socialists towards more moderate positions, and the democratic initiative of Karamanlis and Nea Democratia explain the beginning and the development of legitimation.

Moving beyond these country-specific factors, several broader considerations stand out. At the beginning of the legitimation process, the key decisions are made by founding elites during the installation of the new democratic regime. Subsequently, however, these decisions must be supported and electorally strengthened by the people. Legitimation thus involves two sets of decisions, the first at the elite level and the second at the mass level, the latter being manifested in the electoral success of democratic parties, a mass-level choice that is, of course, highly conditioned by the representational biases inherent in the electoral law and by the ability of democratic parties to control civil society. The electoral success of the party or parties that governed during the democratic installation phase is often very important. For this reason, the breakdown of the UCD in Spain created the most difficult moment of the entire consolidation process, to the point of contributing to an attempted coup in 1981; the ability of the Socialists to replace the UCD with a stable democratic alternative was crucial for the success of the consolidation process. Initially, then, a democratic system is largely created by a few actors or even by only one party. Later on, during the process of legitimation, other actors must be involved, even if to a limited extent. Thus, the virtuous circle of legitimation is primed. Italy and Portugal are the clearest examples of this, with the entry into government of increasing numbers of parties spanning broader segments of the political continuum.[116]

Finally, it is noteworthy that in three out of the four cases the party systems which have been stabilized are of the predominant-party variety. While a thorough explanation of this development is not possible here, one explanatory hypothesis is worthy of mention: it is likely that predominant-party systems emerged in Italy (under the Christian Democrats), Spain (the Socialists), and Portugal (the Social Democrats) as a result of the weakness or self-exclusion of the right (due to its involvement with past authoritarian regimes) and of the extreme left. Greece is an exception to this pattern, in part because its right was never delegitimated through close association with a military-dominated authoritarian regime (indeed, it was a prominent leader of the right who played the central role in establishing the new democracy) and in part because of the bias towards bipolarity inherent in its electoral law.[117]

Patterns of Democratic Consolidation

In the preceding section, our analysis of democratic consolidation was restricted to the key subprocess of legitimation. We have seen that Italy about fifteen years following the inauguration of a new democratic regime could be characterized as having secured exclusive legitimacy—its democratic institutions and practices were regarded as legitimate only in a partial and limited way. In contrast, inclusive legitimacy was achieved in Greece, especially in the aftermath of the Communist–Nea Democratia coalition government, and in Spain, the diminishing challenges to the regime from regional nationalist groups notwithstanding. Finally, Portugal is characterized by a quasi-inclusive legitimacy, due to the continuing commitment to communist orthodoxy on the part of the PCP leadership; declining electoral support for the party, however, is making this limitation of legitimacy increasingly irrelevant. In the case of Spain, the legitimation process was largely sufficient to have consolidated the democratic regime by the mid-1980s. To somewhat lesser degrees, the same occurred in Greece and Portugal. In Italy legitimation alone was insufficient to have consolidated the regime.

Legitimation, however, is only one component of the broader process of democratic consolidation. The Italian case, in particular, clearly indicates that other factors may be relevant: otherwise, how could democracy be consolidated over the long term with a level of legitimacy which was initially so limited? Our analysis now comes full-circle: I contend that the stabilization of electoral behavior, the establishment of the party system, and stabilization of the political class can play an important role in the consolidation of a democratic regime. More specifically, I contend that if the legitimation process has not gone far enough to consolidate a regime, stabilization of the party system may be indispensable for successful completion of the consolidation process. This is what unfolded in Italy, where the legitimation process had (fifteen years after the installation of democracy) succeeded in producing only a limited or exclusive legitimacy, but where party dominance was characteristic of relationships with interest groups. I have referred to this process as party-based consolidation.

By what process does this process culminate in democratic consolidation? Parties, in their efforts to achieve and perpetuate themselves in power, attempt to attract and maintain support from sectors of civil society, at least in part through development of their organizations, interest group relations, and control of state resources. In order to acquire and maintain power (especially control of public sector resources), parties must succeed in the game of democratic competition. Once they seriously enter into this game, however, they find themselves caught within a logic that, from the standpoint of consolidation, represents a self-perpetuating virtuous circle. Partisan competition entails an adjustment of parties (as intermediary representative structures) to civil society. Insofar as civil society has encapsulated the procedural aspects of competition within a framework of democratic norms and values, this adaptation will require substantial modification in the stands and behavioral styles of initially antiregime parties and groups; failure to adapt will mean failure in partisan competition and, therefore, in the party's efforts to achieve and maintain itself in power. Similarly, stability, responsibility, and organizational development may enhance efficacy and effectiveness with regard to governmental policy making and implementation, but it may also appeal to voters and strengthen the party's electoral position and relationships with interest groups. This self-reinforcing virtuous circle can contribute to consolidation, as a side-effect of the pursuit of purely partisan objectives.[118]

In Spain the process unfolded in a very different way. In contrast with the Italian case, the parties were relatively neutral in their gatekeeping regarding interest groups and in general were weaker than parties in Italy: they were weakly structured, and only intermediate levels of stabilization of the party system and political class had been achieved. Within a short time following establishment of the new regime, however, widespread legitimacy was achieved (some small and declining regional pockets of antiregime sentiment notwithstanding). Given the importance of the roles played by party leaders in the achievement of inclusive legitimacy, I have regarded Spain as an example of elite-based consolidation.

In Greece and Portugal, the democratic consolidation processes are indicative of a more mixed pattern. Particularly in Greece, there was a strong stabilization of the party system, characterized by continuity in voting behavior, stabilization of the political class, fairly strong internal party organization, and, at the same time, the occupation of civil society by the incumbent party and a great role played by the public sector, further strengthening the incumbent party. In this respect, Greece more closely resembles Italy. But insofar as Greece secured an inclusive legitimacy by the early 1980s, it is closer to the Spanish case. Combining these two dimensions leads us to categorize Greece as having undergone a process of state-based consolidation. A summary of our conclusions regarding the control dimension in Portugal includes the relatively recent electoral stabilization, some stabilization of the political class, relatively developed party organizations, party dominance of civil society, and a strong role played by the public sector until the end of the 1980s, when a reform of the constitution (1989) paved the way to some development of private enterprise. The legitimation process culminated in what we referred to as quasi-legitimacy, without the complete integration of the Communist Party within the game of democratic competition. Overall, the importance in the consolidation process played by the old corporatist authoritarian tradition leads to the categorization of Portugal as a second example of state consolidation.

These differing consolidation processes were summarized in Figure 10.5. The basic thrust of the argument underpinning this typology is that a limited level of legitimacy, secured by democratic institutions and practices in the early stages of the consolidation process, can be compensated for by strong and stable parties playing a dominant role. While strong, stable parties may not be required for democratic consolidation in regimes that have achieved considerable legitimacy (as typified by the case of Spain), parties and their command of state resources may powerfully influence the character of the consolidation process and the kind of democratic regime which emerges.

Consolidation and Beyond: Italy Once Again

This analysis helps make it possible to determine more precisely when the process of democratic consolidation has been completed. In the absence of a crisis (which can serve as an empirical test of regime consolidation), a democracy can be considered more or less consolidated when either a widespread consensus has emerged affirming the legitimacy of democratic institutions and practices, or when party control over civil society has been stabilized, or when both developments have occurred. Widespread legitimacy was achieved in Greece and Spain by the early 1980s, contributing to the peaceful transfer of power to the socialists in both countries (in 1981 and 1982, respectively). For Portugal, the complete neutralization of the army and the election of the new democracy's first civilian president in 1986 seems to be a salient landmark event. By and large, the consolidation processes in all three countries were complete by the mid-1980s. To this, we could add that party developments in the late 1980s give further evidence of stabilization: the emergence and stabilization of support for the Portuguese Social Democratic Party, the stabilization of electoral behavior in Spain, and the short-lived but symbolically significant coalition between Communists and conservatives in Greece all illustrate that democratic institutions and practices have taken on a stable configuration and that past sources of instability have diminished significantly. Italy's democratic regime, weakly consolidated by the end of the 1950s and early 1960s, was also fully consolidated by the mid-1980s, by which time all criteria in both the legitimacy and control dimensions had been met.

Subsequently, these regimes have evolved in different directions. Portugal and Spain are best characterized by the term *persistence*: the basic contours of the democratic institutions and party systems of these two countries remain largely unaltered since the mid-1980s. A few significant changes have occurred in Greece, and repeated alternations in power have become a distinguishing feature of partisan politics. In Italy, however, the extent of change is so extensive as to imply that a transition toward a new form of democracy is under way. There was a period of crisis in the mid-1970s and a new phase of regime crisis in the late 1980s and early 1990s. The latter was so serious as to lead to a complete restructuring of the party system and some changes in core democratic institutions. Fortunately, diffuse legitimacy has become so widespread that the fate of democracy in Italy seems secure (see Chapter 7 of this volume), but a significantly different democratic regime is coming into existence.

In Spain, the party system remains basically stable. A minor increase in total electoral volatility in 1993 (see Table 10.1) was offset by a perfectly stable level of interbloc volatility (Table 10.2)—suggesting that the salience of the left-right cleavage remains unchanged—and by slight declines in fractionalization (Table 10.3) and the number of effective parties, from 2.9 in 1989 to 2.7 in 1993. The dominant position of the PSOE has been maintained, despite the party's loss of a parliamentary majority (with its share of seats declining from 175 in 1989 to 159) and the increasing blackmail power of regional parties in parliament. Democracy remains fully consolidated, the partial exception of the Basque region notwithstanding.

The basic features of the Portuguese party system also persist. The state-based character of its consolidation process, however, is fading away: since 1989, the PSD government has been implementing a policy of privatization in both the industrial and financial sectors. The government has also undertaken a series of budget policy changes, with spending cuts and subsequent reductions in the size of the public sector deficit contributing to improved prospects for economic growth.[119] Overall, by the late 1980s and early 1990s the role of the state in the Portuguese economy was declining, thereby altering an important earlier characteristic of its democratic regime: heavy state intervention in the economy was giving way to a system in which civil society might have a more active and independent role.

In Greece, high total electoral volatility in the election of October 1993 (17.7%, up from 3.3% in 1990) and the doubling of interbloc volatility (2.1% to 4.2%, see Tables 10.1 and 10.2) were not mirrored by a change in the number of effective parties, despite a change in the electoral law (see Table 10.3 and Figure 10.1). As the result of a split in Nea Democratia[120] and a persisting division in the extreme left, PASOK was voted back into power. Thus, alternation in power seems to have become a key aspect of Greek democracy. Beginning in 1991, the Mitsotakis government initiated policies of deregulation, liberalization, and privatization of many firms in the industrial, financial, and service sectors of the economy.[121] Thus, in Greece as in Portugal, the state-centered characteristics of democracy have begun to erode. Greece has not had the predominant-party system and stable dominant leadership Portugal has experienced; alternation in power in Greece has interrupted this process, and PASOK's return to power put a stop to those economic liberalization policies and may lead to a reversal of some of them.

When we turn to Italy, we see a very different situation. Almost half a century after the reestablishment of Italian democracy, its regime entered a phase of far-reaching change. A period of crisis began in 1987 that led to substantial, though partial, changes, the most radical of which relate to its party system. Even prior to the actual casting of ballots in the 1994 election, the Italian party system had undergone a radical transformation: most of the parties participating in that contest were either brand new or had undergone a major face-lift. The left was the first segment of the political continuum to undergo a profound transformation. In the case of the PCI, the process came to a head with the fall of the Berlin Wall. A new party was created, with a new name (the Democratic Party of the Left, PDS) and new symbols. A segment of the old PCI that held more orthodox communist views created a splinter party, Rifondazione Comunista, that was roughly one-third the size of the PDS. At the same time, the extreme left-wing party Democrazia Proletaria (which, under other names, had occupied the political space to the left of the PCI for almost twenty years) disappeared.

The Christian Democratic party was also radically transformed. Following replacement of its party secretary in 1993 and a long intraparty struggle, the Partito Popolare (PPI) was born in January 1994. The DC's conversion was also preceded and accompanied by schisms, from both left and right. Some of its former leaders entered the rightist Alleanza Nazionale (AN, which was dominated by the formerly neofascist Movimento Sociale Italiano); others formed the Centro Cristiano Democratico and became part of the center-right coalition, Polo delle Libertà; others, under the leadership of Antonio Segni, formed a different group in the summer of 1993; still others formed a fifth party, Cristiano Sociali, and entered into coalition with parties of the left.

Similarly, the Liberal, Republican, and Socialist parties have all suffered schisms and either disappeared completely or survive in segments joined to the PDS-led Alleanza Progressista, the centrist coalition Patto per l'Italia (formed by the PPI and the Patto Segni), or the Polo delle Libertà. The Social Democrats, after changing their party secretary several times, became such a small group that they were eliminated by the majoritarian biases in the new electoral law.

As for the right, partly as a result of its strong performance in the local elections of 1993, the MSI seized the political initiative and forged the Alleanza Nazionale, along with a tiny group from the former DC. The AN, led by MSI party secretary Gianfranco Fini, softened some of its rightist stands. Except for an extremist minority, the party was very careful in conveying a more democratic image. This was accompanied by the recruitment of conservative democratic intellectuals to the party.

In January 1994 a brand new party, Forza Italia, suddenly emerged under the leadership of the television magnate Silvio Berlusconi. Within only a few weeks of its birth, public opinion polls indicated that it would become the largest party in the new parliament. The startling surge of Forza Italia in public opinion surveys was the product of a political vacuum on the center-right, in combination with the massive use of television propaganda. It would be difficult to overemphasize the extent to which Berlusconi's control of private television represented an enormous electoral asset: Berlusconi owned and directly controlled three television networks and had virtual control of several local stations. Exploiting a loophole in the law governing television advertising in election campaigns, he used these media outlets to gain maximal benefit for his own candidacy. His strategy was based on public opinion survey data which revealed how empty and malleable the center to center-right segment of the political spectrum was following the self-delegitimation, schisms, and eventual disappearance of Christian Democracy, coupled with the deep crisis and split in the Socialist Party. The success of Forza Italia represented the meeting of a widespread popular demand for a new political product and an entrepreneur with great advertising expertise and experience in selling new products. This phenomenon is part and parcel of "videocracy," or the power of television to sell even a new political party to the public within a matter of weeks.

Berlusconi's ties to old political and, especially, business elites were also important assets in his efforts to change politics by building his own party. Support from the business elite mainly took the form of support from the rank and file of the business class, however, since the peak association of business officially took a neutral stand. Widespread enthusiasm for Berlusconi became particularly apparent in postelection meetings of the business association. Much of this support was rooted in the fact that Berlusconi was, himself, a businessman who had been motivated to become active in politics by the failure of the traditional parties.

In terms of party organization,[122] the PDS and Rifondazione managed to preserve the structures of the former PCI, especially in Emilia Romagna and Tuscany. The Italian Communist Party's heritage of offices and militants did not disappear, despite the PDS's having decided even before 1991 to reduce the number of party officials and to rely on a leaner organization. It should be noted that all traditional parties implemented similar policies of sacking party functionaries and reducing the size of the party organization, in view of their respective financial difficulties. As a result, in July 1993 parliament passed a law that allowed party functionaries to be pensioned off early.

In contrast with the relatively light party structure of the democratic left, the League developed a strong organization manned by voluntary workers (many of them young) from diverse social backgrounds. It emerged as a markedly hierarchical party with a strong leader and a central office controlling finances, electoral campaigns, and party policy. For the most part, the party organization has been managed with efficiency criteria typical of private business firms, even with regard to its patterns and processes of recruitment. From this perspective, the League may be regarded as a sort of party-firm. These aspects of the League's organization and internal functioning reflect the deep respect for the values of entrepreneurship, efficiency, and the free market which has penetrated Italian political culture, especially in the north.

These same features are also characteristic of Forza Italia. Initial plans for the launching of this party were made in the second half of 1993, and the party came into existence between January and March 1994, shortly before the March elections. The key organizing function was played by the staff of Publitalia, the leading advertising firm in Italy, which is part of Berlusconi's conglomerate, Fininvest. In an extraordinarily short period of time, thirteen thousand Forza Italia clubs (growing out of an odd assortment of ancillary organizations, including the Milan soccer clubs, whose president is Berlusconi) were set up throughout the country. Even more than the League, Forza Italia was a party-firm, at least during the election campaign itself, when the personnel of Berlusconi's business firm performed key functions normally carried out by parties. Only after the election did it turn its attention to institutionalizing itself as an autonomous party, under a strong, undisputed leader.

The new Partito Popolare, despite its direct line of descent from Christian democracy, could no longer depend on the political unity of the Catholic vote, since this was divided among various groups of the left, center, and right. Nonetheless, despite the substantial process of secularization that has taken place in Italy over the past twenty-five years, which has reduced the church's influence, the PPI could rely on support from sectors of the church hierarchy, the Catholic Associations (AC), Comunione e Liberazione (CL), and some sectors of the Catholic workers' association (ACLI).[123]

These changes must be seen in conjunction with, and partly as a response to, new electoral laws both at the local and national level. In fact, the enactment of a new municipal-level electoral law in March 1993 had an immediate polarizing effect in the local by-elections of June and November–December of that same year. The new law provides for the direct election of mayors. In municipalities with fewer than fifteen thousand inhabitants, a plurality of votes is sufficient for election. In larger municipalities, if no candidate receives a majority, a runoff election is held between the two candidates receiving the most votes on the first round. Mayoral elections are linked with those for municipal councils through rules designed to assure a supportive majority for the victorious mayoral candidate. On the whole, the complex local electoral law is majoritarian, with some provisions for proportional compensation of minorities. In any case, the result was a drastic and immediate shift towards a bipolar distribution of mayors and seats on municipal councils.

A new national-level electoral system was approved in August 1993. It first went into effect in the general elections to the Senate and the Chamber of Deputies on March 27–28, 1994. In stark contrast with the

Table 10.9 Changes in the Italian Party System, 1968–1994

	Total Electoral Volatility	Interbloc Volatility	Vote Fraction-alization	Number of Effective Parties
1968	3.4	1.4	.75	3.6
1972	4.9	1.1	.76	3.6
1976	8.2	5.4	.72	3.1
1979	5.3	.7	.74	3.4
1983	8.5	.3	.78	4.0
1987	8.4	1.1	.78	4.1
1992	16.2	5.2	.85	5.8
1994	41.9	5.8	.87	7.3

Note: For total electoral volatility, interbloc volatility, vote fractionalization, and the number of effective parties in previous elections, see Tables 10.1, 10.2, 10.3, and Figure 10.1. In calculating interbloc volatility, the PSDI and the Lista Pannella were regarded as of the center/center-right bloc. Vote fractionalization calculations were based on votes cast in the proportional segment. Finally, it should be noted that if the electoral coalitions (Polo delle Libertà, Patto per l'Italia, and Alleanza Progressista) were used in place of parties in calculating, the number of effective parties would be 3.6.

relatively pure proportional representation system used over the preceding four decades, the new law allocates three-quarters of the seats in both houses on the basis of a single-member-plurality electoral system. The remaining quarter of the seats are allocated on the basis of proportional representation, to partly compensate those parties which did not receive representation on the first (single-member-majority) segment.[124] In addition to the majoritarian biases inherent in all single-member-district systems, a 4 percent minimum nationwide vote is established by law as a prerequisite for receiving representation through the proportional representation segment for the Chamber of Deputies. For the Senate, there is no legal threshold, but since the allocation of proportional representation seats is calculated at the regional level, there is a de facto threshold of 10 percent of votes cast for receiving proportional representation seats. The proportional representation segment of the vote softens the impact of the single-member/plurality segment somewhat, but it is far from sufficient to offset its strong majoritarian bias. This represents a radical change in the electoral system that has had a dramatic impact on the configuration of the Italian party system.

The extent of the transformation of the Italian party system resulting from the 1994 election can be seen in Table 10.9. Several important developments are worthy of note. The first is that party fractionalization significantly increased after 1992. This is the result of a strong territorialization of the vote, coupled with the representational biases in single-member/plurality electoral systems, insofar as a party receiving a relatively small share of the nationwide vote may be the plurality party in a particular region, and would therefore receive a disproportionate share of the seats from that area. Thus, while single-member/plurality systems have strong majoritarian biases in translating popular votes into parliamentary seats, they may permit or even provide an incentive for the fragmentation of party systems along regional lines. This phenomenon has clearly occurred in Italy.

Other significant indicators of the extent and nature of the change which took place in the 1992-94 period can be seen in the total electoral volatility and interbloc volatility scores presented in Table 10.9. The 1994 Italian election exhibited the second-highest total volatility score of any European election in the twentieth century (behind only the 1982 Spanish election). But this figure actually conceals the full extent of change in the Italian party system, since it does not take into consideration that the 1992 election also manifested an extraordinarily high level of total volatility. Thus, given the two-step nature of the Italian party system's transformation, its full extent must be regarded as the most far-reaching change in any European party system over the past century.[125] At the same time, however, the level of interbloc volatility exhibited by Italian voters was relatively moderate. Clearly, the share of voters crossing over the left-right barrier was higher in 1992 and 1994 than in previous elections, but in light of the truly massive shifts among parties *within* each bloc, this shift must be regarded as surprisingly moderate. (This puzzling feature of the nature of electoral change in Italy will be explored more extensively in the second volume of this series.)

The radical transformation of the party system in the 1992–94 period may be seen more clearly in Table 10.10. Certainly one of the most important aspects of this change is the breakdown of the main pillar of the "First Republic," the Christian Democratic Party. The share of votes and seats of the direct descendent of the DC, the Partito Popolare, gives a first impression of the extent of the collapse in electoral support for this once-dominant party: in sharp contrast with the 30-plus percent shares of votes and seats commanded by the party over the preceding decades, the PPI received only 11 percent of the vote on the proportional representation segment of the ballot and only 5 percent of the seats in the Chamber of Deputies. In its place, Forza Italia, the Lega Nord, and the postfascist Alleanza Nazionale are the dominant forces at right of center. Clearly, much of the electoral turnover in 1994 involved an abandonment of the DC by its former supporters. An unpublished survey conducted in the aftermath of the 1994 election by a

Table 10.10 Italian Electoral Results, 1992 and 1994 (Chamber of Deputies)

	1992			1994					
				Plurality Segment Seats		PR Segment Vote Seats		Total Seats	
	Votes (%)	Seats		N	%	N	%	N	%
Rifondazione Comunista	5.6	35		29	6.1	6.0	11	40	6.3
Partito Democ. della Sin.	16.1	107		77	16.2	20.4	38	115	18.2
Rete	1.9	12		9	1.9	1.9	—	9	1.4
Verdi	2.8	16		11	2.3	2.7	—	11	1.7
PSI	13.6	92		15	3.1	2.2	—	15	2.4
Lista Pannella	1.2	7		6	1.3	3.5	—	6	.9
			Cristiano Sociali	6	1.3	0	—	6	.9
PRI	4.4	27							
PSDI	2.7	16	All. Democratica	17	3.6	1.2	—	17	2.7
DC	29.7	206	Part. Popol. Italiano	4	.8	11.1	29	33	5.2
PLI	2.8	17	Patto Segni	—	—	4.6	13	13	2.1
			Centro Crist. Democ.	32	6.7	0	—	32	5.1
			Forza Italia	67	14.1	21.0	30	97	15.4
Lega Nord	8.7	55		111	23.4	8.4	11	122	19.4
MSI	5.4	34	Alleanza Nazionale	86	18.1	13.5	23	109	17.3
Others	5.1	6		5	1.0	3.5	—	5	.8

Note: Arrows indicate transference of some leaders from the old parties to the new ones.

group of sociologists from the University of Milan revealed that Forza Italia was the new choice of 21.2 percent of those who had previously voted for the DC.

But the story of the 1994 party-system restructuring also gives a prominent role to the collapse of the Socialist Party. The University of Milan postelection survey found that about 30 percent of former PSI supporters shifted their votes to Forza Italia in 1994. The origins of the electoral disaster which befell the Socialists, however, can be traced back to the previous decade: they involve an elite-level crisis within the party (to be discussed below), as well as the adoption by the PSI's electorate of moderate, centrist attitudes, facilitating their shift of support to a new centrist party, Forza Italia. At the same time, another sizable segment of the PSI electorate voted for the leftist coalition.

The party system which emerged in 1994 is thus composed of four parties, which received between 15 and 20 percent of the seats in the Chamber of Deputies. Three of the four parties belong to the so-called Polo delle Libertà, formed by Alleanza Nazionale, the Lega Nord, Forza Italia, and the Centro Cristiano Democratico. This right-of-center alliance won 360 seats, or 57.1 percent of the total in the lower house. The leftist alliance, which included the PDS, Rifondazione, Verdi (Greens), La Rete (the anti-Mafia network), the PSI, AD, and Cristiano Sociali, won 213 seats (33.8 percent). The territorialization of the new party system is best evidenced by the League, which received only 8.4 percent of the vote nationwide but was allocated 111 seats (23.4%) in the lower house of parliament—all of them from the northern regions.

Election results for the Senate were somewhat different, and, since Italian governments must receive and maintain majority support in both houses of parliament, this could have significant political implications at some point. In the Senate, the conservative coalition (Polo delle Libertà) won 154 seats out of 315 (48.9%), while the Progressisti were allocated 122 seats (38.7%). Thus, installation of a center-right government requires the additional votes of some senators not belonging to the conservative coalition—most importantly, the twenty-seven senators of the Partito Popolare and the four of the Patto Segni. The difference between the electoral results for the two houses of parliament appear to be related to the higher propensity of younger voters to support centrist and right-wing parties, motivated, in part, by an electoral campaign by Forza Italia that promised to create one million new jobs. In elections for the Senate, only those age 25 and older can vote (as compared with a minimum voting age of 18 for the Chamber of Deputies), thereby excluding these more conservative younger voters.

One final and highly significant aspect of this party-system change is that the Italian political class has undergone a very substantial renewal. Fully 70 percent of those elected to parliament in 1994 had never held national-level office before.

How could such a radical transformation of the party system occur? First of all, it should be recalled that this change took place through a two-step process. The first phase of this process unfolded between 1990 and 1992 and primarily involved the left and the growth of the League. The collapse of Eastern European communism in 1989 played an important role in bringing about the transformation of the communist left. The second stage mainly involved developments to the right of center and occurred following 1992. These developments were set in motion by the dramatic inquiries by magistrates in Milan (and elsewhere) into the illegal funds given to parties and the ill-gotten wealth accumulated by certain party leaders through kick-backs from public sector contracts. While suspicions of corruption were already widespread, the so-called "*mani pulite*" (clean hands) inquiry in Milan, together with similar investigations in Rome, Naples, and other cities from 1992 through early 1994, produced dramatic evidence concerning how deeply rooted and pervasive this phenomenon was throughout the Italian political class.

The result was a delegitimation of the traditional parties and a severing of those parties from their bases of support. This was especially true of the Socialist Party and its leader Craxi, but virtually all the traditional parties were affected. Only the PCI/PDS, which had not been included in national governments, emerged relatively unscathed, but it was still saddled with the failures of Eastern European communism at the time of the election. With the disappearance of the party system's legitimacy, the stalemate was abruptly shattered. It should be noted that these judicial inquiries have produced as a side-effect a new political problem: the politicization of the judiciary.[126] Obviously, the depoliticization of the judiciary will be a significant issue facing future governments, much as depoliticization of the military was an important task facing new democratic regimes in Portugal and certain Latin American countries.

The referendum of April 18, 1993, when the vast majority of Italians chose to change the law for senatorial elections, was an important turning point which broke the stalemate and set in motion a series of far-reaching developments. This popular initiative compelled the recalcitrant Italian political class to adopt the radically different electoral laws discussed above, the effect of which was to magnify and accelerate the processes of change in the party system.

But the change in electoral law, the collapse of communism, and judicial inquiries only explain why change in the party system came about at that precise moment. Political events of this magnitude take place only when certain preconditions have been met. Indeed, scandals and judicial inquiries had besmirched the reputations of parties and party leaders in the 1960s and 1970s, yet the party system remained remarkably stable. What, then, were the basic conditions onto which the two aforementioned developments were grafted?

First, a profound socioeconomic transformation, beginning in the 1960s, led to the political mobilization of the working class, the young, and women. In the 1960s and 1970s, however, the transformation of parties had been blocked, not only by the incomplete democratic legitimacy of the Communist Party, but also by the violence of left-wing and right-wing terrorism. During the 1980s, several changes gradually occurred. Discontent with malfunctioning political institutions began to increase, and civil society progressively became detached from party institutions.[127] At the same time, the cost of politics increased as the result of growing dependence on television for conducting election campaigns (TV first became important in the 1983 election) and of the struggle for power in government between the Socialists and the Christian Democrats. These increasing political expenses forced the leaders of the government coalition to take advantage of their control over the public sector to extract ever greater volumes of "taxes" for party (and personal) use. At the same time, the PCI was making great strides towards the democratic integration of the party, culminating in its transformation into the PDS (and Rifondazione) in 1991.

Other social, economic, and political changes were also relevant to this realignment. In earlier periods, expressions of discontent over the inefficiency of public services had been constrained in the belief that the communist menace required a broad coalition of moderate forces. After 1989, there was no reason to continue to exercise such restraint. Indeed, the PDS became one of the principal channels for the expression of this discontent. Thus, the disappearance of the "enemy" from the international scene had an important impact on domestic politics in Italy insofar as it led many voters to wonder why they should continue to support those parties (especially the DC and PSI) which had been so thoroughly discredited by deep involvement with the aforementioned scandals. These doubts were particularly salient among business entrepreneurs, struggling with the effects of widespread economic crisis made worse by huge public sector deficits, who began to resist the demands of parties for money.

Finally, Italian society had lost its religious connotations, and even Catholics no longer felt the need to rally in support of one powerful party. Indeed, there were now newly available contenders for their votes, such as Forza Italia, which received endorsements from some individuals in the Catholic hierarchy. Thus, the combined effect of economic crisis, the secularization of society, the increasing cost of partisan politics, and the disappearance of a credible communist threat was to make possible the unrestrained expression of dissatisfaction with the existing system. Previously, widespread latent discontent (clearly apparent in the data presented in Chapter 7 of this book) was not translated into actual political behavior, but following the changes that took place in the 1980s, the existing parties were delegitimated and sweeping change in the party system took place.

These changes have also affected the nature of the relationships between parties and civil society that we analyzed earlier in this chapter. Indeed, relationships among interests, parties, and institutions have been substantially altered. Agricultural interests, for example, are now more decisively affected by European Community policies than by domestic politics. Coldiretti, and to a lesser degree Confagricoltura, may still be reservoirs of votes, but in the early 1990s their members came to depend less and less on the DC. The point of no return for Coldiretti came in 1994, when its leaders announced a break with the DC. The interests of industrial entrepreneurs had evolved to such an extent that they (especially large firms, such as FIAT) denounced to the judiciary the system of corruption which had led to Tangentopoli ("kick-back city"). The fears of terrorism and anxiety over the threat posed by communism had disappeared, while at the same time the stresses of the economic crisis were making it increasingly painful to pay kick-backs to parties, especially for firms facing the specter of bankruptcy. In this context, the small firms of Lombardy and the Veneto abandoned their former allegiance to the traditional parties (especially the DC) and began to shift their support—some to the League, for its local policies, its anticentralism, and its antigovernment protests, and others to Forza Italia and Berlusconi. The ties linking trade unions to parties have also become much looser, and have undergone a significant transformation: the trade union agenda is now completely dominated by labor-related issues and demands. The idea of a unitary trade union without party ties has gathered much strength. On the whole, party domination over interests, whether organized or not, slowly diminished during the second half of the 1980s. In the end, the once-dominant traditional parties themselves disappeared.

These changes represent a marked departure from the party-society linkages which had served as the underpinning for Italy's process of democratic consolidation. They may culminate in the establishment of a different democratic regime, especially if relations between the executive and the legislature are modified and if the head of government is directly elected, as some political forces are demanding.

Thus, on the whole, throughout Southern Europe the phase of democratic consolidation through the three models described in this chapter has ended. To what extent these models of consolidation are relevant to other countries, especially in Eastern Europe, is another important question. But that would require further research.

11 Conclusion

P. Nikiforos Diamandouros, Hans-Jürgen Puhle, and Richard Gunther

In the Introduction to this volume, we defined a consolidated democratic regime as one in which all politically significant groups regard its key institutions as the only legitimate framework for political contestation and all groups adhere to its democratic rules of the game. Using the attitudinal and behavioral dimensions implicit in this definition, the contributors to this volume have concluded that democratic regimes in Greece, Italy, Portugal, and Spain had been successfully consolidated by the 1980s. This is not to say that some of these democracies have not had to confront serious problems or have not passed through periods of crisis. In the Basque country of Spain, a militant and violent, but steadily shrinking and increasingly isolated, separatist minority has continued to contest the legitimacy of Spanish democracy. And in Italy, both the party system and some central democratic institutions have undergone extensive change in response to past failures. But in all four countries, support for democracy is widespread at both the mass and elite levels, and the legitimacy of democracy and continued respect for democratic rules of the game have helped these democracies to persist and thrive in the face of even serious challenges.

The Southern European success story stands in stark contrast to the uncertainties and travails which continue to bedevil most other societies which have embarked upon their own journeys towards democratization in recent years. With the exceptions of Uruguay and Costa Rica, democracies in Central and South America are still struggling with transition problems of varying, and often major, magnitude and intensity. If Chile's transition seems to be well on its way to successful completion, Brazil's, the longest on record, continues to be mired in uncertainty and increasing frustration.

The situation is even worse in the countries of Eastern, East-Central, and Southeastern Europe where, as Juan Linz, Alfred Stepan, and

Richard Gunther point out in Chapter 3, the process of democratization has been enormously complicated by the need to negotiate a *simultaneous* transition to democracy and to a market economy. In addition, what they call "stateness" crises have greatly exacerbated the transition problems confronting the former states of the Soviet Union, Yugoslavia, and Czechoslovakia.

Finally, with the exception of South Korea, which seems to have made considerable progress towards consolidation of its democratic political system, most East Asian societies still find themselves in various stages of their uncertain democratic transitions. The tendency to emulate the regionally salient Japanese model and to rely heavily on one dominant party in building their democracies appears to be complicating the process of democratization in these countries.

To be sure, the consolidation processes that unfolded in Southern Europe exhibited significant variation across the four countries. The process was swiftest in Greece, where, depending on the choice of criteria used, democracy became consolidated as early as 1977 or no later than 1981, when a peaceful and impeccable change in governmental incumbency brought the opposition Socialists (PASOK) to power. The Spanish consolidation was almost as fast, reaching completion at the national level in 1982 or 1983, by which time nondemocratic segments of the military had abandoned all aspirations of toppling the new regime and had accepted and even begun to collaborate effectively with a government of the Socialist Party—towards which the military had historically been hostile. The Portuguese experience was severely complicated by the fact that, well into the 1980s, the legitimacy of the democratic regime remained substantially undermined by the competing legitimacy which the military independently derived from its role as a key actor in the transition process and by the reserved powers which it retained. It was not until the constitutional revision of 1982 (which eliminated these reserved powers and the last vestiges of this competing legitimacy) that both processes, transition and consolidation, were largely completed in that country. The final step towards simultaneous completion of both these processes was the constitutional reform of 1989, which removed from the constitution those clauses that prevented democratically elected governments from privatizing the industries and properties seized and nationalized during the revolution of 1974–75 and, thereby, cordoned off a "reserved policy domain" that violated our ideal-type definition of democracy. At about the same time, the PCP formally abandoned its revolutionary program and strategy, thus transforming itself from an antisystem party into a loyal competitor in Portuguese democratic politics. The Italian consolidation process was by far the most protracted. Though its roots lie in the late 1940s, it cannot be said to have reached closure prior to the mid-1970s. Throughout this period, concern over the PCI's commitment to democracy and its perceived antisystem stance constituted the major obstacles to consolidation. The important 1978 agreements, which incorporated the PCI into a de facto parliamentary coalition in support of a minority Christian Democratic government, symbolized the completion of consolidation in Italy.

What accounts for the distinct variation in the consolidation patterns observable in each of the Southern European countries? Which factors facilitated the relative overall success of democratic consolidation in the region, and, conversely, what kinds of factors have stood in the way of consolidation in other recent but less successful democratization processes? The main purpose of this concluding chapter is to address these questions.

Let us begin with a conceptual clarification that has a bearing on the following discussion. Although we regard consolidation as a discrete aspect of the overall democratization process, it should not be understood as being linked to transition in a neatly sequential manner. In empirical reality, the two more often than not overlap, the roots of consolidation being located in the transition period and often extending well beyond the transition. The Greek and Spanish consolidation experiences most closely conform to this pattern. In both cases, different background factors, to be discussed more fully below, contributed decisively to the development, during each country's transition, of the requisite conditions of moderation and restraint on major issues that greatly enhanced the chances of a successful consolidation. And in both countries, consolidation reached closure a few years after the end of their respective transitions—marked by the adoption of a new constitution in Greece and the enactment of a constitution and autonomy statutes in Spain. On the other hand, the experience in Portugal, where the constitutional revisions of 1982 and 1989 represented steps towards the simultaneous completion of both the transition and consolidation processes, suggests that it is possible for the two processes to coincide. The same is likely to be the case in Chile as well, once the institutional barriers that were erected by the Pinochet regime and are contributing to the protractedness of the transition process are lifted or become exhausted.

The Italian case was the most complicated of the lot, and it underscores the fact that empirical reality often resists easy categorization into conceptual boxes or ideal types. If one looks to the role of political parties in the consolidation of Italian democracy, as Leonardo Morlino does in this volume, then it is legitimate to argue that transition and consolidation there were sequentially linked, with the latter commencing after the critical election of 1948. If, however, one views the Italian consolidation experience from the perspective of a broader array of actors (including trade unions), then the origins of the consolidation process have to be moved back by a few years, to overlap with, rather than follow, the transition.

Finally, the Italian and Portuguese cases also serve as powerful reminders that consolidation is not and should not be conceived of as a linear process, moving inexorably towards successful completion. Empirical reality has amply demonstrated in recent years that protractedness, stagnation, temporary reversal, and, quite often, deconsolidation are equally, if not more likely outcomes.

Socioeconomic Modernization, Economic Performance, and Democratic Consolidation

To what extent do socioeconomic structure and short-term economic conditions affect processes of democratic consolidation? There is a long tradition in the social sciences of positing a linkage between socioeconomic factors and democracy.[1] While the relevant literature is too extensive to be surveyed here, it is important to distinguish among three distinct sets of arguments. The first derives from what has been collectively referred to as modernization theory, which, in its minimalist version, focuses on the extent to which socioeconomic development mobilizes individuals politically and enables them to engage in autonomous and self-sustaining participation—as the very definition of democracy requires.[2] A second set of arguments involves the extent to which socioeconomic modernization, over the long term, tends to lessen economic and social polarization in a society, which in turn reduces the socioeconomic bases for political polarization. In accord with the theoretical perspectives advanced in the introductory chapter and elsewhere in this book, socioeconomic and political polarization, and the lack of an adequate level of economic prosperity, are detrimental to prospects for consolidation, particularly in cases where consolidation proceeds primarily along the lines of elite convergence.[3] These first two arguments hypothesize that, other things being equal, higher levels of socioeconomic development should facilitate successful democratic consolidation. A third kind of linkage between economics and democracy focuses on short-term economic performance and on support for political regimes. The hypothesis, in this case, is that regime support and survival are highly contingent on the performance of the economy (growth, stagnation, or recession).[4] The four Southern European cases provide us with considerable variation with regard to both the socioeconomic development and economic performance variables. Hence, our study of consolidation processes within the region makes it possible to test these hypotheses.

With regard to these variables, the Italian experience stands in stark contrast to those of the other three countries, largely because its transition and consolidation were initiated at a time of low socioeconomic development as well as during the major deprivation, devastation, and famine that resulted from the Second World War. Put otherwise, the Italian democratization experience was launched under material conditions that were less propitious for the eventual consolidation of democracy than were those in the other three countries. Conversely, these latter countries had undergone substantial socioeconomic modernization prior to the onset of their transitions, though in different ways and to differing degrees. At the opposite end of the continuum from the Italy of the 1940s was Spain in the 1970s, where socioeconomic transformation was the most impressive, especially when we bear in mind that Spain had previously been regarded as the European country with the deepest and most divisive socioeconomic cleavages. Portugal lagged considerably behind Spain, particularly in the early to mid-1970s. Its modernization had started later and proceeded at a slower pace than in the other countries. In addition, economic inequality was extreme, particularly in the latifundist regions of the south. The processes of socioeconomic change in Greece produce a mixed picture. To be sure, Greek rates of growth in the postwar period were among the highest in the world. Still, the impact of this change was sharply uneven, leaving the country with petty commodity and agrarian sectors among the largest in Europe (and certainly the largest in the European Union), dominated for the most part by labor-intensive practices and low technology. In the aggregate, per capita wealth and overall levels of socioeconomic modernization in the 1970s placed Greece behind Spain on this dimension.

In general, the democratic consolidation experiences of Southern Europe provide evidence confirming the linkage between socioeconomic development and democracy. Regime transition and consolidation processes that unfolded within relatively undeveloped societies were much more problematic and protracted than those which took place within relatively modern and affluent social contexts. It could be argued that to some extent the revolutionary dynamic which gripped Portugal in the early stages of its transition reflected that country's lower level of socioeconomic development and its late encounter with modernity. Patterns of political polarization clearly reflected socioeconomic cleavages, with landless agricultural workers in the latifundist regions of the south spearheading the sometimes turbulent political and economic revolution which characterized the early stages of its transition, while the minifundist majority in the north mobilized to block and eventually reverse the tide of the revolution. The existence of a hard-line, Marxist-Leninist communist party in Portugal and a relatively radical though less rigid communist party in early postwar Italy similarly contributed to significant polarization in these countries and adversely affected their prospects for a smooth consolidation of democracy. By contrast, the subsequent adoption by the Italian Communist Party of more moderate Eurocommunist positions following decades of economic development and increasing prosperity, and the espousal of similar views by the Communist Party in Spain, helped to attenuate class polarization in these countries during the 1970s and 1980s and substantively contributed to the consolidation of their democracies.[5]

These cases reveal that the level of socioeconomic development can affect the consolidation of democracy in another way as well. A low level of socioeconomic modernization can freeze or imprint certain premodern features into political institutions and behavioral patterns in the new democratic regime that may persist well into the future. Democracy and new political parties were established in Italy, for example, at a time when large sectors of its society retained many characteristics more typical of the nineteenth century than the twentieth. In the south, in particular, local-level clientelism (sometimes linked to high levels of corruption), in addition to the persistence of traditional familial and religious values and patterns of political deference, were grafted into the newly emerging party system. This contributed to the factionalism which characterized Italian party politics at least until its radical transformation in 1994. The governmental inefficacy that this factionalized structure engendered, moreover, coupled with growing revulsion over the extent to which corruption permeated the political class, contributed to the gradual erosion of the consensus undergirding the regime and eventually led to the crisis of 1992–94. Thus, while widespread support for democracy in Italy remained unshaken, and processes of political change unfolded through democratic institutions and in strict accord with democratic rules of the game, Italy's party-system "partial regime" became deconsolidated and was radically restructured. In addition, other partial regimes—including the structure of the state, important aspects of the electoral process, and the basic nature of executive-legislative relations—were increasingly challenged by politically significant groups. At the other end of the continuum stood Spain, whose social structures had become considerably more modern by the time democracy was reestablished. Thus, important features of party politics in Spain bore the imprint of what in established Western democracies has been described as "the new campaign politics," in which party organizations have weakened, election campaigns are heavily dependent on television, a personalization or "presidentialization" of party politics is widespread, and relationships between parties and politicized secondary organizations are weak, contentious, or lacking altogether. This notion of imprinting or freezing of new and old social and institutional characteristics into partisan politics in Southern Europe will be explored much more fully in Volume 2 of this series.

The strength of the relationship between economics and politics should not be overestimated, however, despite some scholars' inclination to subordinate political to economic factors in studies of regime transition. Contrary to the hypothesis positing a strong and direct causal link between economic performance and regime support and survival, analyses of Southern Europe presented in this book (as well as in a number of other published studies) do not support this claim. This negative finding holds true for the legitimacy of both the outgoing authoritarian regimes and the newly democratic regimes in Greece, Portugal, and Spain. All three countries, for example, experienced unprecedented economic growth during the late 1960s and early 1970s, and yet there is abundant behavioral and public-opinion-survey evidence that this increased prosperity did not lead Greeks, Portuguese, or Spaniards to support their respective authoritarian regimes. Quite the contrary: the modernization-theory perspective concerning the relationship between economic change and politics fits far better with observable data—as these societies and economies developed, ever larger segments of their populations found continued authoritarian rule increasingly objectionable, and proto-participatory attitudes became widespread. Stronger evidence of the weakness of the relationship between economic performance and political change can be seen in the fact that the periods of political transition and democratic consolidation in all three Southern European countries perfectly coincided with the severe economic crises of the second half of the 1970s and early 1980s, and yet all three became fully consolidated. Furthermore, support for Greece's democratic regime and negative assessments of the colonels' regime remain very high despite the continuing stagnation (and in some sectors decline) of the Greek economy. The same inverse relationship between economic performance and democratic consolidation is true of Uruguay—the only recently redemocratized Latin American country that has been fully consolidated—whose economy has undergone a dismal and protracted long-term decline. This is not to say that there is no significant relationship between economic performance and consolidation processes. There is no doubt that in regions such as Eastern Europe, where economic problems are much more severe than they were in Southern Europe, economic and political change are much more tightly linked. These findings, however, do lead us to challenge simple assertions that successful economic performance, per se, is the bringer of democratic consolidation.

Indeed, an excessive emphasis by governing elites on economic factors over politics can be detrimental to prospects for successful democratic consolidation, insofar as efforts to address serious economic problems by implementing radical economic reforms may, at least over the short term, polarize and destabilize a society at a critical stage of the democratization process. This is especially likely when such restructuring occurs in settings characterized by lower and uneven levels of socioeconomic development. Latin America and especially Eastern Europe serve as good empirical exemplars of these observations. In several Latin American countries, deep socioeconomic cleavages have been exacerbated by economic stabilization plans. To a much greater degree, the simultaneity of the transition to democratic politics and attempts to establish some variant of a market economy in Eastern Europe has contributed to considerable social destabilization and political fragmentation. This has greatly overburdened the transition process, severely complicated the tasks facing decision makers, and significantly delayed and impeded democratic consolidation. In some cases (e.g., Russia), the resulting polarization has been so severe as to raise the specter of retrogression to some less democratic form of politics.

In sharp contrast to the East European and Latin American democratization experiences to date, developments in Southern Europe underscore the advantages deriving from the ability to decouple political from economic restructuring and to postpone the disruptive processes of economic reform until after the consolidation of democracy.[6] By that later time, the regime will probably have acquired a substantial reservoir of legitimacy and support, and democratic norms should have been sufficiently disseminated and internalized as to effectively habituate elites and masses alike to behavior supportive of democracy. These characteristics can contribute decisively to a democratic regime's ability to persist and thrive in the face of the stresses and strains that invariably accompany economic restructuring. The political elites managing the regime transition and consolidation processes in Greece, Portugal, and Spain consciously and deliberately pursued this strategy. Economic restructuring, which entailed drastic increases in unemployment resulting from the closure or privatization of formerly subsidized parastate firms, and the opening up of domestic markets to international competition (policy reforms that will be more extensively surveyed in Volumes 3 and 4 of this series) were postponed until the mid-1980s. By postponing painful economic reforms until after their democratic regimes had been consolidated, governing elites in Southern Europe successfully eschewed the perils of the polarization that would have resulted from attempting economic restructuring at the time of regime change.

To be sure, the possibility of postponing economic reform may not be entirely at the discretion of domestic political elites. When a political regime transition occurs at a time of complete collapse of the economic system, elites may have no alternative but to initiate a radical restructuring of the economy. In this respect, these three Southern European countries found themselves in relatively advantageous circumstances. They were able to delay economic reform, in great part because their economic conditions at the time of regime change were not as dire as those of the East European systems. In addition, unlike most Latin American countries, they were not heavily dependent on international loans. Hence, a debt crisis did not occur simultaneously with the onset of political transition, leading to the forced imposition of austerity programs by international banking institutions. The negative consequences of economic restructuring in Southern Europe were rendered less painful by the profound socioeconomic change which had transformed these countries in the preceding decades and by the existence of a predominantly market economy and a growing, though underdeveloped and underfunded, welfare state—all of which were inherited from the preceding authoritarian regime. Thus, the implications of this relationship between economic and political change for elites currently leading democratization processes are mixed. While we can state that it is desirable to avoid overloading the agenda of political change with potentially disruptive economic reforms, not all governing elites in new democracies are likely to find themselves in a position to postpone economic changes until after democratic consolidation has been completed.

Democratization Trajectories and Democratic Consolidation

As indicated in the Preface and Introduction to this volume, we regard the notion of trajectories as a convenient heuristic device for understanding the differing ways in which transition and consolidation processes unfold. An attentiveness to differences among transition trajectories renders more readily intelligible the subtle interplay and shifting balance between freedom and constraint which, ultimately, constitutes the single most important characteristic of the democratization process. At the same time, it deepens our understanding of the way in which the move from transition to consolidation entails the gradual assertion of constraint and the commensurate loss of freedom of maneuver for the actors involved in these processes.

One determinant of the course of a regime's transition and consolidation trajectory is the behavior of political elites. As stated repeatedly in this volume, transitions represent the one facet of the overall democratization process in which the constraints of the past become most attenuated (though by no means eliminated) and when the course of future developments is most susceptible to intervention by political elites. Indeed, in general it could be said that the less constrained a country's politics, the broader the scope for innovation, for crafting and steering the democratization process in novel directions designed to enhance the chance of a successful consolidation. This increased malleability, however, is a double-edged sword. If not steered in the right direction(s), the greater freedom of movement afforded politics during transition may also result in elite options and decisions which can adversely affect the consolidation trajectory in a given society, possibly even jeopardizing consolidation itself. The Italian experience following the First World War, analyzed by Sidney Tarrow in this volume, may well fall into this category. To a certain extent, so may the initial phase (1974–75) of the Portuguese transition.

There are, however, structural determinants of a regime's prospects for democratic consolidation that are not at all under the control of elites. One of these, as we have seen, is the level of a country's socioeconomic development. Others are previous experiences with democracy, the legacy of the nondemocratic predecessor regime, the particular transition trajectory, and the constellation of partial regimes involved. The initial context within which regime change unfolds, as well as the subsequent course of events, are significantly affected by different legacies. The particular way in which these legacies are brought together, their sequence, overlap, and, more generally, interaction give each trajectory its distinct character and dynamic and account for similarities or variations in different consolidation and, more broadly, democratization stories.

The Historical Legacy

The character of the regime which preceded the nondemocratic political system whose demise triggered the transition to democracy can significantly affect the consolidation process. How democratic, if at all, was that regime? How inclusive or exclusive were its rules governing political participation? How far in the past, relative to the incipient democratic regime, was it situated? What is the thrust and quality of the political learning embedded by that experience in the historical memories of the elites and ordinary citizens called upon to participate in the new democratic game? How positive, neutral, or negative for the democratic experiment is that learning likely to be? The answers to these questions will have a significant, although perhaps distant and diffuse, bearing on the way in which the legacy of the past will influence the trajectory traveled by a particular society on its way to democratic consolidation.

All four Southern European countries established parliamentary institutions during the middle to late nineteenth century and, with the exception of Portugal, experimented with different forms of democratic politics in the first decades of the twentieth century. Outside of certain urban areas, however, their "democracies" were often limited, clientelistic, and segmented. The result was that in all cases the democratic experiments foundered on the hurdles thrown up by late socioeconomic development and by conjunctural factors such as the First World War and its aftermath, the appearance of fascism and Marxism-Leninism as ideologies and models for emulation, and by economic depressions. Given the long duration of the ensuing nondemocratic regimes (more the case in Spain and Portugal than in Italy and Greece), the extent to which the democratic learning generated by this past experience would serve as an agent of democratic socialization was limited: with the high levels of demographic turnover throughout the following decades, such learning would affect only a small segment of the mass population and the elites who eventually became involved in the democratization process in these countries. The experiences derived from this more distant past were, nevertheless, important in one respect: they imparted to both masses and elites powerful historical memories that taught particularly the mistakes and negative outcomes that should be avoided.

The Nondemocratic Predecessor Regime

The empirical findings of several chapters in this volume clearly indicate that the nature of the nondemocratic predecessor regime had a major and immediate bearing on the character of the democratic transition and, thus, on the consolidation trajectory issuing from it. The impact on subsequent transition and consolidation processes of the authoritarian regimes in Greece, Portugal, and Spain, and Mussolini's hybrid nondemocratic regime (mixing authoritarianism with certain totalitarian elements) varied in several ways. First, there were important consequences of the greatly differing durations of these nondemocratic systems. Here the Greek and Portuguese experiences, which lasted seven years and nearly five decades, respectively, stand at opposite ends of the spectrum. The length of their durations had significant implications for a variety of transition-relevant factors, such as continuity versus discontinuity in the political class, and political learning at both the elite and mass levels.

A second variable attribute of the predecessor regime concerns the extent to which the nondemocratic experience contributed to the emergence of what, in this volume, Morlino and José Ramón Montero term "negative legitimation" of democratic politics, namely, the spawning of negative attitudes towards nondemocratic politics among the masses in each country and a preference for democracy as the only viable organizational principle of political life. The harshness of the predecessor regime and, more generally, the lingering memories associated with it are two of the factors capable of shaping such a negative legitimacy for democratic politics.

Third, the degree of pluralism observable in the predecessor regime is of critical importance for democratic consolidation. As Linz, Stepan, and Gunther argue in this volume, the higher degree of pluralism tolerated and even fostered by authoritarian regimes (as compared with posttotalitarian and sultanistic systems) constitutes a positive legacy of critical importance for the success of consolidation. The significant degree of economic and social pluralism engendered by the advent of socioeconomic modernity in Spain and the limited but nonresponsible political pluralism tolerated by the Franco regime in the last two decades of its existence go a long way in explaining the smoothness of the consolidation process in Spain. In particular, they facilitated the reemergence of political parties whose leaders were the key protagonists in the politics of consensus. To a lesser extent, the same holds true for authoritarian Greece and Portugal, and even for fascist Italy, where the institutional independence of the army, the monarchy, and the church vis-à-vis the regime effectively ensured the survival of pluralist structures in that country. The authoritarian legacy of the Southern European countries contrasts sharply with the totalitarian and posttotalitarian experiences in Eastern Europe and the former Soviet

Union and with the sultanistic legacies to be found in Ceausescu's Romania and certain Central American and Caribbean countries currently experimenting with democratization. In all these cases, the relative absence of pluralism or (in other words) the weakness of civil society severely complicates the chances for successful consolidation.

The character of the ruling elites and elite coalitions in the outgoing authoritarian regime constitutes a fourth factor affecting the consolidation trajectories traveled by democratizing countries. Based on their respective analyses of Latin American and Southern European democratic transitions and consolidations, Felipe Agüero and Linz, Stepan, and Gunther point to the degree of military penetration in a given regime as an important determinant of the trajectory to be traveled by the consolidation process in that country. The more the military is entrenched in the authoritarian regime, the greater the probability that the transition and consolidation trajectories in that country will be problematic. Brazil, where the military thoroughly penetrated most institutional loci of power, and Spain, whose overwhelmingly but not completely civilianized character was increasingly evident in the later years of Franco's rule, represent the clearest examples of regimes at either end of this continuum. Portugal, where the military did not belong to the power elite of the regime, constitutes a notable exception unless we regard it as having undergone two transitions, one from the conservative and civilian Salazar-Caetano regime, the other from the revolutionary military governments of 1974–75.

These same authors further argue that the hierarchical versus nonhierarchical nature of the military presence within the predecessor nondemocratic regime had a marked influence on the consolidation trajectory traveled in a given country. An authoritarian regime ruled by a nonhierarchical military elite is more easily displaced from power, with far fewer complications for the consolidation process. Conversely, the problems of extricating the military from politics and eliminating its reserved powers are much more severe if the military hierarchy played dominant roles in the predecessor regime.

The degree of unity or divisiveness of a predecessor regime's ruling elite can also affect the nature of the democratic transition and the prospects for consolidation. As the Spanish experience demonstrates, the presence within this elite of reformers willing to collaborate with moderate members of the opposition forces greatly enhanced the likelihood for a successful transition and consolidation. The Italian case can be said to be similar in its origins but to have been subsequently derailed by the impact of the Cold War on Italian politics.

Finally, the mode of the authoritarian regime's expiration (which is, in turn, linked to the mode and degree of its institutionalization) constitutes an additional factor immediately affecting the trajectory to be followed by democratic consolidation in a given country. As the Portuguese experience demonstrates, expiration that occurs as a result of a nondemocratic regime's abrupt collapse is likely to impart a turbulent, if not radical, quality to the democratization process and to adversely affect the chances for a smooth consolidation by protracting its duration and adding a further dimension of uncertainty to it. By contrast, the Spanish case points to the benefits to be derived from a slow and gradual expiration of the nondemocratic regime, which, being free of convulsive moments, can inject a dimension of moderation into the democratization process and positively influence the prospects for consolidation. Moreover, a gradual transition allows the full array of political forces to organize and participate on an equal basis in the founding election of the new democracy. Subsequently, politics and policy making are likely to be characterized by contestation on an equal playing field and by relatively incremental policy change supported by (at least) a majority and perhaps by a consensus of public opinion. In contrast, abrupt regime termination almost invariably privileges those political forces that had organized and been active in clandestine opposition to the nondemocratic regime; hence, previously disorganized political options will be excluded from power, and the political center of gravity of the governing elite will be temporarily and artificially skewed to one side or the other. Under these circumstances, radical policy change not endorsed by a majority of the general public is a likely outcome. This factor clearly distinguishes the Spanish transition from that of Portugal. Decision making in Spain during the transition involved substantial interparty dialogue that spanned the political spectrum and contributed decisively to the development of a broad-based consensus that was the hallmark of its transition, and which, in turn, greatly facilitated the consolidation of the new regime. The Portuguese transition and consolidation processes, in contrast, were greatly complicated and protracted by efforts to "undo the excesses of the revolution" carried out by the first post-Caetano governments.

The Character of the Transition

The mode of expiration of a nondemocratic regime is, thus, intimately and sequentially linked to the type of democratic transition which it helps bring about. This is especially true in the case of gradual and uneventful expiration in which the elites presiding over the transfer of power have to collaborate with their democratic opponents in order to launch the transition. The Spanish experience, aptly captured by the phrase "*reforma pactada–ruptura pactada*," is the *locus classicus* for this pattern of peaceful and evolutionary change, which contrasts sharply with the discontinuous and radical nature of the Portuguese transition, in which elite collaboration was nonexistent and mass mobilization played a central role in the initial stages of democratization.

Elites versus Masses

To date, the literature on democratic transition and consolidation has focused overwhelmingly on the role of elites. This is largely a reflection of empirical reality and helps underscore the fact that the more successful cases of democratization, so far, have been characterized by a combination of elite preponderance and relative mass quiescence. As the Spanish case illustrates, a strategic demobilization of the masses can be particularly important during those phases of democratization characterized predominantly by elite negotiations: such demobilization reduces the prospects of political polarization resulting from clashes in the streets and contributes to the autonomy of elites, thus enabling them to make the concessions that are essential for consensual resolution of potentially divisive conflicts. Conversely, the major mobilization of the masses associated with the Portuguese transition greatly complicated and delayed that country's consolidation process.

However accurate this initial assessment, it needs to be qualified. As Tarrow points out in his contribution to this volume, the role played by the masses in a given transition can affect the consolidation process in several ways. First, it establishes parameters within which elites can operate. This may take the form of mass action which expands the space and scope of elite action, pushing the elites in directions they may not otherwise have opted to explore. Conversely, as the events of summer 1975 in central and northern Portugal amply demonstrated, mass mobilization can also act as an effective barrier to unpopular elite policies and decisively affect the course of a transition and consolidation trajectory. Second, mass action or the threat of mass mobilization interacts with elite strategies and behavior in important ways. While the key decisions that determine the course of a particular transition may be made through elite negotiations, the resources that elites can command have an important bearing on their prospects for success in bargaining. In the Spanish case, for example, Adolfo Suárez was greatly aided in his efforts to neutralize the right-wing bunker by pointing to the possibility of mass-level unrest and turmoil as the alternative to his proposed reforms. Thus, credible threats of mass action can facilitate the making of elite agreements. A third way in which mass behavior during the transition can affect the consolidation process relates to the common pattern of mass demobilization which often occurs once transition processes have been set in motion. Tarrow's argument in this regard is that mass quiescence during critical moments of the transition may result in what could be termed "missed opportunities" for elite action which could expand the scope of democratic space created by the dynamic of regime change. Mass-level demobilization may also carry over into the posttransition phase in ways that may be detrimental to the quality of democracy, particularly insofar as it culminates in low levels of political participation and secondary-group organization.

Pacts

The importance of pacts in transition and consolidation processes has been widely commented upon in the literature on democratization. By their very nature, pacts are conducive to the generation of compromise and consensus, which privilege positive-sum rather than zero-sum strategies and perspectives and which contribute to the emergence of a climate of moderation that greatly enhances the prospects for successful democratic consolidation. Conversely, the absence of pacts may act as an impediment to the emergence of such a climate of moderation and compromise and as an indicator of a potentially more contested and problematic consolidation. The Portuguese, Spanish, and Uruguayan experiences accord with these observations. The smooth character of the Spanish consolidation has been attributed by many observers in great part to the capacity of the Spanish elites to negotiate important and binding agreements which enhanced the climate of trust, consensus, and moderation that became the salient features of that country's democratization process. In Uruguay, the Naval Club Accord, concluded in mid-1984 between the military and the civilian opposition, served as the centerpiece for a consolidation strategy steeped in the *reforma pactada* logic which prevailed in Spain. Conversely, the absence of pacts in the early stages of the Portuguese transition was the inevitable by-product of the radical and revolutionary turn assumed by events in that country and a reflection of the fact that democratization was being attempted through a strategy of *ruptura* rather than conciliation. The result was a consolidation trajectory qualitatively different from those which prevailed in the other countries; it was marked by uncertainty, turbulence, confrontation, and conflict centering on competing principles of legitimation about the organization of politics, economy, and society in that country.

At the same time, the significance of pacts and their impact on the chances for consolidation should not be overestimated. As the Greek case demonstrates, pacts are not a requisite for successful consolidation. To be sure, the threat of war, which constitutes an idiosyncratic characteristic of the Greek transition, effectively acted as a powerful source of restraint on elites and masses alike and helped ensure the swift and uneventful completion of the transition. Over the longer-run, however, when the immediate threat of war had been drastically reduced, if not eliminated, Greek elites demonstrated significant restraint in substantive policy matters, thereby enabling the consolidation process to proceed smoothly to its conclusion.

Similarly, the frequency, scope, and sequence of pacts, as well as their political consequences, can vary from case to case. In Latin America, pacts negotiated with the outgoing military have tended to form an integral part of the consolidation process. Even in Argentina, where pacts with the military were avoided in the transition after the defeat in war of the old regime, civilian elites had to renegotiate a number of important conditions with the military at a later point—a kind of postponed pact. The Spanish and Greek experiences, however, point in the opposite direction. In the former, given the largely civilianized nature of the late Franco regime, the military did not become party to any negotiations concerning the direction of democratic transition or consolidation. In Greece, the outgoing military sought to obtain such an agreement but was unequivocally rebuffed by the civilian opposition and, given its own weak power position because of the Cyprus crisis which it had brought about, chose not to contest the situation. Thus, as the chapters by Agüero and Linz, Stepan, and Gunther strongly argue, it would appear that the presence or absence of transition or consolidation pacts involving the military is largely a function of the character of the outgoing nondemocratic regime and, specifically, of the degree of military penetration in it.

Some attention has also been paid to the sequential ordering of pacts. Observations drawn primarily from Latin American transition and consolidation experiences point to a pattern of distinct military, political, and socioeconomic pacts that are more or less sequentially linked and which affect the character of the consolidation. The Southern European cases, however, do not provide confirmation of this. As just indicated, in Spain, Greece, and Italy, there were no military pacts. In Portugal, the abrupt collapse and dismantling of the Salazar-Caetano regime precluded pacts. The only pacts involving the military were a later series of partial agreements designed to facilitate the extrication of the revolutionary military government from politics. Neither, with the partial and temporary exception of the Moncloa Pacts in Spain, is it easy to argue that socioeconomic agreements played an important role in defining the Southern European consolidation trajectories. Rather, as was pointed out earlier, such matters tended to be consciously postponed until after the critical political agreements needed to ensure consolidation had been concluded.

One parsimonious interpretation of the substantial variations from one case to another in the sequencing of pacts is that agreements of this kind should appear in the order of the magnitude of the problems confronted in the transition. Seen in the light of the Latin American experiences and the somewhat different Portuguese case, the insistence on according primacy to military pacts appears quite justified, given the central involvement of the military in the democratic transitions of these countries. A second consideration regarding the sequencing of pacts reflects the view that the temporally separate handling of intractable issues is likely to lighten the pressures which the transition generates for elites and masses alike and, thus, to facilitate consolidation. Again, the severity of the problems confronting a democratizing country may be the critical variable. As the East European cases clearly demonstrate, the need to confront simultaneously political problems associated with the legacies of posttotalitarian regimes and a grave socioeconomic situation linked to the collapse of centrally controlled economic systems has severely complicated the democratic transitions in these countries and is undoubtedly leaving its deep imprint on their consolidation trajectories. Conversely, the intractability of the military problem as well as of the foreign debt situation in Latin America point to the wisdom of adopting a sequential logic in the negotiation of pacts as key aspects of the transition and consolidation in the region.

Finally, pacts are sometimes seen as involving a potential paradox distinguishing their short-term impact from their longer-term impact on consolidation. It is often argued that pacts facilitate transitions and the early stages of consolidation by helping to eliminate or mute division over a number of contested issue areas. It is also sometimes argued, however, that pacts usually include exclusionary elements, sometimes placing certain policy areas off-limits for the normal give and take of political contestation, sometimes privileging one sector of society or set of interests at the expense of others. According to this argument, pacts that may have contributed to what we refer to as the "sufficient" consolidation of a new democracy may, over time, preclude the effective rooting or deepening of democracy. In this case, the result may be a democracy which, though consolidated, will remain mired in its own contradictions and, hence, become frozen.[7]

Once again, the Southern European experience does not seem to bear out this hypothesis, which appears to reflect more accurately the

Latin American situation and the intractable problems associated with the deep political and, especially, socioeconomic divisions in that region. Spanish democracy, whose transition and consolidation are widely regarded as the quintessential case of a pacted process, has shown no signs of becoming frozen. Indeed, the extensive policy reforms which the governing Socialists (PSOE) undertook during the 1980s, in such sensitive areas as civil-military relations and especially in economic restructuring, without perceptible negative consequences for the country's democratic structures, seem to constitute evidence of the vigor, resilience, and modernity of Spanish democracy rather than of its being frozen. The boldness of these economic policy reforms is even more striking when one bears in mind that these changes were effected under conditions of severe unemployment, which ranged from 15 percent to 21 percent throughout this period. Several of the cases examined in this book also call into question Adam Przeworski's statement that pacts invariably give rise to situations where extrication of the military from politics will delay and complicate consolidation processes.[8] This assessment is not consistent with the cases of Spain and Uruguay, whose pacts did not give rise to extrication crises. Neither does it fit with the case of Portugal, whose consolidation and transition processes were both greatly complicated and delayed by problems of military extrication, even though the early stages of its transition were not guided by pacts.

Instauration versus Restoration

The character of a consolidation can also be influenced by the extent to which the establishment of a democratic regime represents a case of instauration, as compared with restoration of democratic politics in a given country. Here, the critical factor is the duration of the predecessor nondemocratic regime and its impact on political learning in both elites and masses. Because of the nearly half-century-long duration of the Salazar-Caetano regime in Portugal, the elites who were called upon to manage the transition and to lead the country towards democracy had no prior experience with the rules, norms, and practices of democratic politics. Indeed, the weakness of the civilian political class is reflected in the fact that the early stages of the transition were dominated by military officers. The same inexperience held true of the general public, which constituted the first truly mass electorate in Portuguese history. Discontinuity and a lack of experience with democratic politics were also characteristic of Spanish and Italian elites. Though the duration of the nondemocratic regime in these countries was somewhat or significantly shorter than that of the Portuguese regime (thirty-six years for Spain, twenty-one for Italy), the net result in all three was a sharp discontinuity with respect to democratic learning, practices, and culture at both the elite and the mass levels. By and large, the only impact of previous democratic interludes was through historical memories. In this sense, the Greek case is quite different. The mass electorate and elites who became involved in the transition to democracy in 1974 after the seven-year-long colonels' regime had direct personal memories and experiences with the democratic rules of the game. There was also considerable continuity of the Greek political elite, which sharply distinguished the case of Greece from those of Italy, Portugal, and Spain.

One factor accounting for the swift nature of the Greek transition and consolidation is that poignant memories of the excesses and pathologies of the *democradura* that had prevailed in Greece after the civil war of 1946–49 greatly increased the determination of elites and masses alike to ensure the success of full political democracy. In this sense, however, Greece was not greatly different from Spain: even though relatively few Spaniards had direct personal experience with the collapse of the Second Republic and with the civil war, these traumatic events (recounted in decades of heavy-handed Franquist propaganda) were burned indelibly into the collective historical memories of both masses and elites, especially the latter, and served to constrain partisan clashes and political behavior in general during crucial phases of the transition and consolidation.

Stateness

To the extent that the notion of democracy presupposes the existence of a constituted state, a fundamental challenge to the legitimacy and integrity of the state, which the crisis of stateness represents, can have a major negative impact on the democratization process and greatly complicate transition and consolidation. While, with the partial exception of Spain, the new Southern European and Latin American democracies have been spared this problem, the crisis of stateness constitutes a central and severe complication to democratization in Estonia and other parts of the former Soviet Union, Yugoslavia, and Czechoslovakia. Though much more attenuated, similar challenges loom close to the surface in Albania, Romania, and even Hungary. In all these cases, the crisis of stateness has been greatly exacerbated by elite decisions and options intended to make use of the increased room for political action afforded by the transition. Their impact on the chances for democratic consolidation in these countries has clearly been detrimental.

Estonia and Spain constitute instructive contrasting cases. In the former, the decision by that country's ultranationalist authorities to define Estonian citizenship in such restrictive terms as to exclude from it a large Russian-speaking minority has led that group to openly push for autonomy and to contest the legitimacy of the state. The involvement of the Russian state in this matter, inserting another divisive twist to this story, further undermines the prospects for a successful consolidation of democracy in Estonia. Conversely, the willingness and ability of the Spanish elite to handle the explosive issue of Euskadi and Catalonia through the adoption of a policy of comprehensive decentralization and the construction of the Estado de las Autonomías constitutes a good example of how the enhanced freedom for political action inherent in democratic transitions can be constructively used to defuse a potentially major stateness crisis. Also important is the impact of political elites on the definition of national identities and, in turn, on acknowledgment or rejection of the legitimacy of the state. In Spain, the dominant regional elites sought, in large part successfully, to forge multiple national and regional identities (e.g., in which most inhabitants of Catalonia define themselves as both Catalan *and* Spanish), which are compatible with the continued legitimacy and stability of the multinational Spanish state. Conversely, political elites in the former states of Yugoslavia redefined national identities in ever more exclusionary and therefore potentially conflictual terms as the transition progressed, which culminated in not only the disappearance of democracy but the outbreak of horrific ethnic warfare.

International Factors

Finally, as Geoffrey Pridham argued in this volume, international factors certainly also have an impact, albeit more indirect, on consolidation trajectories. Once again, particular circumstances surrounding each individual Southern European case largely determined the extent of that impact. There is little doubt that the Italian transition and consolidation were adversely affected by the Cold War. Conversely, the Greek, Spanish, and Portuguese consolidation trajectories were the clear beneficiaries of an international and, especially, regional climate more propitious to democratic politics. The strong support for democracy exhibited by such organizations as the European Community and the Council of Europe reinforced new democratic institutions and behavioral norms in each of these countries. The positive, though indirect, impact of the regional international factor on democratization in Southern Europe stands in contrast to the ambivalent and oscillating historical record of the United States with respect to democratization in Latin America. Finally, Eastern Europe provides a striking example of a case in which international factors had a clear and direct impact on democratization. And though this was more immediately related to the launching of the transition, it is also the case that the consolidation trajectories of these societies have been strongly influenced by the collapse of the nondemocratic regimes, which the swiftness of Soviet withdrawal brought about.

In a more diffuse way, the international environment can also affect consolidation through its impact on mass attitudes and behavior. In this respect, tourists and workers returning from Western and Northern Europe can act as carriers of values and behavioral patterns associated with successful democracies. Given the importance of tourism and of the return of emigrant workers for the societies of the New Southern Europe, the significance of these factors, especially because they so directly pertain to the mass level, should not be underestimated. In a sense, precisely because of their diffuse nature, these influences are likely to penetrate behavioral patterns osmotically and to profoundly affect these countries' democratic cultures.

Partial Regimes and Democratic Consolidation

The significance of partial regimes, as defined by Philippe Schmitter in this volume, lies in their dual link to democratic consolidation. Some partial regimes can directly affect the process of democratic consolidation itself. From the standpoint of regime consolidation, the most important are those encompassing the central institutions of representative government and the party system. But the consolidation of a broader array of partial regimes (relating, for example, to interest groups and patterns of interest intermediation or to the management of the territorial order) is, in itself, important insofar as the configurations assumed by various partial regimes have a marked impact on the type of democracy which emerges in each country.

The partial regime made up of a democracy's central representative and decision-making institutions is one which has a direct impact on the process of regime consolidation. As Gianfranco Pasquino argues in this volume, the nature of executive-legislative relations—more specifically, the dispersion or concentration of power in the executive—during consolidation has an important bearing on the prospects for success of that process. Specifically, a stable and more authoritative executive is more conducive to the internalization and institutionalization of rules and practices established during the transition (a key aspect of consolidation) than is a weak, fragmented, or indecisive government. But Pasquino also points out that successfully meeting the challenges associated with different phases of the democratization process may require different patterns of executive-legislative interactions. As he states, "what is good for the transition to a new democratic regime may not be good for consolidation, and what makes a positive contribution to the consolidation process may be disadvantageous in some respects over the long term." Specifically, he points out that open and consultative styles of executive-legislative relations are beneficial during the transition, insofar as they can increase the access of a wide variety of groups to the decision-making process and encourage their involvement in the shaping of new political and institutional structures. Conversely, from the standpoint of regime consolidation, the internalization of behavioral norms and the building up of confidence in new institutions can be facilitated by higher levels of executive stability and decisiveness. Finally, once consolidation has been achieved, some relaxation of party discipline and some curtailment of executive powers might be salutary for the functioning and adaptability of the regime.

In dealing with partial regimes, however, we should be aware that the causal arrows linking them with the transition and consolidation processes point in both directions. We have argued that the nature of executive-legislative relations affects transition and consolidation processes, but it is also clear that the transition and consolidation trajectory followed by a particular country can greatly influence key government and state institutions that emerge in a new democracy. The institutionalization of a constitutional monarchy in Spain and a presidential form of government in Greece, for example, were not historical inheritances or inevitabilities; they were the direct products of the regime-transformation trajectories followed by these two countries. (This theme is elaborated upon more fully in a chapter by Thomas Bruneau, Nikiforos Diamandouros, Richard Gunther, and Arend Lijphart in Volume 2 of this series.)

The partial regime encompassing parties and party systems can also have a major impact on democratic consolidation. As Morlino argues, the structuration of the Italian party system contributed decisively to democratic consolidation in that country in the late 1970s. Similarly, parties played a major role in the legitimation of democracy in Greece, Spain, and Portugal. Morlino's examination of the Spanish party system makes a further point that is of considerable theoretical significance: the consolidation of a party system is not a necessary condition for the consolidation of democracy. A high level of party-system instability and a low level of organizational development by parties characterized the same period of time when Spanish democracy was being decisively consolidated. However, if the key institutions of a democracy have not secured a sufficient level of legitimacy, a stabilized party system and well-developed party organizations can play a crucial role in consolidating democracy: they can stabilize and structure interactions among actors and groups in society, channeling that behavior into democratic institutionalized arenas with the capacity to contain conflict, and habituating individuals and groups into conformity with democratic rules of the game. This process unfolded in Italy, culminating in Italian democracy's consolidation by the late 1970s and early 1980s. Democracy in Italy remains strong and resilient even in the face of the collapse and realignment of its party system and the restructuring of key governmental institutions.

Finally, Schmitter concludes, interest groups did not play leading or central roles in the transition and consolidation processes of any of these four Southern European countries. Indeed, in this phase of the democratization process, interest groups played a rather secondary role compared to parties. On the other hand, the consolidation of the partial regime of interest intermediation is likely to prove highly relevant to the distribution of benefits, to policy-making processes and the performance of government institutions, and to levels of citizen satisfaction with their respective democracies. In short, it affects the quality of democracy issuing from a consolidation trajectory.

Once a new democratic regime has become consolidated, it enters a stage that we refer to as democratic persistence. At this point, entirely new theoretical and practical concerns move to center stage, as the imperatives of transition and consolidation fade into the background of social inquiry. The nature of these concerns will depend upon the developmental trajectory followed by the regime over the years or decades after consolidation, whether it be a continuation of democratic persistence, deconsolidation and breakdown, or deconsolidation and democratic reequilibration.

Two of these alternative paths emerge as logical outgrowths of the fact that formerly consolidated regimes may become deconsolidated over time, as a result of challenges that undermine their capacity for crisis management and usher in a period of destabilization of the regime's core institutions and behavioral norms. It should be stressed that these two scenarios involve processes that are conceptually distinct from that of democratic consolidation. As Linz has observed, deconsolidation processes cannot properly be regarded as merely consolidation in reverse; entirely different sets of actors and causal processes may be central to breakdown or reequilibration scenarios, requiring explanatory hypotheses that are qualitatively different from those employed in this volume.[9]

Once a regime has entered into a process of deconsolidation, one possible outcome is that its defenders will prove unable to prevent its demise. This may result in high levels of political conflict, followed by the instauration of a nondemocratic regime, whether of the authoritarian, sultanistic, or totalitarian variety. It should be noted that consolidated democracies have broken down in this manner only very rarely: the collapse of the Chilean and Uruguayan democracies in 1973 are the only examples that come to mind of an authoritarian takeover terminating a regime that was both democratic and consolidated. Much more numerous are cases of consolidated limited democracies (such as those of Southern Europe in the late nineteenth and early twentieth centuries) or unconsolidated democracies (such as those in several Latin American and East European countries) that undergo such breakdowns and become captive of a seemingly inescapable pendular movement involving variants of democracy and authoritarianism. Indeed, the remarkable stability of consolidated democracies attests to the theoretical and practical importance of the processes that have been analyzed in this volume.

In the second alternative, the democratic forces within the regime will somehow manage to regain their balance and fashion new institutional arrangements capable of giving the regime a new lease on life. In effect, a different regime within the same democratic genus will emerge. The replacement of the French Fourth Republic by the Fifth Republic in 1958 is a notable example of regime change and reequilibration.

The Italian case, in our view, is one that is best understood as one of reequilibration: the Italian party system is in the process of being reconfigured, and the nature of executive-legislative relations is undergoing an as yet unfinished process of reform. The other three cases, Greece, Portugal, and Spain, are examples of consolidation and continuing democratic persistence. Put otherwise, the distinguishing feature of the New Southern Europe, as opposed to the old, is that in all four countries challenges to particular institutional arrangements have, to date, been successfully met within a fully democratic context.

The stage of democratic persistence shifts our analytical focus away from the immediate requisites of consolidation to the longer-term dimensions of the democratization process. These include the structure and dynamics of political institutions and mass-level behavior, the transformation and performance of economic institutions, the evolution of public policy outputs and the role of the state, and profound changes in the cultures and patterns of social relations in these newly democratized societies. In short, democratic persistence is intimately linked with the nature and quality of a democratic regime. The ensuing volumes in this series will systematically address these issues within the context of the New Southern Europe.

Notes

Preface

1. See Samuel P. Huntington, *The Third Wave: Democratization in the Late Twentieth Century* (Norman: University of Oklahoma Press, 1991).

2. See Juan J. Linz, *The Breakdown of Democratic Regimes* [*BDR*]: *Crisis, Breakdown, and Reequilibration* (Baltimore: Johns Hopkins University Press, 1978) (one of four volumes bearing different subtitles, also collected in a single volume, *The Breakdown of Democratic Regimes,* edited by Juan J. Linz and Alfred Stepan).

3. Guillermo O'Donnell, Philippe C. Schmitter, and Laurence Whitehead, eds., *Transitions from Authoritarian Rule: Prospects for Democracy* (Baltimore: Johns Hopkins University Press, 1986; also published in four separate volumes bearing the same title [*TAR*] but individual topical subtitles). A forerunner to these studies which deserves mention is Dankwart Rustow, "Transitions to Democracy: Toward a Dynamic Model," *Comparative Politics* 2, 1970, pp. 337–63.

4. See John Higley and Richard Gunther, eds., *Elites and Democratic Consolidation in Latin America and Southern Europe* (New York: Cambridge University Press, 1992); Ulrike Liebert and Maurizio Cotta, eds., *Parliament and Democratic Consolidation in Southern Europe: Greece, Italy, Portugal, Spain, and Turkey* (London: Pinter, 1990); and Geoffrey Pridham, ed., *Securing Democracy: Political Parties and Democratic Consolidation in Southern Europe* (London: Routledge, 1990). For more general comparative studies focusing on the prospects for democratic consolidation in Latin America, see Enrique A. Baloyra, ed., *Comparing New Democracies: Transition and Consolidation in Mediterranean Europe and the Southern Cone* (Boulder: Westview, 1987); and Scott Mainwaring, Guillermo O'Donnell, and J. Samuel Valenzuela, eds., *Issues in Democratic Consolidation: The New South American Democracies in Comparative Perspective* (Notre Dame, Ind.: University of Notre Dame Press, 1992).

5. For example, Fernando Rodrigo, *El camino hacia la democracia: Militares y política en la transición española* (doctoral diss., Universidad Complutense de Madrid, 1989); Felipe Agüero, *The Assertion of Civilian Supremacy in Post-Authoritarian Contexts: Spain in Comparative Perspective* (Ph.D. diss., Duke Univer-

sity, 1991; forthcoming, as *Soldiers, Civilians, and Democracy,* from Johns Hopkins University Press); Thanos Veremis, "The Military," in Kevin Featherstone and Dimitrios K. Katsoudas, eds., *Political Change in Greece before and after the Colonels* (New York: St. Martin's, 1987); Thomas C. Bruneau and Alex Macleod, *Politics in Contemporary Portugal: Parties and the Consolidation of Democracy* (Boulder: Lynne Rienner, 1986); and Maria Carrilho, *Forças armadas e mudança política em Portugal no séc. 20: Para uma explicação sociológica do papel dos militares* (Lisbon: Estudos Gerais, 1985).

6. For excellent discussions of the deconsolidation of one formerly stable democracy, Colombia, see John A. Peeler, "Elite Settlements and Democratic Consolidation: Colombia, Costa Rica, and Venezuela," in Higley and Gunther, *Elites and Democratic Consolidation*; and Jonathan Hartlyn, "Colombia: The Politics of Violence and Accommodation," in Larry Diamond, Juan J. Linz, and Seymour Martin Lipset, eds., *Democracy in Developing Countries: Latin America* (Boulder: Lynne Rienner, 1989). For a similar analysis of the deconsolidation of democracy in Chile, see Arturo Valenzuela, *BDR: Chile* (see n. 2 above).

7. Arend Lijphart, Thomas C. Bruneau, P. Nikiforos Diamandouros, and Richard Gunther, "A Mediterranean Model of Democracy?: The Southern European Democracies in Comparative Perspective," *West European Politics* 11 (1988); and Liebert and Cotta, *Parliament and Democratic Consolidation.*

8. The institutional affiliations shown for subcommittee members are as of the initial appointments in 1988. The composition of the subcommittee changed slightly in 1991–93, following the resignations of George Th. Mavrogordatos, Yves Mény, and Loukas Tsoukalis and the addition of Geoffrey Pridham (University of Bristol) and Louka Katseli (University of Athens).

9. Social Science Research Council, *Annual Report, 1987–88* (New York: SSRC, 1988), p. 181.

Chapter 1

1. See Samuel P. Huntington, *The Third Wave: Democratization in the Late Twentieth Century* (Norman: University of Oklahoma, 1991).

2. See the reversal of Seymour Martin Lipset's (and Barrington Moore's) basic assumptions about the social requisites of democracy in Terry Lynn Karl and Philippe C. Schmitter, "Modes of Transition in Latin America, Southern and Eastern Europe," *International Social Science Journal* 128, 1991, pp. 269–84. See also the following by Seymour Martin Lipset: "Some Social Requisites of Democracy: Economic Development and Political Legitimacy," *American Political Science Review* 53, 1959, pp. 69–105; Lipset, Kyoung-Ryung Seong, and John Charles Torres, "A Comparative Analysis of Social Requisites of Democracy," *International Social Science Journal* 136, 1993, pp. 155–75; and "The Social Requisites of Democracy Revisited: 1993 Presidential Address," *American Sociological Review* 59, 1994, pp. 1–22.

3. See, for example, the studies assembled in Guillermo O'Donnell, Philippe C. Schmitter, and Laurence Whitehead, eds., *Transitions from Authoritarian Rule [TAR]: Prospects for Democracy* (Baltimore: Johns Hopkins University Press, 1986) and its individually subtitled constituent volumes (see preface n. 3 above); and some of their forerunners, like Dankwart Rustow, "Transitions to Democracy: Toward a Dynamic Model," *Comparative Politics* 2, 1970, pp. 337–

63; Samuel P. Huntington, "Will More Countries Become Democratic?" *Political Science Quarterly* 99, 1984, pp. 193–218; and Leonardo Morlino, *Come cambiano i regimi politici* (Milan: Angeli, 1980). Many of these studies have drawn insights from another classic, Juan J. Linz, "Totalitarian and Authoritarian Regimes," in Fred I. Greenstein and Nelson W. Polsby, eds., *Handbook of Political Science,* vol. 3 (Reading, Mass.: Addison Wesley, 1975), pp. 175–411.

For studies of the military in the politics of regime transition, see Alfred Stepan, *Rethinking Military Politics* (Princeton: Princeton University Press, 1988); Constantine P. Danopoulos, ed., *Military Disengagement From Politics* (London: Routledge, 1988), and *Warriors and Politicians in Modern Greece* (Chapel Hill: Documentary Publications, 1984); Thomas C. Bruneau and Alex Macleod, *Politics in Contemporary Portugal: Parties and the Consolidation of Democracy* (Boulder: Lynne Rienner, 1986); Felipe Agüero, "The Assertion of Civilian Supremacy in Post-Authoritarian Contexts: Spain in Comparative Perspective," (Ph.D. diss., Duke University, 1991; forthcoming, as *Soldiers, Civilians, and Democracy*, from Johns Hopkins University Press), and Agüero, "Regierung und Streitkräfte in Spanien nach Franco," in Walther L. Bernecker and Josef Oehrlein, eds., *Spanien Heute* (Frankfurt: Vervuert, 1991), pp. 167–88; Fernando Rodrigo, "El camino hacia la democracia: Militares y política en la transición española," (Ph.D. diss., Universidad Complutense, Madrid, 1989); and Louis W. Goodman, Johanna S. R. Mendelson, and Juan Rial, eds., *The Military and Democracy: The Future of Civil-Military Relations in Latin America* (Lexington, Mass.: D. C. Heath, 1990).

On elite agreements, see Donald Share, "Transitions to Democracy and Transition through Transaction," *Comparative Political Studies* 19, 1987, pp. 525–48; Donald Share and Scott Mainwaring, "Transitions through Transaction: Democratization in Brazil and Spain," in Wayne Selcher, ed., *Political Liberalization in Brazil* (Boulder: Westview, 1986), pp. 175–215; and Michael G. Burton and John Higley, "Elite Settlements," *American Sociological Review* 52, 1987, pp. 295–307. Impact of international context is discussed in Geoffrey Pridham, ed., *Encouraging Democracy: The International Context of Regime Transition in Southern Europe* (New York: St. Martin's, 1991); and Kenneth Maxwell, ed., *Democracy and Foreign Policy* (Durham, N.C.: Duke University Press, 1992).

For more general studies of regime transitions in Southern Europe, see O'Donnell, Schmitter, and Whitehead, *TAR: Southern Europe*; Geoffrey Pridham, ed., *The New Mediterranean Democracies: Regime Transition in Spain, Greece and Portugal* (London: Frank Cass, 1984); Giuseppe Di Palma, *To Craft Democracies: An Essay on Democratic Transitions* (Berkeley: University of California Press, 1990); John H. Herz, ed., *From Dictatorship to Democracy: Coping with the Legacies of Authoritarianism and Totalitarianism* (Westport, Conn.: Greenwood, 1982); Julián Santamaría, ed., *Transición a la democracia en el sur de Europa y América Latina* (Madrid: Centro de Investigaciones Sociológicas, 1982); Allan M. Williams, ed., *Southern Europe Transformed: Political and Economic Change in Greece, Italy, Portugal and Spain* (New York: Harper and Row, 1984); James Kurth and James Petras, *Mediterranean Paradoxes: Politics and Social Structure in Southern Europe* (Providence, R.I.: Berg, 1993); Enrique Baloyra, ed., *Comparing New Democracies: Transition and Consolidation in Mediterranean Europe and the Southern Cone* (Boulder: Westview, 1987); Juan J. Linz, "Some Comparative

Thoughts on the Transition to Democracy in Portugal and Spain," in Jorge Braga de Macedo and Simon Serfaty, eds., *Portugal since the Revolution: Economic and Political Perspectives* (Boulder: Westview, 1981), pp. 53–87; Giuseppe Di Palma, "Founding Coalitions in Southern Europe: Legitimacy and Hegemony," *Government and Opposition* 15, 1980, pp. 162–89; and Beate Kohler, *Politischer Umbruch in Südeuropa: Portugal, Griechenland, Spanien auf dem Weg zur Demokratie* (Bonn: Institut für Europäische Politik, 1981). Also see John Laughlin, ed., *Southern European Studies Guide* (London: Bowker-Sauer, 1993).

4. For Portugal and Greece, see, for example, Lawrence S. Graham and Douglas L. Wheeler, eds., *In Search of Modern Portugal: The Revolution and Its Consequences* (Madison: University of Wisconsin Press, 1983); Walter Opello, *Portugal's Political Development* (Boulder: Westview, 1985); de Macedo and Serfaty, *Portugal since the Revolution*; Nancy Gina Bermeo, *The Revolution within the Revolution* (Princeton: Princeton University Press, 1986); Richard Clogg, ed., *Parties and Elections in Greece: The Search for Legitimacy* (London: Hurst, 1987); Kevin Featherstone and Dimitrios K. Katsoudas, eds., *Political Change in Greece: Before and after the Colonels* (New York: St. Martin's, 1987); Christos Lyrintzis, "Political Parties in Post-Junta Greece," *West European Politics* 7, 1984, pp. 99–118; and P. Nikiforos Diamandouros, "Politics and Constitutionalism in Greece: The 1975 Constitution in Historical Perspective," in H. E. Chehabi and Alfred Stepan, eds., *Politics, Society, and Democracy* [hereafter *PSD*]*: Comparative Studies* (Boulder: Westview, 1995), pp. 279–96.

5. In addition to the contributions on Spain in the above mentioned classic collections, on the transition, see, for example, José María Maravall, *The Transition to Democracy in Spain* (London: Croom Helm, 1982); Donald Share, *The Making of Spanish Democracy* (New York: Praeger, 1986); Josep M. Colomer, "Transitions by Agreement: Modeling the Spanish Way," *American Political Science Review* 85, 1991, pp. 1283–302; Richard Gunther, Giacomo Sani, and Goldie Shabad, *Spain after Franco: The Making of a Competitive Party System,* 1st ed. (Berkeley: University of California Press, 1986); Mario Caciagli, *Elecciones y partidos en la transición española* (Madrid: CIS, 1986); and Carlos Huneeus, *La Unión de Centro Democrático y la transición a la democracia en España* (Madrid: CIS, 1985).

6. See, for example, the second edition of Gunther, Sani, and Shabad, *Spain after Franco*; Juan J. Linz and José Ramón Montero, eds., *Crisis y Cambio: Electores y partidos en la España de los años ochenta* (Madrid: CEC, 1986); Stanley G. Payne, ed., *The Politics of Democratic Spain* (Chicago: Council on Foreign Relations, 1986); Ramón Cotarelo, ed., *Transición y Consolidación Democrática en España* (Madrid: CIS, 1992); and Richard Gunther, ed., *Politics, Society, and Democracy* [hereafter *PSD*]*: The Case of Spain* (Boulder: Westview, 1993).

7. See, for example, José Luis García Delgado, ed., *Economía Española de la transición y la democracia, 1973–1986* (Madrid: CIS, 1990); Robert M. Fishman, *Working-Class Organization and the Return to Democracy in Spain* (Ithaca: Cornell University Press, 1990); José María Maravall, "From Opposition to Government: The Politics and Policies of the PSOE," in Gabriel Colomé, ed., *Socialist Parties in Europe* (Barcelona: Institut de Ciències Polítiques i Socials, 1992), pp. 6–34; Salvador Giner and Eduardo Sevilla, "Spain: From Corporatism to Corporatism," in Williams, *Southern Europe Transformed*, pp. 113–41; Carlota

Solé, ed., *Corporatismo y diferenciación regional* (Madrid: Ministerio de Trabajo y Seguridad Social, 1987); Manuel Pérez Yruela and Salvador Giner, eds., *El corporatismo en España* (Barcelona: Ariel, 1988); Victor Pérez Díaz, *The Return of Civil Society* (Cambridge: Harvard University Press, 1993); Ricard Gomà and Joan Subirats, "Nuevos escenarios de integración de intereses: Los Consejos Económicos y Sociales locales," *Revista Española de Investigaciones Sociológicas* 44, 1988, pp. 79–94; and Richard Gunther, *Política y cultura en España* (Madrid: Centro de Estudios Constitucionales, 1992).

8. See, for example, Kenneth Maxwell, ed., *Portugal in the 1980s: Dilemmas of Democratic Consolidation* (New York: Greenwood, 1986); Bruneau and Macleod, *Politics in Contemporary Portugal*; Kenneth Maxwell and Michael H. Haltzel, eds., *Portugal: Ancient Country, Young Democracy* (Washington, D.C.: Woodrow Wilson Center Press, 1990); Speros Vryonis, Jr., ed., *Greece on the Road to Democracy: From the Junta to PASOK, 1974–1986* (New Rochelle: A. D. Caratzas, 1991); P. Nikiforos Diamandouros, "Politics and Culture in Greece, 1974–91: An Interpretation," in Richard Clogg, ed., *Greece, 1981–1989: The Populist Decade* (London: Macmillan, 1993); and for a functional equivalent (however institutionally and culturally different) of "corporatism" in Greece, see, for example, Dimitrios A. Sotiropoulos, "State and Party: The Greek State Bureaucracy and the Panhellenic Socialist Movement (PASOK), 1981–1989," (Ph.D. diss., Yale University, 1991).

9. See, for example, Adam Przeworski, *Democracy and the Market: Political and Economic Reforms in Eastern Europe and Latin America* (Cambridge: Cambridge University Press, 1991); Dieter Nohlen and Aldo Solari, eds., *Reforma Política y Consolidación Democrática: Europa y América Latina* (Caracas: Nueva Sociedad, 1988); Karl and Schmitter, "Modes of Transition"; Claus Offe, "Capitalism by Democratic Design? Democratic Theory Facing the Triple Transition in East Central Europe," *Social Research* 58, 1991, pp. 865–92, and *Der Tunnel am Ende des Lichts* (Frankfurt: Campus, 1994); Nancy Bermeo, ed., *Liberalization and Democratization: Change in the Soviet Union and Eastern Europe* (Baltimore: Johns Hopkins University Press, 1992); and Klaus von Beyme, "Transformationstheorie—ein neuer interdisziplinärer Forschungszweig?" *Geschichte und Gesellschaft* 20, 1994, pp. 99–118. A more detailed examination of the problems involved will be provided by Juan J. Linz and Alfred Stepan, *Problems of Democratic Transition and Consolidation: Eastern Europe, Southern Europe, and South America* (Baltimore: Johns Hopkins University Press, forthcoming). For a comparative analysis of the "founding elections" see also Juan J. Linz and Alfred Stepan, "Political Identities and Electoral Sequences: Spain, the Soviet Union, and Yugoslavia," *Daedalus* 121, 1992, pp. 123–39.

10. See Arend Lijphart, *Democracies: Patterns of Majoritarian and Consensus Government in Twenty-One Countries* (New Haven: Yale University Press, 1988), and "The Southern European Examples of Democratization: Six Lessons for Latin America," *Government and Opposition* 25, 1990, pp. 68–84; David Easton, "Democratic Regimes as Sets of Factors Shaping Political Science as a Discipline and a Profession," *Participation* 14, 1990, pp. 4–7; Robert A. Dahl, *Democracy and Its Critics* (New Haven: Yale University Press, 1991); Alan Ware, "Liberal Democracy: One Form or Many?" *Political Studies* 40, 1992, pp. 130–45; and Wolfgang Merkel, "Struktur oder Akteur System oder Handlung: Gibt es einen

Königsweg in der sozialwissenschaftlichen Transformationsforehung?" in Wolfgang Merkel, ed., *Systemwechsel 1. Theorien, Ansätze und Konzeptionen* (Opladen: Leske, 1994), pp. 303–31. More particularly, see Arend Lijphart, Thomas C. Bruneau, P. Nikiforos Diamandouros, and Richard Gunther, "A Mediterranean Model of Democracy?: The Southern European Democracies in Comparative Perspective," *West European Politics* 11, 1988, pp. 7–25; Philippe C. Schmitter and Terry Lynn Karl, "What Democracy Is . . . and Is Not," *Journal of Democracy* 2, 1991, pp. 75–88, and "Exploring Meanings of Democracy to Provide Guidelines for Policy," unpublished manuscript, 1991; Seymour Martin Lipset, Larry Diamond, and Juan J. Linz, "Introduction: Comparing Experiences with Democracy," in Larry Diamond, Juan J. Linz, and Seymour Martin Lipset, eds., *Democracy in Developing Countries,* vol. 1 (Boulder: Lynne Rienner), pp. 9–21; Juan J. Linz, "The Perils of Presidentialism," *Democracy*, Winter 1990, pp. 51–69; "Change and Continuity in the Nature of Contemporary Democracies," in Gary Marks and Larry Diamond, eds., *Reexamining Democracy: Essays in Honor of S. M. Lipset* (Newbury Park, Calif.: Sage, 1992), pp. 182–207; and Juan J. Linz and Arturo Valenzuela, eds., *The Failure of Presidential Democracy: Comparative Perspectives* (Baltimore: Johns Hopkins University Press, 1994).

11. See, among others, Salvador Giner, "La economía política de la Europa meridional: Poder, clases sociales y legitimación," *Sistema* 50–51, 1982; Giovanni Arrighi, ed., *Semiperipheral Development: The Politics of Southern Europe in the Twentieth Century* (Beverly Hills: Sage, 1985); Nicos P. Mouzelis, *Politics in the Semi-Periphery: Early Parliamentarianism and Late Industrialisation in the Balkans and Latin America* (Basingstoke: Macmillan, 1986); Diane Ethier, ed., *Democratic Transition and Consolidation in Southern Europe, Latin America, and Southeast Asia* (London: Macmillan, 1990); and Robert Putnam, *Making Democracy Work: Civic Traditions in Modern Italy* (Princeton: Princeton University Press, 1993). On the general context, see, for example, Jon Elster, *The Cement of Society: A Study of Social Order* (Cambridge: Cambridge University Press, 1991); Rolf Torstendahl, ed., *State Theory and State History* (London: Sage, 1992); Beate Kohler-Koch, ed., *Staat und Demokratie in Europa* (Opladen: Leske, 1992); Fritz W. Scharpf, *Sozialdemokratische Krisenpolitik in Europa* (Frankfurt: Campus, 1987); and Marino Regini, ed., *The Future of Labour Movements* (London: Sage, 1992). On the problem of participation and legitimation in the EC, see Wolfgang Merkel, "Integration and Democracy in the European Community: The Contours of a Dilemma," working paper no. 42, Instituto Juan March, Madrid, 1993.

12. See, particularly, Dietrich Rueschemeyer, Evelyne Huber Stephens, and John D. Stephens, *Capitalist Development and Democracy* (Oxford: Polity Press, 1992).

13. See Philippe C. Schmitter, "The Consolidation of Political Democracy in Southern Europe (and Latin America)," unpublished manuscript, 1985; and Timothy Power and Nancy Powers, "Issues in the Consolidation of Democracy in Latin America and Southern Europe in Comparative Perspective: A Rapporteur's Report," working paper no. 113, Kellogg Institute, Notre Dame, Ind., 1988. And more recently, Juan J. Linz and Alfred Stepan, "Political Crafting of Democratic Consolidation or Destruction: European and South American Comparisons," and Laurence Whitehead, "The Consolidation of Fragile De-

mocracies," in Robert A. Pastor, ed., *Democracy in the Americas: Stopping the Pendulum* (New York: Holmes and Meier, 1989), pp. 41–61, 76–95; Geoffrey Pridham, "Political Actors, Linkages, and Interactions: Democratic Consolidation in Southern Europe," *West European Politics* 13, 1990, pp. 103–17; Guillermo O'Donnell, "Transitions, Continuities, and Paradoxes," and Scott Mainwaring, "Transitions to Democracy and Democratic Consolidation: Theoretical and Comparative Issues," in Scott Mainwaring, Guillermo O'Donnell, and J. Samuel Valenzuela, eds., *Issues in Democratic Consolidation: The New South American Democracies in Comparative Perspective* (Notre Dame, Ind.: University of Notre Dame Press, 1992), pp. 17–56, 294–341; and Hans-Jürgen Puhle, "Transitions, Demokratisierung und Transformationsprozesse in Südeuropa," in Merkel, *Systemwechsel 1*, pp. 173–94. See also some of the latest reflections on the institutional aspects in Guillermo O'Donnell, "Delegative Democracy?" working paper no. 172, Kellogg Institute, Notre Dame, Ind., March 1992; "On the State, Democratization, and Some Conceptual Problems," *World Development* 8, 1993; and Adam Przeworski et al., *Sustainable Democracy*, unpublished manuscript.

14. See John Higley and Richard Gunther, eds., *Elites and Democratic Consolidation in Latin America and Southern Europe* (New York: Cambridge University Press, 1992); Ulrike Liebert and Maurizio Cotta, eds. *Parliament and Democratic Consolidation in Southern Europe: Greece, Italy, Portugal, Spain, and Turkey* (London: Pinter, 1990); Geoffrey Pridham, ed., *Securing Democracy: Political Parties and Democratic Consolidation in Southern Europe* (London: Routledge, 1990); Leonardo Morlino, "Parties, Pressure Groups, and Democratic Consolidation in Italy," in Chehabi and Stepan, *PSD: Comparative Studies*; Philippe C. Schmitter, "The Consolidation of Democracy and Representation of Social Groups," *American Behavioral Scientist* 35, 1991/92, pp. 422–49; "Interest Systems and the Consolidation of Democracies," in Marks and Diamond, *Reexamining Democracy*, pp. 156–81.

15. Juan J. Linz, "Totalitarian and Authoritarian Regimes," pp. 182–83.

16. In Chapter 3 of this volume, Linz, Stepan, and Gunther write that a democratic transition is completed "when the following criteria are met: a government comes to power that is the direct result of a free and popular vote; this government has full authority to generate new policies; and the executive, legislative, and judicial power generated by the new democracy does not have to share power with other bodies de jure."

17. The 1976 Portuguese constitution thus attempted to create an odd mix of democratic principles, some of them procedural and some substantive. In the latter sense, it was more explicit in its defense of socialism than the constitution of the Soviet Union.

18. See, for example, Di Palma, *To Craft Democracies*.

19. See, for example, Schmitter, "Consolidation of Political Democracy."

20. See, for example, Pridham, *Securing Democracy*; Pridham, *Encouraging Democracy*; and Whitehead, "Consolidation of Fragile Democracies."

21. Schmitter, "Consolidation of Political Democracy," p. 10.

22. Whitehead, "Consolidation of Fragile Democracies," p. 79.

23. Przeworski, *Democracy and the Market*, p. 26.

24. See pp. 3, 48–49, and 58–72, respectively, in Mainwaring, O'Donnell, and Valenzuela, *Issues in Democratic Consolidation*.

25. Linz and Stepan set forth a similar definition in their contribution to this volume.

26. Accordingly, the mere *existence* of an American Nazi Party or a Ku Klux Klan in the 1980s or early 1990s does not, by itself, pose a threat to the survival of the system. If affiliation with or support for those groups were substantially greater, however, one could argue that the point might be reached where either the survival of the system could be threatened or the system's basic character could be so significantly altered as to no longer be regarded as democratic. Along these lines, we would conclude that KKK terrorism and institutionalized intimidation in the American South in the late nineteenth and early twentieth centuries led to such a substantial erosion of democratic norms and principles as to call into question the status of the political regime in that region as democratic. From this perspective, the key difference between the 1980s and the American South in the 1920s involves the *level* of support for antisystem alternatives to democracy and, thereby, their capacity to affect the functioning of the system itself.

27. Elsewhere, Pridham refers to this as a "'rooting' of the system in society" (see "Political Actors, Linkages, and Interactions"). Also see Pridham, *Securing Democracy*, esp. pp. 7, 15. In a similar vein, Laurence Whitehead argues that the consolidation process involves internalization of democratic rules of procedure and that its hallmark is that "the many uncertainties of the transition period are progressively diminished as the new assumptions and procedures become better known and understood and more widely accepted. . . . It is unlikely that such a process can ever be fully accomplished in less than a generation" ("The Consolidation of Fragile Democracies," p. 79).

28. For the definition of *limited democracies*, see Michael Burton, Richard Gunther, and John Higley, "Introduction," in Higley and Gunther, *Elites and Democratic Consolidation*.

29. On the lack of democratic consolidation in Peru, see Henry Dietz, "Elites in an Unconsolidated Democracy: Peru during the 1980s," in Gunther and Higley, *Elites and Democratic Consolidation*.

30. For more extensive discussions of consolidation and stability of the Spanish regime, see Richard Gunther, "Spain: The Very Model of the Modern Elite Settlement," in Higley and Gunther, *Elites and Democratic Consolidation*; and the chapters by Agüero and Linz and Stepan in this volume.

31. The inadequacy of "alternation in power" as a criterion for consolidation is further underlined by the fact that the Italian governmental turnover of 1994 occurred not at a high point of regime consolidation and stability (the early to middle 1980s) but rather at a time of deconsolidation and radical restructuring of several important partial regimes—its party system, its electoral system, and possibly the structure of the state. (See Schmitter's definition and discussion of partial regimes in Chapter 9 of this volume.)

32. See Burton, Gunther, and Higley, "Introduction," p. 11; and Gunther, "Spain: Model Elite Settlement," p. 73.

33. See Samuel P. Huntington, *Political Order in Changing Societies* (New Haven: Yale University Press, 1968), p. 12.

34. Indeed, as he was leading his delegation out of the Congress of Deputies, PNV leader Xabier Arzallus admitted that his party had gotten almost everything it had asked for in the course of the negotiations (*Informaciones*, July 24, 1978).

35. That provision expressed "respect for the historic rights of the territories," whose realization would "be accomplished . . . *within the framework of the constitution* and the statutes of autonomy." The PNV objected to the phrase "within the framework of the constitution" on the grounds that the Basque *fueros* (charters of autonomy) were historic rights (*derechos originarios*) that took precedence over the constitution, and that the present constituent elites lacked the authority to "concede" the restoration of those rights. Clearly, this is not an objection to the substantive content of the constitution or its institutions, and yet it did serve as a significant obstacle to regime consolidation for some time.

36. Consistent with this line of reasoning, Juan Linz and Alfred Stepan, in this volume, identify separate attitudinal, behavioral, and structural dimensions of democratic consolidation.

37. See Herbert McClosky, "Consensus and Ideology in American Politics," *American Political Science Review* 58, 1964, pp. 361–82; and James W. Prothro and Charles M. Grigg, "Fundamental Principles of Democracy: Bases of Agreement and Disagreement," *Journal of Politics* 22, May 1960, pp. 276–94.

38. See, for example, Whitehead, "The Consolidation of Fragile Democracies," p. 79.

39. See John A. Peeler, "Elite Settlements and Democratic Consolidation: Colombia, Costa Rica, and Venezuela," in Higley and Gunther, *Elites and Democratic Consolidation*; and Jonathan Hartlyn, *The Politics of Coalition Rule in Colombia* (Cambridge: Cambridge University Press, 1988).

40. See Burton, Gunther, and Higley, "Introduction."

41. See ibid., pp. 30–35; Arend Lijphart, *The Politics of Accommodation* (Berkeley: University of California Press, 1968); Terry Karl, "Petroleum and Political Pacts: The Transition to Democracy in Venezuela," in O'Donnell, Schmitter, and Whitehead, *TAR: Latin America* (n. 3 above); Terry Karl, "Dilemmas of Democratization in Latin America," *Comparative Politics* 23, 1990, p. 11; and O'Donnell and Schmitter, *TAR: Tentative Conclusions about Uncertain Democracies*, p. 37.

42. Negative integration is a process in which leftist parties and their affiliated trade unions moderate their behavior and tone down their radical political aims in an effort to secure improvements in the working and living conditions of their respective working-class clienteles. See Guenther Roth, *The Social Democrats in Imperial Germany* (Totowa, N.J.: Bedminster, 1963), pp. 315–16; Juan J. Linz, "La democrazia italiana di fronte al futuro," in Fabio Luca Cavazza and Stephen R. Graubard, eds., *Il caso italiano* (Milan: Garzanti, 1974); and Leonardo Morlino, "Parties, Groups, and Democratic Consolidation in Italy," in Chehabi and Stepan, *PSD: Comparative Studies*.

43. For an extensive description and analysis of the consolidation of Spanish democracy, see Gunther, "Spain: Model Elite Settlement."

44. This suggests that conceptualizations of transition and consolidation processes that represent them as distinct phases, with one clearly following the latter, are somewhat misleading. In the Spanish case, completion of the transi-

tion (with establishment of national and regional government institutions and free elections within those new institutional frameworks) was largely coterminous with a partial but highly significant consolidation of the new regime. In addition, in the particular case of Spain (but not necessarily elsewhere), the processes of transition and consolidation largely overlapped: the same interparty negotiations that created the basic institutions of the regime also forged the new patterns of elite interaction that lay at the heart of the consolidation process.

45. Particularly important is the PNV's stand, alongside the other parties in the so-called Pacto de Madrid, against ETA terrorism. But while the behavior of the PNV has changed substantially, the party has still not altered its formal stand vis-à-vis the constitution—it is still one of *acatamiento* and not "loyalty."

The progressive incorporation of the PNV within the democratic consensus supporting the regime has unfolded according to a somewhat modified version of "elite convergence." What makes this case somewhat unusual is that, unlike in the typical case of convergence (where excluded, opposition parties moderate their behavior in an effort to come to power), the PNV abandoned its semiloyal stance in order to *retain* power and in response to constructive blackmail pressures exerted by the PSOE. See Goldie Shabad, "Still the Exception? Democratization and Ethnic Nationalism in the Basque Country of Spain," in Richard Gunther, Goldie Shabad, Juan J. Linz, José Ramón Montero, and Hans-Jürgen Puhle, eds., "Electoral Change and Democratic Consolidation in Spain," unpublished manuscript; also see Francisco Llera, "*Conflicto en Euskadi* Revisited," in Gunther, *PSD: The Case of Spain*.

46. Descriptions and analyses of the carry-over of *franquist* norms and values into the current political culture of Spain may be found in José Cazorla, "The Theory and Reality of the Authoritarian Regime, Thirty Years Later," and José Ramón Montero, "Revisiting Democratic Success: Legitimacy and the Meanings of Democracy in Spain," in Gunther, *PSD: The Case of Spain*; and in José Ramón Montero and Mariano Torcal, "La cultura política de los españoles: Pautas de continuidad y cambio," *Sistema* 99, 1990, pp. 39–74. Comparative analysis of democratic values and participatory norms in Spain and the rest of Southern Europe is discussed by Leonardo Morlino and José Ramón Montero in this volume. It should be noted that these apparent defects in Spain's political culture may also reflect frustration and dissatisfaction growing out of over a decade of nearly hegemonic rule at the national level by a single party.

47. See Maurizio Cotta, "Unification and Democratic Consolidation in Italy: An Historical Overview," in Higley and Gunther, *Elites and Democratic Consolidation*. On the transition to democracy in Italy, see Gianfranco Pasquino, "The Demise of the First Fascist Regime and Italy's Transition to Democracy: 1943–1948," in O'Donnell, Schmitter, and Whitehead, *TAR: Southern Europe*.

48. Pasquino, "Italy's Transition to Democracy," p. 64.

49. Morlino, "Parties, Groups, and Democratic Consolidation in Italy," in Chehabi and Stepan, *PSD: Comparative Studies*, p. 273.

50. Ibid., p. 25. Here, he is quoting partly from P. Scoppola, *La proposta politica di De Gasperi* (Bologna: Il Mulino, 1977).

51. Gianfranco Pasquino, "Party Government in Italy: Achievements and Prospects," in R. Katz, ed., *Party Governments: European and American Experiences*

(Berlin: De Gruyter, 1987), p. 216, and cited in Morlino, "Parties, Groups, and Democratic Consolidation in Italy."

52. Cotta, "Unification and Democratic Consolidation in Italy," p. 167.

53. See Linz, "La democrazia italiana," p. 131; and Morlino, "Parties, Groups, and Democratic Consolidation," unpublished manuscript, p. 1.

54. Pasquino, "Italy's Transition to Democracy," p. 69.

55. Lawrence S. Graham, "Redefining the Portuguese Transition to Democracy," in Higley and Gunther, *Elites and Democratic Consolidation,* p. 287. Our brief account of the consolidation of democracy in Portugal is largely based on Graham's analysis.

56. To date, very little has been written on the consolidation of democracy in Greece. Two works that deal with this subject are Nicos Alivizatos, "The Difficulties of 'Rationalization' in a Polarized Political System: The Greek Chamber of Deputies," in Liebert and Cotta, *Parliament and Democratic Consolidation,* pp. 131–53; and P. Nikiforos Diamandouros, "Transition to, and Consolidation of, Democratic Politics in Greece, 1974–1983," in Pridham, *New Mediterranean Democracies,* pp. 50–71. On the Greek transition, which so far has attracted the attention of only a handful of scholars, see Harry J. Psomiades, "Greece: From the Colonels' Rule to Democracy," in Herz, *From Dictatorship to Democracy,* pp. 251–73; Constantine Arvanitopoulos, "The Political Economy of Regime Transition: The Case of Greece" (Ph.D. diss., The American University, Athens, 1989); and P. Nikiforos Diamandouros, "Regime Change and the Prospects for Democracy in Greece: 1974–1983," in O'Donnell, Schmitter, and Whitehead, *TAR: Prospects for Democracy*, pp. 138–64.

57. On Greek foreign policy during the critical period of democratic consolidation, see Theodore A. Couloumbis, "The Structures of Greek Foreign Policy," in Richard Clogg, ed., *Greece in the 1980s* (London: Macmillan, 1983), pp. 95–121; and "Defining Greek Foreign Policy Objectives," in Howard R. Penniman, ed., *Greece at the Polls: The National Elections of 1974 and 1977* (Washington, D.C.: American Enterprise Institute, 1981), pp. 160–84; Christos Rozakis, "La politique étrangère d'un petit pays," *Les Temps Modernes* 473, December 1985, pp. 861–67; Van Coufoudakis, "Greek Foreign Policy, 1945–1985: Seeking Independence in an Interdependent World—Problems and Prospects," in Featherstone and Katsoudas, *Political Change in Greece,* pp. 230–52; and Dimitri C. Konstas, "Greek Foreign Policy Objectives, 1974–1986," in Hellenic Foundation for Defense and Foreign Policy, *Yearbook 1988* (Athens: ELIAMEP, 1989), pp. 93–128.

58. Authoritative analyses of these aspects of PASOK's evolution as a political party include Michalis Spourdalakis, *The Rise of the Greek Socialist Party* (London: Routledge, 1988), and Christos Lyrintzis, "Between Socialism and Populism: The Rise of the Panhellenic Socialist Movement" (Ph.D. diss., London School of Economics and Political Science, 1983).

59. On the Greek military during the transition and consolidation periods, see, among others, Thanos Veremis, "The Military," in Featherstone and Katsoudas, *Political Change in Greece,* pp. 214–29, as well as the more comparative article by Constantine P. Danopoulos, "Democratising the Military: Lessons from Mediterranean Europe," *West European Politics* 14, October 1991, pp. 25–41. On the Greek communist left, see Michalis Papayannakis, "The Crisis in

the Greek Left," in Penniman, *Greece at the Polls,* pp. 130–59; Vassilis Kapetanyannis, "The Communists," in Featherstone and Katsoudas, *Political Change in Greece,* pp. 145–73; and Geoffrey Pridham and Susannah Verney, "The Coalition of 1989–90 in Greece," *West European Politics* 14, October 1991, pp. 42–49.

Chapter 2

1. Portugal, of course, touches only the Atlantic, with nary an inch of it bordering on the Mediterranean. Nevertheless, the climatic influence of the Mediterranean is very strong, above all in the Algarve, but also in the Alentejo and in parts of Ribatejo and Estremadura. See Orlando Ribeiro, *Portugal, o Mediterraneo e o Atlantico*, 2nd ed. (Lisbon: Sá da Costa, 1963). By the same token, large portions of Italy and Spain lie outside the Mediterranean climatic zone, yet it is a dominant feature of both countries.

2. For example, among Roman authors, the two Senecas, Lucan, Martial, and Quintilian were all Spanish-born, as were the emperors Trajan and Hadrian.

3. Wilbert E. Moore, *Economic Demography of Eastern and Southern Europe,* (New York: League of Nations, 1945), p. 26. If Great Britain is included, the average for Western Europe becomes 19.3 percent. Czechoslovakia was omitted from the calculations because its 32.7 percent average concealed sharp divisions between heavily industrialized Bohemia/Moravia and deeply rural Slovakia. Moore gave no figures for the Soviet Union, but according to its 1926 census, 82.2 percent of its active male population still worked in agriculture (B. R. Mitchell, *European Historical Statistics, l750–1970* [New York: Columbia University Press, 1975], p. 161).

4. Another important difference was that, due to the overwhelming demographic predominance of the peasantry in Eastern Europe, and their relatively homogeneous social position, peasant parties of a defensive, interest-group type could be established during the brief periods when democracy prevailed. Less numerous and more heterogeneous, the Southern European peasantry could never successfully support such parties.

5. These themes are elaborated upon much more extensively in Edward E. Malefakis "Southern Europe in the 19th and 20th Centuries: An Historical Overview," working paper no. 35, 1992, Centro de Estudios Avanzados en Ciencias Sociales, Instituto Juan March, Madrid.

6. As no Greek state existed prior to 1821, neither did a regular Greek army. By "military men" I mean Greeks who had served in foreign armies (e.g., Dimitrios Ypsilantis) or lived by the force of arms as "klephts" (e.g., Theodore Kolokotronis). Even after a state was formed, military irregulars played a greater role in Greece than elsewhere, mainly because of the secret operations periodically inaugurated in Greek territory to foster rebellion in the unredeemed lands, and because of the rebel bands the Greek state covertly sponsored there.

7. Large estates predominated in Portugal's lightly populated Alentejo, but it was the far more numerous small holders of the center and north who set the political tone. The rural social structure was even more egalitarian in Greece, where most peasants had acquired some land after the War of Independence.

8. This was the fifth major assassination in Southern Europe since 1897;

besides the three mentioned in this paragraph, Antonio Cánovas del Castillo and Theodore Deliyannis, Trikoupis's populist rival, had also been slain. A sixth victim, Greece's King George I, would be added in 1913.

9. This was especially true for Spain, of course. Salazar managed to soften the isolation of his dictatorship by the statesmanlike image he projected (so intelligent and liberal a man as Dean Acheson likened him to Plato's philosopher-king) and by other means.

10. The points that follow are more fully developed in my article "Spain and Its Francoist Heritage," in John H. Herz, ed., *From Dictatorship to Democracy: Coping with the Legacies of Authoritarianism and Totalitarianism* (Westport, Conn.: Greenwood, 1982), pp. 215–30.

Chapter 3

This chapter is based on a paper presented by Juan J. Linz and Alfred Stepan at the SSRC Subcommittee on Southern Europe's Conference on Problems of Democratic Consolidation in Southern Europe at the Instituto Juan March de Estudios e Investigaciones, Madrid, July 6–8, 1990. That paper led to the writing of Linz and Stepan, *Problems of Democratic Transition and Consolidation: Southern Europe, South America, and Postcommunist Europe* (Baltimore: Johns Hopkins University Press, forthcoming). Richard Gunther extracted material from that manuscript and added his own contributions in writing this chapter.

1. See Linz and Stepan, *Problems of Democratic Transition and Consolidation*

2. See Anatol Lieven, *The Baltic Revolution: Estonia, Latvia, Lithuania, and the Path for Independence* (New Haven: Yale University Press, 1993).

3. See Juan J. Linz, "Totalitarian and Authoritarian Regimes," in Fred I. Greenstein and Nelson W. Polsby, eds., *Handbook of Political Science,* vol. 3 (Reading, Mass.: Addison-Wesley, 1975); see also Richard Snyder, "Explaining Transitions from Neopatrimonial Dictatorships," *Comparative Politics* 24, no. 4, July 1992, pp. 379–99.

4. See Max Weber, *Economy and Society: An Outline of Interpretive Sociology,* ed. by Guenther Roth and Claus Wittich (Berkeley: University of California Press, 1978), pp. 231–32; Houchang Chehabi and Juan J. Linz, *Sultanistic Regimes,* unpublished manuscript; and Linz, "Totalitarian and Authoritarian Regimes."

5. Juan J. Linz, "State Building and Nation Building," *European Review* 1, no. 4, 1993, pp. 355–69.

6. For a more extensive discussion of some of the potential problems of provisional governments, see Yossi Shain and Juan Linz, "The Role of Interim Governments," *Journal of Democracy* 3, no. 1, January 1992, pp. 73–84, and "The Role of Interim Governments in Transitions to Democracy" (paper presented at the annual meeting of the American Political Science Association, Washington, D.C., August 30–September 2, 1991). See also Yossi Shain and Juan J. Linz, eds., *Between States: Interim Governments in Democratic Transitions* (Cambridge: Cambridge University Press, 1995), and Juan Linz, "Il fattore tempo nei mutamenti di regime," *Teoria politica* 2, 1986, pp. 3–47.

7. The bibliography on the Spanish transition is the most extensive of the cases under consideration in this book. An essential source is José Félix Tezanos, Ramón Cotarelo, and Andrés de Blas, eds., *La transición democrática española* (Madrid: Sistema, 1989). Also see the special issue of *Sistema* 68–69,

November 1985; José María Maravall and Julián Santamaría, "Political Change in Spain and the Prospects for Democracy," in Guillermo O'Donnell, Philippe C. Schmitter, and Laurence Whitehead, eds., *Transitions from Authoritarian Rule* [*TAR*]: *Southern Europe* (Baltimore: Johns Hopkins University Press, 1986) (see preface n. 3 above), pp. 70–108; José María Maravall, *La política de la transición 1975–80* (Madrid: Taurus, 1981), published in English as *The Transition to Democracy in Spain* (London: Croom Helm, 1982); Carlos Huneeus, *Là Unión de Centro Democrático y la transición a la democracia en España* (Madrid: Centro de Investigaciones Sociológicas-Siglo XXI de España, 1985); Donald Share, *The Making of Spanish Democracy* (Westport, Conn.: Praeger, 1986); Charles T. Powell, "Reform versus 'Ruptura' in Spain's Transition to Democracy," (Ph.D. diss., Faculty of Modern History, Oxford University, 1989); Richard Gunther, Giacomo Sani, and Goldie Shabad, eds., *Spain after Franco: The Making of a Competitive Party System,* (Berkeley: University of California Press, 1988); and Robert M. Fishman, "Rethinking State and Regime: Southern Europe's Transition to Democracy," *World Politics* 42, April 1990, pp. 422–37, and *Working-Class Organization and the Return to Democracy in Spain* (Ithaca: Cornell University Press, 1990). On the role of the military in the transition, see Fernando Rodrigo Rodríguez, "El camino hacia la democracia: Militares y política en la transición española" (Ph.D diss., Facultad de Ciencias Políticas y Sociológicas, Universidad Complutense, 1989), pp. 21–72; and Felipe Agüero, "The Assertion of Civilian Supremacy in Post-Authoritarian Contexts: Spain in Comparative Perspective," (Ph.D. diss., Duke University, 1991; forthcoming, as *Soldiers, Civilians, and Democracy*, from Johns Hopkins University Press). The consolidation of democracy is examined in Richard Gunther, "Spain: The Very Model of the Modern Elite Settlement," in John Higley and Richard Gunther, eds., *Elites and Democratic Consolidation in Latin America and Southern Europe* (Cambridge: Cambridge University Press, 1992), and Ramón Cotarelo, ed., *Transición politica y consolidación democratica: España (1975–1986)* (Madrid: Centro de Investigaciones Sociológicas, 1992) (628 pages, with contributions by eighteen authors on different aspects of the process; includes a chronology, basic texts, and bibliography. One of the essays by J. Linz places the Spanish transitions in a comparative context.)

8. See Víctor Pérez-Díaz, "The Emergence of Democratic Spain and the 'Invention' of a Democratic Tradition," working paper no. 1, Instituto Juan March, Madrid, June 1990, pp. 19, 20, 21, 23; Victor M. Pérez-Díaz, *The Return of Civil Society: The Emergence of Democratic Spain* (Cambridge: Harvard University Press, 1993), esp. ch. 1; and Paloma Aguilar Fernández, "La memoria histórica de la Guerra Civil Española en el franquismo y la transición" (Ph.D. diss., Instituto Juan March and Universidad Nacional de Educación a Distancia de Madrid, 1995).

9. This account of the political process of the Moncloa Pact is based largely on an interview by Alfred Stepan with Adolfo Suárez, May 24, 1990. Suárez says he initially considered making the stabilization plan an executive decision but rapidly realized it would be more legitimate, and effective, if he could arrive at an agreement with the political parties. This complex consensual process within political society, which was a hallmark of the Spanish transition was, as we

shall see, virtually absent from the major Brazilian and Argentine stabilization plans each of which was drawn up in *secret* by the president and his closest advisors and announced to a shocked nation on television without ever having been discussed in the legislature. For the relationship between the Communist and Socialist parties, the unions, and the Moncloa Pact see Fishman, *Working-Class Organization,* pp. 17, 180, 215–26; see also Joan Trullen i Thomas, *Fundamentos económicos de la transición política española, la política económica de los acuerdos de la Moncloa* (Madrid: Ministerio de Trabajo y Seguridad Social, 1993, with foreword by Ernest Lluch).

10. See Charles T. Powell, *El piloto del cambio: El rey, la monarquía y la transición a la democracia* (Barcelona: Editorial Planeta, 1991); Juan J. Linz, "Innovative Leadership in the Spanish Transition," in Gabriel Sheffer, ed., *Innovative Leadership in International Politics* (Albany: State University of New York Press, 1993); and Joel Podolny, "The Role of Juan Carlos I in the Consolidation of the Parliamentary Monarchy," in Richard Gunther, ed., *Politics, Society, and Democracy: The Case of Spain* (Boulder: Westview, 1993).

11. See, for example, Josep M. Colomer, *El arte de la manipulación política: Votaciones y teoría de juegos en la política española,* (Barcelona: Editorial Anagrama, 1990), and "Transitions by Agreement: Modeling the Spanish Way," *American Political Science Review* (December 1991), pp. 1283–302.

12. See, for example, Juan J. Linz, "Spain and Portugal: Critical Choices," in David S. Landes, ed., *Critical Choices for Americans: Western Europe* (Lexington, Mass.: Lexington Books, 1977), pp. 237–96, and Linz, "Innovative Leadership."

13. See *El papel de las Fuerzas Armadas en la transición española,* special issue of *Revista de Investigaciones Sociológicas* (36, [October–December 1986]).

14. Ricardo García Damborenea, *La encruicijada vasca* (Barcelona: Editorial Argos Vergara, 1984), p. 52; also see Fernando Reinares, "Sociogénesis y evolución del terrorismo en España," in Salvador Giner, ed., *España: Sociedad y política* (Madrid: Espasa Calpe, 1990).

15. See Pablo Lucas Verdú, *La octava ley fundamental* (Madrid: Tecnos, 1976); and Antonio Hernández Gil, *El cambio político español y la constitución* (Barcelona: Planeta, 1981).

16. In the aftermath of its failure in the 1977 election, the Partido Socialista Popular (which elected only six deputies to the constituent Cortes) merged with the much larger Partido Socialista Obrero Español, leaving four statewide political parties.

17. See Gunther, Sani, and Shabad, *Spain after Franco,* pp. 37–177, 311.

18. See Andrea Bonime-Blanc, *Spain's Transition to Democracy: The Politics of Constitution-Making* (Boulder: Westview, 1987); and Richard Gunther, "Constitutional Change in Contemporary Spain," in Keith G. Banting and Richard Simeon, eds., *The Politics of Constitutional Change in Industrial Nations: Redesigning the State* (London: Macmillan, 1985).

19. See Juan J. Linz, "De la crisis de un Estado unitario al Estado de las autonomías," in Fernando Fernández Rodríguez, *La España de las autonomías* (Madrid: Instituto de Estudios de Administración Local, 1985), pp. 527–672; Juan J. Linz, *Conflicto en Euskadi* (Madrid: Espasa Calpe, 1986), and Linz "State

Building and Nation Building." On the negotiation of the Basque Autonomy Statute see the account by two journalists, Kepa Bordegarai and Robert Pastor, *Estatuto Vasco* (San Sebastián: Ediciones Vascas, 1979).

20. Some extreme separatist groups continued to boycott the vote on autonomy, and the overall voter turnout was 13 percent lower than the Spanish average on the constitutional reform; nevertheless, the voter turnout of 54 percent was still politically significant.

21. Sources: Francisco A. Orizo and Alejandro Sánchez Fernández, *El sistema de valors dels catalans* (Barcelona: Institut Catalá d'Etudis Mediterranees, 1991), p. 207; and Centro de Investigaciones Sociológicas, *Los españoles ante el segundo aniversario de la firma del Tratado de Adhesión de España a la Comunidad Europea,* April 1988, p. 53.

22. See Linz, "De la crisis de un Estado unitario," p. 587.

23. Linz, *Conflicto en Euskadi,* p. 698.

24. Among other things, the nationality policy of the Soviet regime institutionalized and deepened ethnic differences through such practices as establishing administrative units that largely corresponded with ethnicity; defining the identities listed on citizens' internal passports on the basis of ethnicity rather than republic of residence; constitutionally acknowledging the right to secede; securing international diplomatic recognition for some republics (Ukraine and Byelorussia); and recruiting leaders of republics from the majority ethnic group and allowing them to build ethnic power bases. In fact, the institutions created by the party-state virtually created some nations that had not existed before.

25. The statewide elections of 1989 were limited in several important ways: First, these were not multiparty elections, so democratic political society in the real sense could not develop; one third of seats in the Congress of Peoples' Deputies were set aside for the Communist Party and were not open to contestation, and nominations for other seats could be dominated by the party. The races in one quarter of the constituencies were contested by only a single candidate. Second, the more important body, the Supreme Soviet, was elected indirectly by the 2,250 members of the Congress of Peoples' Deputies, and this filtering process introduced clearly undemocratic criteria—Boris Yeltsin, for example, won 89 percent of the vote for his congressional seat but was not allowed to take a seat in the Supreme Soviet until another member resigned from that body and turned his seat over to Yeltsin.

26. We shall not present a detailed analysis of the Spanish transition, since it has been examined at great length by Linz and others in the extensive literature published in recent years. We shall therefore deal only with the consolidation of Spanish democracy. See Linz, "Innovative Leadership," pp. 141–86; and Juan J. Linz, Manuel Gómez-Reino, Francisco A. Orizo, and Darío Vila, *Informe sociológico sobre el cambio político en España: 1975–1981* (Madrid: Editorial Euramérica, 1981).

27. "Actitudes y opiniones de los españoles ante la constitución y las instituciones democráticas," working paper no. 1495, Centro de Investigaciones Sociológicas, Madrid, November 1985, p. 32.

28. Before the coup attempt a number of prominent politicians from a range of parties, including the Socialist Party, engaged in "semiloyal" discus-

sions with the military about a possible civil-military caretaker coalitional government. All such ambivalent actions on the part of party activists stopped after the coup. See Paul Preston, *The Triumph of Democracy in Spain* (London: Methuen, 1986), pp. 160–88, esp. 181–84.

29. Agüero, "Assertion of Civilian Supremacy," pp. 300, 309, 356. An excellent discussion of the Socialist governments' reforms can be found on pp. 309–56.

30. For a more extensive conceptual discussion of military prerogatives and military contestation, see Alfred Stepan, *Rethinking Military Politics,* (Princeton: Princeton University Press, 1988), pp. 93–127.

31. Felipe Agüero, "The Military in the Processes of Political Democratization in South America and South Europe: Outcomes and Initial Conditions" (paper presented at the Fifteenth International Congress of the Latin American Studies Association, San Juan, Puerto Rico, September 21–23, 1989), pp. 22, 27. Also see Rodrigo, "El cambio hacia la democracia," pp. 21–34; and Stepan, *Rethinking Military Politics,* pp. 118–21; Stanley G. Payne, *The Franco Regime* (Madison: University of Wisconsin Press, 1987); Amando de Miguel, *Sociología del franquismo* (Barcelona: Editorial Euros, 1975); and Richard Gunther, *Public Policy in a No-Party State: Spanish Planning and Budgeting in the Twilight of the Franquist Era* (Berkeley: University of California Press, 1980).

32. Pérez-Díaz, *Return of Civil Society*, p. 14.

33. See J. M. Maravall, "Economic Reforms in New Democracies: The Southern European Experience," *East South System Transformations,* working paper no. 3, Department of Political Science, University of Chicago, October 1990, p. 3.

34. Laurence Whitehead, "International Aspects of Democratization," in O'Donnell, Schmitter, and Whitehead, *TAR*, p. 22. Also see Geoffrey Pridham's chapter in this volume.

35. Maravall, "Economic Reforms in New Democracies," p. 16.

36. Spanish unemployment data are from Banco de Bilbao, Economic Research Department, *Situación: Review of the Spanish Economy,* int'l ed., no. 10–11, 1986. The Spanish growth rates are derived from *United Nations Statistical Yearbook,* 1976 and 1982, and Economic Intelligence Unit, *Quarterly Reports: Spain* (2nd quarter 1986).

37. Linz and Stepan develop this argument at greater length in "Political Crafting of Democratic Consolidation or Destruction: European and South American Comparisons," in Robert A. Pastor, ed., *Democracy in the Americas: Stopping the Pendulum* (New York: Holmes and Meier, 1989), pp. 42–48.

38. See Arend Lijphart, *Democracies: Patterns of Majoritarian and Consensus Government in Twenty-one Countries* (New Haven: Yale University Press, 1984), pp. 1–36; Gunther, "Constitutional Change in Contemporary Spain," and "Spain: Modern Elite Settlement;" and Bonime-Blanc, *Spain's Transition to Democracy*.

39. "Actitudes y opiniones," pp. 50–51.

40. See Manuel Lucena, "Interpretações do Salazarismo: notas de leitura crítica" *Análise Social,* 20, (1984): 423–51, and "The Evolution of Portuguese Corporatism under Salazar and Caetano," in Lawrence S. Graham and Harry M. Makler, eds., *Contemporary Portugal: The Revolution and Its Antecedents* (Aus-

tin: University of Texas Press, 1979), pp. 47–88; António Costa Pinto, *O Salazarismo e o Fascismo Europeo: Problemas de interpretação nas ciências sociais* (Lisbon: Editorial Estampa, 1992), and "The Salazar 'New State' and European Fascism," working paper no. 91/12, European University Institute, Florence, 1991; and Javier Tusell, *La dictadura de Franco* (Madrid: Alianza Editorial, 1988), pp. 272–305.

41. See Philippe C. Schmitter, "The 'Régime d'Exception' That Became the Rule: Forty-eight Years of Authoritarian Domination in Portugal," in Graham and Makler, *Contemporary Portugal,* pp. 3–46.

42. See Douglas L. Wheeler, "The Military and the Portuguese Dictatorship, 1926–1974: 'The Honor of the Army,'" in Graham and Makler, *Contemporary Portugal,* pp. 221–56.

43. See Scott Mainwaring and Donald Share, "Transition through Transaction: Democratization in Brazil and Spain," in Wayne Selcher, ed., *Political Liberalization in Brazil* (Boulder: Westview Press, 1986), pp. 175–215.

44. For a systematic analysis of how Marcello Caetano, in sharp contrast to the "innovative leadership" of Suárez in Spain, did not take advantage of these favorable conditions for a transacted transition, see Daniel V. Friedheim, "Innovative Leadership: The Failure to Democratize Pre-Revolutionary Portugal" (Yale University, July 1990, mimeographed).

45. See Philippe C. Schmitter, "Liberation by Golpe: Retrospective Thoughts on the Demise of Authoritarian Rule in Portugal," *Armed Forces and Society* 2 (November 1975), pp. 5–33; and María Carrilho, *Forças armadas e mudança política em Portugal no siglo XX: Para uma explicaçâo sociológica do papel dos militares* (Lisbon: Estudios Gerais Série Universitária, 1985), p. 385.

46. See Nancy Gina Bermeo, *The Revolution within the Revolution: Workers Control in Rural Portugal* (Princeton: Princeton University Press, 1986).

47. Kenneth Maxwell, "Regime Overthrow and the Prospects for Democratic Transition in Portugal," in O'Donnell, Schmitter, and Whitehead, *TAR: Southern Europe*, p. 113.

48. José Sánchez Cervelló, "El proceso democrático portugués (1974–1975)," in Hipólito de la Torre, ed., *Portugal y España en el cambio político (1958–1978)* (Mérida: Universidad Nacional de Educación a Distancia, Centro Regional de Extremadura, 1989), pp. 155–63 (quote, p. 162).

49. Sánchez Cervelló, "El proceso democrático portugués," pp. 162–63. The decrees, manifestos, and speeches of the 1974–1975 revolutionary period are published in Henrique Barrilaro Ruas, *A Revolução das Flores: Do 25 de Abril ao Governo Provisório* (Lisbon: Editorial Aster, n.d.).

50. See David B. Goldey, "Elections and the Consolidation of Portuguese Democracy: 1974–1983," *Electoral Studies* 2, no. 3, 1983, pp. 229–40; and Thomas C. Bruneau and Alex Macleod, *Politics in Contemporary Portugal: Parties and the Consolidation of Democracy,* (Boulder: Lynne Rienner, 1986).

51. Quoted in Maxwell, "Regime Overthrow," p. 127.

52. Agüero, "The Military in Democratization," table 5.

53. Lawrence S. Graham, "The Military: Modernization and Changing Perspectives," in Kenneth Maxwell, ed., *Portuguese Defense and Foreign Policy Since Democratization*, special report no. 3 (New York: Camões Center, Research Institute on International Change, Columbia University, 1991), p. 16.

54. Maxwell, "Regime Overthrow," p. 133.

55. See "Plataforma Constitucional Partidos—M.F.A.," in Fernando Ribeiro de Mello, ed., *Dossier 2a República*, vol. 1 (Lisbon: Edições Afrodite, 1976), pp. 235–41.

56. See "Segundo Pacto dos Partidos con o M.F.A.," in Reinaldo Caldeira and María do C'eu Silva, eds., *Constituição Política da República Portuguesa 1976: Proyectos, Votações e Posições dos Partidos* (Lisbon: Livraria Bertrand, 1976), pp. 343–52.

57. Bruneau and Macleod, *Politics in Contemporary Portugal*, p. 40.

58. See Bruneau and Macleod, *Politics in Contemporary Portugal*, pp. 12–25; and Graham, "The Military," pp. 14–28.

59. Bruneau and Macleod, *Politics in Contemporary Portugal*, p. 40.

60. See Jorge Gaspar and Nuno Vitorino, *As Eleições de 25 de Abril: Geografia e Imagem dos Partidos*, (Lisbon: Livros Horizonte, 1976).

61. See Franz-Wilhelm Heimer, Jorge Vala-Salvador, and José Manuel Leite Vargas, "Attitudes toward Democracy in Contemporary Portugal" (paper presented to the European Consortium for Political Research, Paris, April 10–15, 1989); and Bruneau and Macleod, *Politics in Contemporary Portugal*.

62. *Eurobarometre* (1991), pp. 18–31.

63. Arend Lijphart, Thomas C. Bruneau, P. Nikiforos Diamandouros, and Richard Gunther, "A Mediterranean Model of Democracy?: The Southern European Democracies in Comparative Perspective," *West European Politics* 11, 1988, p. 19.

64. Kenneth Maxwell writes "as events in Lisbon turned leftward, for a time U.S policy, dominated by Henry Kissinger, abandoned hope for a democratic outcome and toyed with various counterrevolutionary options—some paramilitary, some involving separatism in the Azores." See Maxwell's "Portuguese Defense and Foreign Policy: An Overview" in Kenneth Maxwell, ed., *Portuguese Defense and Foreign Policy*, p. 6.

65. See Rainer Eisfeld, "Portugal and Western Europe," in *Portugal in the 1980s: Dilemmas of Democratic Consolidation* (New York: Greenwood, 1986), pp. 29–62, esp. 55; and Thomas C. Bruneau, *Politics and Nationhood* (New York: Praeger, 1984), pp. 52–54.

66. See António Costa Pinto, "Dealing with the Legacy of Authoritarianism: Political Purge and Radical Right Movements in Portugal's Transition to Democracy (1974–1976)," in Stein U. Larsen et al., *Modern Europe after Fascism: 1945–1980s* (Bergen: Norwegian University Press, forthcoming).

67. See Maravall, "Economic Reforms in New Democracies," pp. 2–3; and Diana Smith, "Portugal and the Challenge of 1992" (New York: Camões Center, Research Institute on International Change, Columbia University, 1990), p. 6. The colonial wars, however, caused a growing financial crisis of the state as the regime devoted between 30 and 50 percent of its budget to wars in Africa.

68. As Diana Smith points out, by December 1982 Portugal had a budget deficit amounting to 15 percent of its GDP, a balance-of-payments deficit equal to 13.5 percent of GDP, and a foreign debt equivalent to 72 percent of GDP ("Portugal and the Challenge of 1992," p. 9).

69. Thomas C. Bruneau, "Portugal's Unexpected Transition," in Kenneth Maxwell and Michael H. Haltzel, eds., *Portugal: Ancient Country, Young Democra-*

cy (Washington, D.C.: Woodrow Wilson Center Press, 1990), p. 15.

70. Constantine Danopoulos, "Farewell to Man on Horseback—Intervention and Civilian Rule in Modern Greece" (paper presented at a conference on democratic consolidation organized by the Centro de la Realidad Contemporánea, Santiago, Chile, August 10–11, 1989), p. 6.

71. P. Nikiforos Diamandouros "Regime Change and the Prospects for Democracy in Greece: 1974–1983," in O'Donnell, Schmitter, and Whitehead, *TAR: Southern Europe,* pp. 146–47.

72. Diamandouros "Regime Change," p. 157. Also see Diamandouros, "Transition to, and Consolidation of, Democratic Politics in Greece, 1974–1983: A Tentative Assessment," in Geoffrey Pridham, ed., *The New Mediterranean Democracies: Regime Transitions in Spain, Greece, and Portugal* (London: Frank Cass, 1984), pp. 53–56; and Takis Pappas, "Greece: July 24–November 17, 1974" (unpublished manuscript, Yale University, 1988).

73. Thanos Veremis, "Greece: Veto and Impasse, 1967–1974," in Christopher Clapham and George Philip, eds., *The Political Dilemmas of Military Regimes* (London: Croom Helm, 1985), p. 41.

74. On the significance of the distinction between state and regime, see Fishman, "Rethinking State and Regime," pp. 422–40.

75. Diamandouros, "Transition to and Consolidation of Democratic Politics," p. 60.

76. Thanos Veremis, "The Military," in Kevin Featherstone and Dimitrios K. Katsoudas, eds., *Political Change in Greece before and after the Colonels* (London: Croom Helm, 1987), p. 225. A similar argument is made in Constantine Danopoulos, "Farewell to Man on Horseback."

77. On the antidemocratic paraconstitutional features of Greek political life before the 1967 breakdown see P. Nikiforos Diamandouros, "The Politics of Constitution-Making in Postauthoritarian Greece: A Macrohistorical Perspective" (paper presented to the American Political Science Association, annual meeting, 1987).

78. On the political evolution of PASOK and their early maximalism, see P. Nikiforos Diamandouros, "PASOK and State-Society Relations in Postauthoritarian Greece (1974–1988)," in Speros Vryonis, Jr., ed., *Greece on the Road to Democracy: From the Junta to PASOK, 1974–1986* (New Rochelle, N.Y.: Caratzas, 1991), pp. 15–35.

79. See Richard Clogg, *Parties and Elections in Greece: The Search for Legitimacy* (London: C. Hurst, 1987), p. 60.

80. Nikos Alivizatos, "The Difficulties of 'Rationalization' in a Polarized Political System: The Greek Chamber of Deputies," in Ulrike Liebert and Maurizio Cotta, eds., *Parliament and Democratic Consolidation in Southern Europe* (London: Pinter, 1990), p. 134.

81. See Alivizatos, "The Difficulties of 'Rationalization,'" p. 146.

82. Panayote Elias Dimitras, "Greek Public Attitudes: Continuity and Change," *International Journal of Public Opinion Research* 2, summer 1990, pp. 92–115, esp. 103.

83. These theoretical perspectives are set forth in Juan J. Linz and Alfred Stepan, eds., *The Breakdown of Democratic Regimes* (Baltimore: Johns Hopkins University Press, 1978) (see preface n. 2 above).

84. Laurence Whitehead, "International Aspects of Democratization," p. 23.

85. For more extensive and systematic explorations of the impact of international factors on democratic consolidation, see Linz and Stepan, *Problems of Democratic Transition and Consolidation*; and Geoffrey Pridham's chapter in this volume.

86. See Juan J. Linz, "Excursus on Presidential and Parliamentary Democracy," in Linz and Stepan, *Breakdown of Democratic Regimes*, pp. 71–74, and Juan J. Linz, "Presidential or Parliamentary Democracy: Does It Make a Difference?," in Juan J. Linz and Arturo Valenzuela, eds., *The Failure of Presidential Democracy* (Baltimore: Johns Hopkins University Press, 1994), pp. 3–87, esp. 22–24; and Alfred Stepan, "Parliamentarismo X Presidencialismo no Mundo Moderno: Revisão de um Debate Atual," *Estudios Avançados* 4, no. 8, January–April 1990, pp. 96–107. Also see Richard Gunther and Anthony Mughan, "Political Institutions and Cleavage Management," in R. Kent Weaver and Bert A. Rockman, eds., *Do Institutions Matter?: Government Capabilities in the United States and Abroad* (Washington, D.C.: Brookings Institution, 1993).

Chapter 4

I am grateful to Mariano Torcal and the editors of this volume for their helpful comments.

1. For a detailed account of these limits, see Felipe Agüero, "The Military and the Limits to Democratization in South America," in Scott Mainwaring, Guillermo O'Donnell, and Samuel Valenzuela, eds., *Issues in Democratic Consolidation: The New South American Democracies in Comparative Perspective* (Notre Dame, Ind.: University of Notre Dame Press, 1992).

2. Exceptions to this were the Portuguese military, which rose against the old authoritarian regime, and the militaries in the countries which democratized immediately following defeat in World War II, where the Allies swiftly imposed changes in the structures and values of the socialization process of successor armies.

3. Adam Przeworski, "Some Problems in the Study of the Transition to Democracy," in Guillermo O'Donnell, Philippe C. Schmitter, and Laurence Whitehead, eds., *Transitions from Authoritarian Rule* [*TAR*]: *Comparative Perspectives* (Baltimore, Johns Hopkins University Press, 1986) (see preface n. 3 above), p. 52.

4. The importance of elite unity has been highlighted recently in John Higley and Richard Gunther, eds., *Elites and Democratic Consolidation in Latin America and Southern Europe* (Cambridge: Cambridge University Press, 1992). Also see Giuseppe Di Palma, "La consolidación democrática: Una visión minimalista," *Revista Española de Investigaciones Sociológicas* 42, April–June 1988, pp. 67–92; Bolivar Lamounier, "Challenges to Democratic Consolidation in Brazil" (paper prepared for the American Political Science Association, Washington D.C., September 1988); and Daniel H. Levine, "Venezuela since 1958: The Consolidation of Democratic Politics," in Juan J. Linz and Alfred Stepan, eds., *The Breakdown of Democratic Regimes: Latin America* (Baltimore: Johns Hopkins University Press, 1978) (see preface n. 2 above).

5. For an account of the military in the democratization processes of these

countries see Felipe Agüero, "Regierung und Streitkräfte in Spanien nach Franco," in Walther L. Bernecker and Josef Oehrlein, eds., *Spanien Heute* (Frankfurt: Vervuert Verlag, 1991); "Democracia en España y supremacía civil," *Revista Española de Investigaciones Sociológicas* 44, October–December 1988, pp. 23–49; and Thomas C. Bruneau and Alex Macleod, *Politics in Contemporary Portugal: Parties and the Consolidation of Democracy* (Boulder: Lynne Rienner, 1986). For an account of the 1992 military challenges to a unified elite in Venezuela, see Felipe Agüero, "Debilitating Democracy: Political Elites and Military Rebels in Venezuela," in Louis W. Goodman et al., eds., *Lessons of the Venezuelan Experience* (Baltimore: Woodrow Wilson Center Press and Johns Hopkins University Press, 1994).

6. Di Palma would have democrats relax at a much earlier point (see Giuseppe Di Palma, *To Craft Democracies: An Essay on Democratic Transitions* [Berkeley: University of California Press, 1990], ch. 7). Philippe C. Schmitter, in "The Consolidation of Political Democracy in Southern Europe" (unpublished manuscript, June 1988) views the submission of the military to civilian control as occurring during the process of democratic consolidation or after this process is completed with the internal regulation of major political institutions. Leonardo Morlino describes the "neutralization of the military" as critical to democratic consolidation, in "Consolidación democrática: Definición, modelos, hipótesis," *Revista Española de Investigaciones Sociológicas* 35, July–September 1986, pp. 7–61.

7. My definition differs from Huntington's classic concepts of subjective control or objective control of the military, which, in my view, grant to the military either no autonomy or too much (see Samuel P. Huntington, *The Soldier and the State* [New York: Vintage Books, 1957], p. 82–85). My definition is closer to those found in Claude E. Welch, "Civilian Control of the Military: Myth and Reality," in Claude E. Welch, ed., *Civilian Control of the Military* (Albany: State University of New York Press, 1976), and *No Farewell to Arms* (Boulder: Westview, 1987); J. Samuel Fitch, "Toward a Democratic Model of Civil-Military Relations for Latin America" (paper presented to the International Political Science Association, Washington, D.C., August 1988); and Alfred Stepan, *Rethinking Military Politics* (Princeton: Princeton University Press, 1988).

8. Robert A. Dahl, *Polyarchy* (New Haven: Yale University Press, 1971), p. 3. Also see Juan J. Linz, "Totalitarian and Authoritarian Regimes," in Fred Greenstein and Nelson Polsby, eds., *Handbook of Political Science*, vol. 3 (Reading, Mass.: Addison Wesley, 1975), pp. 182–84. Dahl has now explicitly added civilian control over the military to his views on polyarchy: see Robert A. Dahl, *Democracy and Its Critics* (New Haven: Yale University Press, 1989), pp. 244–51. See also Terry Lynn Karl, "Dilemmas of Democratization in Latin America," *Comparative Politics*, October 1990, p. 2; and Philippe C. Schmitter and Terry Lynn Karl, "What Democracy Is . . . and Is Not," *Journal of Democracy* 2, no. 3, summer 1991.

9. In Stepan's scheme, the new situation develops and is observable through a reduction in the levels of military prerogatives and military contestation. See Stepan, *Rethinking Military Politics*.

10. For categories of transition paths, see Philippe C. Schmitter, "Specula-

tions about the Prospective Demise of Authoritarian Regimes and Its Possible Consequences," *Revista de Ciencia Política* (Lisbon) 1–2, 1985; Donald Share, "Transitions to Democracy and Transition through Transaction," *Comparative Political Studies* 19, January 1985, pp. 525–48; and Alfred Stepan, "Paths toward Redemocratization: Theoretical and Comparative Considerations," in O'Donnell, Schmitter, and Whitehead, *TAR: Comparative Perspectives*.

11. See Juan J. Linz, "Transitions to Democracy," *Washington Quarterly* 13, summer 1990, pp. 143–64; and Donald Share, "Two Transitions: Democratization and the Evolution of the Spanish Socialist Left," *West European Politics* 1, 1985, pp. 82–103. For an account of the Spanish case, see Richard Gunther, "Spain: The Very Model of the Modern Elite Settlement," in Higley and Gunther, *Elites and Democratic Consolidation*.

12. Paraguay is the only case in which forceful removal of the authoritarian leader was combined with a leading role in the following period for the official party of the authoritarian regime; see Benjamín Arditi, "Elecciones y partidos en el Paraguay de la transición," *Revista Mexicana de Sociología* 4, 1990, pp. 83–98. In Bolivia, the start of the transition in 1978 was followed by a succession of interim civil and military regimes until democratization resumed in 1982; see Eduardo A. Gamarra, "Bolivia: Disengagement and Democratization," in Constantine P. Danopoulos, ed., *Military Disengagement from Politics* (London: Routledge, 1988). For Brazil see Frances Hagopian and Scott Mainwaring, "Democracy in Brazil: Problems and Prospects," *World Policy Journal*, Summer 1987, pp. 485–514; for Uruguay see Charles Gillespie, "The Role of Civil-Military Pacts in Elite Settlements and Elite Convergence: Democratic Consolidation in Uruguay," in Higley and Gunther, *Elites and Democratic Consolidation*; for Peru see Julio Cotler, "Military Interventions and 'Transfer of Power to Civilians' in Peru," in O'Donnell, Schmitter, and Whitehead, *TAR: Latin America* (see preface n. 3 above); for Ecuador, Fernando Bustamante, "El rol de los términos de la democratización post-militarista en la evolución democrática de los países andinos de América del Sur," *Documento de Trabajo* 328 (Santiago de Chile), 1987; for Chile, Pamela Constable and Arturo Valenzuela, "Chile's Return to Democracy," *Foreign Affairs* 68, no. 5, winter 1989–90, pp. 169–86; and Arturo Valenzuela and Pamela Constable, "Democracy in Chile," *Current History*, February 1991, pp. 53–56.

13. See Harry J. Psomiades, "Greece: From the Colonels' Rule to Democracy," in John H. Herz, ed., *From Dictatorship to Democracy* (Westport, Conn.: Greenwood Press, 1982); Constantine Danopoulos, "From Military to Civilian Rule in Contemporary Greece," *Armed Forces and Society* 10, no. 2, 1984, pp. 229–50; and P. Nikiforos Diamandouros, "Regime Change and the Prospects for Democracy in Greece: 1974–1983," in O'Donnell, Schmitter, and Whitehead, *TAR: Southern Europe*.

14. Thanos Veremis, "The Military," in Kevin Featherstone and Dimitrios K. Katsoudas, eds., *Political Change in Greece: Before and after the Colonels* (New York: St. Martin's, 1987).

15. See James Brown, *Delicately Poised Allies: Greece and Turkey* (London: Brassey's, 1991), ch. 2. Also see, Constantine P. Danopoulos, *Warriors and Politicians in Modern Greece* (Chapel Hill, N.C.: Documentary Publications, 1984).

16. See Diogo Freitas do Amaral, "La Constitución y las Fuerzas Armadas,"

Revista de Estudios Políticos 60–61 (Madrid) 1988; Francisco Pinto Balsemão, "The Constitution and Politics: Options for the Future," in Kenneth Maxwell, ed., *Portugal in the 1980s: Dilemmas of Democratic Consolidation* (New York: Greenwood, 1986); and Bruneau and Macleod, *Politics in Contemporary Portugal.*

17. See Alvaro Vasconcelos, "Portuguese Defense Policy: Internal Politics and Defense Commitments," in John Chipman, ed., *NATO's Southern Allies: Internal and External Challenges* (London: Routledge, 1988); and Thomas C. Bruneau, "Defense Modernization and the Armed Forces in Portugal: Implications for U.S.-Portuguese Relations" (unpublished manuscript, July 1991).

18. For a more complete account of reforms in Spain, see Felipe Agüero, "The Assertion of Civilian Supremacy in Post-Authoritarian Contexts: Spain in Comparative Perspective," (Ph.D. diss., Duke University, 1991; forthcoming, as *Soldiers, Civilians, and Democracy,* from Johns Hopkins University Press).

19. For a comparison between Spain and Portugal, see Juan J. Linz, "Some Comparative Thoughts on the Transition to Democracy in Portugal and Spain," in Simon Serfaty and Jorge Braga de Macedo, eds., *Portugal since the Revolution: Economic and Political Perspectives* (Boulder: Westview, 1981); and Kenneth Maxwell, "The Emergence of Democracy in Spain and Portugal," *Orbis,* Spring 1983.

20. For a review of these cases in greater detail see Agüero, "The Military and the Limits to Democratization." An earlier review, which includes Central American countries, is J. Samuel Fitch, "The Armed Forces and Democracy in Latin America" (paper presented to the Inter-American Dialogue, Working Group on Armed Forces and Democracy, Lima, August 1987).

21. See David Pion-Berlin, "Between Confrontation and Accommodation: Military and Government Policy in Democratic Argentina," *Journal of Latin American Studies* 23, October 1991, pp. 543–71; Deborah L. Norden, "Democratic Consolidation and Military Professionalism: Argentina in the 1980s," *Journal of Interamerican Studies and World Affairs* 32, fall 1990, pp. 151–76; and J. Samuel Fitch and Andrés Fontana, "Military Policy and Democratic Consolidation in Latin America," *Documento CEDES,* 58 (Buenos Aires) 1990.

22. David Pion-Berlin and Ernesto López, "A House Divided: Crisis, Cleavage, and Conflict in the Argentine Army," in Edward C. Epstein, ed., *The New Democracy in Argentina* (New York: Praeger, forthcoming); and Rosendo Fraga, "Permanente inestabilidad: Frágiles relaciones cívico-militares en Argentina" (unpublished manuscript, March 1991).

23. This situation of continuity fully reflected the absence of a *ruptura* side to the accorded transition reforms, a situation well manifested in the fact that the new civilian president had been, only a few years before, a leading figure in the military regime's official political party. Sarney was in fact supported by the military and a civilian coalition dominated by former supporters of the military regime. In stark contrast to the governments of the Spanish monarchy, the dominant elites in the first Brazilian postmilitary government were not even committed to democratic reforms and the pursuit of civilian supremacy. See Hagopian and Mainwaring, "Democracy in Brazil"; and Frances Hagopian, "'Democracy by Undemocratic Means'?: Elites, Political Pacts, and Regime Transition in Brazil," *Comparative Political Studies* 23, July 1990, pp. 147–70.

24. Proposals to shorten President Sarney's term were based on his acciden-

tal and unexpected accession. A compromise arranged by the moderate opposition to the military government had him run for the vice presidency, but President-elect Tancredo Neves died shortly before he was due to assume office, and the presidential sash was then bestowed on Sarney.

25. Jorge Zaverucha, "Do mito da supremacia civil à realidade: Collor e os militares," *Cadernos de Conjuntura* 44, Instituto Universitário de Pesquisas do Rio de Janeiro, IUPERJ, September 1991; *New York Times,* November 19, 1991, p. A3; *Brazil Report,* August 15, 1991; and *Latin American Monitor,* July–August 1991, p. 921. For a different assessment of the Brazilian case, see Wendy Hunter, "Back to the Barracks?: The Military's Political Role in Post-Authoritarian Brazil" (paper presented to the 17th International Congress of the Latin American Studies Association, Los Angeles, September 24–27, 1992). The military played no direct role in the October 1992 temporary suspension of Fernando Collor from the presidency pending an investigation of corruption charges, a test entirely accomplished by the Congress. The persistent pursuit of the case by Congress was, if anything, supported by the military's view that political deals among elites should not preclude the full observance of legal stipulations on the matter.

26. Felipe Agüero, "Chile: South America's Success Story?" *Current History* 92, no. 572, March 1993, pp. 130–35; and Brian Loveman, "¿Misión cumplida?: Civil Military Relations and the Chilean Political Transition," *Journal of Interamerican Studies and World Affairs* 33, fall 1991, p. 35–74.

27. In the 1980 presidential elections, however, the electorate favored APRA's adversary Fernando Belaúnde, rewarding his refusal to participate in the military-supervised 1978 elections, while punishing APRA's collaboration with the military during the transition.

28. The preceding military regime had been a case of "inclusionary corporatism," which did not rely on the kind of brutal repression that characterized authoritarian rule in Argentina, Brazil, Chile, and Uruguay. See Alfred Stepan, *State and Society: Peru in Comparative Perspective* (Princeton: Princeton University Press, 1978); and Angela Cornell and Kenneth Roberts, "Democracy, Counterinsurgency, and Human Rights: The Case of Peru," *Human Rights Quarterly* 12, 1990, pp. 529–53.

29. See Marcial Rubio, *Ministerio de Defensa: Antecedentes y retos* (Lima: APEP–Friedrich Ebert, 1987); Sandra Woy-Hazelton and William A. Hazelton, "Sustaining Democracy in Peru: Dealing with Parliamentary and Revolutionary Changes," in George A. Lopez and Michael Stohl, eds., *Liberalization and Redemocratization in Latin America* (New York: Greenwood, 1987); and Cynthia McClintock, "El Gobierno aprista y la fuerza armada del Perú," in Heraclio Bonilla and Paul W. Drake, eds., *El APRA: De la ideología a la praxis* (Lima: Nuevo Mundo EIRL, 1989).

30. *Latin American Weekly Report: Southern Cone* 19, April 1990, p. 7.

31. See Juan Rial, *Las Fuerzas Armadas en los años 90* (Montevideo: Peitho, 1990).

32. Gunther, "Spain: Modern Elite Settlement." Highlighting the level of elite unity attained, Burton, Gunther, and Higley maintain that democracy was to a large extent already consolidated by this time. See Michael Burton, Richard Gunther, and John Higley, "Elites and Democratic Consolidation in Latin

America and Southern Europe: An Overview," in Higley and Gunther, *Elites and Democratic Consolidation,* pp. 326–27.

33. The initial landmark development in this regard in Spain was the 1984 reform of the organic law of national defense, which eliminated the Council of Chiefs of Staff as the supreme collective organ in the military chain of command and enhanced the powers of the minister of defense over the armed forces. In Portugal, as we saw above, reforms such as those conducted in Spain have been implemented only very recently.

34. Burton, Gunther, and Higley, "Elites and Democratic Consolidation," p. 325. Elite unity does not mean absence of severe disputes; it only means consensual support for democratic procedures. In Greece, for instance, New Democracy and PASOK have sustained vigorous civil confrontations, but support for democracy has been unquestioned. Notable in this regard were Karamanlis's initial postures in favor of the incorporation of the Communist left—banned since the civil war—and his refusal to back the monarchic right in the 1975 referendum.

35. This question was first raised in Juan J. Linz, "The Transition from Authoritarian Regimes to Democratic Political Systems and the Problems of Consolidation of Political Democracy" (paper presented to the Tokyo Round Table of the International Political Science Association, March 29–April 1, 1982). Also see, Stepan, "Paths toward Redemocratization;" O'Donnell and Schmitter, *TAR: Tentative Conclusions about Uncertain Transitions* (see preface n. 3 above); Guillermo O'Donnell, "Introduction to the Latin American Cases," in O'Donnell, Schmitter, and Whitehead, *TAR: Latin America*; and Felipe Agüero, "The Military in the Processes of Political Democratization in South America and Southern Europe: Outcomes and Initial Conditions" (paper presented to the 15th International Congress of the Latin American Studies Association, Miami, December, 1989).

36. See Richard Gunther, *Public Policy in a No-Party State: Spanish Planning and Budgeting in the Twilight of the Franquist Era* (Berkeley: University of California Press, 1980).

37. For instance, none of the winners in the first presidential elections after the demise of military regimes in Peru, Ecuador, Brazil, Argentina, or Chile was the candidate the military preferred.

38. An important military input, however often neglected by analysts, is the moderating effect on the postures of political leaders that results from the perceived threat of a military backlash.

39. Juan Linz observed that, if the armed forces in Spain had been able to expand their prerogatives during the transition, they most certainly would have made the negotiation of the autonomy statutes for the historic regions—an issue critically sensitive for the military—much more difficult if not entirely impossible (Linz, "Some Comparative Thoughts on Transition," p. 32.)

40. This consequence of civilianization in Spain was reinforced by the peculiar position of the head of state. The king, anointed by Franco, his successor as head of state and supreme chief of the armies, provided to the government institutional continuity as well as legitimacy in the eyes of the military. The military, although apprehensive, felt nonetheless reassured, at least initially, by the fact that the transition would be conducted by elites from within Franquism.

Thus, there were few incentives for the military to change the relatively subordinate position in which it found itself at the start of the transition. See Fernando Rodrigo, "El papel de las Fuerzas Armadas españolas durante la transición política: Algunas hipótesis básicas," *Revista Internacional de Sociología* 43, April–June 1985, pp. 349–69, and "El camino hacia la democracia: Militares y política en la transición española," Ph.D. diss., Universidad Complutense de Madrid, 1989. Also see, Rafael Bañón and José Antonio Olmeda, "Las Fuerzas Armadas en España: Institucionalización y proceso de cambio," in Rafael Bañón and José Antonio Olmeda, eds., *La institución militar en el estado contemporáneo* (Madrid: Alianza Editorial, 1985).

41. O'Donnell and Schmitter, *TAR: Tentative Conclusions,* pp. 17–21.

42. Stepan, "Paths toward Redemocratization," p. 65.

43. Scott Mainwaring, "Transitions to Democracy and Democratic Consolidation: Theoretical and Comparative Issues," in Mainwaring, O'Donnell, and Valenzuela, *Issues in Democratic Consolidation,* p. 322. Also see, Scott Mainwaring and Donald Share, "Transitions through Transaction: Democratization in Brazil and Spain," in *Political Liberalization in Brazil* (Boulder: Westview, 1986); and Scott Mainwaring and Eduardo Viola, "Transitions to Democracy: Brazil and Argentina in the 1980s," *Journal of International Affairs* 38, winter 1985, pp. 193–219. The substance of the distinctions made by Mainwaring influenced subsequent classifications offered in Samuel P. Huntington, *The Third Wave: Democratization in the Late Twentieth Century* (Norman: University of Oklahoma Press, 1991), p. 113; and Josep M. Colomer, "Transitions by Agreement: Modeling the Spanish Way," *American Political Science Review* 85, no. 4, 1991, p. 1297.

44. Stepan, "Paths toward Redemocratization," pp. 74–75.

45. See, for instance, Stepan's treatment of these cases in ibid., pp. 76–78.

46. That a very weakened military stayed in power in Argentina for so long after the collapse of the regime speaks also of the weaknesses of the civilian leadership, which did not effectively become organized until the final stages of the presidential race. In this regard, Argentina's experience clearly differs from that of Venezuela. The latter is placed here under the category of civilian controlled transitions, despite the fact that the transition junta was headed by Admiral Wolfgang Larrazábal, who had conducted the coup against the dictator. However, this junta included civilians appointed in agreement with the major parties, and these were most influential in the conduct of transition policies guided by the terms of the pact that party leaders had previously reached. Also, Larrazábal was running as the presidential candidate of one of the major parties. See Felipe Agüero, "The Military and Democracy in Venezuela," in Louis W. Goodman, Johanna S. R. Mendelson, and Juan Rial, eds., *The Military and Democracy: The Future of Civil-Military Relations in Latin America* (Lexington, Mass.: D. C. Heath, 1990).

47. Gary W. Wynia, "The Military's Attempts to Manage the Transition," in Hans Binnendijk, ed., *Authoritarian Regimes in Transition* (Washington, D.C.: Center for the Study of Foreign Affairs, Foreign Service Institute, Department of State, 1987).

48. Linz and Stepan have recently introduced a helpful distinction regarding the strength with which a military faces the transition to democracy: wheth-

er the military is hierarchically or nonhierarchically led affects its bargaining power with civilian elites. The Portuguese military during the transition was mostly led by the group of junior officers who had staged the coup against the authoritarian regime. The Greek military ousted in 1974 had been led by a group of colonels. These militaries encounter greater chances of internal divisions and cannot command the same amount of clout over the military-as-institution as is the case with hierarchically led militaries. See Juan J. Linz and Alfred Stepan, *Problems of Democratic Transition and Consolidation: Southern Europe, South America, and Postcommunist Europe* (Baltimore: Johns Hopkins University Press, forthcoming); and Linz, Stepan, and Gunther's chapter in this volume.

49. J. Samuel Fitch rightly argued that "the ability of civilian governments to maintain a high level of civilian support and strengthen civilian belief in the legitimacy of the constitutional regime is the single most important factor in preventing military intervention" ("The Theoretical Model Underlying the Analysis of Civil-Military Relations in Contemporary Latin American Democracies: Core Assumptions" (paper presented to the Inter-American Dialogue, 1987).

50. Foreign powers provided substantial economic aid to help their allies in Portugal and halt the growth of leftist and communist influence (see Alfred Tovias, "The International Context of Democratic Transition," in Geoffrey Pridham, ed., *The New Mediterranean Democracies: Regime Transition in Spain, Greece, and Portugal* [London: Frank Cass, 1984]). In Spain, substantial wage increases during the transition helped to counter the effects of the crisis (Rafael López Pintor, "Mass and Elite Perspectives in the Process of Transition to Democracy," in Enrique A. Baloyra, ed., *Comparing New Democracies: Transition and Consolidation in Mediterranean Europe and the Southern Cone* [Boulder: Westview, 1987], p. 87).

51. Juan J. Linz and Alfred Stepan, "Political Crafting of Democratic Consolidation or Destruction: European and South American Comparisons," in Robert A. Pastor, ed., *Democracy in the Americas: Stopping the Pendulum* (New York: Holmes and Meier, 1989), p. 46.

52. In Guillermo O'Donnell's view, this statement is not applicable to cases, such as Brazil, in which the previous authoritarian regime was comparatively less repressive and more successful in its economic program. See his "Transições, continuidades e alguns paradoxos," in Fabio Wanderley Reis and Guillermo O'Donnell, eds., *A democracia no Brasil: Dilemas e perspectivas* (São Paulo: Vértice, Editora Revista dos Tribunais, 1988).

53. A vivid, and perhaps extreme, example of this problem was president Alfonsín's decision to resign to allow the assumption of President-elect Carlos Menem four months earlier than it was legally due.

54. See Juan J. Linz and Arturo Valenzuela, eds. *The Failure of Presidential Democracy* (Baltimore: Johns Hopkins University Press, 1994).

55. Carol Graham, "Peru's APRA Party in Power: Impossible Revolution, Relinquished Reform" (paper presented to the Latin American Studies Association International Congress, Miami, December 1989).

56. Gary W. Wynia, "Campaigning for President in Argentina," *Current History,* March 1989, pp. 133–36; and William C. Smith, "Políticas económicas de

choque y transición democrática en Argentina y Brasil," *Revista Mexicana de Sociología* 2, April–June 1988, pp. 65–88.

57. While support for Alfonsín's government declined dramatically in Argentina, attitudes toward democracy remained basically unchanged (see Edgardo Catterberg, "Attitudes towards Democracy in Argentina during the Transition Period," *International Journal of Public Opinion Research* 2, 1990, pp. 158, 165–66). In Peru, the combination of the disastrous economic situation inherited from the policies of Alan García with the escalation in the subversive war led to substantial public support for nondemocratic solutions, such as offered by President Fujimori's decision to break with the constitution.

58. Adolfo Suárez's popularity had declined relative to leaders of both the left and the right. While Suárez got 4.6 in a 0–10 approval scale, rightist leader Manuel Fraga got 5.4 and socialist leader Felipe González 5.9 in a survey conducted in January 1981 by the Centro de Investigaciones Sociológicas in Madrid (Barómetro no. 17, study no. 1,264). There is evidence of the general democratic preference of the public, although in 1980 slightly fewer than half of respondents declared democracy preferable to any other regime, while one-third declined to answer (see José R. Montero and Mariano Torcal, "Voters and Citizens in a New Democracy: Some Trend Data on Political Attitudes in Spain," *International Journal of Public Opinion Research* 2, 1990, p. 126).

59. Richard Clogg, *Parties and Elections in Greece* (London: C. Hurst, 1987), pp. 192–216.

60. See Mario Bacalhau, "Transition of the Political System and Political Attitudes in Portugal," *International Journal of Public Opinion Research* 2, 1990, pp. 141–54; Manuel Braga da Cruz and Miguel Lobo Antunes, "Revolutionary Transition and Problems of Parliamentary Institutionalization: The Case of the Portuguese National Assembly," in *Parliament and Democratic Consolidation in Southern Europe: Greece, Italy, Portugal, Spain, and Turkey* (London: Pinter, 1990); and Bruneau and Macleod, *Politics in Contemporary Portugal*.

61. Pion-Berlin, "Between Confrontation and Accommodation," p. 570.

62. Pion-Berlin, "Between Confrontation and Accommodation."

63. Ibid.

64. Laurence Whitehead, "Democracy by Convergence and Southern Europe: A Comparative Politics Perspective," in Geoffrey Pridham, ed., *Encouraging Democracy: The International Context of Regime Transition in Southern Europe* (New York: St. Martin's, 1991).

65. Angel Viñas, "Spain and NATO: Internal Debate and External Challenges," in Chipman, *NATO's Southern Allies*; Jonathan Story and Benny Pollack, "Spain's Transition: Domestic and External Linkages," in Pridham, *Encouraging Democracy*; and Kenneth Maxwell, ed., *Spanish Foreign and Defense Policy* (Boulder: Westview, 1991).

66. For the international context of defense policy in Portugal, see Alvaro Vasconcelos, "Portuguese Defence Policy: Internal Politics and Defence Commitments," and Walter C. Opello, Jr., "Portugal: A Case Study of International Determinants of Régime Transition," both in Pridham, *Encouraging Democracy*.

67. Susannah Verney and Theodore Couloumbis, "State-International Systems Interaction and the Greek Transition to Democracy in the Mid-1970s," in Pridham, *Encouraging Democracy*; and Thanos Veremis, "Greece and NATO:

Continuity and Change," in Chipman, *NATO's Southern Allies*.

68. Laurence Whitehead, "International Aspects of Democratization," in O'Donnell, Schmitter, and Whitehead, *TAR: Comparative Perspectives*; and Abraham F. Lowenthal, "The United States and Latin American Democracy: Learning from History," in Abraham F. Lowenthal, ed., *Exporting Democracy: The United States and Latin America* (Baltimore: Johns Hopkins University Press, 1991).

69. Heraldo Muñoz, "The Rise and Decline of the Inter-American System: A Latin American View," and James R. Kurth, "The Rise and Decline of the Inter-American System: A U.S. View," in Richard J. Bloomfield and Gregory F. Treverton, eds., *Alternative to Intervention: A New U.S.–Latin American Security Relationship* (Boulder: Lynne Rienner, 1990).

70. Stepan, *Rethinking Military Politics,* pp. 9–10.

71. See Terry Lynn Karl, "Dilemmas of Democratization in Latin America," pp. 1–21.

72. J. Samuel Valenzuela, "Democratic Consolidation in Post-Transitional Settings: Notion, Process, and Facilitating Conditions," in Mainwaring, O'Donnell, and Valenzuela, *Issues in Democratic Consolidation*.

73. Felipe Agüero, "The Assertion of Civilian Supremacy," pp. 408–21.

74. Gunther, "Spain: Modern Elite Settlement."

75. Terry Lynn Karl, "Dilemmas of Democratization in Latin America;" and Terry Lynn Karl and Philippe C. Schmitter, "Modes of Transition in Latin America, Southern Europe, and Eastern Europe," *International Social Science Journal* 128, May 1991, pp. 269–84.

76. Paul W. Zagorski, *Democracy versus National Security: Civil-Military Relations in Latin America* (Boulder: Lynn Rienner, 1992).

Chapter 5

1. See Geoffrey Pridham, "International Influences and Democratic Transition: Problems of Theory and Practice in Linkage Politics," in Geoffrey Pridham, ed., *Encouraging Democracy: The International Context of Regime Transition in Southern Europe* (London: Leicester University Press, 1991), p. 2.

2. Gabriel Almond, "The International-National Connection," *British Journal of Political Science,* April 1989, p. 254.

3. See, for example, Geoffrey Pridham, "Comparative Perspectives on the New Mediterranean Democracies: A Model of Regime Transition?" in Geoffrey Pridham, ed., *The New Mediterranean Democracies: Regime Transition in Spain, Greece, and Portugal* (London: Frank Cass, 1984); also see Guillermo O'Donnell, Philippe C. Schmitter, and Laurence Whitehead, eds., *Transitions from Authoritarian Rule* [*TAR*]: *Prospects for Democracy* (Baltimore: Johns Hopkins University Press, 1986) (see preface n. 3 above); Basilios Evangelos Tsingos, "Underwriting Democracy, Not Exporting It: The European Community and Greece" (Ph.D. diss., Magdalen College, Oxford University, 1994).

4. See Geoffrey Pridham, ed., *Securing Democracy: Political Parties and Democratic Consolidation in Southern Europe* (London: Routledge, 1990), p. 8.

5. Laurence Whitehead, "Democracy by Convergence and Southern Europe: A Comparative Politics Perspective," in Pridham, *Encouraging Democracy*.

6. David Hine, "The Consolidation of Democracy in Postwar Italy," in Pridham, *Securing Democracy*.

7. Laurence Whitehead, "The Consolidation of Fragile Democracies," (paper presented to the European Consortium for Political Research [ECPR], 1988), pp. 6–8.

8. For a fuller discussion of these points, see Geoffrey Pridham, "Southern European Democracies on the Road to Consolidation: A Comparative Assessment of the Role of Political Parties," in Pridham, *Securing Democracy*, pp. 8–16.

9. See David Easton, *A Systems Analysis of Political Life* (New York: John Wiley, 1965).

10. For a discussion of this literature see Pridham, *Encouraging Democracy*, ch. 1 and app., esp. pp. 29–30; and "Democratic Transition and the International Environment: A Research Agenda," (occasional paper no. 1, Centre for Mediterranean Studies, University of Bristol, February 1991).

11. See Robert Leonardi, "The International Context of Democratic Transition in Postwar Italy: Case of Penetration," in Pridham, *Encouraging Democracy*.

12. In fact, the beginning of détente also saw some relaxation of the U.S. position, when Kennedy gave his blessing to the partial turnover in power with the formation of a center-left coalition.

13. See also Geoffrey Pridham, "The Politics of the European Community, Transnational Networks, and Democratic Transition in Southern Europe," in Pridham, *Encouraging Democracy*, pp. 223–32.

14. See Pridham, "Politics of the European Community," esp. pp. 225–28, 233–35.

15. Susannah Verney and Theodore Couloumbis, "State-International Systems Interaction and the Greek Transition to Democracy in the Mid-1970s," in Pridham, *Encouraging Democracy*, p. 117.

16. Ibid., p. 114.

17. Susannah Verney, "Greece and the European Community," in Kevin Featherstone and Dimitrios Katsoudas, eds., *Political Change in Greece* (London: Croom Helm, 1987).

18. Thanos Veremis, "Greece," in Douglas Stuart, ed., *Politics and Security in the Southern Region of the Atlantic Alliance* (London: Macmillan, 1988), pp. 138–39.

19. Nikiforos Diamandouros, "PASOK and State-Society Relations in Post-Authoritarian Greece, 1974–1988," in Spyros Vryonis, ed., *Greece on the Road to Democracy: From the Junta to PASOK, 1974–1986* (New Rochelle, N.Y.: Orpheus, 1991).

20. Susannah Verney, "To Be or Not to Be in the European Community: The Party Debate and Democratic Consolidation in Greece," in Pridham, *Securing Democracy*.

21. Ibid., p. 213.

22. See, for example, James Edward Miller, *The United States and Italy, 1940–50* (Chapel Hill: University of North Carolina Press, 1986); and John Lamberton Harper, *America and the Reconstruction of Italy, 1945–48* (Cambridge: Cambridge University Press, 1986).

23. Alejandro Lorca Corrons, "The Spanish Experience following Acces-

sion" (paper presented to the University Association for Contemporary European Studies, annual conference, 1988).

24. Felipe González, "Europe from the Community of Twelve to European Union: The Objective for 1992" (tenth Jean Monnet lecture, European University Institute, Florence, 1987), p. 13.

25. See *El País,* March 29, 1985, and the rest of the Spanish press of that and subsequent days.

26. *Financial Times,* December 1, 1986, supplement on Spain, p. 1.

27. Pridham, "Politics of the European Community," pp. 224, 226–27.

28. Audrey Brassloff, "Portugal: 1992 and All That," *Journal of the Association for Contemporary Iberian Studies,* autumn 1991, pp. 25–37.

29. Ibid., pp. 30–31.

30. Ibid., p. 33.

31. Pridham, "Politics of the European Community."

32. For a useful attempt at such an exercise, see John C. Thomas, "EC Membership, Economic Adjustment, and Democratic Development: Lessons for the East from the South" (paper presented at the conference of the European Community Studies Association, George Mason University, May 1991).

33. Thomas, "EC Membership," p. 26.

34. Robert McDonald, "Greece after PASOK's Victory," *World Today,* July 1985, pp. 133–34.

35. *Observer,* January 1, 1989.

36. Quoted in Thomas, "EC Membership," p. 24.

37. *Independent,* January 29, 1991.

38. *Times,* January 3, 1986.

39. Thomas, "EC Membership," p. 15.

40. See Geoffrey Pridham, "Italy," in Carol Twitchett and Kenneth J. Twitchett, eds., *Building Europe: Britain's Partners in the EEC* (London: Europa Publications, 1981), p. 88 ff.

41. Peter Jenkins in *Guardian,* June 28, 1971.

42. *Panorama,* June 12, 1979.

43. Dusan Sidjanski, "Transition to Democracy and European Integration: The Role of Interest Groups in Southern Europe," in Pridham, *Encouraging Democracy.*

44. Thomas, "EC Membership," p. 12.

45. David Corkill, "Portugal's Political Transformation: The Election of July 1987," *Parliamentary Affairs,* April 1988, p. 248.

46. See Allan Williams, *Southern Europe Transformed* (London: Harper and Row, 1984).

47. *Economist,* March 11, 1989.

48. Joaquim Molins and Francesc Morata, "Spanish Lobbying in the European Community" (paper presented to the ECPR, 1991), p. 20.

49. *Financial Times,* August 22, 1990.

50. Ibid., August 29, 1990.

51. Report on business in Spain in *Guardian,* December 10, 1987.

52. *Times,* January 2, 1986.

53. *Financial Times,* January 18, 1988.

54. *Economist,* March 11, 1989.

55. Ibid., May 28, 1988.
56. *Financial Times,* October 11, 1989.
57. Ibid., October 24, 1990.
58. *Die Zeit,* October 21, 1988.
59. *Financial Times,* April, 25, 1991.
60. *Die Zeit,* September 19, 1991; and *Times,* September 10, 1991.
61. Pridham, "Italy," pp. 85–86.
62. Michael Ledeen, *Lo zio sam e l'elefante rosso* (Milan: Sugarco, 1987), esp. chs. 3 and 4.
63. Alfred Tovias, "U.S. Policy towards Democratic Transition in Southern Europe," in Pridham, *Encouraging Democracy.*
64. James N. Rosenau, *Linkage Politics: Essays on the Convergence of National and International Systems* (New York: Free Press, 1969), p. 49.
65. See the chapters by Robert Leonardi on Italy and Walter C. Opello on Portugal in Pridham, *Encouraging Democracy.*
66. See the chapter by José Ferreira "International Ramifications of the Portuguese Revolution," in Lawrence S. Graham and Douglas Wheeler, eds., *In Search of Portugal: The Revolution and Its Consequences* (Madison: University of Wisconsin Press, 1982), pp. 287–90.
67. Gianfranco Pasquino, "The Demise of the First Fascist Regime and Italy's Transition to Democracy," in O'Donnell, Schmitter, and Whitehead, *Transitions from Authoritarian Rule,* pp. 65–66.
68. See Pridham, "Italy," pp. 110–13; also see David Hine, "Consolidation of Democracy in Post-War Italy."
69. Constantine P. Danopoulos, "From Balconies to Tanks: Post-Junta Civil-Military Relations in Greece," *Journal of Political and Military Sociology* 13, 1985, p. 92; *Guardian,* December 18, 1986.
70. Geoffrey Pridham, "Linkage Politics Theory and the Greek-Turkish Rapprochement," in Dimitri Constas, ed., *The Greek-Turkish Conflict in the 1990s* (London: Macmillan, 1991).
71. Antonio Marquina, "Spanish Foreign and Defence Policy since Democratization," in Kenneth Maxwell, ed., *Spanish Foreign and Defence Policy* (Boulder: Westview, 1991), p. 36.
72. *Times,* March 14, 1986.
73. Theodore Couloumbis, "The Structures of Greek Foreign Policy," in Richard Clogg, ed., *Greece in the 1980s* (London: Macmillan, 1983), pp. 113–14.
74. Betty A. Dobratz, "Party Preferences and 'Erratic' Issues in Greece," *Political Studies,* June 1990, p. 352.
75. J. Brooks, "Mediterranean Neo-Democracies and the Opinion-Policy Nexus," *West European Politics,* July 1988, pp. 133–34.
76. Molins and Morata, "Spanish Lobbying," pp. 17–19.
77. *Economist,* March 11, 1989; *Times,* November 24, 1988.
78. See, for example, Geoffrey Pridham, "Southern European Socialists and the State: Consolidation of Party Rule or Consolidation of Democracy?" in Tom Gallagher and Allan M. Williams, eds., *Southern European Socialism* (Manchester: Manchester University Press, 1989), pp. 146–47.
79. *Economist,* May 28, 1988.

80. Michael Tsinisizelis, "The 1992 Programme and Greek Public Administration" (paper presented to the Political Studies Association, 1991).
81. *Financial Times,* January 8, 1991.
82. Molins and Morata, "Spanish Lobbying," pp. 20–21.
83. *El País,* January 14, 1988.
84. Pridham, "Italy," p. 101.
85. Joan Botella, "Spanish Communism in Crisis," in Michael Waller and Meindert Fennema, eds., *Communist Parties in Western Europe* (Oxford: Blackwell, 1988).
86. Paul Heywood, "The Spanish Left: Towards a Common Home?" (paper presented at the 1991 meeting of the Political Studies Association).
87. *Guardian,* May 26, 1989.
88. *El País, edición internacional,* November 19, 1990.
89. Carlos Gaspar, "Portuguese Communism since 1976," *Problems of Communism,* January–February 1990, pp. 60–62.
90. Ibid., pp. 58, 60.
91. Maria Patricio and Alan Stoleroff, "The Portuguese Communist Party: Resistance and Adaptation to Change in the Aftermath of Perestroika" (paper presented to the Political Studies Association, 1991).
92. Verney, "To Be or Not to Be," p. 211.
93. Diamandouros, "PASOK and State-Society Relations."
94. Dimitri Kitsikis, "Populism, Eurocommunism, and the KKE," in Waller and Fennema, *Communist Parties,* pp. 106, 109; Susannah Verney, "The New Red Book of the KKE," in *Journal of Communist Studies,* December 1988, pp. 172–73.
95. Verney, "The New Red Book," p. 171.
96. Pridham, "Italy," p. 112.
97. *La Repubblica,* May 26 and 27, 1991.
98. Constantine P. Danopoulos, "Military Rule and Democratization in Mediterranean Europe" (paper presented at 1991 congress of the International Political Science Association), p. 15.
99. Gregory Treverton, *Spain: Domestic Politics and Security Policy* (Adelphi Paper no. 204, International Institute for Strategic Studies, London, 1986), pp. 32–33.
100. See, for example, Carolyn Boyd and James Boyden, "The Armed Forces and the Transition to Democracy in Spain," in Thomas Lancaster and Gary Prevost, eds., *Politics and Change in Spain* (New York: Praeger, 1985).
101. Ken Gladdish, "Portugal: An Open Verdict," in Pridham, *Securing Democracy,* p. 115.
102. Pridham, "Italy," pp. 115–16.
103. Alvaro Vasconcelos, "Portugal in Atlantic-Mediterranean Security," in Douglas T. Stuart, ed., *Politics and Security in the Southern Region of the Atlantic Alliance* (London: Macmillan, 1988), p. 128.
104. Walter C. Opello, Jr., "Portugal: A Case of International Determinants of Regime Transition," in Pridham, *Encouraging Democracy.*
105. José Magone, "Politische Kultur in der europäischen Semi-peripherie: Der Fall Portugal, 1910–90," *Journal für Entwicklungspolitik* 3, 1991.
106. Thomas Bruneau, *Portugal Fifteen Years after the April Revolution* (field

staff reports no. 1, Universities Field Staff International, Indianapolis, 1989–90).

107. José Barroso, "Crónica de opinião pública," *Revista de Ciencia Política* 4, 1984, pp. 143–44.

108. Asteris Huliaras, "Public Opinion and Foreign Policy in Post-1974 Greece" (paper presented to the ECPR, 1989), p. 14.

109. See Pridham, "Linkage Politics Theory."

110. Antonio Sánchez-Gijón, "On Spain, NATO, and Democracy," in Stuart, *Politics and Security*, pp. 96–98.

111. *Financial Times*, January 20, 1986.

112. Ibid., January 18, 1985.

113. Jaime Pastor, "Le mouvement pour la paix en Espagne et le référendum sur l'OTAN" (paper presented at 1989 meeting of the ECPR).

Chapter 6

I am grateful to Nancy Bermeo, Valerie Bunce, Nikiforos Diamandouros, Giuseppe Di Palma, Miriam Golden, Davydd Greenwood, Richard Gunther, Eric Hershberg, Peter Katzenstein, José María Maravall, and Michael Marks for comments on an earlier version. The advice of Joseph LaPalombara has, as usual, been provocative, while Kurt Lebakken provided inspired research assistance.

1. In fact, most of these theorists spoke only in the language of aggregate probabilities and not of single-case determination, as can be discerned in the following syntheses: Samuel P. Huntington, "Will More Countries Become Democratic?" *Political Science Quarterly* 99, 1984, pp. 198–209; Robert Dahl, *Polyarchy: Participation and Opposition* (New Haven: Yale University Press, 1971), ch. 10; and Tatu Vanhanen, *The Emergence of Democracy: A Comparative Study of 119 States, 1850–1979* (Helsinki: Finnish Society of Sciences and Letters, 1984). For a summary of such studies, see Adam Przeworski, "Some Problems in the Study of the Transition to Democracy," in Guillermo O'Donnell, Philippe C. Schmitter, and Laurence Whitehead, eds., *Transitions from Authoritarian Rule [TAR]: Comparative Perspectives* (Baltimore: Johns Hopkins University Press, 1986) (see preface n. 3 above), p. 47.

2. Dankwart A. Rustow, "Transitions to Democracy: Toward a Dynamic Model," *Comparative Politics* 2, 1970, p. 336. On contingent choice, see Terry Karl, "Dilemmas of Democratization in Latin America," *Comparative Politics*, October 1990, p. 1.

3. See Karl, "Dilemmas of Democratization in Latin America," p. 1. Giuseppe Di Palma, in *To Craft Democracies: An Essay on Democratic Transitions*, (Berkeley: University of California Press, 1990, p. 4), writes, "It is a dismal science of politics that passively entrusts political change to exogenous and distant social transformations." It is dismal indeed to discover that stable democratic development usually has to await economic prosperity, but it is unfortunately true in most cases. Di Palma has reflected more recently on the nature of democratic transitions in his article, "Legitimation from the Top to Civil Society: Politico-cultural Change in Eastern Europe," *World Politics*, October 1991. From some quarters, there is even the hint that, since successful transitions are rare and unexpected events, the normal procedures of social science

do not obtain in interpreting them. O'Donnell and Schmitter, in *TAR: Tentative Conclusions about Uncertain Democracies*, p. 4, write, for example: "We believe that . . . 'normal science methodology' is inappropriate in rapidly changing situations, where those very parameters of political action are in flux. This includes transitions from authoritarian rule." But they go on to deduce a far less sweeping methodological inference from this axiom, with which it is easier to agree: "this type of situation should be analyzed with distinctly political concepts, however vaguely delineated and difficult to pin down they may be."

4. O'Donnell and Schmitter, *TAR: Tentative Conclusions*, p. 48. Di Palma, *To Craft Democracies*, pp. 60–61, is even more categorical. He contends that although democratizing elites need to deal at some stage with pressures for political innovation from newly mobilized groups, the latter's "resentful views will surface precisely because a secession is under way."

5. Juan J. Linz and Alfred Stepan, eds., *The Breakdown of Democratic Regimes* [*BDR*]*: Europe* (Baltimore: Johns Hopkins University Press, 1978) (see preface n. 2 above).

6. This approach is the same as one used by "process tracing" in international relations and has the same problems. On this approach see, Alexander George, "Case Studies and Theory Development," in Paul Gordon Lauren, ed., *Diplomacy: New Approaches in History, Theory, and Policy* (New York: Free Press, 1979). Although this approach offers a certain down-to-earth realism, it does not solve the problem in either field of how to unearth the factors that may induce elites to act as they do.

7. Karl, "Dilemmas of Democratization in Latin America," p. 7.

8. For a discussion of the Reform Act of 1832, see Charles Tilly, "Britain Creates the Social Movement," in James Cronin, ed., *Social Conflict and the Political Order in Modern Britain* (New Brunswick, N.J.: Transaction Press, 1982), and "From Mutiny to Mass Mobilization in Great Britain, 1754–1834," working paper no. 109, Center for Studies of Social Change, New School for Social Research, New York, 1991. An additional work now in preparation by Tilly is "Popular Contention in Britain, 1758–1834."

9. In commenting on an earlier version of this passage, Joseph LaPalombara observed that "no serious historian would say that elites were oblivious of civil society." I agree with LaPalombara's point, but unearthing that consciousness and its relationship to both the content of mass mobilization and to the nature of elite strategies would elude many elitist approaches to democratization.

10. There is no space here to survey the rich theoretical and empirical literature on the collective action problem as it relates to social movements. For an introduction to the theory, see Mancur Olson, *The Logic of Collective Action* (Cambridge: Harvard University Press, 1968). For further elaborations and modifications, see John McCarthy and Mayer N. Zald, "Resource Mobilization and Social Movements: A Partial Theory," *American Journal of Sociology* 82, 1977, pp. 1212–41; McCarthy and Zald, *Social Movements in an Organizational Society* (New Brunswick, N.J.: Transaction, 1987); Bert Klandermans, "Mobilization and Participation: Social-Psychological Expansions of Resource Mobilization Theory," *American Sociological Review* 49, 1984, pp. 583–600; and Karl-Dieter Opp, *The Rationality of Political Protest* (Boulder: Westview, 1989). For syntheses and critiques of the theory, see Bert Klandermans and Sidney Tar-

row, "Mobilization into Social Movements: Synthesizing European and American Approaches," in Bert Klandermans, Hanspeter Kriesi, and Sidney Tarrow, eds., *From Structure to Action: Comparing Social Movement Research Across Cultures,* International Social Movement Research, Vol. 1 (Greenwich, Conn.: JAI, 1988).

11. Rustow, "Transitions to Democracy," pp. 352, 356.

12. See Michael Burton, Richard Gunther, and John Higley, "Introduction: Elite Transformations and Democratic Regimes," in John Higley and Richard Gunther, eds., *Elites and Democratic Consolidation in Latin America and Southern Europe* (New York: Cambridge University Press, 1992), p. 3. In a personal communication to the author in 1993, Gunther wrote, "Mass mobilizations may be necessary in order to induce incumbent authoritarian elites to relinquish power, but . . . the consolidation of democracy may require demobilization in order to stabilize the political environment at certain crucial stages." On the critical choices made by the mass public, see Karl, "Dilemmas of Democratization," pp. 5–6.

13. See Karl, "Dilemmas of Democratization," p. 9.

14. Little is gained and much can be lost by enforcing a mechanical dichotomy between elites and masses. It must be remembered that between the highest elites and the most ordinary citizens are gradations of organized professional groups, oppositional groupings, subelites, institutions, and opinion makers. Especially during periods of social and political transition, groups which normally exercise little influence may temporarily gain marginal power, due to the depth of the cleavages created by rapid change and by the divisions within elites as uncertainty grows and once-loyal dependents of the regime perhaps begin to defect. On the importance of defection in the collapse of state socialism in East Germany, see Daniel V. Friedheim, "Regime Collapse in Democratic Transition: The East German Revolution of 1989," paper presented to the Eighth International Conference of Europeanists, Chicago, 1992.

15. For an argument that Spain is the paradigmatic case of elite transaction, see Donald Share, *The Making of Spanish Democracy* (New York: Praeger, 1986). For a counterargument, see Joe Foweraker, *Making Democracy in Spain: Grassroots Struggle in the South, 1955–1975* (Cambridge: Cambridge University Press, 1989), pp. vii–viii. He argues somewhat polemically that a unique focus on the role of elites runs the risk of giving "the credit for the political transformation . . . to those who negotiated its terms in the last year or so of the old regime, rather than to those thousands of individuals who fought and suffered over many years to achieve democratic rights."

16. On Hungary, see László Bruszt and David Stark, "Remaking the Political Field in Hungary: From the Politics of Confrontation to the Politics of Competition," in Ivo Banac, ed., *Eastern Europe in Revolution* (Ithaca: Cornell University Press, 1992); on Poland, see Roman Laba, *The Roots of Solidarity: A Political Sociology of Poland's Working Class Democratization* (Princeton: Princeton University Press, 1990); and, on East Germany, see Susanne Lohmann, "Rationality, Revolution, and Revolt: The Dynamics of Information Cascades," research paper no. 12139, Stanford University Graduate School of Business, 1992.

17. That is, elites not only make self-conscious pacts designed to reform the political system; they also shape and reshape social coalitions around their

collective interests. Nor does the mass level consist only of opposition political groups but of mass collective action, to which these groups are not reducible but with which they interact. An exclusive focus on civil society and lack of attention to how political society develops mars much of the literature on democratization in Eastern Europe.

18. Seymour Martin Lipset, *Political Man: The Social Bases of Politics* (New York: Anchor, 1960), p. 136.

19. See Serge Hughes, *The Fall and Rise of Modern Italy* (New York: Macmillan, 1967), ch. 7.

20. Vanhanen's quantitative indicators of the democratic threshold make this clear (*Emergence of Democracy,* pp. 145–46). He uses a twofold measure derived from Dahl's definition of polyarchy which contains a competition index and a participation index. He writes: "In Italy the governmental system had been parliamentary since 1861, but participation remained very low until 1912, when all men over 30 were enfranchised. Adult male suffrage was introduced in 1919. Political parties developed slowly and therefore competition remained relatively low until the beginning of this century."

21. See Paolo Farneti, "Social Conflict, Parliamentary Fragmentation, Institutional Shift, and the Rise of Fascism: Italy," in Linz and Stepan, *BDR: Europe,* p. 31.

22. Ibid., p. 10.

23. See ibid., pp. 17 and 29. Human error and bad judgment of course played a crucial role in the failures of the Italian parliamentary elite as well. Nitti, whose government showed its weakness when it failed to move against the protagonists of the Fiume adventure, unwittingly signaled further opportunities for hypernationalist agitation in the streets. Giolitti, who never ceased to play his old personalistic game, bided his time waiting for a majority to form around his person. The king, who, according to existing procedures, could come into the picture only on the initiative of the cabinet—which was sharply divided—failed to sign the order to arrest the fascists. Facta, the last Liberal prime minister, failed to contact the king at a crucial moment. And everybody seems to have thought they could use Mussolini to get through a particularly difficult moment of postwar politics, after which most of them assumed he could be dispensed with.

24. See Edward Malefakis, "A Comparative Analysis of Workers' Movements in Spain and Italy," in Richard Gunther, ed., *Politics, Society, and Democracy: The Case of Spain* (Boulder: Westview, 1993), p. 62. Also, see Farneti, "Social Conflict," p. 24.

25. Malefakis, "Comparative Analysis of Workers' Movements," p. 63 ff.

26. Farneti, "Social Conflict," p. 11.

27. Ibid., p. 20.

28. Ibid., pp. 17–18.

29. Ibid., p. 18.

30. Ibid., pp. 13, 15.

31. See ibid., p. 16.

32. Malefakis, "Comparative Analysis of Workers' Movements," p. 65.

33. On Weimar Germany, see Rainer M. Lepsius, "From Fragmented Party Democracy to Government by Emergency Decree and National Socialist Take-

over: Germany," in Linz and Stepan, *BDR: Europe*; on Italy, see Farneti, "Social Conflict," p. 22.

34. Malefakis, "Comparative Analysis of Workers' Movements," pp. 65–66.

35. Farneti, "Social Conflict," pp. 19, 14.

36. See Josep M. Colomer, "Transitions by Agreement: Modelling the Spanish Way," *American Political Science Review* 85, 1991, pp. 1283–1302; and Richard Gunther, "Spain: The Very Model of the Modern Elite Settlement," in Higley and Gunther, *Elites and Democratic Consolidation*.

37. For examples of models assigning primary responsibility to elites, see Di Palma, *To Craft Democracies*; and Share, *Making of Spanish Democracy*. An example of the second type is Terry Karl, "Dilemmas of Democratization." Models emphasizing interplay among factors include Richard Gunther, Giacomo Sani, and Goldie Shabad, *Spain after Franco: The Making of a Competitive Party System* (Berkeley: University of California Press, 1986); and José Maravall, *The Transition to Democracy in Spain* (London: Croom Helm, 1982).

38. Maravall, *Transition to Democracy in Spain*, p. 3.

39. Of course, there are variations and permutations in the story as it is told by various authors. Some (see, for example, José Maravall, *Dictatorship and Political Dissent: Workers and Students in Franco's Spain* [London: Tavistock, 1978]; and Paul Preston, *The Triumph of Democracy in Spain* [London: Methuen, 1986]) emphasize the prolonged struggle both in Spanish society and within the Franquist establishment which made possible the democratic pacts of 1976–79; others (see, for example, Di Palma, *To Craft Democracies*; and Share, *Making of Spanish Democracy*) emphasize the guarantee of mutual political survival as almost the sole turning point in the transition; still others (for example, O'Donnell and Schmitter, *TAR: Tentative Conclusions*) come closest to the image of a regime unraveling from within.

40. Juan J. Linz, "From Great Hopes to Civil War," in Linz and Stepan, *BDR: Europe*.

41. Maravall, in a personal communication to the author in 1993, observed that Moncloa was also important in clarifying several questions about the constitution as well as reflecting the willingness of the unions to make economic sacrifices to assure democracy.

42. See Felipe Agüero, "The Assertion of Civilian Supremacy in Post-Authoritarian Contexts: Spain in Comparative Perspective," (Ph.D. diss., Duke University, 1991; forthcoming, as *Soldiers, Civilians, and Democracy*, from the Johns Hopkins University Press); and Gunther, "Spain: Model Elite Settlement," p. 66.

43. For the 1969–73 period, see Raymond Carr and Juan Pablo Fusi Aizpurua, *Spain: Dictatorship to Democracy* (London: Allen and Unwin, 1979), ch. 9; and Preston, *Triumph of Democracy in Spain*, ch. 2. For the conflicts between the Franquist establishment and important social forces, see Carr and Fusi, *Spain: Dictatorship to Democracy*, ch. 8; and Share, *Making of Spanish Democracy*, ch. 3.

44. Gunther, Sani, and Shabad, *Spain after Franco*, p. 24.

45. The construction of these measures is described in Vanhanen, *Emergence of Democracy*, pp. 33–37.

46. See Sebastian Balfour, *Dictatorship, Workers, and the City: Labour in Greater*

Barcelona since 1939 (Oxford: Oxford University Press, 1989), p. 41 and, esp., ch. 2; and Gunther, Sani, and Shabad, *Spain after Franco,* p. 24–25.

47. Maravall, *Dictatorship and Political Dissent,* p. 24.

48. For an account of these phenomena, see Juan J. Linz and Amando de Miguel, "Los problemas de la retribución y el rendimiento vistos por los empresarios españoles," *Revista de Trabajo* 1, 1963, pp. 35–141; and Preston, *Triumph of Democracy in Spain,* p. 12.

49. The increases cited by Maravall (*Dictatorship and Political Dissent,* p. 8) are remarkable: "Between 1965 and 1968," he writes, "the number of professionals within the active population increased by 66 percent, people employed in the service sector by 51 percent and white collar workers by 49 percent." Maravall's source is José Félix Tezanos, *Estructura de clases y conflictos de poder en la España postfranquista* (Madrid: Edicusa, 1978).

50. By 1973, the number of Spaniards willing to be recorded in favor of representative government had risen to 60 percent of a national sample (cited in Rafael López Pintor, *La opinión pública española: Del franquismo a la democracia* [Madrid: Centro de Investigaciones Sociológicas, 1982], p. 153).

51. Maravall, *Dictatorship and Political Dissent,* p. 121.

52. For example, Maravall (ibid., p. 8) points out that 81 of the 91 members of the Private Council of the Count of Barcelona, the most liberal elite group within the regime, came from what he calls "the financial aristocracy" and that 39 were connected with the seven largest banks.

53. José Maravall and Julián Santamaría, "Political Change in Spain and the Prospects for Democracy," in O'Donnell, Schmitter, and Whitehead, *TAR: Prospects for Democracy,* p. 76.

54. Preston, *Triumph of Democracy in Spain,* pp. 28–29.

55. See ibid., pp. 30–31; and Maravall and Santamaría, "Political Change in Spain," p. 78.

56. The heading of this section refers to the title of Michael Lipsky's landmark article on American urban protest, "Protest as a Resource," *American Political Science Review* 62, 1968, pp. 1144–58.

57. Robert Fishman, *Working-Class Organization and the Return to Democracy* (Ithaca: Cornell University Press, 1990), p. 88.

58. Maravall, *Transition to Democracy in Spain,* p. 37.

59. On the workers' movements in Spain, see Balfour, *Dictatorship, Workers, and the City,* p. 69 ff.; Foweraker, *Making Democracy in Spain,* p. 23 ff.; and Maravall, *Dictatorship and Political Dissent,* ch. 2 and pp. 36–37.

60. On mass collective action, see Maravall, *Dictatorship and Political Dissent,* ch. 3 and p. 37; and Preston, *Triumph of Democracy in Spain,* p. 15.

61. See Maravall, *Dictatorship and Political Dissent,* p. 15; and Preston, *Triumph of Democracy in Spain,* p. 41.

62. For example, the majority of the church hierarchy condemned the new Ley Sindical introduced in 1971, and a document, signed by two hundred priests, condemning the torture of workers was read aloud in 80 percent of the churches of Navarra in the same year. See Preston, *Triumph of Democracy in Spain,* pp. 37–38.

63. Fishman, *Working-Class Organization,* p. 148. Most studies of the Spanish electorate show that it had a large central mode at the moment of the transition

(see Gunther, Sani, and Shabad, *Spain after Franco,* p. 57; and Maravall and Santamaría, "Political Change in Spain," p. 84) rather than the polarized pluralism that some had feared. This moderation extended to the working class, a majority of whom wanted a just society created "through the accumulation of reforms;" only 17 percent wanted "a socialist society within five year's time (Maravall, *Transition to Democracy in Spain,* p. 20).

64. Fishman, *Working-Class Organization,* pp. 216–17.

65. Malefakis, "Comparative Analysis of Workers' Movements," pp. 19, 64–65.

66. Tezanos, *Estructura de clases,* pp. 238 and 243.

67. Preston, *Triumph of Democracy in Spain,* p. 14. For political activities in the universities prior to the end of the 1950s, see Maravall, *Dictatorship and Political Dissent,* p. 104.

68. Maravall, *Dictatorship and Political Dissent,* p. 101.

69. Quoted in ibid., p. 113.

70. See ibid., p. 139 and ch. 5.

71. The episode is treated in detail in Preston, *Triumph of Democracy in Spain,* pp. 30–36.

72. Ibid., p. 31.

73. Ibid., p. 33. Preston further argues (p. 41) that "the most remarkable feature of the Asamblea was the width of the political spectrum that it spanned. The signatories included several prominent members of the Catalan industrial and banking bourgeoisie. It was rumored that the Asamblea had received a telegram of solidarity from a Catalan bishop."

74. See Maravall, *Dictatorship and Political Dissent*; and Foweraker, *Making Democracy in Spain.*

75. Maravall and Santamaría, "Political Change in Spain," p. 82. Also see Gunther, Sani, and Shabad, *Spain after Franco,* p. 74

76. Fishman, *Working-Class Organization,* p. 3.

77. Maravall, *Transition to Democracy in Spain,* p. 14.

78. Gunther, "Spain: Modern Elite Settlement," p. 88.

79. Karl, "Dilemmas of Democratization," p. 15.

80. López Pintor (*La opinión pública española,* p. 92) reports that in 1980 only 8 percent of those polled expressed "much interest" in politics, while 43 percent said they had no interest in politics. The rising tide of working-class militancy in the 1980s is traced by Lynne Marie Wozniak in "Industrial Restructuring and Political Protest in Socialist Spain" (Ph.D. diss., Cornell University, 1991).

81. For a discussion of "imperfect bipartism," see Giorgio Galli and Alfonso Prandi, *Patterns of Political Participation in Italy* (New Haven: Yale University Press, 1970); for a discussion of the PSOE, see Michael Marks, "The Formation of European Policy in Post-Franco Spain" (Ph.D. diss., Cornell University, 1993); and for a discussion of the Italian communists, see Frederic Spotts and Theodor Wieser, *Italy: A Difficult Democracy* (New York: Cambridge University Press, 1986).

Chapter 7

This work benefited greatly from comments and suggestions offered by the members of the Subcommittee on Southern Europe of the Social Science Research Council, and the invaluable assistance of Franco Mattei and Mariano Torcal in the data analysis. Finally, our special thanks to José María Maravall, Giacomo Sani, and Kent Worcester for their careful reading and reactions to the first draft, and once again to Sani and Julián Santamaría who directed the research group with which we collaborated in collecting the data upon which this analysis is based.

1. See Juan J. Linz and Alfred Stepan, *Problems of Democratic Transition and Consolidation: Southern Europe, South America, and Postcommunist Europe* (Baltimore: Johns Hopkins University Press, forthcoming). Also see Juan J. Linz, "The Consolidation of Regimes: A Theoretical Problem Approach," (paper presented at the International Studies Association World Congress, Toronto, 1974); "The Transitions from Authoritarian Regimes to Democratic Political Systems and the Problems of Consolidation of Political Democracy," (roundtable discussion at the International Political Science Association meeting, Tokyo, 1982); Juan J. Linz, "Transitions to Democracy," *Washington Quarterly*, 1, 1990, pp. 143–64; and Leonardo Morlino, "The Changing Relationship between Parties and Society in Italy," *West European Politics*, 7, 1984, pp. 46–66.

2. Guillermo O'Donnell, Philippe C. Schmitter, and Laurence Whitehead, eds., *Transitions from Authoritarian Rule* [*TAR*]: *Southern Europe* (Baltimore: Johns Hopkins University Press, 1986) (see preface n. 3 above); and Philippe C. Schmitter, "The Consolidation of Political Democracy in Southern Europe," unpublished, 1988.

3. See Michael J. Crozier, Samuel P. Huntington, and Joji Watanuki, *The Crisis of Democracy: Report on the Governability of Democracies to the Trilateral Commission* (New York: New York University Press, 1975); Richard Rose, ed., *Challenge to Governance* (Beverly Hills: Sage, 1980); and Anthony King, "Overload: Problems of Governing in the 1970's," *Political Studies*, 23, 1975, pp. 283–96.

4. This survey, directed by Julián Santamaría and Giacomo Sani, was conducted in the spring of 1985. A total of 8570 people were interviewed: 2000 were interviewed by the survey research organization Norma in Portugal, 2488 by the Centro de Investigaciones Sociológicas in Spain, 2074 by DOXA in Italy, and 1998 Greeks were interviewed by the Centre of Social Research. The Portuguese research group was formed by Mario Bacalhau and María José Stock; the Spanish team included Rosa Conde, Ubaldo Martínez, José R. Montero, and Julián Santamaría; the Italians included Giovanna Guidorossi, Renato Mannheimer, Leonardo Morlino, Giacomo Sani, and Maria Weber; and the Greek group consisted of George Th. Mavrogordatos, Ilias Nicolacopoulos, and Constantinos Tsoucalas.

5. See Leonardo Morlino, *Come cambiano i regimi politici. Strumenti di analisi* (Milan: Franco Angeli, 1980). Here we refer to *political* legitimacy, and we will restrict our analysis to this aspect. It would be possible, however, to add two further dimensions: *social* legitimacy and *economic* legitimacy. On the latter, see Juan J. Linz, "Legitimacy of Democracy and the Socio-Economic System," in Mattei Dogan, ed., *Comparing Pluralist Democracies* (Boulder: Westview, 1988), pp. 65–113.

6. Seymour M. Lipset, *Political Man: The Social Bases of Politics* (Garden City, N.Y.: Doubleday, 1959); Gabriel A. Almond and Sidney Verba, *The Civic Culture: Political Attitudes and Democracy in Five Nations* (Princeton: Princeton Uni-

versity Press, 1963); and Juan J. Linz, "Crisis, Breakdown, and Reequilibration," in Juan J. Linz and Alfred Stepan, eds., *The Breakdown of Democratic Regimes* (Baltimore: Johns Hopkins University Press, 1978), pp. 14–124 (see preface n. 2 above).

7. John Schaar, ed., *Legitimacy in the Modern State* (New Brunswick, N.J.: Transaction Books, 1981).

8. Peter McDonough, Samuel H. Barnes, and Antonio López Pina, "The Growth of Democratic Legitimacy in Spain," *American Political Science Review,* 80, 1986, pp. 735–60.

9. See M. Stephen Weatherford, "Measuring Political Legitimacy," *American Political Science Review,* 86, 1992, pp. 149–66.

10. Linz, "Crisis, Breakdown, and Reequilibration" (quote from p. 18); and Linz, "Legitimacy of Democracy."

11. Morlino, *Come cambiano,* p. 152.

12. In Italy, by the time of the 1985 Four Nation Survey, people who would have had personal experience with the previous authoritarian regime as an adult or potentially politically active teenager would have been 58 or older; in Greece and Portugal, all of those over age 27 in 1985 would have had personal experience with authoritarianism; and in Spain, all of those 24 years of age or older would have had direct personal experience with an authoritarian regime.

13. Frederick D. Weil, "The Sources and Structure of Legitimation in Western Democracies: A Consolidated Model Tested with Time-Series Data in Six Countries since World War II," *American Sociological Review,* 54, 1989, pp. 682–706.

14. We gratefully acknowledge suggestions made by Richard Gunther and others which led to revision of this section. In this regard also see Giuseppe Di Palma, *To Craft Democracies: Reflections on Democratic Transitions and Beyond* (Berkeley: University of California Press, 1990); and Linz and Stepan, *Problems of Democratic Transition and Consolidation.*

15. Robert Dahl, *Poliarchy: Participation and Opposition* (New Haven: Yale University Press, 1971) emphasizes the importance of perceived efficacy. It should be pointed out that the efficacy we are discussing here is that of the democratic regime, not the perception of personal political efficacy, which we will consider in the next section of this chapter.

16. Lipset, *Political Man*; Linz, "Crisis, Breakdown, and Reequilibration;" and Juan J. Linz, "I rapporti tra legitimazione ed efficacia di governo," *Mondoperaio,* 3, 1989, pp. 111–16.

17. Edward W. Muller and Thomas O. Jukam, "On the Meaning of Political Support," *American Political Science Review,* 71, 1977, pp. 1561–95.

18. Gerhard Loewenberg, "The Influence of Parliamentary Behavior on Regime Stability," *Comparative Politics,* 3, 1971, pp. 170–95.

19. See, for instance, Weil, "The Sources and Structure of Legitimation," p. 698.

20. See Peter McDonough, Samuel H. Barnes, and Antonio López Pina, "The Nature of Political Support and Legitimacy in Spain," (paper presented at the Eighth International Conference of Europeanists, Chicago, March 1992).

21. The three questions in the survey were phrased in the following way: For *diffuse legitimacy,* "With which of the following statements do you agree? (1)

Democracy is preferable to any other regime; (2) in some cases an authoritarian regime, a dictatorship, is preferable; or (3) for people like me it is all the same." For *legitimacy by default* or *opinions of the past,* "On the basis of what you remember about Salazarism [or Francoism, Fascism, dictatorship], do you think that: (1) it was in part good and in part bad; (2) it was only bad; or (3) all considered, it was good." And for *perceived efficacy,* "With which of the following statements do you agree? (1) Our democracy works well; (2) our democracy has many defects, but it works; (3) our democracy is getting worse, and soon it will not work at all."

22. Among those surveyed who expressed an opinion (i.e., if "don't know" and no answer are left out), support for democracy was even stronger: diffuse legitimacy was 79 percent in Portugal, 78 percent in Spain, 75 percent in Italy, and 89 percent in Greece; and perceived efficacy was 86 percent in Portugal, 77 percent in Spain, 69 percent in Italy, and 85 percent in Greece.

23. In Portugal, Spain, and Italy those labeled by Morlino and Mattei as neodemocrats (i.e., those who accept democratic legitimacy but at the same time have a positive opinion of the past) are the largest group, with 46 percent, 47 percent and 39 percent, respectively. Neoauthoritarians, who prefer an authoritarian regime and have negative opinions about their past, are relatively a higher number than authoritarians (i.e., those who prefer an authoritarian regime and have a positive opinion of their past): 10 percent versus 6 percent in Portugal, 4 percent versus 3 percent in Greece, and 12 percent versus 4 percent in Italy, but 7 percent versus 9 percent in Spain. See Leonardo Morlino and Franco Mattei, "Vecchio e nuovo autoritarismo nell' Europa Mediterranea," *Rivista Italiana di Scienza Politica,* 22, 1992, pp. 142–43.

24. See Juan J. Linz, Manuel Gómez-Reino, Francisco A. Orizo, and Darío Vila, *Informe sociológico sobre el cambio político en España, 1975–1981* (Madrid: Euramérica, 1981), p. 614.

25. This conclusion is strengthened by an examination of the age of those holding authoritarian attitudes. See Morlino and Mattei, "Vecchio e nuovo autoritarismo;" José R. Montero and Mariano Torcal, "Voters and Citizens in a New Democracy: Some Trend Data on Political Attitudes in Spain," *International Journal of Public Opinion Research,* 2, 1990, pp. 116–40; and Franz-Wilhelm Heimer, Jorge Vala-Salvador, and José M. Leite Viegas, "Attitudes towards Democracy in Contemporary Portugal," unpublished paper, 1989.

26. Lipset, *Political Man*; Linz et al., *Informe sociológico*; and Darío Vila and Manuel Gómez-Reino, "El proceso de cambio político en el electorado (1973–80)" (paper delivered at the Seminar on Electoral Surveys and Electoral Behavior, Madrid, 1980).

27. This terminology is based upon a four-part categorization first developed by Lipset in *Political Man* and subsequently applied to the study of the Spanish electorate by Linz et al. in *Informe sociológico.*

28. Eurobarometer surveys posed the question "How satisfied are you with the way democracy works?" This item is similar to that used in the Four Nation Survey, and it measures perceived efficacy. See Hermann Schmitt, "Party Government in Public Opinion: A European Cross-National Comparison," *European Journal of Political Research,* 11, 1983, pp. 353–76. On the low figures for the Italian case, see Giacomo Sani, "The Political Culture of Italy: Continuity and Change," in Gabriel A. Almond and Sidney Verba, eds., *The Civic Culture*

Revisited (Boston: Little, Brown, 1980); and Giovanna Guidorossi and Giacomo Sani, "The Political Culture of Italy: Fragmentation, Isolation, and Alienation from the Fifties to the Eighties" (paper presented to the 13th World Congress of the International Political Science Association, Paris, 1985).

29. Here we have in mind the case of Herri Batasuna, as well as the dynamics of a polarized and fragmented regional party system, in the Basque country. See Juan J. Linz and José R. Montero, eds., *Crisis y cambio: Electores y partidos en la España de los años ochenta* (Madrid: Centro de Estudios Constitucionales, 1986); and Francisco J. Llera, "El sistema de partidos vasco: Distancia ideológica y legitimación política," *Revista Española de Investigaciones Sociológicas,* 28, 1989, pp. 171–206.

30. This is only a very cursory analysis of two different, but very salient phenomena. For more on this see Chapter 10 in this volume.

31. For example, see Mario Bacalhau, *Os Portugueses e a politica quatro anos depois do 25 de april* (Lisbon: Meseta, 1978).

32. Jean-Claude Passeron, "Los silencios: Contribución a la interpretación de las no respuestas en la encuesta de opinión," *Revista Española de Investigaciones Sociológicas,* 17, 1982, pp. 83–136.

33. See Allan Williams, ed., *Southern Europe Transformed: Political and Economic Change in Greece, Italy, Portugal, and Spain.* (London: Harper & Row, 1984); J. Linz, "Europe's Southern Frontier: Evolving Trends toward What?" *Daedalus,* 1979, pp. 175–209; and José M. Maravall, "Economic Reforms in New Democracies: The Southern European Experience" (working paper no. 22, Instituto Juan March de Estudios e Investigaciones, Madrid, 1991).

34. See Chapter 10 in this volume, as well as Thomas C. Bruneau and Alex Mcleod, *Politics in Contemporary Portugal: Parties and the Consolidation of Democracy* (Boulder: Lynn Rienner, 1986).

35. See Thomas C. Bruneau, "Continuity and Change in Portuguese Politics: Ten Years after the Revolution of 25 April 1974," *West European Politics,* 7, 1984, pp. 72–83.

36. One sampling procedure may have undermined the representativeness of the sample: as a cost-saving measure, the quota of respondents residing in the least populous municipalities was drawn from areas close to larger metropolitan centers. Hence, Greeks in isolated rural areas (who, one might suspect, would be less involved with politics) are underrepresented.

37. See Nikiforos Diamandouros, "Greek Political Culture in Transition: Historical Origins, Evolution, Current Trends," in Richard Clogg, ed., *Greece in the 1980s* (London: Macmillan, 1983), pp. 43–69; Panayote E. Dimitras, "Changes in Public Attitudes," in Kevin Featherstone and Dimitrios K. Katsoudas, eds., *Political Change in Greece: Before and After the Colonels* (London: Croom Helm, 1987), pp. 64–84; and Panayote E. Dimitras, "Greek Public Attitudes: Continuity and Change," *International Journal of Public Opinion Research,* 2, 1990, pp. 92–115; Victor S. Papacosma, *Politics and Culture in Greece* (Ann Arbor: Center for Political Studies, University of Michigan, 1988); and P. Kafetzis, "Europe du sud: A la recherche du citoyen et de la politique," unpublished paper, 1988. Survey data have documented the high levels of political interest found in Greece (see *Eurobarometer,* 1991, "Trend Variables, 1974–1990").

38. It is interesting to see some possible relationships between our data on satisfaction with democracy and a few political events. For instance, the continuity of low levels of satisfaction in Italy contrasts with the higher Spanish ones (see Table 7.4), which coincide with the majority cabinet of Socialists, already inaugurated in 1982; at the same time, the decline of satisfaction in Greece overlaps with the difficulties of PASOK and a new cabinet alternation with Nea Democratia after three general elections held in a short span of time; the growth of satisfaction in Portugal is contemporaneous with the formation of the first majority and homogeneous cabinet by Social Democrats.

39. Maravall, "Economic Reforms in New Democracies."

40. Linz, "Transitions to Democracy"; and Juan J. Linz and Alfred Stepan, "Political Crafting of Democratic Consolidation or Destruction: Europe and South American Comparisons," in R. A. Pastor, ed., *Democracy in the Americas: Stopping the Pendulum* (New York: Holmes & Meier, 1989), pp. 41–61.

41. Such a distinction had a behavioral manifestation in voting. A preliminary analysis of attitudes on diffuse legitimacy and perceived efficacy reveals that democratic legitimacy is quite widespread, while voters diverge significantly in their perceptions of the efficacy of their democratic governments. These diverging evaluations of efficacy are strongly related to voters' support for or opposition to government in each country. It goes without saying that the differences are consistent with the dividing line which separates incumbent parties from opposition parties in each country.

42. See McDonough, Barnes, and López Pina, "Growth of Democratic Legitimacy," p. 751.

43. See Linz, "I rapporti tra legitimazione;" Montero and Torcal, "Voters and Citizens in a New Democracy;" José María Maravall and Julián Santamaría, "Political Change in Spain and Prospects for Democracy," in O'Donnell, Schmitter, and Whitehead, *TAR: Southern Europe*, pp. 71–108; and Giuseppe Di Palma, "Government Performance: An Issue and Three Cases in Search of Theory," in Geoffrey Pridham, ed., *The New Mediterranean Democracies: Regime Transition in Spain, Greece, and Portugal* (London: Frank Cass, 1984), pp. 172–87.

44. For data on Spain, see José R. Montero, "Sobre la democracia en España: Legitimidad, apoyos institucionales y significados" (working paper no. 39, Centro de Estudios Avanzados en Ciencias Sociales, Instituto Juan March de Estudios e Investigaciones, Madrid, 1992); for Portugal, see Thomas C. Bruneau, "Popular Support for Democracy in Post-Revolutionary Portugal," in Lawrence S. Graham and Douglas L. Wheeler, eds., *Portugal: The Revolution and Its Consequences* (Madison: University of Wisconsin Press, 1983), pp. 21–42.

45. An interesting partial exception is the negative correlation (Pearson's r = -.30) between religious practice and democratic legitimacy we find in Spain. These correlations are much weaker in the other countries: -.16 in Greece, -.10 in Portugal, and .07 in Italy. The political salience of this cleavage has been documented in many studies: see, for example, Richard Gunther, Giacomo Sani, and Goldie Shabad, *Spain after Franco: The Making of a Competitive Party System* (Berkeley: University of California Press, 1986); Linz et al., *Informe sociológico*; José R. Montero, "Iglesia, secularización y comportamiento político en España," *Revista Española de Investigaciones Sociológicas*, 34, 1986, pp. 131–59;

and Víctor Pérez Díaz, "Iglesia y religión en la España contemporánea," *El Retorno de la Sociedad Civil* (Madrid: Instituto de Estudios Económicos, 1987), pp. 411–66. Another significant exception is the Basque region of Spain, which is not separately examined in this chapter. For surveys of the extent of legitimacy accorded the Spanish constitutional monarchy in the Basque region, see Francisco J. Llera, "*Conflicto en Euskadi* Revisited," in Richard Gunther, ed., *Politics, Society, and Democracy: The Case of Spain* (Boulder: Westview, 1992); and Goldie Shabad, "Still the Exception?: Democratization and Ethnic Nationalism in the Basque Country of Spain," in Richard Gunther, Goldie Shabad, Juan J. Linz, José Ramón Montero, and Hans-Jürgen Puhle, "Electoral Change and Democratic Consolidation in Spain" (unpublished manuscript). Other interesting patterns involve age and income correlates of an index of political alienation, which will be discussed later in this chapter.

46. McDonough, Barnes, and López Pina ("Growth of Democratic Legitimacy") arrive at a similar conclusion for Spain, using panel survey data from 1978 to 1984.

47. "Don't know" response and nonresponses were excluded from the calculations. Marginal distributions among these categories indicate that supportive attitudes were most prevalent in Greece, where 56 percent of respondents fell into the "strong support" category (as compared with 32 percent in Portugal, 28 percent in Spain, and 27 percent in Italy). The "no support" category produces a mirror-image distribution: it included 26 percent of Spanish and Italian respondents, 19 percent of Portuguese, and 13 percent of Greeks.

48. This is, for instance, one of the main conclusions of the research by Ronald Inglehart and Hans D. Klingemann, "Party Identification, Ideological Preference, and the Left-Right Dimension among Western Mass Public," in Ian Budge, Ivor Crewe, and Dennis Farlie, eds., *Party Identification and Beyond: Representations of Voting and Party Competition* (London: John Wiley & Sons, 1976), pp. 243–76; and by Asher Arian and Michael Shamir, "The Primarily Political Functions of the Left-Right Continuum," *Comparative Politics*, 15, 1983, pp. 139–58. Also see, for example, Jean A. Laponce, *Left and Right: The Topography of Political Perceptions* (Toronto: University of Toronto Press, 1981); Giacomo Sani, "A Test of Least-Distance Model of Voting Choice: Italy 1972," *Comparative Political Studies*, 7, 1974, pp. 193–208; Giacomo Sani and José R. Montero, "El espectro político: Izquierda, derecha y centro," in Linz and Montero, *Crisis y cambio*; Hans D. Klingemann, "Measuring Ideologic Conceptualizations," in Samuel H. Barnes, Max Kaase et al., eds., *Political Action: Mass Participation in Five Western Democracies* (Beverly Hills: Sage, 1979), pp. 215–54; and George Th. Mavrogordatos, "Downs Revisited: Spatial Models of Party Competition and Left-Right Measurements," *International Political Science Review*, 8, 1987, pp. 333–42.

49. Among the measures suggested in the literature, we here follow Renato Mannheimer and Giacomo Sani ("Una componente della cultura politica: L'attaccamento al partito in quattro nazioni del sud Europa" unpublished paper, 1987), who utilize two indicators of partisanship: the classical item ("Tell me whether you feel very close, close, neither close nor distant, distant, or very distant . . . for each of the parties shown in this list") and a second version which includes an affective-reactive dimension ("When someone criticizes the party

you have voted for in the last election, how do you normally react?: (1) It bothers me as if they were criticizing me; (2) it does not bother me, but I do not like it; (3) it makes no difference to me"). Party identification is graded accordingly. Uncommitted respondents represent 57 percent of those interviewed in Spain, 52 percent in Portugal, 43 percent in Italy, and 27 percent in Greece. A similar rank-ordering is produced if we examine only responses to the classical partisanship question: those who regarded themselves as very close and close to a party were 48 percent of respondents Spain, 49 percent in Portugal, 52 percent in Italy, and 70 percent in Greece.

50. More recent data, from an Eurobarometer survey conducted in 1989 (see Hermann Schmitt, "Party Attachment and Party Choice in the European Election of June 1989," *International Journal of Public Opinion Research,* 2, 1990, pp. 169–81), shows even lower levels of identification in Spain, where 30 percent declare themselves to be very close to, fairly close to, or merely sympathizers with a party, while in Greece 57 percent do so. In Portugal the identifying percentage is roughly the same, 49; in Italy those identifying with a party are, surprisingly, a larger percentage, 63. For additional contributions on this topic, see Hermann Schmitt, "On Party Attachment in Western Europe and the Utility of Eurobarometer Data," *West European Politics,* 12, 1989, pp. 122–39; Renato Mannheimer and Giacomo Sani, *Il mercato elettorale: Identikit dell'elettore italiano* (Bologna: Mulino, 1987); Renato Mannheimer, "Un componente della decisione di voto: L'identificazione di partito," in *Capire il voto: Contributi per l'analisi del comportamento elettorale in Italia* (Milan: Angeli, 1989); Bradley Richardson, "The Development of Partisan Commitments in Post-Franquist Spain" (research paper, Department of Political Science, Ohio State University, 1990); and Richard Gunther and José R. Montero, "Los anclajes del partidismo: Un análisis comparado del comportamiento electoral en cuatro democracias del sur de Europa," in Pilar del Castillo, eds., *Comportamiento político y electoral en las democracias* (Madrid: Centro de Investigaciones Sociológicas, 1994) pp. 467–548. See also Chapter 10 of this volume.

51. Sani and Montero, "El espectro político," pp. 155, 185. There is no doubt, however, that the relationship between left-right orientation and other values and attitudes deserves to be explored more closely. Its ambiguities have already been underlined by other authors, such as Mavrogordatos, "Downs Revisited;" and Cees Van der Eijk and B. Niemöller, "Theoretical and Methodological Considerations in the Use of Left-Right Scales" (paper presented at the joint sessions of the ECPR, Salzburg, 1983). Sani and Montero, "El espectro político," did that for Spain; Giacomo Sani, "Partiti e atteggiamenti di massa in Spagna e Italia," *Rivista Italiana di Scienza Politica,* 11, 1981, pp. 235–79, for Italy and Spain; Bacalhau, *Os Portugueses e a Politica,* for Portugal; George Th. Mavrogordatos, *Rise of the Green Sun: The Greek Elections of 1981* (occasional paper no. 1, Centre for Contemporary Greek Studies, London, 1983), for Greece; and Jonas Condonines and José Durão Barroso, "La dimension gauche-droite et la compétition entre les partis politiques en Europe du sud (Portugal, Espagne, Grèce)," *Il Politico,* 49, 1984, pp. 405–28, for Portugal, Spain and Greece.

52. The three statements that served as the basis for our index were: (1) "Politicians do not worry about people like me"; (2) "Politics is so complicated

that people like me don't know what is going on"; and (3) "Those in power always follow their personal interests." For a recent analysis of these items see Franco Mattei, "Le dimensioni dell'efficacia politica: Aspetti metodologici," *Rivista Italiana di Scienza Politica,* 17, 1987, pp. 105–33. Our definition of political alienation basically follows Finifter's notion of it, particularly with reference to the dimension of political powerlessness (see Ada Finifter, "Dimensions of Political Alienation," *American Political Science Review,* 64, 1970, pp. 389–410, and *Alienation and the Political System* [New York: John Wiley & Sons, 1972]). This focus on inefficacy is clearly distinct from several related concepts, including the more negative concept of William A. Gamson (*Power and Discontent* [Homewood, Ill.: Dorsey, 1968], pp. 56–57), according to which authorities are regarded as "incompetent and stupid"; various scholars' conceptualizations of "social" alienation; or David C. Schwartz's concept of "estrangement"—the "perception that one does not identify oneself with the political system" (*Political Alienation and Political Behavior* [Chicago: Aldine, 1973], p. 7). See also Jack Citrin, Herbert McClosky, Merrill Shanks, and Paul M. Sniderman, "Personal and Political Sources of Political Alienation," *British Journal of Political Science,* 5, 1975, pp. 1–31; and James D. Wright, *The Dissent of the Governed: Alienation and Democracy in America* (New York: Academic Press, 1970).

53. See Almond and Verba, *Civic Culture*; Giacomo Sani, "The Political Culture of Italy: Continuity and Change," in Almond and Verba, *Civic Culture Revisited*, pp. 273–324; José María Maravall, *La política de la transición*, 2nd ed. (Madrid: Taurus, 1984); Maravall, *Economic Reforms in New Democracies,* pp. 17–18; and Joan Botella, "La cultura política en la España democrática," in Ramón Cotarelo, ed., *Transición política y consolidación democrática: España (1975–1986)* (Madrid: Centro de Investigaciones Sociológicas, 1992), pp. 121–36. For some discussions of political cynicism see John Fraser, "Personal and Political Meaning and Correlates of Political Cynicism," *Midwest Journal of Political Science,* 15, 1971, pp. 347–64; and Robert E. Agger, Marshall N. Goldstein, and Stanley A. Pearl, "Political Cynicism: Measurement and Meaning," *Journal of Politics,* 23, 1961, pp. 477–506.

54. Guillermo O'Donnell sets forth this same hypothesis in his survey of democratization experiences in Latin America. See Guillermo O'Donnell, "Transitions, Continuities, and Paradoxes," in Scott Mainwaring, Guillermo O'Donnell, and J. Samuel Valenzuela, eds., *Issues in Democratic Consolidation: The New South American Democracies in Comparative Perspective* (Notre Dame, Ind.: University of Notre Dame Press, 1992), pp. 31–37.

55. Robert D. Putnam, *The Beliefs of Politicians: Ideology, Conflict, and Democracy in Britain and Italy* (New Haven: Yale University Press, 1973).

56. The first question was, "When faced with an urgent problem in your neighborhood which affects you directly, which of the following would you prefer?: (1) let the authorities decide; (2) call on the authorities; (3) turn to groups or associations; (4) demonstrate with others affected."

57. The second question was, "When the authorities have to solve a problem, which of the following should they do?: (1) it is better that they make quick decisions without consulting the citizens or the associations that represent them; (2) they must always consult the citizens and the associations that represent them even though this might delay the solution of the problem."

58. See, for example, Giovanni Sartori, *The Theory of Democracy Revisited* (Chatham: Chatham House, 1987).

59. This index was based on responses to the following statements: "Political parties only divide people"; "parties criticize one another, but in reality they are all alike"; "parties are useless"; "parties are needed to defend the interests of the various groups and social classes"; "thanks to parties people can participate in political life"; and "without parties there can be no democracy."

60. This is the suggestion of Gianfranco Pasquino in commenting on a previous draft of this chapter.

61. In Chapter 10 of this volume, Morlino presents some additional data with which to address some of these questions. Richard Gunther and José Ramón Montero will undertake an extensive exploration, "The Anchors of Partisanship," in the second volume of this series.

Chapter 8

I am very grateful to Nikiforos Diamandouros and Richard Gunther for their comments, suggestions, and patience in helping me complete this difficult comparative analysis. I would also like to acknowledge the useful comments of the participants in the Madrid (July 1990) and Rome (December 1990) SSRC conferences, especially those of Juan Linz, José Ramón Montero, and Hans-Jürgen Puhle.

1. In particular, see Karl Loewenstein, *Political Reconstruction* (New York: Macmillan, 1946); and Karl Loewenstein, "Reflections on the Value of Constitutions in Our Revolutionary Age," in Arnold J. Zurcher, ed., *Constitutions and Constitutional Trends since World War II* (New York: New York University Press, 1951) reprinted in Harry Eckstein and David E. Apter, eds., *Comparative Politics* (New York: Free Press, 1963), pp. 149–63 (page citations are to the 1963 edition).

2. Anthony King, "Modes of Executive-Legislative Relations: Great Britain, France, and West Germany," *Legislative Studies Quarterly* 1, no. 1, 1976, pp. 11–34.

3. Harry Eckstein, *The Evaluation of Political Performance: Problems and Dimensions,* Sage Professional Papers in Comparative Politics, vol. 2, nos. 1–17 (Beverly Hills: Sage, 1971).

4. Robert A. Dahl, "The Evaluation of Political Systems," in Ithiel de Sola Pool, ed., *Contemporary Political Studies: Toward Empirical Theory* (New York: McGraw-Hill, 1967), pp. 166–81; Gabriel A. Almond, *Political Development: Essays in Heuristic Theory* (Boston: Little, Brown, 1970); and G. Bingham Powell, Jr., *Contemporary Democracies: Participation, Stability, and Violence* (Cambridge: Harvard University Press, 1982).

5. Ulrike Liebert and Maurizio Cotta, eds., *Parliaments and Democratic Consolidation in Southern Europe* (London: Pinter, 1990).

6. Arend Lijphart, Thomas C. Bruneau, P. Nikiforos Diamandouros, and Richard Gunther, "A Mediterranean Model of Democracy?: The Southern European Democracies in Comparative Perspective," *West European Politics* 11, no. 2, 1988, pp. 7–25. An updated and expanded version of this piece will appear in the second volume in this series.

7. Loewenstein, "Reflections on the Value of Constitutions," p. 155.

8. Arend Lijphart, *Democracies: Patterns of Majoritarian and Consensus Government in Twenty-one Countries* (New Haven: Yale University Press, 1984).

9. Maurice Duverger, "A New Political System Model: Semi-Presidential Government," *European Journal of Political Research* 8, no. 2, 1980, p. 166.

10. See Giuliano Amato and Francesca Bruno, "La forma di governo italiana: Dalle idee dei partiti all'assemblea costituente," *Quaderni Costituzionali*, April 1981, pp. 33–85; and Philip Williams, *The French Parliament 1958–1967* (London: George Allen & Unwin, 1968).

11. For the theoretical underpinnings, see Otto Kirchheimer, "Confining Conditions and Revolutionary Breakthroughs," *American Political Science Review* 59, no. 4, 1965, pp. 964–74.

12. See, for example, Guillermo O'Donnell, Philippe C. Schmitter, and Laurence Whitehead, eds., *Transitions from Authoritarian Rule: Prospects for Democracy* (Baltimore: Johns Hopkins University Press, 1986), especially the chapters by Diamandouros, Maxwell, Maravall and Santamaría, and Pasquino (see preface n. 3 above).

13. For Greece, see Antoine Pantélis, *Les grands problèmes de la nouvelle constitution hellènique de 1975* (Paris: Librairie Générale de Jurisprudence, 1979). For Spain, see Giuseppe De Vergottini, *Una costituzione democratica per la Spagna* (Milan: Franco Angeli, 1978); Eduardo García de Enterría and Alberto Predieri, eds., *La costituzione spagnola del 1978* (Milan: Giuffré, 1982); and Antonio López Pina, "Shaping the Constitution," in Howard R. Penniman and Eusebio M. Mujal-Leon, eds., *Spain at the Polls, 1977, 1979, and 1982* (Durham: Duke University Press, 1985), pp. 30–47. For Portugal, see Giuseppe De Vergottini, *Le origini della Seconda Repubblica Portoghese (1974–1976)* (Milan: Giuffré, 1977); Walter C. Opello, Jr., *Portugal's Political Development: A Comparative Approach* (Boulder: Westview, 1985); and Manuel Braga da Cruz and Miguel Lobo Antunes, "Revolutionary Transition and Problems of Parliamentary Institutionalization: The Case of the Portuguese National Assembly," in Liebert and Cotta, *Parliaments and Democratic Consolidation*, pp. 154–83.

14. See P. Nikiforos Diamandouros, "Politics and Constitutionalism in Greece: The 1975 Constitution in Historical Perspective," in H. E. Chehabi and Alfred Stepan, eds., *Politics, Society, and Democracy: Comparative Studies* (Boulder: Westview, 1995).

15. See Richard Gunther, "Electoral Laws, Party Systems, and Elites: The Case of Spain," *American Political Science Review* 83, no. 3, 1989, pp. 835–58.

16. Opello, *Portugal's Political Development*, p. 155.

17. See José Ramón Montero and Joaquím García Morillo, *El control parlamentario* (Madrid: Tecnos, 1984), pp. 186–92.

18. For a critical assessment of this situation, see Jordi Capo Giol, Ramón García Cotarelo, Diego López Garrido, and Joan Subirats, "By Consociationalism to a Majoritarian Parliamentary System: The Rise and Decline of the Spanish Cortes," in Liebert and Cotta, *Parliaments and Democratic Consolidation*, pp. 92–130.

19. Kevin Featherstone, "The 'Party-State' in Greece and the Fall of Papandreou," *West European Politics* 13, no. 1, 1990, pp. 101–15.

20. David Corkill, "Portugal's Political Transformation: The Election of July 1987," *Parliamentary Affairs* 41, no. 2, 1988, p. 247.

21. Ibid., p. 255.

22. Gianfranco Pasquino, "Party Government in Italy: Achievements and Prospects," in Richard S. Katz, ed., *Party Governments: European and American Experiences* (Berlin: de Gruyter, 1987), pp. 200–242.

23. For an excellent analysis of this evolution, see Braga da Cruz and Lobo Antunes, "Revolutionary Transition," in Liebert and Cotta, *Parliaments and Democratic Consolidation,* esp. pp. 170–77.

24. This is clearly indicated in most, if not all, of the contributions in Juan J. Linz and Alfred Stepan, eds., *The Breakdown of Democratic Regimes* (Baltimore: Johns Hopkins University Press, 1978).

25. Lawrence C. Dodd, *Coalitions in Parliamentary Government* (Princeton: Princeton University Press, 1976); and Eric C. Browne and John Dreijmanis, eds., *Government Coalitions in Western Democracies* (New York: Longman, 1982).

26. Richard Clogg, *Parties and Elections in Greece: The Search for Legitimacy* (London: C. Hurst, 1987).

27. See the excellent analysis on Greece by George Th. Mavrogordatos, *Stillborn Republic: Social Coalitions and Party Strategies in Greece, 1922–1936* (Berkeley: University of California Press, 1983); and, on Spain, see Mario Caciagli, *Elecciones y partidos en la transición española* (Madrid: Centro de Investigaciones Sociológicas, 1986).

28. For discussions of what constitutes an executive and of which executives should be studied, see Anthony King, "Executives," in Fred I. Greenstein and Nelson W. Polsby, eds., *Handbook of Political Science,* vol. 5 (Reading, Mass.: Addison-Wesley, 1975), pp. 173–256. For a sample of executives, see Richard Rose and Ezra N. Suleiman, *Presidents and Prime Ministers* (Washington, D.C.: American Enterprise Institute, 1980).

29. Before the 1982 revisions of the constitution, two motions of censure, approved by the absolute majority of deputies within thirty days of each other, were needed.

30. Opello, *Portugal's Political Development,* p. 155.

31. On this, see Maurizio Cotta, "Il sottosistema governo-parlamento," *Rivista Italiana di Scienza Politica* 17, August 1987, pp. 241–83.

32. Loewenstein, "Reflections on the Value of Constitutions," p. 155.

33. On institutional engineering, see Keith G. Banting and Richard Simeon, eds., *Redesigning the State: The Politics of Constitutional Change in Industrial Nations* (Toronto: University of Toronto Press, 1985); and Gianfranco Pasquino, "The Impact of Institutions on Party Government: Tentative Hypotheses," in Francis G. Castles and Rudolf Wildenmann, eds., *Visions and Realities of Party Government* (Berlin: de Gruyter, 1986), pp. 120–42.

Chapter 9

This paper is part of a larger project initially supported by the Research Council of the European University Institute, San Domenico di Fiesole, Italy. I am indebted to my collaborators in that project for all they have contributed to my understanding of the politics of organized class and sectoral interests during democratic transition and consolidation in Greece (George Mavrogordatos), Italy (Marco Maraffi), Portugal (Manuel Lucena and Carlos Gaspar), Spain (Víctor Pérez Díaz), and Turkey (Ilkay Sunar). I have also profited from discussions with Klaus von Beyme, Salvador Giner, Ulrike Liebert, Leonardo Morlino and Giuseppe di Palma in the course of elaborating this project. In its final stages, I was very fortunate in obtaining original data generously provided to me by Jelle Visser of the University of Amsterdam, Franz Traxler of the University of Vienna, and Loek Halman of the University of Brabant. This version also benefited considerably from the rigorous critique and editing of Richard Gunther.

1. The leading expression of this emphasis on parties is Geoffrey Pridham, ed., *Securing Democracy: Political Parties and Democratic Consolidation in Southern Europe* (London: Routledge, 1990). This pioneering comparative effort was followed by a volume on the less orthodox topic of how foreign actors and actions affected the outcomes of these democratizations: Geoffrey Pridham, ed., *Encouraging Democracy: The International Context of Regime Transition in Southern Europe* (Leicester: Leicester University Press, 1991).

2. See Giuseppe di Palma, "Governo di partiti e riproducibilità democratica: Il dilemma delle nuove democrazie," *Rivista Italiana di Scienza Politica,* 13, 1983, pp. 3–36.

3. One implication of this is that typologies of democracy in the future should include material on the system of interest intermediation that is prevalent, instead of being based exclusively on the nature of the party system or structure of executive power. For an effort in this direction, see Peter Lange and Hudson Meadwell, "Typologies of Democratic Systems: From Political Inputs to Political Economy," in Howard Wiarda, ed., *New Directions in Comparative Politics,* 2nd ed. (Boulder: Westview, 1990).

4. For a more extensive discussion of the notion of partial regimes and of the theoretical framework upon which this essay is based, see Philippe C. Schmitter, "The Consolidation of Democracy and Representation of Social Groups," *American Behavioral Scientist* 35, nos. 4–5, March–June 1992, pp. 422–49.

5. This was the central insight of an unjustly ignored article by Dankwart Rustow that has been retrieved by scholars working on contemporary democratization: "Transitions to Democracy," *Comparative Politics* 2, April 1970, pp. 337–63.

6. Philippe C. Schmitter, "Speculations about the Prospective Demise of Authoritarian Rule and Its Possible Consequences" (working paper no. 165, European University Institute, Florence, 1985), pp. 57–58.

7. The United States and, previously, Great Britain furnished the models towards which it was presumed that latecomers would evolve. More recently, lesser-known cases have occasionally been put forth as examples of particularly stable, "consolidated" democratic rule. See, for example, Harry Eckstein's argument about congruence based on Norway: *Division and Cohesion in Democracy* (Princeton: Princeton University Press, 1966).

8. Alternatively, the new regime can simply pull off the shelf a preexisting constitution and, thereby, avoid public deliberation and choice about metarules, as was the case with Argentina and, to a lesser extent, Greece.

9. See Michael Foley, *The Silence of Constitutions* (London: Routledge, 1989), where it is argued that the "gaps" and "abeyances" in constitutions may be more important than the clauses and commitments they specifically contain.

10. Even in Spain, where authorities of the *franquista* regime continued al-

most until the end to exercise severe and systematic repression of parties and politicians representing working-class constituencies but left opposition trade unions and their leaders relatively free to build clienteles and organizations, the communist-led Comisiones Obreras (CC.OO.) did not subsequently play such a leading role.

11. Guillermo O'Donnell and Philippe C. Schmitter, *Transitions from Authoritarian Rule: Tentative Conclusions about Uncertain Democracies* (Baltimore: Johns Hopkins University Press, 1986), p. 48 (see preface n. 3 above).

12. See Nancy Bermeo, *The Revolution within the Revolution: Workers' Control in Rural Portugal* (Princeton: Princeton University Press, 1986); John L. Hammond, *Building Popular Power: Workers' and Neighborhood Movements in the Portuguese Revolution* (New York: Monthly Review Press, 1988); and Charles Downs, *Revolution at the Grassroots: Community Organizations in the Portuguese Revolution* (New York: SUNY, 1989).

13. Spain is the only country in Southern Europe (indeed, one of the few in the world) whose democratic constitution refers explicitly to the functions performed for the polity by trade unions and business associations (Article 7).

14. Juan Linz, in "Stability and Regime Change" (paper presented to the Committee on Political Sociology of IPSA-ISA, Werner-Reimers Stiftung, Bad Homburg, May 18–22, 1981), speaking of Spain, put the point well, if cryptically: "Politics takes precedence over interests." In the past, when manual workers formed a larger proportion of the potential citizenry, trade unions might have been in a better strategic situation during a political transition. Nevertheless, the British Labour Party seems a unique instance of unions taking the lead in forming a lasting political party—and that did not happen during a change in regime type. One could even say that the recent successes of socialist parties in Southern Europe (France, Greece, Spain, Portugal) have been gained at the expense of, rather than because of, the intensity of these parties' linkage with the trade union movement.

15. Even those European countries not undergoing a change in regime type have been experiencing pressures for new forms of decentralized rule. See Yves Mény, *Neuf ans de régionalisation en Europe: Bilan et perspectives (1970–1980)* (Paris: Cujas, 1982), pp. 5–21, where the 1970s are described as "the decade of regionalism."

16. Mancur Olson, *The Logic of Collective Action: Public Goods and the Theory of Groups* (Cambridge: Harvard University Press, 1965).

17. See Schmitter, "Consolidation of Democracy," where I have elaborated more thoroughly these characteristics and why they are significant in determining the partial regimes of interest representation.

18. Carlos Gaspar and Manuel Lucena, "Métamorphoses corporatives: Associations d'intérêts et consolidation de la démocratie au Portugal," unpublished paper. A Portuguese version of this was subsequently published as Manuel Lucena and Carlos Gaspar, "Associações de interesses econômicos e institucionalização de democracia em Portugal," *Analise Social,* 27 (1991), pp. 847–903, 28 (1992), pp. 135–87.

19. In an empirical study of fifty-six sectors in nine democracies, and correcting for outliers, Wolfgang Streeck has concluded that, on the average, business associations outnumber trade unions by 6.7 to 1 ("Interest Hetero-

geneity and Organizing Capacity: Two Class Logics of Collective Action?" *Social Institutions and Economic Performance* [London: Sage, 1992], p. 88).

20. The comparative data come from Jelle Visser, "In Search of Inclusive Unionism," *Bulletin of Comparative Labour Relations* 18, 1990, pp. 16–17.

21. From 1978 to 1984, the coverage of collective contracts in Spain increased from 60 percent to 90 percent of the workforce (see José María Zufiaur, "El sindicalismo español en la transición y la crisis," *Papeles de la Economía Española* 22, 1985, p. 205). There seems to be some double counting in these figures, however. See below, Table 9.6, for revised figures by Franz Traxler.

22. Nonaffiliated representatives won 18 percent of the enterprise elections in 1978 and only 12 percent in 1982 (ibid., p. 208).

23. See Santos Juliá, *La desavenencia: Partidos, sindicatos y huelga general* (Madrid: El País/Aguilar, 1989); and Salvador Aguilar and Jordi Roca, "14-D: Economía política de una huelga" (Fundació Jaume Bofill, Feb. 1989).

24. These relatively high figures are confirmed by a survey of Spanish businessmen in which only 25 percent of small firms, 20 percent of medium-size firms and 4 percent of large firms reported not being affiliated with some association or federation linked to the CEOE. Robert Martinez and Rafael Pardo Avellaneda, "El asociacionismo español en la transición," *Papeles de la Economía Española* 22, 1985, p. 94.

25. Liborio Mattina, *Gli industriali e la democrazia: La Confindustria nella formazione dell'Italia Repubblicana* (Bologna: Il Mulino, 1991).

26. The Chambers are not completely irrelevant, however. In Robert Martinez's survey of Spanish businessmen (Martínez and Avellaneda, "El asociacionismo español"), 20 percent said that they would channel their problems through the *Cámaras*. Seventy-eight percent would work through employer associations (such as the CEOE and its affiliates) and 32 percent would address ministerial authorities directly. His survey also revealed that many respondents were not even aware that they were members of a *cámara*! For a treatment of the role of these semipublic institutions, see Joaquim Molins, "Chambers of Commerce as Interest Groups," *Working Papers* (Barcelona: Institut de Ciències Polítiques i Socials, 1989).

27. Marco Maraffi, "Organized Interests in Democratic Italy, 1945–1963" (unpublished manuscript, June 1988). For a more detailed treatment see Leonardo Morlino, ed., *Costruire la democrazia: Gruppi e partiti in Italia* (Bologna: Il Mulino, 1991).

28. George Th. Mavrogordatos, *Metaxy Pityokampte kai Prokrouste: Hoi epangelmatikes organoseis ste semerine Hellada* (Athens: Odysseas, 1988), pp. 61–63 and table 5. An English-language version of this is available as "Civil Society under Populism," in Richard Clogg, ed., *Greece 1981–89: The Populist Decade* (London: Macmillan, 1993), pp. 47–64.

29. That this decay may be very slow and that surviving interest associations, especially trade unions, may struggle to retain the monopoly status or guaranteed resources they had under the defunct authoritarian regime and its state-corporatist arrangements is well illustrated by the case of Greece after 1973, as well as by the unsuccessful effort of the communist trade union movement in Portugal to impose *unicidade* after the fall of Caetano.

30. In the case of Turkey, this is misleading since the TOB is based on a

chamber system that blankets the national territory with obligatory units. The TISK, which is voluntary and represents only employer interests, has only twelve member associations, all functionally or sectorally based.

31. Sources: Economic and Social Committee of the European Communities, *The Economic and Social Interest Groups of Greece* (Brussels: Editions Delta, 1981); Comité Economique et Social des Communautés Européennes, *Les organisations socio-professionnelles du Portugal* (Brussels: Editions Delta, 1984); Bertrand Hervieu and Rose-Marie Lagrave, eds., *Les Syndicats Agricoles en Europe* (Paris: L'Harmattan, 1992); corrections and amendments from unpublished manuscripts and personal communications from Manuel Lucena, Marco Maraffi, George Mavrogordatos, and Ilkay Sunar.

32. Note, however, that the Confederación Española de la Pequeña y Mediana Empresa (CEPYME) was initially formed independently and only subsequently joined the CEOE. It still sustains a relative independence as an organization within the CEOE and has joined separately several European and international organizations. Note as well that Spain also has a number of regionally based business associations, some quite active and autonomous, although all are linked to the CEOE. The Fomento de Trabajo Nacional (FTN), which, despite its name, represents Catalan industrial interests, was founded long before the CEOE (in 1889) and has furnished several of the CEOE's leaders.

33. After Alessandro Pizzorno, "Scambio politico e identità collettiva nel conflitto di classe," in Colin Crouch and Alessandro Pizzorno, eds., *Conflitti in Europa* (Milano: Etas Libri, 1977), pp. 410–16.

34. The Basque nationalist movement and, especially, ETA are an obvious exception and a great complication to the Spanish consolidation process.

35. Opinion data from another survey conducted in the mid-1980s produced roughly similar results. In Italy, 5.4 percent reported membership in a political party, as opposed to the 5.2 percent shown in Table 9.7 for 1990; in Spain, 2.6 percent versus 1.4 percent; in Portugal 2.4 percent versus 4.7 percent. The surprising finding, however, is the very high proportion of Greeks that reported party membership in this other survey: 15.8 percent. This suggests—but does not prove, given the absence of comparable data—that Greece may be the only country in Southern Europe where party affiliations outnumber associational ones (see Guido Guidorossi and Mario Weber, "Immagine dei partiti e antagonismo politico in Italia, Spagna, Portogallo e Grecia," *Il Politico* 3, no. 2, 1988, p. 239).

36. Leonardo Morlino has called my attention to the fact that, initially, the Italian trade unions organized a single confederation (the Patto di Roma), in 1944. The subsequent convocation of competitive elections led to its fragmentation along party lines.

37. For GSEE, see Mavrogordatos, *Metaxy Pityokampte kai Prokrouste,* pp. 117–26; for GSEBE, see ibid., pp. 166–69; for PASEGES, see ibid., pp. 67–75; for SEB, see ibid., p. 175. Mavrogordatos goes so far as to accuse the PASOK government of pursuing a policy of *Gleichschaltung* with regard to the country's associative structures. In a personal communication, however, Kostas Lavdas of the University of West England has expressed doubts that "the PASOK tried to intervene and manipulate the organizational structure of the SEB," and has stressed that after 1985, when a stabilization program was initiated, this

government actively courted the support of the SEB and tried to strengthen its authority and influence over its members.

38. It should be noted, however, that these close links were not sufficient to prevent the UGT's leading a general strike against a government led by "its own party" in 1988.

39. See A. Gueslin and B. Hervieu, "Un syndicalisme européen est-il possible?" in Bertrand Hervieu and Rose-Marie Lagrave, eds., *Les Syndicats Agricoles en Europe* (Paris: L'Harmattan, 1992), pp. 301–13.

40. This might not be true if one were to include data on the structures and practices of professional associations in Southern Europe—especially those representing the interests of the major liberal professions. This information, alas, is not easily available, but my impression from knowledge of individual cases is that this is the area in which the continuity with previous state-corporatist practices is the greatest and, therefore, in which one is likely to find the most entrenched associational monopolies.

41. The classic monograph on Confindustria is Joseph LaPalombara, *Interest Groups in Italian Politics* (Princeton: Princeton University Press, 1964). Unfortunately, it says relatively little about how the organization acquired its monopoly status and what were its contributions to the consolidation of democracy in Italy. For that, see the more recent Mattina, *Gli industriali e la democrazia*.

42. For further information on the internal structure of the CEOE, see Harry Rijnen, "La CEOE como organización," *Papeles de la Economía Española* 22, 1985, pp. 115–21.

43. See, in addition to a special number of *Papeles de la Economía Española*, "Empresarios, sindicatos y marco institucional," 22, 1985, Salvador Aguilar, "El asociativismo empresarial en la transición postfranquista," *Papers* 24, 1983 (Barcelona), pp. 53–84. In a personal communication, José Fernández Castro has pointed out that a few of the sectoral federations (construction, electrical equipment, and metallurgy) antedated the CEOE and, indeed, played an important role in its foundation, as did the FNT. He also questioned whether the trade union threat was such an important element in determining its relatively high degree of organizational centralization.

44. Kostas Lavdas, in an unusually thorough set of comments on an earlier draft of this essay, suggested that my account of the peak association of Greek business, the SEB, may have underestimated its strategic capacity, especially its autonomy from government interests and its role in aggregating class interests. He also points out that, on several occasions, efforts were made to strike a macrocorporatist bargain in Greece, although they were ultimately unsuccessful. Collective agreements have been reached independently between the SEB and the GSEE, and they have even been respected by nonsignatories. I am indebted to him for these (and other) critical observations.

Chapter 10

1. See, for example, Gerald M. Pomper, "Concepts of Political Parties," *Journal of Theoretical Politics* 4, 1992, pp. 143–59; Giovanni Sartori, *Parties and Party Systems: A Framework for Analysis* (Cambridge: Cambridge University Press, 1976), p. 63; and Anthony Downs, *An Economic Theory of Democracy* (New York: Harper and Row, 1957), p. 25.

2. Kaare Strom, "A Behavioral Theory of Competitive Political Parties," *American Journal of Political Science* 34, 1990, pp. 565–98.

3. Alessandro Pizzorno, *I soggetti del pluralismo: Classi, partiti, sindacati* (Bologna: Il Mulino, 1980), p. 13.

4. Geoffrey Pridham, ed., *Securing Democracy: Political Parties and Democratic Consolidation in Southern Europe* (London: Routledge, 1990), pp. 26–28.

5. Samuel Barnes, "Ideology and the Organization of Conflict: On the Relationship between Political Thought and Behavior," *Journal of Politics* 28, 1966, pp. 513–30.

6. By democratic consolidation, I mean the multifaceted process of adaptation and establishment of the democratic structures, norms, and regime–civil society relationships so that the democratic regime gains persistence and capability to overcome possible challenges. In other words, this term implies the strengthening of the democratic regime to avert possible future crises (Leonardo Morlino, "Consolidamento democratico: Definizione e modelli," *Rivista Italiana di Scienza Politica* 16, 1986, pp. 197–238).

7. Stefano Bartolini, "The Membership of Mass Parties: The Social Democratic Experience, 1889–1978," in Hans Daalder and Peter Mair, eds., *Western European Party Systems: Continuity and Change* (London: Sage Publications, 1983). For alternative measures of volatility, such as area or bloc volatility and volatility of major parties, see Stefano Bartolini and Peter Mair, *Identity, Competition, and Electoral Availability: The Stabilization of European Electorates, 1885–1985* (Cambridge: Cambridge University Press, 1990); For an application of these measures to Italy, see Leonardo Morlino, "The Changing Relationship between Parties and Society in Italy," in Stefano Bartolini and Peter Mair, eds., *Party Politics in Contemporary Western Europe* (London: Frank Cass, 1984).

8. Vladimir O. Key, "A Theory of Critical Elections," *Journal of Politics* 17, 1955, pp. 3–18.

9. For a discussion of the differences between total volatility and interbloc volatility, see Bartolini and Mair, *Identity, Competition, and Electoral Availability*.

10. For a discussion of counting rules and the concept of interparty blackmail, see Sartori, *Parties and Party Systems,* pp. 121, 123.

11. See, for example, George Mavrogordatos, "The Greek Party System: A Case of 'Limited but Polarized Pluralism'?" in Bartolini and Mair, *Party Politics in Western Europe*; and Seraphim Seferiades, "Polarizzazione partitica e non proporzionalità elettorale in Grecia," *Rivista Italiana di Scienza Politica* 16, 1986, pp. 401–37.

12. On this topic see José Ramón Montero, "Las elecciones legislativas," in Ramón Cotarelo, ed., *Transición política y consolidación democrática: España (1975–1986)* (Madrid: Centro de Investigaciones Sociológicas, 1992), p. 252. The Catalan regional party system is much more stable than that of the Basque region. The regional party system of Catalonia may be regarded as a predominant party system, with Convergència i Unió as the main force. The Basque regional party system, however, is characterized by polarized pluralism, with high polarization, fragmentation, and instability.

13. On the changes in Greek electoral law passed in April 1989, see Virginia Perifanaki Rotolo, "Il nuovo sistema elettorale e il voto di preferenza in Grecia," *Il Politico* 55, 1990, pp. 143–66.

14. In Portugal, there are twenty electoral districts: two are large, electing 56 and 39 deputies (Porto and Lisbon, respectively); six are middle sized (between 11 and 17 deputies); and twelve are small (between 4 and 10). In Spain, the fifty provinces, as well as Ceuta and Melilla, serve as electoral districts. Two of these multimember constituencies are large, with 33 and 32 seats (Barcelona and Madrid); two are medium (Sevilla with 12 seats and Valencia with 15); and the remaining forty-eight are small (between 4 and 10) or very small (fewer than 4).

15. See Richard Gunther, "Electoral Laws, Party Systems, and Elites: The Case of Spain," *American Political Science Review* 83, September 1989, pp. 835–58.

16. Ibid., p. 841.

17. Arend Lijphart, *Democracies: Patterns of Majoritarian and Consensus Government in Twenty-one Countries* (New Haven: Yale University Press, 1988), 2nd ed., p. 221. See also the comparison among indices of proportionality in Montero, "Las elecciones legislativas," Table 26. Detailed analyses of the Spanish electoral system can be found in José R. Montero, Francisco J. Llera, and Mariano Torcal, "Sistemas electorales en España: Una recapitulación," *Revista Española de Investigaciones Sociológicas* 58, April–June, pp. 7–56; and José Ramón Montero and Richard Gunther, "Sistemas 'cerrados' y listas 'abiertas': Sobre algunas propuestas de reformas del sistema electoral en España," in José Ramón Montero, Richard Gunther, and José Ignacio Wert, *Perspectivas de reforma del sistema electoral,* Cuadernos y Debates, (Madrid: Centro de Estudios Constitucionales, 1994).

18. For a discussion of elite instability in Portugal, see Pedro Santana Lopes, "PPD/PSD: La dependencia del carisma," *Revista de Estudios Políticos* 60–61, 1988, pp. 173–84. For discussions of instability among Spanish party leaders, see Richard Gunther, "Democratization and Party Building: The Role of Party Elites in the Spanish Transition," in Robert P. Clark and Michael H. Haltzel, eds., *Spain in the 1980s: The Democratic Transition and a New International Role* (Cambridge, Mass.: Ballinger, 1987); and Richard Gunther, "El colapso de UCD," in Juan J. Linz and José Ramón Montero, eds., *Crisis y cambio: Electores y partidos en la España de los años ochenta* (Madrid: Centro de Estudios Constitucionales, 1986).

19. See Barnes, "Ideology and the Organization of Conflict."

20. Alberto Spreafico, "Orientamento politico e identificazione partitica," in Alberto Spreafico and Joseph La Palombara, eds., *Elezioni e comportamento politico in Italia* (Milano: Comunità, 1963), p. 691.

21. The sources for these data are: for Germany, Werner Zohlnhöfer, "Party Identification in the Federal Republic of Germany," in Kurt L. Shell, ed., *The Democratic Political Process* (Waltham, Mass.: Blaisdell, 1969), p. 154; for the United States, Angus Campbell et al., *Elections and the Political Order* (New York: Wiley and Sons, 1966), p. 251; and for France and Norway, Philip Converse and Roy Pierce, *Political Representation in France* (Cambridge: Belknap Press of Harvard University Press, 1986), p. 77.

22. Hermann Schmitt and Renato Mannheimer, "About Voting and Non-Voting in the European Elections of June 1989," *European Journal of Political Research,* 19, 1991, pp. 31–54.

23. This measure is similar to that adopted by Bartolini in "Membership of Mass Parties" (p. 189).

24. José Ramón Montero, "Non-Voting in Spain: Some Quantitative and Attitudinal Aspects," working paper no. 22, Institut de Ciències Polítiques i Socials, Barcelona, 1990, p. 3.

25. The following data on PASOK party membership are taken from Michalis Spourdalakis, "PASOK in the 1990s: Structure, Ideology, Political Strategy," paper presented at the conference The European Socialist Parties, Barcelona, October 8–9, 1990, p. 40.

26. The author is grateful to Takis Pappas for providing membership data for Nea Democratia.

27. Otto Kirchheimer, "The Transformation of the Western European Party Systems," in Joseph La Palombara and Myron Weiner, eds., *Political Parties and Political Development* (Princeton: Princeton University Press, 1966).

28. Piero Ignazi, *Il polo escluso: Profilo del Movimento Sociale Italiano* (Bologna: Il Mulino, 1989), see esp. ch. 2.

29. See Carlo Vallauri, ed., *L'arcipelago democratico: Organizzazione e struttura dei partiti italani negli anni del centrismo (1949–1958)* (Rome: Bulzoni, 1981).

30. Accordingly, we can regard as a partial failure the attempt by Amintore Fanfani (the party's secretary between 1954 and 1959) to create a modern mass party with a large membership, a central organization, and, above all, a diffuse peripheral structure. For a detailed analysis of the organization during those years, see Gianfranco Poggi, ed., *L'organizzazione partitica del PCI e della DC* (Bologna: Il Mulino, 1968).

31. See Alan Zuckerman, *The Politics of Faction: Christian Democratic Rule in Italy* (New Haven: Yale University Press, 1979).

32. See, for example, Poggi, *L'organizzazione partitica*; Massimo Ilardi and Aris Accornero, eds., *Il Partito Comunista Italiano: Struttura e storia dell'organizzazione 1921–1979* (Milan: Annali della Fondazione Feltrinelli, 1982); and Sidney Tarrow, *Peasant Communism in Southern Italy* (New Haven: Yale University Press, 1967).

33. See Giorgio Galli, *Il bipartitismo imperfetto: Comunisti e Democristiani in Italia* (Bologna: Il Mulino, 1966), p. 166; and Francesco Alberoni, ed., *L'attivista di partito* (Bologna: Il Mulino, 1968).

34. Poggi, *L'organizzazione partitica,* p. 132.

35. Franco Cazzola, *Il partito come organizzazione: Studio di un caso, il P.S.I.* (Rome: Edizioni del Tritone, 1970), pp. 41–42.

36. For example, the PLI had only 170,000 members in 1957, the PSDI had between 123,000 and 150,000 in 1958–59, and the PRI had fewer than 50,000 members in 1963.

37. See Samuel Barnes, *Party Democracy: Politics in an Italian Socialist Federation* (New Haven: Yale University Press, 1967); Tarrow, *Peasant Communism*; Alberoni, *L'attivista di partito*; among others.

38. The internal stabilization of the party may have played an important role in its electoral success in 1982, and its subsequent incumbency contributed to its further stabilization (Richard Gunther, "The Spanish Socialist Party: From Clandestine Position to Party of Government," in Stanley Payne, ed., *The Politics*

of Democratic Spain [Chicago: Council on Foreign Relations, 1986], pp. 22–23).

39. For a detailed analysis of party formal organization prior to 1982 see Paloma Román Marugán, *El Partido Socialista Obrero Español en la transición española: Organización y ideología (1975–1982)* (Madrid: Departamento de Ciencia Política y de la Administración, 1987).

40. Hans-Jürgen Puhle, "El PSOE: Un partido dominante y heterogeneo," in Linz and Montero, *Crisis y Cambio,* pp. 336–37.

41. In 1983, there was some relaxation of these constraints: currents of opinion were again acknowledged within the party, and provisions were enacted to provide for increased participation of minorities in party organs (Félix Tezanos, "Continuidad y cambio en el socialismo español: El PSOE durante la transición democrática," in Félix Tezanos, Ramón Cotarelo, and Andrés de Blas, eds., *La transición democrática española* [Madrid: Editorial Sistema: 1989], p. 469).

42. See Félix Tezanos, *Sociología del Socialismo Español* (Madrid: Tecnos, 1983).

43. See Gunther, "El colapso de UCD"; Richard Gunther, "Un análisis preliminar de las alteraciones producidas en 1982 en el sistema español de partidos," *Revista de Estudios Políticos* 45, 1985, pp. 7–41; Carlos Huneeus, *La Unión de Centro Democrático y la transición a la democracia en España* (Madrid: Centro de Investigaciones Sociológicas, 1985); and Mario Caciagli, "La parábola de la Unión de Centro Democrático," in Tezanos, Cotarelo, and de Blas, *La transición democrática española.*

44. The organization of the AP is examined in Lourdes López Nieto, *Alianza Popular: Estructura y evolución electoral de un partido conservador (1976–1982)* (Madrid: Centro de Investigaciones Sociológicas, 1988).

45. See José Ramón Montero, "Los fracasos políticos y electorales de la derecha política española," in Tezanos, Cotarelo, and de Blas, *La transición democrática española,* p. 517.

46. See Richard Gunther, Giacomo Sani, and Goldie Shabad, *Spain after Franco: The Making of a Competitive Party System* (Berkeley: University of California Press, 1986); Richard Gunther, "Los partidos comunistas de España," in Linz and Montero, *Crisis y cambio*; and Juan Carlos González Hernández, "El Partido Comunista de España en el proceso de transición política," in Tezanos, Cotarelo, and de Blas , *La transición democrática española.*

47. See Juan J. Linz, *Conflicto en Euskadi* (Madrid: Espasa Calpe 1986); and Francisco J. Llera, "*Conflicto en Euskadi* Revisited," in Richard Gunther, ed., *Politics, Society, and Democracy: The Case of Spain* (Boulder: Westview, 1993).

48. See, among others, Vinicio Alves da Costa e Sousa, "O Partido Comunista Portugues (subsidio para um estudo sobre os seus adeptos)," *Estudos Politicos e Sociais* 11, 1983, pp. 497–543; Thomas C. Bruneau and Alex MacLeod, *Politics in Contemporary Portugal: Parties and the Consolidation of Democracy* (Boulder: Lynne Rienner, 1986); José Pacheco Pereira, "A Case of Orthodoxy: The Communist Party of Portugal," in Michael Waller and Meindert Fennema, eds., *Communist Parties in Western Europe: Decline or Adaptation* (Oxford: Basil Blackwell, 1988); and Carlos Gaspar, "Portuguese Communism since 1976: Limited Decline," *Problems of Communism* 3, 1990, pp. 45–63.

49. See Bruneau and MacLeod, *Politics in Contemporary Portugal*; and Maria

José Stock, *Os partidos do poder dez anos depois de '25 April* (Evora: Universidade de Evora, 1986).

50. See Bruneau and MacLeod, *Politics in Contemporary Portugal*, ch. 4; Stock, *Os partidos do poder*.

51. See Richard A. H. Robinson, "The Evolution of the Portuguese Socialist Party, 1973–86, in International Perspective," *Portuguese Studies Review* 1, 1991–92, pp. 6–26.

52. See Stock, *Os partidos do poder*; and Bruneau and MacLeod, *Politics in Contemporary Portugal*.

53. On the first years of the Portuguese party system see Joaquim Aguiar, *A ilusão do poder: Analise do sistema partidario portugues 1976–1982* (Lisbon: Publicaçoes Dom Quixote, 1983).

54. See Vassilis Kapetanyannis, "The Communists," in Kevin Featherstone and Dimitrios K. Katsoudas, eds., *Political Change in Greece* (London: Croom Helm, 1987).

55. See Constantine Calligas, "The Centre: Decline and Convergence," in Featherstone and Katsoudas, *Political Change in Greece*.

56. Christos Lyrintzis, "Political Parties in Post-Junta Greece: A Case of 'Bureaucratic Clientelism'?" in Geoffrey Pridham, ed., *The New Mediterranean Democracies: Regime Transition in Spain, Greece, and Portugal* (London: Frank Cass, 1984), p. 106.

57. See P. Nikiforos Diamandouros, "PASOK and State-Society Relations in Post-Authoritarian Greece (1974–1986)," in Speros Vryonis, ed., *Greece on the Road to Democracy: From the Junta to PASOK 1974–1986* (New Rochelle: Caratzas, 1991).

58. Dimitrios A. Sotiropoulos, "State and Party: The Greek State Bureaucracy and the Panhellenic Socialist Movement (PASOK), 1981–1989," (Ph.D. diss., Yale University, 1991), p. 93.

59. See Michalis Spourdalakis, *The Rise of the Greek Socialist Party* (London: Routledge, 1988).

60. Sotiropoulos, "State and Party," ch. 3.

61. Spourdalakis, *The Rise of the Greek Socialist Party*, p. 249; and Richard Clogg, *Parties and Elections in Greece: The Search for Legitimacy* (Durham: Duke University Press, 1987).

62. Samuel P. Huntington, *Political Order in Changing Societies* (New Haven: Yale University Press, 1968), p. 20.

63. Hans Daalder (in "Parties, Elites, and Political Developments in Western Europe," in La Palombara and Weiner, *Political Parties and Political Development*, p. 75) regards this as the most important aspect of these relationships.

64. The nature of these relationships is more fully developed and applied to the Italian case in Morlino, "Democracy between Consolidation and Crisis: Southern Europe," unpublished manuscript.

65. Paolo Farneti, ed., "Introduzione," *Il sistema politico italiano* (Bologna: Il Mulino, 1973), pp. 31–40.

66. See Joseph La Palombara, *Interest Groups in Italian Politics* (Princeton: Princeton University Press, 1964).

67. For a definition of "negative integration" and relevant bibliography, see note 42 in Chapter 1 of this volume.

68. Marco Maraffi stresses the role of Fanfani in the construction of the public sector (*Politica ed economia in Italia: La vicenda dell'impresa pubblica dagli anni trenta agli anni cinquanta* [Bologna: Il Mulino, 1991], esp. chs. 7 and 8.

69. See Gianfranco Pasquino, *Crisi dei partiti e governabilità* (Bologna: Il Mulino, 1980), p. 95; and Luigi Graziano, *Clientelismo e sistema politico: Il caso dell'Italia* (Milan: Angeli, 1980). A much more detailed analysis of relationships between interest groups and parties in Italy during the 1940s and 1950s is in Morlino, "Democracy between Consolidation and Crisis."

70. See Víctor Pérez Díaz, *El retorno de la sociedad civil: Respuestas sociales a la transición política, la crisis económica y los cambios culturales de España, 1975–1985* (Madrid: Instituto de Estudios Económicos, 1987), ch. 13.

71. For an overview of agricultural organizations see Gloria de La Fuente Blanco, *Las organizaciones agrarias españolas: El asociacionismo sindical de los agricultores y ganaderos españoles en la perspectiva de la Unidad Europea* (Madrid: Instituto de Estudios Económicos, 1991).

72. Pérez Díaz, *El retorno de la sociedad civil,* p. 164.

73. See López Nieto, *Alianza Popular*; and Pérez Díaz, *El retorno de la sociedad civil,* p. 163.

74. For additional studies of business and the attitudes of the business elite, see Robert Martínez and Rafael Pardo Avellaneda, "El asociacionismo empresarial español en la transición," *Papeles de la Economía Española* 22, 1985; Harry Rijnen, "La CEOE como organización," ibid.; and Miguel Jerez Mir, *Business and Politics in Spain: From Francoism to Democracy* (Barcelona: Institut de Ciències Polítiques i Socials, 1992).

75. See Pérez Díaz, *El retorno de la sociedad civil,* ch. 8; and Robert Fishman, *Working-Class Organization and the Return to Democracy in Spain* (Ithaca: Cornell University Press, 1990), esp. p. 163.

76. On this topic, see Manuel Pérez Yruela and Salvador Giner, eds., *El corporativismo en España* (Barcelona: Editorial Ariel, 1988); and Faustino Miguélez and Carlos Prieto, eds., *Las relaciones laborales en España* (Madrid: Siglo XXI de España, 1991).

77. See the special 1989 issue of *Papeles de Economía Española* on this topic; and Pablo Martín Acena and Francisco Comín, *INI. 50 años de industrialización de España* (Madrid: Espasa Calpe, 1989).

78. Richard Gillespie ("Regime Consolidation in Spain: Party, State, and Society," in Pridham, *Securing Democracy,* p. 132) reports that 25,000 such appointments were made between 1984 and 1987. Also see Pérez Díaz, *El retorno de la sociedad civil,* p. 71; and Cotarelo, ed., *Transición política y consolidación democrática,* p. 307.

79. Pérez Díaz, *El retorno de la sociedad civil,* p. 70.

80. Jorge Avilar de Lima, "As organizaçoes agricolas socioprofessionais em Portugal e a integração europeia (1974–85)," *Analise Social* 26, 1991, pp. 209–39; and Manuel de Lucena and Carlos Gaspar, "Metamorfoses corporativas? Associaçoes de interesses económicos e institucionalização da democracia em Portugal (II)," *Analise Social,* 27, 1992, pp. 135–87.

81. Manuel de Lucena and Carlos Gaspar, "Metamorfoses corporativas? Associaçoes de interesses económicos e institucionalização da democracia em Portugal (I)," *Analise Social,* 26, 1991, pp. 847–903.

82. José Manuel Taborda Barreto, "A formação das centrais sindicais e do sindicalismo contemporâneo em Portugal," (Ph.D. diss., University of Lisbon, 1991), p. 459.

83. See Alan Stoleroff, "Reflexoes sobre a evolução do sindicalismo e do movimento operario na era dos governos Cavaco Silva," *Vertice* 31, 1990, pp. 45–55; Alan Stoleroff, "Sindicalismo e relaçoes industriais em Portugal," *Sociologia* 4, 1988, pp. 147–64; Toborda Barreto, *A formação das centrais sindicais*; and Lucena and Gaspar, "Metamorfoses corporativas (I)."

84. See Alvaro de Vasconcelos, "Sociedade, partidos e estado em Portugal," unpublished paper, table 5.

85. See George Mavrogordatos, "From Dictatorship to Populism: Organized Interests in Greece," unpublished manuscript, 1988.

86. See Sotiropoulos, "State and Party"; and Spourdalakis, *The Rise of the Greek Socialist Party*, p. 242.

87. Thus, bipolarization has a double edge. On the one hand, it can help to stabilize parties and electoral behavior by promoting party organization and identification. On the other hand, it intensifies political conflict and increases its potential for radicalization and the violation of democratic norms.

88. Burton, Gunther, and Higley refer to this as an "unconsolidated democracy." See "Introduction," in John Higley and Richard Gunther, eds., *Elites and Democratic Consolidation in Latin America and Southern Europe* (Cambridge: Cambridge University Press, 1992), esp. p. 5.

89. See Juan J. Linz, "Transitions to Democracy," *Washington Quarterly* 1, 1990. pp. 143–64; Morlino, "Consolidamento democratico;" and Chapters 1, 3, and 7 in this volume.

90. A number of these indicators are proposed by Juan J. Linz in "Crisis, Breakdown, and Reequilibration," in Juan J. Linz and Alfred Stepan, eds., *The Breakdown of Democratic Regimes* (Baltimore: Johns Hopkins University Press, 1978) (see Preface n. 2 above); and also by Leonardo Morlino, *Como cambian los régimenes políticos* (Madrid: CEC, 1985). The importance of antiregime parties in the consolidation process is also stressed in Higley and Gunther, *Elites and Democratic Consolidation*. Also see Chapter 1 in this volume.

91. See John H. Herz, ed., *From Dictatorship to Democracy: Coping with the Legacies of Authoritarianism and Totalitarianism* (Westport, Conn.: Greenwood, 1982); Nikiforos Diamandouros, "Regime Change and the Prospects for Democracy in Greece: 1974–1983," and Kenneth Maxwell, "Regime Overthrow and the Prospects for Democratic Transition in Portugal," in Guillermo O'Donnell, Philippe C. Schmitter, and Laurence Whitehead, eds., *Transitions from Authoritarian Rule* (Baltimore: Johns Hopkins University Press, 1986) (see Preface n. 3 above).

92. See Leonardo Morlino and Franco Mattei, "Vecchio e nuovo autoritarismo nell' Europa Mediterranea," *Rivista Italiana di Scienza Politica* 22, 1992, pp. 137–60; and Chapter 7 in this volume.

93. See Ignazi, *Il polo escluso*.

94. See Franco Ferraresi, ed., *La destra radicale* (Milan: Feltrinelli, 1984); and Rosario Minna, "Il terrorismo di destra," in Della Porta, ed., *Terrorismi in Italia* (Bologna: Il Mulino, 1984).

95. Jaime Nogueira Pinto, "A direita e o 25 de Abril: Ideologia, estrategia, e evolução politica," in Mário Baptista Coello, ed., *Portugal: O sistema politico e constitucional 1974–87* (Lisbon: Instituto de Ciencias Sociais, 1989), p. 196; and Bruneau and MacLeod, *Politics in Contemporary Portugal,* p. 77.

96. José Ramón Montero, "El sub-triunfo de la derecha: Los apoyos electorales de AP-PDP," in Linz and Montero, *Crisis y cambio,* p. 370.

97. See Gunther, Sani, and Shabad, *Spain after Franco,* p. 194; and López Nieto, *Alianza Popular.*

98. See Puhle, "El PSOE," p. 332; Román Marugán, *El Partido Socialista,* p. 509; Donald Share, *Dilemmas of Social Democracy: The Spanish Socialist Workers Party in the 1980s* (Westport, Conn.: Greenwood, 1989), ch. 3; and Richard Gunther, "The Spanish Socialist Party: From Clandestine Opposition to Party of Government," in Stanley G. Payne, ed., *The Politics of Democratic Spain* (Chicago: Chicago Council on Foreign Relations, 1986).

99. Diamandouros, "PASOK and State-Society Relations." Also see Clogg, *Parties and Elections in Greece,* Appendix and p. 217; Kevin Featherstone, "PASOK and the Left," in Featherstone and Katsoudas, eds., *Political Change in Greece,* p. 119; Spourdalakis, *The Rise of the Greek Socialist Party,* p. 180; and George Th. Mavrogordatos, "The Rise of the Green Sun: The Greek Election of 1981," (occasional paper 1, Centre of Contemporary Greek Studies, King's College, London, 1983).

100. See María José Stock, "O centrismo politico em Portugal: Evolução do sistema de partidos, genese do 'Bloco Central' e analise dos dois parceiros da coligação," *Analise Social* 21, 1985; and Robinson, "The Evolution of the Portuguese Socialist Party."

101. See Pietro Di Loreto, *Togliatti e la doppiezza: Il PCI tra democrazia e insurrezione 1944–49* (Bologna: Il Mulino, 1991); and Marcello Flores and Nicola Gallerano, *Sul PCI: Un'interpretazione storica* (Bologna: Il Mulino, 1992); and Piero Ignazi, *Dal PCI al PDS* (Bologna: Il Mulino, 1992).

102. See Juan Carlos González Hernández, "El Partido Comunista de España"; Gunther, Sani, and Shabad, *Spain after Franco*; Gunther, "Los partidos comunistas de España"; and Eusebio Mujal-León, *Communism and Political Change in Spain* (Bloomington: Indiana University Press, 1981).

103. Gunther, Sani, and Shabad, *Spain after Franco,* p. 166.

104. Clogg, *Parties and Elections in Greece,* p. 171.

105. Kapetanyannis, "The Communists."

106. Bruneau and MacLeod, *Politics in Contemporary Portugal,* p. 49.

107. Bruneau and MacLeod, *Politics in Contemporary Portugal*; Pacheco Pereira, "A Case of Orthodoxy"; and Gaspar, "Portuguese Communism since 1976."

108. See Linz, *Conflicto en Euskadi*; and Llera, "*Conflicto en Euskadi* Revisited."

109. Recent survey data revealed high levels of satisfaction within these regions with "how autonomy works": 48 percent of Catalans expressed their satisfaction, as did 44 percent of Basques. See José Ramón Montero and Mariano Torcal, "Autonomías y Comunidades Autónomas en España: Preferencia, dimensiones y orientaciones políticas," *Revista de Estudios Políticos* 70, 1990, p. 69.

110. See Llera, "*Conflicto en Euskadi* Revisited"; Fernando Reinares, "Democratización y terrorismo en el caso español," in Tezanos, Cotarelo, and de Blas, *La transición democrática española.*

111. Sartori, *Parties and Party Systems.*

112. From an elitist perspective, legitimation is closer to convergence than to settlement. However, settlements can also play key roles in initiating the longer-term legitimation process. See Richard Gunther, "Spain: The Very Model of Modern Elite Settlement," and other chapters in Higley and Gunther, *Elites and Democratic Consolidation.* Also see John Higley and Michael G. Burton, "The Elite Variable in Democratic Transitions and Breakdowns," *American Sociological Review* 54, 1989, pp. 17–32; and G. Lowell Field, John Higley, and Michael G. Burton, "A New Elite Framework for Political Sociology," *Revue Européenne des Sciences Sociales: Cahiers Vilfredo Pareto* 28, 1990, pp. 149–82.

113. For greater detail on this, see Morlino, "Democracy between Consolidation and Crisis."

114. See José María Maravall, *La política de la transición 1975–80* (Madrid: Taurus, 1981); Víctor Pérez Díaz, *La emergencia de la España democrática: La "invención" de una tradición y la dudosa institucionalización de una democracia,* (working paper, Instituto Juan March de Estudios e Investigaciones, Madrid, April 1991); and Gunther, "Spain: Modern Elite Settlement."

115. Pérez Díaz, *El retorno de la sociedad civil.*

116. See Leonardo Morlino, "Consolidamento democratico: alcune ipotesi esplicative," *Rivista Italiana di Scienza Politica* 16, 1986, pp. 439–59.

117. See T. J. Pempel, ed., *Uncommon Democracies: The One-Party Dominant Regime* (Ithaca: Cornell University Press, 1990).

118. This process is similar in many ways to what Burton, Gunther, and Higley have referred to as elite convergence. (See "Introduction," in *Elites and Democratic Consolidation.*)

119. See Organization for Economic Cooperation and Development, *Economic Surveys: Portugal* (Paris: OECD, 1990–91, 1991–92, and 1993).

120. Following deep disagreements within the Mitsotakis cabinet over foreign and domestic policies, a new conservative party was born, Politike Anoixe (Political Spring), which attracted 4.9 percent of the vote and won ten parliamentary seats in 1993.

121. See OECD, *Economic Surveys: Greece* (Paris: OECD, 1990–91, 1991–92, and 1993).

122. The following disscussion of party organization is based upon research conducted by a group under the direction of Leonardo Morlino. Preliminary (pre-1990) results from this research have been published in Richard Katz and Peter Mair, eds., *How Parties Organize: Adaptation and Change in Party Organization in Western Democracies* (London: Sage, 1994). A more complete presentation of these results will be published in Leonardo Morlino, *Il mutamento partitico in Italia* (Bologna: Il Mulino, forthcoming).

123. See Roberto Cartocci, "Rilevare la secolarizzazione: indicatori a geometria variabile," *Rivista Italiana de Scienza Politica,* 23, 1993, pp. 119–52.

124. In Senate elections, the voter has one vote to cast, and a party that elects a senator through the single-member/majority segment of the ballot has the votes that were cast for its victorious candidate subtracted from its total in the

calculation of seats to be allocated in the proportional representation segment. In elections for the Chamber of Deputies, the voter has two votes: one for the single-member district and another for the proportional list at the constituency level. In calculating the seats to be allocated to each party, the votes cast for the proportional representation lists are considered and the votes received by the *second place* candidate in the single-member constituency are subtracted from the total of the proportional votes won by the party of the candidate who has gained the seat in the single-member constituency. The remainder following this subtraction is the basis upon which the allocation of the proportional representation seats is calculated.

125. For a compendium of data concerning electoral volatility since 1885, see Bartolini and Mair, *Identity, Competition, and Electoral Availability*.

126. As Linz has noted, the politicization of neutral powers is often symptomatic of democratic crises. See Linz, "Crisis, Breakdown, and Reequilibration."

127. See Morlino, "The Changing Relationship between Parties and Society"; and Chapter 7 in this volume.

Chapter 11

1. Classic statements of this relationship can be found in Seymour Martin Lipset, "Some Social Requisites of Democracy," *American Political Science Review* 53, 1959, pp. 69–105, and Lipset, "Economic Development and Democracy," in his *Political Man: The Social Bases of Politics* (New York: Doubleday, 1960). More recent formulations of this argument include Lipset, "The Social Requisites of Democracy Revisited," *American Sociological Review,* 59, 1994, pp. 1–22; Seymour Martin Lipset, Kyoung-Ryung Seong, and John Charles Torres, "A Comparative Analysis of the Social Requisites of Democracy," *International Social Science Journal,* 136, 1993, pp. 155–75; and Dietrich Rueschemeyer, Evelyne Huber Stephens, and John D. Stephens, *Capitalist Development and Democracy* (Oxford: Polity Press, 1992).

2. The hypothesis that socioeconomic development enables citizens to be politically autonomous and active can be found in Daniel Lerner, *The Passing of Traditional Society* (New York: Free Press, 1958); and Karl Deutsch, *Nationalism and Social Communication* (Cambridge: MIT Press, 1953), and Deutsch, "Social Mobilization and Political Development," *American Political Science Review* 55, September 1961, pp. 493–511.

3. See Michael Burton, Richard Gunther, and John Higley's introduction to John Higley and Richard Gunther, eds., *Elites and Democratic Consolidation in Latin America and Southern Europe* (Cambridge: Cambridge University Press, 1992), p. 29.

4. One notable exponent of this approach is Adam Przeworski, who, in his overview of regime transitions, asserts, "As everyone agrees, the eventual survival of the new democracies will depend to a large extent on their economic performance" (*Democracy and the Market: Political and Economic Reforms in Eastern Europe and Latin America* [Cambridge: Cambridge University Press, 1991], p. 95).

5. In the case of the Spanish Communist Party, it is clear that this ideological conversion was motivated at least in part by the party's growing awareness that

Spain's economy and society had changed. See the analysis of Spanish society and its implications for the appeal of communism in the Spanish Communist Party's *Noveno Congreso del Partido Comunista de España, 19–23 abril, 1978* (Barcelona: Editorial Crítica, 1978).

6. On this point, see Nancy Bermeo, "Sacrifice, Sequence, and Strength in Successful Dual Transitions: Lessons from Spain," *Journal of Politics* 56, August 1994, pp. 610–27; and P. Nikiforos Diamandouros, "The Southern European NICs," *International Organization* 20, 2, 1986, pp. 547–56.

7. See Terry Lynn Karl and Philippe C. Schmitter, "Modes of Transition and Types of Democracy in Latin America, Southern and Eastern Europe," unpublished paper, p. 55; and Terry Lynn Karl, "Dilemmas of Democratization in Latin America," *Comparative Politics* 23, 1, 1990, pp. 1–21.

8. The following quotation nicely captures Przeworski's thinking on this matter: "Whenever the *ancien régime* negotiates its way out of power, the optimal strategy of democratization is inconsistent: It requires compromises *ex ante*, resolution *ex post*. Transitions by extrication leave institutional traces: most important, the autonomy of the armed forces. These traces can be effaced, but transitions are more problematic and longer in countries where they result from negotiated agreements with the old regime" (*Democracy and the Market*, p. 94).

9. For one appropriate approach to the study of these phenomena, see Juan J. Linz, *The Breakdown of Democratic Regimes: Crisis, Breakdown, and Reequilibration* (Baltimore: Johns Hopkins University Press, 1978).

Contributors

Felipe Agüero is assistant professor of political science at Ohio State University, and recently a fellow at the Institute of Advanced Studies, Princeton. His publications include *Soldiers, Civilians, and Democracy: Post-Franco Spain in Comparative Perspective.*

P. Nikiforos Diamandouros is professor of comparative politics at the University of Athens, and co-chair of the Social Science Research Council's Subcommittee on Southern Europe. His previous works include "Prospects for Democracy in Southeastern Europe," " Politics and Constitutionalism in Greece," and *Cultural Dualism and Political Change in Postauthoritarian Greece.*

Richard Gunther is professor of political science at Ohio State University, and co-chair of the Social Science Research Council's Subcommittee on Southern Europe. His previous publications include *Elites and Democratic Consolidation in Latin America and Southern Europe; Politics, Society, and Democracy: The Case of Spain; Spain after Franco;* and *Public Policy in a No-Party State.*

Juan J. Linz is Sterling Professor of Political and Social Science at Yale University and recipient of the Premio Príncipe de Asturias. Among his many publications are *The Breakdown of Democratic Regimes; Informe sociológico sobre el cambio político en España, 1975–1981;* "Totalitarian and Authoritarian Regimes"; *Conflicto en Euskadi;* and *The Failure of Presidential Democracy.*

Edward Malefakis is professor of history at Columbia University. His previous publications include *Agrarian Reform and Peasant Revolution in*

Spain: Origins of the Civil War and *Southern Europe in the Nineteenth and Twentieth Centuries: An Historical Overview.*

José Ramón Montero is professor of political science at the Universidad Autónoma de Madrid and at the Centro de Estudios Avanzados en Ciencias Sociales, Madrid. His previous publications include *La CEDA: El catolicismo social y político en la segunda República; El control parlamentario;* and, as co-editor with Juan J. Linz, *Crisis y Cambio: Electores y partidos en la España de los años ochenta.*

Leonardo Morlino is professor of political science and dean of the Facoltà di Scienze Politiche of the University of Florence. He is author of *Como cambian los régimenes políticos, Dalla democrazia al autoritarismo, Costruire la democrazia,* and *Between Consolidation and Crisis.*

Gianfranco Pasquino is professor of political science at the University of Bologna and adjunct professor of political science at the Bologna Center of Johns Hopkins University. He co-authored *Euroministri: Il governo dell'Europa* and co-edited and contributed to *The End of Post-War Politics in Italy.*

Geoffrey Pridham is professor of European politics and director of the Centre for Mediterranean Studies, University of Bristol. His recent publications include *Democratisation in Eastern Europe: Domestic and International Perspectives,* which he co-edited with Tatu Vanhanen, and *Building Democracy? The International Dimensions in Eastern Europe.*

Hans-Jürgen Puhle is professor of political science at the Johann Wolfgang Goethe-Universität, Frankfurt am Main. His previous books include *Politische Agrarsbewegungen, Politik in Uruguay, Preussen im Rückblick,* and *Bürger in der Gesellschaft der Neuzeit.*

Philippe C. Schmitter is professor of political science at Stanford University and former vice president of the American Political Science Association. His publications include *Transitions from Authoritarian Rule, Private Interest Government,* and *Essaying the Consolidation of Democracies.*

Alfred Stepan is rector of Central European University in Budapest. His publications include *Authoritarian Brazil, Democratizing Brazil, Rethinking Military Politics,* and *The Military and Politics.*

Sidney Tarrow is Maxwell Upson Professor of Government at Cornell. His previous works include *Peasant Communism in Southern Italy, Between Center and Periphery, Democracy and Disorder,* and *Power in Movement.*

Index